ATHENAEUS

II

LCL 208

ATHENAEUS

THE LEARNED BANQUETERS

BOOKS III.106e–V

EDITED AND TRANSLATED BY

S. DOUGLAS OLSON

HARVARD UNIVERSITY PRESS
CAMBRIDGE, MASSACHUSETTS
LONDON, ENGLAND
2006

LOEB CLASSICAL LIBRARY® is a registered trademark
of the President and Fellows of Harvard College

Library of Congress Catalog Card Number 2006041321
CIP data available from the Library of Congress

ISBN-13: 978-0-674-99621-2
ISBN-10: 0-674-99621-6

Composed in ZephGreek and ZephText by
Technologies 'N Typography, Merrimac, Massachusetts.
Printed and bound by Edwards Brothers,
Ann Arbor, Michigan, on acid-free paper.

CONTENTS

PREFACE

For a general introduction to Athenaeus and *The Learned Banqueters*, and to my citation conventions, see the beginning of Volume I. I would like to reiterate my gratitude to Dean Steven Rosenstone of the College of Liberal Arts at the University of Minnesota for his continuing support of my research. Thanks are also due my research assistant Timothy Beck, as well as Christy Marquis, whose work on the text of Books 1–5 was generously supported by a grant from the Graduate Research Partnership Program. This volume is dedicated to my guardian, guide, and friend Barbara Lehnhoff, for whose unfailing support, good humor, and kind advice I will always be grateful.

ABBREVIATIONS

Berve	H. Berve, *Das Alexanderreich auf prosopographischer Grundlage* ii *Prosopographie* (Munich, 1926)
Billows	R. A. Billows, *Antigonos the One-Eyed and the Creation of the Hellenistic State* (Berkeley, Los Angeles, and London, 1990)
Bradford	A. S. Bradford, *A Prosopography of Lacedaimonians from the Death of Alexander the Great, 323 B.C., to the Sack of Sparta by Alaric, A.D. 396* (Vestigia 27: Munich, 1977)
Braund and Wilkins	D. Braund and J. Wilkins (eds.), *Athenaeus and His World: Reading Greek Culture in the Roman Empire* (Exeter, 2000)
FGE	D. L. Page (ed.), *Further Greek Epigrams* (Cambridge, 1981)
FGrH	F. Jacoby (ed.), *Die Fragmente der Griechischen Historiker* (Leiden, 1923–69)
FHG	C. and T. Müller, *Fragmenta Historicorum Graecorum* (5 vols.: Paris, 1841–70)
GGM	C. Müller, *Geographi Graeci Minores* (3 vols.: Paris, 1855–61)
GPh	A. S. F. Gow and D. L. Page (eds.), *The Greek Anthology: The Garland of Philip* (Cambridge, 1968)

ABBREVIATIONS

HE	A. S. F. Gow and D. L. Page (eds.), *The Greek Anthology: Hellenistic Epigrams* (Cambridge, 1965)
IG	*Inscriptiones Graecae*
K–A	see *PCG*
PA	J. Kirchner, *Prosopographia Attica* (Berlin, 1901–3)
PAA	J. Traill (ed.), *Persons of Ancient Athens* (Toronto, 1994–)
PCG	R. Kassel and C. Austin (eds.), *Poetae Comici Graeci* (Berlin and New York, 1983–)
PMG	D. L. Page (ed.), *Poetae Melici Graeci* (Oxford, 1962)
Poralla	P. Poralla, *A Prosopography of Lacedaimonians froom the Earliest Times to the Death of Alexander the Great (X–323 B.C.)*[2] (revised by A. S. Bradford: Chicago, 1985)
SH	H. Lloyd-Jones and P. Parsons (eds.), *Supplementum Hellenisticum* (Texte und Kommentar, Band 11: Berlin and New York, 1983)
SSR	G. Giannantoni, *Socratis et Socraticorum Reliquiae* (4 vols.; n.p., 1990)
Stephanis	I. E. Stephanis, Διονυσιακοὶ Τεχνίται (Herakleion, 1988)
SVF	J. van Arnim (ed.), *Stoicorum Veterum Fragmenta* (3 vols.; Leipzig, 1921, 1903)
TrGF	B. Snell et al. (eds.), *Tragicorum Graecorum Fragmenta* (Göttingen, 1971–)
West, *AGM*	M. L. West, *Ancient Greek Music* (Oxford, 1992)

THE CHARACTERS

ATHENAEUS, the narrator; also a guest at the dinner party
TIMOCRATES, Athenaeus' interlocutor

AEMILIANUS MAURUS, grammarian (e.g. 3.126b)
ALCEIDES OF ALEXANDRIA, musician (1.1f; 4.174b)
AMOEBEUS, citharode (14.622d–e)
ARRIAN, grammarian (3.113a)
CYNULCUS, Cynic philosopher whose given name is
    Theodorus (e.g. 1.1d; 3.97c)
DAPHNUS OF EPHESUS, physician (e.g. 1.1e; 2.51a)
DEMOCRITUS OF NICOMEDIA, philosopher (1.1e; 3.83c)
DIONYSOCLES, physician (3.96d, 116d)
GALEN OF PERGAMUM, physician (e.g. 1.1e–f, 26c)
LARENSIUS, Roman official and also host of the party
    (e.g. 1.2b–3c; 2.50f)
LEONIDAS OF ELIS, grammarian (1.1d; 3.96d)
MAGNUS (e.g. 3.74c)
MASURIUS, jurist, poet, musician (e.g. 1.1c; 14.623e)
MYRTILUS OF THESSALY, grammarian (e.g. 3.83a)
PALAMEDES THE ELEATIC, lexicographer (9.379a)
PHILADELPHUS OF PTOLEMAIS, philosopher (1.1d)*
PLUTARCH OF ALEXANDRIA, grammarian (e.g. 1.1c–d;
    3.83b)
PONTIANUS OF NICOMEDIA, philosopher (1.1d; 3.109b)

CHARACTERS

Rufinus of Nicaea, physician (1.1f)*
Ulpian of Tyre, grammarian and also symposiarch
   (e.g. 1.1d–e; 2.49a)
Varus, grammarian (3.118d)
Zoilus, grammarian (e.g. 1.1d; 7.277c)

* Neither Philadelphus nor Rufinus is said to speak anywhere in the preserved text of *The Learned Banqueters*, and most likely some of the anonymous speeches in 1.2a–3.73e (represented in the Epitome manuscripts only) belong to them.

THE LEARNED BANQUETERS

Γ

106e Ἑξῆς εἰσεκομίσθη ταγηνιστὰ ἥπατα περιειλημένα
τῷ καλουμένῳ ἐπίπλῳ, ὃν Φιλέταιρος ἐν Τηρεῖ ἐπί-
πλοιον εἴρηκεν. εἰς ἃ ἀποβλέψας ὁ Κύνουλκος, λέγε
f ἡμῖν, ἔφη, ὦ σοφὲ Οὐλπιανέ, | εἴ που κεῖται οὕτως τὸ
ἧπαρ ἐντετυλιγμένον. καὶ ὅς· ἐὰν πρότερον δείξῃς σὺ
παρὰ τίνι ὁ ἐπίπλους εἴρηται ἐπὶ τοῦ λίπους καὶ τοῦ
ὑμένος. ἀντικορυσσομένων οὖν τούτων ὁ Μυρτίλος
ἔφη· ὁ μὲν ἐπίπλους παρ' Ἐπιχάρμῳ ἐν Βάκχαις·

καὶ τὸν ἀρχὸν ἐπικαλύψας ἐπιπλόῳ.

107 καὶ ἐν Θεαροῖς· ||

< . . . > ὀσφύος τε πέρι κἠπιπλόου.

καὶ ὁ Χῖος δὲ Ἴων ἐν ταῖς Ἐπιδημίαις ἔφη· τῷ ἐπίπλῳ
ἐπικαλύψας. ἀπέχεις, φίλη κεφαλὴ Οὐλπιανέ, τὸν ἐπί-
πλουν, ἵν' ἤδη ποτὲ αὐτῷ ἐντυλιχθεὶς κατακαυθῇς καὶ
πάντας ἡμᾶς ζητήσεων ἀπαλλάξῃς. τὸ δὲ μαρτύριον
τοῦ οὕτως διεσκευασμένου ἥπατος δίκαιος εἶ σὺ ἀπο-
μνημονεῦσαι, προειρημένου σοι πάλαι ὅτε περὶ τῶν
ὠτίων καὶ ποδῶν ἐζητοῦμεν, <ὅτι> Ἄλεξις ἐν Κρατείᾳ

2

BOOK III (continued)

Immediately after this, fried livers were brought in wrapped in what is called *epiplous* ("omentum, caul"),[1] which Philetaerus in *Tereus* (fr. 16) refers to as *epiploios*. Cynulcus looked at them and said: Tell us, wise Ulpian, if liver wrapped this way is attested anywhere. And he said: If you first show me in what author *epiplous* is used for the fat and the caul! As the two of them were butting heads, Myrtilus said: The word *epiplous* is found in Epicharmus' *Bacchants* (fr. 16):

and covering the leader with an *epiplous*.

And in *Envoys* (fr. 69):

around a tailbone and an *epiplous*.

Ion of Chios too said in his *Travels* (*FGrH* 392 F 5): covering it with the *epiplous*. You are reserving the *epiplous*, my dear Ulpian, so that you can eventually be wrapped in it and burned, freeing us all of your questions. But you ought to cite the evidence for liver prepared this way, since you noted earlier,[2] when we were exploring the question of ears and feet, that Alexis uses the word in *Crateia or The*

---

[1] The membrane that lines the walls of the abdominal cavity and encloses the viscera.   [2] At 3.95a.

ἢ Φαρμακοπώλῃ εἴρηκε. πᾶσα δ' ἡ ἐκλογὴ χρησίμη
b οὖσα εἰς πολλά, ἐπεὶ τὰ | νῦν διὰ μνήμης οὐ κρατεῖς,
αὐτὸς ἐγὼ διεξελεύσομαι. φησὶ δ' οὕτως ὁ κωμικός·

πρῶτον μὲν ⟨οὖν⟩ ὄστρεια παρὰ Νηρεῖ τινι
ἰδὼν γέροντι φυκί' ἠμφιεσμένα
ἔλαβον ἐχίνους τ'· ἔστι γὰρ προοίμιον
δείπνου χαριέντως ταῦτα πεπρυτανευμένου.
τούτων δ' ἀπολυθείς, κειμένων ἰχθυδίων
μικρῶν, τρεμόντων τῷ δέει τί πείσεται,
θαρρεῖν κελεύσας ἕνεκ' ἐμοῦ ταῦτ', οὐδὲ ἓν
c φήσας ἀδικήσειν, ἐπριάμην γλαῦκον μέγαν. |
ἔπειτα νάρκην ἔλαβον, ἐνθυμούμενος
ὅτι δεῖ γυναικὸς ἐπιφερούσης δακτύλους
ἁπαλοὺς ὑπ' ἀκάνθης μηδὲ ἓν τούτους παθεῖν.
ἐπὶ τὸ τάγηνον φυκίδας, ψήττας τινάς,
καρῖδα κυφήν, κωβιόν, πέρκην, σπάρον,
ἐπόησά τ' αὐτὸ ποικιλώτερον ταῶ.
κρεάδι' ⟨ἄττα⟩, ποδάρια, ῥύγχη τινά,
d ὠτάρι' ὑεῖ', ἡπάτιον ἐγκεκαλυμμένον· |
αἰσχύνεται γὰρ πελιδνὸν ὂν τῷ χρώματι.
τούτοις μάγειρος οὐ πρόσεισ' οὐδ' ὄψεται·
οἰμώξεται γὰρ νὴ Δί'. ἀλλ' ἐγὼ σοφῶς
ταῦτ' οἰκονομήσω καὶ γλαφυρῶς καὶ ποικίλως
οὕτω, πῶ γὰρ τοὖψον αὐτός, ὥστε τοὺς
δειπνοῦντας εἰς τὰ λοπάδι' ἐμβάλλειν πῶ

---

[3] Properly the Old Man of the Sea (cf. 1.6e–f); here an aged
fish-seller.   [4] An unidentified shark of some sort.

4

Pharmacist. Because the entire quotation is useful for a number of purposes and you cannot recall it at the moment, I will recite the whole piece myself. The comic poet says the following (fr. 115):

First of all, then, I spotted oysters wrapped
in seaweed in the stall of some old Nereus,[3]
and I bought them and some sea-urchins; for these
are the prelude to a well-organized dinner.
After I took care of them, some tiny fish were
lying there, trembling in fear of what was going to
    happen to them.
I told them not to worry about me, declared
that I would do them no harm, and purchased a large
    glaukos[4].
Next I bought an electric eel, keeping in mind
that when a woman lays her soft fingers on it,
they shouldn't suffer any harm from its sting.
For the frying-pan I got wrasses, some flatfish,
a curved shrimp, a goby, a sea-perch, and a sea-
    bream;
and I made the pan more colorful than a peacock.
Some chunks of meat, pigs' feet, some snouts,
pigs' ears, a small liver wrapped up
(for it was ashamed of its livid color);
no cook is going to get near these items or even look
    at them.
Because he'll be sorry if he does, by Zeus! Instead,
    I'll
take care of them so wisely, elegantly, and subtly—
because I do my own cooking—that
I'll make the guests chew on the casserole-dishes

ATHENAEUS

ἐνίοτε τοὺς ὀδόντας ὑπὸ τῆς ἡδονῆς.
τὰς σκευασίας πάντων δὲ καὶ τὰς † σκευάσεις †
e   τούτων ἕτοιμός εἰμι δεικνύειν, λέγειν, |
προῖκα προδιδάσκειν, ἂν θέλῃ τις μανθάνειν.

ὅτι δ' ἔθος τῷ ἐπίπλῳ περικαλύπτεσθαι τὰ ἡπάτια,
Ἡγήσανδρος ὁ Δελφὸς ἐν Ὑπομνήμασί φησι Μετά-
νειραν τὴν ἑταίραν ὡς ἐν τοῖς κεκαλυμμένοις ἡπατίοις
αὐτὴ πνευμόνιον ἔλαβε καὶ ὡς περιελοῦσα τὸ στέαρ
εἶδεν, ἀνέκραγεν·

ἀπόλωλα· πέπλων μ' ὤλεσαν περιπτυχαί.

μήποτε δὲ καὶ Κρώβυλος ὁ κωμῳδιοποιὸς αἰσχυνόμενον εἶπε τὸ τοιοῦτο ἧπαρ ὥσπερ καὶ Ἄλεξις, ἐν
f   Ψευδυποβολιμαίῳ λέγων οὕτως· |

καὶ πλεκτάνην στιφρὰν σφόδρ' ἐν τούτοις τέ που
αἰσχυνόμενον ἧπαρ καπρίσκου σκατοφάγου.

ἡπάτιον δ' εἴρηκεν Ἀριστοφάνης ἐν Ταγηνισταῖς καὶ
Ἀλκαῖος ἐν Παλαίστρᾳ Εὔβουλός τ' ἐν Δευκαλίωνι.
δασυντέον ⟨δὲ⟩ λέγοντας τὸ ἧπαρ· καὶ γὰρ ἡ συν-
αλοιφή ἐστιν παρ' Ἀρχιλόχῳ διὰ δασέος. φησὶ γάρ·

108   ⟨ . . . ⟩ χολὴν γὰρ οὐκ ἔχεις ἐφ' ἥπατι. ||

ἐστὶ δὲ καὶ ἰχθύς τις ἥπατος καλούμενος, ὅν φησιν

---

5 Quoted at 3.96c.
6 *eph' hēpati*. If the word had a smooth breathing, the text
would read *ep' ēpati*.

6

occasionally out of sheer pleasure.
As for my recipes for everything and my [corrupt],
I'm prepared to show them off, describe them,
even teach them for free, if anyone wants to learn
    them.

As for it being customary for livers to be wrapped in omentum, Hegesander of Delphi says in his *Commentaries* (fr. 29, *FHG* iv.419) that when the courtesan Metaneira took a lung from a platter of wrapped livers and removed the fat and saw it, she cried (adesp. tr. fr. 91):

I am lost! The folds of my garments ruined me!

Perhaps Crobylus the comic poet too claimed that liver prepared this way is ashamed, as Alexis did (fr. 115.17, above), when he said the following in *Falsely Suppositious* (fr. 7):

and a very stout tentacle, and somewhere among
    those items
an ashamed liver of a shit-eating boar.

Aristophanes uses the word *hēpation* ("small liver") in *Frying-Pan Men* (fr. 520.4)[5], as do Alcaeus in *The Wrestling School* (Alc. Com. fr. 25) and Eubulus in *Deucalion* (fr. 23). The word should be pronounced *hēpar*, with a rough breathing; and in fact a coalescence with a rough breathing is found in Archilochus (fr. 234 West[2]), since he says:

for you have no bile in your liver.[6]

There is also a fish called the *hēpatos*. The same Eubulus

‹ὁ› αὐτὸς Εὔβουλος ἐν Λάκωσιν ἢ Λήδᾳ οὐκ ἔχειν
χολήν·

οὐκ ᾤου ‹σύ› με
χολὴν ἔχειν, ὡς δ' ἡπάτῳ μοι διελέγου;
ἐγὼ δέ γ' εἰμὶ τῶν μελαμπύγων ἔτι.

Ἡγήσανδρος δ' ἐν Ὑπομνήμασιν ἐν τῇ κεφαλῇ φησι
τὸν ἥπατον δύο λίθους ἔχειν τῇ μὲν αὐγῇ καὶ τῷ
χρώματι παραπλησίους τοῖς ‹ἐν τοῖς› ὀστρείοις, τῷ
δὲ σχήματι ῥομβοειδεῖς.

Ταγηνιστῶν δ' ἰχθύων μνημονεύει Ἄλεξις ἐν Δη-
b μητρίῳ | καθάπερ κἀν τῷ προκειμένῳ δράματι. Εὔ-
βουλος Ὀρθάννῃ·

πᾶσα δ' εὔμορφος γυνὴ
ἐρῶσα φοιτᾷ τηγάνων τε σύντροφα
τριβαλλοπανόθρεπτα μειρακύλλια,
ὁμοῦ δὲ τευθὶς καὶ Φαληρικὴ κόρη
σπλάγχνοισιν ἀρνείοισι συμμεμιγμένη
πηδᾷ, χορεύει, πῶλος ὡς ὑπὸ ζυγοῦ.
ῥιπὶς δ' ἐγείρει φύλακας Ἡφαίστου κύνας
θερμὴν παροξύνουσα τηγάνου πνοήν·
c ὀσμὴ δὲ πρὸς μυκτῆρας ἠρεθισμένη |
ᾄσσει· μεμαγμένη δὲ Δήμητρος κόρη
κοίλην φάραγγα δακτύλου πιέσματι

---

[7] I.e. any capacity for anger.
[8] A "black-butt" is someone as tough as Heracles; cf. Ar. *Lys.*
802–3; Fraenkel on A. *Ag.* 115.

claims in *Spartans or Leda* (fr. 61) that it lacks bile:

> Didn't you think
> I had any bile,[7] when you were talking to me like I'm
> a *hēpatos*?
> In fact, I'm still one of the black-butts.[8]

Hegesander says in the *Commentaries* (fr. 37, *FHG* iv.420) that the *hēpatos* has two stones in its head that resemble those found in oysters[9] in their luster and color, but are rhombus-shaped.

Alexis mentions frying-pan fish in *Demetrius* (fr. 51), as well as in the play cited above (fr. 115.12). Eubulus in *Orthannēs* (fr. 75):

> Every well-built woman
> who's in love comes, as do the nurslings of frying-
> pans,
> pan-nourished-Triballian young men;[10]
> and along with them a squid and a Phalerian girl[11]
> mixed with sheep entrails
> leap and dance like a colt escaping the yoke.
> A fan rouses up Hephaestus' watchdogs[12],
> stimulating the warm breath of the frying-pan;
> and the smell, stirred up, rushes toward
> the nostrils. The kneaded daughter of Demeter[13]
> has a hollow cleft made in her by a finger's

[9] Pearls.

[10] The Triballians were a Thracian tribe whose name was borrowed by a group of wild young Athenians (D. 54.39).

[11] A riddling reference to small-fry from the Bay of Phaleron.

[12] The coals of the fire, which have been sleeping quietly.

[13] A barley-cake.

9

σύρει τριήρους ἐμβολὰς μιμουμένη,
δείπνου πρόδρομον ἄριστον.

ἤσθιον δὲ καὶ ταγηνιστὰς σηπίας. Νικόστρατος ἢ
Φιλέταιρος ἐν Ἀντύλλῳ φησίν·

οὔποτ᾽ αὖθις
σηπίαν ἀπὸ τηγάνου
τολμήσαιμι φαγεῖν μόνος.

Ἡγήμων δ᾽ ἐν Φιλίννῃ καὶ γόνον ἐκ ταγήνου ἐσθίοντας ποιεῖ ἐν τούτοις·

μάλα ταχέως αὐτῶν πρίω <μοι> πουλύπουν
d   καὶ δὸς καταφαγεῖν, κἀπὸ τηγάνου γόνον. |

Ἐπὶ τούτοις οὐχ ἡσθεὶς ὁ Οὐλπιανός, ἀνιαθεὶς δέ,
ἀποβλέψας ὡς ἡμᾶς καὶ τὰ ἐξ Ὀρθάννου Εὐβούλου
ἰαμβεῖα εἰπών·

ὡς εὖ νεναυάγηκεν ἐπὶ τοῦ τηγάνου
ὁ θεοῖσιν ἐχθρὸς

Μυρτίλος· ὅτι γὰρ οὐδὲν τούτων πριάμενός ποτε ἔφα-
γεν εὖ οἶδα, τῶν τινος οἰκετῶν αὐτοῦ εἰπόντος μοί ποτε
τὰ ἐκ Πορνοβοσκοῦ Εὐβούλου ἰαμβεῖα τάδε·

τρέφει με Θετταλός τις ἄνθρωπος βαρύς,
e   πλουτῶν, φιλάργυρος δὲ κἀλιτήριος, |
ὀψοφάγος, ὀψωνῶν δὲ μέχρι τριωβόλου.

ἐπεὶ δὲ πεπαιδευμένος ἦν ὁ νεανίσκος καὶ οὐχὶ παρὰ

pressure so that she resembles a trireme's ram,
and is the best prelude to a dinner.

They also ate fried cuttlefish. Nicostratus or Philetaerus
says in *Antyllus* (Nicostr. fr. 6):

> Might I never again
> venture to eat a squid
> from a frying-pan by myself!

Hegemon in *Philinnē* (fr. 1) represents people eating
small-fry out of a frying-pan in the following verses:

> Very quickly buy me an octopus with this money
> and give it to me to eat, along with small-fry from a
>   frying-pan!

Ulpian was not pleased at these remarks but annoyed;
he looked straight at us and recited the iambic lines from
Eubulus' *Orthannēs* (fr. 76):

> What a fine shipwreck on the frying-pan
> for the god-detested

Myrtilus! For I am certain that he never purchased any of
these items and ate them, since one of his slaves once
quoted me the following iambic lines from Eubulus' *The
Pimp* (fr. 87):

> My master is an overbearing Thessalian,
> a wealthy man but a miser, a sinner,
> and a glutton—but one who spends only three obols
>   when he shops for food.

Since the boy had been educated—not while he belonged

τῷ Μυρτίλῳ γε, ἀλλὰ παρὰ ἄλλῳ τινί, ὡς ἐπυνθανό-
μην αὐτοῦ πῶς εἰς τὸν Μυρτίλον ἐνέπεσεν, ἔφη μοι τὰ
ἐκ Νεοττίδος Ἀντιφάνους τάδε·

> παῖς ὢν μετ᾽ ἀδελφῆς εἰς Ἀθήνας ἐνθάδε
> ἀφικόμην ἀχθεὶς ὑπό τινος ἐμπόρου,
> Σύρος τὸ γένος ὤν. περιτυχὼν δ᾽ ἡμῖν ὁδὶ
> κηρυττομένοις ὀβολοστάτης ὢν ἐπρίατο,

f
> ἄνθρωπος ἀνυπέρβλητος εἰς πονηρίαν, |
> τοιοῦτος οἷος μηδὲν εἰς τὴν οἰκίαν
> μηδ᾽ ὢν ὁ Πυθαγόρας ἐκεῖνος ἤσθιεν,
> ὁ τρισμακαρίτης, εἰσφέρειν ἔξω θύμου.

Ἔτι τοῦ Οὐλπιανοῦ τοιαῦτά τινα παίζοντος ὁ Κύνουλκος ἀνέκραγεν· ἄρτου δεῖ καὶ οὐ τοῦ Μεσσαπίων
βασιλέως λέγω τοῦ ἐν Ἰαπυγίᾳ, περὶ οὗ καὶ σύγ-
γραμμά ἐστι Πολέμωνι. μνημονεύει δ᾽ αὐτοῦ καὶ Θουκυδίδης ἐν ἑβδόμῃ καὶ Δημήτριος ὁ κωμῳδιοποιὸς ἐν
109   τῷ ἐπιγραφομένῳ δράματι Σικελίᾳ διὰ τούτων· ||

> (Α.) ἐκεῖθεν εἰς τὴν Ἰταλίαν ἀνέμῳ νότῳ
> διεβάλομεν τὸ πέλαγος εἰς Μεσσαπίους·
> Ἄρτος δ᾽ ἀναλαβὼν ἐξένισεν ἡμᾶς καλῶς.
> (Β.) ξένος γε χαρίεις † ἦν ἐκεῖ μέγας καὶ
> λαμπρὸς ἦν †.

οὐ τούτου οὖν τοῦ Ἄρτου ὁ νῦν καιρὸς ἦν, ἀλλὰ τῶν
εὑρημένων ὑπὸ τῆς Σιτοῦς καλουμένης Δήμητρος καὶ

to Myrtilus, however, but while he was with someone else—when I asked him how he got mixed up with Myrtilus, he recited me the following verses from Antiphanes' *Neottis*[14] (fr. 166):

> When I was a child, I was brought here
> to Athens, along with my sister, by a trader;
> I'm Syrian by birth. This loan-shark here
> came along while we were being auctioned off, and
>   bought us.
> He's as bad as they come,
> the sort of person who brings nothing into his house,
> not even what the famous Pythagoras,
> bless his soul, used to eat, except for thyme.

While Ulpian was still making jokes like these, Cynulcus shouted: We need bread (*artos*)—and I'm not referring to the king of the Messenians in Iapygia, who is the subject of a treatise by Polemon (fr. 89 Preller)! Thucydides also mentions him in Book VII (33.4), as does the comic poet Demetrius in his play entitled *Sicily* (Demetr. Com. I fr. 1), as follows:

> (A.) From there we took advantage of a south wind
> and crossed the sea to Italy, to the Messapians.
> Artos took us in and entertained us very well.
> (B.) A lovely host † was there large and shining
>   was † !

This was not the moment for this Artos, then, but for the loaves invented by Demeter, called Mistress Grain

---

[14] Probably a courtesan's name.

ATHENAEUS

Ἰμαλίδος[1]· οὕτως γὰρ ἡ θεὸς παρὰ Συρακοσίοις τι-
μᾶται, ὡς <ὁ> αὐτὸς Πολέμων ἱστορεῖ ἐν τῷ Περὶ τοῦ
Μορύχου. ἐν δὲ τῷ πρώτῳ τῶν Πρὸς Τίμαιον ἐν
b Σκώλῳ φησὶ τῷ Βοιωτιακῷ Μεγαλάρτου | καὶ Μεγα-
λομάζου ἀγάλματα ἱδρῦσθαι. ἐπεὶ δὲ ἤδη ἄρτοι εἰσε-
κομίζοντο καὶ πλῆθος ἐπ’ αὐτοῖς παντοδαπῶν βρωμάτων, ἀποβλέψας εἰς αὐτὰ ἔφη·

> τοῖς ἄρτοις ὅσας
> ἱστᾶσι παγίδας οἱ ταλαίπωροι βροτοί,

φησὶν Ἄλεξις ἐν τῇ Εἰς τὸ Φρέαρ. ἡμεῖς οὖν εἴπωμέν
τι καὶ περὶ ἄρτων.

Προφθάσας δ’ αὐτὸν ὁ Ποντιανὸς ἔφη· Τρύφων ὁ
Ἀλεξανδρεὺς ἐν τοῖς Φυτικοῖς ἐπιγραφομένοις ἄρτων
ἐκτίθεται γένη, εἴ τι κἀγὼ μέμνημαι, ζυμίτην, ἄζυμον,
c σεμιδαλίτην, | χονδρίτην, συγκομιστόν—τοῦτον δ’
εἶναί φησι καὶ διαχωρητικώτερον τοῦ καθαροῦ—, τὸν
ἐξ ὀλυρῶν, τὸν ἐκ τιφῶν, τὸν ἐκ μελινῶν. γίνεται μέν,
φησίν, ὁ χονδρίτης ἐκ τῶν ζειῶν· ἐκ γὰρ κριθῆς
χόνδρον μὴ γίνεσθαι. παρὰ δὲ τὰς ὀπτήσεις ὀνομάζεσθαι ἰπνίτην, οὗ μνημονεύειν Τιμοκλέα ἐν Ψευδο-
λῃσταῖς οὕτως·

> καταμαθὼν δὲ κειμένην σκάφην
> θερμῶν ἰπνιτῶν ἤσθιον.

[1] Ἰμαλίδος Schweighäuser: Σιμαλίδος A: Σιμαλία CE

14

and Abundance; for the Syracusans honor the goddess with these titles, as the same Polemon records in his *On Morychus* (fr. 74 Preller). And in Book I of his *Response to Timaeus* (fr. 39 Preller) he reports that in Boeotian Scolus statues have been erected of Megalartos ("Large Loaf of Bread") and Megalomazos ("Large Barley-Cake").[15] Since loaves of bread were now being brought in, and a large quantity of food of various sorts along with them, he fixed his eyes on them and said:

How many traps
wretched mortals set to catch loaves of bread!,

as Alexis puts it in his *Into the Well* (fr. 86). So let us have some discussion about bread.

Pontianus began to speak before the other could get any further, and said: Tryphon of Alexandria in his work entitled *On Plants* (fr. 117 Velsen) lists the types of bread, if I remember correctly, as yeast bread, unleavened bread, durum wheat bread, groat bread, bread made of unsieved flour—he reports that this is more laxative than bread made of sieved flour—bread made of emmer, of einkorn, and of millet. He claims that groat bread is made of rice-wheat, because groats are not produced from barley.[16] "Oven bread" gets its name from the fact that it is baked. Timocles mentions it in his *Fake Bandits* (fr. 35), as follows:

When I learned that a pan of warm
oven bread was lying there, I ate it.

---

[15] Cf. 10.416b–c.   [16] A strange claim; perhaps something has gone wrong with the text.

Ἐσχαρίτης. τούτου μνημονεύει Ἀντίδοτος ἐν Πρωτο-
χόρῳ·

d   λαβόντα θερμοὺς ἐσχαρίτας, πῶς γὰρ οὔ; |
    τούτους ἀνειλίττοντα βάπτειν εἰς γλυκύν.

καὶ Κρώβυλος ἐν Ἀπαγχομένῳ·

        καὶ σκάφην λαβών τινα
τῶν ἐσχαριτῶν τῶν καθαρῶν.

Λυγκεὺς δ᾽ ὁ Σάμιος ἐν τῇ Πρὸς Διαγόραν Ἐπιστολῇ
συγκρίνων τὰ Ἀθήνησι γινόμενα τῶν ἐδωδίμων πρὸς
τὰ ἐν Ῥόδῳ φησίν· ἔτι δὲ σεμνυνομένων παρ᾽ ἐκείνοις
τῶν ἀγοραίων ἄρτων, ἀρχομένου μὲν τοῦ δείπνου καὶ
μεσοῦντος οὐθὲν λειπομένους ἐπιφέρουσιν· ἀπειρηκό-
e   των δὲ καὶ πεπληρωμένων | ἡδίστην ἐπεισάγουσι
διατριβὴν τὸν διάχριστον ἐσχαρίτην καλούμενον, ὃς
οὕτω κέκραται τοῖς μειλίγμασι καὶ τῇ μαλακότητι καὶ
τοιαύτην ἐνθρυπτόμενος ἔχει πρὸς τὸν γλυκὺν συναυ-
λίαν ὥστε προσβιαζόμενος θαυμαστόν τι συντελεῖ·
καθάπερ ἀνανήφειν πολλάκις γίνεται τὸν μεθύοντα,
τὸν αὐτὸν τρόπον ὑπὸ τῆς ἡδονῆς ἀναπεινῆν γίνεται
τὸν ἐσθίοντα.

    Ἀταβυρίτην. Σώπατρος ἐν Κνιδίᾳ·

ἀταβυρίτης δ᾽ ἄρτος ἦν πλησίγναθος.

f   Ἀχαίνας. τούτου τοῦ ἄρτου μνημονεύει Σῆμος | ἐν
ὀκτῇ Δηλιάδος λέγων ταῖς Θεσμοφόροις γίνεσθαι.

Brazier bread. Antidotus mentions this in *The Chorus-Leader* (fr. 3):

He took warm loaves of brazier bread—why wouldn't he?—
unrolled them, and dipped them in grape-must.

Also Crobylus in *The Man Who Tried To Hang Himself* (fr. 2):

and after taking a tray
of brazier bread made of sifted flour.

Lynceus of Samos in his *Letter to Diagoras* (fr. 14 Dalby), in the course of comparing the food produced in Athens to that in Rhodes, says: Moreover, since the bread sold in the market in their country is magnificent, they serve it in enormous quantities at the beginning of the meal and the middle. But once the guests are full and refuse it, they bring in next, as a delicious bit of fun, what is called "anointed brazier bread." This is made so soft and sweet, and goes so well with the grape-must it is dipped into, that something amazing happens, quite against one's will; for just as it frequently happens that a drunk becomes sober again, so in a similar way anyone who eats this enjoys it so much that he grows hungry again.

Ataburitēs. Sopater in *The Girl from Cnidus* (fr. 9):

There was jaw-filling *ataburitēs* bread.

Achaïnai. Semus mentions this bread in Book VIII of his *History of Delos* (*FGrH* 396 F 14) and says that it is pro-

---

[17] Demeter (one of whose epithets was Achaia) and her daughter, Persephone/Pherrephatta.

εἰσὶ δὲ ἄρτοι μεγάλοι, καὶ ἑορτὴ καλεῖται Μεγαλάρτια ἐπιλεγόντων τῶν φερόντων·

ἀχαΐνην στέατος ἔμπλεων τράγον.

Κριβανίτην. τούτου μνημονεύει Ἀριστοφάνης ἐν Γήρᾳ· ποιεῖ δὲ λέγουσαν ἀρτόπωλιν διηρπασμένων αὐτῆς τῶν ἄρτων ὑπὸ τῶν τὸ γῆρας ἀποβαλλόντων·

(Α.) τουτὶ τί ἦν τὸ πρᾶγμα; (Β.) θερμούς, ὦ τέκνον.
(Α.) ἀλλ᾽ ἦ παραφρονεῖς; (Β.) κριβανίτας, ὦ τέκνον.
(Α.) τί κριβανίτας; (Β.) πάνυ δὲ λευκούς, ὦ τέκνον. ‖

110

Ἐγκρυφίαν. τούτου μνημονεύει Νικόστρατος ἐν Ἱεροφάντῃ καὶ ὁ ὀψοδαίδαλος Ἀρχέστρατος, οὗ κατὰ καιρὸν τὸ μαρτύριον παραθήσομαι.

Δίπυρον. Εὔβουλος ἐν Γανυμήδει.

(Α.) διπύρους τε θερμούς. (Β.) οἱ δίπυροι δ᾽ εἰσὶν τίνες;
(Α.) ἄρτοι τρυφῶντες·

Ἀλκαῖος Γανυμήδει.

---

[18] Aristotle *HA* 506ª24, 611ᵇ18 uses this adjective to describe a deer of some sort, and Semos (or Athenaeus) may have misunderstood its significance.

[19] Literally "hidden (bread)," i.e. bread baked within the coals.

18

duced for the Thesmophoroi[17]. The loaves are large, and the festival is called the Megalartia ("Large Loaf Festival"); and those who carry them recite:

an *achaïna*[18] he-goat full of lard.

Baking-shell bread. Aristophanes mentions this in *Old Age* (fr. 129). He represents a female bread-vendor, whose loaves have been stolen by the men who have shed their old age, as saying:

(A.) What's going on? (B.) Warm ones, my child!
(A.) What—are you crazy? (B.) Made in a baking
    shell, my child!
(A.) What do you mean, "in a baking shell"? (B.) Very
    white, my child!

Enkruphia.[19] Nicostratus mentions this in his *Initiatory Priest* (fr. 12), as does the glutton Archestratus (fr. 5.15 Olson–Sens = *SH* 135.15), whose evidence I will cite at the appropriate moment.[20]
Dipuros.[21] Eubulus in *Ganymede* (fr. *17).

(A.) And warm *dipuroi*. (B.) What are *dipuroi*?
(A.) Sumptuous bread.

Thus Alcaeus in *Ganymede* (Alc. Com. fr. 2).[22]

[20] See 3.111f.
[21] Literally "twice fired," i.e. "twice baked"; cf. English "biscuit" and German "Zwieback."
[22] Pollux 7.23 assigns the quotation that precedes this notice to Alcaeus' *Ganymede* rather than to Eubulus' play of the same name, and the passage from Eubulus has apparently fallen out of the text.

Λάγανον. τοῦτο ἐλαφρόν τ᾽ ἐστὶ καὶ ἄτροφον, καὶ μᾶλλον αὐτοῦ ἔτι ἡ ἀπανθρακὶς καλουμένη. μνημονεύει δὲ τοῦ μὲν Ἀριστοφάνης ἐν Ἐκκλησιαζούσαις φάσκων·[2]

λάγανα πέττεται,

b τῆς δ᾽ ἀπανθρακίδος | Διοκλῆς ὁ Καρύστιος ἐν πρώτῳ Ὑγιεινῶν οὑτωσὶ λέγων· ἡ δ᾽ ἀπανθρακίς ἐστι τῶν λαγάνων ἀπαλωτέρα. ἔοικε δὲ καὶ οὗτος ἐπ᾽ ἀνθράκων γίνεσθαι, ὥσπερ καὶ ὁ παρ᾽ Ἀττικοῖς ἐγκρυφίας· ὃν καὶ Ἀλεξανδρεῖς τῷ Κρόνῳ ἀφιεροῦντες προτιθέασιν ἐσθίειν τῷ βουλομένῳ ἐν τῷ τοῦ Κρόνου ἱερῷ. Ἐπίχαρμος δ᾽ ἐν Ἥβης Γάμῳ κἂν Μούσαις—τοῦτο δὲ τὸ δρᾶμα διασκευή ἐστι τοῦ προκειμένου—ἄρτων ἐκτίθεται γένη κριβανίτην, ὅμωρον, σταιτίτην, ἐγκρίδα, ἀλειφατίτην, ἡμιάρτιον. ὧν καὶ Σώφρων ἐν Γυναικείοις | Μίμοις μνημονεύει λέγων οὕτως· δεῖπνον ταῖς θείαις[3] κριβανίτας καὶ ὁμώρους καὶ ἡμιάρτιον Ἑκάτᾳ. οἶδα δ᾽, ἄνδρες φίλοι, ὅτι Ἀττικοὶ μὲν διὰ τοῦ ρ στοιχείου λέγουσι καὶ κρίβανον καὶ κριβανίτην, Ἡρόδοτος δ᾽ ἐν δευτέρᾳ τῶν Ἱστοριῶν ἔφη· κλιβάνῳ διαφανεῖ. καὶ ὁ Σώφρων δὲ ἔφη· τίς σταιτίτας ἢ κλιβανίτας ἢ ἡμιάρτια πέσσει; ὁ δ᾽ αὐτὸς μνημονεύει καὶ πλακίτα τινὸς ἄρτου ἐν Γυναικείοις· εἰς νύκτα μ᾽ † αἰτιᾷ σὺν ἄρτῳ πλακίτᾳ. καὶ τυρῶντος δ᾽ ἄρτου μνη-

c

---

[2] The traditional text of the play has λαγῶ᾽ ἀναπηγνύασι, πόπανα πέττεται.   [3] θειαῖς Blomfield

Wafer bread. This is light and thin, something even more true of what is called an *apanthrakis*[23]. Aristophanes mentions it in *Assemblywomen* (823), where he says:

Wafer bread is being baked.

Diocles of Carytus mentions the *apanthrakis* in Book I of his *On Matters of Health* (fr. 191 van der Eijk), where he says the following: The *apanthrakis* is more delicate than wafer bread. This type too is probably produced on top of coals, like what Attic authors refer to as an *enkruphia*. The inhabitants of Alexandria offer it to Cronus and put it out in his temple for anyone who wants some to eat. Epicharmus in *The Wedding of Hebe* (fr. 46, unmetrical) and in *Muses*—the latter play is a revised version of the former (*The Wedding of Hebe* test. ii)—lists as types of bread: baking-shell bread, *homōron*,[24] spelt bread, honey-and-oil-cake,[25] oil bread, and half-loaf. Sophron too mentions these in his *Women's Mimes* (fr. 26) and says the following: a dinner for the aunts, baking-shell bread and *homōroi*, and a half-loaf for Hecate. I am aware, my friends, that Attic authors say *kribanos* ("baking shell") and *kribanitēs* ("baking-shell bread") with a *rho*, whereas Herodotus in Book II (92.5) of his *Histories* said: a red-hot *klibanos*. Sophron (fr. 27) also said: Who is baking spelt bread or *klibanitai* or half-loaves? The same author mentions a type of bread called a *plakita* in his *Women's Mimes* (fr. 28): At night she [corrupt] me with *plakita*-bread. Sophron also

---

[23] Literally "off-the-charcoal (bread)." For wafer bread, see also 8.363a.   [24] Perhaps to be identified with what Hsch. o 817 calls *homoura* ("boiled durum wheat, containing honey and sesame seed"); cf. 14.646d with n.

d μονεύει ὁ Σώφρων ἐν | τῇ ἐπιγραφομένῃ Πενθερᾷ
οὕτως· συμβουλεύω τ᾽ ἐμφαγεῖν· ἄρτον γάρ τις τυρῶν-
τα τοῖς παιδίοις ἴαλε. Νίκανδρος δ᾽ ὁ Κολοφώνιος ἐν
ταῖς Γλώσσαις τὸν ἄζυμον ἄρτον καλεῖ δάρατον.
Πλάτων δ᾽ ὁ κωμῳδιοποιὸς ἐν Νυκτὶ Μακρᾷ τοὺς
μεγάλους ἄρτους καὶ ῥυπαροὺς Κιλικίους ὀνομάζει
διὰ τούτων·

> κᾆθ᾽ ἧκεν ἄρτους πριάμενος
> μὴ τῶν καθαρύλλων, ἀλλὰ μεγάλους Κιλικίους.

e ἐν δὲ τῷ Μενελάῳ ἐπιγραφομένῳ ἀγελαίους | τινὰς
ἄρτους καλεῖ. αὐτοπύρου δ᾽ ἄρτου μέμνηται Ἄλεξις ἐν
Κυπρίῳ·

> τὸν δ᾽ αὐτόπυρον ἄρτον ἀρτίως φαγών.

Φρύνιχος δ᾽ ἐν Ποαστρίαις αὐτοπυρίτας αὐτοὺς καλῶν φησιν·

> αὐτοπυρίταισί τ᾽ ἄρτοις καὶ λιπῶσι στεμφύλοις.

ὀρίνδου δ᾽ ἄρτου μέμνηται Σοφοκλῆς ἐν Τριπτολέμῳ
ἤτοι τοῦ ἐξ ὀρύζης γινομένου ἢ ἀπὸ τοῦ ἐν Αἰθιοπίᾳ
f γιγνομένου σπέρματος, ὅ ἐστιν ὅμοιον σησάμῳ. |
κολλάβου δ᾽ ἄρτου Ἀριστοφάνης ἐν Ταγηνισταῖς·

> < . . . > λαμβάνετε κόλλαβον ἕκαστος.

καὶ πάλιν·

---

25 Cf. 14.645e.

mentions cheese-bread in the mime entitled *The Mother-in-Law* (fr. 13), as follows: And I suggest you eat a bit; for someone sent cheese-bread for the children. Nicander of Colophon in his *Glossary* (fr. 184 Schneider) refers to unleavened bread as *daratos*. The comic poet Plato in *The Long Night* (fr. 92) calls large loaves made of dirty wheat Cilicians, in the following verses:

> and then he's come and bought not some
> clean little loaves, but big Cilicians.

In his play entitled *Menelaus* (fr. 78) he refers to certain loaves as *agelaioi*.[26] Alexis mentions whole-wheat (*autopuros*) bread in *The Man from Cyprus* (fr. 126):

> after eating the whole-wheat bread just now.

Phrynichus in *Female Grass-Cutters* (fr. 40) calls them *autopuritai* when he says:

> whole-wheat (*autopuritaisi*) loaves and oily olive
> pomace.

Sophocles in *Triptolemus* (fr. 609) mentions *orindos* bread, which is made either from rice or from the grain that grows in Ethiopia and resembles sesame. Aristophanes mentions wheat rolls in *Frying-Pan Men* (fr. 522):

> Each of you take a wheat roll!

And again (fr. 520.6–8):[27]

[26] Literally "herd (bread), gregarious (bread)"; probably small loaves baked together in a single pan.

[27] Cited at greater length at 3.96c; cf. 9.374f.

ἢ δέλφακος ὀπωρινῆς
ἠτριαίαν φέρετε δεῦρο μετὰ κολλάβων
χλιαρῶν.

γίνονται δ᾽ οἱ ἄρτοι οὗτοι ἐκ νέου πυροῦ, ὡς Φιλύλλιος
ἐν Αὔγῃ παρίστησιν·

αὐτὸς φέρων πάρειμι πυρῶν ἐκγόνους τριμήνων
γαλακτόχρωτας κολλάβους θερμούς.

μακωνίδων δ᾽ ἄρτων μνημονεύει Ἀλκμὰν ἐν τῷ πέμ-
111 πτῳ οὕτως· ‖

κλῖναι μὲν ἑπτὰ καὶ τόσαι τράπεσδαι
μακωνιᾶν ἄρτων ἐπιστεφοίσαι
λίνω τε σασάμω τε κὴν πελίχναις
† πεδεστε † χρυσοκόλλα.

ἐστὶ ⟨δὲ⟩ βρωμάτιον διὰ μέλιτος καὶ λίνου.
Τοῦ δὲ κολλύρας καλουμένου ἄρτου Ἀριστοφάνης
ἐν Εἰρήνῃ·

κολλύραν μεγάλην καὶ κόνδυλον ὄψον ἐπ᾽ αὐτῇ.

καὶ ἐν Ὁλκάσι·

καὶ κολλύραν † τοῖσι περῶσι † διὰ τοὺν
b   Μαραθῶνι τρόπαιον. |

ὁ δὲ ὀβελίας ἄρτος κέκληται ἤτοι ὅτι ὀβολοῦ πι-
πράσκεται, ὡς ἐν τῇ Ἀλεξανδρείᾳ, ἢ ὅτι ἐν ὀβελίσκοις
ὤπτατο. Ἀριστοφάνης Γεωργοῖς·

> Or bring us here the stomach
> of a late-summer pig, along with some hot
> wheat rolls!

This type of bread is produced from recently harvested wheat, as Philyllius demonstrates in *Augē* (fr. 4):

> I'm here in person, bearing the offspring of three-
> month wheat,
> warm wheat rolls the color of milk.

Alcman mentions poppy-seed bread in Book V (*PMG* 19), as follows:

> Seven couches, and an equal number of tables
> covered with poppy-seed bread,
> flax seed, and sesame seed, and in the cups
> [corrupt] *chrusokolla*.

This is a type of food made with honey and flax seed.

Aristophanes refers to the loaf of bread called a *kollura* in *Peace* (123):

> a big *kollura* and a knuckle-sandwich to go with it.

Also in *Merchantships* (fr. 429):

> and a *kollura* [corrupt] on account of the victory
> monument at Marathon.

Obelias-bread got its name either from the fact that it is sold for an obol, as in Alexandria, or because it is baked on small spits (*obeliskoi*). Aristophanes in *Farmers* (fr. 105):

εἶτ' ἄρτον ὀπτῶν τυγχάνει τις ὀβελίαν.

Φερεκράτης Ἐπιλήσμονι·

 † ὦλεν † ὀβελίαν σποδεῖν, ἄρτου δὲ μὴ
 προτιμᾶν.

ἐκαλοῦντο δὲ καὶ ὀβελιαφόροι οἱ ἐν ταῖς πομπαῖς
παραφέροντες αὐτοὺς ἐπὶ τῶν ὤμων. Σωκράτης ἐν
ἕκτῳ Ἐπικλήσεων τὸν ὀβελίαν φησὶν ἄρτον Διόνυσον
εὑρεῖν ἐν ταῖς στρατείαις.

 Ἐτνίτας ἄρτος ὁ προσαγορευόμενος λεκιθίτας, ὥς
c φησιν | Εὐκράτης. πανὸς ἄρτος· Μεσσάπιοι. καὶ τὴν
πλησμονὴν πανίαν καὶ πάνια τὰ πλήσμια· Βλαῖσος
ἐν Μεσοτρίβᾳ καὶ Δεινόλοχος ἐν Τηλέφῳ Ῥίνθων τε
ἐν Ἀμφιτρύωνι. καὶ Ῥωμαῖοι δὲ πᾶνα τὸν ἄρτον καλοῦσι.

 Ναστὸς ἄρτος ζυμίτης καλεῖται μέγας, ὥς φησι
Πολέμαρχος καὶ Ἀρτεμίδωρος, Ἡρακλέων δὲ πλακοῦντος εἶδος. Νικόστρατος δ' ἐν Κλίνῃ·

 ναστὸς τὸ μέγεθος τηλικοῦτος, δέσποτα,
d λευκός· τὸ γὰρ πάχος ὑπερέκυπτε τοῦ κανοῦ. |
 ὀσμὴ δέ, τοὐπίβλημ' ἐπεὶ περιῃρέθη,
 ἄνω 'βάδιζε καὶ μέλιτι μεμιγμένη
 ἀτμίς τις εἰς τὰς ῥῖνας· ἔτι γὰρ θερμὸς ἦν.

κνηστὸς ἄρτος ποιὸς παρὰ Ἴωσι, Ἀρτεμίδωρος ὁ

---

[28] Sc. in the east; cf. 1.33d n.

26

Then someone happens to be baking *obelias*-bread.

Pherecrates in *The Absent-Minded Man* (fr. 61):

> [corrupt] to devour an *obelias*, but to pay no attention
>   to bread.

The men who carried these on their shoulders in their processions were referred to as *obeliaphoroi*. Socrates says in Book VI of his *Appellations* (fr. 15, *FHG* iv.499) that Dionysus discovered bread during his campaigns.[28]

Etnitas[29]-bread is what is generally called legume bread, according to Eucrates (*FHG* iv.407). *Panos* is "bread"; thus the Messapians. And *pania* is "satiety," while the foods that fill one up are *pánia*; thus Blaesus in *Mesotribas* (fr. 1), Deinolochus in *Telephus* (fr. 6), and Rhinthon in *Amphitryon* (fr. 1). The Romans also refer to bread as *pana*.[30]

Nastos is the term for a large loaf of leavened bread, according to Polemarchus and Artemidorus[31]; but Heracleon (p. 6 Berndt) says that it is a type of flatcake. Nicostratus in *The Couch* (fr. 13):

> A *nastos* as large as this, master,
>   and white; for it was so big around that it peeked up
>   out of the sacrificial basket.
> The smell of it, when the cover was removed,
> rose straight to my nostrils, along with a sort of
> steam mixed with honey; because it was still warm.

Knēstos is a type of bread known to the Ionians, according

---

[29] Cognate with *etnos*, "legume soup."
[30] Latin *panis*.

Ἐφέσιός φησιν ἐν Ἰωνικοῖς Ὑπομνήμασι.

Θρόνος ἄρτου ὄνομα. Νεάνθης ὁ Κυζικηνὸς ἐν δευτέρᾳ Ἑλληνικῶν γράφων οὕτως· ὁ δὲ Κόδρος τό-μον ἄρτου τὸν καλούμενον θρόνον λαμβάνει καὶ κρέας καὶ τῷ πρεσβυτάτῳ νέμουσι.

Βάκχυλος δ᾽ ἐστὶν ἄρτος σποδίτης παρ᾽ Ἠλείοις
e καλούμενος, ὡς | Νίκανδρος ἐν δευτέρῳ Γλωσσῶν ἱστορεῖ. μνημονεύει δ᾽ αὐτοῦ καὶ Δίφιλος ἐν Διαμαρ-τανούσῃ οὕτως·

ἄρτους σποδίτας κρησερίτας περιφέρειν.

ἄρτου δ᾽ εἶδός ἐστι καὶ ὁ ἀποπυρίας καλούμενος, ἐπ᾽ ἀνθράκων δ᾽ ὀπτᾶται. καλεῖται δ᾽ οὗτος ὑπό τινων ζυμίτης. Κρατῖνος Μαλθακοῖς· † πρῶτον ἀποπυρίαν ἔχω ζυμηταμιαδου πλεους κνεφαλλον †.

Ἀρχέστρατος δ᾽ ἐν τῇ Γαστρονομίᾳ περὶ ἀλφίτων
f καὶ ἄρτων οὕτως ἐκτίθεται· |

πρῶτα μὲν οὖν δώρων μεμνήσομαι ἠυκόμοιο
Δήμητρος, φίλε Μόσχε· σὺ δ᾽ ἐν φρεσὶ βάλλεο
σῇσιν.
ἔστι γὰρ οὖν τὰ κράτιστα λαβεῖν βέλτιστά τε
πάντων,
εὐκάρπου κριθῆς καθαρῶς ἠσσημένα πάντα,
ἐν Λέσβῳ, κλεινῆς Ἐρέσου περικύμονι μαστῷ,
112   λευκότερ᾽ αἰθερίης χιόνος· θεοὶ εἴπερ ἔδουσιν ‖

---

31 See 1.5b n.   32 Literally "seat, chair."
33 A legendary king of Athens.

to Artemidorus of Ephesus in his *Notes on Ionia* (*FGrH* 438 F 1).

Thronos[32] is the name of a type of bread; thus Neanthes of Cyzicus, writing as follows in Book II of the *History of Greece* (*FGrH* 84 F 1): Codrus[33] takes the slice of bread referred to as the *thronos* and some meat, and they treat it as the oldest man's portion.

Bakchulos is the term the Eleans use for bread baked in the ashes, according to Nicander in Book II of the *Glossary* (fr. 121 Schneider). Diphilus too mentions it in *The Woman Who Was Quite Mistaken* (fr. 25), as follows:

> to carry around loaves of ash bread made of sifted
> flour.

The so-called *apopurias*[34] is also a type of bread, which is baked on top of the coals. Some authorities refer to this as *zumitēs* ("yeast bread"). Cratinus in *Soft Men* (fr. 106, corrupt and unmetrical): first of all I have an *apopuria* [obscure].

Archestratus in his *Gastronomy* (fr. 5 Olson–Sens = *SH* 135) expounds on barley-meal and baked bread as follows:

> First of all, then, my dear Moschus, I will mention
>   the gifts of fair-haired
> Demeter; you must internalize all of this.
> The best one can get and the finest of all,
> all sifted clean from highly productive barley,
> are in Lesbos, on the wave-girt breast where famous
>   Eresus is located,
> whiter than heavenly snow. If the gods eat

[34] Literally "from the fire (bread)."

29

ATHENAEUS

ἄλφιτ᾽, ἐκεῖθεν ἰὼν Ἑρμῆς αὐτοῖς ἀγοράζει.
ἐστὶ δὲ κἂν Θήβαις ταῖς ἑπταπύλοις ἐπιεικῆ
κἂν Θάσῳ ἔν τ᾽ ἄλλαις πόλεσίν τισιν, ἀλλὰ
    γίγαρτα
φαίνονται πρὸς ἐκεῖνα· σαφεῖ τάδ᾽ ἐπίστασο
    δόξῃ.
στρογγυλοδίνητος δὲ τετριμμένος εὖ κατὰ χεῖρα
κόλλιξ Θεσσαλικός σοι ὑπαρχέτω, ὃν καλέουσι |
κεῖνοι κριμνίτην, οἱ δ᾽ ἄλλοι χόνδρινον ἄρτον.
εἶτα τὸν ἐν Τεγέαις σεμιδάλεος υἱὸν ἐπαινῶ
ἐγκρυφίην. τὸν δ᾽ εἰς ἀγορὴν ποιεύμενον ἄρτον
αἱ κλεειναὶ παρέχουσι βροτοῖς κάλλιστον Ἀθῆναι.
ἐν δὲ φερεσταφύλοις Ἐρυθραῖς ἐκ κλιβάνου
    ἐλθὼν
λευκὸς ἁβραῖς θάλλων ὥραις τέρψει παρὰ
    δεῖπνον.

b

ταῦτ᾽ εἰπὼν ὁ τένθης Ἀρχέστρατος καὶ τὸν τῶν ἄρτων
| ποιητὴν ἔχειν συμβουλεύει Φοίνικα ἢ Λυδόν· ἠγνόει
γὰρ τοὺς ἀπὸ τῆς Καππαδοκίας ἀρτοποιοὺς ἀρίστους
ὄντας. λέγει δ᾽ οὕτως·

c

ἔστω δ᾽ ἤ σοι ἀνὴρ Φοῖνιξ ἢ Λυδὸς ἐν οἴκῳ,
ὅστις ἐπιστήμων ἔσται σίτοιο κατ᾽ ἦμαρ
παντοίας ἰδέας τεύχειν, ὡς ἂν σὺ κελεύῃς.

---

[35] Cf. 3.113b.

30

barley groats, it is from there that Hermes goes and
  buys them for them.
They are also fairly good in seven-gated Thebes
and in Thasos and some other cities, although these
  resemble
grape-stones compared with the Lesbian sort. You
  should regard this as absolutely certain.
Get yourself a Thessalian loaf that has been kneaded
  until it is round
and thoroughly worked by hand; the Thessalians
call this coarse-meal bread, but others call it groat
  bread.
Next after that I praise the Tegean son of Wheat
  Flour,
Ash Cake. But as for bread made for sale in the
  marketplace,
famous Athens supplies mortals with the best.
And in Erythrae with its grape-clusters a white loaf
  that has come
from the oven fully risen, just at the moment it is
  ready to be eaten, will give pleasure at dinner.

After making these remarks, the glutton Archestratus (fr. 6
Olson–Sens = *SH* 136) also suggests that one have a Phoenician or Lydian as one's breadmaker, because he was unaware that Cappadocian breadmakers are the best.[35] He
puts it thus:

Be sure to have in your house either a Phoenician or
  a Lydian,
who will know about cereal products, and can make
  every sort of them
on a daily basis in accord with your orders.

31

Τῶν δ' Ἀττικῶν ἄρτων ὡς διαφόρων μνημονεύει
καὶ Ἀντιφάνης ἐν Ὀμφάλῃ οὕτως·

πῶς γὰρ ἄν τις εὐγενὴς γεγὼς
δύναιτ' ἂν ἐξελθεῖν ποτ' ἐκ τῆσδε στέγης;
ὁρῶν μὲν ἄρτους λευκοσωμάτους ἱπνὸν
d καταμπέχοντας ἐν πυκναῖς διεξόδοις, |
ὁρῶν δὲ μορφὴν κριβάνοις ἠλλαγμένους,
μίμημα χειρὸς Ἀττικῆς, οὓς δημόταις
Θεαρίων ἔδειξεν.

οὗτός ἐστι Θεαρίων ὁ ἀρτοποιὸς οὗ μνημονεύει Πλάτων ἐν Γοργίᾳ συγκαταλέγων αὐτῷ καὶ Μίθαικον
οὕτως γράφων· οἵτινες ἀγαθοὶ γεγόνασιν ἢ εἰσὶ σωμάτων θεραπευταὶ ἔλεγές μοι πάνυ σπουδάζων, Θεα-
e ρίων ὁ ἀρτοκόπος καὶ Μίθαικος | ὁ τὴν ὀψοποιίαν
συγγεγραφὼς τὴν Σικελικὴν καὶ Σάραμβος ὁ κάπη-
λος, ὅτι οὗτοι θαυμάσιοι γεγόνασι σωμάτων θεραπευ-
ταί, ὁ μὲν ἄρτους θαυμαστοὺς παρασκευάζων, ὁ δὲ
ὄψον, ὁ δὲ οἶνον. καὶ Ἀριστοφάνης ἐν Γηρυτάδῃ καὶ
Αἰολοσίκωνι διὰ τούτων·

ἥκω Θεαρίωνος ἀρτοπώλιον
λιπών, ἵν' ἐστὶ κριβάνων ἑδώλια.

Κυπρίων δὲ ἄρτων μνημονεύει Εὔβουλος ὡς διαφόρων
f ἐν Ὀρθάννῃ διὰ τούτων· |

---

36 PAA 501987.

Antiphanes refers to Attic bread as particularly good in *Omphalē* (fr. 174), as follows:

> For how could any decent
> person ever leave this house,
> when he sees these white-bodied loaves filling
> the kitchen and moving constantly in and out of it,
> and when he sees their form changed by the baking-
>   shells,
> a creation of an Attic hand, put on display
> for his demesmen by Thearion?

This Thearion[36] is the breadmaker Plato mentions in his *Gorgias* (518b), where he includes him in a list along with Mithaecus and writes as follows: As for those who have been or are now good caretakers of our bodies, you told me in all seriousness: "Thearion the baker, Mithaecus the author of the Sicilian cookbook,[37] and Sarambus the bartender, because they have been marvellous caretakers of our bodies, the first by providing amazing bread, the second fine food, and the third wine." Also Aristophanes in *Gerytades* (fr. 177) and in *Aeolosicon* (fr. 1), as follows:

> I've come from Thearion's bakery,
> where the abodes of the baking-shells are.

Eubulus refers to Cyprian bread as particularly good in *Orthannēs* (fr. 77), as follows:

[37] A new Sicilian and South Italian style of cooking, which relied on the heavy use of spices and cheese, became popular in Athens around the end of the 5th century.

δεινὸν μὲν ἰδόντα παριππεῦσαι
Κυπρίους ἄρτους· μαγνῆτις γὰρ
λίθος ὡς ἕλκει τοὺς πεινῶντας.

τῶν δὲ κολλικίων ἄρτων—οἱ αὐτοὶ δ᾽ εἰσὶ τοῖς κολ-
λάβοις—Ἔφιππος ἐν Ἀρτέμιδι μνημονεύει οὕτως·

παρ᾽ Ἀλεξάνδρου δ᾽ ἐκ Θετταλίας
κολλικοφάγου κρίβανος ἄρτων.

Ἀριστοφάνης δ᾽ ἐν Ἀχαρνεῦσιν·

113   ὦ χαῖρε, κολλικοφάγε Βοιωτίδιον. ‖

Τούτων οὕτω λεχθέντων ἔφη τις τῶν παρόντων
γραμματικῶν, Ἀρριανὸς ὄνομα· ταῦτα σιτία Κρονικά
ἐστιν, ὦ ἑταῖροι. ἡμεῖς γὰρ

οὔτ᾽ ἀλφίτοισι χαίρομεν·
πλήρης γὰρ ἄρτων ἡ πόλις·

οὔτε τῷ τῶν ἄρτων τούτων καταλόγῳ. ἐπεὶ δὲ καὶ ἄλλῳ
Χρυσίππου τοῦ Τυανέως συγγράμματι ἐνέτυχον ἐπιγραφομένῳ Ἀρτοποιικῷ καὶ πεῖραν ἔσχον τῶν αὐτόθι
ὀνομασθέντων παρὰ πολλοῖς τῶν φίλων, ἔρχομαι καὶ
αὐτὸς λέξων τι περὶ ἄρτων. ὁ ἀρτοπτίκιος ἄρτος κα-
b   λούμενος κλιβανικίου καὶ φουρνακίου | διαφέρει. ἐὰν
δ᾽ ἐκ σκληρᾶς ζύμης ἐργάζῃ αὐτόν, ἔσται καὶ λαμπρὸς καὶ εὔβρωτος πρὸς ξηροφαγίαν· εἰ δ᾽ ἐξ ἀνειμέ-

---

[38] "Rolls"; see 3.110f.

34

It's difficult to see Cyprian bread
and ride on past; for it attracts
hungry people like a magnet.

Ephippus mentions the type of bread known as *kollikia*—
these are the same as *kollaboi*[38]—in *Artemis* (fr. 1), as follows:

from Alexander,[39] from *kollix*-eating
Thessaly, a baking shell full of bread.

Aristophanes in *Acharnians* (872):

Greetings, little *kollix*-eating Boeotian!

After these remarks were complete, one of the grammarians present, whose name was Arrian, said: These
breadstuffs are very out of date[40], gentlemen; for we
(adesp. com. fr. *106)

neither take any pleasure in barley groats—
for the city is full of bread—

nor in this catalogue of these types of bread. But because I
encountered another treatise by Chrysippus of Tyana entitled *Breadmaking*, and thus developed some familiarity
with the items mentioned here by a number of our friends,
I myself as well am come to say something about bread.
The so-called *artoptikios*-bread is better than the type produced in baking shells or ovens. If you make it with dry
yeast, it will be light-colored and good to eat dry,[41] whereas

---

[39] Alexander II, king of Macedon 370/69–367 BCE, who inter-
vened briefly—and unsuccessfully—in Thessaly in 369.

[40] Literally "as old as Cronus."

[41] I.e. with no broth or sauce.

νης, ἔσται μὲν ἐλαφρός, οὐ λαμπρὸς δέ. κλιβανίκιος
δὲ καὶ φουρνάκιος χαίρουσιν ἁπαλωτέρᾳ τῇ ζύμῃ.
παρὰ δὲ τοῖς Ἕλλησι καλεῖταί τις ἄρτος ἁπαλὸς
ἀρτυόμενος γάλακτι ὀλίγῳ καὶ ἐλαίῳ καὶ ἁλσὶν ἀρκε-
τοῖς. δεῖ δὲ τὴν ματερίαν ἀνειμένην ποιεῖν. οὗτος δὲ ὁ
ἄρτος λέγεται Καππαδόκιος, ἐπειδὴ ἐν Καππαδοκίᾳ
κατὰ τὸ πλεῖστον ἁπαλὸς ἄρτος γίνεται. τὸν δὲ τοι-
c οῦτον | ἄρτον οἱ Σύροι λαχμὰν προσαγορεύουσι, καί
ἐστιν οὗτος ἐν Συρίᾳ χρηστότατος γινόμενος διὰ τὸ
θερμότατος τρώγεσθαι καί ἐστιν < . . . > ἄνθει παραπλήσιος. ὁ δὲ βωλητῖνος καλούμενος ἄρτος πλάττεται
μὲν ὡς βωλήτης, καὶ ἀλείφεται ἡ μάκτρα ὑποπασσο-
μένης μήκωνος, ἐφ᾽ ᾗ ἐπιτίθεται ἡ ματερία, καὶ ἐν τῷ
ζυμοῦσθαι οὐ κολλᾶται τῇ καρδόπῳ. ἐπειδὰν δ᾽ ἐμ-
βληθῇ εἰς τὸν φοῦρνον, ὑποπάσσεται τῷ κεράμῳ
χόνδρος τις καὶ τότ᾽ ἐπιτίθεται ὁ ἄρτος καὶ ἕλκει
d χρῶμα κάλλιστον, ὅμοιον | τῷ φουμώσῳ τυρῷ. ὁ δὲ
στρεπτίκιος ἄρτος συναναλαμβάνεται γάλακτι ὀλίγῳ,
καὶ προσβάλλεται πέπερι καὶ ἔλαιον ὀλίγον· εἰ δὲ μή,
στέαρ. εἰς δὲ τὸ καλούμενον ἀρτολάγανον ἐμβάλλεται
οἰνάριον ὀλίγον καὶ πέπερι γάλα τε καὶ ἔλαιον ὀλίγον
ἢ στέαρ. εἰς δὲ τὰ καπύρια τὰ καλούμενα τράκτα
μίξεις ὥσπερ καὶ εἰς ἄρτον.

Ταῦτ᾽ ἐκθεμένου τἀριστάρχεια δόγματα τοῦ Ῥωμαίων μεγαλοσοφιστοῦ ὁ Κύνουλκος ἔφη· Δάματερ
σοφίας· οὐκ ἐτὸς ἄρα ψαμμακοσίους ἔχει μαθητὰς ὁ

---

42 A Latin loan-word, = *materia*.

if you make it with dissolved yeast, it will rise more but will not be light-colored. Baking-shell bread and oven bread do well with softer yeast. The Greeks use the term "soft" for a type of bread prepared with a little milk, oil, and just enough salt; you need to make the dough[42] soft and spongy. This type of bread is called Cappadocian, since soft bread is for the most part produced in Cappadocia. The Syrians refer to this type of bread as *lachma*[43]; it is particularly good when produced in Syria, since it is eaten very warm and is . . . resembling a flower. The so-called *bolētinus* bread is moulded into the shape of a boletus mushroom. The kneading-trough is greased, poppy-seed is sprinkled on the bottom, and the dough is put into it and does not stick to the trough while it rises. When it is put into the oven, some roughly milled grain is sprinkled on the bottom of the pan, and the bread is then put into it and acquires a fine color, like that of smoked[44] cheese. Twisted bread contains a little milk, and some pepper and a bit of oil (or else lard) is added to it. A small quantity of wine, pepper, and milk, and a little oil is added to what is called *artolaganon* ("bread-wafer"). Mix up the same ingredients for *kapuria* (also called *tracta*[45]) as for bread.

After this great Roman scholar expounded these Aristarchean[46] opinions, Cynulcus said: By Demeter, what learning![47] There is a reason why the amazing Blepsias[48]

---

[43] An Aramaic word.   [44] A Latin loan-word, = *fumosus*.

[45] A Latin word (cognate with *traho*) for a long piece of dough used to produce pastry.   [46] A reference to the immensely learned Aristarchus of Samothrace, head of the Library in Alexandria *c*.153–144 BCE.   [47] Probably a poetic fragment, given the unexpected use of Doric *Damater*.

e θαυμάσιος | Βλεψίας καὶ πλοῦτον ἀπηνέγκατο τοσοῦ-
τον ἐκ τῆς καλῆς ταύτης σοφίας ὑπὲρ Γοργίαν καὶ
Πρωταγόραν. ὅθεν ὀκνῶ μὰ τὰς θεὰς εἰπεῖν πότερον
αὐτὸς οὐ βλέπει ἢ οἱ ἑαυτοὺς μαθητὰς αὐτῷ παρα-
διδόντες πάντες ἕνα ἔχουσιν ὀφθαλμόν, ὡς μόλις διὰ
τὸ πλῆθος ὁρᾶν. μακαρίους οὖν αὐτούς, μᾶλλον δὲ
μακαρίτας εἶναί φημι τοιαύτας δείξεις τῶν διδασκά-
λων ποιουμένων. πρὸς ὃν ὁ Μάγνος φιλοτράπεζος ὢν
καὶ τὸν γραμματικὸν τοῦτον ὑπερεπαινῶν διὰ τὴν
f ἐκτένειαν ἔφη· |

οὗτοι ἀνιπτόποδες χαμαιευνάδες ἀερίοικοι,

κατὰ τὸν κωμικὸν Εὔβουλον,

ἀνόσιοι λάρυγγες,
ἀλλοτρίων κτεάνων παραδειπνίδες,

οὐ χὡ προπάτωρ ὑμῶν Διογένης πλακοῦντά ποτε
ἐσθίων ἐν δείπνῳ λάβρως πρὸς τὸν πυνθανόμενον
ἔλεγεν ἄρτον ἐσθίειν καλῶς πεποιημένον; ὑμεῖς δ᾿

ὦ λοπαδάγχαι,

κατὰ τὸν αὐτὸν ποιητὴν Εὔβουλον,

---

48 A mocking nickname (cognate with *blepō*, "see"; cf. below)
used by Cynulcus to refer to Arrian.
49 Two of the most famous late 5th-/early 4th-century sophists.
50 *ou blepei*, punning on Blepsias (above).
51 The idea is apparently that Arrian's disciples resemble the

has countless disciples and has made so much money from this marvellous learning of his, outdoing Gorgias and Protagoras.[49] I am therefore reluctant, by the goddesses, to say whether he himself is blind[50], or whether those who surrender themselves to him as disciples all have only one eye, as a result of which they can barely see, because there are so many of them.[51] I accordingly refer to them as "blessed"—or rather as "of blessed memory"—if their teachers put on displays like this. In response, Magnus, who was a great lover of dinner parties and liked to heap lavish praise on this grammarian[52] because of his eagerness for his subject, said:

> You of the unwashed feet, who make your beds on
>   the ground and whose roof is the open sky,

as the comic poet Eubulus (fr. 137, encompassing the lines that follow as well) puts it,

> unholy gullets,
> who dine on other people's goods—

didn't your forefather Diogenes[53] once, when he was greedily eating a cake at a dinner party, say to a man who questioned him that he was eating nicely-made bread? But you,

> O snatchers of casserole dishes,

> as the same poet, Eubulus, puts it,

mythical Graeae, all three of whom shared a single eye (as well as a single tooth).

[52] Arrian; the attack that follows is directed at Cynulcus.

[53] Diogenes of Sinope, the original Cynic; cf. 2.49a with n.

λευκῶν ὑπογαστριδίων,

ἑτέροις οὐ παραχωροῦντες φθέγγεσθε καὶ τὰς ἡσυ-
114 χίας οὐκ ἄγετε, ἕως ‖ ἄν τις ὑμῖν ὡς κυνιδίοις ἄρτων ἢ
ὀστέων προσρίψῃ. πόθεν ὑμῖν εἰδέναι ὅτι καὶ κύβοι,
οὐχ οὓς ἀεὶ μεταχειρίζεσθε, ἄρτοι εἰσὶ τετράγωνοι,
ἡδυσμένοι ἀννήθῳ καὶ τυρῷ καὶ ἐλαίῳ, ὥς φησιν
Ἡρακλείδης ἐν Ὀψαρτυτικῷ; παρεῖδε δὲ τοῦτον ὁ
Βλεψίας, ὥσπερ καὶ τὸν θάργηλον, ὅν τινες καλοῦσι
θαλύσιον—Κράτης δ' ἐν δευτέρῳ Ἀττικῆς Διαλέκτου
θάργηλον καλεῖσθαι τὸν ἐκ τῆς συγκομιδῆς πρῶτον
γινόμενον ἄρτον—καὶ τὸν σησαμίτην. οὐχ ἑώρακε δὲ
οὐδὲ τὸν ἀνάστατον καλούμενον, ὃς ταῖς ἀρρηφόροις
b γίνεται. ἐστὶ δὲ καὶ ὁ | πυραμοῦς ἄρτος διὰ σησάμων
πεττόμενος καὶ τάχα ὁ αὐτὸς τῷ σησαμίτῃ ὤν. μνημονεύει δὲ πάντων τούτων Τρύφων ἐν πρώτῳ Φυτικῶν,
καθάπερ καὶ τῶν θιαγόνων ὀνομαζομένων· οὗτοι δ'
εἰσὶν ἄρτοι θεοῖς πεττόμενοι ἐν Αἰτωλίᾳ. δράμικες δὲ
καὶ ἀράξεις παρ' Ἀθαμᾶσιν ἄρτοι τινὲς οὕτως καλοῦνται. καὶ οἱ γλωσσογράφοι δὲ ἄρτων ὀνόματα καταλέ-
γουσι. Σέλευκος μὲν δράμιν ὑπὸ Μακεδόνων οὕτως
καλούμενον, δάρατον δ' ὑπὸ Θεσσαλῶν· ἐνίταν δέ
c φησι ἄρτον εἶναι λεκιθίτην, ἐρικίτας δὲ καλεῖσθαι |
τὸν ἐξ ἐρηριγμένου καὶ ἀσήστου πυροῦ γιγνόμενον
καὶ χονδρώδους. Ἀμερίας δὲ καλεῖ ξηροπυρίταν τὸν
αὐτόπυρον ἄρτον· ὁμοίως δὲ καὶ Τιμαχίδας. Νίκαν-

---

54 Another allusion to the root-meaning of the name Blepsias
(see 3.113e n.), like "he has failed to note" below.

full of white belly-steaks,

you talk without letting anyone else get a word in; you are
not quiet until you are thrown some bread or bones, like
puppies. How could you be aware that dice (not the type
you always have in your hands!) are square loaves of bread
seasoned with anise, cheese, and oil, according to Heracleides in the *Art of Cooking*? Blepsias overlooked[54] this
type, as well as the *thargēlos*, which some authorities refer
to as *thalusios*—Crates in Book II of the *Attic Dialect*
(*FGrH* 362 F 6 = fr. 106 Broggiato) reports that the first
bread produced after the harvest is called *thargēlos*—and
sesame bread. He has also failed to note the so-called
anastatos bread, which is produced for the *arrhēphoroi*[55].
There is *puramous* bread too, which is baked with sesame seeds and is perhaps the same as sesame bread.
Tryphon mentions all of these in Book I of *On Plants* (fr.
116 Velsen), as well as what are called *thiagonoi*; this is a
type of bread baked for the gods in Aetolia.[56] *Dramikes*
and *araxeis* are the Athamanians' names for certain varieties of bread. The glossographers also list names of breads.
Seleucus (fr. 50 Müller) mentions what the Macedonians call *dramis* but the Thessalians refer to as *daratos*[57],
and says that *etnitas* is bread made of legumes, and that
erikitas is the term for bread made of coarse-ground,
rough, unsifted wheat. Amerias (p. 12 Hoffmann) refers to
whole-wheat bread as *xēropuritē* ("dry-wheat"), as does
Timachidas (fr. 29 Blinkenberg). Nicander (fr. 136 Schnei-

---

[55] A group of Athenian girls who lived on the Acropolis for a
year and carried out various sacred rites.
[56] See below, where this bit of information is attributed to
Nicander.   [57] Cf. 3.110d.

ATHENAEUS

δρος δὲ θιαγόνας φησὶν ἄρτους ὑπ' Αἰτωλῶν καλεῖσθαι τοὺς τοῖς θεοῖς γινομένους. Αἰγύπτιοι δὲ τὸν ὑποξίζοντ' ἄρτον κυλλᾶστιν καλοῦσιν. μνημονεύει δ' αὐτοῦ Ἀριστοφάνης Δαναῖσι·

καὶ τὸν κυλλᾶστιν φθέγγου καὶ τὸν Πετόσιριν.

μνημονεύουσιν αὐτοῦ καὶ Ἑκαταῖος καὶ Ἡρόδοτος καὶ Φανόδημος ἐν ἑβδόμῃ Ἀτθίδος. ὁ δὲ Θυατειρηνὸς
d Νίκανδρος | τὸν ἐκ τῆς κριθῆς ἄρτον γινόμενον ὑπὸ τῶν Αἰγυπτίων κυλλᾶστίν φησι καλεῖσθαι. τοὺς δὲ ῥυπαροὺς ἄρτους φαιοὺς ὠνόμασεν Ἄλεξις ἐν Κυπρίῳ οὕτως·

(Α.) ἔπειτα πῶς ἦλθες; (Β.) μόλις
ὀπτωμένους κατέλαβον. (Α.) ἐξόλοι'. ἀτὰρ
πόσους φέρεις; (Β.) ἑκκαίδεκ'. (Α.) οἶσε δεῦρο
⟨ . . . ⟩
(Β.) λευκοὺς μὲν ὀκτώ, τῶν δὲ φαιῶν τοὺς ἴσους.

βλῆμα δέ φησι καλεῖσθαι τὸν ἐντεθρυμμένον ἄρτον καὶ θερμὸν Σέλευκος. Φιλήμων δ' ἐν πρώτῳ Παντοδα-
e πῶν Χρηστηρίων πύρνον φησὶ καλεῖσθαι | τὸν ἐκ πυρῶν ἀσήστων γινόμενον ἄρτον καὶ πάντα ἐν ἑαυτῷ ἔχοντα, βλωμιαίους τε ἄρτους ὀνομάζεσθαι λέγει τοὺς ἔχοντας ἐντομάς, οὓς Ῥωμαῖοι κοδράτους λέγουσι, βραττίμην τε καλεῖσθαι τὸν πιτυρίτην ἄρτον, ὃν εὐκο-

---

[58] A pseudo-historical Egyptian priest, who along with King

42

der) claims that the loaves of bread produced for the gods are called *thiagones* by the Aetolians. The Egyptians refer to their sour bread as *kullastis*. Aristophanes mentions it in *Danaids* (fr. 267):

Use the words *kullastis* and *Petosiris*[58]!

Hecataeus (*FGrH* 1 F 322), Herodotus (2.77.4), and Phanodemus in Book VII of his *History of Attica* (*FGrH* 325 F 7) also mention it. Nicander of Thyateira (*FGrH* 343 F 10) says that the Egyptians call barley bread *kullastis*. Alexis uses the term "gray" for dirty loaves of bread[59] in *The Man from Cyprus* (fr. 125), as follows:

      (A.) So how did your errand go? (B.) I got them just as they were being baked. (A.) Damn you! But how many have you brought? (B.) 16. (A.) Bring
        them here . . .
  (B.) Eight white loaves, and an equal number of the
      gray ones.

Seleucus (fr. 40 Müller) says that warm bread crumbled into liquid is called *blēma*. Philemon says in Book I of *A Complete List of Sacrificial Offerings* that *purnos* is the name for bread that is made from unsifted flour and contains all parts of the grain; he also reports that incised loaves, which the Romans refer to as *kodratoi*[60], are called *blōmiaioi*, and that *brammitē* is the term for bran bread,

Nechepso eventually came to be identified as authors of a late Hellenistic astrological work.

  [59] I.e. loaves made from flour that was particularly full of bran and various impurities; cf. Pl. Com. fr. 92, quoted at 3.110d.

  [60] Latin *quadrati*.

νον[4] ὀνομάζουσιν Ἀμερίας καὶ Τιμαχίδας. Φιλητᾶς δ᾽
ἐν τοῖς Ἀτάκτοις σποδέα[5] καλεῖσθαί τινα ἄρτον, ὃν
ὑπὸ τῶν συγγενῶν μόνον καταναλίσκεσθαι.

Καὶ μάζας δ᾽ ἔστιν εὑρεῖν ἀναγεγραμμένας παρά
τε τῷ Τρύφωνι καὶ παρ᾽ ἄλλοις πλείοσιν. παρ᾽ Ἀθη-
f ναίοις μὲν φύστην τὴν μὴ | ἄγαν τετριμμένην, ἔτι δὲ
καρδαμάλην καὶ βήρηκα καὶ τολύπας καὶ Ἀχίλλειον·
καὶ ἴσως αὕτη ἐστὶν ἡ ἐξ Ἀχιλλείων κριθῶν γινομένη·
θριδακίνας τε καὶ οἰνοῦτταν καὶ μελιτοῦτταν καὶ κρί-
νον ‹ . . . › καλούμενον καὶ σχῆμά τι χορικῆς
ὀρχήσεως παρ᾽ Ἀπολλοφάνει ἐν Δαλίδι. αἱ δὲ παρ᾽
Ἀλκμᾶνι θριδακίσκαι λεγόμεναι αἱ αὐταί εἰσι ταῖς
Ἀττικαῖς θριδακίναις. λέγει δὲ οὕτως ὁ Ἀλκμάν·

‹ . . . › θριδακίσκας τε καὶ κριβανωτώς.

115 Σωσίβιος δ᾽ ἐν τρίτῳ Περὶ Ἀλκμᾶνος ‖ κρίβανά φησι
λέγεσθαι πλακοῦντάς τινας τῷ σχήματι μαστοειδεῖς.
ὑγίεια δὲ καλεῖται ἡ διδομένη ἐν ταῖς θυσίαις μᾶζα
ἵνα ἀπογεύσωνται. καὶ Ἡσίοδος δὲ μᾶζάν τιν᾽ ἀμολ-
γαίαν καλεῖ·

μᾶζά τ᾽ ἀμολγαίη γάλα τ᾽ αἰγῶν σβεννυμενάων,

---

[4] εὔκονον τευκονον A
[5] σποδέα Schweighäuser: σπολέα A: σπολεύς CE

---

[61] Perhaps *teukonos*; the manuscripts have both forms of the
word, and one or the other must be expelled.

which Amerias (p. 10 Hoffmann) and Timachidas (fr. 26 Blinkenberg) call *eukonos*[61]. Philetas in his *Miscellany* (fr. 11 Dettori) reports that *spodeus* is the name of a type of bread consumed only by one's relatives.

Barley-cakes[62] can also be found in the records produced by Tryphon (fr. 118 Velsen) and many others. The Athenians have the *phustē*,[63] which is not worked very hard, as well as pepper-cress cake, *bērēx*, ball-of-wool cake,[64] the Achilleion—this is perhaps the type made with Achilleian barley[65]—lettuce cake, wine cake, honey cake, lily cake . . . the same term is used for a choral dance-step by Apollophanes in *Dalis* (fr. 2). What Alcman calls *thridakiskai* are the same as Attic lettuce cakes (*thridakinai*). Alcman (*PMG* 94) says the following:

> lettuce cakes (*thridakiskai*) and baking-shell bread
> (*kribanōtoi*).

Sosibius in Book III of *On Alcman* (*FGrH* 595 F 6b) says that *kribana* are a type of cake shaped like a breast.[66] The barley-cake of which everyone at sacrifices is offered a taste is called a "health." Hesiod (*Op.* 590) too refers to a type of barley-cake as an *amolgaia*:

> and an *amolgaiē* barley-cake and milk from she-goats
> running dry.

[62] Unlike wheat bread, barley-cakes were not baked but merely kneaded into shape.   [63] Cf. 4.137e, 147c.

[64] For the *bērēx* and the ball-of-wool cake, cf. 4.140a (where the former is referred to in the Doric form *barax*).

[65] A particularly fine variety of barley.

[66] See 14.646a (where the word is given in a slightly different form) for a more complete version of Sosibius' note.

τὴν ποιμενικὴν λέγων καὶ ἀκμαίαν· ἀμολγὸς γὰρ τὸ
ἀκμαιότατον. παραιτητέον δὲ καταλέγειν—οὐδὲ γὰρ
οὕτως εὐτυχῶς μνήμης ἔχω—ἃ ἐξέθετο πόπανα καὶ
b   πέμματα Ἀριστομένης ὁ Ἀθηναῖος ἐν τρίτῳ | τῶν
Πρὸς τὰς Ἱερουργίας. ἔγνωμεν δὲ καὶ ἡμεῖς τὸν ἄνδρα
τοῦτον νεώτεροι πρεσβύτερον. ὑποκριτὴς δὲ ἦν ἀρχαίας κωμῳδίας ἀπελεύθερος τοῦ μουσικωτάτου βασιλέως Ἀδριανοῦ, καλούμενος ὑπ᾽ αὐτοῦ Ἀττικοπέρδιξ.
καὶ ὁ Οὐλπιανὸς ἔφη· ὁ δ᾽ ἀπελεύθερος παρὰ τίνι
κεῖται; εἰπόντος δέ τινος καὶ δρᾶμα ἐπιγράφεσθαι
Φρυνίχου Ἀπελευθέρους, Μένανδρον δ᾽ ἐν Ῥαπιζο-
μένῃ καὶ ἀπελευθέραν εἰρηκέναι καὶ ἐπισυνάπτοντος
< . . . > πάλιν ἔφη· τίνι δὲ διαφέρει ἐξελευθέρου; ταῦτα
c   μὲν οὖν ἔδοξε κατὰ τὸ παρὸν | ἀναβαλέσθαι.

Καὶ ὁ Γαληνὸς μελλόντων ἡμῶν ἐφάπτεσθαι τῶν
ἄρτων, οὐ πρότερον, ἔφη, δειπνήσομεν, ἕως ἂν καὶ
παρ᾽ ἡμῶν ἀκούσητε ὅσα εἰρήκασι περὶ ἄρτων ἢ
πεμμάτων ἔτι τε ἀλφίτων Ἀσκληπιαδῶν παῖδες. Δίφιλος μὲν ὁ Σίφνιος ἐν τῷ Περὶ τῶν Προσφερομένων
τοῖς Νοσοῦσι καὶ τοῖς Ὑγιαίνουσιν, ἄρτοι, φησίν, οἱ
ἐκ πυρῶν κριθίνων εἰσὶ πολυτροφώτεροι καὶ εὐοικονομητότεροι καὶ τὸ ὅλον κρείττονες, εἶθ᾽ οἱ σεμιδαλῖται,
μεθ᾽ οὓς οἱ ἀλευρῖται, εἶθ᾽ οἱ συγκομιστοὶ ἐξ ἀσήστων
d   ἀλεύρων | γινόμενοι· οὗτοι γὰρ πολυτροφώτεροι εἶναι

---

[67] The meaning of the word is in fact obscure, although it is
probably cognate with *amolgē*, "milking"; see West's n. on the line
from Hesiod.   [68] Stephanis #361.

He means the type that is eaten by shepherds and is the best there is, since whatever is at its very best is called *amolgos*.[67] I must beg off offering a list—my memory is not that good—of the various sacrificial cakes described by Aristomenes of Athens[68] in Book III of his *On Sacrifices* (*FGrH* 364 F 1). I got to know this fellow when I was quite young and he was older; he was an Old Comic actor and a freedman (*apeleutheros*) of the highly cultivated emperor Hadrian[69], who called him "the Attic Partridge." And Ulpian said: In what author is the word "freedman" attested? Someone replied that a play by Phrynichus was entitled *Freedmen*[70], and that Menander uses the term "freedwoman" in *The Girl Who Was Beaten with a Stick* (fr. 332); and he added . . . (Ulpian) answered: How does this word differ from *exeleutheros*? It was decided to put these questions off for the moment.[71]

As we were about to begin consuming the bread, Galen said: We are not going to dine until I tell you what some of the children of the Asclepiadae[72] have to say about bread and cakes, as well as barley-meal. Diphilus of Siphnos in his *On Food for the Sick and the Healthy* says: Wheat bread is more nutritious, more easily digested, and generally superior to barley bread, first bread of top-quality flour, then after this bread made of ordinary flour, then finally whole-wheat bread made of unsifted flour; for these appear to be the most nutritious. Philistion of Locris (fr. 9

[69] Reigned 117–138 AD.

[70] The play was also called *Tragic Actors* (*Suda* φ 763), under which title Athenaeus cites it repeatedly (e.g. 7.287b; 14.654b).

[71] The matter is not, in fact, ever taken up again.

[72] The physicians.

ATHENAEUS

δοκοῦσι. Φιλιστίων δ' ὁ Λοκρὸς τῶν χονδριτῶν τοὺς
σεμιδαλίτας πρὸς ἰσχύν φησι μᾶλλον πεφυκέναι· μεθ'
οὓς τοὺς χονδρίτας τίθησιν, εἶτα τοὺς ἀλευρίτας. οἱ δὲ
ἐκ γύρεως ἄρτοι γινόμενοι κακοχυλότεροί τέ εἰσι καὶ
ὀλιγοτροφώτεροι. πάντες δ' οἱ θερμοὶ ἄρτοι τῶν ἐψυγ-
μένων εὐοικονομητότεροι πολυτροφώτεροί τε καὶ εὐ-
χυλότεροι, ἔτι δὲ πνευματικοὶ καὶ εὐανάδοτοι. οἱ δ'
ἐψυγμένοι πλήσμιοι, δυσοικονόμητοι. οἱ δὲ τελείως
παλαιοὶ καὶ κατεψυγμένοι ἀτροφώτεροι στατικοί τε
e κοιλίας καὶ κακόχυλοι. ὁ δ' | ἐγκρυφίας ἄρτος βαρὺς
δυσοικονόμητός τε διὰ τὸ ἀνωμάλως ὀπτᾶσθαι. ὁ δὲ
ἰπνίτης καὶ καμινίτης δύσπεπτοι καὶ δυσοικονόμητοι.
ὁ δὲ ἐσχαρίτης καὶ ἀπὸ τηγάνου διὰ τὴν τοῦ ἐλαίου
ἐπίμιξιν εὐεκκριτώτερος, διὰ δὲ τὸ κνισὸν κακοστο-
μαχώτερος. ὁ δὲ κλιβανίτης πάσαις ταῖς ἀρεταῖς
περιττεύει· εὔχυλος γὰρ καὶ εὐστόμαχος καὶ εὔπεπτος
καὶ πρὸς ἀνάδοσιν ῥᾷστος· οὔτε γὰρ ἱστάνει κοιλίαν
οὔτε παρατείνει. Ἀνδρέας δὲ ὁ ἰατρὸς ἄρτους τινάς
φησιν ἐν Συρίᾳ γίνεσθαι ἐκ συκαμίνων, ὧν τοὺς
f φαγόντας τριχορρυεῖν. Μνησίθεος δέ φησι τὸν | ἄρ-
τον τῆς μάζης εὐπεπτότερον εἶναι καὶ τοὺς ἐκ τῆς
τίφης μᾶλλον ἱκανῶς τρέφειν· πέττεσθαι γὰρ αὐτοὺς
καὶ οὐ μετὰ πολλοῦ πόνου. τὸν δ' ἐκ τῶν ζειῶν ἄρτον
ἄδην φησὶν ἐσθιόμενον βαρὺν εἶναι καὶ δύσπεπτον·
διὸ οὐχ ὑγιαίνειν τοὺς αὐτὸν ἐσθίοντας. εἰδέναι δὲ
116 ὑμᾶς δεῖ ‖ ὅτι τὰ μὴ πυρωθένταἢ τριφθέντα σιτία φύ-

[73] Cf. 3.110a.

48

Wellmann) says that bread made with top-quality flour promotes physical strength more than bread made of coarse-ground flour does; he ranks bread made with coarse-ground flour second, and bread made with ordinary flour after that. Bread made with very fine meal produces worse *chulē* ("digestive juice") and is less nourishing. Warm bread of all sorts is more easily digested and more nourishing than bread that has cooled, and produces better *chulē*; it also promotes pneumatic action and is easily assimilated. Bread that has cooled is filling and not easily digested. Bread that is quite old and very cold is less nourishing, arrests the movement of the bowels, and produces bad *chulē*. *Enkruphias*-bread[73] is heavy and difficult to digest because it is baked unevenly. Oven bread and kiln bread are difficult to break down and digest. Brazier bread and bread made in a frying-pan are easier to excrete, because oil has been mixed into them, but are harder on the stomach because of their greasiness. Baking-shell bread is rich in good characteristics of all sorts, for it produces good *chulē*, is easy on the stomach, and is easily digested, broken down, and assimilated, because it neither arrests the movement of the bowels nor distends them. Andreas the physician (fr. 41 von Staden) says that a type of bread is produced in Syria from mulberries, and that anyone who eats it loses his hair. Mnesitheus (fr. 28 Bertier) says that bread is more easily broken down than barley-cake, and that bread made of einkorn supplies more adequate nutrition, since it is broken down without difficulty. As for bread made of rice-wheat, he says that if one eats it until one is full, it is heavy and difficult to break down, and that as a result those who eat it are unhealthy. You ought to be aware that breadstuffs that are neither baked nor kneaded pro-

49

ATHENAEUS

σας καὶ βάρη καὶ στρόφους καὶ κεφαλαλγίας ποιεῖ.

Μετὰ τὰς τοσαύτας διαλέξεις ἔδοξεν ἤδη ποτὲ καὶ δειπνεῖν, καὶ περιενεχθέντος τοῦ καλουμένου ὡραίου ὁ Λεωνίδης ἔφη· Εὐθύδημος ὁ Ἀθηναῖος, ἄνδρες φίλοι, ἐν τῷ Περὶ Ταρίχων Ἡσίοδόν φησι περὶ πάντων τῶν ταριχευομένων τάδ᾽ εἰρηκέναι·

     † ἄμφακες μὲν πρῶτον στόμα καὶ κριται αντα
       καὶ θιοην †
     γναθμὸν <ὃν> ηὐδάξαντο δυσείμονες
b   ἰχθυβολῆες, |
     οἷς ὁ ταριχόπλεως ἅδε Βόσπορος, οἵ θ᾽
      ὑπόγαστρα
     τμήγοντες τετράγωνα ταρίχια τεκταίνονται.
     ναὶ μὴν οὐκ ἀκλεὲς θνητοῖς γένος ὀξυρρύγχου,
     ὃν καὶ ὅλον καὶ τμητὸν Ἀλεξανδρεῖς ἐκόμισσαν.
c   θύννων δ᾽ ὡραίων Βυζάντιον ἔπλετο μήτηρ |
     καὶ σκόμβρων κυβίων τε καὶ εὐχόρτου †
      λικιβάττεω †,
     καὶ Πάριον κολιῶν κυδρὴ τροφὸς ἔσκε πολίχνη·
     Ἰόνιον δ᾽ ἀνὰ κῦμα φέρων Γαδειρόθεν ἄξει
     Βρέττιος ἢ Καμπανὸς ἢ ἐξ ἀγαθοῖο Τάραντος
     ὀρκύνοιο τρίγωνα, τά τ᾽ <ἐν> στάμνοισι τεθέντα
     ἀμφαλλὰξ δείπνοισιν ἐνὶ πρώτοισιν ὀπηδεῖ.

d   ταῦτα τὰ ἔπη ἐμοὶ μὲν δοκεῖ τινος μαγείρου εἶναι |

---

74 Literally "peak-season (saltfish)."

duce flatulence, a heavy feeling, cramps, and headaches.

After these lengthy discussions, the decision was finally made to dine. After the so-called *horaion*[74] made its way around the company, Leonides said: Euthydemus of Athens, my friends, reports in his *On Saltfish* (*SH* 455) that Hesiod has the following to say about preserved fish of every sort:

† First of all a two-edged mouth [corrupt], †
which the ill-dressed fishermen refer to as "the jaw";
the saltfish-rich Bosporus takes pleasure in these, as
    do those
who cut up the belly-sections to make squares of
    preserved fish.
Certainly the family of the sharp-nosed one[75] is not
    inglorious among mortals;
the inhabitants of Alexandria take it home both whole
    and in pieces.
Byzantium is the mother of peak-season tuna
and of mackerel, gobies, and fattening [corrupt];
and the city of Parion is a glorious nurse of Spanish
    mackerel.
Bearing them over the Ionian wave from Cadiz
or lovely Tarentum, a Bruttian or Campanian will
    bring
triangular chunks of tuna which, tightly packed in
    jars,
accompany the beginning of dinner.

In my opinion, these verses were composed by a cook

---

[75] Presumably the sturgeon.

μᾶλλον ἢ τοῦ μουσικωτάτου Ἡσιόδου. πόθεν γὰρ
εἰδέναι δύναται Πάριον ἢ Βυζάντιον, ἔτι δὲ Τάραντα
καὶ Βρεττίους καὶ Καμπανοὺς πολλοῖς ἔτεσι τούτων
πρεσβύτερος ὤν; δοκεῖ οὖν μοι αὐτοῦ τοῦ Εὐθυδήμου
εἶναι τὰ ποιήματα. καὶ ὁ Διονυσοκλῆς ἔφη· ὅτου μέν
ἐστι τὰ ποιήματα, ὦ ἀγαθὲ Λεωνίδη, ὑμῶν ἐστι κρί-
νειν τῶν δοκιμωτάτων γραμματικῶν· ἀλλ' ἐπεὶ περὶ
ταρίχων ἐστὶν ὁ λόγος, περὶ ὧν οἶδα καὶ παροιμίαν
μνήμης ἠξιωμένην ὑπὸ τοῦ Σολέως Κλεάρχου·

e   σαπρὸς τάριχος | τὴν ὀρίγανον φιλεῖ,

ἔρχομαι κἀγὼ λέξων τι περὶ αὐτῶν, τὰ τῆς τέχνης.
Διοκλῆς μὲν ὁ Καρύστιος ἐν τοῖς Ὑγιεινοῖς ἐπιγραφομένοις τῶν ταρίχων φησὶ τῶν ἀπιμέλων κράτιστα
εἶναι τὰ ὡραῖα, τῶν δὲ πιόνων τὰ θύννεια. Ἱκέσιος δ'
ἱστορεῖ οὐκ εἶναι εὐεκκρίτους κοιλίας οὔτε πηλαμύδας
οὔτε τὰ ὡραῖα, τὰ δὲ νεώτερα τῶν θυννείων τὴν αὐτὴν
ἀναλογίαν ἔχειν τοῖς κυβίοις μεγάλην τε εἶναι διαφορὰν πρὸς πάντα τὰ ὡραῖα λεγόμενα. ὁμοίως δὲ λέγει
καὶ τῶν Βυζαντίων ὡραίων πρὸς τὰ ἀφ' ἑτέρων τόπων
f   λαμβανόμενα καὶ οὐ μόνον τῶν θυννείων, | ἀλλὰ καὶ
τῶν ἄλλων τῶν ἁλισκομένων ἐν Βυζαντίῳ. τούτοις
προσέθηκεν ὁ Ἐφέσιος Δάφνος· Ἀρχέστρατος μὲν ὁ
περιπλεύσας τὴν οἰκουμένην γαστρὸς ἕνεκα καὶ τῶν
ὑπὸ τὴν γαστέρα φησί·

---

[76] Tarentum was founded in the late 8th century. Byzantium in

rather than by the extremely accomplished Hesiod; for how can he know about Parion or Byzantium, or about Tarentum[76], Bruttians, and Campanians, given that he is many years older than they are? I therefore believe that the poem is by Euthydemus himself. And Dionysocles said: The question of who wrote this poem, my good Leonides, is up to you distinguished grammarians to decide. But as our subject is saltfish, about which I know a proverb that Clearchus of Soli (fr. 82 Wehrli) thought worthy of mention:

Rotten saltfish likes marjoram,[77]

I too intend to say something about it, on technical matters. Diocles of Carystus in his work entitled *On Matters of Health* (fr. 233 van der Eijk) claims that the best lean saltfish is *horaion*, whereas the best fatty saltfish is made from tuna. Hicesius reports that neither *pēlamudes* ("small tuna") nor *horaia* are easily excreted from the bowels, and that the saltfish made from younger tuna is comparable to *kubion* ("cube-saltfish") and much better than all the varieties referred to as *horaia*. He makes similar remarks about Byzantine *horaion* in comparison to that got elsewhere, and not just about *horaion* made from tuna, but about that made from all the other fish caught in Byzantium as well. To these remarks Daphnis of Ephesus added: Archestratus (fr. 39 Olson–Sens = *SH* 169), who circumnavigated the inhabited world for the sake of his belly and the portions of his anatomy below the belly, says:

the first half of the 7th century, around or a little after the time of the historical Hesiod.   [77] Sc. to cover the smell. The same proverb is cited again at 3.119e.

καὶ Σικελοῦ θύννου τέμαχος ⟨ . . . ⟩

117   τμηθὲν ὅτ᾽ ἐν βίκοισι ταριχεύεσθαι ἔμελλεν. ‖
σαπέρδῃ δ᾽ ἐνέπω κλαίειν μακρά, Ποντικῷ ὄψῳ,
καὶ τοῖς κεῖνον ἐπαινοῦσιν· παῦροι γὰρ ἴσασιν
ἀνθρώπων, ὅ τι φαῦλον ἔφυ καὶ κεδνὸν ἔδεσμα.
ἀλλὰ τριταῖον ἔχειν σκόμβρον πρὶν ἐς ἁλμυρὸν
   ὕδωρ
ἐλθεῖν ἀμφορέως ἐντὸς νέον ἡμιτάριχον.

b   ἂν δ᾽ ἀφίκῃ κλεινοῦ Βυζαντίου εἰς πόλιν ἁγνήν, |
ὡραίου φάγε μοι τέμαχος πάλιν· ἔστι γὰρ
   ἐσθλὸν
καὶ μαλακόν.

παρέλιπεν δ᾽ ὁ τένθης Ἀρχέστρατος συγκαταλέξαι
ἡμῖν καὶ τὸ παρὰ Κράτητι τῷ κωμῳδιοποιῷ ἐν Σαμί-
οις λεγόμενον ἐλεφάντινον τάριχος, περὶ οὗ φησιν·

σκυτίνῃ ποτ᾽ ἐν χύτρᾳ τάριχος ἐλεφάντινον
ἧψε ποντιὰς χελώνη πευκίνοισι κύμασι,
καρκίνοι ποδάνεμοί τε καὶ τανύπτεροι λύκοι
† υσοριμαχειν † ἄνδρες οὐρανοῦ καττύματα.

c   παῖ ᾽κεῖνον, | ἄγχ᾽ ἐκεῖνον. ἐν Κέῳ τίς ἡμέρα;

ὅτι δὲ διαβόητον ἦν τὸ τοῦ Κράτητος ἐλεφάντινον
τάριχος μαρτυρεῖ Ἀριστοφάνης ἐν Θεσμοφοριαζού-
σαις διὰ τούτων·

---

78 The first four lines are a series of *adunata* presented in the
form of a riddle. According to Photius ε 972, citing Eup. fr. 288

and a slice of Sicilian tuna . . .
cut up when it was about to be pickled in jars.
But I say to hell with *saperdē*, a Pontic dish,
and those who praise it; for few people
know which food is wretched and which is excellent.
But get a mackerel on the third day, before it goes
    into the saltwater
within a transport jar as a piece of recently cured,
    half-salted fish.
And if you come to the holy city of famous
    Byzantium,
I urge you again to eat a steak of peak-season tuna;
    for it is very good
and soft.

But the gluttonous Archestratus failed to include for us in his catalogue what Crates the comic poet in *Samians* (fr. 32) refers to as ivory saltfish, about which he says:

Once upon a time a sea-tortoise stewed ivory saltfish
in a cookpot made of leather with pinewood waves,
and wind-footed crabs and long-winged wolves
[corrupt] men scraps of heavenly shoe-leather.
Hit him! Choke him! What day is it on Ceos?[78]

That Crates' ivory saltfish was notorious is proven by Aristophanes in *Women Celebrating the Thesmophoria* (fr. 347, from *Thesmophoriazusae* II), in the following verses:

("for no one knows what day it is on Ceos"), the Ceans had no fixed calendar, and everyone there kept track of the days however he wished.

ἦ μέγα τι βρῶμ᾽ † ἐστὶ ἡ † τρυγῳδοποιο-
   μουσική,
ἡνίκα Κράτης τό τε τάριχος ἐλεφάντινον
λαμπρὸν ἐνόμιζεν ἀπόνως παρακεκλημένον
ἄλλα τε τοιαῦθ᾽ ἕτερα μυρί᾽ ἐκιχλίζετο.

Ὠμοτάριχον δέ τινα κέκληκεν Ἄλεξις ἐν Ἀπεγλαυκωμένῳ. ὁ δ᾽ αὐτὸς ποιητὴς ἐν Πονήρᾳ περὶ σκευα-
d σίας ταρίχων μάγειρόν τινα παράγει | λέγοντα τάδε·

ὅμως ⟨δὲ⟩ λογίσασθαι πρὸς ἐμαυτὸν βούλομαι
καθεζόμενος ἐνταῦθα τὴν ὀψωνίαν,
ὁμοῦ τε συντάξαι τί πρῶτον οἰστέον
ἡδυντέον τε πῶς ἕκαστόν ἐστί μοι.
⟨ . . . ⟩ τάριχος πρῶτον ὡραῖον τοδί.
διωβόλου τοῦτ᾽ ἐστί. πλυτέον εὖ μάλα.
εἶτ᾽ εἰς λοπάδιον ὑποπάσας ἡδύσματα
ἐνθεὶς τὸ τέμαχος, λευκὸν οἶνον ἐπιχέας,
e ἐπεσκέδασα τοὔλαιον εἶθ᾽ ἕψων ποῶ |
μυελὸν ἀφειλόν τ᾽ ἐπιγανώσας σιλφίῳ.

ἐν δὲ Ἀπεγλαυκωμένῳ συμβολάς τις ἀπαιτούμενός
φησι·

   (Α.) παρ᾽ ἐμοῦ δ᾽, ἐὰν μὴ καθ᾽ ἓν ἕκαστον πάντα
      † δ᾽ ὡς †,
   χαλκοῦ μέρος δωδέκατον οὐκ ἂν ἀπολάβοις.

---

[79] See also Nicostr. fr. 1.2, quoted at 4.133c.

Certainly a great bit of food † is the † production of
   comic poetry,
when Crates both considered his saltfish "ivory"
and "shining" and "summoned without effort,"
and made a million other such jokes.

Alexis refers to something called raw-saltfish in *The
Man Who Had a Cataract* (fr. 15.4, cited below).[79] The
same poet in *The Miserable Woman* (fr. 191) introduces a
cook who says the following about how saltfish is prepared:

All the same, I want to sit down here
and privately reckon up the food I've bought,
and simultaneously organize what I ought to serve
   first
and how I need to season each item.
. . . First there's this *horaion* saltfish here;
it cost two obols. It has to be thoroughly rinsed;
then I sprinkle some spices into the casserole-dish;
put the slice of fish inside; pour white wine over it;
drizzle oil on top; stew it until it's
soft as marrow; and take it out after I've glazed it
   with silphium.

In *The Man Who Had a Cataract* (Alex. fr. 15), someone
being asked to pay his share of the expenses for a dinner
party says:

(A.) Unless [corrupt] every item individually, you
   wouldn't get a penny[80] out of me.

---

[80] Literally "one-twelfth of a *chalkous*," which was a bronze
coin = one-eighth of an obol, and thus an exceedingly small
amount of money.

(Β.) δίκαιος ὁ λόγος. (Α.) ἀβάκιον, ψῆφον. λέγε.

(Β.) ἔστ᾽ ὠμοτάριχος πέντε χαλκῶν. (Α.) λέγ᾽

f   ἕτερον. |

(Β.) μῦς ἑπτὰ χαλκῶν. (Α.) οὐδὲν ἀσεβεῖς

    οὐδέπω.

λέγε. (Β.) τῶν ἐχίνων ὀβολός. (Α.) ἀγνεύεις ἔτι.

(Β.) ἆρ᾽ ἦν μετὰ ταῦθ᾽ ἡ ῥάφανος, ἣν ἐβοᾶτε;

    (Α.) ναί·

χρηστὴ γὰρ ἦν. (Β.) ἔδωκα ταύτης δύ᾽ ὀβολούς.

118   (Α.) τί γὰρ ἐβοῶμεν; (Β.) τὸ κύβιον τριωβόλου. ‖

(Α.) † ονεῖλκε χειρῶν γε † οὐκ ἐπράξατ᾽ οὐδὲ ἕν.

(Β.) οὐκ οἶσθας, ὦ μακάριε, τὴν ἀγοράν, ὅτι

κατεδηδόκασιν τὰ λάχαν᾽ <αἱ> τρωξαλλίδες.

(Α.) διὰ τοῦτο <τὸ> τάριχος τέθεικας διπλασίου;

(Β.) ὁ ταριχοπώλης ἐστίν· ἐλθὼν πυνθάνου.

γόγγρος δέκ᾽ ὀβολῶν. (Α.) οὐχὶ πολλοῦ. λέγ᾽

    ἕτερον.

(Β.) τὸν ὀπτὸν ἰχθὺν ἐπριάμην δραχμῆς. (Α.)

    παπαῖ,

ὥσπερ πυρετὸς ἀνῆκεν, εἶτ᾽ † ἐν ἐπιτέλει †.

(Β.) πρόσθες τὸν οἶνον, <ὃν> μεθυόντων

    προσέλαβον

ὑμῶν, χοᾶς τρεῖς, δέκ᾽ ὀβολῶν ὁ χοῦς.

b Ἰκέσιος δ᾽ ἐν δευτέρῳ Περὶ Ὕλης πηλαμύδας | κύβια
εἶναί φησι μεγάλα. κυβίων δὲ μνημονεύει Ποσείδιπ-

---

81 Addressed to a slave.
82 "Bronze pieces," i.e. small coins.

(B.) Fair enough. (A.) Bring an abacus and some
   counting pebbles![81] Go ahead!
(B.) There's raw-saltfish for five *chalkoi*. (A.) Next
   item!
(B.) Mussels for seven *chalkoi*.[82] (A.) You haven't
   committed any sacrilege so far.
Next item! (B.) An obol for the sea-urchins. (A.)
   You're still clean.
(B.) Wasn't what came after that the cabbage you
   kept shouting for? (A.) Yeah—
it was good. (B.) I paid two obols for it.
(A.) So why did we shout for it? (B.) The cube-
   saltfish cost three obols.
(A.) Didn't he charge anything for [corrupt]?
(B.) My dear sir, you don't know how matters are in
   the marketplace;
the locusts have consumed the vegetables.
(A.) Is that why you've charged double for the
   saltfish?
(B.) That's the saltfish-dealer; go ask him about it.
Conger eel for ten obols. (A.) That's not much. Next
   item!
(B.) I purchased the roast fish for a drachma. (A.)
   Damn!
It dropped like a fever, then [corrupt].
(B.) Add the wine I bought when you
were drunk: three *choes*, at ten obols per *chous*.[83]

Hicesius in Book II of *On Raw Materials* says that *pēlamudes* are large pieces of cube-saltfish. Posidippus men-

---

[83] A *chous* is a liquid measure equal to about 3.2 litres.

πος ἐν Μεταφερομένῳ. Εὐθύδημος ἐν τῷ Περὶ Ταρίχων τὸν δελκανόν φησιν ἰχθὺν ὀνομάζεσθαι ἀπὸ Δέλ-
κωνος τοῦ ποταμοῦ, ἀφ᾽ οὗπερ καὶ ἁλίκεσθαι, καὶ
ταριχευόμενον εὐστομαχώτατον εἶναι. Δωρίων δ᾽ ἐν
τῷ Περὶ Ἰχθύων τὸν⁶ λεβίαν ὀνομάζων φησὶ λέγειν
τινὰς ὡς <ὁ> αὐτός ἐστι τῷ δελκανῷ, τὸν δὲ κορακῖνον
ὑπὸ πολλῶν λέγεσθαι σαπέρδην καὶ εἶναι κράτιστον
τὸν ἐκ τῆς Μαιώτιδος λίμνης. θαυμαστοὺς δὲ εἶναι
c λέγει | καὶ τοὺς περὶ Ἄβδηρα ἁλισκομένους κεστρεῖς,
μεθ᾽ οὓς τοὺς περὶ Σινώπην, καὶ ταριχευομένους εὐ-
στομάχους ὑπάρχειν. τοὺς δὲ προσαγορευομένους φησὶ μύλλους ὑπὸ μέν τινων καλεῖσθαι ἀγνωτίδια, ὑπὸ
δέ τινων πλατιστάκους ὄντας τοὺς αὐτούς, καθάπερ
καὶ τὸν χελλαρίην· καὶ γὰρ τοῦτον ἕνα ὄντα ἰχθὺν
πολλῶν ὀνομασιῶν τετυχηκέναι· καλεῖσθαι γὰρ καὶ
βάκχον καὶ ὀνίσκον καὶ χελλαρίην. οἱ μὲν οὖν μεί-
ζονες αὐτῶν ὀνομάζονται πλατίστακοι, οἱ δὲ μέσην
ἔχοντες ἡλικίαν μύλλοι, οἱ δὲ βαιοὶ τοῖς μεγέθεσιν
d ἀγνωτίδια. μνημονεύει δὲ τῶν μύλλων καὶ | Ἀριστο-
φάνης ἐν Ὁλκάσι·

σκόμβροι, κολίαι, λεβίαι, μύλλοι, σαπέρδαι,
    θυννίδες.

Ἐπὶ τούτοις σιωπήσαντος τοῦ Διονυσοκλέους ὁ

⁶ τὸν λεπτηνὸν Α

tions cube-saltfish in *The Man Who Tried To Change*[84] (fr. 17). Euthydemus in his *On Saltfish* says that the fish known as the *delkanos* gets its name from the Delcon river, where it is caught, and that when preserved, it is very easy on the stomach. When Dorion mentions the *lebias* in his *On Fish*, he says that some authorities identify it with the *delkanos*, and notes that many people call the *korakinos* a *saperdēs* and that it is best when taken from the Sea of Azov. He also reports that the gray mullets caught around Abdera are outstanding;[85] that after them come those caught around Sinope; and that when preserved, they are easy on the stomach. He says that some authorities refer to the fish called *mulloi* as *agnōtidia*, while others call them *platistakoi*, which are the same creature, as is the *chellariēs*. This is only one fish, but has been given many names, since it is also known as a *bakchos*, *oniskos*, and *chellariēs*. The large ones are called *platistakoi*; those that are not yet full-grown are *mulloi*; and the small ones are *agnōtidia*. Aristophanes also mentions *mulloi* in *Merchantships* (fr. 430):

> mackerel, Spanish mackerel, *lebiai*, *mulloi*, *saperdai*,
>   tuna.

Dionysocles kept quiet,[86] and the grammarian Varus

---

[84] I.e. to sobriety from a profligate style of life? The title is elsewhere given in the plural.

[85] A bit of information apparently drawn from Archestr. fr. 44 Olson–Sens (cited at 7.307b).

[86] Dionysocles (also a physician) spoke briefly at 3.116d–f, and the implication would seem to be that he might have been expected to respond somehow to Daphnus.

61

γραμματικὸς ἔφη Οὔαρος· ἀλλὰ μὴν καὶ Ἀντιφάνης ὁ
ποιητὴς ἐν Δευκαλίωνι ταρίχων τῶνδε μέμνηται·

> τάριχος ἀντακαῖον εἴ τις βούλετ᾽ ἢ
> Γαδειρικόν, Βυζαντίας δὲ θυννίδος
> † εὐφροσύναις † ὀσμαῖσι χαίρει.

καὶ ἐν Παρασίτῳ·

> τάριχος ἀντακαῖον ἐν μέσῳ
> πῖον, ὁλόλευκον, θερμόν.

e Νικόστρατός τε ἢ Φιλέταιρος ἐν Ἀντύλλῳ· |

> Βυζάντιόν ‹τε› τέμαχος ἐπιβακχευσάτω,
> Γαδειρικόν θ᾽ ὑπογάστριον παρεισίτω.

καὶ προελθών·

> ἀλλ᾽ ἐπριάμην παρ᾽ ἀνδρός, ὦ γῆ καὶ θεοί,
> ταριχοπώλου πάνυ καλοῦ τε κἀγαθοῦ
> τιλτὸν μέγιστον, ἄξιον δραχμῆς, δυοῖν
> ὀβολοῖν, ὃν οὐκ ἂν καταφάγοιμεν ἡμερῶν
> τριῶν ἂν ἐσθίοντες οὐδὲ δώδεκα·
f ὑπερμέγεθες γάρ ἐστιν. |

ἐπὶ τούτοις ὁ Οὐλπιανὸς ἀποβλέψας εἰς τὸν Πλούταρ-
χον ἔφη· μήποτ᾽ οὗτις ἐν τούτοις, ὦ οὗτος, τοὺς παρ᾽
ὑμῖν τοῖς Ἀλεξανδρεῦσι κατέλεξε Μενδησίους, ὧν
οὐδ᾽ ἂν μαινόμενος κύων γεύσαιτο ἄν ποτε, ἢ τῶν

responded: Well, the poet Antiphanes as well mentions these types of saltfish in *Deucalion* (fr. 78):

> If anyone wants sturgeon-saltfish or
> the kind that comes from Cadiz, and takes pleasure
> in † festivities † the smell of Byzantine tuna.

And in *The Parasite* (fr. 184):

> In the middle is sturgeon-saltfish,
> fat, all-white, warm.

Also Nicostratus or Philetaerus in *Antyllus* (Nicostr. fr. 5, encompassing both quotations):

> And let a slice of Byzantine fish burst in like a
>   bacchant,
> and a belly-slice from Cadiz enter next to it!

And further on:

> But I purchased, O earth and gods, from
> a quite distinguished saltfish-seller
> a very large piece of scaled saltfish worth a drachma
> for two obols[87]. We couldn't finish it
> if we ate non-stop for three days—or 12;
> because it's enormous.

Ulpian looked at Plutarch and said in response: It seems, sir, that none of these authors mentioned the Mendesian fish you Alexandrians enjoy, which not even a mad dog

[87] = one-third of a drachma.
[88] For Egyptian half-fresh, see 3.121b–c. The Egyptian sheat-fish is included in what Athenaeus identifies as a list of Nile fish in Archipp. fr. 26 (quoted at 7.312a).

καλῶν σου ἡμινήρων ἢ τῶν ταριχηρῶν σιλούρων. καὶ
119 ὁ Πλούταρχος, ὁ μὲν ἡμίνηρος, ‖ ἔφη, τί διαφέρει τοῦ
προκαταλελεγμένου ἡμιταρίχου, ⟨οὗ⟩ ὁ καλὸς ὑμῶν
Ἀρχέστρατος μέμνηται; ἀλλ᾽ ὅμως ὠνόμασεν ἡμίνηρον ὁ Πάφιος Σώπατρος ἐν Μυστάκου Θητείῳ οὕτως·

> ἐδέξατ᾽ ἀντακαῖον, ὃν τρέφει μέγας
> Ἴστρος Σκύθαισιν ἡμίνηρον ἡδονήν.

καὶ τὸν Μενδήσιον οὕτως ὁ αὐτὸς καταλέγει·

> Μενδήσιός θ᾽ ὡραῖος ἀκρόπαστος εὖ,
> ξανθαῖσιν ὀπτὸς κέφαλος ἀκτῖσιν πυρός.

b ταῦτα δὲ τὰ βρώματα ὅτι πολλῷ ἡδίω ἐστὶ τῶν | παρὰ
σοὶ περισπουδάστων κόττα καὶ λέπιδι, οἱ πειραθέντες
ἴσασι. λέγε οὖν ἡμῖν καὶ σὺ εἰ καὶ ἀρσενικῶς ὁ
τάριχος λέγεται παρ᾽ Ἀττικοῖς· παρὰ γὰρ Ἐπιχάρμῳ
οἴδαμεν. ὃν ζητοῦντα προφθάσας ὁ Μυρτίλος ἔφη·
Κρατῖνος μὲν ἐν Διονυσαλεξάνδρῳ·

> ἐν σαργάναις ἄξω ταρίχους Ποντικούς.

Πλάτων Διὶ Κακουμένῳ·

> ὥσθ᾽ ἅττ᾽ ἔχω ταῦτ᾽ ἐς ταρίχους ἀπολέσω.

---

89 Quoted at 3.117a.

90 Cf. 9.385a, where the words appear in the form *kottana* and
lepidin and are compared somehow to oil-and-vinegar sauce.

91 I.e. rather than in the more common neuter form. In
the passages from Cratinus and Sophocles cited below, the word

would care to taste, or your delicious half-fresh fish or your preserved Egyptian sheatfish[88]. And Plutarch said: How is half-fresh fish different from the half-salted fish referred to earlier, which your fine Archestratus (fr. 39.7 Olson–Sens = *SH* 169.7)[89] mentions? Be that as it may, Sopater of Paphos used the word "half-fresh" in *Mustakos' Wage* (fr. 11), as follows:

> He received a sturgeon, which the mighty Danube
> nourishes as a half-fresh pleasure for Scythians.

The same author (fr. 22) mentions Mendesian fish, as follows:

> and a peak-season Mendesian, lightly and carefully
>   salted,
> (and) a mullet roasted with the yellow rays of fire.

That these foods are much more delicious than the *kotta* and *lepidi* so eagerly sought after in your country[90], those who have tried them know. Tell us, then, whether the word "saltfish" is also used in the masculine by Attic authors;[91] for we know that it appears in Epicharmus (fr. 159).[92] He was pondering the question, but before he could speak, Myrtilus said: Cratinus in *Dionysalexandros* (fr. 44):

> I'll bring Pontic saltfish (masc.) in baskets.

Plato in *Zeus Abused* (fr. 49):

> so that I'd lose everything I have on saltfish (masc.).

could be emended to neuter, and the fragment of Hermippus is problematic in any case. But the masculine is metrically guaranteed in the other fragments.   [92] Cf. 3.119d.

c Ἀριστοφάνης Δαιταλεῦσιν· |

οὐκ αἰσχυνοῦμαι τὸν τάριχον τουτονὶ
πλύνων ἅπασιν ὅσα σύνοιδ᾽ αὐτῷ κακά.

Κράτης Θηρίοις·

καὶ τῶν ῥαφάνων ἕψειν χρή,
ἰχθῦς τ᾽ ὀπτᾶν τούς τε ταρίχους, ἡμῶν δ᾽ ἀπὸ
χεῖρας ἔχεσθαι.

ἰδίως δ᾽ ἐσχημάτισται παρ᾽ Ἑρμίππῳ ἐν Ἀρτοπώλισι·

< . . . > καὶ τάριχος πίονα.

Σοφοκλῆς τ᾽ ἐν Φινεῖ·

νεκρὸς τάριχος εἰσορᾶν Αἰγύπτιος.

d ὑποκοριστικῶς δ᾽ εἴρηκεν Ἀριστοφάνης ἐν Εἰρήνῃ·[7] |

ἀγόρασόν τι χρηστὸν εἰς ἀγρὸν ταρίχιον.

καὶ Κηφισόδωρος ἐν Ὑί·

κρεᾴδιόν τι φαῦλον ἢ ταρίχιον.

Φερεκράτης ἐν Αὐτομόλοις·

ἡ γυνὴ δ᾽ ἡμῶν ἑκάστῳ λέκιθον ἕψουσ᾽ ἢ φακῆν

---

[7] The traditional text of Aristophanes has ἐμπολήσαντες ("after purchasing") for Athenaeus' unmetrical ἀγόρασον ("buy!").

Aristophanes in *Banqueters* (fr. 207):

I won't be ashamed to wash[93] this saltfish (masc.)
with all the bad deeds I know it's guilty of.

Crates in *Wild Beasts* (fr. 19):

You should stew some cabbages,
and roast fish and saltfish (masc.)—and keep your
hands off us!

The word appears in an unusual form in Hermippus' *Female Breadsellers* (fr. 10):[94]

and fatty saltfish.

Sophocles in *Phineus* (fr. 712):

seemingly as dead as Egyptian saltfish[95] (masc.).

Aristophanes uses it in the diminutive in *Peace* (563):

Buy a little piece of good saltfish to take into the
country!

Also Cephisodorus in *The Pig* (fr. 8):

a nasty little chunk of meat or a little piece of saltfish.

Pherecrates in *Deserters* (fr. 26):

Our wife is waiting for each of us, making us some
pea soup

---

[93] The verb also has the colloquial sense "abuse, reproach," which the second verse plays on.

[94] The noun is neuter, but the adjective is masculine; probably intended as a solecism.

[95] In fact, the word probably means "mummy" here.

67

ἀναμένει καὶ σμικρὸν ὀπτῶσ᾽ ὀρφανὸν ταρίχιον.

καὶ Ἐπίχαρμος δ᾽ ἀρσενικῶς εἴρηκεν ὁ τάριχος. Ἡρόδοτος δ᾽ ἐν ἐνάτῃ οὕτως· οἱ τάριχοι ἐπὶ τῷ πυρὶ
e κείμενοι ἐπάλλοντο καὶ ἤσπαιρον. καὶ αἱ | παροιμίαι
δὲ κατὰ τὸ ἄρρεν λέγουσι·

τάριχος ὀπτὸς εὐθὺς ἂν ἴδῃ τὸ πῦρ.
σαπρὸς τάριχος τὴν ὀρίγανον φιλεῖ.
οὐκ ἂν πάθοι τάριχος ὧνπερ ἄξιος.

Ἀττικοὶ δὲ οὐδετέρως λέγουσι, καὶ γίνεται ἡ γενικὴ
τοῦ ταρίχους. Χιωνίδης Πτωχοῖς·

ἆρ᾽ ἂν φάγοιτ᾽ ἂν καὶ ταρίχους, ὦ θεοί;

καὶ ἐπὶ δοτικῆς·

ἐπὶ τῷ ταρίχει τῷδε τοίνυν κόπτετον.

ἡ δὲ δοτικὴ ταρίχει ὡς ξίφει. Μένανδρος Ἐπιτρέπου-
f σιν | ⟨καὶ ἐπὶ αἰτιατικῆς·⟩[8]

ἐπέπασα ⟨ . . . ⟩
ἐπὶ τὸ τάριχος ἅλας, ἐὰν οὕτω τύχῃ.

ὅτε δὲ ἀρσενικόν ἐστιν, ἡ γενικὴ οὐκέτι ἕξει τὸ σ.
τοσαύτην δ᾽ Ἀθηναῖοι σπουδὴν ἐποιοῦντο περὶ τὸ
τάριχος ὡς καὶ πολίτας ἀναγράψαι τοὺς Χαιρεφίλου

---

[8] add. Schweighäuser

or lentil soup, and roasting a tiny little piece of
orphan saltfish.

Epicharmus (fr. 159) too uses the word "saltfish" in the
masculine. Herodotus in Book IX (120.1), as follows: The
saltfish lying on the fire began to leap about and struggle.
The proverbs as well have the word in the masculine:[96]

Saltfish is roasted as soon as it sees the fire.
Rotten saltfish likes marjoram.[97]
Saltfish would not suffer what it deserves.

But Attic authors use it in the neuter, and the genitive is
tarichous. Chionides in *Beggars* (fr. 5):

Wouldn't you eat some saltfish (*tarichous*), gods?

Also in the dative (Chionid. fr. *6):

Well, the two of them gnawed at this saltfish
(*tarichei*).

The dative is *tarichei*, like *xiphei*[98]. Menander in *Men at
Arbitration* also used it in the accusative (fr. 5 K–T):

If this is how it is,
I sprinkled . . . salt on saltfish (*tarichos*).

When the word is masculine, the genitive no longer has the
sigma.[99] The Athenians were so serious about saltfish that
they enrolled the sons of Chairephilus the saltfish-seller[100]

---

[96] The masculine and neuter forms of the word are identical,
but in each case the noun is modified by a masculine adjective.
[97] Cf. 3.116e with n.   [98] From neuter *xiphos*, "sword."
[99] I.e. the form is *tarichou* rather than *tarichous*.

τοῦ ταριχοπώλου υἱούς, ὥς φησιν Ἄλεξις ἐν Ἐπι-
δαύρῳ οὕτως·

120   τοὺς Χαιρεφίλου δ᾽ υἱεῖς Ἀθηναίους, ὅτι ‖
εἰσήγαγεν τάριχος, οὓς καὶ Τιμοκλῆς
ἰδὼν ἐπὶ τῶν ἵππων δύο σκόμβρους ἔφη
ἐν τοῖς σατύροις εἶναι.

μνημονεύει αὐτῶν καὶ Ὑπερείδης ὁ ῥήτωρ. Εὐθύνου δὲ
τοῦ ταριχοπώλου μέμνηται Ἀντιφάνης ἐν Κουρίδι
οὕτως·

ἐλθών τε πρὸς τὸν τεμαχοπώλην, περίμενε,
παρ᾽ οὗ φέρειν εἴωθα. κἂν οὕτω τύχῃ,
Εὔθυνος < . . . > ἀπολογίζων αὐτόθι
b   χρηστόν τι περίμεινον, κέλευσον μὴ τεμεῖν. |

Φειδίππου δὲ—καὶ γὰρ οὗτος ταριχοπώλης—Ἄλεξις
ἐν Ἱππίσκῳ κἂν Σωράκοις·

Φείδιππος ἕτερός τις ταριχηγὸς ξένος.

Ἐσθιόντων δ᾽ ἡμῶν τὸ τάριχος καὶ πολλῶν ὁρμὴν
ἐχόντων ἐπὶ τὸ πιεῖν ὁ Δάφνος ἔφη ἀνατείνας τὼ
χεῖρε· Ἡρακλείδης ὁ Ταραντῖνος, ἄνδρες φίλοι, ἐν τῷ
ἐπιγραφομένῳ Συμποσίῳ φησί· ληπτέον σύμμετρον

---

100 *PA* 15187; the Pheidippus attacked in Alex. fr. 6 (quoted
below, where see n.) was one of his sons. See also 8.339d–e, citing
inter alia a fragment of Timocles' *Icarians*.
101 *PAA* 433922.   102 *PA* 14163.

as citizens, according to Alexis in *Epidaurus* (fr. 77), as follows:

> (. . . made) the sons of Chairephilus Athenians,
>   because
> he imported saltfish. When Timocles
> saw them on their horses, he said that two mackerels
> were among the satyrs.

Hyperides the orator (fr. 183 Jensen) also mentions them. Antiphanes refers to Euthynus the saltfish-seller[101] in *The Barber* (fr. 126), as follows:

> Go to the fellow who sells fish-steaks, the one from
>   whom I
> normally make my purchases, and wait there. And if
>   it works out this way,
> Euthynus . . . making some convenient excuse
> wait around there, and tell him not to cut it up.

Alexis mentions Pheidippus[102]—he was also a saltfish-seller—in *The Brooch*[103] (fr. 6) and *Storage Boxes* (fr. 221):

> another fellow, Pheidippus the foreign saltfish-
>   importer.

As we were eating the saltfish and many of us were growing eager to have a drink, Daphnis stretched out his hands[104] and said: Heracleides of Tarentum, my friends, says in his work entitled *The Symposium* (fr. 69 Guar-

---

[103] Athenaeus occasionally refers to the play elsewhere as *Agonis* (a courtesan's name) *or The Brooch* (8.339c; 15.678e).

[104] Here apparently a gesture intended to keep the rest of the guests from doing anything until Daphnis had his say.

71

τροφὴν πρὸ τοῦ πίνειν καὶ μάλιστα τὰς εἰθισμένας
c προπαρατίθεσθαι | περιφοράς. ἐκ διαστήματος γὰρ
εἰσφερομένας ἐναλλάττειν τὰ ἀπὸ τοῦ οἴνου προσ-
καθίζοντα τῷ στομάχῳ καὶ δηγμῶν αἴτια καθιστά-
μενα. οἴονται δέ τινες ταῦτ᾽ εἶναι καὶ κακοστόμαχα—
λέγω δὴ λαχάνων καὶ ταρίχων γένη—δηκτικόν τι
κεκτημένα, εὐθετεῖν δὲ τὰ κολλώδη καὶ ἐπιστύφοντα
βρώματα, ἀγνοοῦντες ὅτι πολλὰ τῶν τὰς ἐκκρίσεις
ποιούντων εὐλύτους ἐκ τῶν ἐναντίων εὐστόμαχα καθ-
έστηκεν· ἐν οἷς ἐστι καὶ τὸ σίσαρον καλούμενον (οὗ
d μνημονεύει Ἐπίχαρμος ἐν Ἀγρωστίνῳ, | ἐν Γῇ καὶ
Θαλάσσῃ, καὶ Διοκλῆς ἐν πρώτῳ Ὑγιεινῶν), ἀσπάρα-
γος, τεῦτλον τὸ λευκόν (τὸ γὰρ μέλαν καθεκτικόν
ἐστιν ἐκκρίσεων), κόγχαι, σωλῆνες, μύες θαλάττιοι,
χῆμαι, κτένες, τάριχος τέλειος καὶ μὴ βρομώδης, καὶ
ἰχθύων εὐχύλων γένη. προπαρατίθεσθαι δ᾽ ἐστὶν ὠφέ-
λιμον τὴν λεγομένην φυλλίδα καὶ τευτλίον, ἔτι δὲ
τάριχος, εἰς τὰς ὁρμὰς εἰς ταῦτα < . . . > μὴ ὁμοίως
τῶν πολυτρόφων ἀπολαύειν. τὰς δὲ ἀθρόους ἐν ἀρχῇ
πόσεις ἐκκλιτέον· δύσκλητοι † γὰρ εἰς τὴν πλείονα
τῶν ὑγρῶν προσφοράν. Μακεδόνες δ᾽, ὥς φησιν
e Ἔφιππος | ὁ Ὀλύνθιος ἐν τῷ Περὶ τῆς Ἀλεξάνδρου
καὶ Ἡφαιστίωνος Ταφῆς, οὐκ ἠπίσταντο πίνειν εὐ-
τάκτως, ἀλλ᾽ εὐθέως ἐχρῶντο μεγάλαις προπόσεσιν,
ὥστε μεθύειν ἔτι παρακειμένων τῶν πρώτων τραπεζῶν

---

[105] Hephaestion (Berve i #357) was one of Alexander the

dasole): You should consume a moderate amount of food before drinking, especially the items commonly served before the symposium begins. For when such foods are introduced only after an interval, they counteract the wine's effect, thus oppressing the stomach and causing serious pain. Some authorities believe that these foods—I am referring to the different types of vegetables and saltfish—are hard on the stomach, since they have a tendency to irritate it, and maintain that glutinous and astringent foods are more suitable. This is because they are unaware that many foods that promote easy bowel movements are, to the contrary, easy on the stomach; these include what is referred to as *sisaros* ("parsnip")—Epicharmus mentions it in *The Rustic* (fr. 3) and *Earth and Sea* (fr. 24), as does Diocles in Book I of *On Matters of Health* (fr. 198 van der Eijk)—asparagus, white beet (for the black variety hinders excretion), conchs, razor-shells, sea-mussels, clams, scallops, good saltfish that does not stink, and the types of fish that produce good *chulē*. It is helpful to serve what is referred to as *phullis* ("salad") and beets beforehand, as well as saltfish, to encourage (the guests) regarding these items . . . and similarly not to enjoy foods that are very rich. You should avoid drinking a great deal at the beginning, because † they have a bad reputation in regard to the excessive consumption of liquids. According to Ephippus of Olynthus in his *On the Burial of Alexander and Hephaestion*[105] (*FGrH* 126 F 1), the Macedonians did not know how to drink in an orderly way, but engaged in large toasts at the very beginning; the result was that they got

Great's closest friends. He died in Ecbatana in autumn 324 BCE, less than a year before the death of Alexander himself.

καὶ μὴ δύνασθαι τῶν σιτίων ἀπολαύειν. Δίφιλος δ᾽ ὁ
Σίφνιός φησι· τὰ ταρίχη τὰ ἐκ τῶν θαλασσίων καὶ
λιμναίων καὶ ποταμίων γινόμενά ἐστιν ὀλιγότροφα,
ὀλιγόχυλα, καυσώδη, εὐκοίλια, ἐρεθιστικὰ ὀρέξεως.
κράτιστα δὲ τῶν μὲν ἀπιόνων κύβια καὶ ὡραῖα καὶ τὰ
τούτοις ὅμοια γένη, τῶν δὲ πιόνων τὰ θύννεια καὶ
f   κορδύλεια. | τὰ δὲ παλαιὰ κρείσσονα καὶ δριμύτερα
καὶ μάλιστα τὰ Βυζάντια. τὸ δὲ θύννειον, φησί, γίνεται ἐκ τῆς μείζονος πηλαμύδος, ὧν τὸ μικρὸν ἀνα-
λογεῖ τῷ κυβίῳ, ἐξ οὗ γένους ἐστὶ καὶ τὸ ὡραῖον. ἡ δὲ
121   σάρδα προσέοικε τῷ κολίᾳ μεγέθει. ‖ ὁ δὲ σκόμβρος
κούφως καὶ ταχέως ἀποχωρῶν τοῦ στομάχου. ὁ κολί-
ας δὲ σκιλλωδέστερος, δηκτικώτερος καὶ κακοχυλότε-
ρος, τρόφιμος· κρείσσων δὲ ὁ Ἀμυνκλανὸς καὶ Σπανὸς
ὁ Σαξιτανὸς λεγόμενος· λεπτότερος γὰρ καὶ γλυκύτε-
ρος. Στράβων δ᾽ ἐν τρίτῳ Γεωγραφικῶν πρὸς ταῖς
Ἡρακλέους φησὶ νήσοις κατὰ Καρχηδόνα τὴν καινὴν
πόλιν εἶναι Σεξιτανίαν, ἐξ ἧς καὶ τὰ ταρίχη ἐπωνύμως
λέγεσθαι, καὶ ἄλλην Σκομβροαρίαν ἀπὸ τῶν ἁλισκο-
b   μένων σκόμβρων, ἐξ ὧν τὸ ἄριστον σκευάζεσθαι |
γάρον. οἱ δὲ λεγόμενοι μελάνδρυαι, ὧν καὶ Ἐπίχαρμος μνημονεύει ἐν Αὐτομόλῳ Ὀδυσσεῖ οὕτως·

---

106 I.e. the dinner tables, as opposed to the "second tables," on
which the symposium food was served.
107 New Carthage was located near the extreme southern end
of the eastern coast of what is today Spain. The Island of Heracles

drunk while the first tables[106] were still lying beside them, and were unable to enjoy the food. Diphilus of Siphnos says: Saltfish produced from sea-, lake- and river-creatures does not contain much nutrition or produce much *chulē*, generates heat, is easy on the bowels, and stimulates the appetite. The best varieties of lean saltfish are cube-, *horaia* and the like, while the best varieties of fatty saltfish are made of tuna and *kordulos*. The older saltfish is, the better and more pungent it becomes, especially Byzantine saltfish. He claims that tuna-saltfish is made from the larger variety of *pēlamus*, while the small *pēlamus* is suited for cube-saltfish; this type is also used to make *horaion*. The *sarda* is the same size as the Spanish mackerel. The mackerel moves lightly and rapidly out of the stomach. The Spanish mackerel has a more squill-like taste, is more pungent, produces worse *chulē*, and is nourishing. The best varieties are the Amynclanian and the Spanish type called Saxitanian, because they are lighter and sweeter. Strabo in Book III (156) of his *Geography* says that Sexitania, from which the saltfish gets its name, is near the Islands of Heracles opposite New Carthage[107]; he adds (III.159) that there is another city, called Scombroaria from the mackerel *(skombroi)* caught there, from which the best *garum*[108] is made. The so-called *melandruai*, which Epicharmus mentions in *Odysseus the Deserter* (fr. 101), as follows:

(also known as Scombroaria; Athenaeus or his source has garbled the geographical details) lay in front of the bay that formed the city's harbor.

[108] Fermented fish-sauce.

ποτιφόριμον τὸ τέμαχος ἦς,
ὑπομελανδρυῶδες.

μέλανδρυς δὲ τῶν μεγίστων θύννων εἶδός ἐστιν, ὡς
Πάμφιλος ἐν τοῖς Περὶ Ὀνομάτων παρίστησι, καί
ἐστι τὰ τεμάχη αὐτοῦ λιπαρώτερα. τὸ δὲ ὠμοτάριχον,
φησὶν ὁ Δίφιλος, † κητεμε † τινὲς λέγουσι, καί ἐστι
βαρὺ καὶ γλοιῶδες, προσέτι δὲ καὶ δύσπεπτον. ὁ δὲ
ποτάμιος κορακῖνος, ὃν πέλτην τινὲς καλοῦσιν, ὁ ἀπὸ
c   τοῦ Νείλου, ὃν οἱ κατὰ τὴν Ἀλεξάνδρειαν | ἰδίως
ἡμίνηρον ὀνομάζουσιν, ὑποπίμελος μέν ἐστι καὶ ἥκι-
στα κακόχυλος, σαρκώδης, τρόφιμος, εὔπεπτος, εὐ-
ανάδοτος, κατὰ πάντα τοῦ μύλλου κρείσσων. τὰ μέντοι τῶν ἰχθύων καὶ τῶν ταρίχων ᾠὰ πάντα δύσπεπτα,
δύσφθαρτα, μᾶλλον δὲ τὰ τῶν λιπαρωτέρων καὶ μει-
ζόνων· σκληρότερα γὰρ μένει καὶ ἀδιαίρετα. γίνεται
δὲ εὐστόμαχα μετὰ ἁλῶν σβεσθέντα καὶ ἐποπτη-
θέντα. πάντας δὲ χρὴ τοὺς ταρίχους πλύνειν, ἄχρι ἂν
τὸ ὕδωρ ἄνοσμον καὶ γλυκὺ γένηται. ὁ δ᾽ ἐκ θαλάσ-
d   σης ἑψόμενος τάριχος | γλυκύτερος γίνεται, θερμοί τε
οἱ τάριχοι ἡδίονές εἰσιν. Μνησίθεος δ᾽ ὁ Ἀθηναῖος ἐν
τῷ Περὶ Ἐδεστῶν, οἱ ἁλυκοί, φησίν, καὶ γλυκεῖς
χυμοὶ πάντες ὑπάγουσι τὰς κοιλίας, οἱ δ᾽ ὀξεῖς καὶ
δριμεῖς λύουσι τὴν οὔρησιν, οἱ δὲ πικροὶ μᾶλλον μέν
εἰσιν οὐρητικοί, λύουσι δ᾽ αὐτῶν ἔνιοι καὶ τὰς κοιλίας·
οἱ δὲ στρυφνοὶ < . . . > τὰς ἐκκρίσεις. Ξενοφῶν δὲ ὁ
μουσικώτατος ἐν τῷ ἐπιγραφομένῳ Ἱέρωνι ἢ Τυραν-

The fish-steak was suitable,
rather like *melandrus*.

A *melandrus* is one of the largest kinds of tuna, as Pamphilus shows in his *On Names* (fr. XXII Schmidt), and the steaks cut from it are oilier. According to Diphilus, some authorities refer to raw-saltfish as † *kēteme*[109] †, and it is heavy and glutinous, as well as difficult to digest. The river-*korakinos* caught in the Nile, which some authorities refer to as a *peltē*, and for which the inhabitants of Alexandria use the local term "half-fresh,"[110] is rather fatty, produces a minimal amount of bad *chulē*, and is meaty, nourishing, easily digested and assimilated, and better than the mullet in every respect. All fish eggs, however, including those in saltfish, are difficult to digest and dissolve, especially those from fatter and larger fish, because they remain harder and unseparated. But they become easy on the stomach if they are plunged into salt and then roasted. All saltfish needs to be rinsed until the water has no smell and no taste of salt. Saltfish stewed in sea-water is sweeter; and it tastes better warm. Mnesitheus of Athens says in his *On Edible Substances* (fr. 22 Bertier): All salty and sweet juices[111] set the bowels in motion; sharp and pungent juices stimulate urination; and some bitter juices are more diuretic, while others also loosen the bowels. But astringent juices . . . excretions. The refined Xenophon in his work entitled *Hieron or The Tyrant's Life* (1.22–3) condemns foods of

---

[109] Corrupt; whatever the word is, it may well be cognate with *kētos* ("large fish"), which the zoologist Sostratus at 7.303b–c (cf. Archestr. fr. 35.3 Olson–Sens, quoted at 7.301f) says was a name for an extremely large tuna.   [110] Cf. 3.118f.

[111] Or "humours."

νικῷ διαβάλλων τὰ τοιαῦτα βρώματά φησι· "τί γάρ",
e ἔφη ὁ Ἱέρων, "τὰ πολλὰ ταῦτα μηχανήματα | κατανε-
νοήκατε ἃ παρατίθεται τοῖς τυράννοις, ὀξέα καὶ δρι-
μέα καὶ στρυφνὰ καὶ τὰ τούτων ἀδελφά;" "πάνυ μὲν
οὖν", ἔφη ὁ Σιμωνίδης, καὶ πάνυ γέ μοι δοκοῦντα
παρὰ φύσιν εἶναι ταῦτα ἀνθρώπῳ." ἄλλο τι οἴει, "ἔφη
ὁ Ἱέρων, ταῦτα ἐδέσματα εἶναι ἢ μὴ διὰ κακῆς καὶ
ἀσθενούσης ψυχῆς ἐπιθυμήματα; ἐπεὶ οἵ γε ἡδέως
ἐσθίοντες καὶ σύ που οἶσθα ὅτι οὐδὲν προσδέονται
τούτων τῶν σοφισμάτων." ἐπὶ τούτοις λεχθεῖσιν ὁ
Κύνουλκος πιεῖν ᾔτησε δηκόκταν, δεῖν λέγων ἁλμυ-
f ροὺς λόγους γλυκέσιν | ἀποκλύζεσθαι νάμασι. πρὸς
ὃν ὁ Οὐλπιανὸς σχετλιάσας καὶ τύψας τῇ χειρὶ τὸ
προσκεφάλαιον ἔφη· μέχρι πότε βαρβαρίζοντες οὐ
παύσεσθε; ἢ ἕως ἂν καταλιπὼν τὸ συμπόσιον οἴχω-
μαι, πέττειν ὑμῶν τοὺς λόγους οὐ δυνάμενος; καὶ ὅς·
ἐν Ῥώμῃ τῇ βασιλευούσῃ διατρίβων τὰ νῦν, ὦ λῷστε,
ἐπιχωρίῳ κέχρημαι κατὰ τὴν συνήθειαν φωνῇ. καὶ
γὰρ παρὰ τοῖς ἀρχαίοις ποιηταῖς καὶ συγγραφεῦσι
122 τοῖς σφόδρα ἑλληνίζουσιν ἔστιν εὑρεῖν καὶ Περσικὰ ‖
ὀνόματα κείμενα διὰ τὴν τῆς χρήσεως συνήθειαν, ὡς
τοὺς παρασάγγας καὶ τοὺς ἀστ‹άνδας ἢ ἀγγ›άρους
καὶ τὴν σχοῖνον ἢ τὸν σχοῖνον· μέτρον δ' ἐστὶ τοῦτο

---

112 A Latin word (sc. *aqua*), hence Ulpian's angry response, for
water that had been "boiled down" (*decoquo*) and then suddenly
chilled.   113 Cf. Pl. *Phdr.* 243d.   114 Cf. 3.98c n.

this sort, saying: Well then, said Hieron, have you noticed all these concoctions served to tyrants: acidic sauces, bitter sauces, astringent sauces, and their cousins? Certainly, said Simonides; they seem to me to be utterly unnatural for a human being. Hieron said: Do you think that these foods represent anything other than the cravings of a sick, ugly soul? For I imagine that you are aware that people who enjoy eating have no need for fancy items like these. In response to these remarks, Cynulcus asked to drink some *decocta*[112], saying that he needed to wash salty words out of his ears with sweet streams.[113] Ulpian became indignant with him, pounded his pillow with his fist, and said: How long are you going to continue using barbarisms? Until I leave the symposium and go home, unable to stomach your words? And he said: Since I am currently spending my time in the imperial city of Rome, my very good sir, I have grown accustomed to using the local language. For even in the ancient poets and prose-authors who write the purest Greek one can find Persian words that appear because they are in common usage, such as "parasangs"[114], *astandai* or *angaroi*[115], and *schoinos*, whether masculine or feminine; the latter is a measure of distance, which is referred to in this way by many people even today.[116] I am also

[115] Two different words for couriers who travelled along the Persian royal road; but the text is conjectural.

[116] A *schoinos* (literally "rope") was apparently in origin an Egyptian unit, which according to Hdt. 2.6.3 was equal to 60 stades or 2 parasangs. The word itself is neither Persian nor Egyptian; but Callimachus (fr. 1.18) also refers to a "Persian *schoinos*," and the crucial point for the average Greek-speaker was probably that the unit was associated with the barbarian East, a fact that confused the etymological issue.

ὁδοῦ μέχρι νῦν οὕτως παρὰ πολλοῖς καλούμενον.
μακεδονίζοντάς τ᾽ οἶδα πολλοὺς τῶν Ἀττικῶν διὰ τὴν
ἐπιμιξίαν. βέλτιον δ᾽ ἦν μοι

αἷμα ταύρειον πιεῖν,
ὁ Θεμιστοκλέους γὰρ θάνατος αἱρετώτερος,

ἢ εἰς σὲ ἐμπεσεῖν. οὐ γὰρ ἂν εἴποιμι Ταύρειον ὕδωρ
πιεῖν, ὅπερ σὺ οὐκ οἶσθα τί ἐστιν· οὐδὲ γὰρ ἐπίστασαι
b ὅτι καὶ παρὰ τοῖς ἀρίστοις τῶν | ποιητῶν καὶ συγγρα-
φέων εἴρηταί τινα καὶ φαῦλα. Κηφισόδωρος γοῦν ὁ
Ἰσοκράτους τοῦ ῥήτορος μαθητὴς ἐν τῷ τρίτῳ τῶν
Πρὸς Ἀριστοτέλην λέγει ὅτι εὕροι τις ἂν ὑπὸ τῶν
ἄλλων ποιητῶν ἢ καὶ σοφιστῶν ἓν ἢ δύο γοῦν πονηρῶς εἰρημένα, οἷα παρὰ μὲν Ἀρχιλόχῳ τὸ πάντ᾽ ἄνδρ᾽
ἀποσκολύπτειν, Θεοδώρῳ δὲ τὸ κελεύειν μὲν πλέον
ἔχειν, ἐπαινεῖν δὲ τὸ ἴσον, Εὐριπίδη τε τὸ τὴν γλῶτταν
ὀμωμοκέναι φάναι καὶ Σοφοκλεῖ τὸ ἐν Αἰθίοψιν εἰρη-
c μένον· |

τοιαῦτά τοί σοι πρὸς χάριν τε κοὐ βίᾳ
λέγω. σὺ δ᾽ αὐτός, ὥσπερ οἱ σοφοί, τὰ μὲν
δίκαι᾽ ἐπαίνει, τοῦ δὲ κερδαίνειν ἔχου.

καὶ ἀλλαχοῦ δ᾽ ὁ αὐτὸς ἔφη μηδὲν εἶναι ῥῆμα σὺν
κέρδει κακόν· Ὁμήρῳ δὲ τὸ τὴν Ἥραν ἐπιβουλεῦσαι

---

117 The Athenian general and statesman Themistocles (*PAA*
502610; *c*.525–459 BCE) was said to have committed suicide by
drinking bull's blood rather than fulfil a promise to help subject

aware that many Attic authors use Macedonian vocabulary because of their dealings with this people. It would be better for me (Ar. *Eq.* 83–4)

> to drink bull's *(taureion)* blood,
> because Themistocles' death[117] is preferable

to getting entangled with you. (I would not say "to drink Taureian water," since you have no idea what this is.)[118] For you do not realize that some unelevated remarks are made by even the best poets and prose-authors. Cephisodorus the student of the orator Isocrates, for example, says in Book III of his *Reply to Aristotle* (fr. 5 Radermacher) that one can find at least one or two vulgar remarks made by the other poets and philosophers, such as the phrase "to remove every man's skin"[119] in Archilochus (fr. 39 West², unmetrical), and "to encourage the accumulation of wealth, but praise equality" in Theodorus (*SH* 754, unmetrical); or having someone say "my tongue has sworn an oath"[120] in Euripides (*Hipp.* 612); or what Sophocles says in *Ethiopians* (fr. 28):

> I am making these remarks to you to please you
> and not because I must. But as for you yourself, do
>   what wise people do,
> and praise what is right but cling to making a profit!

And elsewhere (*El.* 61) the same author said that no speech made with profit in mind is bad. Likewise Hera's

---

Greece to the authority of the Persian king (D.S. 11.58.2–3). Cf. 1.29f–30a with n.   [118] See 3.122e–f.   [119] I.e. "to give every man an erection"?   [120] Sc. "but my mind has not." A notorious verse; cf. Ar. *Th.* 275–6 with Austin–Olson ad loc.

τῷ Διὶ καὶ τὸν Ἄρη μοιχεύειν· ἐφ' οἷς πάντες κατηγο-
ροῦσιν αὐτῶν. εἰ οὖν κἀγώ τι ἥμαρτον, ὦ καλλίστων
ὀνομάτων καὶ ῥημάτων θηρευτά, μὴ χαλέπαινε. κατὰ
d γὰρ τὸν Μιλήσιον Τιμόθεον τὸν ποιητήν· |

οὐκ ἀείδω τὰ παλαιά,
τὰ γὰρ ἀμὰ κρείσσω·
νέος ὁ Ζεὺς βασιλεύει,
τὸ πάλαι δ' ἦν Κρόνος ἄρχων·
ἀπίτω Μοῦσα παλαιά.

Ἀντιφάνης τ' ἐν Ἀλκήστιδι ἔφη·

ἐπὶ τὸ καινουργεῖν φέρου,
οὕτως, ἐκείνως, τοῦτο γινώσκων ὅτι
ἓν καινὸν ἐγχείρημα, κἂν τολμηρὸν ᾖ,
e πολλῶν παλαιῶν ἐστι χρησιμώτερον. |

ὅτι δὲ καὶ οἱ ἀρχαῖοι οἴδασι τὸ οὕτω λεγόμενον ὕδωρ,
ἵνα μὴ πάλιν ἀγανακτήσῃς δηκόκταν μου λέγοντος,
δείξω. κατὰ γὰρ Φερεκράτους Ψευδηρακλέα·

εἴποι τις ἂν τῶν πάνυ δοκησιδεξίων.
ἐγὼ δ' ἂν ἀντείποιμι· μὴ πολυπραγμόνει,
ἀλλ' εἰ δοκεῖ σοι, πρόσεχε τὸν νοῦν κἀκροῶ.

ἀλλὰ μὴ φθονήσῃς, ἔφη ὁ Οὐλπιανός, δέομαι, μηδὲ
τοῦ Ταυρείου ὕδατος ὁποῖόν ἐστι δηλῶσαι· τῶν γὰρ
f τοιούτων[9] ἐγὼ διψῶ. καὶ ὁ Κύνουλκος, | ἀλλὰ προπίνω

---

[9] τοιούτων φωνῶν A

82

plotting against Zeus in Homer (*Il.* 14.159ff) and Ares'
illicit love-affair (*Od.* 8.266ff). And everyone condemns
them for these passages. So if I made a mistake, O mighty
hunter of the loveliest words and phrases, do not be angry
with me. For to quote the Milesian poet Timotheus (*PMG*
796):

> I do not sing the old songs,
> for mine are better.
> A new Zeus is king;
> Cronus was in power long ago.
> Away with the ancient Muse!

And Antiphanes said in *Alcestis* (fr. 30):

> Aim to do something new
> in one way or another; and recognize that
> a single novel undertaking, even if too bold,
> is more useful than many old ones.

I intend to prove that the ancients know of water referred
to this way (I am trying to prevent your being annoyed with
me again for saying "*decocta*"). For to quote Pherecrates'
Fake Heracles (fr. 163):

> . . . one of these apparently very clever people might
>   say.
> And I would respond: Don't make trouble,
> but if you're willing, pay attention and listen.

Ulpian said: Please—don't begrudge us a clarification as to
what Taureian water is;[121] for I am thirsty for information
like this. And Cynulcus said: Then I drink your health, and

[121] Cf. 3.122a.

σοι, ἔφη, φιλοτησίαν (διψᾷς γὰρ λόγων) παρ᾽ Ἀλέξιδος λαβὼν ἐκ Πυθαγοριζούσης·

ὕδατος ἀπέφθου κύαθον· ἂν δ᾽ ὠμὸν πίῃ,
βαρὺ καὶ κοπῶδες.

τὸ δὲ Ταύρειον ὕδωρ ὠνόμασεν, ὦ φίλε, Σοφοκλῆς
Αἰγεῖ ἀπὸ τοῦ περὶ Τροιζῆνα ποταμοῦ Ταύρου, παρ᾽ ᾧ
123 καὶ κρήνη τις ‖ Ὑόεσσα καλεῖται. ἐπίστανται δ᾽ οἱ
παλαιοὶ καὶ τὸ πάνυ ψυχρὸν ὕδωρ ἐν ταῖς προπόσεσιν, ἀλλ᾽ οὐκ ἐρῶ, ἐὰν μὴ καὶ σύ με διδάξῃς εἰ ἔπινον
θερμὸν ὕδωρ ἐν ταῖς εὐωχίαις οἱ ἀρχαῖοι. εἰ γὰρ οἱ
κρατῆρες ἀπὸ τοῦ συμβεβηκότος τῆς ὀνομασίας ἔτυχον οὗτοί τε κερασθέντες παρέκειντο πλήρεις, οὐ ζέον
τὸ ποτὸν παρεῖχον, λεβήτων τρόπον ὑποκαιόμενοι. ὅτι
γὰρ οἴδασι θερμὸν ὕδωρ Εὔπολις μὲν ἐν Δήμοις
παρίστησι·

τὸ χαλκίον
θέρμαινέ θ᾽ ἡμῖν καὶ θύη πέττειν τινὰ
b   κέλευ᾽, ἵνα σπλάγχνοισι ‖ συγγενώμεθα.

Ἀντιφάνης δ᾽ ἐν Ὀμφάλῃ·

ἐν χύτρᾳ δέ μοι
ὅπως ὕδωρ ἕψοντα μηδέν᾽ ὄψομαι.

---

122 Viz. that something was mixed (kerannumi) in them, as
what follows makes clear, although Cynulcus seems to be arguing
that what was mixed in a mixing-bowl was not wine and water but

(because you are thirsty for words) I have borrowed the cup of friendship I do it with from Alexis' *The Female Pythagorean* (fr. 202):

> a ladleful of boiled water; but if one drinks it raw,
> it's heavy and debilitating.

As for Taureian water, my friend, Sophocles in *Aegeus* (fr. 19) derived the name from the Taurus river near Troezen, beside which is a spring called Hyoessa. The ancients also know of the use of very cold water in their toasts; but I am not going to tell you about this, unless you inform me as to whether the ancients drank warm water at their feasts. For if their mixing bowls *(kratēres)* got their name from the circumstances,[122] and if, after they were mixed up, they were set down beside them full, they did not serve their drinks boiling hot by lighting a fire under the mixing-bowls, as one does with cauldrons. For Eupolis in *Demes* (fr. 99.41–3) establishes that they are familiar with warm water:

> Warm up
> the bronze pot for us and tell someone to bake
> sacrificial cakes, so that we can associate with[123]
> entrails.

Antiphanes in *Omphale* (fr. 175):

> I don't want to see
> anyone boiling water in a cookpot for me;

hot and cold substances (as in a bathtub), so that whatever was served must have been lukewarm at best.

[123] I.e. in context "eat."

οὐ γὰρ κακὸν ἔχω μηδ' ἔχοιμ'. ἐὰν δ' ἄρα
στρέφῃ με περὶ τὴν γαστέρ' ἢ τὸν ὀμφαλόν,
παρὰ Φερτάτου δακτύλιός ἐστί μοι δραχμῆς.

ἐν δ' Ἀλειπτρίᾳ—φέρεται τὸ δρᾶμα καὶ ὡς Ἀλέξιδος—·

c   ἐὰν δὲ τοὐργαστήριον ποιῆτε περιβόητον, |
κατασκεδῶ, νὴ τὴν φίλην Δήμητρα, τὴν
        μεγίστην
ἀρύταιναν ὑμῶν ἐκ μέσου βάψασα τοῦ λέβητος
ζέοντος ὕδατος· εἰ δὲ ⟨μή⟩, μηδέποθ' ὕδωρ πίοιμι
ἐλευθέριον.

Πλάτων δ' ἐν τετάρτῳ Πολιτείας· ἐπιθυμία ⟨ἂν⟩ ἐν τῇ
ψυχῇ εἴη; οἷον δίψα ἐστὶ δίψα ἆρά γε θερμοῦ ποτοῦ ἢ
ψυχροῦ ⟨ἢ πολλοῦ ἢ⟩ ὀλίγου ἢ καὶ ἑνὶ λόγῳ ποιοῦ
τινος πώματος; ἢ ἐὰν μέν τις θερμότης τῷ δίψει
προσῇ, τὴν τοῦ θερμοῦ ἐπιθυμίαν προσπαρέχοιτ' ἄν,
ἐὰν δὲ ψυχρότης, τὴν τοῦ ψυχροῦ, ἐὰν δὲ διὰ πλήθους
d   παρουσίαν | πολλὴ ἡ δίψα ᾖ, τὴν τοῦ πολλοῦ παρέξε-
ται, ἐὰν δὲ ὀλίγη, τὴν τοῦ ὀλίγου· αὐτὸ δὲ τὸ διψῆν οὐ
μή ποτε ἄλλου γένηται ἐπιθυμία ἢ οὗπερ πέφυκεν,
αὐτοῦ πώματος, καὶ αὖ τὸ πεινῆν βρώματος; Σῆμος δὲ
ὁ Δήλιος ἐν δευτέρᾳ Νησιάδος ἐν Κιμώλῳ τῇ νήσῳ
φησὶ ψυχεῖα κατεσκευάσθαι θέρους ὀρυκτά, ἔνθα χλι-

---

124 The quotation is truncated at the beginning and garbled in
the middle, where Plato actually claims that the presence of heat
or cold produces a desire for the opposite.

86

because I don't have any trouble and I don't want
    any. But if
I develop a cramp in my stomach or my gut,
I've got a ring from Phertatos that cost a drachma.

And in *The Female Oiler* (Antiph. fr. 26)—the play is also
attributed to Alexis—:

If you make our workshop notorious,
by our beloved Demeter, I'll dump the biggest
ladle over you after I've filled it with boiling water
from the middle of the cauldron. And if I don't, may I
    never drink the water
of freedom.

Plato in Book IV of the *Republic* (437d–e):[124] Could there
be desire in the soul? Thus, is thirst actually thirst for
something warm to drink, or something cold, or for more,
or less, or simply put for any particular sort of drink? Or is
it the case that, if heat is associated with the thirst, it adds
the desire for something warm to it, whereas if cold is associated with the thirst, it adds the desire for something cold;
and if the thirst is great, because quantity is present, it will
add the desire for drinking a great deal; and if the thirst is
minimal, it will add the desire for only a little to drink? But
the thirst itself could never be a desire for anything except
that which it arises from, that is for wanting something to
drink, just as hunger is a desire for food? Semus of Delos in
Book II of his *History of the Island* (*FGrH* 396 F *3) says
that on the island of Cimolus during the summer cooling-
pits are prepared, in which they deposit jars full of warm

ερου ὕδατος πλήρη κεράμια καταθέντες κομίζονται
χιόνος οὐδὲν διάφορον. τὸ δὲ χλιαρὸν ὕδωρ Ἀθηναῖοι
e μετάκερας καλοῦσιν, ὡς Σώφιλος ἐν Ἀνδροκλεῖ. |
Ἄλεξις δ' ἐν Λοκροῖς·

> αἱ δὲ παῖδες παρέχεον
> ἡ μὲν τὸ θερμόν, ἡ δ' ἑτέρα ⟨τὸ⟩ μετάκερας.

καὶ Φιλήμων ἐν Κορινθίᾳ. Ἄμφις δ' ἐν Βαλανείῳ·

> ἀνεβόησ' ὕδωρ ἐνεγκεῖν θερμόν, ἄλλος
> μετάκερας.

Μέλλοντος δὲ τοῦ κυνικοῦ τούτοις ἐπισωρεύειν τινὰ
ὁ Ποντιανὸς ἔφη· οἴδασιν, ὦ φίλτατοι ἀνδρῶν, οἱ
ἀρχαῖοι καὶ τὴν τοῦ πάνυ ψυχροῦ πόσιν. Ἄλεξις γοῦν
ἐν Παρασίτῳ φησί·

> καὶ γὰρ βούλομαι
f ὕδατός σε γεῦσαι· πρᾶγμα δ' ἐστί | μοι μέγα
> φρέατος ἔνδον ψυχρότερον Ἀραρότος.

ὀνομάζει δὲ καὶ Ἕρμιππος ἐν Κέρκωψι φρεατιαῖον
ὕδωρ οὕτως ⟨ . . . ⟩. ὅτι δὲ καὶ χιόνα ἔπινον ἐν
Μανδραγοριζομένῃ ἔφη Ἄλεξις·

> εἶτ' οὐ περίεργόν ἐστιν ἄνθρωπος φυτὸν
> ὑπεναντιωτάτοις τε πλείστοις χρώμενον;

---

[125] Cf. 2.41d, where this information is attributed to Eratosthenes.
[126] Araros was one of Aristophanes' sons and a comic poet

water; when they take them out they are the same temperature as snow. The Athenians refer to warm water as *metakeras*, according to Sophilus in *Androcles* (fr. 1).[125] Alexis in *Locrians* (fr. 141):

> One of the slave-girls
> was pouring in hot water, the other one warm
> (*metakeras*) water.

Also Philemon in *The Girl from Corinth* (fr. 40). Amphis in *The Bathhouse* (fr. 7):

> One man called for someone to bring him hot water,
> another called for warm (*metakeras*).

As the Cynic was about to heap some further examples on top of these, Pontianus said: The ancients, most dear sirs, are also familiar with drinking very cold water. For example, Alexis says in *The Parasite* (fr. 184):

> For in fact I want
> you to taste some water; I have a remarkable
> well inside, which is more frigid than Araros.[126]

Hermippus also refers to well-water in *The Cercopes* (fr. 40), as follows . . . And that they drank snow is asserted by Alexis in *The Woman Who Ate Mandrake* (fr. 145):

> Aren't human beings strange creatures,
> engaging in so many activities directly contradictory
> to one another?

in his own right. The charge of frigidity refers to his alleged use of overly extravagant compounds, forced puns, and the like; cf. Olson on Ar. *Ach.* 138–40.

124 ἐρῶμεν ἀλλοτρίων, παρορῶμεν συγγενεῖς. ‖
    ἔχοντες οὐδὲν εὐποροῦμεν τοῖς πέλας,
    ἐράνους φέροντες οὐ φέρομεν ἀλλ᾽ ἢ κακῶς.
    τἀκ τῆς τροφῆς δὲ τῆς καθ᾽ ἡμέραν πάλιν
    γλιχόμεθα μὲν τὴν μᾶζαν ἵνα λευκὴ παρῇ,
    ζωμὸν δὲ ταύτῃ μέλανα μηχανώμεθα
    τὸ καλόν τε χρῶμα δευσοποιῷ χρῴζομεν.
    καὶ χιόνα μὲν πίνειν παρασκευάζομεν,
    τὸ δ᾽ ὄψον ἂν μὴ θερμὸν ᾖ, διασύρομεν.
    καὶ τὸν μὲν ὀξὺν οἶνον ἐκπυτίζομεν,
b   ἐπὶ ταῖς ἀβυρτάκαισι δ᾽ ἐκβακχεύομεν. |
    οὐκοῦν, τὸ πολλοῖς τῶν σοφῶν εἰρημένον,
    τὸ μὴ γενέσθαι μὲν κράτιστόν ἐστ᾽ ἀεί,
    ἐπὰν γένηται δ᾽, ὡς τάχιστ᾽ ἔχειν τέλος.

Δεξικράτης δ᾽ ἐν τῷ ἐπιγραφομένῳ Ὑφ᾽ Ἑαυτῶν Πλα-
νωμένοίς φησιν·

    εἰ δὲ μεθύω καὶ χιόνα πίνω καὶ μύρον
    ἐπίσταμ᾽ ὅ τι κράτιστον Αἴγυπτος ποεῖ.

Εὐθυκλῆς δ᾽ ἐν Ἀσώτοις ἢ Ἐπιστολῇ·

    πρῶτος μὲν οἶδεν εἰ χιών ἐστ᾽ ὠνία,
    πρῶτον δ᾽ ἐκεῖνον σχαδόνα δεῖ πάντως φαγεῖν.

c   οἶδεν δὲ καὶ ὁ καλὸς Ξενοφῶν ἐν Ἀπομνημονεύμασι |
τὴν διὰ χιόνος πόσιν. Χάρης δ᾽ ὁ Μιτυληναῖος ἐν ταῖς
Περὶ Ἀλέξανδρον Ἱστορίαις καὶ ὅπως δεῖ χιόνα δια-
φυλάσσεσθαι εἴρηκε, διηγούμενος περὶ τῆς πολιορ-

We fall in love with members of other households,
    but neglect our families;
although we're poor, we seem rich to our neighbors;
when we loan someone money, we do it clumsily.
And as for what we eat every day,
we're eager for our barley-cake to be white;
but we make the broth that goes with it black,
and we stain its lovely color with dye.
We arrange to drink snow;
but if our food isn't hot, we make nasty remarks
    about it.
And we spit out sour wine,
but get ecstatic about sour sauces.
So, as many wise men have said,
it's always best not to have been born,
and once you're born, to die as quickly as possible.

Dexicrates says in the play entitled *The Self-Deceivers* (fr. 1):

If I'm drunk, and I drink snow, and I know
that Egypt produces the best perfumed oil.

Euthycles in *Profligates or The Letter* (fr. 1):

He's the first to know if snow is for sale,
and he absolutely has to be the first to eat
    honeycomb.

The excellent Xenophon as well shows familiarity with the use of snow in drinking in his *Memorabilia* (2.1.30). Chares of Mitylene in his *Histories of Alexander* (*FGrH* 125 F 16) also tells us how to preserve snow, when he de-

κίας τῆς ἐν Ἰνδοῖς πόλεως Πέτρας, ὀρύξαι φάσκων
τὸν Ἀλέξανδρον ὀρύγματα τριάκοντα ψυχεῖα, ἃ πλη-
ρώσαντα χιόνος παρεμβαλεῖν δρυὸς κλάδους· οὕτω
γὰρ παραμένειν πλείω χρόνον τὴν χιόνα. ὅτι δὲ καὶ
τὸν οἶνον ἔψυχον ὑπὲρ τοῦ ψυχρότερον αὐτὸν πίνειν
d Στράττις φησὶν ἐν Ψυχασταῖς· |

οἶνον γὰρ πιεῖν
οὐδ᾿ ἂν εἷς δέξαιτο θερμόν, ἀλλὰ πολὺ
τοὐναντίον
ψυχόμενον ἐν τῷ φρέατι ⟨καὶ⟩ χιόνι μεμιγμένον.

καὶ ὁ Λύσιππος ἐν Βάκχαις·

(Α.) Ἕρμων. (Ερ.) τί ἔστι; (Α.) πῶς ἔχομεν; (Ερ.)
τί δ᾿ ἄλλο γ᾿ ἢ
ὁ πατὴρ ἄνωθεν ἐς τὸ φρέαρ, ἐμοὶ δοκεῖν,
ὥσπερ τὸν οἶνον τοῦ θέρους καθεῖκέ με.

Δίφιλος δ᾿ ἐν Μνηματίῳ φησίν·

ψῦξον τὸν οἶνον, Δωρί.

e Πρωταγορίδης δ᾿ ἐν δευτέρῳ τῶν Κωμικῶν Ἱστοριῶν |
τὸν Ἀντιόχου τοῦ βασιλέως κατὰ τὸν ποταμὸν διηγούμενος πλοῦν λέγει τι καὶ περὶ ἐπιτεχνήσεως ψυ-
χρῶν ὑδάτων ἐν τούτοις· τὴν γὰρ ἡμέραν ἡλιάζοντες
αὐτό, ἀπηθοῦντες[10] τὸ παχύτατον τὸ λοιπὸν ἐξαι-
θριάζουσιν ἐν ὑδρίαις κεραμέαις ἐπὶ τῶν μετεωρο-
τάτων μερῶν τῆς οἰκήσεως, δι᾿ ὅλης τε τῆς νυκτὸς δύο

scribes the siege of the Indian city of Petra and says that Alexander dug 30 cooling pits, which he filled with snow and then threw oak branches on top; for this way the snow lasts longer. That they also chilled wine in order to drink it colder is asserted by Strattis in *Men Who Keep Cool* (fr. 60):

> No one would
> be willing to drink warm wine, but quite the
>   opposite,
> wine that's chilled in a well and mixed with snow.

Also Lysippus in *Bacchants* (fr. 1):

> (A.) Hermon! (Hermon) What is it? (A.) How're we
>   doing? (Hermon) Nothing's going on—except
> that my father, it seems to me, lowered
> me into the well, like our wine in the summer!

Diphilus says in *The Little Monument* (fr. 56):

> Chill the wine, Doris!

Protagorides in Book II of his *Comic Histories* (*FGrH* 853 F 3), in his description of King Antiochus' voyage down the river,[127] offers some information about how they produce cold water, as follows: For during the day they set it out in the sun, strain off the sediment, and then expose it to the air in earthenware water-jugs on the highest parts of their houses; and all night long two slaves sprinkle the jars

---

[127] I.e. the Nile. The King Antiochus in question is probably Antiochus IV (reigned 175–164 BCE).

---

[10] τῆς νυκτὸς ἀπηθοῦντες ACE

παῖδες ὕδατι τὰ τεύχη καταρραίνουσιν. ὄρθρου δὲ
καθαιροῦντες καὶ τὴν ὑποστάθμην πάλιν ὑποσπῶντες
λεπτόν τε ποιοῦντες αὐτὸ καὶ πρὸς ὑγίειαν οἷον ἄρι-
f στον ἐν ἀχύροις τιθέασιν | τὰς ὑδρίας, εἶθ᾽ οὕτως
χρῶνται χιόνος οὐδ᾽ ἡντινοῦν χρείαν ἔχοντες. λακκαίου δὲ ὕδατος μνημονεύει Ἀναξίλας ἐν Αὐλητῇ οὕτως·

(Α.) ὕδατός τε λακκαίου. (Β.) παρ᾽ ἐμοῦ τουτί γέ
σοι
νόμιζ᾽ ὑπάρχειν.

125 καὶ πάλιν· ‖

ἴσως τὸ λακκαῖόν γ᾽ ὕδωρ ἀπόλωλεν.

Ἀπολλόδωρος δ᾽ ὁ Γελῷος καὶ τοῦ λάκκου αὐτοῦ,
ὥσπερ ἡμεῖς λέγομεν, μνημονεύει ἐν Ἀπολειπούσῃ
οὕτως·

ἀγωνιῶσα τόν τε τοῦ λάκκου κάδον
λύσασα καὶ τὸν τοῦ φρέατος εὐτρεπεῖς
τὰς ἱμονιὰς πεποίηκα.

Τούτων ὁ Μυρτίλος ἀκούσας ἔφη· ἐγὼ δ᾽ ὢν φιλοτάριχος, ὦ ἑταῖροι, χιόνος πιεῖν βούλομαι κατὰ Σιμωνίδην. καὶ ὁ Οὐλπιανός, κεῖται μὲν ὁ φιλοτάριχος,
b ἔφη, παρ᾽ Ἀντιφάνει ἐν Ὀμφάλῃ οὕτως· |

οὐ φιλοτάριχος οὐδαμῶς εἴμ᾽, ὦ κόρη.

Ἄλεξις δ᾽ ἐν Γυναικοκρατίᾳ καὶ ζωμοτάριχόν τινα
κέκληκεν ἐν τούτοις·

with water. Just before daybreak they bring them down,
drain the sediment off again, making the water as light and
healthy as it can be, and deposit the water-jugs in heaps of
chaff; then they use it as it is and have no need whatsoever
for snow. Anaxilas mentions cistern-water in *The Pipe-Player* (fr. 3, encompassing both quotations), as follows:

> (A.) . . . and cistern-water. (B.) Consider this my gift
> to you.

And again:

> Perhaps he's used up his cistern-water.

Apollodorus of Gela mentions the cistern itself, using the
same word we do,[128] in *The Woman Who Left Her Husband* (fr. 1), as follows:

> In her distress, she untied the cistern-bucket
> and the well-bucket, and put the ropes
> to good use.

When Myrtilus heard these remarks, he said: Because
I am fond of saltfish *(philotarichos)*, my friends, I want to
drink snow, as Simonides said. And Ulpian said: The word
philotarichos is attested in Antiphanes' *Omphale* (fr. 176),
as follows:

> I'm not at all fond of saltfish *(philotarichos)*, my girl.

And Alexis in *Women in Power* (fr. 43) refers to someone as
"like saltfish-broth" *(zōmotarichos)*, in the following lines:

---

[128] I.e. *lakkos* ~ Latin *lacus*.

ὁ δὲ Κίλιξ ὅδ᾽ Ἱπποκλῆς,
ὁ ζωμοτάριχος ὑποκριτής.

τὸ δὲ κατὰ Σιμωνίδην τί ἐστιν οὐκ οἶδα. οὐ γὰρ μέλει
σοι, ἔφη ὁ Μυρτίλος, ἱστορίας, ὦ γάστρων. κνισολοιχὸς γάρ τις εἶ ⟨καὶ⟩ κατὰ τὸν Σάμιον ποιητὴν Ἄσιον
c τὸν παλαιὸν ἐκεῖνον[11] κνισοκόλαξ. Καλλίστρατος ἐν |
ἑβδόμῳ Συμμίκτων φησὶν ὡς ἐστιώμενος παρά τισι
Σιμωνίδης ὁ ποιητὴς κραταιοῦ καύματος ὥρᾳ καὶ τῶν
οἰνοχόων τοῖς ἄλλοις μισγόντων εἰς τὸ ποτὸν χιόνος,
αὐτῷ δὲ οὔ, ἀπεσχεδίασε τόδε τὸ ἐπίγραμμα·

τῇ ῥά ποτ᾽ Οὐλύμποιο περὶ πλευρὰς ἐκάλυψεν
    ὠκὺς ἀπὸ Θρήκης ὀρνύμενος Βορέης,
ἀνδρῶν δ᾽ ἀχλαίνων ἔδακεν φρένας, αὐτὰρ †
d   ἐκάμφθη † |
ζωὴ Πιερίην γῆν ἐπιεσσαμένη,
ἔν τις ἐμοὶ καὶ τῆς χεάτω μέρος. οὐ γὰρ ἔοικε
    θερμὴν βαστάζειν ἀνδρὶ φίλῳ πρόποσιν.

πιόντος οὖν αὐτοῦ πάλιν ἐζήτει ὁ Οὐλπιανός· ποῦ
κεῖται ὁ κνισολοιχὸς καὶ τίνα ἐστὶ τὰ τοῦ Ἀσίου ἔπη

---

11 ἐκεῖνον καὶ A

129 *PAA* 538357; Stephanis #1281. Otherwise unknown; but
the claim that he is a Cilician (and thus not an Athenian) is most
likely only comic slander.
130 Quoted in full at 3.125d–e.
131 Although the end of the third line is corrupt (Brunck suggested ἐκρύφθη, "was hidden," while Porson proposed ἐθάφθη,

BOOK III

The Cilician Hippocles[129] here,
the actor who resembles saltfish-broth
    (*zōmotarichos*).

But what "as Simonides said" means, I have no idea. Yes,
said Myrtilus, because you do not care about history, you
glutton. For you are a fat-licker (*knisoloichos*) and, to
quote the well-known ancient Samian poet Asius, a "fat-
flatterer" (fr. 14.2 West[2])[130]. Callistratus in Book VII of
the *Miscellanies* (*FGrH* 348 F 2) says that the poet Simonides was being entertained by some people during a
period of severe heat, and when the slaves in charge of
the wine mixed snow into the other guests' drinks but not
into his, he extemporized the following epigram (*FGE*
1032–7):

That with which the swift North Wind, setting out
        from Thrace,
    once veiled Olympus' flanks,
and which gnawed at the minds of men who lacked
        cloaks, but † was bent †
    alive, clothing itself with Pierian earth[131]—
Someone pour me a share of this! For it is
        inappropriate
    to raise a warm toast to a man who is a friend.

As he was drinking, Ulpian posed another question: Where
is the word *knisoloichos* ("fat-licker") attested? And what

"was buried"), the point must be that the snow was buried in pits
in the foothills of Olympus for use during the summer; cf. 3.124c.
The setting for the anecdote is thus apparently the house of a
wealthy Thessalian.

97

ATHENAEUS

τὰ περὶ τοῦ κνισοκόλακος; τὰ μὲν οὖν τοῦ Ἀσίου, ἔφη
ὁ Μυρτίλος, ἔπη ταῦτ᾿ ἐστί·

χωλός, στιγματίης, πολυγήραος, ἶσος ἀλήτῃ
ἦλθε κνισοκόλαξ, εὖτε Μέλης ἐγάμει,
e   ἄκλητος, ζωμοῦ κεχρημένος· ἐν δὲ μέσοισιν |
ἥρως εἱστήκει βορβόρου ἐξαναδύς.

ὁ δὲ κνισολοιχός ἐστι παρὰ μὲν Σωφίλῳ ἐν Φιλάρχῳ
οὕτως·

ὀψοφάγος εἶ καὶ κνισολοιχός.

ἐν δὲ τοῖς ἐπιγραφομένοις Συντρέχουσι κνισολοιχίαν
εἴρηκεν ἐν τούτοις·

ὁ πορνοβοσκὸς γὰρ μ᾿ ὑπὸ κνισολοιχίας
χορδήν τιν᾿ αἱματῖτιν αὐτῷ σκευάσαι
f   ἐκέλευσε ταυτηνί με. |

τοῦ κνισολοιχοῦ δὲ καὶ Ἀντιφάνης μνημονεύει ἐν
Βομβυλιῷ. ὅτι δὲ ἔπινον καὶ γλυκὺν οἶνον μεταξὺ
ἐσθίοντες, Ἄλεξίς φησιν ἐν Δρωπίδῃ·

εἰσῆλθεν ἡ ἑταίρα φέρουσα τὸν γλυκὺν
ἐν ἀργυρῷ ποτηρίῳ πετάχνῳ τινί,

---

132 Viz. of the underworld; cf. Ar. *Ra.* 145, 273.
133 Literally "someone who eats (only) *opson*," the generic
term for any side-dish designed to add interest to the main course
of bread, barley-cake, porridge, or the like; cf. 4.138a.
134 A personal name. In fact, Alexis refers not to "sweet wine"

98

are the verses by Asius about the fat-flatterer (*knisokolax*)? Myrtilus said: The verses by Asius (fr. 14 West²) are as follows:

> Lame, tattooed, extremely old, no different from a
>   beggar,
> a *knisokolax* came, when Meles was celebrating his
>   wedding;
> he was uninvited but wanted some broth. And he
>   stood
> in their midst like a hero risen from the muck.[132]

The word *knisoloichos* ("fat-licker") is found in Sophilus' *Philarchus* (fr. 8), as follows:

> You're a gourmand[133] and a *knisoloichos*.

And in the play entitled *Men Who Agree* (fr. 6) he uses the word *knisoloichia* ("fat-licking," i.e. "greed"), in the following lines:

> For the pimp, as a result of his *knisoloichia*,
> ordered me to prepare him a blood-sausage;
> and here it is.

Antiphanes as well mentions the *knisoloichos* in *The Bumblebee* (fr. 65). Alexis in *Dropides*[134] (fr. 60) attests that they drank sweet wine while eating:

> The courtesan came in carrying the grape-must
> in a silver *petachnon*-goblet[135],

(*glukus oinos*) but to unfermented grape juice (*glukus*).

[135] Athenaeus comments on this type of cup at 11.496a, where see n.

ἀστειοτάτῳ τὴν ὄψιν, οὔτε τρυβλίῳ
οὔτε φιάλῃ, μετεῖχε δ᾽ ἀμφοῖν τοῖν ῥυθμοῖν.

Ἑξῆς ἐπεισηνέχθη πλακοῦς ἐκ γάλακτος ἰτρίων τε
126 καὶ μέλιτος, ὃν Ῥωμαῖοι λίβον ‖ καλοῦσι. καὶ ὁ
Κύνουλκος ἔφη· ἐμπίπλασο, Οὐλπιανέ, χθωροδλάψου
πατρίου, ὃς παρ᾽ οὐδενὶ τῶν παλαιῶν μὰ τὴν Δήμητρα
γέγραπται πλὴν εἰ μὴ ἄρα παρὰ τοῖς τὰ Φοινικικὰ
συγγεγραφόσι Σαγχουνιάθωνι καὶ Μώχῳ, τοῖς σοῖς
πολίταις. καὶ ὁ Οὐλπιανός,

ἀλλ᾽ ἐμοὶ μέν, (ἔφη) ὦ κυνάμυια, μελιπήκτων
ἅλις,

ἡδέως δ᾽ ἂν χόνδρου φάγοιμι τῶν ὀστρακίδων ἢ τῶν
κοκκάλων ἀφθόνως ἔχοντος. καὶ κομισθέντος, δότε,
ἔφη, μυστίλην· οὐ γὰρ ἂν εἴποιμι μύστρον, παρ᾽
οὐδενὶ δὲ τῶν πρὸ ἡμῶν εἰρημένον. ἐπιλήσμων εἶ, ἔφη,
b ὦ θαυμάσιε, ὁ Αἰμιλιανός. οὐ σὺ | μέντοι τὸν Κολοφώ-
νιον Νίκανδρον ἀεὶ τεθαύμακας τὸν ἐποποιὸν ὡς φι-
λάρχαιον καὶ πολυμαθῆ; καὶ ὡς τὸ πέπερι ὀνομά-
σαντα παρέθου; οὗτος τοίνυν αὐτὸς ἐν τῷ προτέρῳ τῶν
Γεωργικῶν ἐμφανίζων τὴν τοῦ χόνδρου χρῆσιν καὶ
μύστρον ὠνόμασε διὰ τούτων·

---

136 Latin *libum*.　　　137 A Homeric term of abuse (*Il.*
21.394, 421), used here because Cynulcus is himself a "Dog." Cf.
4.157a, where the word is applied to a prostitute who attends a
Cynic drinking party.　　　138 Pine-nuts; see the discussion of
the various names for them at 2.57b–c.

a very nice-looking one; it was neither a bowl
    (trublion)
nor a libation-bowl *(phialē),* but a combination of the
    two shapes.

Immediately after this, a flat-cake made of milk, wafer
bread, and honey, which the Romans refer to as a *libon,*[136]
was brought in. Cynulcus said: Stuff yourself, Ulpian, on
your ancestral *chthōrodlapsus*, a word found in no ancient
author, by Demeter, except perhaps your fellow-citizens
Sanchuniathon (*FGrH* 794 F 5a) and Mochos (*FGrH* 784
F *36), who composed histories of Phoenicia. And Ulpian
said:

Well, I've had enough honey cakes, you dogfly[137].
    (adesp. com. fr. *107)

But I would be happy to eat some wheat pudding full of
ostrachides or pine-kernels.[138] After this was brought, he
said: Give me a *mustilē*[139]! Since I refuse to use the word
mustron, which is not found in any author before our time.
Aemilianus said: You have grown forgetful, and I am astonished at you. Have you not, now, always expressed admira-
tion for the epic poet Nicander of Colophon as someone
fond of archaic usages and extremely learned? And did you
not cite him for his use of the word "pepper"?[140] Well, he
himself in the first of his two books of *Georgics*, in his description of how wheat pudding is made, uses the word
mustron in the following verses (fr. 68 Schneider):

[139] Like a *mustron* (below), a piece of bread hollowed out and
used as a spoon to eat soup, porridge, or the like.
[140] At 2.66e.

ἀλλ᾽ ὁπότ᾽ ἢ ἐρίφοιο νεοσφάγος ἠὲ καὶ ἀρνὸς
ἠὲ αὐτοῦ ὄρνιθος ἐφοπλίζηαι ἐδωδήν,

c χίδρα μὲν ἐντρίψειας ὑποστρώσας ἐνὶ κοίλοις |
ἄγγεσιν, εὐώδει δὲ μιγῇ ἀνάφυρσον ἐλαίῳ.
ζωμὸν δὲ βρομέοντα † καταντλας † < . . . >
< . . . >   πνῖγε δὲ πῶμα
ἀμφιβαλών· φωκτὸν γὰρ ἀνοιδαίνει βαρὺ
κρίμνον·
ἠρέμα δὲ χλιάον κοίλοις ἐκδαίνυσο μύστροις.

διὰ τούτων, ὦ θαυμασιώτατε, ὑπογράφει ὁ Νίκανδρος
τὴν χρείαν τοῦ τε χόνδρου καὶ τῆς ἐπτισμένης κριθῆς,
ἐπιχεῖν κελεύων ἀρνὸς ἢ ἐρίφου ζωμὸν ἢ ὄρνιθος. τὰ
d μὲν οὖν χίδρα, φησίν, ἔντριψον | μὲν ἐν θυείᾳ, μίξας δ᾽
ἔλαιον αὐτοῖς ἀναφύρασον, ἡνίκ᾽ ἂν ἕψηται. τὸν ἐκ
τῆς τοιᾶσδε σκευῆς ἀναβρομοῦντα ζωμὸν πυκνότερον
τῇ ζωμηρύσει καταμίγνυε, μηδὲν ἕτερον ἐπεγχέων,
ἀλλ᾽ αὐτὸν ἀπ᾽ αὐτοῦ ἀρυόμενος πρὸς τὸ μηδὲν ὑπερ-
ζέσαι τοῦ πιμελεστέρου. διὸ καί φησι, κατάπνιγε τὸ
ὑπερζέον ἐπιθεὶς πῶμα· τὸ <γὰρ> κρίμνον οὕτω φωκτὸν γινόμενον ἀνοιδεῖ. τελευταῖον δὲ πράως χλιαρὸν
γενόμενον κοίλοις προσφέρου τοῖς μύστροις. ἀλλὰ
e μὴν καὶ Ἱππόλοχος ὁ Μακεδὼν ἐν τῇ Πρὸς | Λυγκέα
Ἐπιστολῇ, δι᾽ ἧς ἐμφανίζει Μακεδονικόν τι δεῖπνον
πολυτελείᾳ τὰ πάντα πανταχοῦ γενόμενα ὑπερβαλόν,
μνημονεύει ὡς ἑκάστῳ τῶν δειπνούντων δοθέντων μύστρων χρυσῶν. ἐπεὶ δὲ φιλάρχαιος εἶναι θέλεις καὶ
οὐδὲν φὴς φθέγξεσθαι ὃ μὴ τῆς Ἀττικῆς ἐστι φωνῆς,

But when you prepare a freshly slaughtered kid
or a lamb or even a bird for eating,
grind some rough-milled wheat and sprinkle it into
    hollow
vessels, and mix it up together with fragrant oil.
When the broth is seething † dumping it down (?) †
. . .   and smother it by
clamping on a lid; for the heavy barley-meal swells as
    it cooks.
And after it has cooled down, feast on it with hollow
    mustra.

In these verses, admirable sir, Nicander outlines how
wheat pudding and crushed barley should be prepared,
recommending that you pour lamb-, kid- or bird-broth
over it. As for the rough-milled wheat, he says, grind it in a
mortar, and then add oil to it and mix it up when it begins to
boil. When the broth begins to seethe more vigorously, ag-
itate it with the ladle; do not add anything else to it, but lift
and stir it so that none of the fattier portion boils over. This
is why he says "Smother it when it boils over by putting
a lid on;" because the barley-meal swells when cooked
this way. And finally, when it has cooled a bit, eat it with
hollow *mustra*. Moreover, Hippolochus of Macedon in his
Letter to Lynceus, in which he describes a Macedonian
dinner party that outdid any held anywhere for extravagance, notes that all the guests were given gold *mustra*.[141]
But since you wish to be known for your love of antiquity
and deny that you use any non-Attic vocabulary, my very

[141] See 4.129c, where the letter is quoted directly.

ὦ φίλτατε, τί ἐστιν ὃ λέγει Νικοφῶν ὁ τῆς ἀρχαίας κωμῳδίας ποιητὴς ἐν τοῖς Χειρογάστορσιν; ἐγὼ γὰρ καὶ τοῦτον εὑρίσκω μνημονεύοντα τῶν μύστρων ὅταν λέγῃ·

μεμβραδοπώλαις, ἀνθρακοπώλαις,
ἰσχαδοπώλαις, διφθεροπώλαις,
ἀλφιτοπώλαις, μυστριοπώλαις,
f   βιβλιοπώλαις, | κοσκινοπώλαις,
ἐγκριδοπώλαις, σπερματοπώλαις.

τίνες γὰρ ἂν εἶεν οἱ μυστριοπῶλαι ⟨ἀλλ'⟩ ἢ οἱ τὰ μύστρα πωλοῦντες; μαθὼν οὖν ἐκ τούτων, ὦ καλέ μου Συραττικέ, τὴν τοῦ μύστρου χρῆσιν ἐμφοροῦ τοῦ χόνδρου, ἵνα μὴ λέγῃς·

ἄκικύς εἰμι κὠλιγοδρανέω.

127 τεθαύμακα δὲ καὶ πῶς οὐκ ἐζήτησας, ὁ δὲ ‖ χόνδρος πόθεν; Μεγαρόθεν ἢ Θετταλικός; ὅθεν καὶ Μυρτίλος ἐστίν. καὶ ὁ Οὐλπιανός, παύομαι, ἔφη, ἐσθίων, ἕως ἂν με διδάξῃς παρὰ τίσιν εἴρηνται οὗτοι οἱ χόνδροι. καὶ ὁ Αἰμιλιανὸς ἔφη· ἀλλ' οὐ φθονήσω σοι· ὁρῶν γὰρ λαμπροτάτην δείπνου παρασκευὴν βούλομαί σε δίκην ἀλεκτρυόνος ἐμφορηθέντα τοῦ χόνδρου κορύξασθαι καὶ διδάσκειν ἡμᾶς περὶ ὧν μέλλομεν ἐδεσμάτων μεταλαμβάνειν. καὶ ὃς δυσχεράνας ἔφη· πόθεν σοι καὶ τὰ ἐδέσματα; μὴ γὰρ ἀναπαύσασθαι ἔστι ζη-
b   τοῦντα ἀεί | τι πρὸς τοὺς ὀψιμαθεῖς τούτους σοφιστάς;

104

good friend, what is it that Nicophon the Old Comic poet says in his *Men Who Live From Hand to Mouth* (fr. 10)? For I find that he too mentions *mustra* when he says:

> small-fry-sellers, charcoal-sellers,
> dried-fig-sellers, hide-sellers,
> barley-groat-sellers, spoon-sellers *(mustriopōlai)*,
> book-sellers, sieve-sellers,
> oil-and-honey-cake-sellers, seed-sellers.

For who could spoon-sellers *(mustriopōlai)* be, other than people who sell spoons *(mustra)*? So now that you have learned about the usage of the word *mustron* from these examples, my good Syro-Atticist, fill yourself with the wheat porridge, so that you don't say:

> I'm weak and feeble.[142]

I am also astonished that you did not ask, "Where does wheat pudding come from? From Megara or from Thessaly, which is Myrtilus' home-country?" And Ulpian said: I am not going to eat any more, until you instruct me as to which authors mention these wheat puddings. And Aemilianus said: Well, I will not begrudge you this. For when I see this brilliantly prepared dinner, I am happy to have you play the rooster and, once you are full of pudding, raise your crest and offer us some instruction about the foods *(edesmata)* we are about to partake of. And he got annoyed and said: Where did you get this word *edesmata*? Will I never be able to stop constantly posing questions for these scholars who failed to get an education when they were

---

[142] The first portion of an adespoton (tragic? or paratragic?) iambic trimeter line.

ἀλλὰ μήν, ἔφη, καὶ περὶ τούτου σοι τὸν λόγον, ὁ
Αἰμιλιανός, ἀποδώσω. λέξω δὲ πρῶτον περὶ τοῦ χόνδρου Ἀντιφάνους παρατιθέμενος ἐξ Ἀντείας τάδε·

(Α.) ἐν ταῖς σπυρίσι δὲ τί ποτ᾽ ἔνεστι, φίλτατε;
(Β.) ἐν ταῖς τρισὶν μὲν χόνδρος ἀγαθὸς
 Μεγαρικός.
(Α.) οὐ Θετταλικὸν τὸν χρηστὸν εἶναί φασι δέ;
(Β.) < . . . > τῆς <δὲ> Φοινίκης < . . . >
c σεμίδαλις, ἐκ πολλῆς σφόδρ᾽ ἐξεττημένη. |

τὸ δ᾽ αὐτὸ τοῦτο δρᾶμα φέρεται καὶ ὡς Ἀλέξιδος ἐν
ὀλίγοις σφόδρα διαλλάττον. ἐν δὲ Πονήρᾳ πάλιν ὁ
Ἄλεξις·

καὶ χόνδρος ἔνδον ἐστὶ Θετταλικὸς πολύς.

χόνδρον δὲ εἴρηκε τὸ ῥόφημα Ἀριστοφάνης ἐν Δαιτα-
λεῦσιν οὕτως·

ἢ χόνδρον ἕψων εἶτα μυῖαν ἐμβαλὼν
ἐδίδου ῥοφεῖν ἄν.

καὶ σεμιδάλεως δὲ μέμνηται, εἰ καὶ μὴ τὰ μαρτύρια
d κρατῶ, Στράττις ἐν Ἀνθρωπορέστῃ καὶ Ἄλεξις | ἐν
Ἰσοστασίῳ. τὴν γενικὴν δὲ σεμιδάλιδος εἴρηκεν ὁ
Στράττις ἐν τῷ αὐτῷ δράματι οὕτω·

---

143 In fact, the first two quotations clearly use the word *chon-
dros* in the sense "rough-milled wheat, wheat-groats" rather than
"pudding made of rough-milled wheat," as above.

young? Very well, said Aemilianus, I will offer you some account of this word as well. But first I will discuss wheat pudding,[143] by citing the following lines from Antiphanes' *Anteia* (fr. 36):

> (A.) What in the world is in these baskets, my good
>   friend?
> (B.) Fine Megarian wheat groats are in three of them.
> (A.) Don't people say that the Thessalian variety is
>   best?
> (B.) . . . of Phoenicia . . .
> durum wheat, very finely sifted.

This same play is also assigned to Alexis with changes in only a very few places. Alexis again in *The Miserable Woman* (fr. 196):

> And a large quantity of Thessalian wheat-groats is
>   inside.

Aristophanes in *Banqueters* (fr. 208) refers to wheat pudding as something gulped down, as follows:

> Or when he cooked wheat pudding, he would throw a
>   fly in
> and offer it to someone to gulp down.

Durum wheat *(semidalis)* is also mentioned, although I cannot cite the specific passages, by Strattis in his *Man-Breaker* (fr. 2, including the quotation that follows) and by Alexis in *Isostasion*[144] (fr. 102.4).[145] Strattis uses the genitive form *semidalidos* in the same play, as follows:

---

[144] "Equal in weight (to gold)"; probably a prostitute's name.
[145] Quoted in full at 4.134c–d.

τῶν δὲ διδύμων ἐκγόνων Σεμιδάλιδος.

τὰ δὲ ἐδέσματα ὠνόμασεν Ἀντιφάνης ἐν Διδύμοις
οὑτωσί·

ἀπέλαυσα πολλῶν καὶ καλῶν ἐδεσμάτων,
πιών τε προπόσεις τρεῖς ἴσως ἢ τέτταρας
ἐστρηνίων πως, καταβεβρωκὼς σιτία
ἴσως ἐλεφάντων τεττάρων.

e ἐχέτω τέλος καὶ ἥδε ἡ βίβλος ἐπὶ τοῖς λόγοις τοῖς |
περὶ τῶν ἐδεσμάτων ἔχουσα τὴν καταστροφήν· ἀρχὴν
γὰρ τοῦ δείπνου ἀπὸ τῶν ἑξῆς ποιησόμεθα. —οὐ πρό-
τερόν γε, ὦ Ἀθήναιε, πρὶν ἡμῖν διελθεῖν καὶ τὸ τοῦ
Ἱππολόχου τὸ Μακεδονικὸν συμπόσιον. —ἀλλ' εἰ τοῦτό σοι φίλον, ὦ Τιμόκρατες, οὕτω παρασκευαζώμεθα.

the twin offspring of Durum Wheat *(Semidalidos)*.

Antiphanes used the word *edesmata* ("foods") in *Twins* (fr. 82), as follows:

> I enjoyed many fine foods *(edesmata)*;
> and after I drank three toasts, or maybe four,
> I ran a bit wild, since I'd consumed enough food
> for four elephants or so.

Let this book come to an end and have its conclusion with this discussion about *edesmata*; and we will begin our dinner party with what comes next. —Not until you give us a complete account of Hippolochus' Macedonian symposium, Athenaeus! —If this is what you want, Timocrates, let us arrange it that way.

Δ

128 Ἱππόλοχος ὁ Μακεδών, ἑταῖρε Τιμόκρατες, τοῖς
χρόνοις μὲν γέγονε κατὰ Λυγκέα καὶ Δοῦριν τοὺς
Σαμίους, Θεοφράστου δὲ τοῦ Ἐρεσίου μαθητάς, συν-
θήκας δ᾽ εἶχε ταύτας πρὸς τὸν Λυγκέα, ὡς ἐκ τῶν
αὐτοῦ μαθεῖν ἔστιν Ἐπιστολῶν, πάντως αὐτῷ δηλοῦν
εἴ τινι συμπεριενεχθείη δείπνῳ πολυτελεῖ, τὰ ὅμοια
κἀκείνου ἀντιπροπίνοντος αὐτῷ. ἑκατέρων οὖν σῴζον-
ται δειπνητικαί τινες ἐπιστολαί, Λυγκέως μὲν τὸ Λα-
b μίας | τῆς Ἀττικῆς αὐλητρίδος ἐμφανίζοντος δεῖπνον
Ἀθήνησι γενόμενον Δημητρίῳ τῷ βασιλεῖ, ἐπίκλην δὲ
Πολιορκητῇ (ἐρωμένη δ᾽ ἦν ἡ Λάμια τοῦ Δημητρίου),
τοῦ δ᾽ Ἱππολόχου τοὺς Καράνου τοῦ Μακεδόνος ἐμ-
φανίζοντος γάμους. καὶ ἄλλαις δὲ περιετύχομεν τοῦ
Λυγκέως ἐπιστολαῖς πρὸς τὸν αὐτὸν γεγραμμέναις
Ἱππόλοχον, δηλούσαις τό τε Ἀντιγόνου τοῦ βασιλέως
δεῖπνον Ἀφροδίσια ἐπιτελοῦντος Ἀθήνησι καὶ τὸ

---

1 Duris (tyrant of Samos and a historian) lived c.340–260 BCE.
The comic poet and bon-vivant Lynceus was his brother; for
Lynceus' connection with Theophrastus, cf. 4.130d.

BOOK IV

Hippolochus of Macedon, my friend Timocrates, was a contemporary of Lynceus and Duris of Samos[1], who were pupils of Theophrastus of Eresos[2] (Thphr. fr. 18.10). He had an agreement of the following sort with Lynceus, as one can learn from his *Letters*, which was that he was to describe for him without fail any expensive dinner party he participated in; Lynceus offered him the same courtesy in return. Dinner-party letters by both men are preserved; Lynceus describes a dinner party given in Athens for King Demetrius, nicknamed Poliorcetes ("Besieger of Cities"),[3] by Lamia the Athenian pipe-girl[4] (Lamia was Demetrius' lover); while Hippolochus describes the wedding feast put on by Caranus of Macedon. I have also encountered other letters by Lynceus written to the same Hippolochus, which offer accounts of the dinner parties given by King Antigonus when he was celebrating the Aphrodisia festival

[2] Theophrastus (*c.*372/1–*c.*287/6 BCE) was Aristotle's successor as head of his school.

[3] Demetrius (Berve i #257; 336–283 BCE) was the son of Antigonus the One-Eyed (Berve i #87). Cf. 3.100e–f, 101e–f, where Athenaeus also mentions the letters describing the dinner parties given by Antiochus and Ptolemy referred to below.

[4] *PAA* 601325; cf. 3.101e.

Πτολεμαίου τοῦ βασιλέως. <οὐ> δώσομεν δέ σοι ἡμεῖς
c καὶ αὐτὰς τὰς ἐπιστολάς. | ἐπεὶ δὲ ἡ τοῦ Ἱππολόχου
σπανίως εὑρίσκεται, ἐπιδραμοῦμαί σοι τὰ ἐν αὐτῇ
γεγραμμένα διατριβῆς ἕνεκα νῦν καὶ ψυχαγωγίας.

Ἐν Μακεδονίᾳ, ὡς ἔφην, τοῦ Καράνου γάμους
ἑστιῶντος οἱ μὲν συγκεκλημένοι ἄνδρες ἦσαν εἴκοσιν·
οἷς καὶ κατακλιθεῖσιν εὐθέως ἐδόθησαν φιάλαι ἀργυραῖ ἑκάστῳ μία δωρεά. προεστεφανώκει δὲ καὶ ἕκαστον πρὶν εἰσελθεῖν στλεγγίδι χρυσῇ· πέντε χρυσῶν
d ἑκάστῃ δ᾽ ἦν τὸ τίμημα. ἐπεὶ δ᾽ ἐξέπιον τὰς | φιάλας,
ἐν χαλκῷ πίνακι τῶν Κορινθίων κατασκευασμάτων
ἄρτος ἑκάστῳ ἰσόπλατυς ἐδόθη, ὄρνεις τε καὶ νῆσσαι,
προσέτι δὲ καὶ φάτται καὶ χὴν καὶ τοιαύτη τις ἄλλη
ἀφθονία σεσωρευμένα, καὶ ἕκαστος λαβὼν αὐτῷ πίνακι τοῖς κατόπιν διεδίδου παισίν. ἄλλα δ᾽ ἐσθίειν
περιεφέρετο πολλὰ καὶ ποικίλα, καὶ μετὰ ταῦτα ἀργυροῦς πίναξ ἕτερος, ἐφ᾽ ᾧ πάλιν ἄρτος μέγας καὶ χῆνες
καὶ λαγῳοὶ καὶ ἔριφοι καὶ ἕτεροι ἄρτοι πεπονημένοι
καὶ περιστεραὶ καὶ τρυγόνες πέρδικές τε καὶ ὅσον
e ἄλλο πτηνῶν πλῆθος ἦν. | ἐπεδώκαμεν οὖν, φησί, καὶ
ταῦτα τοῖς δούλοις καὶ ὡς ἅδην εἴχομεν βρώσεως
ἐχερνιψάμεθα. καὶ στέφανοι εἰσηνέχθησαν πολλοὶ
παντοδαπῶν ἀνθέων ἐπὶ πᾶσί τε χρυσαῖ στλεγγίδες,
ὁλκὴν ἴσαι τῷ πρώτῳ στεφάνῳ. ἐπὶ δὲ τούτοις εἰπὼν ὁ
129 Ἱππόλοχος ὡς Πρωτέας ‖ ἀπόγονος ἐκείνου Πρωτέου

5 Presumably Antiochus I (reigned 295/4–261 BCE) and Ptolemy II Philadelphus (reigned 285/3–246 BCE).

112

in Athens, and by King Ptolemy.[5] I will not offer you the letters themselves; but since the one by Hippolochus is rarely encountered, I will run through its contents for you now to provide some amusement and diversion.[6]

When Caranus gave his wedding feast in Macedon, as I said, 20 men attended as his guests; the moment they lay down, each of them was given a silver libation-bowl to keep. Even before they came in, he had garlanded them all with gold tiaras, each worth five gold coins. After they drank the contents of their libation-bowls, each man was given a loaf of bread on a bronze platter of Corinthian workmanship (the loaf was as big as the platter), along with chickens and ducks, as well as ring-doves, a goose, and an immense pile of other such items; each man took the food and handed it, platter and all, to the slaves standing behind him. Many other elaborate dishes made their way around the group, and after them came another platter, this one of silver, upon which was again a large loaf of bread, geese, hares, kids, other fancy types of bread, pigeons, turtle-doves, partridges, and an enormous collection of other birds. So we gave these items as well, he says, to the slaves; and when we had had enough to eat, we washed our hands. Numerous garlands made of flowers of every kind were brought in, with gold tiaras that weighed as much as the first garlands attached to all of them. Following this, Hippolochus reports, Proteas, a descendant of the famous

---

[6] The character Athenaeus is the narrator until 4.134d, when Plutarch begins to speak and we abruptly return to the dinner party in Larensius' house.

Λανίκης υἱοῦ, ἥτις ἐγεγόνει τροφὸς Ἀλεξάνδρου τοῦ
βασιλέως, ἔπινε πλεῖστον (ἦν γὰρ πολυπότης ὡς καὶ
ὁ πάππος αὐτοῦ Πρωτέας ὁ συγγενόμενος Ἀλεξάνδρῳ) καὶ ὅτι πᾶσι προῦπιεν, ἑξῆς γράφει καὶ ταῦτα·
ἤδη δὲ ἡμῶν ἡδέως ἀπηλλοτριωμένων τοῦ σωφρονεῖν
ἐπεισβάλλουσιν αὐλητρίδες καὶ μουσουργοὶ καὶ σαμ-
βυκίστριαί τινες Ῥόδιαι, ἐμοὶ μὲν γυμναὶ δοκῶ, πλὴν
ἔλεγόν τινες αὐτὰς ἔχειν χιτῶνας, ἀπαρξάμεναί τε
b ἀπῆλθον. καὶ ἐπεισῆλθον ἄλλαι φέρουσαι | ληκύθους
μύρου ἑκάστη δύο συνδεδεμένας ἱμάντι χρυσῷ, τὴν
μὲν ἀργυρᾶν, τὴν δὲ χρυσῆν, κοτυλιαίας, καὶ ἑκάστῳ
προσέδωκαν. ἔπειτ᾽ εἰσφέρεται πλοῦτος ἀντὶ δείπνου,
πίναξ ἀργυροῦς ἐπὶ πάχος οὐκ ὀλίγον περίχρυσος,
ὅσος δέξασθαι μέγεθος χοίρου τινὸς ὀπτοῦ καὶ σφόδρα μεγάλου, ὃς ὕπτιος ἐπέκειτο τὴν γαστέρα δεικνὺς
ἄνω πλήρη οὖσαν πολλῶν ἀγαθῶν· ἦσαν γὰρ ἐν αὐτῷ
συνωπτημέναι κίχλαι καὶ νῆτται καὶ συκαλλίδων
c πλῆθος ἄπειρον καὶ ᾠῶν ἐπικεχυμέναι | λέκιθοι καὶ
ὄστρεα καὶ κτένες· καὶ ἑκάστῳ πεπυργωμένα αὐτοῖς
πίναξιν ἐδόθη. μετὰ δὲ ταῦτα πιόντες ἐλάβομεν ἕκαστος ἔριφον ζέοντα ἐφ᾽ ἑτέρῳ πάλιν πίνακι τοιούτῳ
σὺν μύστροις χρυσοῖς. ὁρῶν οὖν τὴν δυσχωρίαν ὁ
Κάρανος κελεύει σπυρίδας ἡμῖν καὶ ἀρτοφόρα διὰ
ἱμάντων ἐλεφαντίνων πεπλεγμένα δοθῆναι, ἐφ᾽ οἷς

---

7 Berve i #664. Proteas belonged to Alexander's inner circle of
Macedonian nobles, and the king is supposed to have died after a
drinking contest with him; see 10.434a–b.

Proteas[7] the son of Lanice[8] (who was King Alexander's nurse), drank more than anyone else—he was a heavy drinker, like his grandfather Proteas, the contemporary of Alexander—and toasted them all. Immediately after this he writes the following: We had now happily escaped sobriety, when some pipe-girls, female singers, and Rhodian *sambukē*[9]-girls came in—they looked naked to me, although some of the guests claimed that they were wearing tunics—and after playing a prelude, they went out again. Other girls came in after them, each carrying two perfume-flasks, one made of gold and the other of silver, and each with a capacity of one *kotulē*[10] and tied together with a gold cord, and they gave a pair to all of us. Then a fortune was served instead of dinner: a silver platter covered with heavy gold plate, and large enough to hold a huge roast piglet lying on its back and displaying its belly, which was full of many delicious items; for inside it were roast thrushes, ducks, and an immense quantity of warblers, as well as pea soup poured over hard-boiled eggs, as well as oysters and scallops. These items were all stacked on top of one another and were given to each guest, along with the platters. After this we drank, and each of us received a piping hot kid on yet another platter of the same sort, accompanied by gold spoons.[11] When Caranus saw that we were running into trouble, he ordered us to be given baskets and breadtrays woven out of strips of ivory; we were so delighted

[8] Berve i #462.

[9] A primitive arched harp, also referred to as an *iambukē*; cf. 14.633f–4b, 637b; West, *AGM* 75–7.

[10] Approximately one cup.

[11] Cf. 3.126e.

ἡσθέντες ἀνεκροταλίσαμεν τὸν νυμφίον ὡς καὶ τῶν
δοθέντων ἡμῖν ἀνασεσωσμένων. ἔπειτα στέφανοι πάλιν καὶ διλήκυθον μύρου χρυσοῦν καὶ ἀργυροῦν ἰσό-
d σταθμον | τοῖς προτέροις. ἡσυχίας δὲ γενομένης ἐπ-
εισβάλλουσιν ἡμῖν οἱ κἀν τοῖς Χύτροις τοῖς Ἀθήνησι
λειτουργήσαντες. μεθ᾽ οὓς εἰσῆλθον ἰθύφαλλοι καὶ
σκληροπαῖκται καί τινες καὶ θαυματουργοὶ γυναῖκες
εἰς ξίφη κυβιστῶσαι καὶ πῦρ ἐκ τοῦ στόματος ἐκριπί-
ζουσαι γυμναί. ἐπεὶ δὲ καὶ τούτων ἀπηλλά- γημεν,
ἐκλαμβάνει πάλιν ἡμᾶς θερμός τις καὶ ζωρότερος
πότος, οἴνων ὄντων ἡμῖν Θασίων καὶ Μενδαίων καὶ
Λεσβίων, χρυσίδων πάνυ μεγάλων ἑκάστῳ προσ-
ενεχθεισῶν. καὶ μετὰ τὸν πότον ὑελοῦς πίναξ δίπηχύς
e | που τὴν διάμετρον ἐν θήκῃ κατακείμενος ἀργυρᾷ
πλήρης ἰχθύων ὀπτῶν πάντα γένη συνηθροισμένων,
ἅπασί τε προσεδόθη καὶ ἀργυροῦν ἀρτοφόρον ἄρτων
Καππαδοκίων, ὧν τὰ μὲν ἐφάγομεν, τὰ δὲ τοῖς θερά-
πουσιν ἐπεδώκαμεν. καὶ νιψάμενοι τὰς χεῖρας ἐστεφα-
νούμεθα καὶ πάλιν στλεγγίδας ἐλάβομεν χρυσᾶς,
διπλασίους τῶν πρότερον, καὶ ἄλλο διλήκυθον μύρου.
ἡσυχίας δὲ γενομένης ἐξαλλόμενος τῆς κλίνης ὁ Πρωτέας αἰτεῖ σκύφον χοαῖον καὶ πληρώσας οἴνου Θα-
f σίου ὀλίγον τι | ἐπιρράνας ὕδατος ἐξέπιεν ἐπειπών·

ὁ πλεῖστα πίνων πλεῖστα κεὐφρανθήσεται.

12 Probably a chorus of some sort; cf. 4.130d; Plu. *Mor.* 841f;
D.L. 3.56.   13 Three of the finest local varieties of Greek
wine; cf. 1.28d–9f.

with these that we applauded the bridegroom, since our gifts had been preserved for us. Then there were more garlands and a pair of gold and silver perfume-flasks that weighed as much as the first set. When things quieted down, we were visited by the men who perform at the Festival of Pots in Athens.[12] They were followed in by ithyphallic dancers and clowns, and by naked female acrobats who did tumbling tricks among swords and blew fire from their mouths. When we were finished with them, our attention was captured next by a strong hot drink; we had Thasian, Mendaean, and Lesbian wines[13] at our disposal, and each of us was brought an enormous gold drinking-cup. After we finished drinking, we were all presented with a glass platter about two cubits[14] in diameter lying in a silver frame and full of a collection of roast fish of every sort, as well as with a silver bread-tray full of Cappadocian bread[15]; we ate some of this food and gave the rest to our slaves. Afterward we washed our hands, garlanded ourselves, and were given another set of gold tiaras twice as large as the previous ones, along with another set of perfume-flasks. When things quieted down, Proteas leapt up from his couch and asked for a bowl that could hold a *chous*[16]. He filled the bowl with Thasian wine, sprinkled a few drops of water into it,[17] drank the contents, and said:

He who drinks the most will also be the happiest.[18]

[14] Approximately three feet; see 2.50b n.

[15] See 3.112b–c.

[16] See 3.118a n.

[17] On the pretext of mixing it.

[18] Cf. E. fr. 576 "He of mortals who does the most errs the most."

καὶ ὁ Κάρανος ἔφη· ἐπεὶ πρῶτος ἔπιες, ἔχε πρῶτος καὶ
τὸν σκύφον δῶρον· τοῦτο δὲ καὶ τοῖς ἄλλοις ὅσοι ἂν
πίωσιν ἔσται γέρας. ἐφ᾽ οἷς λεχθεῖσιν

οἱ δ᾽ ἐννέα πάντες ἀνέσταν

ἁρπάζοντες κάλλος ἄλλον φθάνοντες. εἷς δὲ τῶν συν-
δειπνούντων ἡμῖν ἄθλιος οὐ δυνάμενος πιεῖν ἀνακαθί-
σας ἔκλαιεν ἄσκυφος γενόμενος, καὶ ὁ Κάρανος αὐτῷ
130 χαρίζεται κενὸν τὸ ἔκπωμα. ἐπὶ ‖ τούτοις χορὸς εἰσῆλθεν ἀνθρώπων ἑκατὸν ἐμμελῶς ᾀδόντων γαμικὸν
ὕμνον, μεθ᾽ οὓς ὀγχηστρίδες διεσκευασμέναι τρόπον
Νηρηίδων, αἱ δὲ νυμφῶν. τοῦ πότου δὴ προϊόντος καὶ
τῆς ὥρας ὑποσκιαζούσης ἀναπετάννυουσι τὸν οἶκον,
ἐν ᾧ κύκλῳ ὀθόναις διείληπτο πάντα λευκαῖς· καὶ
ἀναπετασθεισῶν Ναΐδες ἐφάνησαν λάθρα κατὰ μηχανὰς σχασθέντων τῶν φραγμάτων καὶ Ἔρωτες καὶ
Ἀρτέμιδες καὶ Πᾶνες καὶ Ἑρμαῖ καὶ τοιαῦτα πολλὰ
εἴδωλα ἀργυροῖς δᾳδουχοῦντα λαμπτῆρσι. θαυμαζόν-
b των | δ᾽ ἡμῶν τὴν τεχνιτείαν Ἐρυμάνθιοι τῷ ὄντι
σύαγροι κατὰ πινάκων τετραγώνων χρυσομίτρων σι-
βύναις ἀργυραῖς διαπεπερονημένοι περιεφέροντο ἑκά-
στῳ· καὶ τὸ θαυμάσιον, ὅτι παρειμένοι καὶ καρηβα-
ροῦντες ὑπὸ τῆς μέθης ὁπότε τι τῶν ἀγομένων θεασαί-
μεθα πάντες ἐξενήφομεν, ὀρθοὶ τὸ δὴ λεγόμενον ἀνι-
στάμενοι. ἔναττον οὖν οἱ παῖδες εἰς τὰς εὐτυχεῖς

---

19 Sc. from which the curtains hung; but the Greek is obscure.

BOOK IV

And Caranus said: Since you were the first to drink your wine, you are also the first to have your bowl as a gift. But the same prize awaits any of the others who drink theirs. In response to these words (*Il.* 7.161)

all nine arose,

each man trying to grab his bowl more quickly than anyone else could. But one unhappy member of our group, who was unable to drink his wine, sat up and began to weep because he failed to get a bowl, until Caranus emptied the cup and made him a present of it. After this a chorus of 100 men came in singing a wedding hymn in harmony; they were followed by dancing-girls, some dressed like Nereids, others like nymphs. As the drinking continued and the evening shadows began to spread, they opened up the room, which had been entirely surrounded by white linen curtains. After these were pulled up and the lattice-work[19] was withdrawn in some mysterious way, Naiads appeared, along with Erotes, Artemises, Pans, Hermeses, and many figures of this type holding torches in silver lampstands. As we were expressing amazement about how this had been done, virtual Erymanthian boars[20] spitted on silver spears were brought around for all the guests on square platters with gold rims. What is amazing is that, although we were weak and our heads were heavy because of how drunk we were, whenever we saw one of the items that were brought in, we all grew sober and "stood up straight," as the saying goes. For the slaves kept on piling our lucky baskets full

[20] A reference to the enormous boar that lived around Mt. Erymanthus, which Heracles captured as one of his labors (e.g. S. *Tr.* 1097; [Apollod.] *Bib.* 2.5.4.)

119

σπυρίδας, ἕως ἐσάλπισε τὸ εἰωθὸς τοῦ τελευταίου
δείπνου σημεῖον· οὕτω γὰρ τὸ Μακεδονικὸν οἶσθα
ἔθος ἐν ταῖς πολυανθρώποις εὐωχίαις γινόμενον. καὶ ὁ
c Κάρανος ἄρξας πότου | μικροῖς ἐκπώμασι περισοβεῖν
ἐκέλευε τοῖς παισίν. ἐπίνομεν οὖν εὐμαρῶς ὥσπερ
ἀντίδοτον ἐκ τῆς προτέρας ἀκρατοποσίας λαμβάνον-
τες. ἐν τούτῳ δὲ ὁ γελωτοποιὸς εἰσῆλθε Μανδρογένης,
ἐκείνου Στράτωνος τοῦ Ἀττικοῦ, ὥς φασιν, ἀπόγονος
καὶ πολλοὺς κατέρρηξεν ἡμῶν γέλωτας· καὶ μετὰ
ταῦτα ὠρχεῖτο μετὰ τῆς γυναικὸς ἔτη οὔσης ὑπὲρ τὰ
ὀγδοήκοντα. καὶ τελευταῖαι ἐπεισῆλθον ἐπιδόρπιαι
τράπεζαι, τραγήματά τ' ἐν πλεκτοῖς ἐλεφαντίνοις ἐπε-
δόθη πᾶσι καὶ πλακοῦντες ἕκαστα γένη, Κρητικῶν
d καὶ τῶν σῶν, ἑταῖρε Λυγκεῦ, | Σαμιακῶν καὶ Ἀττικῶν
αὐταῖς ταῖς ἰδίαις τῶν πεμμάτων θήκαις. μετὰ δὲ
ταῦτα ἐξαναστάντες ἀπηλλαττόμεθα νήφοντες νὴ
τοὺς θεοὺς διὰ τὸν φόβον τοῦ πλούτου ὃν ἐλάβομεν.
σὺ δὲ μόνον ἐν Ἀθήναις μένων εὐδαιμονίζεις τὰς
Θεοφράστου θέσεις ἀκούων, θύμα καὶ εὔζωμα καὶ
τοὺς καλοὺς ἐσθίων στρεπτούς, Λήναια καὶ Χύτρους
θεωρῶν. ἡμεῖς δ' ἐκ τοῦ Καράνου δείπνου πλοῦτον
ἀντὶ μερίδων εὐωχηθέντες νῦν ζητοῦμεν οἱ μὲν οἰκίας,
οἱ δὲ ἀγρούς, οἱ δὲ ἀνδράποδ' ὠνήσασθαι.

e   Εἰς | ταῦτα, ὦ ἑταῖρε Τιμόκρατες, ἀποβλέπων τίνι

---

[21] An allusion to the sip of unmixed wine drunk at the beginning of the symposium in honor of the "good divinity"; cf. 2.38d
with n.

until the customary trumpet-blast that marks the end of dinner sounded; because, as you know, this is the Macedonian custom at feasts attended by a large number of people. Caranus began the drinking with small cups and ordered the slaves to make their way rapidly around the group. We accordingly started drinking at an easy pace, as if we were taking an antidote for the unmixed wine we drank earlier.[21] As this was going on, the clown Mandrogenes,[22] who people claim is a descendant of the famous Straton of Athens,[23] came in and made us break into laughter repeatedly; after that he danced with his wife, who was over 80 years old. Finally the after-dinner tables came in, and everyone was given symposium snacks in ivory baskets, along with flat-cakes of every kind—the Cretan types, your Samian types, my dear Lynceus, and the Attic types—along with the special cake-containers for each. After this we got up and left; and we were sober, by the gods, as a result of our anxiety about the riches we got. You, on the other hand, simply remain in Athens and consider yourself happy because you listen to Theophrastus' theses (Thphr. fr. 76), and eat thyme, rocket, and your fine twist-bread[24], and are a spectator at the Lenaia and the Festival of Pots.[25] Whereas we, who were feasted on wealth from Caranus' dinner party rather than on leftovers, are currently looking for houses, land, or slaves to buy.

When you take account of all this, my friend

[22] Stephanis #1600.
[23] *PA* 12968; Stephanis #2314; cf. 14.614d (another reference to this section of the letter).
[24] Cf. 3.113d.

συγκρῖναι ἔχεις τῶν Ἑλληνικῶν δείπνων τὸ προκεί-
μενον τοῦτο συμπόσιον; ὁπότε καὶ Ἀντιφάνης ὁ κωμῳδιοποιὸς ἐν Οἰνομάῳ ἢ Πέλοπι διαπαίζων ἔφη·

τί δ' ἂν Ἕλληνες μικροτράπεζοι,
φυλλοτρῶγες δράσειαν; ὅπου
τέτταρα λήψῃ κρέα μίκρ' ὀβολοῦ.
παρὰ δ' ἡμετέροις προγόνοισιν ὅλους
βοῦς ὤπτων, σῦς, ἐλάφους, ἄρνας·
f   τὸ τελευταῖον δ' ὁ | μάγειρος ὅλον
τέρας ὀπτήσας μεγάλῳ βασιλεῖ
θερμὴν παρέθηκε κάμηλον.

ὁ Ἀριστοφάνης δ' ἐν Ἀχαρνεῦσι καὶ αὐτὸς τῶν βαρβάρων ἐμφανίζων τὴν μεγαλειότητά φησιν·

(Πρ.) εἶτ' ἐξένιζε παρετίθει θ' ἡμῖν ὅλους
131   ἐκ κριβάνου βοῦς. (Δι.) καὶ τίς εἶδε πώποτε ||
βοῦς κριβανίτας; τῶν ἀλαζονευμάτων.
(Πρ.) καὶ ναὶ μὰ Δί' ὄρνιν τριπλάσιον
Κλεωνύμου
παρέθηκεν ἡμῖν· ὄνομα δ' ἦν αὐτῷ φέναξ.

Ἀναξανδρίδης δ' ἐν Πρωτεσιλάῳ διασύρων τὸ τῶν
Ἰφικράτους γάμων συμπόσιον, ὅτε ἤγετο τὴν Κότυος

---

25 Cf. 4.129d with n.

BOOK IV

Timocrates, to what Greek dinner party can the symposium just described be compared? Since the comic poet
Antiphanes says mockingly in *Oenomaus or Pelops* (fr.
170):

> What could leaf-eating Greeks
> with their scanty tables accomplish? A land where
> you'll get four little chunks of meat for an obol!
> Whereas in our ancestors' time they roasted
> whole oxen, pigs, deer, and lambs;
> and to top it all off, the cook would roast
> and serve the Great King, as a surprise,
> 　　　a whole hot camel!

Aristophanes in *Acharnians* (85–9) as well describes the
barbarians' magnificence and says:

> (Ambassador) Then he entertained us and served us
> 　　whole
> oxen prepared in a baking shell. (Dicaeopolis) Who
> 　　ever saw
> oxen prepared in a baking shell? What bullshit!
> (Ambassador) And, by Zeus, he served us a bird
> three times as big as Cleonymus[26]; it was called a
> 　　"cheat-bird."

Anaxandrides in *Protesilaus* (fr. 42) mocks the symposium
that was part of Iphicrates' wedding feast when he married

---

[26] *PAA* 579410, an Athenian politician attacked by Aristophanes *inter alia* for his alleged gluttony and duplicity. See Olson
ad loc.

τοῦ Θρᾳκῶν βασιλέως θυγατέρα, φησί·

(A.) κἂν ταῦτα ποιῇθ' ὥσπερ φράζω,
λαμπροῖς δείπνοις δεξόμεθ' ὑμᾶς,
οὐδὲν ὁμοίοις τοῖς Ἰφικράτους
τοῖς ἐν Θρᾴκῃ· καίτοι φασὶν
b   βουβαυκαλόσαυλα | γενέσθαι.
κατὰ τὴν ἀγορὰν μὲν ὑπεστρῶσθαι
στρώμαθ' ἁλουργῆ μέχρι τῆς ἄρκτου·
δειπνεῖν δ' ἄνδρας βουτυροφάγους,
αὐχμηροκόμας μυριοπληθεῖς·
τοὺς δὲ λέβητας χαλκοῦς εἶναι,
μείζους λάκκων δωδεκακλίνων·
αὐτὸν δὲ Κότυν περιεζῶσθαι
ζωμόν τε φέρειν ἐν χοῖ χρυσῇ,
καὶ γευόμενον τῶν κρατήρων
πρότερον μεθύειν τῶν πινόντων.
αὐλεῖν δ' αὐτοῖς Ἀντιγενείδαν,
Ἀργᾶν δ' ᾄδειν καὶ κιθαρίζειν
Κηφισόδοτον τὸν Ἀχαρνῆθεν,
c   μέλπειν | δ' ᾠδαῖς
τοτὲ μὲν Σπάρτην τὴν εὐρύχορον,
τοτὲ δ' αὖ Θήβας τὰς ἑπταπύλους,
τὰς ⟨θ'⟩ ἁρμονίας μεταβάλλειν.
φερνάς τε λαβεῖν δύο μὲν ξανθῶν

---

[27] Iphicrates son of Timotheus of the deme Rhamnous (*PAA* 542925) was an important Athenian general. Cotys took the

BOOK IV

the daughter of Cotys king of the Thracians,[27] and says:

> (A.) And if you behave just as I explain,
> we'll welcome you with a brilliant dinner party
> quite unlike the one Iphicrates
> celebrated in Thrace; although they say
>   it was a huge, swank, swaggering affair.
> Purple bedding was spread as high as
> the Great Bear throughout the marketplace;
> butter-eating men were dining,
> dirty-haired hordes;
> the cauldrons were made of bronze
> and were larger than 12-couch cisterns;
> and Cotys himself wore an apron,
> served broth in a gold pitcher,
> and got drunk before the drinkers did,
> by tasting the mixing-bowls.
> Antigeneides played the pipes for them;
> Argas sang;[28] and Cephisodotus
> of Acharnae played the lyre
> and celebrated with his songs
> now Sparta of the broad dancing-places,
> now seven-gated Thebes,
>   and varied his harmonies.
> As a dowry he got two herds

throne in 384 or 383, and Iphicrates probably married into the
family a few years earlier, before Cotys was awarded Athenian citi-
zenship (cf. D. 23.118). The bride may actually have been Cotys'
sister rather than his daughter, as Athenaeus and other late
sources claim. See J.K. Davies, *Athenian Propertied Families
600–300 B.C.* (Oxford, 1971) 248–50; and cf. 6.248e with n.;
12.531e–2a.

ἵππων ἀγέλας αἰγῶν τ᾽ ἀγέλην
χρυσοῦν τε σάκος
    < . . . > φιάλην τε λεπαστήν,
χιόνος τε πρόχουν κέρχνων τε σιρὸν
βολβῶν τε χύτραν δωδεκάπηχυν
    καὶ πουλυπόδων ἑκατόμβην.
ταῦτα μὲν οὕτως φασὶ ποιῆσαι
Κότυν ἐν Θρᾴκῃ, γάμον Ἰφικράτει.
τούτων δ᾽ ἔσται πολὺ σεμνότερον
καὶ λαμπρότερον παρὰ δεσποσύνοις
τοῖς ἡμετέροις. τί | γὰρ ἐλλείπει
δόμος ἡμέτερος, ποίων ἀγαθῶν;
οὐ σμύρνης ἐκ Συρίας ὀσμαὶ
λιβάνου τε πνοαί; τερενόχρωτες
μαζῶν ὄψεις, ἄρτων, ἀμύλων,
πουλυποδείων, χολίκων, δημοῦ,
φυσκῶν, ζωμοῦ, τεύτλων, θρίων,
λεκίθου, σκορόδων, ἀφύης, σκόμβρων,
ἐνθρυμματίδων, πτισάνης, ἀθάρης,
κυάμων, λαθύρων, ὤχρων, δολίχων,
μέλιτος, τυροῦ, χορίων, πυρῶν,

d

---

[28] Antigeneidas son of Satyrus of Thebes (Stephanis #196) and
Argas (Stephanis #292) were famous musicians in the first half of
the 4th century. Cephisodotus (*PAA* 567705; Stephanis #1393) is
otherwise unknown.   [29] Or perhaps "a gold shield," although "wine-strainer" makes better sense with what follows.

[30] For this type of bowl, the exact shape of which is obscure,
see 11.484f–6a.   [31] For chilling wine; see 3.123d–5d.

of bay horses and a herd of goats,
a gold wine-strainer[29],
   . . . a limpet-shaped libation-bowl,[30]
a pitcher of snow,[31] a storage pit full of millet,
a 12-cubit cookpot of hyacinth bulbs,
   and an enormous quantity of octopi.[32]
That's how, people say, Cotys arranged
these matters in Thrace, as a wedding for Iphicrates.
What goes on in our masters' house, on the other
   hand,
will be much grander and more brilliant
than this. For what does our house
lack, or what category of goods does it want?
Are there no scents of Syrian myrrh
or wafts of frankincense? Tender-skinned
barley-cakes can be seen; and bread, milk-and-honey-
   cakes,
little octopi, intestine sausages, beef fat,
phuskai[33], broth, beets, fig-leaf pastries,
pea soup, garlic, small-fry, mackerel,
enthrummatides[34], barley gruel, wheat gruel,
fava beans, vetch, *ōchroi*[35], long beans,
honey, cheese, membrane pudding[36], wheat,

[32] Hyacinth bulbs and octopi were regarded as aphrodisiacs, which must be part of the point. [33] Another type of sausage, made of wheat flour and meat (Suda ϕ 865), or of barley flour, fat, and blood (*EM* p. 802.56–8). Cf. 4.138e.

[34] Cakes of some sort, perhaps identical with *thrummatides* (thus Hsch. θ 794; cf. 4.132a, 147b); cf. Antiph. fr. 181.4–5; Phot. θ 238. [35] An unidentified type of vetch.

[36] Made with milk and honey; see 14.646e with n.

καρύων, χόνδρου,
κάραβοι ὀπτοί, τευθίδες ὀπταί,
κεστρεὺς ἐφθός, σηπίαι ἐφθαί,
μύραιν' ἐφθή, κωβιοὶ ἐφθοί,
e   θυννίδες ὀπταί, φυκίδες | ἐφθαί,
βάτραχοι, πέρκαι,
συνόδοντες, ὄνοι, βατίδες, ψῆτται,
γαλεός, κόκκυξ, θρίσσαι, νάρκαι,
ῥίνης τεμάχη, σχαδόνες, βότρυες,
σῦκα, πλακοῦντες, μῆλα, κράνειαι,
ῥόαι, ἔρπυλλος, μήκων, ἀχράδες,
κνῆκος, ἐλᾶαι, στέμφυλ', ἄμητες,
πράσα, γήτειον, κρόμμυα, φυστή,
βολβοί, καυλοί, σίλφιον, ὄξος,
μάραθ', ᾠά, φακῆ, τέττιγες, ὀποί,
κάρδαμα, σήσαμα, κήρυκες, ἅλες,
πίνναι, λεπάδες, μύες, ὄστρεια,
κτένες, ὄρκυνες· καὶ πρὸς τούτοις
ὀρνιθαρίων ἄφατον πλῆθος,
f   νηττῶν, φαττῶν· | χῆνες, στρουθοί,
κίχλαι, κόρυδοι, κίτται, κύκνοι,
πελεκάν, κίγκλοι, γέρανος— (Β.) τουδὶ
τοῦ χάσκοντος διατειναμένη
διὰ τοῦ πρωκτοῦ καὶ τῶν πλευρῶν
  διακόψειεν τὸ μέτωπον.
(Α.) οἶνοι δέ † σοι λευκὸς
γλυκὺς αὐθιγενὴς ἡδὺς καπνίας.

128

nuts, wheat pudding,
roasted crayfish, roasted squid,
stewed mullet, stewed cuttlefish,
stewed moray eel, stewed gobies,
roasted tuna, stewed wrasse,
angler-fish, perch,
four-toothed sea-bream, hake, skate, turbots,
thresher shark, gurnard, sprats, electric rays,
monkfish steaks, honeycombs, grape clusters,
figs, flat-cakes, apples, cornel cherries,
pomegranates, thyme, poppy seed, wild pears,
saffron, olives, olive pomace, milk cakes,
a leek, a *gēteion*[37], onions, a *phustē*[38],
hyacinth bulbs, silphium stalk, silphium, vinegar,
fennel, eggs, lentil soup, cicadas, fig juice,
cress, sesame seeds, trumpet-shells, salt,
pinnas, limpets, mussels, oysters,
scallops, *orkunes*[39]. And in addition
an enormous quantity of little birds,
ducks, and ring-doves; also geese, sparrows,
thrushes, larks, jays, swans,
a pelican, wagtails, a crane— (B.) May the crane
stretch out its head through the asshole
and ribs of this fellow here with the open mouth
    and split his forehead open!
(A.) And wines † for you white,
sweet, local, pleasant, and smoky.

---

[37] An unidentified vegetable related to the onion; see Arnott on Alex. fr. 132.7 (quoted at 4.170b).

[38] A barley-cake of some sort; cf. Moer. φ 10; *EM* p. 803.1.

[39] Some sort of tuna; cf. Olson–Sens on Archestr. fr. 35.3.

Λυγκεὺς δ᾽ ἐν Κενταύρῳ διαπαίζων τὰ Ἀττικὰ
δεῖπνά φησι·

    (Α.) μάγειρ᾽, ὁ θύων ἔσθ᾽ ὁ δειπνίζων τ᾽ ἐμὲ
Ῥόδιος, ἐγὼ δ᾽ ὁ κεκλημένος Περίνθιος·
οὐδέτερος ἡμῶν ἤδεται τοῖς Ἀττικοῖς
132   δείπνοις. (Β.) ἀηδία γάρ ἐστιν Ἀττική; ‖
    (Α.) ὥσπερ ξενική. παρέθηκε πίνακα γὰρ μέγαν,
ἔχοντα μικροὺς πέντε πινακίσκους ἄνω·
τούτων ὁ μὲν ἔχει σκόροδον, ὁ δ᾽ ἐχίνους δύο,
ὁ δὲ θρυμματίδα γλυκεῖαν, ὁ δὲ κόγχας δέκα,
ὁ δ᾽ ἀντακαίου μικρόν. ἐν ὅσῳ δ᾽ ἐσθίω,
ἕτερος ἐκεῖν᾽, ἐν ὅσῳ δ᾽ ἐκεῖνος, τοῦτ᾽ ἐγὼ
ἠφάνισα. βούλομαι δέ γ᾽, ὦ βέλτιστε σύ,
b   κἀκεῖνο καὶ τοῦτ᾽, ἀλλ᾽ ἀδύνατα βούλομαι· ⎮
οὔτε στόματα γὰρ οὔτε χεῖρας πέντ᾽ ἔχω.
ὄψιν μὲν οὖν ἔχει τὰ τοιαῦτα ποικίλην,
ἀλλ᾽ οὐθέν ἐστι τοῦτο πρὸς τὴν γαστέρα·
κατέπασα γὰρ τὸ χεῖλος, οὐκ ἐνέπλησα δέ.
τί οὖν; ἔχεις ὄστρεια; (Β.) πολλά. (Α.) πίνακά
    μοι
τούτων παραθήσεις αὐτὸν ἐφ᾽ ἑαυτοῦ μέγαν.
ἔχεις ἐχίνους; (Β.) ἕτερος ἔσται σοι πίναξ·
αὐτὸς γὰρ αὐτὸν ἐπριάμην ὀκτὼ ὀβολῶν.
    (Α.) ὀψάριον αὐτὸ τοῦτο παραθήσεις μόνον,

---

40 See 4.131d n.

Lynceus makes fun of Attic dinner parties in *The Centaur* (fr. 1) and says:

(A.) Cook, the man who's making the sacrifice and
    having me to dinner
is from Rhodes, and I, his guest, am from Perinthos;
neither of us likes Attic
dinner parties. (B.) Is it possible to dislike Attic food?
(A.) Just like any food that's not one's own. You're
    served a big platter
with five little platters on top;
one holds a garlic clove, another two seaurchins,
the third a sweet *thrummatis*[40], the fourth ten
    shellfish,
and the fifth a little piece of sturgeon. While I'm
    eating this,
the other fellow is eating that; and while he's eating
    that,
I'm making this disappear. But, my good sir, I want
both this and that—and what I want is impossible,
because I don't have five mouths or five hands.
This sort of arrangement makes an impressive
    appearance,
but that doesn't do your stomach any good;
I get my lips dirty, but I'm not full.
Anyway—have you got oysters? (B.) Lots. (A.) Serve
    me
a large platter of these all by itself.
Have you got sea-urchins? (B.) You'll have another
    platter, with these;
because I bought them myself for eight obols.
(A.) Serve this dish separately, by itself,

131

c   ἵνα ταὐτὰ πάντες, μὴ τὸ μὲν ἐγώ, τὸ δ᾽ ἕτερος. |

Δρομέας δ᾽ ὁ παράσιτος ἐρωτήσαντός τινος αὐτόν, ὡς
φησιν ὁ Δελφὸς Ἡγήσανδρος, πότερον ἐν ἄστει γίνεται βελτίω δεῖπνα ἢ ἐν Χαλκίδι, τὸ προοίμιον εἶπε τῶν
ἐν Χαλκίδι δείπνων χαριέστερον εἶναι τῆς ἐν ἄστει
παρασκευῆς, τὸ πλῆθος τῶν ὀστρέων καὶ τὴν ποικιλίαν προοίμιον εἰπὼν δείπνου. Δίφιλος δ᾽ ἐν Ἀπολειπούσῃ μάγειρόν τινα παράγων ποιεῖ τάδε λέγοντα·

d   (Α.) πόσοι τὸ πλῆθός εἰσιν οἱ κεκλημένοι |
     εἰς τοὺς γάμους, βέλτιστε, καὶ πότερ᾽ Ἀττικοὶ
     ἅπαντες, ἢ κἀκ τοὐμπορίου τινές; (Β.) τί δαὶ
     τοῦτ᾽ ἐστὶ πρὸς σὲ τὸν μάγειρον; (Α.) τῆς τέχνης
     ἡγεμονία τις ἐστὶν αὐτῆς, ὦ πάτερ,
     τὸ τῶν ἐδομένων τὰ στόματα προειδέναι.
     οἷον Ῥοδίους κέκληκας· εἰσιοῦσι δὸς
     εὐθὺς ἀπὸ θερμοῦ τὴν μεγάλην αὐτοῖς σπάσαι,
     ἀποζέσας σίλουρον ἢ λεβίαν, ἐφ᾽ ᾧ
e   χαριεῖ πολὺ μᾶλλον ἢ μυρίνην προσεγχέας. |
     (Β.) ἀστεῖον ὁ σιλουρισμός. (Α.) ἂν Βυζαντίους,
     ἀψινθίῳ † σφοιη † δεῦσον ὅσα γ᾽ ἂν παρατιθῇς,
     κάθαλα ποήσας πάντα κἀσκοροδισμένα.
     διὰ γὰρ τὸ πλῆθος τῶν παρ᾽ αὐτοῖς ἰχθύων

---

41 *PAA* 374610; otherwise unknown.
42 Athens.

> so that everyone eats the same food, not me one
>   thing and the other fellow something else.

According to Hegesander of Delphi (fr. 10, *FHG* iv.415),
when someone asked the parasite Dromeas[41] whether the
dinner parties were better in the city[42] or in Chalcis, he
said that the prelude to the dinner parties in Chalcis was
more delightful than what was prepared in the city, referring to the large quantities of different types of shellfish as
"the prelude to dinner." Diphilus brings a cook onstage in
The Woman Who Wanted To Leave Her Husband (fr. 17)
and represents him as saying the following:

> (A.) How many guests have been invited
> to the wedding feast, my good man? And are they all
> Athenians, or are some from the merchants' quarter?
>   (B.) What's this
> to you? You're the cook. (A.) A fundamental part
> of my art itself, old sir,
> is having advance knowledge of the palates of the
>   diners.
> You've invited Rhodians, for example. The minute
>   they come in,
> offer them the big cup full of hot wine to suck down,
> and stew a sheatfish or a *lebias* until it's perfect; you'll
>   give him
> more pleasure this way than if you poured perfumed
>   wine over his hands.
> (B.) Very clever, this sheatfish-izing! (A.) If you've
>   invited people from Byzantium,
> soak whatever you serve [corrupt] in wormwood,
> and season it all with salt and garlic;
> the fact that they have so many fish in their country

πάντες βλιχανώδεις εἰσὶ καὶ μεστοὶ λάπης.

Μένανδρος δ' ἐν Τροφωνίῳ·

ξένου τὸ δεῖπνόν ἐστιν ὑποδοχή τινος.
ποδαποῦ; διαφέρει τῷ μαγείρῳ τοῦτο γάρ.
οἷον τὰ † μὲν νησιωτικὰ ταυτὶ ξενύδρια,

f ἐν προσφάτοις ἰχθυδίοις τεθραμμένα |
καὶ παντοδαποῖς, τοῖς ἁλμίοις μὲν οὐ πάνυ
ἁλίσκετ', ἀλλ' οὕτως παρέργως ἅπτεται,
τὰς δ' ὀνθυλεύσεις καὶ τὰ κεκαρυκευμένα
μᾶλλον προσεδέξατ'. Ἀρκαδικὸς τοὐναντίον
ἀθάλαττος ἐν τοῖς λοπαδίοις ἁλίσκεται.
Ἰωνικὸς πλούταξ· ὑποστάσεις πῶ,

133 κάνδαυλον, ὑποβινητιῶντα βρώματα. ‖

ἐχρῶντο γὰρ οἱ παλαιοὶ καὶ τοῖς εἰς ἀναστόμωσιν
βρώμασιν ὥσπερ ταῖς ἁλμάσιν ἐλάαις, ἃς κολυμ-
βάδας καλοῦσιν. Ἀριστοφάνης γοῦν ἐν Γήρᾳ φησίν·

ὦ πρεσβῦτα, πότερα φιλεῖς τὰς δρυπεπεῖς
    ἑταίρας
ἢ τὰς ὑποπαρθένους ἁλμάδας ὡς ἐλάας
στιφράς;

Φιλήμων δ' ἐν Μετιόντι ἢ Ζωμίῳ·

---

43 Literally "treated with *karuk(k)ē*," a spicy blood-based
Lydian sauce; cf. 4.160a, 172b, 173c–d; 12.516c.
44 Another proverbially rich Lydian dish; cf. 1.9a; 4.172b

means they're all clammy and full of phlegm.

Menander in *Trophonius* (fr. 351):

> The dinner party is being given for some foreigner;
> but where's he from? Because this matters to a cook.
> These guests from the island †, for example,
> who're brought up on fresh fish
> of every kind, aren't much attracted
> to salted foods, but consume them rather
>   indifferently;
> whereas they're more well-disposed to dishes that are
>   stuffed
> and richly sauced.[43] An Arcadian, on the other hand,
> isn't familiar with the sea and can be trapped in
>   casserole-dishes.
> A rich Ionian fool—I make thick soups
> and *kandaulos*[44], lecherous foods.

For the ancients used to eat foods intended to whet their appetites, such as brined olives, which they refer to as *kolumbades* ("swimmers"). Aristophanes, for example, says in *Old Age* (fr. 148):

> Old man, do you like the tree-ripened[45] prostitutes
> or the preadolescent ones, who are as firm as
> brined olives?

Philemon in *The Man Who Was in Pursuit or Brothlet* (fr. 42):

(spelled in the late form *kandulos* in both places); 12.516c–17e; Arnott on Alex. fr. 178.1.
   [45] I.e. "fully mature," and thus "full of wrinkles"; cf. 2.56a–d.

(Α.) ἰχθὺς τί σοι
ἐφαίνεθ᾽ οὑφθός; (Β.) μικρὸς ἦν, ἀκήκοας;
b   ἅλμη τε λευκὴ καὶ παχεῖ᾽ ὑπερβολῇ, |
κοὐχὶ λοπάδος προσῶζεν οὐδ᾽ ἡδυσμάτων.
(Α.) ἐβόων <δ᾽> ἅπαντες "ὡς ἀγαθὴν ἅλμην
   ποεῖς".

ἤσθιον δὲ καὶ τέττιγας καὶ κερκώπας ἀναστομώσεως
χάριν. Ἀριστοφάνης Ἀναγύρῳ·

πρὸς θεῶν· ἔραμαι τέττιγα φαγεῖν
καὶ κερκώπην θηρευσαμένη
καλάμῳ λεπτῷ.

ἐστὶν δ᾽ ἡ κερκώπη ζῷον ὅμοιον τέττιγι καὶ τιτιγονίῳ,
ὡς Σπεύσιππος παρίστησιν ἐν τετάρτῳ Ὁμοίων. μνημονεύει αὐτῶν Ἐπίλυκος ἐν Κωραλίσκῳ. Ἄλεξις ἐν
c Θράσωνί φησι· |

σοῦ δ᾽ ἐγὼ λαλιστέραν
οὐπώποτ᾽ εἶδον οὔτε κερκώπην, γύναι,
οὐ κίτταν, οὐκ ἀηδόν᾽, <οὐ χελιδόνα,>
οὐ τρυγόν᾽, οὐ τέττιγα.

Νικόστρατος δ᾽ ἐν Ἅβρᾳ·

πίναξ ὁ πρῶτος τῶν μεγάλων ἡγήσεται,

---

[46] Speusippus (below) identified this as another insect similar
to a cicada, but Athenaeus' treatment of the word makes it clear
that he had no idea how the two could be distinguished.

(A.) What did you think of
the stewed fish? (B.) It was small, do you
    understand?
Also the brine-sauce was white and way too thick;
and there wasn't any smell of the casserole-dish or of
    spices.
(A.) But they all kept shouting "What a nice brine-
    sauce you make!"

They also ate cicadas *(tettiges)* and *kerkōpai*[46] to whet their
appetites. Aristophanes in *Anagyrus* (fr. 53):[47]

By the gods, I long to eat
a cicada *(tettix)* and a *kerkōpē* after I've caught them
with a thin reed.

The *kerkōpē* is a creature that resembles the cicada *(tettix)*
and the *titigonion*[48], as Speusippus establishes in Book IV
of *Similar Things* (fr. 10 Tarán). Epilycus mentions them in
The Young Girl (fr. 5). Alexis says in *Thrason*[49] (fr. 96):

I've never seen
a greater chatterbox than you, woman—no *kerkōpē*
or jay or nightingale or swallow
or turtledove or cicada *(tettix)!*

Nicostratus in *The Slave-Girl*[50] (fr. 1):

The first platter will lead the way for the main dishes,

[47] The first half of the first verse is a parody of E. *Hipp.* 219.
[48] Not attested elsewhere, but probably a diminutive form of a
word cognate with *tettix*.   [49] A personal name, perhaps of a
soldier ("Mr. Bold").   [50] For the word, see Photius α 50. Alternatively, the title might be the personal name Habra.

137

ἔχων ἐχῖνον, ὠμοτάριχον, κάππαριν,
θρυμματίδα, τέμαχος, βολβὸν ἐν ὑποτρίμματι.

Ὅτι δ᾽ ἤσθιον διὰ ἀναστόμωσιν καὶ τὰς δι᾽ ὄξους
d   καὶ νάπυος γογγυλίδας σαφῶς παρίστησι | Νίκαν-
δρος ἐν δευτέρῳ Γεωργικῶν λέγων οὕτως·

γογγυλίδος δισσὴ γὰρ ἰδ᾽ ἐκ ῥαφάνοιο γενέθλη
μακρή τε στιφρή τε φαείνεται ἐν πρασιῇσι.
καὶ τὰς μέν θ᾽ αὔηνον ἀποπλύνας βορέῃσι,
προσφιλέας χειμῶνι καὶ οἰκουροῖσιν ἀεργοῖς·
θερμοῖς δ᾽ ἱκμανθεῖσαι ἀναζώουσ᾽ ὑδάτεσσι.
τμῆγε δὲ γογγυλίδος ῥίζας κατακαρφέα φλοιὸν
ἦκα καθηράμενος λεπτουργέας, ἠελίῳ δὲ
e   αὐήνας ἐπὶ τυτθόν, ὅτ᾽ ἐν ζεστῷ ἀποβάπτων |
ὕδατι, δριμείῃ πολέας ἐμβάπτισον ἄλμῃ·
ἄλλοτε δ᾽ αὖ λευκὸν γλεῦκος συστάμνισον ὄξει
ἶσον ἴσῳ, τὰς δ᾽ ἐντὸς ἐπιστύψας ἁλὶ κρύψαις.
πολλάκι δ᾽ ἀσταφίδας προχέας τριπτῆρι λεήναις
σπέρματά τ᾽ ἐνδάκνοντα σινήπυος. εἰν ἑνὶ δὲ
τρὺξ
ὄξεος ἱκμάζουσα καὶ † ὠμοτέρην ἐπὶ κόρσην
f   ὥριον ἁλμαίην ἄμυσαι κεχρηόσι δαίτης †. |

---

51 See 4.131d n.   52 Three additional verses from the
beginning of the fragment are quoted at 9.369b (and cf. 9.366d).
    53 The word normally means "cabbage," although Nicander
would appear to be using it to refer to root-vegetable closely related to a turnip. Cf. 2.57a, where Athenaeus claims that the
comic poet Callias used it to mean "radish."

with a sea-urchin, raw-saltfish, a caper,
a *thrummatis*[51], a fish-steak, and a hyacinth bulb in
    sauce.

That they also ate turnips in vinegar and mustard to
whet their appetites is clearly established by Nicander in
Book II of the *Georgics* (fr. 70.4–18 Schneider), where he
says the following:[52]

For two varieties of turnip (*goggulis*) and
    rhaphanos[53],
both large and firm, are seen in our vegetable
    gardens.
Wash the latter and dry them in the north winds;
in the winter they are welcome to those who remain
    idle indoors,
and when they are soaked in warm water they revive.
But cut turnip roots into fine slices after you
gently wash the dry outer skin; dry them
for a little while in the sun; and then dip a number of
    them
in boiling water and plunge them into a bitter brine-
    sauce.
Alternatively, mix equal amounts of white grape-must
    and vinegar
together in a jar, place them inside, and cover them
    with salt.
Often you could grind up raisins and pungent
mustard-seed with a pestle and pour it over them. At
    the same time
moist vinegar lees [corrupt and obscure] . . .

Δίφιλος δ' ἢ Σώσιππος ἐν Ἀπολειπούσῃ·

       (Α.) ἔστιν ἔνδον ὄξος ὀξύ σοι;
(Β.) ὑπολαμβάνω, παιδάριον, ὀπὸν εἰλήφαμεν.
ἄριστα τούτοις πάντα πιέσω καὶ πυκνά.
ἡ φυλλὰς ἡ δριμεῖα περιοισθήσεται·
τῶν πρεσβυτέρων γὰρ ταῦτα τῶν ἡδυσμάτων
ἀναστομοῖ τάχιστα τἀσθητήρια,
τό τε νωκαρῶδες καὶ κατημβλυωμένον
ἐσκέδασε κἀποίησεν ἡδέως φαγεῖν. ‖

134

Ἄλεξις δ' ἐν Ταραντίνοις ἐν τοῖς συμποσίοις φησὶ
τοὺς Ἀττικοὺς καὶ ὀρχεῖσθαι ὑποπιόντας·

       (Α.) τοῦτο γὰρ νῦν ἐστί σοι
ἐν ταῖς Ἀθήναις ταῖς καλαῖς ἐπιχώριον·
ἅπαντες ὀρχοῦντ' εὐθύς, ἂν οἴνου μόνον
ὀσμὴν ἴδωσιν. (Β.) συμφορὰν λέγεις ἄκραν.
(Α.) φαίης ἄν, εἰς συμπόσιον εἰσελθὼν ἄφνω.
καὶ τοῖς μὲν ἀγενείοις ἴσως ἔπεστί τις
χάρις· ἀλλ' ἐπὰν δὴ τὸν γόητα Θεόδοτον
ἢ τὸν παραμασύντην ἴδω τὸν ἀνόσιον ∣
βαυκιζόμενον τὰ λευκά τ' ἀναβάλλονθ' ἅμα,

b

---

54 The items in question are presumably barley-cakes, which
were vigorously kneaded before being served.

Diphilus or Sosippus in *The Woman Who Wanted To Leave Her Husband* (Diph. fr. 18):

> (A.) Do you have any sharp vinegar inside?
> (B.) I assume, slave, that we have rennet.
> I'll press these[54] so they're all good and tight for
>   them.
> The bitter salad will be brought around;
> because these spices rapidly excite
> the sense organs of old men,
> and dispel their lethargy and
> stolidity, and make them happy to eat.

Alexis says in *Men from Tarentum* (fr. 224) that the Athenians danced at their symposia after they had a bit to drink:

> (A.) Because this is now your
> local custom in lovely Athens:
> they all start dancing immediately, if they get even a
>   glimpse
> of the smell of wine. (B.) You're describing a terrible
>   misfortune.
> (A.) You'd say it was, if you accidentally found
>   yourself at a symposium!
> For young men there's perhaps a bit of charm
> in it. But when I see the charlatan
> Theodotus[55] or the filthy parasite
> dancing like a woman and rolling his eyes so the
>   whites show,

---

[55] *PAA* 505150; otherwise unknown and perhaps merely a character in the play, like the "filthy parasite" mentioned below.

ἥδιστ᾽ ἂν ἀναπήξαιμ᾽ ἐπὶ τοῦ ξύλου λαβών.

μήποτε δὲ καὶ Ἀντιφάνης ἐν Καρσὶ κατὰ τὸ Ἀττικὸν
ἔθος[1] κωμῳδεῖ τινα τῶν σοφῶν ὡς παρὰ δεῖπνον ὀρχούμενον λέγων οὕτως·

　　　　　　οὐχ ὁρᾷς ὀρχούμενον
ταῖς χερσὶ τὸν βάκηλον; οὐδ᾽ αἰσχύνεται
ὁ τὸν Ἡράκλειτον πᾶσιν ἐξηγούμενος,
c　　ὁ τὴν Θεοδέκτου μόνος ἀνευρηκὼς τέχνην, |
ὁ τὰ κεφάλαια συγγράφων Εὐριπίδῃ.

τούτοις οὐδ᾽ ἀναρμόστως ἄν τις ἐπενέγκαι τὰ Ἐρίφῳ
τῷ κωμικῷ ἐν Αἰόλῳ εἰρημένα τάδε·

λόγος γάρ ἐστ᾽ ἀρχαῖος οὐ κακῶς ἔχων·
οἶνον λέγουσι τοὺς γέροντας, ὦ πάτερ,
πείθειν χορεύειν οὐ 'θέλοντας.

Ἄλεξις δ᾽ ἐν τῷ ἐπιγραφομένῳ Ἰσοστάσιόν φησιν·

　　(Α.) ἀπὸ συμβολῶν ἔπινον, ὀρχεῖσθαι μόνον
d　βλέποντες, ἄλλο δ᾽ οὐδέν, ὄψων ὀνόματα |
καὶ σιτίων ἔχοντες. (Β.) ὄψων; (Α.) Κάραβος

---

[1] ἔθος τῆς ὀρχήσεως A

---

[56] For the stocks *(xulon)*, see Olson on Ar. *Pax* 479–80. But the
verb (literally "peg him up") is more appropriate for the method of
execution called *apotumpanismos* (cf. 4.166c with n.), in which a
malefactor was fastened to a plank (usually *sanis*) and allowed to
die slowly; cf. Austin–Olson on Ar. *Th.* 930–1.

I'd be delighted to take him and clap him in the
 stocks.[56]

Perhaps Antiphanes as well is referring to the custom in
Attica in *Men from Caria* (fr. 111) when he mocks one of
the sophists for dancing at a dinner party, saying the following:

>   Don't you see the
> pansy dancing with his hands? He's not ashamed—
> the man who explains Heracleitus to everyone,
> and is the only person able to make sense of
>   Theodectas' art[57]
> and the author of summaries of Euripides.

It would not be inappropriate to add the following remarks
made by the comic poet Eriphus in *Aeolus* (fr. 1):

> Because there's an old saying, and a good one:
> they say, aged sir, that wine persuades old men
> to dance even when they don't want to.[58]

Alexis says in the play entitled *Isostasion* (fr. 102):

> (A.) They were sharing the expense of the drinking,
>   with an eye to
> dancing and nothing else; and their names were
>   drawn
> from fancy dishes and grainstuffs. (B.) Fancy dishes?
>   (A.) Crayfish

---

[57] Theodectas was a tragic poet (*TrGF* 72), Heraclitus a
presocratic philosopher (D–K 22).
[58] For the proverb, cf. 10.428a.

καὶ Κωβιός, Σεμίδαλις.

Ἀττικὸν δὲ δεῖπνον οὐκ ἀχαρίτως διαγράφει Μάτρων ὁ παρῳδός, ὅπερ διὰ τὸ σπάνιον οὐκ ἂν ὀκνή-
σαιμι ὑμῖν, ἄνδρες φίλοι, ὁ Πλούταρχος ἔφη, ἀπο-
μνημονεῦσαι·

δεῖπνά μοι ἔννεπε, Μοῦσα, πολυτρόφα καὶ μάλα
    πολλά, ἃ Ξενοκλῆς ῥήτωρ ἐν Ἀθήναις δείπνισεν
e   ἡμᾶς· |
ἦλθον γὰρ κἀκεῖσε, πολὺς δέ μοι ἕσπετο λιμός.
οὗ δὴ καλλίστους ἄρτους ἴδον ἠδὲ μεγίστους,
λευκοτέρους χιόνος, ἔσθειν δ᾽ ἀμύλοισιν ὁμοίους·
τάων καὶ Βορέης ἠράσσατο πεσσομενάων.
αὐτὸς δὲ Ξενοκλῆς ἐπεπωλεῖτο στίχας ἀνδρῶν,
στῆ δ᾽ ἄρ᾽ ἐπ᾽ οὐδὸν ἰών· σχεδόθεν δέ οἱ ἦν
    παράσιτος
f Χαιρεφόων, πεινῶντι λάρῳ ὄρνιθι ἐοικώς, |
νήστης, ἀλλοτρίων εὖ εἰδὼς δειπνοσυνάων.
τέως δὲ μάγειροι μὲν φόρεον πλῆσάν τε
    τραπέζας,
οἷς ἐπιτετράφαται μέγας οὐρανὸς ὀπτανιάων,

---

[59] Much of the language is borrowed direct from epic or adapts epic formulae.

[60] Xenocles (*PAA* 732385) and Stratocles (*PA* 12938; Berve i #724; mentioned below; cf. 6.252f n.) were important late 4th-century Athenian politicians.

[61] A notorious parasite mentioned repeatedly in late 4th-century Athenian sources; cf. 4.164f–5a; 6.242f–4a; etc. A letter by

and Goby; Durum Wheat.

The parodist Matro (fr. 1 Olson–Sens = *SH* 534) describes an Attic dinner party in quite a witty fashion;[59] I would not hesitate to quote the piece to you, my friends, said Plutarch, on account of its rarity.

Dinners describe to me, Muse, much-nourishing and
    numerous,
which Xenocles the orator[60] dined us on in Athens—
for I went there as well, and a great hunger
    accompanied me—
where indeed I saw very large and lovely loaves of
    bread,
whiter than snow, with a taste that resembled wheat-
    paste cakes;
the North Wind fell in love with them as they were
    baking.
Xenocles himself went about, inspecting the ranks of
    men,
and came and stood on the threshold. Close by him
    was the parasite
Chaerephon,[61] a man resembling a hungry sea-gull,
starving, and well acquainted with other people's
    dining.
The cooks accordingly began to bring tables and load
    them up;
to them has been entrusted the great vault of the
    cookhouses,

him that contained an extended description of a dinner party was preserved in the Library in Alexandria (Call. fr. 434, cited at 6.244a).

ἠμὲν ἐπισπεῦσαι δείπνου χρόνον ἠδ᾽ ἀναμεῖναι.
ἔνθ᾽ ἄλλοι πάντες λαχάνοις ἐπὶ χεῖρας ἴαλλον,
ἀλλ᾽ ἐγὼ οὐ πιθόμην, ἀλλ᾽ ἤσθιον εἴδατα
    πάντα, ‖
βολβοὺς ἀσπάραγόν τε καὶ ὄστρεα μυελόεντα,
ὠμοτάριχον ἐῶν χαίρειν, Φοινίκιον ὄψον.
αὐτὰρ ἐχίνους ῥῖψα κάρη κομόωντας ἀκάνθαις,
οἱ δὲ κυλινδόμενοι καναχὴν ἔχον ἐν ποσὶ παίδων
ἐν καθαρῷ, ὅθι κύματ᾽ ἐπ᾽ ἠιόνος κλύζεσκε·
πολλὰς δ᾽ ἐκ κεφαλῆς προθελύμνους εἷλκον
    ἀκάνθας.
ἡ δὲ Φαληρικὴ ἦλθ᾽ ἀφύη, Τρίτωνος ἑταίρη,
ἄντα παρειάων σχομένη ῥυπαρὰ κρήδεμνα ‖

       *   *   *

τοὺς δ᾽ ὁ Κύκλωψ ἐφίλει καὶ ἐν οὔρεσιν
    ἐξεπεφύκει

       *   *   *

πίννας ἦλθε φέρων † καὶ ἄμυλα † ἠχήεντα,
ἃς κατὰ φυκότριχος πέτρης λευκὸν τρέφει ὕδωρ.

       *   *   *

ψῆττά τε χονδροφυὴς καὶ τρίγλη μιλτοπάρῃος.
τῇ δ᾽ ἐγὼ ἐν πρώτοις ἐπέχον κρατερώνυχα χεῖρα,

that they might both hasten the dinner-hour and
    patiently await its coming.
Then all the others were putting forth their hands
    upon vegetables;
however I did not follow their example, but was
    eating every sort of food—
hyacinth bulbs, asparagus, and marrowy oysters—
although having nothing to do with shoulder-cuts of
    saltfish, a Phoenician dish.
As for the sea-urchins with their long, spiny hair, I
    cast them away,
and they produced an uproar as they rolled about
    among the boys' feet,
in an open space, where the sea's waves always wash;
and I pulled many spines out by their roots from my
    face.
The Phaleric small-fry, Triton's companioness,
    arrived,
holding before her cheeks a dirty veil.

        *   *   *

these the Cyclops used to love, and produced them in
    the mountains.

        *   *   *

(A cook) came carrying fan-mussels † and echoing
    wheat-paste cakes †,
which the clear water nourishes (as they hang) down
    from a rock with seaweed hair

        *   *   *

and the cartilaginous flat-fish, and the carmine-
    cheeked red mullet.
I was among the first to put a strong-clawed hand to
    it,

οὐδ' ἔφθην τρώσας μιν, ἄασε <δὲ> Φοῖβος
    Ἀπόλλων.
ὡς <δὲ> ἴδον Στρατοκλῆ, κρατερὸν μήστωρα
c   φόβοιο, |
τρίγλης ἱπποδάμοιο κάρη μετὰ χερσὶν ἔχοντα,
ἂψ δ' ἑλόμην χάρμῃ, λαιμὸν δ' ἄπληστον ἄμυξα.
ἦλθε δὲ Νηρῆος θυγάτηρ, Θέτις ἀργυρόπεζα,
σηπίη εὐπλόκαμος, δεινὴ θεὸς αὐδήεσσα,
ἣ μόνη ἰχθὺς ἐοῦσα τὸ λευκὸν καὶ μέλαν οἶδε.
καὶ Τιτυὸν εἶδον, λίμνης ἐρικυδέα γόγγρον,
κείμενον ἐν λοπάδεσσ'· ὁ δ' ἐπ' ἐννέα κεῖτο
    τραπέζας.
d   τῷ δὲ μετ' ἴχνια βαῖνε θεὰ λευκώλενος ἰχθὺς |
ἔγχελυς, ἣ Διὸς εὔχετ' ἐν ἀγκοίνῃσι μιγῆναι,
ἐκ Κωπῶν, ὅθεν ἐγχέλεων γένος ἀγροτεράων,
παμμεγέθης, ἣν οὔ κε δύ' ἀνέρες ἀθλητῆρες,
οἷοι ἄρ' Ἀστυάναξ τε καὶ Ἀντήνωρ ἐγένοντο,
ῥηιδίως ἐπ' ἄμαξαν ἀπ' οὔδεος ὀχλίσσειαν·
τρισπίθαμοι γὰρ ταί γε καὶ ἐννεαπήχεες ἦσαν
εὖρος, ἀτὰρ μῆκός γε γενέσθην ἐννεόργυιοι.
πολλὰ δ' ἄναντα κάταντα κατὰ στίχος ἦλθ' ὁ
    μάγειρος,
e   σείων ὀψοφόρους πίνακας κατὰ δεξιὸν ὦμον. |
τῷ δ' ἅμα τεσσαράκοντα μέλαιναι χύτραι
    ἔποντο,
αὐτὰρ ἀπ' Εὐβοίης λοπάδες τόσαι ἐστιχόωντο.

---

[62] Astyanax (Moretti #470, 474, 479; see 10.413a–b with n.)

although I did not wound it before the others; for
    Phoebus Apollo led me wrong.
But when I saw Stratocles, the powerful raiser of fear,
holding the head of the horse-mastering red mullet in
    his hands,
I snatched it back with martial ardor, and scratched
    his insatiable gullet.
The daughter of Nereus, silver-footed Thetis, arrived,
the cuttlefish fair-tressed, a fearful goddess able to
    speak,
the only fish who knows white from black.
I also saw Tityus, the famed conger eel of the sea,
lying in stewing-pots; he lay over nine tables.
In his tracks came a white-armed goddess-fish,
the eel, who claims to have spent time in the arms of
    Zeus.
She was from Copais, whence comes the race of wild
    eels,
and was very large; not even two athletes,
men such as Astyanax and Antenor[62] were,
could easily have lifted her onto a cart from the earth;
for they were three spans and nine cubits
wide, and nine fathoms in length.
The cook went repeatedly up and down the ranks,
brandishing serving-platters loaded with side-dishes
    over his right shoulder.
Forty black cookpots followed along with him,
while from Euboea an equal number of casserole-
    dishes were drawn up in a line.

and Antenor (*PAA* 131460; Moretti #488; see 13.578f–9a), both of
Miletus, were famous late 4th-century pancratiasts.

Ἶρις δ' ἄγγελος ἦλθε ποδήνεμος, ὠκέα τευθίς,
πέρκη τ' ἀνθεσίχρως καὶ ὁ δημοτικὸς
    μελάνουρος,
ὃς καὶ θνητὸς ἐὼν ἔπετ' ἰχθύσιν ἀθανάτοισιν.
οἴη δ' αὖ θύννου κεφαλὴ θαλαμηιάδαο
νόσφιν ἀφειστήκει, κεχολωμένη εἵνεκα τευχέων
f   αἰρομένων· τὸ δὲ πῆμα θεοὶ θέσαν ἀνθρώποισι. |
ῥίνη δ', ἣν φιλέουσι περισσῶς τέκτονες ἄνδρες,
τρηχεῖ', ἀλλ' ἀγαθὴ κουροτρόφος· ἦ γὰρ ἔγωγε
ἧς σαρκὸς δύναμαι γλυκερώτερον ἄλλο ἰδέσθαι.
ὀπταλέος δ' εἰσῆλθε πελώριος ἱππότα κεστρεύς,
οὐκ οἶος· ἅμα τῷ γε δυώδεκα σαργοὶ ἕποντο·
κυανόχρως δ' ἀμίας ἐπὶ τοῖς μέγας, ὅς τε
    θαλάσσης
136   πάσης βένθεα οἶδε, Ποσειδάωνος ὑποδμώς, ‖
καρῖδές θ', αἳ Ζηνὸς Ὀλυμπίου εἰσὶν ἀοιδοί,
αἳ δὴ γήραϊ κυφαὶ ἔσαν, χρησταὶ δὲ πάσασθαι.
χρύσοφρυς, ὃς κάλλιστος ἐν ἄλλοις ἵσταται
    ἰχθύς,
κάραβος, ἀστακὸς αὖτε λιλαίετο θωρήσσεσθαι
ἐν μακάρων δείπνοις. τοῖς δαιτυμόνες χέρ'
    ἐφέντες
ἐν στόμασίν ⟨τ'⟩ ἔθεσαν καὶ ἀπήγαγον ἄλλυδις
    ἄλλον.
b   τῶν δ' ἄρ' ἔλοψ κρειῶν δουρικλυτὸς ἡγεμόνευεν, |
οὗ πλήρης περ ἐὼν κρατερῶς παλάμῃ ἐπορέχθην

BOOK IV

Iris the wind-footed messenger came in, the swift
    squid,
and the sea-perch with her brightly colored flesh, and
    the popular saddled bream,
which, although mortal, follows immortal fish.
Only the head of the tuna, Son of Fish-lair,
stood apart, angry on account of the gear
taken from him; the gods made this a grief for men.
Also the monkfish, of which craftsmen are
    extraordinarily fond;
it is rough but good for nourishing young men. I
    myself
can envision other foods more pleasant than its flesh.
An enormous horseman, the roasted gray mullet,
    came in,
but not alone; twelve sargues followed along with it.
After these came a large, blue-hued bonito, who
    knows
the depths of the entire sea and is Poseidon's servant,
and prawns, which are the singers of Olympian Zeus;
they were bent with old age, but were good for
    eating.
A gilthead, which is the loveliest fish among them all,
(and) a crayfish; a lobster too was eager to take a
    valiant part
in the banquets of the blessed. The diners laid their
    hands on these foods,
and put them in their mouths and took them off in
    various directions.
Lord Sturgeon, famous for his spear, was their leader;
although full, I reached out forcefully for him with
    my hand,

γεύσασθ᾽ ἱμείρων· τὸ δέ γ᾽ ἀμβροσίη μοι ἔδοξεν,
οἵην δαίνυνται μάκαρες θεοὶ αἰὲν ἐόντες.
μύραιναν δ᾽ ἐπέθηκε φέρων, τὸ κάλυμμα
    τραπέζης,
ζώνην θ᾽, ἣν φορέεσκεν ἀγαλλομένη περὶ δειρήν,
εἰς λέχος ἡνίκ᾽ ἔβαινε Δρακοντιάδῃ μεγαθύμῳ.

c   σάνδαλα δ᾽ αὖ παρέθηκεν ἀειγενῆ ἀθανατάων, |
βούγλωσσόν <θ᾽>, ὃς ἔναιεν ἐν ἄλμῃ
    μορμυρούσῃ,
κίχλας δ᾽ ἐξείης ἡβήτορας ὑψιπετήεις
καὶ πέτρας κάτα βοσκομένας, ὑάδας θ᾽
    ὑδατινούς.
ἐν δ᾽ ἀναμὶξ σαργοί τε καὶ ἵππουροι γλάνιές τε,
μόρμυρος, † ἄντα δ᾽ ἦν μεγάλη † σπάρος· οὓς ὁ
    μάγειρος
σίζοντας παρέθηκε φέρων, κνίσωσε δὲ δῶμα.
τῶν ἔλεγεν δαίνυσθαι· ἐμοὶ δέ γε θηλυτεράων

d   εἶναι βρώματ᾽ ἔδοξεν, ἐπεὶ ῥ᾽ ὅρμαινον ἐπ᾽ ἄλλα. |
κεῖτο δέ τις βατάνη, τῆς οὐδεὶς ἥπτετο δειπνῶν,
ἐν καθαρῷ ὅθι περ λοπάδων διεφαίνετο χῶρος,
ἐξ ἧς κόσσυφος ἦλθε μόνος γεύσασθαι ἕτοιμος·

eager to have a taste. This seemed to me to be
    ambrosia
of the sort the blessed gods who live forever dine
    upon.
(A cook) brought and served a moray eel, the table's
    veil,
along with her belt, which she used to wear with
    pride about her neck
when she went off to bed with the great-hearted Son
    of Serpent.
Next he served eternal sandals belonging to
    goddesses,
that is to say a *bouglōssos,* which haunted the roiling
    brine,
and immediately after these plump thrush-fish, high-
    flying
and feeding among the rocks, watery pig-fish,
and a jumble of sargues, dolphin-fish, and eels;
a marmora, † and opposite it was a great † bream.
    These the cook
brought and served sizzling, and filled the house with
    steam.
He told us to eat some of them; but to me these
    seemed to be
women's food, for I was inclined toward other foods.
A casserole-dish, which no-one was laying hands on
    as he dined, lay there
in a clear spot, where a space appeared among the
    cookpots,
and out of it came a single blackbird, ready to be
    tasted.

οὐ μὴν οὐδ' ἄρ' ἄθικτος ἔην, πόθεον δὲ καὶ
   ἄλλοι.
κωλῆν δ' ὡς εἶδον, ὡς ἔτρεμον· ἐν δὲ σίναπυ
† κεῖτ' ἀγχοῦ γλυκὺ πλείονα χρυσὸς ὢν
   ἀπερύκων. †
γευσάμενος δ' ἔκλαιον, ὅ τ' αὔριον οὐκέτι ταῦτα
e ὄψομαι, ἀλλά με τυρῷ δεῖ καὶ μάζῃ ὀτρηρῇ |

      *   *   *

νηδὺς δ' οὐχ ὑπέμεινε, βιάζετο γὰρ ἀδέεσσι·
δάμνα μιν ζωμός τε μέλας ἀκροκώλιά θ' ἐφθά.
παῖς δέ τις ἐκ Σαλαμῖνος ἄγεν τρισκαίδεκα
   νήσσας,
λίμνης ἐξ ἱερῆς, μάλα πίονας, ἃς ὁ μάγειρος
θῆκε φέρων ἵν' Ἀθηναίων κατέκειντο φάλαγγες.
Χαιρεφόων δ' ἐνόησεν ἅμα πρόσσω καὶ ὀπίσσω
f ὄρνιθας γνῶναι καὶ ἐναίσιμα σιτίζεσθαι. |
ἤσθιε δ' ὥστε λέων, παλάμῃ δ' ἔχε τὸ σκέλος
   ἀμνοῦ,
ὄφρα οἱ οἴκαδ' ἰόντι πάλιν ποτιδόρπιον εἴη.
χόνδρος δ' ἡδυπρόσωπος, ὃν Ἥφαιστος κάμεν
   ἕψων,
Ἀττικῷ ἐν κεράμῳ πέσσων τρισκαίδεκα μῆνας.
αὐτὰρ ἐπεὶ δόρποιο μελίφρονος ἐξ ἔρον ἕντο,
χεῖρας νιψαμένοισιν ἀπ' Ὠκεανοῖο ῥοάων
137 ὡραῖος παῖς ἦλθε φέρων μύρον ἴρινον ἡδύ, ‖

Nor was it in fact untouched, and others as well
    desired it.
But when I saw the ham, how I began to tremble; in
    mustard
† it lay nearby sweet more being gold keeping off †.
I began to wail when I tasted it, since I would no
    longer see these foods
on the morrow, but on cheese and servile bread
    would have to

      *   *   *

My stomach did not endure this, for it was hard-
    pressed by fullness;
black broth and boiled pigs' trotters were overcoming
    it.
A slave brought thirteen ducks from Salamis,
from the sacred sea, very fat ones, which the cook
served where the ranks of Athenians were reclining.
Chaerephon looked back and forth at the same time
to recognize the birds and feed on what was allotted
    him.
He ate like a lion and held a lamb's leg in his hand,
in order that it might serve as his dinner when he
    went home.
Also sweet-faced wheat porridge, which Hephaestus
    worked to boil,
cooking it for thirteen months in an Attic pot.
But when they had put away desire for delightful
    dinner
and had washed their hands, from the streams of
    Ocean
came a lovely boy, bringing sweet iris-scented oil.

ἄλλος δ' αὖ στεφάνους ἐπὶ δεξιὰ πᾶσιν ἔδωκεν,
οἳ ῥόδον ἀμφεπλέκοντο διάνδιχα κοσμηθέντες.
κρητὴρ δὲ Βρομίου ἐκεράννυτο, πίνετο δ' οἶνος
Λέσβιος, οὗ δὴ πλεῖστον ἀνὴρ ὑπὲρ ἄνδρα
      πεπώκει.

b   δεύτεραι αὖτε τράπεζαι ἐφωπλίζοντο γέμουσαι· |
ἐν δ' αὐταῖσιν ἐπῆν ἄπιοι καὶ πίονα μῆλα,
ῥοιαί τε σταφυλαί τε, θεοῦ Βρομίοιο τιθῆναι
            *   *   *

πρόσφατος, ἥν θ' ἁμάμαξυν ἐπίκλησιν καλέουσι.
τῶν δ' ἐγὼ οὐδενὸς ἦσθον ἁπλῶς, μεστὸς δ'
      ἀνεκείμην.
ὡς δὲ ἴδον ξανθὸν γλυκερὸν μέγαν ἔγκυκλον,
      ἄνδρες,

c   Δήμητρος παῖδ' ὀπτὸν ἐπεισελθόντα πλακοῦντα, |
πῶς ἂν ἔπειτα πλακοῦντος ἐγὼ θείου ἀπεχοίμην;
οὐδ' εἴ μοι δέκα μὲν χεῖρες, δέκα δὲ στόματ'
      εἶεν,
γαστὴρ δ' ἄρρηκτος, χάλκεον δέ μοι ἦτορ ἐνείη.
πόρναι δ' εἰσῆλθον, κοῦραι δύο θαυματοποιοί,
ἃς Στρατοκλῆς ἤλαυνε ποδώκεας ὄρνιθας ὥς.

Ἄλεξις δ' ἐν Συντρέχουσιν ἐπισκώπτων τὰ Ἀττικὰ
δεῖπνά φησιν·

d   ἔγωγε δύο λαβεῖν μαγείρους βούλομαι |

Another distributed garlands to everyone from right
    to left;
they were intertwined with roses, ornamented in two
    ways.
A bowl of Bromius was mixed and Lesbian wine
was drunk; each man had drunk more of this than his
    neighbor.
Next the second tables, loaded with food, were fitted
    out.
On them were pears and fat apples,
pomegranates and grape clusters, the nurses of
    Bromius

*   *   *

freshly picked, which they call by the nickname
    hamamaxus.
I ate none of these foods whatsoever, but lay there
    stuffed.
But, gentlemen, when I saw the tawny, sweet, big,
    circular,
roasted child of Demeter entering—that is, the flat-
    cake—
how then could I keep away from the divine flat-
    cake?
Not even did I have ten hands and ten mouths,
and were my stomach impervious and my heart
    within made of bronze.
Whores came in, two wonder-working girls,
whom Stratocles was driving like fast-legged birds.

Alexis mocks Attic dinner parties in *Men Who Agree* (fr.
216), saying:

I want to hire the two cleverest

οὓς ἂν σοφωτάτους δύνωμ᾽ ἐν τῇ πόλει.
μέλλοντα δειπνίζειν γὰρ ἄνδρα Θετταλὸν
οὐκ Ἀττικηρῶς οὐδ᾽ ἀπηκριβωμένως
† λιμῷ παρελθεῖν ἃ δεῖ καθ᾽ ἓν
ἕκαστον αὐτοῖς παρατιθέντα μεγαλείως δέ †.

εὐτράπεζοι δ᾽ εἰσὶν ὄντως οἱ Θετταλοί, καθὰ καὶ Ἐρι-
φός φησιν ἐν Πελταστῇ οὕτως·

τάδ᾽ οὐ Κόρινθος οὐδὲ Λαΐς, ὦ Σύρε,
οὐδ᾽ εὐτραπέζων Θετταλῶν ξένων τροφαί,
ὧν οὐκ ἄμοιρος ἥδε χεὶρ ἐγίνετο. |

ὁ δὲ τοὺς εἰς Χιωνίδην ἀναφερομένους Πτωχοὺς ποιήσας τοὺς Ἀθηναίους φησίν, ὅταν τοῖς Διοσκούροις
ἐν πρυτανείῳ ἄριστον προτιθῶνται, ἐπὶ τῶν τραπεζῶν
τιθέναι τυρὸν καὶ φυστὴν δρυπεπεῖς τ᾽ ἐλάας καὶ
πράσα, ὑπόμνησιν ποιουμένους τῆς ἀρχαίας ἀγωγῆς.
Σόλων δὲ τοῖς ἐν πρυτανείῳ σιτουμένοις μᾶζαν παρέχειν κελεύει, ἄρτον δὲ ταῖς ἑορταῖς προσπαρατιθέναι,
μιμούμενος τὸν Ὅμηρον. καὶ γὰρ ἐκεῖνος τοὺς ἀρι-
στεῖς συνάγων πρὸς τὸν Ἀγαμέμνονα | φύρετο δ᾽
ἄλφιτα φησίν. Χρύσιππός τ᾽ ἐν τετάρτῳ Περὶ τοῦ

---

63 Corinth was well-known for its prostitutes, at least two of
whom were named Laïs; cf. 13.570d–e (citing Anaxandr. fr. 9),
586e and 592c (both citing the same speech by Lysias); Ar. Pl. 179.
Syrus is a common comic slave-name.
64 A reference to the ritual of *theoxenia*, in which a god was entertained at a banquet; cf. 6.239b–c (citing Diod. Com. fr. 2); Pi.

cooks I can find in the city.
Because when you're going to entertain a Thessalian
not in the Attic way or with precisely measured
    portions,
† with hunger to evade what's necessary one
item at a time served to them but magnificently †.

The Thessalians do in fact set a fine table, as Eriphus says in *The Peltast* (fr. 6), putting it thus:

This isn't Corinth or Laïs,[63] Syrus,
or the food served by gourmandizing Thessalian
    hosts,
which this hand never lacked a share of.

The author of *The Beggars*, which is attributed to Chionides (fr. 7), says that when the Athenians serve lunch to the Dioscuri in the Prytaneion[64], they place cheese, a barley-cake (*phustē*)[65], tree-ripened olives, and leeks on the tables, as a reminder of their ancient way of life. But Solon (fr. 89 Ruschenbusch) orders them to provide those who get their meals in the Prytaneion[66] with a barley-cake, and to add a loaf of bread on festival days. He is imitating Homer (*Cypr.* fr. dub. 38 Bernabé); for when he assembles the nobles to meet Agamemnon, he says that barley groats were kneaded. Chrysippus in Book IV of *On the Good and*

O. 3.1. Nothing else is known about the meal given in honor of the Dioscuri in Athens. For the Prytaneion, see 1.32a n.

   [65] Cf. 3.114e–f.

   [66] I.e. various state officials, official state guests, and citizens who had for one reason or another been honored with perpetual maintenance there, such as the descendants of the tyrannicides Harmodius and Aristogeiton.

Καλοῦ καὶ τῆς Ἡδονῆς φησιν· ἐν Ἀθήναις δὲ ἱστο-
ροῦσιν οὐ πάνυ ἀρχαίων δυεῖν γινομένων δείπνων ἐν
Λυκείῳ τε καὶ Ἀκαδημείᾳ, τοῦ μὲν εἰς τὴν Ἀκαδήμειαν
εἰσενέγκαντος ὀψοποιοῦ λοπάδα πρὸς ἑτέραν τινὰ
χρείαν τὸν κέραμον κατᾶξαι πάντα τοὺς ἱεροποιοὺς
ὡς[2] οὐκ ἀστείας παρεισδύσεως γινομένης, δέοντος
ἀπέχεσθαι τούτων <τῶν> μακρόθεν· τὸν δ᾽ ἐν τῷ Λυκείῳ κρέας[3] εἰς τάριχος διασκευάσαντα μαστιγωθῆ-
ναι ὡς παρασοφιζόμενον πονηρῶς. Πλάτων ‖ δ᾽ ἐν
δευτέρῳ Πολιτείας οὕτως ἑστιᾷ τοὺς αὑτοῦ νεοπολί-
τας, γράφων· "ἄνευ ὄψου," ἔφη, "ὡς ἔοικας, ποιεῖς τοὺς
ἄνδρας ἑστιωμένους." "ἀληθῆ," "ἦν δ᾽ ἐγώ," λέγεις.
ἐπελαθόμην ὅτι καὶ ὄψον ἕξουσιν, ἅλας τε δηλονότι
καὶ ἐλαίας καὶ τυρόν· καὶ βολβοὺς καὶ λάχανά γε οἷα
δὴ ἐν ἀγροῖς ἑψήματα ἑψήσονται. καὶ τραγήματά που
παραθήσομεν αὐτοῖς τῶν τε σύκων καὶ ἐρεβίνθων καὶ
κυάμων, καὶ μύρτα καὶ φηγοὺς σποδιοῦσι πρὸς τὸ
πῦρ μετρίως ὑποπίνοντες. καὶ οὕτως διάγοντες τὸν
βίον ǀ ἐν εἰρήνῃ μετὰ ὑγιείας, ὡς εἰκός, γηραιοὶ
τελευτῶντες ἄλλον τοιοῦτον βίον τοῖς ἐκγόνοις παρα-
δώσουσιν."

Ἑξῆς δὲ λεκτέον καὶ περὶ τῶν Λακωνικῶν συμποσίων. Ἡρόδοτος μὲν οὖν ἐν τῇ ἐνάτῃ τῶν Ἱστοριῶν

---

[2] ὡς μακρόθεν ACE   [3] κρέας ταριχηρὸν ACE

---

67 Two of Athens' gymnasia, and the spots where the schools of
Aristotle and Plato, respectively, were located.

Pleasure (xxviii fr. 3, *SVF* iii.198–9) says: It is a matter of historical record that two dinner parties, neither particularly ancient, take place in Athens, in the Lyceum and the Academy,[67] and that when a cook brought a casserole-dish intended for another purpose into the Academy, the officials in charge of the rite smashed all his pots, on the grounds that the introduction was contrary to civic practice and that it was necessary to avoid these foreign manners, while the cook who prepared meat in the Lyceum so that it resembled saltfish was whipped for making an unfortunate attempt at excessive cleverness. And Plato in Book II of his *Republic* (372c–d) feasts the citizens of his new state this way when he writes: "Apparently," he said, "you're describing your men as feasting without any *opson*[68]!" "You're right," I said. "I forgot that they'll also have *opsa*: salt, of course, and olives, and cheese; and they'll stew hyacinth bulbs and whatever wild vegetables can be cooked this way. As for snacks, I suppose, we'll serve them some figs, chickpeas, and fava beans; and they'll toast myrtle berries and acorns in the fire as they drink a little wine. So they'll live in peace and good health and, most likely, die as old men and pass a similar lifestyle on to their descendants."

The next topic that requires discussion is Spartan symposia. Now Herodotus in Book IX (82) of his *Histories*[69]

---

[68] See 3.125e n.; 4.141b.

[69] The Greek has been Atticized and many details of the narrative modified. A very similar anecdote, but involving different characters, is preserved at 4.150b–c. Mardonius was Xerxes' most important commander.

περὶ τῆς Μαρδονίου παρασκευῆς λέγων καὶ μνημο-
νεύσας Λακωνικῶν συμποσίων φησί· Ξέρξης φεύγων
ἐκ τῆς Ἑλλάδος Μαρδονίῳ τὴν παρασκευὴν κατέλιπε
τὴν αὐτοῦ. Παυσανίαν οὖν ἰδόντα τὴν τοῦ Μαρδονίου
παρασκευὴν χρυσῷ καὶ ἀργύρῳ καὶ παραπετάσμασι
c   ποικίλοις κατεσκευασμένην | κελεῦσαι τοὺς ἀρτοποι-
οὺς καὶ ὀψοποιοὺς κατὰ ταὐτὰ καθὼς Μαρδονίῳ δεῖπνον παρασκευάσαι. ποιησάντων δὲ τούτων τὰ κελευσθέντα τὸν Παυσανίαν ἰδόντα κλίνας χρυσᾶς καὶ
ἀργυρᾶς ἐστρωμένας καὶ τραπέζας ἀργυρᾶς καὶ
παρασκευὴν μεγαλοπρεπῆ δείπνου ἐκπλαγέντα τὰ
προκείμενα κελεῦσαι ἐπὶ γέλωτι τοῖς ἑαυτοῦ διακόνοις
παρασκευάσαι Λακωνικὸν δεῖπνον. καὶ παρασκευ-
ασθέντος γελάσας ὁ Παυσανίας μετεπέμψατο τῶν
d   Ἑλλήνων τοὺς στρατηγοὺς | καὶ ἐλθόντων ἐπιδείξας
ἑκατέρου τῶν δείπνων τὴν παρασκευὴν εἰπεν· "ἄνδρες
Ἕλληνες, συνήγαγον ὑμᾶς βουλόμενος ἐπιδεῖξαι τοῦ
Μήδων ἡγεμόνος τὴν ἀφροσύνην, ὃς τοιαύτην δίαιταν
ἔχων ἦλθεν ὡς ἡμᾶς οὕτω ταλαίπωρον ἔχοντας." φασὶ
δέ τινες καὶ ἄνδρα Συβαρίτην ἐπιδημήσαντα τῇ
Σπάρτῃ καὶ συνεστιαθέντα ἐν τοῖς φιδιτίοις εἰπεῖν·
"εἰκότως ἀνδρειότατοι ἁπάντων εἰσὶ Λακεδαιμόνιοι·
ἕλοιτο γὰρ ‹ἄν› τις εὖ φρονῶν μυριάκις ἀποθανεῖν ἢ
e   οὕτως εὐτελοῦς | διαίτης μεταλαβεῖν."

    Πολέμων δ' ἐν τῷ Παρὰ Ξενοφῶντι Κανάθρῳ τοῦ
παρὰ Λάκωσι καλουμένου δείπνου κοπίδος μνημονεύοντα Κρατῖνον ἐν Πλούτοις λέγειν·

describes Mardonius' personal property and mentions Spartan symposia, saying: When Xerxes was fleeing Greece, he left his personal property to Mardonius. So when Pausanias saw Mardonius' property, which was adorned with gold and silver and embroidered tapestries, he ordered the bakers and cooks to prepare a dinner exactly as they did for Mardonius. They did what they were told; and when Pausanias saw the gold and silver couchs covered with bed-clothes, the silver tables, and the ostentatious preparations for dinner, he was astonished at what lay before him, and as a joke he ordered his own attendants to prepare a Spartan dinner. When it was ready, Pausanias laughed and sent for the Greek generals. When they arrived, he showed them how each dinner had been prepared and said: "Greek sirs, I assembled you because I wanted to show you the folly of the Median commander who, although he lives like this, attacked us, who are so poor. " Some authorities also report that a Sybarite[70] who had spent time in Sparta and eaten with them in the public messes said: "It's no surprise that the Spartans are the bravest men there are; anyone with any sense would rather die a million times than share such a miserable life!"

Polemon in his *On the Carriage Fitted with Wickerwork in Xenophon* (fr. 86 Preller, referring to X. *Ages.* 8.7) [reports] that Cratinus mentions the Spartan dinner called a *kopis* in *Gods of Wealth* (fr. 175), where he says:

[70] The city of Sybaris in Southern Italy was notorious for wealth and luxury.

ἆρ᾽ ἀληθῶς τοῖς ξένοισιν ἔστιν, ὡς λέγουσ᾽, ἐκεῖ
πᾶσι τοῖς ἐλθοῦσιν ἐν τῇ κοπίδι θοινᾶσθαι
   καλῶς;
ἐν δὲ ταῖς λέσχαισι φύσκαι
προσπεπατταλευμέναι

f   κατακρέμανται τοῖσι πρεσβύταισιν ἀποδάκνειν |
   ὀδάξ;

καὶ Εὔπολις ἐν Εἵλωσι·

   αἴ κα γένηται τοῦδε σάμερον κοπίς.

δεῖπνον δ᾽ ἐστὶν ἰδίως ἔχον ἡ κοπίς, καθάπερ καὶ τὸ
καλούμενον αἶκλον. ἐπὴν δὲ κοπίζωσι, πρῶτον μὲν δὴ
σκηνὰς ποιοῦνται παρὰ τὸν θεόν, ἐν δὲ ταύταις στι-
βάδας ἐξ ὕλης, ἐπὶ δὲ τούτων δάπιδας ὑποστρων-
νύουσιν, ἐφ᾽ αἷς τοὺς κατακλιθέντας εὐωχοῦσιν οὐ
μόνον τοὺς ἐκ τῆς ἡμεδαπῆς ἀφικνουμένους, ἀλλὰ καὶ
τοὺς ἐπιδημήσαντας τῶν ξένων. θύουσι δ᾽ ἐν ταῖς
139 κοπίσιν αἶγας, ἄλλο δ᾽ οὐδὲν ἱερεῖον· ‖ καὶ τῶν κρεῶν
διδόασι μοίρας πᾶσι καὶ τὸν καλούμενον φυσίκιλλον,
ὅς ἐστιν ἀρτίσκος ἐγκρίδι παραπλήσιος, γογγυλώτε-
ρος δὲ τὴν ἰδέαν. διδόασι τῶν συνιόντων ἑκάστῳ
τυρὸν χλωρὸν καὶ γαστρὸς καὶ φύσκης τόμον καὶ
τραγήματα σῦκά τε ξηρὰ καὶ κυάμους καὶ φασήλους
χλωρούς. κοπίζει δὲ καὶ τῶν ἄλλων Σπαρτιατῶν ὁ
βουλόμενος. ἐν δὲ τῇ πόλει κοπίδας ἄγουσι καὶ τοῖς
Τιθηνιδίοις καλουμένοις ὑπὲρ τῶν παίδων· κομίζουσι
γὰρ αἱ τιτθαὶ τὰ ἄρρενα παιδία κατὰ τὸν καιρὸν

Is it true, as people say, that every stranger
who goes there is offered a fine feast at the *kopis*?
And that sausages *(phuskai)*[71] hang from pegs
in the public buildings for old men to bite off with
    their teeth?

Also Eupolis in *Helots* (fr. 147):

if a *kopis* is held this very day.[72]

A *kopis* is a distinct sort of dinner, as is the so-called *aiklon*.
When they hold a *kopis*, they begin by erecting tents in the
god's sanctuary; they make beds of brushwood inside and
spread carpets over them, and provide a feast for anyone
who lies down on them, not just visitors from our country[73]
but any foreigners who are present. They sacrifice goats at
the *kopides* but nothing else; they give everyone a share of
the meat as well as the so-called *phusikillos*, which is a
small loaf of bread that resembles an *enkris* ("oil-and-
honey-cake")[74] but is more rounded. They offer everyone
who attends green cheese and a slice of stomach-sausage
and large-intestine-sausage; for snacks they offer dried
figs, fava beans, and green *phasēloi*.[75] Any other Spartiate
who wishes to participate can do so as well. They also celebrate *kopides* in their city at what is called the Tithēnidia,
which is celebrated for the sake of their children; because
their nurses *(tithai)* take the boys into the countryside at

---

[71] See 4.131d n., and cf. below.

[72] Spoken in Doric dialect (appropriate for a Spartan).

[73] Probably Rome, in which case Polemon (who was from
Ilium) is momentarily no longer being quoted.

[74] Cf. 3.110b with n.   [75] See 2.56a with n., where this
information is specifically said to be drawn from Polemon.

b τοῦτον εἰς ἀγρὸν πρὸς | τὴν Κορυθαλίαν καλουμένην
Ἄρτεμιν, ἧς τὸ ἱερὸν παρὰ τὴν καλουμένην Τίασσόν
ἐστιν ἐν τοῖς πρὸς τὴν Κλήταν μέρεσι. ⟨καὶ ταύτας⟩
τὰς κοπίδας παραπλησίως ταῖς λελεγμέναις ἐπιτε-
λοῦσι. θύουσι δὲ καὶ τοὺς γαλαθηνοὺς ὀρθαγορίσκους
καὶ παρατιθέασιν ἐν τῇ θοίνῃ τοὺς ἱπνίτας ἄρτους. ὅτι
αἶκλον ὑπὸ μὲν τῶν ἄλλων Δωριέων καλεῖται τὸ δεῖπνον. Ἐπίχαρμος γοῦν ἐν Ἐλπίδι φησίν·

> ἐκάλεσε γάρ τύ τις
> ἐπ' αἶκλον ἀέκων· τὺ δὲ ἑκὼν ᾤχεο τρέχων.

c τὰ αὐτὰ εἴρηκε καὶ ἐν Περιάλλῳ. | ἐν δὲ τῇ Λακεδαί-
μονι τοῖς εἰσιοῦσιν εἰς τὸ φιδίτιον μετὰ δεῖπνον τὸ
καλούμενον αἶκλον εἰσφέρουσιν ἄρτους ἐν ἀρριχίδι
καὶ κρέας ἑκάστῳ, καὶ τῷ νέμοντι τὰς μοίρας ἀκο-
λουθῶν ὁ διάκονος κηρύττει τὸ αἶκλον προστιθεὶς τοῦ
πέμψαντος τὴν ὀνομασίαν.

Ταῦτα μὲν ὁ Πολέμων· πρὸς ὃν ἀντιλέγων Δίδυμος
ὁ γραμματικός—καλεῖ δὲ τοῦτον Δημήτριος ὁ Τροι-
ζήνιος βιβλιολάθαν διὰ τὸ πλῆθος ὧν ἐκδέδωκε συγ-
γραμμάτων· ἐστὶ γὰρ τρισχίλια πρὸς τοῖς πεντα-
d κοσίοις—φησὶ τάδε· Πολυκράτης, | φησί, ἐν τοῖς
Λακωνικοῖς ἱστορεῖ ὅτι τὴν μὲν τῶν Ὑακινθίων θυσίαν οἱ Λάκωνες ἐπὶ τρεῖς ἡμέρας συντελοῦσι καὶ διὰ
τὸ πένθος τὸ γενόμενον περὶ τὸν Ὑάκινθον οὔτε στε-
φανοῦνται ἐπὶ τοῖς δείπνοις οὔτε ἄρτον εἰσφέρουσιν,

---

[76] Cf. Paus. 3.18.6.   [77] Cf. 4.140b.

166

this time to Artemis Koruthalia, whose temple is located beside [the torrent-stream] known as Tiassos in the area called Cleta.[76] They celebrate these *kopides* in a way similar to those discussed earlier, but they also sacrifice suckling pigs *(orthagoriskoi)*[77] and serve oven-bread[78] at the meal. This dinner is referred to as an *aiklon* by the other Dorians. Epicharmus, for example, says in *Hope*[79] (fr. 34):

> For someone against his will
> invited you to an *aiklon*, but you went willingly on the
> run.

He makes the same assertions in *Periallos* (fr. 109). But in Sparta they bring people who enter the common mess after dinner what is referred to as an *aiklon*, which consists of loaves of bread in a wicker basket and a piece of meat for each person; and the attendant follows the man who is distributing the portions and announces the *aiklon*, adding the name of the donor.

This is what Polemon has to say. Didymus the grammarian—Demetrius of Troezen (*SH* 376) calls him "the book-forgetter," because of the large number of treatises he published (there are over 3500)—contradicts him, saying the following (p. 44 Schmidt): Polycrates, he says, records in his *History of Sparta* (*FGrH* 588 F 1) that the Spartans celebrate the Hyacinthia festival for three days, and because of the grief felt for Hyacinthus[80] they neither wear garlands at their dinner parties nor serve bread, but

---

[78] Cf. 3.109c.   [79] The title is more often given as *Hope or Wealth*.   [80] Hyacinthus, a son of the legendary King Amyclas of Sparta, was accidentally killed by his lover Apollo (e.g. [Apollod.] *Bib.* 1.3.3).

ἀλλὰ πέμματα καὶ τὰ τούτοις ἀκόλουθα διδόασι. καὶ
τὸν εἰς τὸν θεὸν παιᾶνα οὐκ ᾄδουσιν οὐδ' ἄλλο τι
τοιοῦτον[4] οὐδὲν καθάπερ ἐν ταῖς ἄλλαις θυσίαις ποιοῦσιν, ἀλλὰ μετ' εὐταξίας πολλῆς δειπνήσαντες ἀπ-
e έρχονται. τῇ δὲ μέσῃ τῶν τριῶν ἡμερῶν | γίνεται θέα
ποικίλη καὶ πανήγυρις ἀξιόλογος καὶ μεγάλη· παῖδές
τε γὰρ κιθαρίζουσιν ἐν χιτῶσιν ἀνεζωσμένοις καὶ
πρὸς αὐλὸν ᾄδοντες πάσας ἅμα τῷ πλήκτρῳ τὰς
χορδὰς ἐπιτρέχοντες ἐν ῥυθμῷ μὲν ἀναπαίστῳ, μετ'
ὀξέος δὲ τόνου τὸν θεὸν ᾄδουσιν· ἄλλοι δ' ἐφ' ἵππων
κεκοσμημένων τὸ θέατρον διεξέρχονται· χοροί τε νεανίσκων παμπληθεῖς εἰσέρχονται καὶ τῶν ἐπιχωρίων
τινὰ ποιημάτων ᾄδουσιν, ὀρχησταί τε τούτοις ἀνα-
f μεμιγμένοι τὴν κίνησιν ἀρχαϊκὴν ὑπὸ τὸν αὐλὸν | καὶ
τὴν ᾠδὴν ποιοῦνται. τῶν δὲ παρθένων αἱ μὲν ἐπὶ
καννάθρων[5] φέρονται πολυτελῶς κατεσκευασμένων,
αἱ δ' ἐφ' ἁμίλλαις ἁρμάτων ἐζευγμένων πομπεύουσιν,
ἅπασα δ' ἐν κινήσει καὶ χαρᾷ τῆς θεωρίας ἡ πόλις
καθέστηκεν. ἱερεῖά τε παμπληθῆ θύουσι τὴν ἡμέραν
ταύτην καὶ δειπνίζουσιν οἱ πολῖται πάντας τοὺς γνω-
ρίμους καὶ τοὺς δούλους τοὺς ἰδίους· οὐδεὶς δ' ἀπο-
λείπει τὴν θυσίαν, ἀλλὰ κενοῦσθαι συμβαίνει τὴν
πόλιν πρὸς τὴν θέαν. τῆς δὲ κοπίδος μνημονεύει καὶ
140 Ἀριστοφάνης ‖ ἢ Φιλύλλιος ἐν ταῖς Πόλεσιν, Ἐπί-
λυκός τε ἐν Κωραλίσκῳ λέγων οὕτως·

---

[4] τοιοῦτον εἰσάγουσιν A
[5] καννάθρων καμαρωτῶν ξυλίνων ἁρμάτων ACE

instead offer sacrificial cakes and the foods that go with them. And they do not sing the paean to the god[81] or do anything else of this sort, as they do at their other festivals, but eat in a very orderly fashion and then leave. On the middle day of the three there is an elaborate show and a large festival assembly that deserves mention. Boys play the lyre with their tunics pulled up high and sing accompanied by the pipe, running their picks over all the strings and singing to the god in anapaestic rhythm and a high pitch; and others pass through the theater mounted on horses in trappings. Numerous choruses of young men come in and sing some of their local poems, and dancers mixed in with them move in the ancient style, accompanied by the pipe and the song. Some of the unmarried girls are carried in expensively ornamented carriages fitted with wickerwork, while others process on two-horse racing chariots; and the whole city is full of movement and the pleasure of the festival. They also sacrifice a large number of animals on this day, and the citizens offer dinner to everyone they know, as well as to their own slaves. No one misses the celebration, and the city empties out to attend the show. Aristophanes or Philyllius (fr. 15) mentions the *kopis* in *Cities*,[82] as does Epilycus in *The Young Girl* (fr. 4), saying the following:[83]

[81] Apollo.

[82] Cf. 3.86e and 9.381a for confusion over the authorship of the play. Aristophanes is not otherwise known to have written a *Cities*, and Pollux and Hesychius consistently assign the comedy to Philyllius.

[83] The passage is in Doric dialect, appropriate for a Spartan.

ποττὰν κοπίδ', οἰῶ, σῶμαι·
ἐν Ἀμύκλαισιν παρ' Ἀπέλλω
βάρακες πολλοὶ κάρτοι
καὶ δωμός τοι μάλα ἁδύς,

διαρρήδην λέγων μάζας ἐν ταῖς κοπίσι παρατίθεσθαι—τοῦτο γὰρ αἱ βάρακες δηλοῦσιν, οὐχὶ τολύπας,
ὥς φησι Λυκόφρων, ἢ τὰ προφυράματα τῶν μαζῶν,
ὡς Ἐρατοσθένης—καὶ ἄρτους δὲ καὶ ζωμόν τινα καθ-
ηδυσμένον περιττῶς. τίς δέ ἐστιν ἡ κοπὶς σαφῶς
b ἐκτίθεται Μόλπις ἐν τῇ Λακεδαιμονίων Πολιτείᾳ |
γράφων οὕτως· ποιοῦσι δὲ καὶ τὰς καλουμένας κοπί-
δας· ἐστὶν δ' ἡ κοπὶς δεῖπνον, μᾶζα, ἄρτος, κρέας,
λάχανον ὠμόν, ζωμός, σῦκον, τράγημα, θέρμος. ἀλλὰ
μὴν οὐδ' ὀρθαγορίσκοι λέγονται, ὥς φησιν ὁ Πολέμων, οἱ γαλαθηνοὶ χοῖροι, ἀλλ' ὀρθαγορίσκοι, ἐπεὶ
πρὸς τὸν ὄρθρον πιπράσκονται, ὡς Περσαῖος ἱστορεῖ
ἐν τῇ Λακωνικῇ Πολιτείᾳ καὶ Διοσκουρίδης ἐν δευτέρῳ Πολιτείας καὶ Ἀριστοκλῆς ἐν τῷ προτέρῳ καὶ
c οὗτος τῆς Λακώνων Πολιτείας. ἔτι φησὶν ὁ Πολέμων |
καὶ τὸ δεῖπνον ὑπὸ τῶν Λακεδαιμονίων αἶκλον προσαγορεύεσθαι, παραπλησίως ἁπάντων Δωριέων οὕτως
αὐτὸ καλούντων. Ἀλκμὰν μὲν γὰρ οὕτω φησί·

κἠπὶ τᾷ μύλᾳ δρυφῆται κἠπὶ ταῖς συναικλίαις,

οὕτω τὰ συνδείπνια καλῶν. καὶ πάλιν·

---

[84] For barakes/bērēkes and ball-of-wool cakes, cf. 3.114f.
[85] Cf. 4.139b.

I'm hurrying to the *kopis*, I think.
In Apollo's temple at Amyclae
there are many *barakes*, loaves of bread,
and quite delicious broth.

He thus says explicitly that barley-cakes are served at the *kopides*—because this is what *barakes* refers to, not to a ball-of-wool cake,[84] as Lycophron claims, or the material kneaded up in advance to make barley-cakes, as Eratosthenes (pp. 233–4 Bernhardy) says—along with loaves of bread and some type of very tasty broth. What a *kopis* is is clearly expressed by Molpis in his *Constitution of the Spartans* (*FGrH* 590 F 1), writing as follows: They also hold the so-called *kopides*. A *kopis* is a dinner that features barley-cakes, bread, meat, wild vegetables, broth, figs, snacks, and lupine seeds. Yet the suckling pigs are not called *orthagoriskoi*, as Polemon claims,[85] but *orthragoriskoi*, because they are sold shortly before dawn (*orthros*),[86] as Persaeus records in his *Spartan Constitution* (*FGrH* 584 F 1 = fr. 455, *SVF* i.101–2), along with Dioscurides in Book II of *The State* (*FGrH* 594 F 2) and Aristocles as well in Book I of his *Constitution of the Spartans* (*FGrH* 586 F 1). Polemon (fr. 86, continued) further asserts that the Spartans refer to the dinner as an *aiklon*, and that nearly all the Dorians use this name for it. Alcman (*PMG* 95(a)), for example, says the following:

He tears his cheeks at the mill and at the *sunaikliai*,

by which he means their common meals. Again (*PMG* 95(b)):

[86] The other element in the name is supposed to be cognate with *agora* ("marketplace").

αἶκλον Ἀλκμάων ἁρμόξατο.

αἶκλον δ᾽ οὐ λέγουσιν οἱ Λάκωνες τὴν μετὰ τὸ δεῖπνον
μοῖραν, ἀλλ᾽ οὐδὲ τὰ διδόμενα τοῖς φιδίταις μετὰ τὸ
δεῖπνον· ἄρτος γάρ ἐστι καὶ κρέας. ἀλλ᾽ ἐπαίκλα μὲν
d λέγεται ταῦτα, ὄντα οἷον ἐπιχορηγήματα τοῦ | συν-
τεταγμένου τοῖς φιδίταις αἴκλου· παρὰ γὰρ τοῦτο
οἶμαι τὴν φωνὴν πεποιῆσθαι. καί ἐστιν ἡ παρασκευὴ
τῶν λεγομένων ἐπαίκλων οὐχ ἁπλῆ, καθάπερ ὁ Πολέμων ὑπείληφεν, ἀλλὰ διττή· ἣν μὲν γὰρ τοῖς παισὶ
παρέχουσι, πάνυ τις εὔκολός ἐστι καὶ εὐτελής· ἄλφιτα
γάρ ἐστιν ἐλαίῳ δεδευμένα, ἅ φησι Νικοκλῆς ὁ Λά-
κων κάπτειν αὐτοὺς μετὰ τὸ δεῖπνον ἐν φύλλοις δάφνης, παρὸ καὶ καμματίδας μὲν προσαγορεύεσθαι τὰ
φύλλα, αὐτὰ δὲ τὰ ψαιστὰ κάμματα. ὅτι δὲ ἔθος ἦν
e τοῖς | πάλαι καὶ φύλλα δάφνης τραγηματίζεσθαι
Καλλίας ἢ Διοκλῆς ἐν τοῖς Κύκλωψί φησιν οὕτως·

φυλλὰς ἡ δείπνων κατάλυσις ἥδε καθάπερ
σχημάτων.

ἦν δ᾽ εἰς τὰ τῶν ἀνδρῶν φιδίτια κομίζουσι, σκευοποι-
εῖται ἔκ τινων ζῴων ὡρισμένων, παραχορηγοῦντος
αὐτὰ τοῖς φιδίταις ἑνὸς τῶν εὐπορούντων, ἔσθ᾽ ὅτε δὲ
καὶ πλειόνων. ὁ δὲ Μόλπις καὶ ματτύην φησὶ προσαγορεύεσθαι τὰ ἐπαίκλα. περὶ δὲ τῶν ἐπαίκλων Περσαῖος ἐν τῇ Λακωνικῇ Πολιτείᾳ οὑτωσὶ γράφει· καὶ

87 For the doubts about the authorship of the play, cf. 12.524f;
15.667d; contrast 7.285e, 286b; 11.487a.

Alcman prepared an *aiklon*.

The Spartans do not use the term *aiklon* for the food distributed after the dinner or for what is given out to the members of a mess-group after the dinner; this is bread and meat. These items are instead referred to as *epaikla*, since they are, as it were, additions to the *aiklon* arranged for the members of the mess; because I believe that this is the source of the word. Nor is the food prepared for the *epaikla* under discussion here of a single type, as Polemon (fr. 86, continued) assumes, but of two types. For what they give the boys is very simple and cheap, since it is merely barley groats kneaded up with oil; Nicocles of Sparta (*FGrH* 587 F 1) reports that they gulp it down (*kaptein*) after dinner wrapped in laurel leaves, as a result of which the leaves are called *kammatides* and the cakes themselves *kammata*. That it was the custom of people long ago to snack on laurel leaves is asserted by Callias (fr. 7) or Diocles in *Cyclops*,[87] as follows:

> This foliage represents an end to our dinner party as well as our dancing.

The food they bring into the men's messes, on the other hand, is prepared from specific animals that one of the wealthy members (or occasionally a number of them) supplies for his mess-mates. Molpis (*FGrH* 590 F *2b*) claims that the *epaikla* are also referred to as a *mattuē*.[88] Persaeus writes the following about *epaikla* in his *Spartan Constitu-*

---

[88] See the extended discussion of this term at 14.662f–4f, esp. 664e–f, where Molpis is cited again.

f   εὐθὺς τοὺς μὲν | εὐπόρους ζημιοῖ εἰς ἐπαίκλα· ταῦτα δέ
ἐστιν μετὰ δεῖπνον τραγήματα· τοῖς δ᾽ ἀπόροις ἐπι-
τάττει κάλαμον ἢ στιβάδα ἢ φύλλα δάφνης φέρειν,
ὅπως ἔχωσι τὰ ἐπαίκλα κάπτειν μετὰ δεῖπνον· γίνεται
γὰρ ἄλφιτα ἐλαίῳ ἐρραμένα. τὸ δ᾽ ὅλον ὥσπερ πολί-
τευμά τι τοῦτο δὴ συνίσταται μικρόν. καὶ γὰρ ὄντινα
δεῖ πρῶτον κατακεῖσθαι ἢ δεύτερον ἢ ἐπὶ τοῦ σκιμ-
ποδίου καθῆσθαι, πάντα τοιαῦτα ποιοῦσιν εἰς ἐπαί-
141   κλα. τὰ ὅμοια ἱστορεῖ καὶ Διοσκουρίδης. ‖ περὶ δὲ τῶν
καμματίδων καὶ τῶν καμμάτων Νικοκλῆς οὕτως γρά-
φει· διακούσας δὲ πάντων ὁ ἔφορος ἤτοι ἀπέλυσεν ἢ
κατεδίκασεν. ὁ δὲ νικήσας ἐζημίωσεν ἐλαφρῶς ἤτοι
κάμμασιν ἢ καμματίσιν. ἐστὶ δὲ τὰ μὲν κάμματα
ψαιστά, αἱ δὲ καμματίδες αἷς κάπτουσι τὰ ψαιστά.
περὶ δὲ τοῦ τῶν φιδιτίων δείπνου Δικαίαρχος τάδε
ἱστορεῖ ἐν τῷ ἐπιγραφομένῳ Τριπολιτικῷ· τὸ δεῖπνον
πρῶτον μὲν ἑκάστῳ χωρὶς παρατιθέμενον καὶ πρὸς
b   ἕτερον κοινωνίαν οὐδεμίαν ἔχον· εἶτα μᾶζαν μὲν |
ὅσην ἂν ἕκαστος ᾖ βουλόμενος, καὶ πιεῖν πάλιν ὅταν
ᾖ θυμὸς ἑκάστῳ κώθων παρακείμενός ἐστιν. ὄψον δὲ
ταὐτὸν ἀεί ποτε πᾶσίν ἐστιν, ὕειον κρέας ἐφθόν, ἐνίοτε
δ᾽ ⟨οὐδ᾽⟩ ὀτιμενοῦν πλὴν † ὄψον † τι μικρὸν ἔχον
σταθμὸν ὡς τέταρτον μάλιστα, καὶ παρὰ τοῦτο ἕτερον
οὐδὲν πλὴν ὅ γε ἀπὸ τούτων ζωμὸς ἱκανὸς ὢν παρὰ
πᾶν τὸ δεῖπνον ἅπαντας αὐτοὺς παραπέμπειν, κἂν

---

89 The subject must be an early Spartan statesman or lawgiver,
presumably Lycurgus (Poralla #499).

tion (FGrH 584 F 2 = fr. 454, *SVF* i.101): At once he[89] imposes an assessment on the rich for *epaikla*; these are the snacks eaten after dinner. He assigns the poor, on the other hand, to bring reeds, a bed of cut branches, or some laurel leaves, so that they can gulp down *(kaptein)* their *epaikla* after dinner; these consist of barley-groats worked together with oil. This whole affair is organized like a small state; because if someone is required to lie down first or second,[90] or to sit on the stool, they use the same arrangements for the *epaikla*. Dioscurides *(FGrH* 594 F *3)* reports the same. As for the *kammatides* and the *kammata*, Nicocles *(FGrH* 587 F 2) writes the following: The ephor listened to them all and either acquitted or convicted them. Anyone who won his case imposed a light penalty in *kammata* or *kammatides*;[91] *kammata* are barley-cakes *(psaista)*, while *kammatides* are what they use to gulp *(kaptousi)* the barley-cakes down. As for the dinner eaten by the members of the mess, Dicaearchus records the following in his work entitled *The Tristatesman* (fr. 72 Wehrli): The dinner is initially served to each man separately, and nothing is shared with anyone else. Then there is a barley-cake as large as each of them wants; and, moreover, a cup is set beside each man to drink from whenever he wishes. Everyone is always given the same *opson*, some stewed pork; and sometimes it is nothing at all except a little bit of [corrupt] that weighs a quarter-unit at most. Beyond that there is nothing else except the broth made from the meat, which is enough to supply them all during

[90] As a mark of honor.

[91] Sc. because money was not yet in use; cf. .3.74f–5a.

ἆρα ἐλάα τις ἢ τυρὸς ἢ σῦκον, ἀλλὰ κἄν τι λάβωσιν
ἐπιδόσιμον, ἰχθὺν ἢ λαγὼν ἢ φάτταν ἤ τι τοιοῦτον.
c εἶτ᾽ ὀξέως ἤδη δεδειπνηκόσιν ὕστερα περιφέρεται |
ταῦτα τὰ ἐπαῖκλα καλούμενα. συμφέρει δ᾽ ἕκαστος εἰς
τὸ φιδίτιον ἀλφίτων μὲν ὡς τρία μάλιστα ἡμιμέδιμνα
Ἀττικά, οἴνου δὲ χοεῖς ἕνδεκά τινας ἢ δώδεκα, παρὰ
δὲ ταῦτα τυροῦ σταθμόν τινα καὶ σύκων, ἔτι δὲ εἰς
ὀψωνίαν περὶ δέκα τινὰς Αἰγιναίους ὀβολούς. Σφαῖ-
ρος δ᾽ ἐν τρίτῳ Λακωνικῆς Πολιτείας γράφει· φέρουσι
δὲ καὶ ἐπαῖκλα αὐτοῖς οἱ φιδῖται· καὶ τῶν μὲν ἀγρευ-
ομένων ὑφ᾽ αὑτῶν ἐνίοτε οἱ πολλοί, οὐ μὴν ἀλλ᾽ οἵ γε
πλούσιοι καὶ ἄρτον καὶ ὧν ἂν ὥρα ἐκ τῶν ἀγρῶν ὅσον
d εἰς αὐτὴν τὴν συνουσίαν, | νομίζοντες καὶ τὸ πλείονα
τῶν ἱκανῶν παρασκευάζειν περιττὸν εἶναι, μὴ μέλ-
λοντά γε προσφέρεσθαι. Μόλπις δέ φησι· μετὰ δὲ τὸ
δεῖπνον εἴωθεν ἀεί τι παρά τινος κομίζεσθαι, ἐνίοτε δὲ
καὶ παρὰ πλειόνων, παρ᾽ αὑτοῖς κατ᾽ οἶκον ἠρτυμένη
ματτύη, ὃ καλοῦσιν ἐπαῖκλον. τῶν δὲ κομιζομένων
οὐδεὶς οὐθὲν ἀγοράσας εἴωθεν φέρειν· οὔτε γὰρ ἡδονῆς οὐδ᾽ ἀκρασίας γαστρὸς οὕνεκεν κομίζουσιν, ἀλλὰ
τῆς αὑτῶν ἀρετῆς ἀπόδειξιν τῆς κατὰ τὴν θήραν
e ποιούμενοι. πολλοὶ δὲ καὶ ποίμνια αὑτῶν τρέφοντες |
ἀφθόνως μεταδιδόασι τῶν ἐκγόνων. ἔστι δ᾽ ἡ ματτύα
φάτται, χῆνες, τρυγόνες, κίχλαι, κόσσυφοι, λαγώ,
ἄρνες, ἔριφοι. οἱ δὲ μάγειροι σημαίνουσι τοὺς ἀεί

---

92 About 12 bushels; cf. 2.67f n. This must be the amount contributed per month or the like.

the whole dinner, and perhaps an olive, some cheese, or a fig, or if they are given something extra, a fish, a hare, a ring-dove, or the like. They eat quickly, and then after this the so-called *epaikla* are passed around. Each man contributes at most about three Attic half-*medimnoi*[92] of barley groats to the mess, perhaps 11 or 12 *choes*[93] of wine, and in addition a certain weight of cheese and figs, and about 10 Aeginetan obols[94] to buy *opson*. Sphaerus writes in Book III of the *Spartan Constitution* (*FGrH* 585 F 1): The members of the mess also bring *epaikla* to them. On occasion average people bring some game they have caught, whereas the rich bring bread and as much of whatever is in season in their fields as is enough for a single meeting, since they regard preparing more than enough as excessive, if it is not going to be consumed. Molpis (*FGrH* 590 F *2c) says: After the dinner, it was customary that something always be provided by someone, and on occasion by a number of people, specifically a *mattuē* they had prepared at home, which they refer to as an *epaiklon*. It was not the custom for anyone to purchase any of the items that were provided and bring it; for they do not supply these items for pleasure's sake or because their bellies are out of control, but as a way of demonstrating their own prowess in hunting. And many of them who keep flocks offer a generous share of the lambs and kids. The *mattua* consists of ring-doves, geese, turtledoves, thrushes, blackbirds, hares, lambs, and kids. Whenever individuals supply

93 About 10 gallons; cf. 3.118a n.
94 The Spartans did not have their own coinage, and Aeginetan money was widely used throughout the Greek world; cf. 4.143b.

τι κομίζοντας εἰς μέσον, ἵνα πάντες εἰδῶσι τὴν τῆς
θήρας φιλοπονίαν καὶ τὴν εἰς αὐτοὺς ἐκτένειαν.
Δημήτριος δ᾽ ὁ Σκήψιος ἐν τῷ πρώτῳ τοῦ Τρωικοῦ
Διακόσμου τὴν τῶν Καρνείων φησὶν ἑορτὴν παρὰ
Λακεδαιμονίοις μίμημα εἶναι στρατιωτικῆς ἀγωγῆς.

f τόπους μὲν γὰρ εἶναι ἐννέα τῷ ἀριθμῷ, | σκιάδες δὲ
οὗτοι καλοῦνται σκηναῖς ἔχοντες παραπλήσιόν τι· καὶ
ἐννέα καθ᾽ ἕκαστον ἄνδρες δειπνοῦσι, πάντα τε ἀπὸ
κηρύγματος πράσσεται, ἔχει τε ἑκάστη σκιὰς φρα-
τρίας τρεῖς καὶ γίνεται ἡ τῶν Καρνείων ἑορτὴ ἐπὶ
ἡμέρας ἐννέα.

Τὴν δὲ τῆς διαίτης τῆς τοιαύτης σκληρότητα ὕστερον καταλύσαντες οἱ Λάκωνες ἐξώκειλαν εἰς τρυφήν.
Φύλαρχος γοῦν ἐν τῇ πέμπτῃ καὶ εἰκοστῇ τῶν Ἱστοριῶν τάδε γράφει περὶ αὐτῶν· Λακεδαιμόνιοι εἰς μὲν
142 τὰ φιδίτια οὐκ ἤρχοντο κατὰ τὸ πάτριον ἔθος· ‖ ὅτε δὲ
καὶ παραγένοιντο, μικρὰ < . . . > συμπεριενεχθεῖσι
νόμου χάριν παρεσκευάζετο καὶ πάλιν αὐτοῖς στρω-
μναί τε τοῖς μεγέθεσιν οὕτως ἐξησκημέναι πολυτελῶς
καὶ τῇ ποικιλίᾳ διαφόρως ὥστε τῶν ξένων ἐνίους τῶν
παραληφθέντων ὀκνεῖν τὸν ἀγκῶνα ἐπὶ τὰ προσ-
κεφάλαια ἐρείδειν. οἱ δὲ πρότερον ἐπὶ τοῦ κλιντηρίου
ψιλοῦ διακαρτεροῦντες[6] παρ᾽ ὅλην τὴν συνουσίαν, ὅτε
τὸν ἀγκῶνα ἅπαξ ἐρείσειαν < . . . > εἰς δὲ τὴν
προειρημένην τρυφὴν ἦλθον ποτηρίων τ᾽ ἐκθέσεις
b πολλῶν καὶ βρωμάτων παντοδαπῶς πεποιημένων |

---

[6] διακαρτεροῦντες τῆς κλίνης ACE

something, the cooks announce their names in the middle of the group, so that everyone can be aware of the hard work they have put into the hunting and the effort they have gone to for the others. Demetrius of Scepsis in Book I of his *Trojan Catalogue* (fr. 1 Gaede) says that the Spartans' Carneia festival imitates their military way of life. For there are a total of nine places, referred to as "canopies" because they contain something that resembles tents. Nine men eat dinner at each of these; everything is done in response to a herald's order; each canopy contains three phratries[95]; and the Carneia festival lasts for nine days.

The Spartans later abandoned a way of life as austere as this and drifted into luxury. Phylarchus, for example, writes the following about them in Book XXV of his *Histories* (*FGrH* 81 F 44): The Spartans stopped going to the common messes as their forefathers had. When they did attend, accommodating themselves to the situation out of respect for the law, tiny . . . were prepared for them; moreover, their bedding was so generously large and elaborately embroidered, that some of the foreigners who were there as guests were hesitant to rest their elbows on the pillows. In the old days, they put up with a bare couch throughout the whole party, once they rested their elbow on it . . . they arrived at the sort of luxury discussed above, and at the display of numerous cups and the serving of food prepared in

---

[95] Literally "brotherhoods," traditional kinship-groups attested in both Dorian states such as Sparta and Ionian states such as Athens. Here the point is that each Spartan phratry was represented by three men at one of the canopies.

παραθέσεις, ἔτι δὲ μύρων ἐξηλλαγμένων, ὡς δ᾽ αὕτως
οἴνων καὶ τραγημάτων. καὶ τούτων ἦρξαν οἱ μικρὸν
πρὸ Κλεομένους βασιλεύσαντες Ἄρευς καὶ Ἀκρότα-
τος αὐλικὴν ἐξουσίαν ζηλώσαντες· οὓς τοσοῦτον αὖθις ὑπερῆράν τινες τῶν ἰδιωτῶν τῶν ἐν Σπάρτῃ γενο-
μένων κατ᾽ ἐκεῖνον τὸν χρόνον τῇ πολυτελείᾳ τῇ καθ᾽
αὑτούς, ὥστε δοκεῖν τὸν Ἄρεα καὶ τὸν Ἀκρότατον
εὐτελείᾳ πάντας ὑπερβεβληκέναι τοὺς ἀφελεστάτους
τῶν πρότερον. Κλεομένης δὲ πολὺ διενέγκας τῷ τε
c   συνιδεῖν πράγματα, καίτοι νέος ὤν, καὶ κατὰ τὴν |
δίαιταν ἀφελέστατος γέγονεν. ἤδη γὰρ τηλικούτων
πραγμάτων ἡγούμενος ἔμφασιν τοῖς παραλαμβανο-
μένοις πρὸς τὴν θυσίαν ἐποίει, διότι τὰ παρὰ ἐκείνοις
τῶν παρ᾽ αὐτὸν οὐδὲν καταδεέστερον εἴη παρασκευα-
ζόμενα. πολλῶν δὲ πρεσβειῶν παραγινομένων πρὸς
αὐτὸν οὐδέποτε ἐνωρίστερον τοῦ κατειθισμένου συν-
ῆγεν καιροῦ πεντακλίνου τε διεστρώννυτο οὐδέποτε
πλεῖον· ὅτε δὲ μὴ παρείη πρεσβεία, τρίκλινον. καὶ
πρόσταγμα οὐκ ἐγίνετο δι᾽ ἐδεάτρου τίς εἴσεται καὶ
d   κατακλιθήσεται πρῶτος, ἀλλ᾽ | ὁ πρεσβύτατος ἡγεῖτο
ἐπὶ τὰς κλίνας, εἰ μή τιν᾽ αὐτὸς προσκαλέσαιτο. κατελαμβάνετο δὲ ἐπὶ τὸ πολὺ μετὰ τοῦ ἀδελφοῦ κατακείμενος ἢ μετά τινος τῶν ἡλικιωτῶν. ἐπί τε τῷ τρί-
ποδι ψυκτὴρ χαλκοῦς ἐπέκειτο καὶ κάδος καὶ σκαφίον
ἀργυροῦν δύο κοτύλας χωροῦν καὶ κύαθος, ἡ δ᾽ ἐπίχυ-
σις χαλκή. πιεῖν δὲ οὐ προσεφέρετο, εἰ μή τις αἰτή-

---

96 Areus (Bradford p. 43) reigned c.309–265 BCE. Acrotatus

every way and of extraordinary perfumes, as well as wines and snacks. These changes were initiated by Areus and Acrotatus, who were kings shortly before Cleomenes[96] and adopted the excessive style of life typical of royal courts. They in turn were so far outdone in personal extravagance by some private Spartan citizens of the same period, that Areus and Acrotatus appeared to have exceeded all the simplest men of the past in their frugality. Cleomenes was quite exceptional in his understanding of political affairs, even though he was a young man, and he lived a very simple life. Despite the fact that he was now responsible for important matters, he created the impression among the men he invited to sacrificial feasts that the food in their own houses was not prepared any worse than what he ate. And although many embassies visited him, he never convened a meeting before the customary hour and never had more than five couches spread;[97] when no embassy was present, there only three. There was no announcement by a steward as to who was going to sit or lie down first; instead, the oldest man led the way to the couches, unless he himself asked someone else to do so. [Cleomenes] was generally found reclining with his brother or one of the men of his own age.[98] There was a bronze wine-cooler that sat on its tripod, a wine-jar, a silver bowl with a capacity of two *kotulai*[99], and a ladle; the pitcher was made of bronze. No one was offered anything to drink unless he asked for it.

(Bradford p. 22) was his son and successor, who died in battle at Megalopolis *c*.262. Cleomenes III (Bradford p. 240; discussed below) became king *c*.235.   [97] Creating room for ten men, two per couch.   [98] Sc. rather than with a younger lover.
    [99] About a pint; see 4.129b n.

σειεν· ἐδίδοτο δὲ κύαθος εἷς πρὸ τοῦ δείπνου, αὐτῷ δὲ
πολὺ πρώτῳ· καὶ ὅτε προσνεύσειεν ἐκεῖνος, οὕτως
ᾔτουν καὶ οἱ λοιποί. τὰ δὲ παρατιθέμενα ἐπὶ μὲν
e τραπεζίου ἦν τοῦ τυχόντος, | τὰ δὲ λοιπὰ ὥστε μήθ᾿
ὑπεραίρειν μήτ᾿ ἐλλείπειν, ἀλλ᾿ ἱκανὰ ἅπασι γίνεσθαι
καὶ μὴ προσδεῖσθαι τοὺς παρόντας. οὔτε γὰρ οὕτως
ᾤετο δεῖν ὥσπερ ἐν τοῖς φιδιτίοις δέχεσθαι ζωμῷ καὶ
κρεᾳδίοις ἀφελῶς οὔτε πάλιν οὕτως ὑπερτείνειν ὡς εἰς
τὸ μηθὲν δαπανᾶν, ὑπερβάλλοντα τὸ σύμμετρον τῆς
διαίτης· τὸ μὲν γὰρ ἀνελεύθερον ἐνόμιζε, τὸ δ᾿ ὑπερή-
φανον. ὁ δ᾿ οἶνος ἦν μικρῷ βελτίων, ὅτε παρείησάν
τινες. ἐπεὶ δὲ δειπνήσειαν, ἐσιώπων πάντες, ὅ τε παῖς
f ἐφειστήκει κεκραμένον ἔχων τὸ ποτὸν | καὶ τῷ αἰτοῦν-
τι προσέφερε. τὸν αὐτὸν δὲ τρόπον καὶ μετὰ τὸ δεῖπνον οὐ πλεῖον ἐδίδοτο δύο κυάθων καὶ τοῦτο προσ-
νεύσαντι προσεφέρετο. ἀκρόαμα δὲ οὐδὲν οὐδέποτε
παρεισεπορεύετο, διετέλει δ᾿ αὐτὸς προσομιλῶν πρὸς
ἕκαστον καὶ πάντας ἐκκαλούμενος εἰς τὸ τὰ μὲν ἀκού-
ειν, τὰ δὲ λέγειν αὐτούς, ὥστε τεθηρευμένους ἀποτρέ-
χειν ἅπαντας. διακωμῳδῶν δ᾿ Ἀντιφάνης τὰ Λακω-
νικὰ δεῖπνα ἐν τῷ ἐπιγραφομένῳ δράματι Ἄρχων
143 φησὶν οὕτως· ‖

ἐν Λακεδαίμονι
γέγονας· ἐκείνων τῶν νόμων μεθεκτέον
ἐστίν. βάδιζ᾿ ἐπὶ δεῖπνον εἰς τὰ φιδίτια,
ἀπόλαυε τοῦ ζωμοῦ, † φόρει τοὺς βύστακας.
μὴ καταφρόνει, μηδ᾿ ἕτερ᾿ ἐπιζήτει καλά,

One ladleful was offered before the dinner, to Cleomenes well before the others; when he nodded to them, the rest of the group asked for theirs. The food was served on a little table and was quite ordinary; beyond that, the aim was for there to be neither too much nor too little, so that everyone had enough and no one who was present had to ask for anything additional. Because he felt it unnecessary either to entertain them as in the common messes with nothing but broth and chunks of meat, or on the other hand, to go so far as to spend money pointlessly, exceeding the moderation in which he lived; he considered the former course stingy, the latter insolently proud. The wine was slightly better when other people were present. They all remained quiet while they ate, and a slave stood over them holding the wine, which had already been mixed, and provided it to anyone who asked. So too after dinner, no one was offered more than two ladlesful, and he only got those if he nodded his head. No musical entertainment was ever brought in, and Cleomenes himself spent his time talking to each of his guests and urging them all to say or listen to this or that. The result was that they were all captivated by him when they left. Antiphanes satirizes Spartan dinner parties in the play entitled *The Archon* (fr. 46), saying the following:

> You were born
> in Sparta, so you ought to stick to
> their customs. Go to dinner in the common mess,
> enjoy the broth † and wear a mustache!
> Don't be haughty or seek other pleasures,

ἐν τοῖς δ᾽ ἐκείνων ἔθεσιν ἴσθ᾽ ἀρχαικός.

Περὶ δὲ τῶν Κρητικῶν συσσιτίων Δωσιάδας ἱστορῶν ἐν τῇ τετάρτῃ τῶν Κρητικῶν γράφει οὕτως· οἱ δὲ
Λύττιοι συνάγουσι μὲν τὰ κοινὰ συσσίτια οὕτως.
b ἕκαστος τῶν γινομένων καρπῶν ἀναφέρει τὴν | δεκά-
την εἰς τὴν ἑταιρίαν καὶ τὰς τῆς πόλεως προσόδους,
ἃς διανέμουσιν οἱ προεστηκότες τῆς πόλεως εἰς τοὺς
ἑκάστων οἴκους. τῶν δὲ δούλων ἕκαστος Αἰγιναῖον
φέρει στατῆρα κατὰ κεφαλήν. διῄρηνται δ᾽ οἱ πολῖται
πάντες καθ᾽ ἑταιρίας, καλοῦσι δὲ ταύτας ἀνδρεῖα. τὴν
δὲ ἐπιμέλειαν ἔχει τοῦ συσσιτίου γυνὴ τρεῖς ἢ τέτταρας τῶν δημοτικῶν προσειληφυῖα πρὸς τὰς ὑπηρεσίας. ἑκάστῳ δ᾽ αὐτῶν ἀκολουθοῦσι δύο θεράποντες
ξυλοφόροι· καλοῦσι δ᾽ αὐτοὺς καλοφόρους. εἰσὶ δὲ
πανταχοῦ κατὰ τὴν Κρήτην οἶκοι δύο ταῖς συσσιτί-
c αις, ὧν τὸν μὲν | καλοῦσιν ἀνδρεῖον, τὸν δ᾽ ἄλλον ἐν ᾧ
τοὺς ξένους κοιμίζουσι κοιμητήριον προσαγορεύουσι.
κατὰ δὲ τὸν συσσιτικὸν οἶκον πρῶτον μὲν κεῖνται δύο
τράπεζαι ξενικαὶ καλούμεναι, αἷς προσκαθίζουσι τῶν
ξένων οἱ παρόντες· ἑξῆς δ᾽ εἰσὶν αἱ τῶν ἄλλων. παρατίθεται δὲ τῶν παρόντων ἴσον μέρος ἑκάστῳ· τοῖς δὲ
νεωτέροις ἥμισυ δίδοται κρέως, τῶν δ᾽ ἄλλων οὐθενὸς
ἅπτονται. εἶτα ποτήριον ἐν ἑκάστῃ τραπέζῃ παρατίθεται κεκραμένον ὑδαρῶς· τοῦτο κοινῇ πάντες πίνουσιν
d οἱ κατὰ τὴν κοινὴν τράπεζαν, καὶ δειπνήσασιν | ἄλλο
παρατίθεται. τοῖς δὲ παισὶ κοινὸς κέκραται κρατήρ.
τοῖς δὲ πρεσβυτέροις ἐὰν βούλωνται πλεῖον πιεῖν

but act old-fashioned in the same way they do!

Dosiades offers a report about the Cretan *sussitia* ("common messes") in Book IV of his *History of Crete* (*FGrH* 458 F 2), writing as follows: The inhabitants of Lyttus organize their common *sussitia* in the following way. Each man contributes one-tenth of the crops his land produces to the group, along with the state revenues the city magistrates divide among the various households. The slaves all contribute one Aeginetan *stater* per head.[100] All the citizens are divided into groups, which they refer to as *andreia* ("men's associations"). A woman is put in charge of the mess and is given three or four public slaves as assistants. Each of them is accompanied by two common slaves, whose job is to carry wood; they refer to them as *kalophoroi* ("wood-bearers"). Everywhere throughout Crete there are two houses for the common messes, one of which they refer to as the *andreion*, while the name they use for the other, where they have visitors sleep *(koimizousi)*, is the *koimētērion*. In the mess-house there are, first of all, two tables set up; these are referred to as *xenikai* ("guest-[tables]"), and any foreigners present sit at them. After them are the tables for the others. Everyone is served an equal portion of whatever food there is, although the young men are given only a half-portion of meat and do not touch anything else. Then a cup of heavily diluted wine is set on each table, and everyone who shares a table drinks from this in common; after they eat, another cup is served. A shared mixing-bowl of wine and water is prepared for the boys; the old men are permitted to drink more if they

[100] See 4.141c n.

ἐξουσία δέδοται. ἀπὸ δὲ τῆς τραπέζης τὰ βέλτιστα
τῶν παρακειμένων ἡ προεστηκυῖα τῆς συσσιτίας
γυνὴ φανερῶς ἀφαιροῦσα παρατίθησι τοῖς κατὰ πόλεμον ἢ κατὰ σύνεσιν δεδοξασμένοις. ἀπὸ δὲ τοῦ δείπνου πρῶτον μὲν εἰώθασι βουλεύεσθαι περὶ τῶν κοι-
νῶν, εἶτα μετὰ ταῦτα μέμνηνται τῶν κατὰ πόλεμον
πράξεων καὶ τοὺς γενομένους ἄνδρας ἀγαθοὺς ἐπαι-
νοῦσι, προτρεπόμενοι τοὺς νεωτέρους εἰς ἀνδραγα-
e θίαν. | Πυργίων δ' ἐν τρίτῳ Κρητικῶν Νομίμων, ἐν
τοῖς συσσιτίοις, φησίν, οἱ Κρῆτες καθήμενοι συσσι-
τοῦσι· καὶ[7] ὅτι οἱ νεώτατοι αὐτῶν ἐφεστᾶσι διακονοῦν-
τες· καὶ ὅτι μετ' εὐφημίας σπείσαντες τοῖς θεοῖς
μερίζουσι τῶν παρατιθεμένων ἅπασι. ἀπονέμουσι δὲ
καὶ τοῖς υἱοῖς κατὰ τὸν θᾶκον τὸν τοῦ πατρὸς ὑφιζά-
νουσιν ἐξ ἡμισείας τῶν τοῖς ἀνδράσι παρατιθεμένων·
τοὺς δ' ὀρφανοὺς ἰσομερεῖς εἶναι. παρατίθεται δ' αὐ-
f τοῖς ἀβαμβάκευτα τῇ κράσει | καθ' ἕκαστα τῶν νενο-
μισμένων. ἦσαν δὲ καὶ ξενικοὶ θᾶκοι καὶ τράπεζα
τρίτη δεξιᾶς εἰσιόντων εἰς τὰ ἀνδρεῖα, ἣν Ξενίου τε
Διὸς Ξενίαν τε προσηγόρευον.

Ἡρόδοτος δὲ συγκρίνων τὰ τῶν Ἑλλήνων συμπόσια πρὸς τὰ παρὰ Πέρσαις φησίν· ἡμέρην δὲ Πέρσαι ἀπασέων μάλιστα ἐκείνην τιμᾶν νομίζουσι τῇ
ἕκαστος ἐγένετο. ἐν ταύτῃ δὲ πλέω δαῖτα τῶν ἄλλων
δικαιεῦσι προτίθεσθαι· ἐν τῇ οἱ εὐδαίμονες αὐτῶν
144 βοῦν καὶ ὄνον καὶ ἵππον καὶ κάμηλον προτιθέαται ‖
ὅλους ὀπτοὺς ἐν καμίνοις· οἱ δὲ πένητες αὐτῶν τὰ

want. The woman in charge of the mess makes a show of
removing the best food that has been served from the table
and giving it to the men who have won a good reputation in
war or for their intelligence. After dinner it is their custom
to discuss public matters first; then after this they recall
deeds done in war and praise brave men from the past, as a
way of encouraging the younger ones to distinguish themselves. Pyrgion says in Book III of *Cretan Customs* (*FGrH*
467 F 1) that the Cretans sit in their common messes and
eat together; the youngest ones stand beside them and
serve. After they pour a libation to the gods in silence, they
give everyone a share of the food that has been served.
They give the boys, who sit beside their fathers' chairs, half
of what is served to the men. Orphans, on the other hand,
get a full share, although their food is served without any of
the usual seasonings mixed in. There were also chairs re-
served for guests, and a third table on the right-hand side
as one entered the mess, which they referred to as "the table of Zeus the Stranger" and "the Stranger's table."

  Herodotus (1.133)[101] compares Greek symposia to
those the Persians celebrate, saying: The Persians think it
appropriate to show the most honor to the day one was
born. On that day they consider it right to serve a larger
meal than on other days; on it the wealthy ones serve an ox,
a donkey, a horse, and a camel, all roasted whole in ovens,
whereas the poor serve small herd-animals. They do not

---

[101] The Greek has been inconsistently Atticized and there are
a number of minor deviations from the traditional text.

---

7 συσσιτοῦσι· καὶ ὅτι ἀβαμβάκευστα τοῖς ὀρφανοῖς
παρατίθεται· καὶ A

λεπτὰ τῶν προβάτων προτίθενται. σίτοισί τε ὀλίγοισι
χρέονται, ἐπιφορήμασι δὲ πολλοῖσι καὶ οὐκ ἀλέσι.
καὶ διὰ τοῦτό φασι Πέρσαι τοὺς Ἕλληνας σιτεομέ-
νους πεινῶντας παύεσθαι, ὅτι σφίσιν ἀπὸ δείπνου
παραφορέεται οὐδὲν λόγου ἄξιον· εἰ δέ τι παρα-
φέροιτο, ἐσθίοντας ἂν οὐ παύεσθαι. οἴνῳ δὲ κάρτα
προσκέαται· καί σφιν οὐκ ἐμέσαι ἔξεστιν, οὐκ οὐρῆ-
σαι ἀντίον ἄλλου. ταῦτα μέν νυν οὕτω φυλάσσεται.
b μεθυσκόμενοι δὲ εἰώθασι βουλεύεσθαι τὰ | σπουδαι-
ότατα τῶν πρηγμάτων· τὸ δ᾽ ἂν ἅδῃ σφίσι βουλευο-
μένοισι, τοῦτο τῇ ὑστεραίῃ νήφουσι προτιθεῖ ὁ στε-
γέαρχος ἐν τοῦ ἂν ἐόντες βουλεύωνται. καὶ ἢν μὲν ἅδῃ
καὶ νήφουσι, χρέονται αὐτῷ· εἰ δὲ μή, μετιεῖσιν. τὰ δ᾽
ἂν νήφοντες προβουλεύσωνται, μεθυσκόμενοι ἐπιδια-
γινώσκουσι.

Περὶ δὲ τῆς τρυφῆς τῶν ἐν Πέρσαις βασιλέων
Ξενοφῶν ἐν Ἀγησιλάῳ οὕτω γράφει· τῷ μὲν γὰρ
Πέρσῃ πᾶσαν γῆν περιέρχονται μαστεύοντες τί ἂν
ἡδέως πίοι, μυρίοι δὲ τεχνῶνται τί ἂν ἡδέως φάγοι·
c ὅπως γε | μὴν καταδάρθοι οὐδ᾽ ἂν εἴποι τις ὅσα
πραγματεύονται. Ἀγησίλαος δὲ διὰ τὸ φιλόπονος
εἶναι πᾶν μὲν τὸ παρὸν ἡδέως ἔπινε, πᾶν δὲ τὸ
συντυχὸν ἡδέως ἤσθιεν· εἰς δὲ τὸ ἀσμένως κοιμη-
θῆναι πᾶς τόπος ἱκανὸς ἦν αὐτῷ. ἐν δὲ τῷ Ἱέρωνι
ἐπιγραφομένῳ λέγων περὶ τῶν τοῖς τυράννοις παρα-
σκευαζομένων καὶ τῶν τοῖς ἰδιώταις εἰς τροφάς φησιν
οὕτως· "καὶ οἶδά γε," ἔφη, "ὦ Σιμωνίδη, ὅτι τούτῳ κρί-
νουσιν οἱ πλεῖστοι ἥδιον ἡμᾶς καὶ πίνειν καὶ ἐσθίειν

eat much bread or cakes, but consume many side-dishes, not all at the same time. This is why the Persians say that the Greeks stop eating while they are still hungry, because the Greeks are not served anything worth eating after dinner; but if anything like this *were* served, they would *not* stop eating. They are very fond of wine, and are not allowed to vomit or urinate in front of another person. These are the customs they keep. It is their practice to consider the most serious matters when they are drunk. Whatever they decide, the next day the master of the house where they have their discussions sets it before them when they are sober. If the idea also pleases them when they are sober, they adopt it; otherwise they let it go. As for proposals they make when they are sober, they take a careful look at them while drunk.

As regards the luxury of the Persian kings, Xenophon writes as follows in *Agesilaus* (9.3): Men travel through the Persian king's entire territory for him, trying to find wines he would enjoy drinking; countless people produce foods he might like to eat; and it is impossible to describe how much trouble is taken to ensure that he goes to sleep. But because Agesilaus liked to work hard, he enjoyed drinking whatever was available, and enjoyed eating whatever there was; and as for going happily to sleep, any place was good enough for him. In his work entitled *Hieron* (1.17–20), in his discussion of the foods prepared for tyrants and for private citizens to eat, he says the following: "I am also aware, Simonides," said [Hieron], "that the reason most people believe that we get more pleasure from eating and drink-

τῶν ἰδιωτῶν, ὅτι δοκοῦσι καὶ αὐτοὶ ἥδιον ἂν δειπνῆσαι
d τὸ | ἡμῖν παρατιθέμενον δεῖπνον ἢ τὸ ἑαυτοῖς· τὸ γὰρ
τὰ εἰωθότα ὑπερβάλλον, τοῦτο παρέχει τὰς ἡδονάς.
διὸ καὶ πάντες ἄνθρωποι ἡδέως προσδέχονται τὰς
ἑορτὰς πλὴν[8] οἱ τύραννοι· ἔκπλεω γὰρ αὐτοῖς ἀεὶ
παρεσκευασμέναι οὐδεμίαν ἐν ταῖς ἑορταῖς ἐπίδοσιν
ἔχουσιν αὐτῶν αἱ τράπεζαι· ὥστε ταύτῃ πρῶτον τῇ
εὐφροσύνῃ τῆς ἐλπίδος μειονεκτοῦσι τῶν ἰδιωτῶν.
ἔπειτα", ἔφη, "ἐκεῖνο εὖ οἶδα ὅτι καὶ σὺ ἔμπειρος εἶ, ὅτι
ὅσῳ ἂν πλείω τις παραθῆται τὰ περιττὰ τῶν ἱκανῶν,
e τοσούτῳ καὶ θᾶσσον[9] κόρος | ἐμπίπτει τῆς ἐδωδῆς.
ὥστε καὶ τῷ χρόνῳ τῆς ἡδονῆς μειονεκτεῖ ὁ παρατιθέμενος πολλὰ τῶν μετρίως διαιτωμένων." "ἀλλὰ ναὶ μὰ
Δία," ἔφη ὁ Σιμωνίδης, "ὅσον ἂν χρόνον ἡ ψυχὴ προσ-
ίηται, τοῦτον πολὺ μᾶλλον ἥδονται οἱ ταῖς πολυτε-
λεστέραις παρασκευαῖς τρεφόμενοι τῶν τὰ εὐτελέ-
στερα παρατιθεμένων." Θεόφραστος δ᾽ ἐν τῷ Πρὸς
Κάσανδρον Περὶ Βασιλείας (εἰ γνήσιον τὸ σύγγραμ-
μα· πολλοὶ γὰρ αὐτὸ φασιν εἶναι Σωσιβίου, εἰς ὃν
Καλλίμαχος ὁ ποιητὴς ἐπίνικον ἐλεγειακὸν ἐποίησεν)
τοὺς Περσῶν φησι βασιλεῖς ὑπὸ τρυφῆς προκηρύτ-
τειν τοῖς ἐφευρίσκουσί τινα καινὴν ἡδονὴν ἀργυρίου
πλῆθος. Θεόπομπος δ᾽ ἐν τῇ τριακοστῇ καὶ πέμπτῃ
f τῶν Ἱστοριῶν τὸν | Παφλαγόνων φησὶ βασιλέα Θῦν
ἑκατὸν πάντα παρατίθεσθαι δειπνοῦντα ἐπὶ τὴν τράπεζαν ἀπὸ βοῶν ἀρξάμενον· καὶ ἀναχθέντα αἰχμάλω-
τον ὡς βασιλέα καὶ ἐν φυλακῇ ὄντα πάλιν τὰ αὐτὰ
παρατίθεσθαι ζῶντα λαμπρῶς. διὸ καὶ ἀκούσαντα

190

ing than private citizens do is because they think they
would enjoy eating the dinner we are served more than the
one served to themselves. Because whatever exceeds what
one is used to provides pleasure. This is why everyone except tyrants eagerly awaits festivals; for the fact that their
tables are always full means that they offer nothing extra
on festival days. As a result, in this delight one gets from
anticipation, first of all, they have less than private citizens
do. And then," he said, "I'm sure you've experienced this,
that to the extent someone's served more than he needs, he
becomes that much more rapidly full of food. As a result,
someone served many dishes is at a disadvantage compared to those who live moderately in how long his pleasure lasts." "But by Zeus," said Simonides, "as long as their
appetite holds out, surely those who eat the more expensive food get much more pleasure than those who are
served less expensive things!" Theophrastus in his *To
Cassander on Kingship* (fr. 603)—if the treatise is authen-
tic; many authorities attribute it to Sosibius (*FGrH* 595 T
3), for whom the poet Callimachus (fr. 384) wrote a victory
ode in elegiacs—says that the Persian kings are so addicted
to luxury that they make a public offer of a substantial
amount of money to anyone who discovers a new pleasure. Theopompus in Book XXXV of his *Histories* (*FGrH*
115 F 179) says that when the Paphlagonian king Thys
had dinner, 100 of everything was set on his table, starting
with oxen; when he was brought inland as a prisoner to
the King and was under guard, the same foods were still
being served to him and he was living splendidly. When

---

8 πλὴν οὐχ A: ἀλλ᾽ οὐχ CE
9 θᾶσσον μᾶλλον ACE

145 Ἀρταξέρξην ‖ εἰπεῖν ὅτι οὕτως αὑτῷ δοκοίη ζῆν ὡς
ταχέως ἀπολούμενος. ὁ δ᾽ αὐτὸς Θεόπομπος ἐν τῇ
τετάρτῃ καὶ δεκάτῃ τῶν Φιλιππικῶν, ὅταν, φησί,
βασιλεὺς εἴς τινας ἀφίκηται τῶν ἀρχομένων, εἰς τὸ
δεῖπνον αὐτοῦ δαπανᾶσθαι εἴκοσι τάλαντα, ποτὲ δὲ
καὶ τριάκοντα· οἱ δὲ καὶ πολὺ πλείω δαπανῶσιν·
ἑκάσταις γὰρ τῶν πόλεων κατὰ τὸ μέγεθος ὥσπερ ὁ
b   φόρος καὶ | τὸ δεῖπνον ἐκ παλαιοῦ τεταγμένον ἐστίν.
Ἡρακλείδης δ᾽ ὁ Κυμαῖος ὁ τὰ Περσικὰ συγγράψας
ἐν τῷ δευτέρῳ τῶν ἐπιγραφομένων Παρασκευαστικῶν,
καὶ οἱ θεραπεύοντες, φησί, τοὺς Περσῶν βασιλεῖς
δειπνοῦντας ἅπαντες λελουμένοι διακονοῦσιν ἐσθῆτας
καλὰς ἔχοντες καὶ διατρίβουσι σχεδὸν τὸ ἥμισυ τῆς
ἡμέρας περὶ τὸ δεῖπνον. τῶν δὲ τοῦ βασιλέως συνδείπνων οἱ μὲν ἔξω δειπνοῦσιν, οὓς καὶ ὁρᾶν ἔξεστι
παντὶ τῷ βουλομένῳ, οἱ δὲ εἴσω μετὰ βασιλέως. καὶ
οὗτοι δὲ οὐ συνδειπνοῦσιν αὐτῷ, ἀλλ᾽ ἔστιν οἰκήματα
δύο καταντικρὺ ἀλλήλων, ἐν ᾧ ⟨θ᾽⟩ ὁ βασιλεὺς τὸ
ἄριστον ποιεῖται καὶ ἐν ᾧ οἱ σύνδειπνοι· καὶ ὁ βασι-
c   λεὺς ἐκείνους ὁρᾷ διὰ τοῦ παρακαλύμματος | τοῦ ἐπὶ
τῇ θύρᾳ, ἐκεῖνοι δ᾽ αὐτὸν οὐχ ὁρῶσιν. ἐνίοτε μέντοι
ἐπειδὰν ἑορτὴ ᾖ, ἐν ἑνὶ οἰκήματι ἅπαντες δειπνοῦσιν,
ἐν ᾧ καὶ ὁ βασιλεύς, ἐν τῷ μεγάλῳ¹⁰. ὅταν δὲ βασιλεὺς πότον ποιῆται, ποιεῖται δὲ πολλάκις, συμπόται
αὐτῷ εἰσιν ὡς μάλιστα δώδεκα. καὶ ὅταν δειπνήσω-
σιν, ὅ τε βασιλεὺς αὐτὸς καθ᾽ ἑαυτὸν καὶ οἱ σύνδειπνοι, καλεῖ τοὺς συμπότας τούτους τις τῶν εὐνού-

Artaxerxes heard this, he accordingly said that he thought that Thys was living in a way that suggested he was expecting to die soon.[102] The same Theopompus says in Book XIV of his *History of Philip* (*FGrH* 115 F 113): Whenever the King visits any of his subjects, they spend 20 talents on his dinner, or sometimes 30; others spend even more than this. Because since ancient times his dinner has been assigned to each city in proportion to its size, like the tribute. Heracleides of Cumae, the author of the *History of Persia*, says in Book II of the work entitled *Preparations* (*FGrH* 689 F 2): When the Persian kings are dining, all their attendants bathe and wear fine clothing while they serve them, and they spend nearly half the day dealing with the dinner. Some of those who dine with the King eat outside, and anyone who wants to can see them, whereas others eat inside with the King. But even they do not eat in his company; instead, there are two rooms opposite one another, and the King has lunch in one and his guests in the other. The King can see them through the curtain that covers the door, but they cannot see him. Occasionally, however, when a festival is going on, they all dine in a single room, that is the large one, which the King occupies. Whenever the King has a drinking party (and he does this often), a dozen people generally join him. After they are done with dinner, the King all alone by himself and his guests separately, one of the eunuchs summons the men who are go-

---

[102] The location of the incident in Book XXXV of the *Histories* places it in the mid-340s BCE, in which case the Persian king in question must be Artaxerxes III (reigned 359/8–338).

---

[10] μεγάλῳ οἴκῳ ACE

χων. καὶ ὅταν εἰσέλθωσι, συμπίνουσιν μετ' αὐτοῦ, οὐ
τὸν αὐτὸν οἶνον κἀκεῖνοι, καὶ οἱ μὲν χαμαὶ καθήμενοι,
d ὁ δ' ἐπὶ κλίνης | χρυσόποδος κατακείμενος· καὶ ὑπερ-
μεθυσθέντες ἀπέρχονται. τὰ δὲ πλεῖστα ὁ βασιλεὺς
μόνος ἀριστᾷ καὶ δειπνεῖ. ἐνίοτε δὲ καὶ ἡ γυνὴ αὐτῷ
συνδειπνεῖ καὶ τῶν υἱῶν ἔνιοι. καὶ παρὰ τὸ δεῖπνον
ᾄδουσί τε καὶ ψάλλουσιν αἱ παλλακαὶ αὐτῷ, καὶ μία
μὲν ἐξάρχει, αἱ δὲ ἄλλαι ἀθρόως ᾄδουσι. τὸ δὲ δεῖπνον, φησί, τὸ βασιλέως καλούμενον ἀκούσαντι μὲν
δόξει μεγαλοπρεπὲς εἶναι, ἐξεταζόμενον δὲ φανεῖται
οἰκονομικῶς καὶ ἀκριβῶς συντεταγμένον καὶ τοῖς
e ἄλλοις Πέρσαις τοῖς ἐν δυναστείᾳ οὖσι κατὰ | τὸν
αὐτὸν τρόπον. ἐστὶ μὲν γὰρ τῷ βασιλεῖ χίλια ἱερεῖα
τῆς ἡμέρας κατακοπτόμενα· τούτων δ' εἰσὶ καὶ ἵπποι
καὶ κάμηλοι καὶ βόες καὶ ὄνοι καὶ ἔλαφοι καὶ τὰ
πλεῖστα πρόβατα· πολλοὶ δὲ καὶ ὄρνιθες ἀναλίσκον-
ται, οἵ τε στρουθοὶ οἱ Ἀράβιοι—ἐστὶν δὲ τὸ ζῷον
μέγα—καὶ χῆνες καὶ ἀλεκτρυόνες. καὶ μέτρια μὲν
αὐτῶν παρατίθεται ἑκάστῳ τῶν συνδείπνων τοῦ βασιλέως, καὶ ἀποφέρεται ἕκαστος αὐτῶν ὅ τι ἂν καταλί-
πηται ἐπὶ τῷ ἀρίστῳ. τὰ δὲ πλεῖστα τούτων τῶν
f ἱερείων καὶ τῶν σιτίων οὓς τρέφει βασιλεὺς | τῶν τε
δορυφόρων καὶ τῶν πελταστῶν, τούτοις ἐκφέρεται εἰς
τὴν αὐλήν· οὗ ἡμιδεῆ ἅπαντα μερίδας ποιήσαντες τῶν
κρεῶν καὶ τῶν ἄρτων ἴσας διαιροῦνται. ὥσπερ δὲ οἱ
μισθοφόροι ἐν τῇ Ἑλλάδι μισθὸν ἀργύριον λαμβάνουσιν, οὕτως οὗτοι τὰ σιτία παρὰ τοῦ βασιλέως εἰς
ὑπόλογον λαμβάνουσιν. οὕτω δὲ καὶ παρὰ τοῖς ἄλλοις

ing to drink with him. After they come in, they drink in his company, although not the same wine; they do this sitting on the floor, whereas he lies on a couch with gold feet. And after they get very drunk, they leave. The King usually eats lunch and dinner alone, but from time to time his wife and some of his sons eat with him. During dinner, his concubines sing and play the harp, and one of them takes the lead, while the others sing in unison.[103] What is referred to as the "King's Dinner," he says, will seem magnificent if one hears it described, but if it is examined carefully, it will be clear that it has been arranged in a careful, economical fashion, like the meals given by other Persian high officials. 1000 sacrificial victims are butchered for the King every day; these include horses, camels, oxen, donkeys, and deer, although the majority are sheep and goats. Many birds are also consumed, including ostriches[104]—the creature is a large one—geese, and chickens. Each of the King's guests is served a modest portion of this food and takes home whatever is left over for the next day's lunch. But the majority of the sacrificial meat and breadstuffs is taken out into the courtyard for the bodyguards and light-armed troops the King supports. There they split up all the half-eaten meat and bread into shares and divide them equally. And just as mercenary soldiers in Greece get their wages in silver, so these men get food from the king in return for their services. So too in the houses of the other Persians

[103] I.e. as a chorus.
[104] Literally "Arabian sparrows."

ATHENAEUS

Πέρσαις τοῖς ἐν δυναστείᾳ οὖσιν ἀθρόα πάντα τὰ
σιτία ἐπὶ τὴν τράπεζαν παρατίθεται· ἐπειδὰν δὲ οἱ
σύνδειπνοι δειπνήσωσι, τῶν ἀπὸ τῆς τραπέζης κατα-
λειπομένων—καταλείπεται δὲ τὰ πλεῖστα κρέα καὶ
ἄρτοι—ὁ τῆς τραπέζης ἐπιμελούμενος δίδωσιν ἑκάστῳ
τῶν οἰκετῶν, καὶ ταῦτα λαβὼν τὴν καθ᾽ ἡμέραν ἔχει
146 τροφήν. ‖ παρὰ γὰρ τὸν βασιλέα φοιτῶσιν οἱ ἐντιμό-
τατοι τῶν συνδείπνων ἐπὶ τὸ ἄριστον μόνον διὰ τὸ
παρῃτῆσθαι, ἵνα μὴ δὶς πορεύωνται, ἀλλὰ καὶ αὐτοὶ
τοὺς συνδείπνους ὑποδέχωνται. Ἡρόδοτος δέ φησιν
ἐν τῇ ἑβδόμῃ ὡς οἱ ὑποδεχόμενοι Ἑλλήνων τὸν βασιλέα καὶ δειπνίζοντες Ξέρξην ἐς πᾶν κακοῦ ἀφίκοντο
οὕτως ὥστε ἐκ τῶν οἴκων ἀνάστατοι ἐγίνοντο· ὅκου
Θασίοισιν ὑπὲρ τῶν ἐν τῇ ἠπείρῳ πολίων τῶν σφε-
τέρων δεξαμένοις τὴν Ξέρξεω στρατιὰν καὶ δειπνί-
b σασι τετρακόσια | τάλαντα ἀργυρίου Ἀντίπατρος τῶν
ἀστῶν ἀνὴρ ἐδαπάνησε· καὶ γὰρ ἐκπώματα ἀργυρᾶ
καὶ χρυσᾶ καὶ κρατῆρας παρετίθεντο, καὶ ταῦτα μετὰ
τὸ δεῖπνον < . . . > εἰ δὲ Ξέρξης δὶς ἐσιτέετο μεταλαμβάνων καὶ ἄριστον, ἀνάστατοι ἂν ἐγεγόνεσαν αἱ
πόλεις. καὶ ἐν τῇ ἐνάτῃ δὲ τῶν Ἱστοριῶν φησι· βασι-
λήιον δεῖπνον βασιλεὺς προτίθεται. τοῦτο δὲ παρα-
σκευάζεται ἅπαξ τοῦ ἐνιαυτοῦ ἐν ἡμέρῃ τῇ ἐγένετο ὁ
βασιλεύς. οὔνομα δὲ τῷ δείπνῳ Περσιστὶ μὲν τυκτά,

---

105 The Greek has been substantially reworked and inconsistently Atticized.
106 During the Persian invasion of 480 BCE.

who hold high positions, all the food is placed on the table together; when the guests are done eating, the man in charge of the table gives some of the food left on it—and most of the meat and bread is left over—to the individual members of the household, which is how they get their provisions for the day. The most distinguished guests therefore visit the King only for lunch, because they ask to be excused from coming twice, so that they themselves can entertain dinner guests. Herodotus says in Book VII (118)[105] that the Greeks who entertained King Xerxes[106] and offered him dinner were reduced to such straits that they lost their homes; since when the Thasians entertained Xerxes' army and provided it with dinner in order to protect their cities on the mainland, Antipater, who was one of the citizens, spent 400 talents of silver on their behalf. For (cf. Hdt. 7.119.2) they set silver and gold goblets and mixing-bowls beside them, and after dinner these items . . . [107] And (cf. Hdt. 7.120) if Xerxes had eaten twice, by also having lunch, the cities would have been ruined. He also says in Book IX (110.2) of the *Histories*: The King was holding the royal dinner. This is prepared once each year on the King's birthday; the dinner is called *tukta* in Persian, which means *teleion* ("perfect, complete") in Greek.[108] On this

[107] The sense of the missing words can be inferred from Hdt. 7.119.3 "they would seize all the implements and march off with them, leaving nothing, but treating this as plunder."

[108] Herodotus did not know Persian and has certainly got the translation wrong. *-kt-* is impossible for a genuine Iranian word; but if *tukta* represents anything, it may be cognate with Middle Persian *taxt* ("throne") and *taxtag* ("board, flat surface"; cf. the Jewish Aramaic loan-word *takhtaka*, "low table or stool").

c Ἑλληνιστὶ δὲ τέλειον. τότε καὶ τὴν κεφαλὴν | σμᾶται
μοῦνον καὶ Πέρσαις δωρέεται. ὁ δὲ μέγας Ἀλέξανδρος
δειπνῶν ἑκάστοτε μετὰ τῶν φίλων, ὡς ἱστορεῖ Ἔφιππος ὁ Ὀλύνθιος ἐν τῷ Περὶ τῆς Ἀλεξάνδρου καὶ
Ἡφαιστίωνος Μεταλλαγῆς, ἀνήλισκε τῆς ἡμέρας
μνᾶς ἑκατόν, δειπνούντων ἴσως ἑξήκοντα ἢ ἑβδομήκοντα φίλων. ὁ δὲ Περσῶν βασιλεύς, ὥς φησι Κτη-
σίας καὶ Δίνων ἐν τοῖς Περσικοῖς, ἐδείπνει μὲν μετὰ
ἀνδρῶν μυρίων πεντακισχιλίων, καὶ ἀνηλίσκετο εἰς τὸ
δεῖπνον τάλαντα τετρακόσια. γίνεται δὲ ταῦτα Ἰτα-
d λικοῦ | νομίσματος ἐν μυριάσι διακοσίαις τεσσα-
ράκοντα, αὗται δὲ εἰς μυρίους πεντακισχιλίους μερι-
ζόμεναι ἑκάστῳ ἀνδρὶ γίνονται ἀνὰ ἑκατὸν ἑξήκοντα
Ἰταλικοῦ νομίσματος. ὥστ᾽ εἰς ἴσον καθίστασθαι τῷ
τοῦ Ἀλεξάνδρου ἀναλώματι· ἑκατὸν γὰρ μνᾶς ἀνή-
λισκεν, ὡς ὁ Ἔφιππος ἱστόρησε. Μένανδρος δ᾽ ἐν
Μέθῃ τοῦ μεγίστου δείπνου δαπάνημα τάλαντον τί-
θησι λέγων οὕτως·

εἶτ᾽ οὐχ ὅμοια πράττομεν καὶ θύομεν;
e ὅπου γε τοῖς θεοῖς μὲν ἠγορασμένον |
δραχμῶν ἄγω προβάτιον ἀγαπητὸν δέκα,
αὐλητρίδας δὲ καὶ μύρον καὶ ψαλτρίας,
† Μενδαῖον Θάσιον, ἐγχέλεις, τυρόν, μέλι,
μικροῦ ταλάντου, γίνεται τε κατὰ λόγον.

---

109 See 3.120e (where the work is assigned a slightly different
title) with n.

day alone he smears perfume on his head and gives the Persians presents. Whenever Alexander the Great had dinner with his friends, according to Ephippus of Olynthus in his *On the Deaths of Alexander and Hephaestion*[109] (*FGrH* 126 F 2), he spent 100 minas[110] per day, and perhaps 60 or 70 of his friends were there. According to Ctesias (*FGrH* 688 F 39) and Dinon in his *History of Persia* (*FGrH* 690 F 24), the Persian king used to dine with 15,000 men and spent 400 talents on the meal. This amounts to 2,400,000 denarii[111]; if this is divided among 15,000 men, it comes out to 160 denarii per man. The figure is thus equal to what Alexander spent; because he spent 100 minas, according to Ephippus. Menander in *Drunkenness* (fr. 224.1–6)[112] sets the cost of a very large dinner at one talent, saying the following:

> So doesn't how we do in life match the way we
>   sacrifice?
> Since I'm bringing the gods a nice little
> goat purchased for 10 drachmas,
> whereas the cost of the dancing-girls, perfume, harp-
>   girls,
> † Mendaean and Thasian wine, eels, cheese, and
>   honey
> is minimal—a talent. And it's reasonable . . .

[110] = 10,000 drachmas, or about 167 drachmas per person, if there were 60 guests.

[111] A denarius was a silver Roman coin equal in value to one Attic drachma, of which there were 6000 in a talent.

[112] Quoted at greater length at 8.364d–e.

ὡς γὰρ ὑπερβολῆς τινος ἀναλώματος τάλαντον ὠνόμασε. καὶ ἐν Δυσκόλῳ δέ φησιν οὕτως·

      ὡς θύουσι δ' οἱ τοιχωρύχοι·
κοίτας φέρονται σταμνί' οὐχὶ τῶν θεῶν
ἔνεκ', ἀλλ' ἑαυτῶν. ὁ λιβανωτὸς εὐσεβὲς |
καὶ τὸ πόπανον· τοῦτ' ἔλαβεν ὁ θεὸς ἐπὶ τὸ πῦρ
ἅπαν ἐπιτεθέν· οἱ δὲ τὴν ὀσφῦν ἄκραν
καὶ τὴν χολήν, ὅτι ἔστ' ἄβρωτα, τοῖς θεοῖς
ἐπιθέντες αὐτοὶ τἆλλα καταπίνουσι.

Φιλόξενος δ' ὁ Κυθήριος ἐν τῷ ἐπιγραφομένῳ Δείπνῳ—εἴπερ τούτου καὶ ὁ κωμῳδιοποιὸς Πλάτων ἐν τῷ
Φάωνι ἐμνήσθη καὶ μὴ τοῦ Λευκαδίου Φιλοξένου—
τοιαύτην ἐκτίθεται παρασκευὴν δείπνου·

εἰς δ' ἔφερον διπλόοι
    παῖδες λιπαρῶπα τράπεζαν
ἄμμ', ἑτέραν δ' ἑτέροις,
    ἄλλοις δ' ἑτέραν, μέχρι οὗ
        πλήρωσαν οἶκον· ||
ταὶ δὲ πρὸς ὑψιλύχνους
    ἔστιλβον αὐγὰς
εὐστέφανοι λεκάναις
    παροψίσι τ' ὀξυβάφων
      † πλήρεις † σύν τε χλιδῶσαι

---

113 The poem (cited repeatedly by Athenaeus, including at
9.409e, where a few additional verses from the end of this fragment are given) is written in an extravagantly "dithyrambic" style,

He thus refers to a talent as a quite exorbinate amount to spend. So too in *The Difficult Man* (Men. *Dysc.* 447–53) he says the following:

> Look how the bastards sacrifice!
> They bring hampers and wine-jars, not to please the
>   gods
> but themselves. The incense and the sacrificial cake
> are a matter of piety—the god can have that, and it's
>   all
> placed on the fire. They also put on the tail-bone
> and the gall bladder for the gods—because they're
> inedible. But they guzzle down the rest themselves!

Philoxenus of Cythera in his poem entitled *The Dinner* (*PMG* 836(b))—assuming that he rather than Philoxenus of Leucas is the man mentioned by the comic poet Plato in *Phaon* (fr. 189.4, quoted at 1.5b)—describes preparations of the following sort for a dinner:[113]

> A pair of slaves brought in
>   a bright-faced table
> for us, and another for some others,
>   and for some others another, until
>   they filled the room.
> The tables reflected the gleam
>   of the high-hung lamps,
> and were covered with bowls
>   and † full of † shallow saucers
>   for the side-dishes, and luxuriant

and the text as it is preserved here is full of gaps and seriously corrupt.

παντοδαποῖσι τέχνας
  εὑρήμασι πρὸς βιοτάν,
    ψυχὰς δελεασματίοισι·
πάρφερον ἐν κανέοις
  μάζας χιονόχροας ἄλλοι·
⟨τοῖς⟩ δ' ἔπι πρῶτα παρῆλθ'
  οὐ κάκκαβος, ὦ φιλότας,
    ἀλλ' † ἀλλοπλατεῖς † τὸ μέγιστον
† πάντ' ἔπαθεν λιπαροντες
  εγχελεα τινες ἄριστον
γόγγροι τοιωνητεμων †
  πλῆρες θεοτερπές. ἐπ' αὐτῷ
δ' ἄλλο παρῆλθε τόσον,
  βατὶς δ' ἐνέην ἰσόκυκλος· |
μικρὰ δὲ κακκάβι' ἧς
  ἔχοντα τὸ μὲν γαλεοῦ
    τι, ναρκίον ἄλλο ⟨ . . . ⟩
⟨ . . . ⟩ παρῆς ἕτερον
  πίων ἀπὸ τευθιάδων
    καὶ σηπιοπουλυποδείων
⟨ . . . ⟩ ἁπαλοπλοκάμων·
  θερμὸς μετὰ ταῦτα παρῆλθεν
ἰσοτράπεζος ὅλος
  † μνήστης συνόδων πυρὸς ⟨ . . . ⟩
⟨ . . . ⟩ ἔπειτα βαθμοὺς
  ἀτμίζων ἐπὶ τῷδ' ἐπιπυσται †

with every sort of clever
        invention for enjoying life,
                lures for the appetite.
Other slaves served us barley-cakes,
        whose skin was white as snow, in baskets;
what came to us first after these
        was not a cookpot, my love,
                but [corrupt] the biggest
† everything he suffered shiny-ing
        eelish-some lunch
conger-eel-of-such-cutting †
        full and capable of pleasing a god. After it,
another of the same size arrived,
        and a perfectly round ray was in it.
There were small cookpots,
        one of which contained a bit of thresher shark,
                another a little electric ray . . .
. . . There was another one,
        rich, made of squid
                and cuttlefish-octopi
. . . with soft tentacles.
        After them arrived a whole
hot four-toothed sea-bream as big as the table
        † of wedded fire . . .
. . . then stairs
        emitting steam after this [corrupt] †

τευθίδες, ὦ φίλε, καὶ
    ξανθαὶ μελικαρίδες αἱ
        κοῦφαι παρῆλθον.
θρυμματίδες δ᾽ ἐπὶ ταύ-
    ταις εὐπέταλοι χλοεραί
        τε † δηφαρυγες
πυριων τε † στεγαναὶ
    φυσταὶ μέγαθος κατὰ κάκ-
c   καβον γλυκυόξεες < . . . > |
ὀμφαλὸς θοίνας καλεῖται
    παρά γ᾽ ἐμὶν καὶ τίν, σάφ᾽ οἶδα.
† εσταδα † ναὶ μὰ θεοὺς
    ὑπερμέγεθές τι θέμος
        θύννου μόλεν ὀπτὸν ἐκεῖθεν
† θερμὸν ὅθεν γλυφις †
    τετμημένον εὐθὺς ἐπ᾽ αὐτὰς
τὰς ὑπογαστρίδας. <αἷς>
    διανεκέως ἐπαμύνειν
εἴπερ ἐμίν τε μέλοι
    καὶ τίν, μάλα κεν κεχαροίμεθ᾽.
ἀλλ᾽ ὅθεν ἐλλίπομεν,
    θοίνα παρέῃς † ὅτε παλάξαι
δύνατ᾽ ἐπικρατέως †
    ἔγωγ᾽ ἔτι, κοὔ κε λέγοι τις
πάνθ᾽ ἃ παρῆν ἐτύμως
    ἄμμιν, † παρέπεσαι † δὲ θερμὸν
σπλάγχνον· ἔπειτα δὲ νή-
d   στις δέλφακος οἰκετικᾶς |

204

Squid, my friend, and the
      golden-brown bent
            honey cakes arrived.
After these were *thrummatides*[114]
        that divided easily into segments, and fresh
              [corrupt]
and [corrupt] frosted
      sweet-and-sour *phustai* the size
          of a cookpot.
This is referred to as "the navel of the feast"
      by us and you, I'm sure.
[corrupt], by the gods,
      came an enormous
             serving of roast tuna from there
† hot whence [corrupt] †
      cut up immediately after the
underbellies themselves. If
      defending these perpetually
were up to us
      and you, we would be quite happy.
But where we fell short,
      the feast was there, † when to sprinkle
it was possible with great force †
      I still, at any rate; and no one could truthfully
recount everything that was there
      for us, but [corrupt] hot
entrails. And then the jejunum
      of a pig raised in the house

---

[114] For *thrummatides* and *phustai* (below), see 4.131d n. and 3.114e–f n., respectively.

καὶ νωτί᾽ ἐσῆλθε καὶ ὀσ-
    φὺς καὶ μινυρίγματα θερμά·
καὶ κεφάλαιον ὅλον
    διαπτυχὲς ἐφθὸν † ἀπερ-
        πευθηνος ἀλεκτοτρόφου †
            πνικτᾶς ἐρίφου παρέθηκε,
εἶτα δίεφθ᾽ ἀκροκώ-
    λια σχελίδας τε μετ᾽ αὐτῶν
λευκοφορινοχρόους,
    ῥύγχη κεφάλαια πόδας
        τε χναυμάτιόν τε σεσιλ-
            φιωμένον·
ἐφθά τ᾽ ἔπειτα κρέ᾽ ὀπ-
    τά ‹τ› ἄλλ᾽ ἐρίφων τε καὶ ἀρνῶν,
ἅ θ᾽ ὑπερωμόκρεως
    χορδὰ γλυκίστα
μιξεριφαρνογενής,
    ἃν δὴ φιλέοντι θεοί.
τουτ‹ . . . ›, ὦ φιλότας,
    ἔσθοις κε· λαγῷά τ᾽ ἔπειτ᾽ |
        ἀλεκτρυόνων τε νεοσσοί.
περδίκων φάσσεων
    τε † χύδαν ἤδη δὲ παρεβάλλετο θερμὰ
    πολλὰ †

e

came in, along with slices off the back,
     a tail-bone, and some hot warbles[115].
And he served us a whole
     stewed head, split in two
          [corrupt]
               of a smothered she-kid.
After this came boiled
     trotters, accompanied by ribs
the color of white skin,
     snouts, heads, and feet,
         and a morsel flavored
            with silphium.
And then other meat, stewed
     and roasted, of kids and lambs,
and the most delicious sausage,
     made of meat cut from above the shoulder
from a mix of kids and lambs,
     which the gods are fond of.
This . . . , my dear,
     you would eat. And then hare-meat
         and cockerels.
Of partridges and ringdoves
     † in heaps now but were set beside us many hot †

[115] Roasted songbirds?

καὶ μαλακοπτυχέων
    ἄρτων· ὁμοσύζυγα δὲ
        ξανθόν τ᾽ ἐπεισῆλ-
            θεν μέλι καὶ γάλα σύμπακ-
                τον, τό κε τυρὸν ἅπας τις
ἦμεν ἔφασχ᾽ ἁπαλόν,
    κἠγὼν ἐφάμαν· ὅτε δ᾽ ἤδη
βρωτύος ἠδὲ ποτᾶ-
    τος ἐς κόρον ἦμεν ἑταῖροι,
τῆνα μὲν ἐξαπάει-
    ρον δμῶες, ἔπειτα δὲ παῖ-
        δες νίπτρ᾽ ἔδοσαν κατὰ χειρῶν.

Σωκράτης δὲ ὁ Ῥόδιος ἐν τρίτῳ Ἐμφυλίου Πολέμου τὸ Κλεοπάτρας ἀναγράφων συμπόσιον τῆς
f τελευταίας | Αἰγύπτου βασιλευσάσης, γημαμένης δ᾽
Ἀντωνίῳ τῷ Ῥωμαίων στρατηγῷ[11], φησὶν οὕτως·
ἀπαντήσασα τῷ Ἀντωνίῳ ἡ Κλεοπάτρα ἐν Κιλικίᾳ
παρεσκεύασεν αὐτῷ βασιλικὸν συμπόσιον, ἐν ᾧ πάντα χρύσεα καὶ λιθοκόλλητα περιττῶς ἐξειργασμένα
ταῖς τέχναις· ἦσαν δέ, φησί, καὶ οἱ τοῖχοι ἀλουργέσι
καὶ διαχρύσοις ἐμπεπετασμένοι ὕφεσι. καὶ δώδεκα
τρίκλινα διαστρώσασα ἐκάλεσε τὸν Ἀντώνιον μεθ᾽ ὧν
148 ἐβούλετο ἡ Κλεοπάτρα. ‖ τοῦ δὲ τῇ πολυτελείᾳ τῆς
ὄψεως ἐκπλαγέντος ὑπομειδιάσασα ταῦτ᾽ ἔφη πάντα
δωρεῖσθαι αὐτῷ καὶ εἰς αὔριον παρεκάλει συνδειπνῆ-
σαι πάλιν ἥκοντα μετὰ τῶν φίλων καὶ τῶν ἡγεμόνων·

---

[11] στρατηγῷ ἐν Κιλικίᾳ A: βασιλεῖ ἐν Κιλικίᾳ CE

and of softly folded
>> bread. And a mixture
>>>> of blond honey and curdled milk
>>>>> came in; everyone said
> that the cheese was tender,
>> and I agreed. And when now
> those of us in the group reached satiety
>> of food and drink,
> servants removed those things; then slaves
>> poured washing-water over our hands.

Socrates of Rhodes in Book III of his *Civil War* (*FGrH* 192 F 1) describes the drinking party given by Cleopatra, the last queen of Egypt,[116] who married the Roman general Antonius,[117] saying the following: When Cleopatra met Antonius in Cilicia, she prepared a royal drinking party for him, all the vessels for which were made of gold, set with gems, and elaborately worked. And he says that the walls were hung with purple tapestries through which ran threads of gold. Cleopatra spread bed-clothes over couches in 12 *triclinia*[118] and invited Antonius to come with anyone he wanted. When he expressed astonishment at the expensive display, she smiled slightly, said that all these objects were a gift for him, and invited him to come and dine with her again on the next day along with his friends and commanders. Then she arranged for this party

[116] Cleopatra VII (reigned 51–30 BCE). The events referred to here took place in 41/0 in the city of Tarsus.

[117] Marcus Antonius, who had defeated Cassius and Brutus at Philippi in 42 BCE and was now in control of the eastern half of the Empire and of Gaul.

[118] Banquet rooms fitted with three couches.

ὅτε καὶ πολλῷ κρεῖττον διακοσμήσασα τὸ συμπόσιον
ἐποίησε φανῆναι τὰ πρῶτα μικρά, καὶ πάλιν καὶ
ταῦτα ἐδωρήσατο. τῶν δ᾽ ἡγεμόνων ἐφ᾽ ᾗ ἕκαστος
κατέκειτο κλίνῃ καὶ τὰ κυλικεῖα καθὼς ταῖς στρωμναῖς ἐμεμέριστο, ἑκάστῳ φέρειν ἐπέτρεψε. καὶ κατὰ
b τὴν ἄφοδον τοῖς μὲν ἐν ἀξιώμασι φορεῖα σὺν | τοῖς
κομίζουσι, τοῖς πλείοσι δὲ καταργύροις σκευαῖς κεκο-
σμημένους ἵππους, πᾶσι δὲ λαμπτηροφόρους παῖδας
Αἰθίοπας παρέστησε. τῇ δὲ τετάρτῃ τῶν ἡμερῶν τα-
λαντιαίους εἰς ῥόδα μισθοὺς διέδωκε, καὶ κατεστρώθη
ἐπὶ πηχυαῖα βάθη τὰ ἐδάφη τῶν ἀνδρώνων ἐμπεπε-
τασμένων δικτύων τοῖς ἕλιξιν. ἱστορεῖ δὲ καὶ αὐτὸν
τὸν Ἀντώνιον ἐν Ἀθήναις μετὰ ταῦτα διατρίψαντα
περίοπτον ὑπὲρ τὸ θέατρον κατασκευάσαντα σχεδίαν
χλωρᾷ πεπυκασμένην ὕλῃ, ὥσπερ ἐπὶ τῶν Βακχικῶν
c ἄντρων γίνεται, | ταύτης τύμπανα καὶ νεβρίδας καὶ
παντοδαπὰ ἄλλ᾽ ἀθύρματα Διονυσιακὰ ἐξαρτήσαντα
μετὰ τῶν φίλων ἐξ ἑωθινοῦ κατακλινόμενον μεθύσκε-
σθαι, λειτουργούντων αὐτῷ τῶν ἐξ Ἰταλίας μεταπεμ-
φθέντων ἀκροαμάτων συνηθροισμένων ἐπὶ τὴν θέαν
τῶν Πανελλήνων. μετέβαινε δ᾽ ἐνίοτε, φησίν, καὶ ἐπὶ
τὴν ἀκρόπολιν ἀπὸ τῶν τεγῶν λαμπάσι δᾳδουχου-
μένης πάσης τῆς Ἀθηναίων πόλεως. καὶ ἔκτοτε ἐκέλευσεν ἑαυτὸν Διόνυσον ἀνακηρύττεσθαι κατὰ τὰς
d πόλεις ἁπάσας. | καὶ Γάιος δὲ ὁ αὐτοκράτωρ ὁ Καλ-
λίκολα προσαγορευθεὶς διὰ τὸ ἐν στρατοπέδῳ γεννη-
θῆναι οὐ μόνον ὠνομάζετο νέος Διόνυσος, ἀλλὰ καὶ

to be far more elaborate, making the equipment for the first seem insignificant; and once again she presented everything to him as a gift. The couches on which his individual commanders reclined and the cup-stands, along with the bed-clothes, were also divided up, and she gave each of them a share to take home. When they left, she provided litters and bearers for the men of high rank, and horses decked out with silver-plated trappings for the majority of them; and she furnished them all with Ethiopian slaves carrying torches. On the fourth day she distributed a talent's worth of money to pay for roses, and the floors of the banquet rooms were covered a cubit deep with them braided into a mesh and spread out over everything. He also reports that when Antonius himself spent some time in Athens after this, he had a roughly framed hut built in a conspicuous spot above the Theater and covered with green brushwood, as they do with Bacchic "caves"; and he hung drums, fawnskins, and other Dionysiac paraphernalia of all sorts in it. He lay inside with his friends, beginning at dawn, and got drunk; musicians summoned from Italy entertained him, and the whole Greek world gathered to watch. Sometimes, he says, Antonius moved up onto the Acropolis, and the entire city of Athens was illuminated by the lamps that hung from the ceilings. He also gave orders that from then on he was to be proclaimed as Dionysus throughout all the cities. So too the emperor Gaius,[119] who was called Caligula because he was born in an army camp, was not only referred to as a new Dionysus, but actually

---

[119] Reigned 37–41 CE. The explanation of his nickname that follows is slightly garbled: Caligula is derived from Latin *caliga*, a type of military boot Gaius wore in the camps as a boy.

211

τὴν Διονυσιακὴν πᾶσαν ἐνδύνων στολὴν προήει καὶ
οὕτως ἐσκευασμένος ἐδίκαζεν.

Εἰς ταῦτα ἔστιν ἀποβλέποντας τὰ ὑπὲρ ἡμᾶς ἀγα-
πᾶν τὴν Ἑλληνικὴν πενίαν, λαμβάνοντας πρὸ ὀφθαλ-
μῶν καὶ τὰ παρὰ Θηβαίοις δεῖπνα, περὶ ὧν Κλείταρ-
χος ἐν τῇ πρώτῃ τῶν Περὶ Ἀλέξανδρον Ἱστοριῶν,
διηγούμενος καὶ ὅτι ὁ πᾶς αὐτῶν πλοῦτος ηὑρέθη
e   μετὰ | τὴν ὑπ᾽ Ἀλεξάνδρου τῆς πόλεως κατασκαφὴν
ἐν ταλάντοις τετρακοσίοις τεσσαράκοντα, φησὶν ὅτι
τε μικρόψυχοι ἦσαν καὶ τὰ περὶ τὴν τροφὴν λίχνοι,
παρασκευάζοντες ἐν τοῖς δείπνοις θρῖα καὶ ἑψητοὺς
καὶ ἀφύας καὶ ἐγκρασιχόλους καὶ ἀλλᾶντας καὶ σχε-
λίδας καὶ ἔτνος· οἷσι Μαρδόνιον εἱστίασε μετὰ τῶν
ἄλλων πεντήκοντα Περσῶν Ἀτταγῖνος ὁ Φρύνωνος,
ὅν φησιν Ἡρόδοτος ἐν τῇ ἐνάτῃ μεγάλως[12] παρεσκευ-
f   άσθαι. ἡγοῦμαι <δ᾽> ὅτι οὐκ ἂν περιεγένοντο | οὐδ᾽ ἂν
ἐδέησε τοῖς Ἕλλησι περὶ Πλαταιὰς παρατάττεσθαι
ἀπολωλόσιν ἤδη ὑπὸ τῶν τοιούτων τροφῶν.

Ἀρκαδικὸν δὲ δεῖπνον διαγράφων ὁ Μιλήσιος
Ἑκαταῖος ἐν τῇ τρίτῃ τῶν Γενεαλογιῶν μάζας φησὶν
εἶναι καὶ ὕεα κρέα. Ἁρμόδιος δὲ ὁ Λεπρεάτης ἐν τῷ
Περὶ τῶν Κατὰ Φιγάλειαν Νομίμων, ὁ κατασταθείς,
φησί, παρὰ Φιγαλεῦσι σίταρχος ἔφερε τῆς ἡμέρας
οἴνου τρεῖς χόας καὶ ἀλφίτων μέδιμνον καὶ τυροῦ
πεντάμνουν καὶ τἆλλα τὰ πρὸς τὴν ἄρτυσιν τῶν ἱερεί-

---

[12] μεγάλως πλούτῳ A

put on the full Dionysiac outfit, and went out in public and sat in judgment dressed that way.

When we consider these things, which are far beyond what we have, we can appreciate Greek poverty if we have before our eyes the dinner parties given by the Thebans, which Cleitarchus describes in Book I of his *Histories of Alexander* (*FGrH* 137 F 1). He explains there that after the city was destroyed by Alexander,[120] its wealth was found to total 440 talents; but he says that they were petty-minded and greedy where food was concerned, and for their dinner parties they prepared fig-leaf pastries, boiled small-fry, sprats and anchovies, sausages, ribs, and pea-soup. This is the food on which Attaginus the son of Phrynon feasted Mardonius and 50 other Persians, although Herodotus claims in Book IX (16.1) that Attaginus made elaborate preparations. But I think that they could not have won and that it would not even have been necessary for the Greeks to have drawn up their troops against them at Plataea, if they had already been devastated by food like this.

Hecataeus of Miletus offers a sketch of an Arcadian dinner in Book III of his *Genealogies* (*FGrH* 1 F 9), saying that it consisted of barley-cakes and pork. Harmodius of Lepreum says in his *On the Customs in Phigaleia* (*FGrH* 319 F 1): The man who was appointed *sitarchos* ("commissary officer, quartermaster") in Phigaleia used to supply three *choes*[121] of wine every day, along with a *medimnos*[122] of barley groats, five minas[123] of cheese, and whatever was

---

[120] In 335 BCE; Thebes had revolted from Macedonian authority and was made an example of.   [121] About three gallons; cf. 3.118a n.   [122] About eight bushels; cf. 2.67f n.

[123] Four to five pounds.

149   ων ἁρμόττοντα. ‖ ἡ δὲ πόλις παρεῖχεν ἑκατέρῳ τῶν
χορῶν τρία πρόβατα καὶ μάγειρον ὑδριαφόρον τε καὶ
τραπέζας καὶ βάθρα πρὸς τὴν καθέδραν καὶ τὴν
τοιαύτην ἅπασαν παρασκευήν, τὴν δὲ τῶν περὶ τὸν
μάγειρον σκευῶν ὁ χορηγός. τὸ δὲ δεῖπνον ἦν τοιοῦτο·
τυρὸς καὶ φυστὴ μᾶζα νόμου χάριν ἐπὶ χαλκῶν κανῶν
τῶν παρά τισι καλουμένων μαζονόμων, ἀπὸ τῆς χρείας εἰληφότων τὴν ἐπωνυμίαν· ὁμοῦ δὲ τῇ μάζῃ καὶ τῷ
τυρῷ σπλάγχνον καὶ ἅλες προσφαγεῖν. καθαγισάν-
b   των | δὲ ταῦτα ἐν κεραμέᾳ κοτταβίδι πιεῖν ἑκάστῳ
μικρόν, καὶ ὁ προσφέρων ἂν εἶπεν "εὐδειπνίας." εἶτα
δ᾽ εἰς τὸ κοινὸν ζωμὸς καὶ περίκομμα, πρόσχερα δὲ
ἑκάστῳ δύο κρέα. ἐνόμιζον δ᾽ ἐν ἅπασι τοῖς δείπνοις,
μάλιστα δὲ τοῖς λεγομένοις μαζῶσι—τοῦτο γὰρ ἔτι
καὶ νῦν ἡ Διονυσιακὴ σύνοδος ἔχει τοὔνομα—τοῖς
ἐσθίουσι τῶν νέων ἀνδρικώτερον ζωμόν τ᾽ ἐγχεῖν
πλείω καὶ μάζας καὶ ἄρτους παραβάλλειν. γενναῖος
γὰρ ὁ τοιοῦτος ἐκρίνετο καὶ ἀνδρώδης ὑπάρχειν· θαυ-
c   μαστὸν γὰρ ἦν | καὶ περιβόητον παρ᾽ αὐτοῖς ἡ πολυ-
φαγία. μετὰ δὲ τὸ δεῖπνον σπονδὰς ἐποιοῦντο οὐκ
ἀπονιψάμενοι τὰς χεῖρας, ἀλλ᾽ ἀποματτόμενοι τοῖς
ψωμοῖς καὶ τὴν ἀπομαγδαλίαν ἕκαστος ἀπέφερε, τοῦτο ποιοῦντες ἕνεκα τῶν ἐν ταῖς ἀμφόδοις γινομένων

---

124 The man charged with paying and outfitting a chorus for a
state-sponsored festival. What is described here is probably a
post-performance celebration.

needed to season the sacrificial meat. The city supplied each chorus with three sheep or goats, a cook, a slave to haul water, and tables, benchs to sit on, and all the equipment of this sort, while the *choregos*[124] supplied the cook's utensils. The dinner was of the following sort: cheese and lightly-kneaded barley-cakes[125] served, as the law required, in bronze baskets referred to by some authorities as *mazonomoi* ("barley-cake dispensers"), which got their name from the use to which they were put; in addition to the barley-cakes and the cheese, there were entrails and salt to eat with them. After they dedicated these items, each guest was given a little wine to drink in an earthenware *cottabus*-basin; the man who served it would say "Enjoy your dinner!" After this, there was broth and hash, which everyone shared, and two pieces of meat *proschera*[126] for each person. At all their dinners, but especially those referred to as *mazones*[127]—this name is still used today for the Dionysiac guild—it was their custom to pour more broth into the bowls of the young men who ate more heartily, and to serve them more barley-cakes and bread. This is because they considered such individuals noble and manly, since gluttony was regarded as something that deserved respect and acclaim. After the dinner, they made libations; but rather than washing their hands first, they wiped themselves clean with pieces of bread, which they took with them when they left. They did this because of the frightening events that occurred in the

---

[125] A *phustē*; cf. 3.114e–f.

[126] The meaning of the word is obscure ("ready at hand," i.e. "for him alone," in contrast to the food the company shared?).

[127] Cognate with *maza*, "barley-cake."

νυκτερινῶν φόβων. ἀπὸ δὲ τῶν σπονδῶν παιὰν ᾄδεται.
ὅταν δὲ τοῖς ἥρωσι θύωσι, βουθυσία μεγάλη γίνεται
καὶ ἑστιῶνται πάντες μετὰ τῶν δούλων· οἱ δὲ παῖδες ἐν
ταῖς ἑστιάσεσι μετὰ τῶν πατέρων ἐπὶ λίθων καθήμε-
d νοι γυμνοὶ συνδειπνοῦσιν. | Θεόπομπος δ' ἐν τῇ ἕκτῃ
καὶ τεσσαρακοστῇ τῶν Φιλιππικῶν, οἱ Ἀρκάδες, φησίν, ἐν ταῖς ἑστιάσεσιν ὑποδέχονται τοὺς δεσπότας
καὶ τοὺς δούλους, καὶ μίαν πᾶσι τράπεζαν παρασκευ-
άζουσι καὶ τὰ σιτία πᾶσιν εἰς τὸ μέσον παρατιθέασι
καὶ κρατῆρα τὸν αὐτὸν πᾶσι κιρνᾶσι.

Παρὰ δὲ Ναυκρατίταις, ὥς φησιν Ἑρμείας ἐν τῷ
e δευτέρῳ τῶν Περὶ τοῦ Γρυνείου Ἀπόλλωνος, | ἐν τῷ
πρυτανείῳ δειπνοῦσι γενεθλίοις Ἑστίας Πρυτανίτιδος
καὶ Διονυσίοις, ἔτι δὲ τῇ τοῦ Κωμαίου Ἀπόλλωνος
πανηγύρει, εἰσιόντες πάντες ἐν στολαῖς λευκαῖς, ἃς
μέχρι καὶ νῦν καλοῦσι πρυτανικὰς ἐσθῆτας. καὶ κατακλιθέντες ἐπανίστανται εἰς γόνατα τοῦ ἱεροκήρυκος
τὰς πατρίους εὐχὰς καταλέγοντος συσπένδοντες. μετὰ δὲ ταῦτα κατακλιθέντες λαμβάνουσιν ἕκαστος οἴνου κοτύλας δύο πλὴν τῶν ἱερέων τοῦ τε Πυθίου
Ἀπόλλωνος καὶ τοῦ Διονύσου· τούτων γὰρ ἑκατέρῳ
διπλοῦς ὁ οἶνος μετὰ καὶ τῶν ἄλλων μερίδων δίδοται.
f ἔπειτα ἑκάστῳ παρατίθεται ἄρτος καθαρὸς | εἰς πλά-
τος πεποιημένος, ἐφ' ᾧ ἐπίκειται ἄρτος ἕτερος, ὃν
κριβανίτην καλοῦσι, καὶ κρέας ὕειον καὶ λεκάριον
πτισάνης ἢ λαχάνου τοῦ κατὰ καιρὸν γινομένου ᾠά τε

---

[128] The idea is apparently that the bread was left at crossroads

streets at night.[128] After the libations, a paean is sung. But when they sacrifice to the heroes, they slaughter a large number of cattle, and everyone feasts with his slaves; their children dine along with them at their feasts, sitting without a cloak on stones next to their fathers. Theopompus says in Book XLVI of his *History of Philip* (*FGrH* 115 F 215): The Arcadians entertain both the masters and the slaves at their feasts, and they prepare a single table for everyone, put the food in the midst of them all, and mix wine in one mixing-bowl for everyone.

In Naucratis, according to Hermeias in Book II of his *On Gryneian Apollo* (fr. 2, *FHG* ii.80–1), a dinner is held in the prytaneion on the birthday of Hestia Prytanitis and during festivals of Dionysus, as well as at the festival of Apollo Komaios; they all come in wearing white robes, which they refer to even today as "prytanic clothing." They lie down, and then rise again to their knees and join in a libation as the sacred herald recites the ancestral prayers. After this they lie down, and each of them gets two *kotulai*[129] of wine, except for the priests of Pythian Apollo and Dionysus, each of whom is given twice as much wine, as well as his portion of everything else. Then each man is served a flat loaf of good bread, with another loaf of bread, which they refer to as *kribanitēs* ("baking-shell bread")[130], on top, along with some pork, a little dish of barley-gruel or whatever vegetable is in season, two eggs, a wheel of

---

shrines of the sinister nocturnal goddess Hecate, in the hope that she would furnish her suppliants with protection during their journey home.

[129] About two cups; cf. 4.129b with n.
[130] Cf. 3.109f.

δύο καὶ τυροῦ τροφαλὶς σῦκά τε ξηρὰ καὶ πλακοῦς καὶ
στέφανος. καὶ ὃς ἂν ἔξω τι τούτων ἱεροποιὸς παρα-
σκευάσῃ ὑπὸ τῶν τιμούχων ζημιοῦται. ἀλλὰ μὴν οὐδὲ
τοῖς σιτουμένοις ἐν πρυτανείῳ ἔξωθεν προσεισφέρειν
τι βρώσιμον ἔξεστι, μόνα δὲ ταῦτα καταναλίσκουσι,
150 τὰ ὑπολειπόμενα τοῖς οἰκέταις μεταδιδόντες. ‖ ταῖς δ᾽
ἄλλαις ἡμέραις πάσαις τοῦ ἐνιαυτοῦ ἔξεστι τῶν σι-
τουμένων τῷ βουλομένῳ ἀνελθόντι εἰς τὸ πρυτανεῖον
δειπνεῖν, οἴκοθεν παρασκευάσαντα αὑτῷ λάχανόν τι ἢ
τῶν ὀσπρίων καὶ τάριχος ἢ ἰχθύν, κρέως δὲ χοιρείου
βραχύτατον, καὶ τούτων μεταλαμβάνων ⟨ . . . ⟩
κοτύλην οἴνου. γυναικὶ δὲ οὐκ ἔξεστιν εἰσιέναι εἰς τὸ
πρυτανεῖον ἢ μόνῃ τῇ αὐλητρίδι. οὐκ εἰσφέρεται δὲ
οὐδὲ ἀμὶς εἰς τὸ πρυτανεῖον. ἐὰν δέ τις Ναυκρατιτῶν
γάμους ἑστιᾷ, ὡς ἐν τῷ γαμικῷ νόμῳ γέγραπται,
b ἀπείρηται ᾠὰ καὶ μελίπηκτα | δίδοσθαι. τίς δὲ ἡ
τούτων αἰτία, Οὐλπιανὸς ἡμᾶς διδάσκειν δίκαιος.

Λυκέας δ᾽ ἐν τοῖς Αἰγυπτιακοῖς προκρίνων τὰ Αἰ-
γυπτιακὰ δεῖπνα τῶν Περσικῶν, Αἰγυπτίων ἐπιστρα-
τευσάντων, φησίν, ἐπὶ Ὦχον τὸν Περσῶν βασιλέα
καὶ νικηθέντων, ἐπεὶ ἐγένετο αἰχμάλωτος ὁ τῶν Αἰγυπτίων βασιλεύς, ὁ Ὦχος αὐτὸν φιλανθρώπως ἄγων
ἐκάλεσε καὶ ἐπὶ δεῖπνον. τῆς οὖν παρασκευῆς γενομένης λαμπρᾶς ὁ Αἰγύπτιος κατεγέλα ὡς εὐτελῶς τοῦ

---

131 The challenge is never taken up.
132 Ochos is the proper Persian personal name for Artaxerxes

cheese, some dried figs, a cake, and a garland. If the official in charge of the rite provides anything beyond this, the magistrates fine him. Moreover, those who eat in the prytaneion are not allowed to bring in any other food from outside, but can only consume the items mentioned above; they give the leftovers to their slaves. On every other day of the year, anyone eligible for maintenance there who wishes can come into the prytaneion for dinner and bring with him food he prepared for himself at home, such as a vegetable, some beans or lentils, fresh or salted fish, or a little bit of pork. And while partaking of them . . . a *kotulē* of wine. No woman may enter the prytaneion except the pipe-girl. A pisspot may not be brought into the prytaneion. If one of the inhabitants of Naucratis gives a wedding feast, according to the law about weddings, he is forbidden to serve eggs or honey cake. But Ulpian is the right person to tell us why this is so.[131]

Lyceas in his *History of Egypt* (*FGrH* 613 F 4) expresses a preference for Egyptian dinners over Persian ones when he says: The Egyptians mounted an expedition against Ochos the king of Persia and were defeated.[132] When the Egyptian king was captured, Ochos treated him humanely and actually invited him to dinner. Although the meal was magnificent, the Egyptian laughed at the Persian

---

III (reigned 359/8–338 BCE). The Egyptian king referred to below is Tachos (reigned *c*.362–360 BCE), who was actually deposed when he was out of the country during an invasion of Syria, and who fled to Persia for safety and was thus Artaxerxes' guest rather than his prisoner, explaining the kindness with which he was treated. The anecdote is modeled on the story about Pausanias told at Hdt. 9.82 and quoted at 4.138c–d.

Πέρσου διαιτωμένου. "εἰ δὲ θέλεις εἰδέναι," ἔφη, "ὦ
c βασιλεῦ, | πῶς δεῖ σιτεῖσθαι τοὺς εὐδαίμονας βασι-
λέας, ἐπίτρεψον τοῖς ἐμοῖς ποτε γενομένοις μαγείροις
παρασκευάσαι σοι Αἰγύπτιον δεῖπνον." καὶ κελεύσαντος, ἐπεὶ παρεσκευάσθη, ἡσθεὶς ὁ Ὦχος τῷ δείπνῳ,
"κακὸν κακῶς σε," ἔφη, "ὦ Αἰγύπτιε, ἀπολέσειαν οἱ
θεοί, ὅστις δεῖπνα τοιαῦτα καταλιπὼν ἐπεθύμησας
θοίνης εὐτελεστέρας." τίνα δ᾽ ἦν τὰ Αἰγύπτια δεῖπνα
Πρωταγορίδης ἐν τῷ πρώτῳ Περὶ Δαφνικῶν Ἀγώνων
διδάσκει ἡμᾶς λέγων οὕτως· τρίτη δέ ἐστιν ἰδέα
d δείπνων Αἰγυπτιακὴ | τραπεζῶν μὲν οὐ παρατιθεμέ-
νων, πινάκων δὲ περιφερομένων.

Παρὰ δὲ Γαλάταις φησὶ Φύλαρχος ἐν τῇ ἕκτῃ ἐπὶ
ταῖς τραπέζαις ἄρτους πολλοὺς κατακεκλασμένους
παρατίθεσθαι χύδην καὶ κρέατα ἐκ τῶν λεβήτων, ὧν
οὐδεὶς γεύεται εἰ μὴ πρότερον θεάσηται τὸν βασιλέα
εἰ ἥψατο τῶν παρακειμένων. ἐν δὲ τῇ τρίτῃ ὁ αὐτὸς
Φύλαρχος Ἀριάμνην φησὶ τὸν Γαλάτην πλουσιώτα-
τον ὄντα ἐπαγγείλασθαι ἑστιᾶσαι Γαλάτας πάντας
e ἐνιαυτὸν καὶ τοῦτο συντελέσαι | ποιήσαντα οὕτως.
κατὰ τόπους τῆς χώρας τὰς ἐπικαιροτάτας τῶν ὁδῶν
διέλαβε σταθμοῖς ἐπί τε τούτοις ἐκ χαράκων καὶ
καλάμων τῶν οἰσυΐνων[13] ἐπεβάλλετο σκηνὰς χωρού-
σας ἀνὰ τετρακοσίους ἄνδρας καὶ πλείους ἔτι, καθὼς
ἂν ἐκποιῶσιν οἱ τόποι τό τ᾽ ἀπὸ τῶν πόλεων δέξασθαι
καὶ τῶν κωμῶν μέλλον ἐπιρρεῖν πλῆθος. ἐνταῦθα δὲ
λέβητας ἐπέστησε κρεῶν παντοδαπῶν μεγάλους, οὓς
πρὸ ἐνιαυτοῦ καὶ πρὸ τοῦ μέλλειν μεταπεμψάμενος

for living inexpensively. "If you would like to know, O King," he said, "how wealthy kings ought to eat, let the men who used to be my cooks prepare an Egyptian dinner." The order was given and the preparations made, and Ochos enjoyed the meal and said: "You deserve whatever bad end the gods bring you to, Egyptian, since you left dinners like these behind and wanted to feast on something cheaper!" Protagorides informs us about what Egyptian dinners were like in Book I of *On the Games at Daphne* (*FGrH* 853 F 1), saying the following: The third type of dinner is the Egyptian, in which tables are not set beside the guests, and trays are brought around instead.

Among the Celts, according to Phylarchus in Book VI (*FGrH* 81 F 9), many loaves of bread are broken into pieces and placed on the tables in a heap along with chunks of meat from the cauldrons; but no one tastes anything until he sees that the king has touched the food he was served. In Book III the same Phylarchus (*FGrH* 81 F 2) says that Ariamnes the Celt, who was extremely wealthy, announced that he would feast all the Celts for a year, and did this by making the following arrangements. He set stations along the most convenient roads in various parts of the country and installed shelters in them made of poles and willow branches and large enough to hold 400 men or more, so that the places would be sufficiently spacious to accommodate the crowds likely to stream there from the cities and villages. He installed large cauldrons full of meat of every kind in them; he summoned craftsmen from other cities the previous year, in advance of when he intended to

---

13 καὶ τῶν καλάμων τῶν τε οἰσυΐνων ACE

f τεχνίτας ἐξ ἄλλων | πόλεων ἐχαλκεύσατο. θύματα δὲ
καταβάλλεσθαι ταύρων καὶ συῶν καὶ προβάτων τε
καὶ ⟨τῶν⟩ λοιπῶν κτηνῶν ἑκάστης ἡμέρας πολλά,
πίθους τε οἴνου παρεσκευάσθαι καὶ πλῆθος ἀλφίτων
πεφυραμένων. καὶ οὐ μόνον, φησίν, οἱ παραγινόμενοι
τῶν Γαλατῶν ἀπὸ τῶν κωμῶν καὶ τῶν πόλεων ἀπέλαυ-
ον, ἀλλὰ καὶ οἱ παριόντες ξένοι ὑπὸ τῶν ἐφεστηκότων
παίδων οὐκ ἠφίεντο ἕως ἂν μεταλάβωσι τῶν παρασκευασθέντων.

Θρᾳκίων δὲ δείπνων μνημονεύει Ξενοφῶν ἐν ἑβδόμῳ Ἀναβάσεως τὸ παρὰ Σεύθῃ διαγράφων συμπό-
151 σιον ἐν τούτοις· ‖ ἐπειδὴ δὲ εἰσῆλθον ἐπὶ τὸ δεῖπνον
πάντες (τὸ δὲ δεῖπνον ἦν καθημένοις κύκλῳ), ἔπειτα δὲ
τρίποδες εἰσηνέχθησαν πᾶσιν. οὗτοι δὲ ὅσον εἴκοσι
κρεῶν μεστοὶ νενεμημένων καὶ ἄρτοι ζύμητες μεγάλοι
προσπεπερονημένοι ἦσαν πρὸς τοῖς κρέασι. μάλιστα
δ᾽ αἱ τράπεζαι κατὰ τοὺς ξένους αἰεὶ ἐτίθεντο· νόμος
γὰρ ἦν. καὶ πρῶτος τοῦτ᾽ ἐποίει Σεύθης· ἀνελόμενος
τοὺς παρ᾽ αὑτῷ κειμένους ἄρτους διέκλα κατὰ μικρὰ
καὶ διερρίπτει οἷς αὑτῷ ἐδόκει καὶ τὰ κρέα ὡσαύτως,
b ὅσον μόνον γεύσασθαι ἑαυτῷ καταλιπών. | καὶ οἱ
ἄλλοι δὲ κατὰ τὰ αὐτὰ ἐποίουν, καθ᾽ οὓς καὶ αἱ
τράπεζαι ἔκειντο. Ἀρκὰς δέ τις Ἀρύστας ὄνομα, φαγεῖν δεινός, τὸ μὲν διαρριπτεῖν εἴα χαίρειν, λαβὼν δ᾽
εἰς τὴν χεῖρα ὅσον τριχοίνικον ἄρτον καὶ κρέα θέμε-
νος ἐπὶ τὰ γόνατα ἐδείπνει. κέρατα δὲ οἴνου περιέφε-
ρον καὶ πάντες ἐδέχοντο. ὁ δὲ Ἀρύστας ἐπεὶ παρ᾽

do this, and had these forged. Large numbers of bulls, pigs, sheep and goats, and other animals were sacrificed every day; and casks of wine had been prepared and an immense quantity of barley groats mixed up in advance. Nor was it just the Celts, he says, who came there from their villages and cities who benefitted; because the slaves in charge of the meal refused to let any foreigners who passed by get away until they had their share of the food being served.

Xenophon mentions Thracian dinners in Book VII (3.21–32, condensed) of the *Anabasis*, where he describes the drinking party given by Seuthes, as follows: After everyone came in to dinner (the meal was eaten sitting in a circle), tables were brought in for the whole group. There were about 20 of these, covered with portions of meat; and large loaves of leavened bread had been attached to the meat on skewers. The tables were quite consistently placed in front of the foreigners[133], because this was their custom. Seuthes was the first to do the following: he picked up the loaves of bread that were lying next to him and began to break them into little pieces and throw them about to whomever he wanted. He did the same with the meat, leaving himself only enough for a taste; the others who had tables set before them followed his example. But an Arcadian named Arystas, who had an incredible appetite, wanted nothing to do with flinging food around, but grabbed a huge[134] loaf of bread and some meat, set them on his lap, and started eating. They were bringing drinking-horns full of wine around, and everyone was taking them. But when the cupbearer came to Arystas with the

[133] I.e. the Greeks.
[134] Literally "three-*choinix*," i.e. "gallon-sized" (cf. 3.98e n.).

αὐτὸν φέρων τὸ κέρας ὁ οἰνοχόος ἦν, εἶπεν ἰδὼν τὸν
Ξενοφῶντα οὐκ ἔτι δειπνοῦντα· "ἐκείνῳ," ἔφη, "δός· σχο-
λάζει γὰρ ἤδη, ἐγὼ δ' οὔπω." ἐνταῦθα μὲν δὴ γέλως
c ἐγένετο. | ἐπεὶ δὲ προυχώρει ὁ πότος, εἰσῆλθεν ἀνὴρ
Θρᾷξ ἵππον ἔχων λευκὸν καὶ λαβὼν κέρας μεστόν,
"προπίνω σοι, ὦ Σεύθη," ἔφη, "καὶ τὸν ἵππον δωροῦμαι,
ἐφ' οὗ καὶ διώκων ὃν ἂν θέλῃς αἱρήσεις καὶ ἀποχωρῶν
οὐ μὴ δείσῃς τὸν πολέμιον." ἄλλος παῖδα εἰσαγαγὼν
οὕτως ἐδωρήσατο προπίνων καὶ ἄλλος ἱμάτια τῇ γυ-
ναικί, καὶ Τιμασίων προπίνων φιάλην τε ἀργυρᾶν καὶ
ταπίδα ἀξίαν δέκα μνῶν. Γνήσιππος δέ τις Ἀθηναῖος
d ἀναστὰς εἶπεν ὅτι ἀρχαῖος εἴη νόμος κάλλιστος τοὺς |
μὲν ἔχοντας διδόναι τῷ βασιλεῖ τιμῆς ἕνεκα, τοῖς δὲ
μὴ ἔχουσι διδόναι τὸν βασιλέα. Ξενοφῶν δὲ ἀνέστη
θαρσαλέως καὶ δεξάμενος τὸ κέρας εἶπεν· "ἐγώ σοι, ὦ
Σεύθη, δίδωμι ἐμαυτὸν καὶ τοὺς ἐμοὺς τούτους ἑταίρους φίλους εἶναι πιστοὺς καὶ οὐδένα ἄκοντα. καὶ νῦν
πάρεισιν οὐδέν σε προσαιτοῦντες, ἀλλὰ καὶ πονεῖν
ὑπὲρ σοῦ καὶ προκινδυνεύειν βουλόμενοι." καὶ ὁ Σεύ-
θης ἀναστὰς συνέπιε καὶ συγκατεσκεδάσατο μετ' αὐ-
e τοῦ τὸ κέρας. μετὰ δὲ ταῦτα εἰσῆλθον κέρασί τε οἵοις |
σημαίνουσιν αὐλοῦντες καὶ σάλπιγξιν ὠμοβοείαις
ῥυθμούς τε καὶ οἰονεὶ μάγαδιν σαλπίζοντες.

Ποσειδώνιος δὲ ὁ ἀπὸ τῆς στοᾶς ἐν ταῖς Ἱστορίαις,
αἷς συνέθηκεν οὐκ ἀλλοτρίως ἧς προῄρητο φιλοσο-

---

135 *PAA* 279700; otherwise unknown.

horn, Arystas saw that Xenophon was no longer eating and said: "Give it to him! He has time on his hands now, whereas I don't!" This provoked some laughter. As the drinking proceeded, a Thracian came in with a white horse, took a horn full of wine, and said: "I drink to you, Seuthes, and present you with this horse. When you're riding him, you'll catch anyone you want to chase; and if you retreat, you'll have no need to fear your enemy!" Another man brought in a slave and presented him to Seuthes in the same way, drinking his health; a third offered him robes for his wife; and Timasion toasted him and presented him with a silver libation-bowl and a carpet worth ten minas. An Athenian named Gnesippus[135] stood up and said that it was an old and admirable custom for wealthy men to show the king honor by offering him gifts, and for the king in turn to provide presents for the poor. Xenophon got his courage up, stood up, took the drinking horn, and said: "The gift I have to offer you, Seuthes, is that I and my companions here will be your reliable and willing friends. They're not here now with any requests for you; instead, they wish to work hard for you and run risks on your behalf." And Seuthes stood up and joined Xenophon in taking a drink and dumping out the rest of the contents of the horn. After this, men came in playing pipe-music on the horns they use for signals and trumpeting rhythmically with two tones at the same time on trumpets made of the horns of wild oxen.[136]

Posidonius the Stoic in his *Histories* (*FGrH* 87 F *15 = fr. 67 Edelstein–Kidd), which he compiled by recording

---

[136] Literally "as if they were playing a *magadis*," a pipe capable of producing two tones at once; cf. 4.182d.

φίας πολλὰ παρὰ πολλοῖς ἔθιμα καὶ νόμιμα ἀναγράφων, Κελτοί, φησί, τὰς τροφὰς προτίθενται χόρ-
τον ὑποβάλλοντες καὶ ἐπὶ τραπεζῶν ξυλίνων μικρὸν
ἀπὸ τῆς γῆς ἐπηρμένων. ἡ τροφὴ δ᾽ ἐστὶν ἄρτοι μὲν
ὀλίγοι, κρέα δὲ πολλὰ ἐν ὕδατι καὶ ὀπτὰ ἐπ᾽ ἀνθράκων
152 ἢ ὀβελίσκων. ‖ προσφέρονται δὲ ταῦτα καθαρείως
μέν, λεοντωδῶς δέ, ταῖς χερσὶν ἀμφοτέραις αἴροντες
ὅλα μέλη καὶ ἀποδάκνοντες, ἐὰν δὲ ᾖ τι δυσαπόσπα-
στον, μαχαιρίῳ μικρῷ παρατέμνοντες, ὃ[14] ἐν ἰδίᾳ
θήκῃ παράκειται. προσφέρονται δὲ καὶ ἰχθῦς οἵ τε
παρὰ τοὺς ποταμοὺς οἰκοῦντες καὶ παρὰ τὴν ἐντὸς καὶ
τὴν ἔξω θάλασσαν, καὶ τούτους δὲ ὀπτοὺς μετὰ ἁλῶν
καὶ ὄξους καὶ κυμίνου· τοῦτο δὲ καὶ εἰς τὸ ποτὸν
ἐμβάλλουσιν. ἐλαίῳ δ᾽ οὐ χρῶνται διὰ σπάνιν καὶ διὰ
b τὸ ἀσύνηθες ἀηδὲς αὐτοῖς φαίνεται. | ὅταν δὲ πλείονες
συνδειπνῶσι, κάθηνται μὲν ἐν κύκλῳ, μέσος δὲ ὁ
κράτιστος ὡς ἂν κορυφαῖος χοροῦ, διαφέρων τῶν
ἄλλων ἢ κατὰ τὴν πολεμικὴν εὐχέρειαν ἢ κατὰ γένος
ἢ κατὰ πλοῦτον. ὁ δ᾽ ὑποδεχόμενος παρ᾽ αὐτόν, ἐφεξῆς
δ᾽ ἑκατέρωθε κατ᾽ ἀξίαν ἧς ἔχουσιν ὑπεροχῆς. καὶ οἱ
μὲν τοὺς θυρεοὺς ὁπλοφοροῦντες ἐκ τῶν ὀπίσω παρ-
εστᾶσιν, οἱ δὲ δορυφόροι κατὰ τὴν ἀντικρὺ καθήμενοι
κύκλῳ καθάπερ οἱ δεσπόται συνευωχοῦνται. τὸ δὲ
ποτὸν οἱ διακονοῦντες ἐν ἀγγείοις περιφέρουσιν ἐοι-
c κόσι μὲν | ἀμβίκοις, ἢ κεραμέοις ἢ ἀργυροῖς. καὶ γὰρ
τοὺς πίνακας ἐφ᾽ ὧν τὰς τροφὰς προτίθενται τοιούτους

14 ὃ τοῖς κολεοῖς ACE

numerous usages and customs among many peoples that were germane to the philosophy he had adopted, says: The Celts throw hay on the ground and serve their meals on wooden tables barely raised off of it. The food consists of a few loaves of bread and large quantities of meat that is either boiled or roasted on the coals or on spits. They consume the meat in a simple if lion-like way, taking whole joints in both hands and biting it off; if a piece proves difficult to tear away, they cut it off with a small knife that lies beside them in its own sheath. Those who live along the rivers or beside the interior or exterior sea[137] also consume fish, which they eat roasted with salt, vinegar, and cumin. They also add cumin to their wine. They do not use oil, because it is scarce and because their lack of familiarity with it makes the taste seem unpleasant to them. Whenever a group of them has dinner together, they sit in a circle, and whoever is most important sits in the middle, like the leader of a dramatic chorus, whether he is distinguished from the others by his skill in warfare, the family he comes from, or his wealth. The host sits next to him; after that they sit in order on either side according to how prominent they are. Armed men bearing oblong shields stand behind the guests, and their bodyguards sit opposite them in a circle, just like their masters, and eat together. The servants bring the wine around in vessels that resemble spouted cups[138] and are made of either earthenware or silver. The platters on which they serve the food are similar;

[137] The Mediterranean Sea and the Atlantic Ocean, respectively.

[138] See 11.480d, where the word for this vessel appears in a slightly different form.

ἔχουσιν· οἱ δὲ χαλκοῦς, οἱ δὲ κάνεα ξύλινα καὶ
πλεκτά. τὸ δὲ πινόμενόν ἐστι παρὰ μὲν τοῖς πλου-
τοῦσιν οἶνος ἐξ Ἰταλίας καὶ τῆς Μασσαλιητῶν χώρας
παρακομιζόμενος, ἄκρατος δ᾽ οὗτος· ἐνίοτε δὲ ὀλίγον
ὕδωρ παραμίγνυται· παρὰ δὲ τοῖς ὑποδεεστέροις ζύ-
θος πύρινον μετὰ μέλιτος ἐσκευασμένον, παρὰ δὲ τοῖς
πολλοῖς καθ᾽ αὑτό· καλεῖται δὲ κόρμα. ἀπορροφοῦσι
d δὲ ἐκ τοῦ αὐτοῦ ποτηρίου κατὰ | μικρόν, οὐ πλεῖον
κυάθου· πυκνότερον δὲ τοῦτο ποιοῦσι. περιφέρει δὲ ὁ
παῖς ἐπὶ τὰ δεξιὰ καὶ τὰ λαιά· οὕτως διακονοῦνται. καὶ
τοὺς θεοὺς προσκυνοῦσιν ἐπὶ τὰ δεξιὰ στρεφόμενοι.
ἔτι ὁ Ποσειδώνιος διηγούμενος καὶ τὸν Λουερνίου τοῦ
Βιτύιτος πατρὸς πλοῦτον τοῦ ὑπὸ Ῥωμαίων καθαιρε-
θέντος, φησὶ δημαγωγοῦντα αὐτὸν τοὺς ὄχλους ἐν
ἅρματι φέρεσθαι διὰ τῶν πεδίων καὶ σπείρειν χρυσίον καὶ ἀργύριον ταῖς ἀκολουθούσαις τῶν Κελτῶν
μυριάσι φράγμα τε ποιεῖν δωδεκαστάδιον τετράγω-
e νον, ἐν | ᾧ πληροῦν μὲν ληνοὺς πολυτελοῦς πόματος,
παρασκευάζειν δὲ τοσοῦτο βρωμάτων πλῆθος ὥστε
ἐφ᾽ ἡμέρας πλείονας ἐξεῖναι τοῖς βουλομένοις εἰσερ-
χομένοις τῶν παρασκευασθέντων ἀπολαύειν ἀδιαλεί-
πτως διακονουμένοις. ἀφορίσαντος δ᾽ αὐτοῦ προ-
θεσμίαν ποτὲ τῆς θοίνης ἀφυστερήσαντά τινα τῶν
βαρβάρων ποιητὴν ἀφικέσθαι καὶ συναντήσαντα
μετὰ ᾠδῆς ὑμνεῖν αὐτοῦ τὴν ὑπεροχήν, ἑαυτὸν δ᾽

---

139 I.e. *curmi* (attested also at Dsc. 2.110, and in a pair of in-

but others use bronze platters or baskets made of wood or wickerwork. The rich drink wine imported from Italy or Massaliote territory; it is consumed unmixed, although occasionally they put a little water into it. Poorer people drink wheat-beer with honey added, or in most cases without it; they refer to this as *korma*.[139] They sip it a bit at a time from the same vessel, which does not hold more than a fraction of a cup[140]; but they do this repeatedly. The slave carries the cup around from left to right and right to left; this is how they are served. They also turn from right to left when they prostrate themselves before their gods. Posidonius (*FGrH* 87 F 18 = fr. 67 Edelstein–Kidd, continued) again, in his description of the wealth of Louernius the father of Bituis,[141] who was deposed by the Romans, says that when Louernius was trying to gain influence among the common people, he traveled through the plains in a chariot and scattered gold and silver coins to the countless Celts who followed him. He also built an enclosure 12 stades square, filled vats inside it with expensive wine, and prepared so much food that for many days anyone who wanted to could come in and enjoy it, and the food was served constantly. He eventually called an end to the feast; but a barbarian poet arrived late and, when he met him, sang a hymn about his preeminence and lamented

scriptions); probably cognate with Latin *cremor* ("a thick juice produced by boiling grain"). For beer, see 1.16c n.

[140] Literally "a *kuathos*" ("ladleful"), which in Attica was a standard measure = one-sixth of a *kotulē*.   [141] Louernius was king of the Avernians, and the events referred to here took place at the very end of the 120s BCE. Strabo 4.191 (probably also drawing on Posidonius) gives the name in the form Louerius.

ἀποθρηνεῖν ὅτι ὑστέρηκε, τὸν δὲ τερφθέντα θυλάκιον
f   αἰτῆσαι χρυσίου καὶ ῥῖψαι αὐτῷ παρατρέχοντι. | ἀν-
ελόμενον δ' ἐκεῖνον πάλιν ὑμνεῖν λέγοντα διότι τὰ
ἴχνη τῆς γῆς ἐφ' ἧς ἁρματηλατεῖ χρυσὸν καὶ εὐεργ-
εσίας ἀνθρώποις φέρει. ταῦτα μὲν οὖν ἐν τῇ τρίτῃ
καὶ εἰκοστῇ ἱστόρησεν. ἐν δὲ τῇ πέμπτῃ περὶ Πάρθων
διηγούμενός φησιν· ὁ δὲ καλούμενος φίλος τραπέζης
μὲν οὐ κοινωνεῖ, χαμαὶ δ' ὑποκαθήμενος ἐφ' ὑψηλῆς
κλίνης κατακειμένῳ τῷ βασιλεῖ τὸ παραβληθὲν ὑπ'
αὐτοῦ κυνιστὶ σιτεῖται καὶ πολλάκις διὰ τὴν τυχοῦ-
153 σαν αἰτίαν ἀποσπασθεὶς τοῦ χαμαιπετοῦς δείπνου ‖
ῥάβδοις καὶ ἱμᾶσιν ἀστραγαλωτοῖς μαστιγοῦται καὶ
γενόμενος αἱμόφυρτος τὸν τιμωρησάμενον ὡς εὐερ-
γέτην ἐπὶ τὸ ἔδαφος πρηνὴς προσπεσὼν προσκυνεῖ.
ἐν δὲ τῇ ἕκτῃ καὶ δεκάτῃ περὶ Σελεύκου διηγούμενος
τοῦ βασιλέως, ὡς εἰς Μηδίαν ἀνελθὼν καὶ πολεμῶν
Ἀρσάκει ἠχμαλωτίσθη ὑπὸ τοῦ βαρβάρου καὶ ὡς
πολὺν χρόνον παρὰ τῷ Ἀρσάκει διέτριψεν ἀγόμενος
βασιλικῶς, γράφει καὶ ταῦτα· παρὰ Πάρθοις ἐν τοῖς
b   δείπνοις ὁ βασιλεὺς τήν τε κλίνην ἐφ' ἧς | μόνος
κατέκειτο μετεωροτέραν τῶν ἄλλων καὶ κεχωρισμένην
εἶχε καὶ τὴν τράπεζαν μόνῳ καθάπερ ἥρωι πλήρη
βαρβαρικῶν θοιναμάτων παρακειμένην. ἱστορῶν δὲ
καὶ περὶ Ἡρακλέωνος τοῦ Βεροιαίου, ὃς ὑπὸ τοῦ

---

142 To tear the victim's flesh more efficiently.

that he himself had not come in time. Louernius was
pleased and asked for a bag of gold coins, which he threw
to the man as he ran alongside his chariot. The poet picked
it up and sang another hymn, saying that the tracks in
the earth made by Louernius' chariot were bearing gold
and benefactions for mankind. Posidonius recorded these
events in Book XXIII. But in Book V (*FGrH* 87 F 5 = fr. 57
Edelstein–Kidd), in his discussion of the Parthians, he
says: The man referred to as the king's "friend" does not
share his food, but sits on the ground below the king, who
lies on a high couch, and eats whatever is thrown to him,
like a dog. Often for one reason or another he is dragged
away from his dinner on the ground and beaten with rods
or whips to which knucklebones have been attached.[142] Afterwards he bows down with his face to the earth, covered
with blood, and worships the man who punished him as his
benefactor. And in Book XVI (*FGrH* 87 F 12 = fr. 64
Edelstein–Kidd), in his description of how King Seleucus
went inland into Media and made war on Arsaces, was captured by the barbarian, and spent a long time with Arsaces,
and was treated as royalty,[143] he writes the following: At
Parthian dinner parties, the king reclined alone on his
couch, which was higher than the others and separate from
them; a table full of barbarian dishes was set beside him
alone, as if he were a hero. And in his account of Heracleon of Beroea, who after King Antiochus (nicknamed

[143] The Seleucid king in question is Demetrius II, who was
captured by the Parthian king Mithridates I (referred to, like
Demetrius, by the name of his royal house, the Arsacids) in 139
BCE and remained with him as a captive for ten years.

Γρυποῦ καλουμένου Ἀντιόχου τοῦ βασιλέως προ-
αχθεὶς μικροῦ δεῖν τῆς βασιλείας ἐξέβαλε τὸν εὐερ-
γέτην, γράφει ἐν τῇ ⟨τετάρτῃ⟩ καὶ τριακοστῇ τῶν
Ἱστοριῶν τάδε· ἐποιεῖτό τε τῶν στρατιωτῶν τὰς κατα-
κλίσεις ἐπὶ τοῦ ἐδάφους ἐν ὑπαίθρῳ ἀνὰ χιλίους
c δειπνίζων. τὸ ‖ δὲ δεῖπνον ἦν ἄρτος μέγας καὶ κρέας,
τὸ δὲ ποτὸν κεκραμένος οἶνος οἷος δήποτε ὕδατι ψυ-
χρῷ. διηκόνουν δὲ ἄνδρες μαχαιροφόροι καὶ σιωπὴ ἦν
εὔτακτος. ἐν δὲ τῇ δευτέρᾳ, ἐν τῇ Ῥωμαίων, φησίν,
πόλει ὅταν εὐωχῶνται ἐν τῷ τοῦ Ἡρακλέους ἱερῷ,
δειπνίζοντος τοῦ κατὰ καιρὸν θριαμβεύοντος, καὶ ἡ
παρασκευὴ τῆς εὐωχίας Ἡρακλεωτική ἐστι. διοινο-
χοεῖται μὲν γὰρ οἰνόμελι, τὰ δὲ βρώματα ἄρτοι μεγάλοι καὶ καπνιστὰ κρέα ἑφθὰ καὶ τῶν προσφάτως
d καθιερευθέντων ‖ ὀπτὰ δαψιλῆ. παρὰ δὲ Τυρρηνοῖς δὶς
τῆς ἡμέρας τράπεζαι πολυτελεῖς παρασκευάζονται
ἀνθιναί τε στρωμναὶ καὶ ἐκπώματα ἀργυρᾶ παντοδαπά, καὶ δούλων πλῆθος εὐπρεπῶν παρέστηκεν ἐσθή-
σεσι πολυτελέσι κεκοσμημένων. Τίμαιος δ᾽ ἐν τῇ
πρώτῃ τῶν Ἱστοριῶν καὶ τὰς θεραπαίνας φησὶ παρ᾽
αὐτοῖς μέχρι οὗ ἂν αὐξηθῶσι γυμνὰς διακονεῖσθαι.

Μεγασθένης δ᾽ ἐν τῇ δευτέρᾳ τῶν Ἰνδικῶν τοῖς
Ἰνδοῖς φησιν ἐν τῷ δείπνῳ παρατίθεσθαι ἑκάστῳ
e τράπεζαν, ‖ ταύτην δ᾽ εἶναι ὁμοίαν ταῖς ἐγγυθήκαις,
καὶ ἐπιτίθεσθαι ἐπ᾽ αὐτῇ τρυβλίον χρυσοῦν, εἰς ὃ
ἐμβάλλειν αὐτοὺς πρῶτον μὲν τὴν ὄρυζαν ἑφθὴν ὡς
ἄν τις ἑψήσειε χόνδρον, ἔπειτα ὄψα πολλὰ κεχειρουρ-

Grypus)[144] put him in a prominent position, nearly expelled his benefactor from his kingship, he writes the following in Book XXXIV (*FGrH* 87 F *24 = fr. 75 Edelstein–
Kidd): When he gave his troops dinner, he used to have
them lie down on the ground in the open air in groups of
1000. The dinner consisted of a large loaf of bread and
meat; they drank whatever wine was available mixed with
cold water. Men wearing daggers acted as their servants,
and there was an orderly silence. In Book II (*FGrH* 87 F 1
= fr. 53 Edelstein–Kidd) he says: Whenever they hold a
feast in Heracles' temple in Rome and the man celebrating a triumph at the moment serves as host, the preparations for the dinner are themselves Heraclean; for a great
deal of honeyed wine is poured, and the food consists of
large loaves of bread, stewed smoked meat, and substantial
roasted portions of the animals that have just been sacrificed. In Etruria, sumptuous tables are set twice a day,
along with couches spread with brightly colored cloths and
silver drinking vessels of every type; and a crowd of good-
looking slaves dressed in expensive clothing stands nearby.
Timaeus in Book I of his *Histories* (*FGrH* 566 F 1a) says
that their slave-girls work in the nude until they grow
up.[145]

Megasthenes says in Book II of his *History of India*
(*FGrH* 715 F 2) that at an Indian dinner a table resembling a cup-stand is set beside each guest. A gold bowl is
put on top of it, and first they place some rice that has been
boiled in the same way one would boil wheat pudding into
it, and then on top of this many other fine dishes prepared

[144] Antiochus VIII (reigned 125/1–96 BCE).
[145] Cf. 12.517d.

233

γημένα ταῖς Ἰνδικαῖς σκευασίαις. Γερμανοὶ δέ, ὡς
ἱστορεῖ Ποσειδώνιος ἐν τῇ τριακοστῇ, ἄριστον προσφέρονται κρέα μεληδὸν ὠπτημένα καὶ ἐπιπίνουσι
γάλα καὶ τὸν οἶνον ἄκρατον. Καμπανῶν δέ τινες παρὰ
f   τὰ συμπόσια μονομαχοῦσι. | Νικόλαος δ' ὁ Δαμασκη-
νός, εἷς τῶν ἀπὸ τοῦ περιπάτου φιλοσόφων, ἐν τῇ
δεκάτῃ πρὸς ταῖς ἑκατὸν τῶν Ἱστοριῶν Ῥωμαίους
ἱστορεῖ παρὰ τὸ δεῖπνον συμβάλλειν μονομαχίας,
γράφων οὕτως· τὰς τῶν μονομάχων θέας οὐ μόνον ἐν
πανηγύρεσι καὶ θεάτροις ἐποιοῦντο Ῥωμαῖοι, παρὰ
Τυρρηνῶν παραλαβόντες τὸ ἔθος, ἀλλὰ κἀν ταῖς ἑστιάσεσιν. ἐκάλουν γοῦν τινες πολλάκις ἐπὶ δεῖπνον τοὺς
φίλους ἐπί τε ἄλλοις καὶ ὅπως ἂν δύο ἢ τρία ζεύγη
ἴδοιεν μονομάχων, ὅτε καὶ κορεσθέντες δείπνου καὶ
μέθης εἰσεκάλουν τοὺς μονομάχους. καὶ ὁ μὲν ἅμα
154   ἐσφάττετο, αὐτοὶ δ' ἐκρότουν ἐπὶ τούτῳ ἡδόμενοι. ‖
ἤδη δέ τις κἀν ταῖς διαθήκαις γέγραφεν γυναῖκας
εὐπρεπεστάτας μονομαχῆσαι ἃς ἐκέκτητο, ἕτερος δὲ
παῖδας ἀνήβους ἐρωμένους ἑαυτοῦ. ἀλλὰ γὰρ οὐκ
ἠνέσχετο ὁ δῆμος τὴν παρανομίαν ταύτην, ἀλλ' ἄκυ-
ρον τὴν διαθήκην ἐποίησεν. Ἐρατοσθένης δ' ἐν πρώτῳ Ὀλυμπιονικῶν τοὺς Τυρρηνούς φησι πρὸς αὐλὸν
πυκτεύειν.

    Ποσειδώνιος δ' ἐν τρίτῃ καὶ εἰκοστῇ τῶν Ἱστοριῶν,
Κελτοί, φησίν, ἐνίοτε παρὰ τὸ δεῖπνον μονομαχοῦσιν.
b   ἐν γὰρ τοῖς ὅπλοις ἀγερθέντες σκιαμαχοῦσι | καὶ
πρὸς ἀλλήλους ἀκροχειρίζονται, ποτὲ δὲ καὶ μέχρι
τραύματος προΐασιν καὶ ἐκ τούτου ἐρεθισθέντες, ἐὰν

234

according to Indian recipes. The Germans, according to Posidonius in Book XXX (*FGrH* 87 F 2 = fr. 73 Edelstein–Kidd), eat whole joints of roasted meat for lunch, and drink milk and unmixed wine along with it. Some Campanians fight duels at their drinking parties. Nicolaus of Damascus, one of the Peripatetic philosophers, records in Book CX of his *Histories* (*FGrH* 90 F 78) that the Romans stage gladiator fights at dinner, writing as follows: The Romans used to put on gladiatorial displays not just at festivals and in their theaters—they took the custom over from the Etruscans—but also at their feasts. Some of them, at any rate, would frequently invite their friends to dinner with the promise that, among other things, they were going to see two or three pairs of gladiators; after they had enough to eat and drink, they would call the gladiators in. While one of the men was being butchered, they were applauding in delight at what was going on. There was once a man who actually put it in his will that some beautiful women he had purchased were to fight a duel, while another specified that pre-adolescent boys he had used for sex were to do so. But the people did not put up with this depravity and declared the will invalid. Eratosthenes says in Book I of *Olympic Victors* (p. 252 Bernhardy) that the Etruscans box to pipe-music.

Posidonius says in Book XXIII of his *Histories* (*FGrH* 87 F 16 = fr. 68 Edelstein–Kidd): The Celts sometimes fight duels at dinner. For they have their weapons with them when they assemble, and they engage in imaginary battles or pretend to fight one another from a distance. But sometimes they go so far as to wound one another, and this

μὴ ἐπισχῶσιν οἱ παρόντες, καὶ ἕως ἀναιρέσεως ἔρ-
χονται. τὸ δὲ παλαιόν, φησίν, ὅτι παρατεθέντων κω-
λήνων τὸ μηρίον ὁ κράτιστος ἐλάμβανεν· εἰ δέ τις
ἕτερος ἀντιποιήσαιτο, συνίσταντο μονομαχήσοντες
μέχρι θανάτου. ἄλλοι δ᾽ ἐν θεάτρῳ λαβόντες ἀργύριον
ἢ χρυσίον, οἱ δὲ οἴνου κεραμίων ἀριθμόν τινα, καὶ
πιστωσάμενοι τὴν δόσιν καὶ τοῖς ἀναγκαίοις | φίλοις
διαδωρησάμενοι ὕπτιοι ἐκταθέντες ἐπὶ θυρεῶν κεῖνται,
καὶ παραστάς τις ξίφει τὸν λαιμὸν ἀποκόπτει. Εὐφορίων δ᾽ ὁ Χαλκιδεὺς ἐν Ἱστορικοῖς Ὑπομνήμασιν
οὕτω γράφει· παρὰ δὲ τοῖς Ῥωμαίοις προτίθεσθαι
πέντε μνᾶς τοῖς ὑπομένειν βουλομένοις τὴν κεφαλὴν
ἀποκοπῆναι πελέκει, ὥστε τοὺς κληρονόμους κομίσα-
σθαι τὸ ἆθλον· καὶ πολλάκις ἀπογραφομένους πλείους δικαιολογεῖσθαι καθ᾽ ὃ δικαιότατός ἐστιν ἕκαστος
αὐτῶν ἀποτυμπανισθῆναι.

Ἕρμιππος | δ᾽ ἐν πρώτῳ Περὶ Νομοθετῶν τῶν
μονομαχούντων εὑρετὰς ἀποφαίνει Μαντινεῖς Δημώ-
νακτος ἑνὸς τῶν πολιτῶν συμβουλεύσαντος, καὶ ζη-
λωτὰς τούτων γενέσθαι Κυρηναίους. Ἔφορος δ᾽ ἐν
ἕκτῃ Ἱστοριῶν, ἤσκουν, φησί, τὰ πολεμικὰ οἱ Μαντινεῖς καὶ Ἀρκάδες, τήν τε στολὴν τὴν πολεμικὴν καὶ
τὴν ὅπλισιν τὴν ἀρχαίαν ὡς εὑρόντων ἐκείνων ἔτι καὶ
νῦν Μαντινικὴν ἀποκαλοῦσι. πρὸς δὲ τούτοις καὶ
ὁπλομαχίας μαθήσεις ἐν Μαντινείᾳ πρῶτον εὑρέθη-
σαν Δημέου | τὸ τέχνημα καταδείξαντος. ὅτι δὲ ἀρ-
χαῖον ἦν τὸ περὶ τοὺς μονομάχους καὶ Ἀριστοφάνης
εἴρηκεν ἐν Φοινίσσαις οὕτως·

makes them angry; if the bystanders do not restrain them, they do not stop until someone is dead. In the old days, he says, whole joints of meat were served, and whoever was most powerful got the thigh; if someone else claimed it, they fought a duel to the death. Others collected silver or gold coins in the theater, or perhaps a certain number of jars of wine; after they extracted guarantees that their will would be carried out, and divided up what they had got among their relatives, they would lie stretched out on their back on top of their shield, and someone would stand beside them and slit their throat with his sword. Euphorion of Chalcis in his *Historical Notes* (fr. 4, *FHG* iii.72 = fr. 173 van Groningen) writes as follows: In Rome five minas are offered to anyone willing to allow his head to be cut off with an ax, on the condition that his heirs get the prize; often too many people put their names on the list and they argue about which of them is most deserving of execution.

Hermippus declares in Book I of *On Lawgivers* (fr. 83 Wehrli) that gladiators were invented by the Mantineans on the advice of Demonax, who was one of the citizens, and that the Cyreneans imitated them. Ephorus says in Book VI of the *Histories* (*FGrH* 70 F 54): The Mantineans and Arcadians were devoted to the arts of war, and even today people refer to war-gear and the ancient style of armor as "Mantinean," on the ground that they invented them. In addition, lessons in hoplite fighting were first invented in Mantineia, and the art was taught by Demeas. That fighting involving individual combatants (*monomachoi*) was an ancient custom is asserted by Aristophanes in *Phoenician Women* (fr. 570), as follows:

ἐς Οἰδίπου δὲ παῖδε, διπτύχω κόρω,
Ἄρης κατέσκηψ᾽, ἔς τε μονομάχου πάλης
ἀγῶνα νῦν ἑστᾶσιν.

ἔοικεν δὲ πεποιῆσθαι τὸ ὄνομα οὐκ ἐκ τοῦ μάχη, ἀλλ᾽
ἐκ ῥήματος τοῦ μάχεσθαι μᾶλλον συγκεῖσθαι. ὁπότε
γὰρ τὸ μάχη συντιθέμενον τὸ τέλος εἰς -ος τρέπει, ὡς
ἐν τῷ σύμμαχος, πρωτόμαχος, ἐπίμαχος, ἀντίμαχος,

f   < . . . > φιλόμαχον | γένος ἐκ Περσέος

παρὰ Πινδάρῳ, τηνικαῦτα προπαροξύνεται· ὁπότε δὲ
παροξύνεται, τὸ μάχεσθαι ῥῆμα περιέχει, ὡς ἐν τῷ
πυγμάχος, ναυμάχος,

    < . . . > αὐτόν σε πυλαμάχε πρῶτον

παρὰ Στησιχόρῳ, ὁπλομάχος, τειχομάχος, πυργο-
μάχος. ὁ δὲ κωμῳδιοποιὸς Ποσείδιππος ἐν Πορνο-
βοσκῷ φησιν·

155   ὁ μὴ πεπλευκὼς οὐδὲν ἑόρακεν κακόν· ‖
τῶν μονομαχούντων ἐσμὲν ἀθλιώτεροι.

ὅτι δὲ καὶ οἱ ἔνδοξοι καὶ οἱ ἡγεμόνες ἐμονομάχουν καὶ
ἐκ προκλήσεως τοῦτ᾽ ἐποίουν ἐν ἄλλοις εἰρήκαμεν.
Δίυλλος δ᾽ ὁ Ἀθηναῖος ἐν τῇ ἐνάτῃ τῶν Ἱστοριῶν

---

146 Perhaps in the portions of Books 1–3 that survive only in
the Epitome.
147 E.g. in *Iliad* 3, where Paris and Menelaus fight for Helen.

Ares swooped down upon the twin children of
    Oedipus,
the two-fold youths; and they stand ready now
for a contest of single-combat (*monomáchou*) battle.

The word does not appear to have been formed from
machē ("battle"), but to be instead a compound from *machesthai* ("to fight"). For whenever a compound of *machē*
ends in *-os*, as for example *súmmachos* ("ally"), *prōtóma-
chos* ("champion"), *epímachos* ("assailable"), *antímachos*
("adversial"), or

    a war-loving (*philómachos*) race descended from
        Perseus

in Pindar (fr. 164), it has an acute accent on the second-
to-last syllable. But when it has an acute on the next-to-
the-last syllable, it contains the word *machesthai*, as for
example in *pugmáchos* ("fist-fighter, boxer"), *naumáchos*
("fighting at sea"),

    you yourself first, O fighter in the gate (*pulaimáchos*)

in Stesichorus (*PMG* 242), *hoplomáchos* ("fighting in
armor"), *teichomáchos* ("fighting from a wall") and *purgo-
máchos* ("fighting from a tower"). The comic poet Posidippus says in *The Pimp* (fr. 23):

    Anyone who hasn't sailed has never seen trouble;
    we're more wretched than gladiators
        (*monomachoúntōn*).

We have explained elsewhere[146] that prominent individuals and commanders used to fight duels and did so in response to a challenge.[147] Diyllos of Athens says in Book IX

239

ATHENAEUS

φησιν ὡς Κάσανδρος ἐκ Βοιωτίας ἐπανιὼν καὶ θάψας
τὸν βασιλέα καὶ τὴν βασίλισσαν ἐν Αἰγαίαις καὶ μετ᾽
αὐτῶν τὴν Κύνναν τὴν Εὐρυδίκης μητέρα καὶ τοῖς
ἄλλοις τιμήσας οἷς προσήκει καὶ μονομαχίας ἀγῶνα
ἔθηκεν, εἰς ὃν κατέβησαν τέσσαρες τῶν στρατιωτῶν.

b   Δημήτριος δ᾽ ὁ Σκήψιος ἐν τῷ πέμπτῳ καὶ δεκάτῳ |
τοῦ Τρωικοῦ Διακόσμου, παρὰ Ἀντιόχῳ, φησί, τῷ
βασιλεῖ τῷ μεγάλῳ προσαγορευθέντι ἐν τῷ δείπνῳ
πρὸς ὅπλα ὠρχοῦντο οὐ μόνον οἱ βασιλέως φίλοι,
ἀλλὰ καὶ αὐτὸς ὁ βασιλεύς. ἐπεὶ δὲ καὶ εἰς Ἡγησι-
άνακτα τὸν Ἀλεξανδρέα ἀπὸ Τρῳάδος τὸν τὰς Ἱστορίας γράψαντα ἡ τῆς ὀρχήσεως τάξις ἐγένετο, ἀναστὰς εἶπε· "πότερον, ὦ βασιλεῦ, κακῶς ὀρχούμενόν με
θεάσασθαι βούλει ἢ καλῶς ἀπαγγέλλοντός μου ἴδια
ποιήματα θέλεις ἀκροάσασθαι;" κελευσθεὶς οὖν λέγειν

c οὕτως ᾖσε τὸν βασιλέα ὥστ᾽ | ἐράνου τε ἀξιωθῆναι
καὶ τῶν φίλων εἷς γενέσθαι. Δοῦρις δ᾽ ὁ Σάμιος ἐν τῇ
τῶν Ἱστοριῶν ἑβδόμῃ καὶ δεκάτῃ Πολυσπέρχοντά
φησιν, εἰ μεθυσθείη, καίτοι πρεσβύτερον ὄντα ὀρχεῖσθαι, οὐδενὸς Μακεδόνων ὄντα δεύτερον οὔτε κατὰ
τὴν στρατηγίαν οὔτε κατὰ τὴν ἀξίωσιν, καὶ ἐνδυό-

---

148 Philip III Arrhidaeus (Berve i. #781) and Eurydice (or
Adea; Berve i #23), members of the Macedonian royal family who
opposed Polyperchon (see 4.155c, where he is referred to as
Polysperchon, with n.) and Olympias (Alexander the Great's
mother), and allied themselves with Cassander. Philip was murdered on Olympias' orders in 317, and Eurydice was forced to

240

of his *Histories* (*FGrH* 73 F 1) that when Cassander returned from Boeotia after burying the king and queen in
Aegae,[148] and Eurydice's mother Cynna along with them,
he showed them the other appropriate honors and also
held a gladiatorial contest, which four of his soldiers entered.

Demetrius of Scepsis says in Book XV of his *Trojan Catalogue* (fr. 7 Gaede): When King Antiochus the Great[149] at
a dinner party ordered them to do so, it was not just the
king's friends who began to dance bearing arms, but the
king himself. When it was the turn of Hegesianax of Alexandria Troas, the author of the *Histories* (*FGrH* 45 T 3), to
dance, he stood up and said: "King, do you want to watch
me dance poorly, or would you like to listen to me do a
good job of reciting some of my own works?" He was ordered to speak and pleased the king so much that he was
judged worthy of a grant of money and joined Antiochus'
circle. Duris of Samos says in Book XVII of his *Histories*
(*FGrH* 76 F 12) that whenever Polysperchon[150] got drunk,
he would start dancing, even though he was quite an old
man and second to none of the Macedonians in his gen-
eralship or the esteem in which he was held; he used to

commit suicide; after Cassander (Berve i #414) emerged trium-
phant over Olympias and Polyperchon in 316, he had Philip and
Eurydice buried in the Macedonian royal tombs in Aegae in an
attempt to rehabilitate their image. Cynna/Cynane (Alexander's
half-sister, Berve i #456; referred to below) was murdered by
Alcetas in 322 on Perdiccas' orders.

[149] Antiochus III (reigned 222–187 BCE).   [150] One of
Alexander the Great's commanders and successors (Berve i #654);
the correct form of his name appears to be Polyperchon.

241

μενον αὐτὸν κροκωτὸν καὶ ὑποδούμενον Σικυώνια δια-
τελεῖν ὀρχούμενον. Ἀγαθαρχίδης δ᾽ ὁ Κνίδιος ἐν
ὀγδόῃ Ἀσιατικῶν ἱστορεῖ ὡς οἱ ἑστιῶντες Ἀλέξανδρον τὸν Φιλίππου τῶν φίλων τὸ μέλλον παρατεθή-
d σεσθαι τῶν τραγημάτων περιεχρύσουν· | ὅτε δὲ θέλοι-
εν ἀναλίσκειν, περιελόντες τὸν χρυσὸν ἅμα τοῖς
ἄλλοις ἐξέβαλλον, ἵνα τῆς μὲν πολυτελείας οἱ φίλοι
θεαταὶ γίνωνται, οἱ δ᾽ οἰκέται κύριοι. ἐπιλελησμένοι δ᾽
ἦσαν οὗτοι, ὡς καὶ Δοῦρις ἱστορεῖ, ὅτι καὶ Φίλιππος
ὁ τοῦ Ἀλεξάνδρου πατὴρ ποτήριον χρυσοῦν ὁλκὴν
ἄγον πεντήκοντα δραχμὰς κεκτημένος τοῦτο ἐλάμβανε κοιμώμενος ἀεὶ καὶ πρὸς κεφαλὴν αὐτοῦ κατετίθετο.
Σέλευκος δὲ Θρᾳκῶν φησί τινας ἐν τοῖς συμποσίοις
e ἀγχόνην παίζειν βρόχον | ἀρτήσαντας ἔκ τινος
ὕψους[15], πρὸς ὃν κατὰ κάθετον ὑποτίθεσθαι λίθον
εὐπερίτρεπτον τοῖς ἐπιβαίνουσι. διαλαγχάνειν οὖν αὐτοὺς καὶ τὸν λαχόντα ἔχοντα δρεπάνιον ἐπιβαίνειν τῷ
λίθῳ καὶ τὸν τράχηλον εἰς τὸν βρόχον ἐντιθέναι·
παρερχόμενον δὲ ἄλλον ἐγείρειν τὸν λίθον· καὶ ὁ
κρεμάμενος ὑποτρέχοντος τοῦ λίθου, ἐὰν μὴ ταχὺ
φθάσας ἀποτέμῃ τῷ δρεπάνῳ, τέθνηκε, καὶ οἱ ἄλλοι
γελῶσι παιδιὰν ἔχοντες τὸν ἐκείνου θάνατον.
f   Ταῦτ᾽ εἰπεῖν εἶχον, ἄνδρες φίλοι | καὶ συμπόται

---

15 ὕψους στρογγύλον ACE

put on a saffron-colored robe and Sicyonian shoes[151] and
dance and dance. Agatharchides of Cnidus reports in Book
VIII of his *History of Asia* (*FGrH* 86 F 2) that when
the friends of Alexander son of Philip[152] had a feast for
him, they would gild whatever was going to be served as
snacks.[153] When they wanted to eat something, they would
remove the gold and throw it away with everything else;
the result was that their friends got to admire the expense to which they went, but the profit went to the slaves.
These people had forgotten something else, which Duris
(*FGrH* 76 F 37b)[154] records, which is that Alexander's father Philip owned a gold drinking cup that weighed 50
drachmas, which he always took and set beside his head
when he slept. Seleucus (*FGrH* 341 F *4 = fr. 80 Müller)
claims that there are Thracians who play a symposium
game that involves hanging, in which they attach a rope to
something high and place a stone that moves easily when
one stands on it directly beneath it. Then they draw lots;
the man whose lot is drawn gets up on the stone, holding a
small sickle, and puts his neck in the noose. Someone else
comes along and makes the stone move. The stone slips
out from under him, and if the man who is hanging does
not cut the rope quickly enough with his sickle, he is dead,
and the others laugh and regard his death as a great joke.

   This is the information I can offer you, my friends and
far and away the foremost drinking companions of the

---

[151] More often worn by women; cf. Macho 158 (quoted at
8.349e); Herod. 7.57 with Headlam's n.　　[152] Alexander the
Great.　　[153] Here the reference is clearly to nuts or beans,
whose husks were thrown onto the floor for slaves to clean up.

   [154] Cf. 6.231b–c.

τῶν Ἑλλήνων πολὺ πρῶτοι, περὶ ἀρχαίων συμποσίων
ἐπιστάμενος. ἀκριβῶς δ᾽ ὁ σοφὸς Πλάτων ἐν τῷ πρώτῳ Νόμων περὶ συμποσίων διηγεῖται λέγων οὕτως·
καὶ οὔτ᾽ ἂν ἐπ᾽ ἀγρῶν ἴδοις οὔτ᾽ ἐν ἄστεσιν ὅσων
Σπαρτιάταις μέλει συμπόσια οὐδ᾽ ὁπόσα τούτοις ξυν-
156 επόμενα πάσας ἡδονὰς κινεῖ κατὰ δύναμιν. ‖ οὐδ᾽
ἔστιν ὅστις ἂν ἀπαντῶν κωμάζοντί τινι μετὰ μέθης
οὐκ ἂν τὴν μεγίστην δίκην εὐθὺς ἐπιθείη καὶ οὐδ᾽ ἂν
Διονύσια πρόφασιν ἔχοντ᾽ αὐτὸν ῥύσαιτο, ὥσπερ ἐν
ἁμάξαις εἶδον παρ᾽ ὑμῖν ἐγώ, καὶ ἐν Τάραντι δὲ παρὰ
τοῖς ἡμετέροις ἀποίκοις πᾶσαν τὴν πόλιν ἐθεασάμην
περὶ τὰ Διονύσια μεθύουσαν. ἐν Λακεδαίμονι οὐκ ἔστ᾽
οὐδὲν τοιοῦτον.

Καὶ ὁ Κύνουλκος, ἀλλ᾽ ὡς ὤφελον, ἔφη, τὴν Θρᾴκι-
ον ταύτην παίξας παιδιὰν διεφθάρης· ἀνέτεινες γὰρ
b ἡμᾶς ὥσπερ νηστείαν ἄγοντας καὶ περιμένοντας | τὸ
ἀνατέλλον ἄστρον, οὗ φασι μὴ φανέντος οἱ τὴν χρη-
στὴν ταύτην φιλοσοφίαν εὑρόντες νόμιμον εἶναι μηδενὸς γεύεσθαι. ἐγὼ δ᾽ ὁ τάλας κατὰ τὸν κωμῳ-
διοποιὸν Δίφιλον·

κεστρεὺς ἂν εἴην ἕνεκα νηστείας ἄκρας.

---

155 Literally "in the carts"; cf. Alex. fr. 9.5 (quoted at 10.431e).
156 See 4.166e n.

Greeks, from my knowledge of ancient symposia. The wise Plato offers some accurate remarks about drinking parties in Book I of the *Laws* (637a–b), saying the following: And neither in the country nor in the cities the Spartiates control would you see drinking parties or the activities that accompany them and encourage pleasures of all sorts as much as they can. There's not one man of them who wouldn't immediately impose the harshest penalty possible on anyone he caught wandering drunk through the streets, and a festival of Dionysus wouldn't save him, if he offered it as an excuse, as I've seen happen in your country in the wine-market[155]; among our own colonists in Tarentum, I've seen the whole city drunk during Dionysia-time.[156] In Sparta there's nothing like this.

Cynulcus said: How I wish you had played this Thracian game and died! You have made us as tense as people who are fasting and waiting for the rising star, which has to appear, they say, before those who invented this fine philosophy[157] are allowed to taste any food. Miserable me, as the comic poet Diphilus (fr. 53.2)[158] puts it—

I might as well be a mullet as a result of this extended fasting.[159]

[157] The sect in question is unidentified, although earlier commentators took the reference to be to the Jews.

[158] Cf. 7.307f–8a, where the fragment is quoted in a more complete form and assigned to *Lemnian Women*.

[159] The mullet was also known as the "faster" (*nēsteus*), supposedly because no food was ever found in its belly; cf. the texts collected at 7.307c–8b.

ἐπελάθεσθε δὲ καὶ ὑμεῖς τῶν τοῦ ποιητοῦ καλῶν, ὃς ἔφη·

οὐ μὲν γάρ τι χέρειον ἐν ὥρῃ δεῖπνον ἑλέσθαι.

καὶ ὁ καλὸς δ᾽ Ἀριστοφάνης ἐν Κωκάλῳ ἔφη·

c   ἀλλ᾽ ἐστίν, ὦ πάτερ, κομιδῇ μεσημβρία, |
     ἡνίκα γε τοὺς νεωτέρους δειπνεῖν χρεών.

ἐμοί τε πολλῷ ἦν ἄμεινον κατὰ τὸ Παρμενίσκου τῶν Κυνικῶν Συμπόσιον δειπνεῖν ἢ ἐνθάδε πάντα ὥσπερ τοὺς πυρέσσοντας περιφερόμενα ὁρᾶν. γελασάντων δὲ ἡμῶν ἔφη τις· ἀλλ᾽ ὦ λῷστε ἀνδρῶν, μὴ φθονήσῃς ἡμῖν τὸ Παρμενίσκειον ἐκεῖνο διελθεῖν συμπόσιον. καὶ ὃς μετέωρον αὐτὸν παραναστήσας ἔφη· ὄμνυμι δ᾽ ὑμῖν, ἄνδρες, κατὰ τὸν ἡδὺν Ἀντιφάνη, ὃς ἐν τῇ Παρεκδιδομένῃ ἔφη·

    ὄμνυμι δ᾽ ὑμῖν, ἄνδρες, αὐτὸν τὸν θεόν,
d   ἐξ οὗ τὸ μεθύειν πᾶσιν ἡμῖν γίγνεται, |
     ἦ μὴν ἑλέσθαι τοῦτον ἂν ζῆν τὸν βίον
     ἢ τὴν Σελεύκου τοῦ βασιλέως ὑπεροχήν.
     ῥοφεῖν φακῆν ἐσθ᾽ ἡδὺ μὴ δεδοικότα,
     μαλακῶς καθεύδειν ἄθλιον δεδοικότα.

ἀλλ᾽ ὅ γε Παρμενίσκος οὕτως ὑπήρξατο· Παρμενίσκος Μόλπιδι χαίρειν. πλεονάζων ἐν ταῖς προσφωνήσεσι πρὸς σὲ περὶ τῶν ἐπιφανῶν κλήσεων ἀγωνιῶ μή ποτε εἰς πληθώραν ἐμπεσὼν μεμψιμοιρήσῃς. διὸ καὶ μεταδοῦναί σοι βούλομαι τοῦ παρὰ Κέβητι τῷ

You forgot the fine words of the poet, who said (*Od.* 17.176):

For there's no disadvantage in having dinner on time.

The noble Aristophanes as well says in *Cocalus* (fr. 360):

But, aged sir, it's exactly noon,
which is when younger men need to have dinner.

In my opinion, it would be much better to dine in the way described in Parmeniscus' *Cynics' Drinking Party* than to see all the food going around in a circle here, like a man suffering from a fever. We laughed, and someone said: My very good sir, please do not begrudge us a full account of Parmeniscus' drinking party! And he raised himself up high and said: I swear to you, gentlemen, to quote the delightful Antiphanes, who said in *The Girl Who Was Secretly Given in Marriage* (fr. 185):

I swear to you, gentlemen, by the god himself,
who's making it possible for us all to get drunk,
that I would certainly prefer to live like this
than to be as exalted as King Seleucus.
Gulping down lentil soup with no fear is quite
    pleasant,
whereas sleeping in fear in a soft bed is miserable.

But Parmeniscus began as follows: Parmeniscus to Molpis (*FGrH* 590 T 1): Greetings. Since I frequently address you regarding the distinguished invitations I receive, I feel some anxiety lest you criticize me because you have grown full of such matters. I therefore wish to share with you the dinner I had at the house of Cebes of Cyzicus. So

247

ATHENAEUS

e Κυζικηνῷ δείπνου· προπιὼν δ᾽ | ὑσώπου τὴν ὥραν
ἐπάναγε ἐπὶ τὴν ἑστίασιν. Διονυσίων γὰρ ὄντων Ἀθήνησι παρελήφθην πρὸς αὐτόν. κατέλαβον δὲ κυνικοὺς
μὲν ἀνακειμένους ἕξ, ἕνα δὲ κύνουλκον Καρνεῖον τὸν
Μεγαρικόν. τοῦ δείπνου δὲ χρονίζοντος λόγος ἐγένετο
ποῖον τῶν ὑδάτων ἥδιστόν ἐστιν. καὶ τῶν μὲν ἐγκω-
μιαζόντων τὸ ἀπὸ τῆς Λέρνης, ἄλλων δὲ τὸ ἀπὸ τῆς
Πειρήνης, ὁ Καρνεῖος κατὰ Φιλόξενον εἶπε τὸ "κατὰ
χειρῶν". καὶ τῆς τραπέζης παρατεθείσης ἐδειπνοῦμεν

καὶ τὴν μὲν ἐξηντλοῦμεν φακῆν, ἡ δ᾽ ἐπεισέρρει.

f εἶτα | πάλιν φακοὶ προσηνέχθησαν ὄξει βεβρεγμένοι,
καὶ ὁ Διτρέφης δραξάμενος ἔφη·

Ζεῦ, μὴ λάθοι σε τῶνδ᾽ ὃς αἴτιος φακῶν.

καὶ ἄλλος ἐξῆς ἀνεβόησε·

φακός σε δαίμων καὶ φακὴ τύχη λάβοι.

(ἐμοὶ δὲ κατὰ τὸν κωμικὸν Δίφιλον, φησὶν δ᾽ οὗτος ἐν
Πελιάσι·

---

160 A strong-smelling medicinal herb, presumably intended to
settle Molpis' over-full stomach.
161 I.e. a Cynic master; cf. 1.1d with n.
162 At a normal party the topic would have been wine.
163 Peirene was a famous fountain in Corinth (cf. 2.43b), but
Lerna was a marsh in the Argive plain, and the reference to it as a
source of fine drinking water is most likely a joke.
164 Sc. to wash them before dinner is served.
165 An (unmetrical) parody of adesp. tr. fr. 89.

248

drink some hyssop[160] and direct your attention to the feast. It was Dionysia-time in Athens when I was invited to visit him. I found six Cynics lying there and one hound-master[161], Carneius of Megara. Dinner was delayed, and a conversation began about what sort of water tastes best.[162] Some of them praised the water from Lerna, others that from Peirene;[163] but Carneius quoted Philoxenus (*PMG* 836(b).40, quoted at 4.147e) and spoke for the water "poured over one's hands."[164] The table was set beside us and we began eating;

> The moment we drained one bowl of lentil soup,
>   another flowed in.[165]

Then lentils were served again, this time soaked in vinegar; and Diitrephes took a handful and said:

> Zeus, may the man responsible for this pea-vishness
>   not evade your notice![166]

And immediately another guest shouted out:

> Might a pea-vish fate and a pea-vish destiny take
>   you![167]

(My reaction[168] is that of the comic poet Diphilus, who says in *The Daughters of Pelias* (fr. 64):

---

[166] A parody of E. *Med.* 332, with *phakoi* ("lentils," here translated "pea" for the sake of the pun, as again below) substituted for the original *kakoi* ("evils"). [167] A parody of adesp. tr. fr. 92, with forms of *kakos* ("evil") twice replaced by an invented adjective formed from *phakos* ("lentil").

[168] Like the quotation from Theopompus below, an interjection by Cynulcus rather than part of Parmeniscus' letter.

(A.) τὸ δειπνάριον ἀνθηρὸν ἦν, γλαφυρὸν
σφόδρα·

157   φακῆς κατ᾽ ἄνδρα τρύβλιον μεστὸν μέγα. ‖
(B.) πρώτιστον οὐκ ἀνθηρόν. (A.) ἐπὶ ταύτῃ
φέρων
εἰς τὸ μέσον ἐπεχόρευσε σαπέρδης μέγας
ὑπό τι δυσώδης οὗτος † ηρος ἀνθίαν,
ὃν πολλὰ ταῖς κίχλαις ἤδη λέγει. †)

γέλωτος οὖν ἐπιρραγέντος παρῆν ἡ θεατροτορύνη
Μέλισσα καὶ ἡ κυνάμυια Νίκιον· αὗται δ᾽ ἦσαν τῶν
οὐκ ἀσήμων ἑταιρίδων. ἀποβλέψασαι οὖν αὗται εἰς τὰ
παρακείμενα καὶ θαυμάσασαι ἐγέλων. καὶ ἡ Νίκιον
ἔφη·" οὐδεὶς ὑμῶν, ἄνδρες γενειοσυλλεκτάδαι, ἰχθὺν
b   ἐσθίει; ἢ καθάπερ | ὁ πρόγονος ὑμῶν Μελέαγρος ὁ
Γαδαρεὺς ἐν ταῖς Χάρισιν ἐπιγραφομέναις ἔφη τὸν
Ὅμηρον Σύρον ὄντα τὸ γένος κατὰ τὰ πάτρια ἰχθύων
ἀπεχομένους ποιῆσαι τοὺς Ἀχαιοὺς δαψιλείας πολλῆς
οὔσης κατὰ τὸν Ἑλλήσποντον; ἢ μόνον ἀνέγνωτε
συγγραμμάτων αὐτοῦ τὸ περιέχον λεκίθου καὶ φακῆς
σύγκρισιν; ὁρῶ γὰρ πολλὴν παρ᾽ ὑμῖν τῆς φακῆς τὴν
σκευήν· εἰς ἣν ἀποβλέπουσα συμβουλεύσαιμ᾽ ἂν ὑμῖν
c   κατὰ τὸν Σωκρατικὸν Ἀντισθένην ἐξάγειν ἑαυτοὺς |
τοῦ βίου τοιαῦτα σιτουμένους." πρὸς ἣν ὁ Καρνεῖος
ἔφη· "Εὐξίθεος ὁ Πυθαγορικός, ὦ Νίκιον, ὥς φησι

---

169 An unidentified fish; perhaps some sort of mackerel.
170 Another unidentified fish.   171 Or "theater-stirrer";
obscure, but doubtless not a compliment.

(A.) The little dinner was splendid, very elegant:
a big bowl full of lentil soup for each man.
(B.) For starters, that's not very splendid. (A.) After
    this
a big *saperdē*[169] abruptly danced into our midst;
it smelled rather bad † [corrupt] an *anthias*[170]
about which it makes many remarks now to the
    wrasses. †)

There was accordingly a burst of laughter, after which Me-
lissa the theater-ladle[171] and Nicion the dog-fly[172]—they
were well-known courtesans—appeared. They looked at
the food and began to laugh in astonishment. Nicion said:
"Don't any of you, beard-gathering sirs, eat fish? Or is it as
your ancestor Meleager of Gadara[173] said about Homer in
his work entitled *The Graces* (fr. II Riese), that because
he was a Syrian by birth he followed the customs of his
country[174] and represented the Achaeans as avoiding fish,
even though there was an abundant supply of them in the
Hellespont? Or is the only treatise by him you've read the
one that includes a comparison of bean soup and lentil
soup? Because I see that a lot of lentil soup has been prepared for you; and when I see it, my advice to you would
be, to quote Socrates' associate Antisthenes (*SSR* V.A F
133), to export yourselves from life, if this is how you eat."
Carneius said to her: "According to Clearchus the Peripatetic in Book II of the *Lives* (fr. 38 Wehrli), Nicion,
Euxitheus the Pythagorean used to say that all men's souls

---

[172] See 3.126a n.
[173] A Cynic poet and philosopher (*fl.* 100 BCE).
[174] Cf. 8.346c–d.

Κλέαρχος ὁ περιπατητικὸς ἐν δευτέρῳ Βίων, ἔλεγεν
ἐνδεδέσθαι τῷ σώματι καὶ τῷ δεῦρο βίῳ τὰς ἁπάντων
ψυχὰς τιμωρίας χάριν, καὶ διείπασθαι τὸν θεὸν ὡς εἰ
μὴ μενοῦσιν ἐπὶ τούτοις, ἕως ἂν ἑκὼν αὐτοὺς λύσῃ,
πλείοσι καὶ μείζοσιν ἐμπεσοῦνται τότε λύμαις. διὸ
πάντας εὐλαβουμένους τὴν τῶν κυρίων ἀνάτασιν φο-
d   βεῖσθαι τοῦ ζῆν ἑκόντας ἐκβῆναι μόνον τε τὸν ἐν | τῷ
γήρᾳ θάνατον ἀσπασίως προσίεσθαι, πεπεισμένους
τὴν ἀπόλυσιν τῆς ψυχῆς μετὰ τῆς τῶν κυρίων γίγνε-
σθαι γνώμης. τούτοις τοῖς δόγμασιν ἡμεῖς πειθόμεθα."
"ὑμῖν δὲ φθόνος οὐδὲ εἷς ἑλέσθαι ἕν τι τῶν τριῶν ἔχειν
κακῶν. οὐ γὰρ ἐπίστασθε, ὦ ταλαίπωροι, ὅτι αἱ βαρεῖαι αὗται τροφαὶ φράττουσι τὸ ἡγεμονικὸν καὶ οὐκ
ἐῶσι τὴν φρόνησιν ἐν αὑτῇ εἶναι."

Θεόπομπος οὖν ἐν πέμπτῃ Φιλιππικῶν φησι· τὸ
γὰρ ἐσθίειν πολλὰ καὶ κρεοφαγεῖν τοὺς μὲν λογι-
e   σμοὺς | ἐξαιρεῖ καὶ τὰς ψυχὰς ποιεῖται βραδυτέρας,
ὀργῆς δὲ καὶ σκληρότητος καὶ πολλῆς σκαιότητος
ἐμπίπλησι. καὶ ὁ θαυμάσιος δὲ Ξενοφῶν φησιν ὡς
ἡδὺ μὲν μᾶζαν καὶ κάρδαμα φαγεῖν πεινῶντι, ἡδὺ δὲ
ὕδωρ ἀρυσάμενον ἐκ ποταμοῦ διψῶντα πιεῖν. Σωκράτης δὲ καὶ πολλάκις κατελαμβάνετο διαπεριπατῶν
ἑσπέρας βαθείας πρὸ τῆς οἰκίας καὶ πρὸς τοὺς πυνθανομένους "τί τηνικάδε;" ἔλεγεν ὄψον συνάγειν πρὸς τὸ
f   δεῖπνον. |

175 The three most common means of suicide, the noose, the
sword, and a leap from a high place?

are imprisoned in their bodies and their life here in order
to punish them, and that the god has decided that if they do
not abide by his terms until he chooses to release them,
they will be afflicted with more indignities and more serious ones. We should therefore all be on guard against the
inflexibility of our masters and be afraid to leave life volun-
tarily; the only death we should happily accept is the one
that comes with old age, when we can be confident that our
soul is released with the consent of our masters. These are
the doctrines we follow." "But no one begrudges *you* pick-
ing one of the three evils[175] for your own. You don't realize,
you wretches, that these heavy foods impede the authori-
tative part of the soul[176] and prevent your good sense from
being fully conscious."

(Theopompus[177] therefore says in Book V of the *History of Philip* (*FGrH* 115 F 57): Eating large amounts
of food and consuming meat ruins our powers of reason-
ing, makes the soul more sluggish, and fills it with anger,
harshness, and considerable clumsiness. The marvelous
Xenophon (cf. *Cyr.* 1.2.11) as well says that a hungry man
enjoys eating a barley-cake and cress, and a thirsty man is
happy to get water from a river to drink. Socrates (*SSR*
I.C.159) was often caught walking around in front of his
house late at night; when people asked him "Why are you
doing this now?", he said he was collecting some *opson* for
his dinner.[178])

[176] I.e. the reason; a standard term in Stoic philosophy.
[177] Another interjection by Cynulcus.
[178] Sc. by giving himself an appetite.

ATHENAEUS

"Ἡμῖν δὲ αὐτάρκης μερὶς ἦν ἂν παρ' ὑμῶν λάβωμεν, καὶ οὐ χαλεπαίνομεν ὡς ἔλαττον φερόμενοι,
καθάπερ ὁ παρὰ Ἀντικλείδῃ Ἡρακλῆς. φησὶ γὰρ
οὗτος ἐν τῷ δευτέρῳ τῶν Νόστων· μετὰ τὸ συντελέσαι
τοὺς ἄθλους Ἡρακλέα Εὐρυσθέως θυσίαν τινὰ ἐπιτελοῦντος συμπαραληφθέντα καὶ τῶν τοῦ Εὐρυσθέως
υἱῶν τὰς μερίδας ἑκάστῳ παρατιθέντων, τῷ δ' Ἡρα-
158 κλεῖ ταπεινοτέραν ‖ παραθέντων, ὁ Ἡρακλῆς ἀτιμά-
ζεσθαι ὑπολαβὼν ἀπέκτεινε τρεῖς τῶν παίδων Περι-
μήδην, Εὐρύβιον, Εὐρύπυλον. οὐ τοιοῦτοι οὖν τὸν
θυμὸν ἡμεῖς, εἰ καὶ πάντα Ἡρακλέους ζηλωταί."

τραγικὸν γὰρ ἡ φακῆ 'στιν, Ἀρχάγαθος ἔφη
† πο γεγραφέναι †
ῥοφοῦντ' Ὀρέστην τῆς νόσου πεπαυμένον,

φησὶ Σώφιλος ὁ κωμῳδιοποιός. στωικὸν δὲ δόγμα
ἐστὶν ὅτι τε πάντα εὖ ποιήσει ὁ σοφὸς καὶ φακῆν
φρονίμως ἀρτύσει. διὸ καὶ Τίμων ὁ Φλιάσιος ἔφη·

b καὶ τὸ φακῆν ἕψειν ὃς μὴ φρονίμως μεμάθηκεν, ⎪

ὡς οὐκ ἄλλως δυναμένης ἑψηθῆναι φακῆς εἰ μὴ κατὰ
τὴν Ζηνώνειον ὑφήγησιν, ὃς ἔφη·

εἰς δὲ φακῆν ἔμβαλλε δυωδέκατον κοριάννου.

---

179 I.e. (as befits Cynic doctrine) as a model of individual freedom asserting itself against social convention. The quotation from
Parmeniscus apparently ends at this point.

254

"Whatever share we get from you is enough for us, and we don't become angry because we got a smaller portion, as Anticleides' *Heracles* did. For he says in Book II of his *Homecomings* (*FGrH* 140 F 3): After Heracles completed his labors, he was included in the party when Eurytheus made a sacrifice. Eurystheus' sons were serving each person his portion, and they served Heracles one of the poorer ones; he assumed that he was being insulted and and killed three of the boys, Perimedes, Eurybius, and Eurypylus. Our temperament is different, even if we imitate Heracles in every way."[179]

> For lentil soup is fit for tragedy, as Archagathos said
> † [corrupt] to have depicted Orestes gulping it down
>   when he'd recovered from his sickness,

says the comic poet Sophilus (fr. 10). It is Stoic doctrine that the wise man will do everything well, including seasoning his lentil soup in a thoughtful way. This is why Timon of Phlius (*SH* 787) said:

> who hasn't even learned to cook lentil soup in a
>   thoughtful way,

as if lentil soup could not be cooked in any way except in accord with the teachings of Zeno[180] (*SH* 788), who said:

> Throw one-twelfth of a coriander seed into your
>   lentil soup.

[180] Zeno of Citium (335–263 BCE), the original Stoic philosopher and a stern ascetic; see 4.160f n.

καὶ Κράτης δ᾽ ὁ Θηβαῖος ἔλεγεν·

> μὴ πρὸ φακῆς λοπάδ᾽ αὔξων
> εἰς στάσιν ἄμμε βάλῃς,

Χρύσιππός τε ἐν τῷ Περὶ τοῦ Καλοῦ γνώμας τινὰς
ἡμῖν εἰσφέρων φησί·

> μηδέποτ᾽ ἐλαίαν ἔσθι᾽, ἀκαλήφην ἔχων.
> χειμῶνος ὥρᾳ βολβοφακῆν· βαβαί, βαβαί.
> c   βολβοφακῆ δ᾽ οἷον ἀμβροσίη ψύχους |
> κρυόεντος.

ὁ χαρίεις τε Ἀριστοφάνης ἐν Γηρυτάδῃ ἔφη·

> πτισάνην διδάσκεις αὐτὸν ἕψειν ἢ φακῆν;

καὶ ἐν Ἀμφιαράῳ·

> ὅστις φακῆν ἥδιστον ὄψων λοιδορεῖς.

Ἐπίχαρμος δ᾽ ἐν Διονύσοις·

> ⟨ . . . ⟩ χύτρα δὲ φακέας ἥψετο.

Ἀντιφάνης Ὁμοίαις·

> εὖ δ᾽ ἐγίγνεθ᾽ ὅτι φακῆν
> ἕψειν μ᾽ ἐδίδασκε τῶν ἐπιχωρίων τις εἷς.

οἶδα δὲ καὶ τὴν Ὀδυσσέως τοῦ φρονιμωτάτου καὶ
d   συνετωτάτου ἀδελφὴν Φακῆν καλουμένην, ἣν ἄλλοι |

Likewise Crates of Thebes (*SH* 353) said:

> Don't set us to arguing
> by praising a casserole-dish over lentil soup.

And Chrysippus in his *On the Good* (fr. 709a, *SVF* iii.178) offers us some maxims, saying:

> Never eat an olive if you have a nettle.
> Hyacinth-bulb-and-lentil soup in the winter season—
>   damn!, damn!
> Hyacinth-bulb-and-lentil soup is like ambrosia when
>   the weather's freezing cold.

The witty Aristophanes as well said in *Gerytades* (fr. 165):

> Are you teaching him to cook barley gruel or lentil
>   soup?

And in *Amphiaraus* (fr. 23):

> you who speak badly of lentil soup, the most delicious
>   dish.

Epicharmus in *Dionysuses* (fr. 30):

> A pot of lentil soup was cooking.

Antiphanes in *Women Who Looked Like Each Other* (fr. 171):

> It turned out fine, because one
> of the locals taught me how to cook lentil soup.

I am also aware that the sister of the supremely thoughtful and intelligent Odysseus was named *Phakē* ("Lentil Soup"), although some other authorities refer to her as

τινὲς Καλλιστὼ ὀνομάζουσιν, ὡς ἱστορεῖν Μνασέαν
τὸν Πατρέα ἐν τρίτῳ Εὐρωπιακῶν φησιν Λυσίμαχος
ἐν τρίτῳ Νόστων.

Ἐπὶ τούτοις γελάσαντος πάνυ ἔκλαμπρον τοῦ
Πλουτάρχου οὐκ ἐνέγκας ὁ κύων παροραθεῖσαν τὴν
περὶ τῆς φακῆς πολυμάθειαν, ἀλλ᾽ ὑμεῖς γε, ἔφη, οἱ
ἀπὸ τῆς καλῆς Ἀλεξανδρείας, ὦ Πλούταρχε, σύν-
τροφοί ἐστε τῷ φακίνῳ βρώματι καὶ πᾶσα ὑμῶν ἡ
πόλις πλήρης ἐστὶ φακίνων· ὧν καὶ Σώπατρος ὁ
Φάκιος παρῳδὸς μέμνηται ἐν δράματι Βακχίδι λέγων
e   οὕτως· |

οὐκ ἂν δυναίμην εἰσορῶν χαλκήλατον
μέγαν κολοσσὸν φάκινον ἄρτον ἐσθίειν.

ἐπεὶ τί δεῖ βροτοῖσι,

κατὰ τὸν σὸν Εὐριπίδην, γραμματικώτατε,

πλὴν δυοῖν μόνον,
Δήμητρος ἀκτῆς πώματός θ᾽ ὑδρηχόου,
ἅπερ πάρεστι καὶ πέφυχ᾽ ἡμᾶς τρέφειν;
ὧν οὐκ ἀπαρκεῖ πλησμονή· τρυφῇ δέ τοι
ἄλλων ἐδεστῶν μηχανὰς θηρεύομεν.

---

[181] At *Od.* 15.363 her name is Ctimenē.
[182] Sopater was actually from Paphos, but Cynulcus mockingly
substitutes an invented ethnic formed from the word for "lentil."

Callisto,[181] as Mnaseas of Patra records in Book III of the *Account of Europe* (fr. 3 Cappelletto), according to Lysimachus in Book III of the *Homecomings* (*FGrH* 382 F 11).

Plutarch laughed rather loudly at these remarks; and the Cynic, who could not bear someone looking askance at the immense learning he displayed in regard to lentil soup, said: But you people from lovely Alexandria, Plutarch, grew up on food made of lentils, and your whole city is full of dishes that incorporate them. The parodist Sopater of Phacus[182] mentions them in his play *Bacchis* (fr. 1),[183] where he says the following:

> When I gaze at this huge bronze statue,[184]
> it would be impossible for me to eat lentil bread.

> Since what do mortals need,

to quote your Euripides (fr. 892), my most learned grammarian,

> except two items only,
> Demeter's grain and some water poured out for us to
>   drink,
> which we have and whose nature it is to nourish us?
> But being full of them is not enough, and our taste
>   for luxury
> makes us search for ways to produce other sorts of
>   food.

[183] Variant titles for the play are attested at 4.160a; 14.644c, 656f.

[184] Perhaps a reference to the "colossal" statue of Helios in Rhodes.

κἂν ἄλλοις δέ φησιν ὁ σκηνικὸς οὗτος φιλόσοφος·

> ἀρκεῖ μετρία βιοτά μοι
> f σώφρονος τραπέζης, |
> τὸ δ' ἄκαιρον ἅπαν ὑπερβάλ-
> λον τε μὴ προσείμαν.

καὶ ὁ Σωκράτης δ' ἔλεγεν τῶν ἄλλων ἀνθρώπων διαφέρειν καθ' ὅσον οἱ μὲν ζῶσιν ἵν' ἐσθίωσιν, αὐτὸς δ'
ἐσθίει ἵνα ζῇ. Διογένης τε πρὸς τοὺς ἐγκαλοῦντας
αὐτῷ ἀποτριβομένῳ ἔλεγεν· "εἴθ' ἠδυνάμην καὶ τὴν
γαστέρα τρίψας τῆς πείνης καὶ τῆς ἐνδείας παύσα-
σθαι." ὁ δ' Εὐριπίδης ἐν Ἱκέτισι περὶ τοῦ Καπανέως
159 φησίν· ||

> Καπανεὺς ὅδ' ἐστίν· ᾧ βίος μὲν ἦν πολύς,
> ἥκιστα δ' ὄλβῳ γαῦρος ἦν· φρόνημα δὲ
> οὐδέν τι μεῖζον εἶχεν ἢ πένης ἀνήρ,
> ψέγων[16] τραπέζαις εἴ τις[17] ἐξογκοῖτ' ἄγαν,
> τἀρκοῦν ἐπαινῶν[18]· οὐ γὰρ ἐν γαστρὸς βορᾷ
> τὸ χρηστὸν εἶναι, μέτρια δ' ἐξαρκεῖν ἔφη.

οὐκ ἦν γὰρ τοιοῦτος ὁ Καπανεὺς οἷον ὁ καλὸς Χρύ-
σιππος διαγράφει ἐν τῷ Περὶ τῶν Μὴ Δι' Αὑτὰ Αἱρε-
τῶν λέγων ὧδε· ἐπὶ τοσοῦτόν τινες ἐκπίπτουσι πρὸς τὸ
b φιλάργυρον ὥστε ἱστορῆσθαι πρὸς τῇ τελευτῇ | τινα
μὲν καταπιόντα οὐκ ὀλίγους χρυσοῦς ἀποθανεῖν, τὸν
δὲ ἕτερον ῥαψάμενον εἴς τινα χιτῶνα καὶ ἐνδύντα

---

16 μισῶν τραπέζας 6.250f: φεύγων τραπέζαις Eur.

And elsewhere this stage-philosopher says (E. fr. 893):

> The moderate way of life produced by
> a modest table is enough for me;
> I'd prefer to have nothing to do
>   with any inappropriate excess.

Socrates too used to say that he was different from other people to the extent that they lived to eat, whereas he ate to live. And when people found fault with Diogenes for masturbating, he would say: "If only I could rub my belly too, and stop being hungry and in need!" Euripides says about Capaneus in *Suppliant Women* (861–6):

> That's Capaneus. He was rich,
> but was not at all proud of his wealth; he gave
> himself no more airs than a poor man,
> and found fault with anyone who boasted too much
>   about what he ate,
> praising simple sufficiency. The good life, he said,
> doesn't consist in food for the belly; modest fare is
>   enough.

Capaneus was not like the man the noble Chrysippus depicts in his *On Things Not To Be Chosen for Their Own Sake* (x fr. 2, SVF iii.195), where he says the following: Some people descend so far into miserliness that tales are told of how at the end of his life one man swallowed a large number of gold coins and died, while another sewed his money up into a tunic, put it on, and told his family to bury

---

[17] ὅστις Eur.
[18] τἀρκοῦντ᾽ ἀτίζων Eur.

αὐτὸν ἐπισκῆψαι τοῖς οἰκείοις θάψαι οὕτως μήτε καύ-
σαντας μήτε θεραπεύσαντας. οὗτοι γὰρ καὶ οἱ τοιοῦτοι μονονουχὶ βοῶντες ἀποθνήσκουσιν·

> ὦ χρυσέ, δεξίωμα κάλλιστον βροτοῖς,
> ὡς οὔτε μήτηρ ἡδονὰς τοίας ἔχει,
> οὐ παῖδες ἐν δόμοισιν[19], οὐ φίλος πατήρ,
c οἵας σὺ χοὶ σὲ δώμασιν κεκτημένοι. |
> εἰ δ᾽ ἡ Κύπρις τοιοῦτον ὀφθαλμοῖς ὁρᾷ,
> οὐ θαῦμ᾽ ἔρωτας μυρίους αὐτὴν ἔχειν.

τοιαύτη τις ἦν ἡ φιλοχρηματία παρὰ τοῖς τότε· περὶ
ἧς Ἀνάχαρσις πυνθανομένου, "τινὸς πρὸς τί οἱ Ἕλληνες χρῶνται τῷ ἀργυρίῳ;", εἶπεν· "πρὸς τὸ ἀριθμεῖν."
Διογένης δ᾽ ἐν τῇ ἑαυτοῦ Πολιτείᾳ νόμισμα εἶναι
νομοθετεῖ ἀστραγάλους. καλῶς γὰρ καὶ ταῦτα ὁ Εὐριπίδης εἴρηκε·

> μὴ πλοῦτον εἴπῃς· οὐχὶ θαυμάζω θεόν,
> ὃν χὼ κάκιστος ῥᾳδίως ἐκτήσατο.

d Χρύσιππος | δ᾽ ἐν τῇ εἰσαγωγῇ τῇ Εἰς τὴν Περὶ
Ἀγαθῶν καὶ Κακῶν Πραγματείαν νεανίσκον φησί
τινα ἐκ τῆς Ἰωνίας σφόδρα πλούσιον ἐπιδημῆσαι
ταῖς Ἀθήναις πορφυρίδα ἠμφιεσμένον ἔχουσαν χρυσᾶ κράσπεδα. πυνθανομένου δέ τινος αὐτοῦ, "ποδαπός
ἐστιν;", ἀποκρίνασθαι ὅτι "πλούσιος. μήποτε τοῦ
αὐτοῦ μνημονεύει καὶ Ἄλεξις ἐν Θηβαίοις λέγων ὧδε·

---

[19] All other witnesses have ἀνθρώποισιν for Athenaeus' ἐν
δόμοισιν.

him just as he was, without burning his corpse or preparing it for the grave. Because these men and others like them all but shout when they die (E. fr. 324[185]):

> O gold, the item mortals are happiest to receive!
> Neither a mother nor children in one's house
> nor a beloved father provides the sort of pleasure
> that you and those who have you in their houses do.
> If Cypris casts golden glances with her eyes,
>   it's no wonder she's attended by countless gods of
>   love.

This is how greedy people were in those days. Anacharsis (fr. A45B Kindstrand) referred to their greed when someone asked him "What do the Greeks use money for?", and he said: "They count it." Diogenes in his own *Republic* ordains that the currency there is to be knucklebones. Because Euripides (fr. 20[186]) is quite right when he says the following:

> Don't mention wealth! I have no respect for a god
> the worst person can easily get control of.

Chrysippus in the introduction to his treatise *On Good and Bad Things* (xvii fr. 2, *SVF* iii.196) says that an extremely wealthy young man from Ionia visited Athens wearing a purple robe with a gold fringe. When someone asked "Where did that come from?", he said: "From all the money I've got." Perhaps Alexis is referring to the same person when he says the following in *Thebans* (fr. 94):

[185] Identified by Stobaeus as coming from *Danae*.
[186] Identified by Stobaeus as coming from *Aeolus*.

263

ATHENAEUS

(A.) ἐστὶν δὲ ποδαπὸς τὸ γένος οὗτος; (B.)
πλούσιος.
τούτους δὲ πάντες φασὶν εὐγενεστάτους
e ⟨εἶναι⟩, πένητας δ' εὐπάτριδας οὐδεὶς ὁρᾷ. |

Ταῦτ' εἰπὼν ὁ Κύνουλκος, ἐπεὶ μὴ ἐκροταλίσθη,
θυμωθείς, ἀλλ' ἐπειδὴ οὗτοι, ἔφη, ὦ συμποσίαρχε,
ὑπὸ λογοδιαρροίας ἐνοχλούμενοι μὴ πεινῶσιν ἢ τὰ
περὶ τῆς φακῆς λεχθέντα χλευάζουσιν, ἐν νῷ ἔχοντες
τὰ εἰρημένα Φερεκράτει ἐν Κοριαννοῖ·

(A.) φέρε δὴ κατακλινῶ· σὺ δὲ τράπεζαν ἔκφερε
καὶ κύλικα κἀντραγεῖν, ἵν' ἥδιον πίω.
(B.) ἰδοὺ κύλιξ σοι καὶ τράπεζα καὶ φακοί.
f (A.) μή μοι φακούς, μὰ τὸν Δί'· οὐ γὰρ ἥδομαι. |
ἢν γὰρ τράγῃ τις, τοῦ στόματος ὄζει κακόν.

ἐπεὶ οὖν διὰ τοῦτο φυλάττονται οἱ σοφοὶ οὗτοι τοὺς
φακούς, ἀλλ' ἡμῖν γε ποίησον δοθῆναι ἄρτον, μεθ' ὧν
μηδὲν τῶν πολυτελῶν, ἀλλὰ κἂν τὴν πολυθρύλητον
ἔχῃς φακὴν ἢ τὸν καλούμενον κόγχον. γελασάντων δὲ
πάντων καὶ ἐπὶ τῷ κόγχῳ μάλιστα, ἀπαίδευτοί ἐστε,
ἔφη, ἄνδρες δαιτυμόνες, οὐκ ἀναγινώσκοντες βιβλία
160 ‖ ἃ μόνα παιδεύει τούς γε ἐπιθυμοῦντας τῶν καλῶν·
λέγω δὲ τὰ Τίμωνος τοῦ Πυρρωνείου[20]. οὗτος γὰρ

[20] Πυρρωνείου τῶν σίλλων A

---

[187] Presumably referring to Ulpian, although Larensius (the
host of the party) is the next character to speak.

(A.) What sort of family is this fellow from? (B.) He's
rich.
Everyone agrees that they're the noblest people
there are; no one's ever seen a pauper from a
distinguished background.

When Cynulcus got no applause for these remarks, he
became angry and said: It's because these people, symposiarch,[187] are too troubled by their verbal diarrhea to be hungry, or else they don't take seriously what I said about lentil soup, since they are thinking of Pherecrates' words in
Corianno (fr. 73):

(A.) Alright, I'd like to lie down. You—bring out a
table
and a cup and something to eat, so I can enjoy my
drinking more!
(B.) Here's a cup for you and a table and some lentils.
(A.) Don't serve me lentils, by Zeus! I don't like
them;
if you eat them, your breath stinks.

Since, therefore, these wise men are on guard against lentils for this reason, arrange for us to be given bread, and
nothing expensive along with it, but perhaps the famous
lentil soup, if you have any, or what is referred to as
conchos.[188] Everyone laughed, especially at the mention of
conchos, and he said: You are uneducated, my fellow
diners, since you do not read the only books that educate
those who desire what is good. I am referring to those that
contain the works of Pyrrhon's student Timon; for he is the

[188] Cf. Latin *conchis* (a type of bean boiled in its pod).

ἔστιν ὃς καὶ τοῦ κόγχου μνημονεύει ἐν τῷ δευτέρῳ τῶν
Σίλλων λέγων οὕτως·

οὔτε μοι ἡ Τείη μᾶζ' ἀνδάνει οὔτε καρύκκη
ἡ Λυδῶν, λιτῇ δὲ καὶ ἀναλέῃ ἐνὶ κόγχῳ
Ἑλλήνων ἡ πᾶσ' ἀπερισσοτρύφητος ὀιζύς.

διαφόρων γὰρ οὐσῶν καὶ τῶν ἐκ Τέω μαζῶν (ὡς καὶ
τῶν ἐξ Ἐρετρίας, ὡς Σώπατρος ἐν Βακχίδος Μνη-
b στῆρσι· φησὶν γάρ· |

Ἐρέτριαν ὡρμήθημεν εἰς λευκάλφιτον)

καὶ τῶν Λυδίων καρυκκῶν προκρίνει ἀμφοτέρων ὁ
Τίμων τὸν κόγχον.
    Πρὸς ταῦτα ὁ καλὸς ἡμῶν ἑστιάτωρ Λαρήνσιος καὶ
αὐτὸς ἔφη· ὦ ἄνδρες κύνες, οἱ < . . . >[21] κατὰ τὴν
Στράττιδος τοῦ κωμῳδιοποιοῦ Ἰοκάστην, ἥτις ἐν ταῖς
ἐπιγραφομέναις Φοινίσσαις φησίν·

παραινέσαι δὲ σφῶν τι βούλομαι σοφόν·
ὅταν φακῆν ἕψητε, μὴ 'πιχεῖν μύρον.

c καὶ ὁ Σώπατρος δέ, οὗ τὰ νῦν μέμνησαι, ἐν Νεκυίᾳ |
μνημονεύει οὕτως·

Ἴθακος Ὀδυσσεύς, τοὐπὶ τῇ φακῇ μύρον,
πάρεστι· θάρσει, θυμέ.

[21] κυνοσσόοι Schweighäuser

one who mentions *conchos* in Book II of his *Silloi* (*SH* 777), where he says the following:

> I take no pleasure in Tean barley-cake or Lydian
> *karukkē*[189]; in a simple, dry *conchos*
> consists the entire, scarcely luxurious woe of the
>   Greeks.

Because although barley-cakes from Teos are particularly good—as are those from Eretria, according to Sopater in *The Suitors of Bacchis* (fr. 3),[190] for he says:

> We set off to Eretria of the white barley groats—

and Lydian *karukkai* are as well, Timon prefers *conchos* to both of them.

   In response, our noble host Larensius himself said: Cynic sirs, who . . . to quote the comic poet Strattis' *Jocasta*, who says in the play entitled *Phoenician Women* (fr. 47):[191]

> I want to give the two of you some wise advice:
> when you cook lentil soup, don't pour perfume into
>   it![192]

Likewise Sopater, whom you referred to just a moment ago, mentions the saying in *Raising the Dead* (fr. 13), as follows:

> Ithacan Odysseus is here—the perfume's
> in the lentil soup! Cheer up, heart!

[189] See 4.132f n.   [190] For the title, see 4.158d n.
[191] A parody of E. *Ph.* 460–1.   [192] The proverb (see below) is roughly equivalent to "Don't throw good money after bad," as the references to it at Cic. *Att.* 1.19.2 and Gell. *NA* 13.29.5 show: no amount of perfume can make lentil soup smell good.

Κλέαρχος δὲ ὁ ἀπὸ τοῦ περιπάτου ἐν τοῖς Περὶ Παροιμιῶν ὡς παροιμίαν ἀναγράφει τὸ "ἐπὶ τῇ φακῇ μύρον", ἧς μέμνηται καὶ ὁ ἐμὸς προπάτωρ Οὐάρρων ὁ
Μενίππειος ἐπικαλούμενος· καὶ οἱ πολλοὶ τῶν γραμματικῶν τῶν Ῥωμαϊκῶν οὐχ ὁμιλήσαντες πολλοῖς
Ἑλληνικοῖς ποιηταῖς καὶ συγγραφεῦσιν οὐκ ἴσασιν
d ὅθεν εἴληφεν ὁ Οὐάρρων τὸ ἰαμβεῖον. σὺ | δέ μοι
δοκεῖς, ὦ Κύνουλκε (τούτῳ γὰρ χαίρεις τῷ ὀνόματι, οὐ
λέγων ὃ ἐκ γενετῆς σε ἡ μήτηρ κέκληκε), κατὰ τὸν
σὸν Τίμωνα εἶναι

    < . . . > μύκλος καλός²² τε μέγας τε,

οὐκ ἐπιστάμενος ὅτι κόγχος παρὰ προτέρῳ μνήμης
τετύχηκεν Ἐπιχάρμῳ ἐν τῇ Ἑορτᾷ καὶ Νάσοις Ἀντι-
φάνει τε τῷ κωμικῷ, ὃς ὑποκοριστικώτερον αὐτὸν
ὠνόμασεν ἐν Γάμῳ οὕτως·

    κογχίον τε μικρὸν ἀλλᾶντός τε προστετμημένον.

e   Ἑξῆς ἁρπάσας τὸν λόγον ὁ Μάγνος, ὁ μὲν πάντα |
ἄριστος, ἔφη, Λαρήνσιος ὀξέως καὶ καλῶς ἀπήντησε
τῷ γάστριδι κυνὶ περὶ τοῦ κόγχου. ἐγὼ δὲ κατὰ τοὺς
τοῦ Παφίου Σωπάτρου Γαλάτας,

    παρ' οἷς ἔθος ἐστίν, ἡνίκ' ἂν προτέρημά τι
    ἐν τοῖς πολέμοις λάβωσι, θύειν τοῖς θεοῖς

---

²² μύκλος καλός Lloyd-Jones–Parsons, following Kaibel and
Wilamowitz: μοι καλός A

Clearchus of the Peripatetic school in his *On Proverbs* (fr. 83 Wehrli) records "The perfume's in the lentil soup" as a proverb, and my ancestor Varro, nicknamed the Menippean, mentions it too.[193] Most Roman grammarians, being unacquainted with many Greek poets and prose-authors, do not know Varro's source for the line. But you, Cynulcus—for you like this name and never refer to the one your mother has called you by since you were born[194]—seem to me to be, as your Timon (*SH* 789) puts it,

> a big, handsome donkey,

given that you are unaware that *conchos* is mentioned by an earlier author, Epicharmus, in his *Festival* (fr. 38) and *Islands* (fr. 94), as well as by the comic poet Antiphanes, who used a diminutive form of the word in *The Marriage*[195] (fr. 72), as follows:

> and a tiny little *conchos* and a slice cut from the
> sausage.

Immediately after this Magnus seized the floor and said: The universally excellent Larensius has responded acutely and properly to this gluttonous dog regarding *conchos*. I, on the other hand, to quote Sopater of Paphos' *Celts* (fr. 6),

> whose custom is, whenever they enjoy some
> success in their wars, to sacrifice their prisoners

---

[193] The proverb was in fact the title of the work (frr. 549–51 Astbury)   [194] Cf. 1.1d. Cynulcus' real name is eventually revealed to be Theodorus (15.669e, 692b).

[195] Called *The Wedding Feast* at 3.95a.

ATHENAEUS

τοὺς αἰχμαλώτους, ⟨τοὺς⟩ Γαλάτας μιμούμενος
κἀγὼ κατακαύσειν ηὐξάμην τοῖς δαίμοσι
διαλεκτικοὺς τρεῖς τῶν παρεγγεγραμμένων.
f καὶ μὴν φιλοσοφεῖν φιλολογεῖν τ᾽ ἀκηκοὼς |
ὑμᾶς ἐπιμελῶς καρτερεῖν θ᾽ αἱρουμένους
τὴν πεῖραν ὑγιῆ λήψομαι τῶν δογμάτων,
† προσθ τον † καπνίζων· εἶτ᾽ ἐὰν ὀπτωμένων
ἴδω τιν᾽ ὑμῶν συσπάσαντα τὸ σκέλος,
Ζηνωνικῷ πραθήσεθ᾽ οὗτος κυρίῳ
ἐπ᾽ ἐξαγωγῇ, τὴν φρόνησιν ἀγνοῶν.

μετὰ παρρησίας γὰρ ἐρῶ πρὸς αὐτούς· εἰ αὐτάρκειαν
161 ἀσπάζῃ, φιλόσοφε, τί οὐ τοὺς Πυθαγορικοὺς ‖ ἐκείνους ζηλοῖς, περὶ ὧν φησιν Ἀντιφάνης μὲν ἐν Μνή-
μασι τάδε·

τῶν Πυθαγορικῶν δ᾽ ἔτυχον ἄθλιοί τινες
ἐν τῇ χαράδρᾳ τρώγοντες ἅλιμα καὶ κακὰ
τοιαῦτα συλλέγοντες ⟨ἐν τῷ κωρύκῳ⟩.

κἂν τῷ κυρίως Κωρύκῳ δ᾽ ἐπιγραφομένῳ φησί·

πρῶτον μὲν ὥσπερ πυθαγορίζων ἐσθίει
ἔμψυχον οὐδέν, τῆς δὲ πλείστης τοὐβολοῦ
b μάζης μελαγχρῆ μερίδα λαμβάνων λέπει. |

Ἄλεξις δ᾽ ἐν Ταραντίνοις·

---

196 The disciples of Zeno (for whom, see 4.158b n.) allegedly
subsisted on little more than bread and water; cf. D.L. 7.27, quoting Philem. fr. 88 and Posidipp. fr. 16.

270

to the gods. In imitation of the Celts,
I for my part vowed to immolate for the gods
three fake philosophers.
I've certainly heard the group of you earnestly opting
to philosophize, philologize, and practice endurance;
so I'm going to test the health of your doctrines
[corrupt] by smoking. Then, while you're roasting,
if I see that one of you drew his leg back,
he'll be sold to a Zenonian master[196]
for export, since he's ignorant of true thought.

For I am going to speak freely to them: If you are eager for
mere sufficiency[197], philosopher, why do you not imitate
the well-known disciples of Pythagoras, about whom Antiphanes says the following in *Monuments* (fr. 158):

Some miserable Pythagoreans happened
to be eating sea orach in the ravine and collecting
nasty foods of that sort in their leather bags.

And in the play properly entitled *The Leather Bag* (fr. 133),
he says:

First of all, he acts like a Pythagorean and eats
nothing that's alive, but buys a black piece of
the biggest barley-cake he can get for an obol and
    gnaws on it.

Alexis in *Men from Tarentum* (fr. 223, encompassing both
quotations):

[197] Cf. 4.157f (where Cynulcus is, however, only quoting one
of Parmeniscus' characters), 164a.

271

(A.) οἱ πυθαγορίζοντες γάρ, ὡς ἀκούομεν,
οὔτ᾽ ὄψον ἐσθίουσιν οὔτ᾽ ἄλλ᾽ οὐδὲ ἓν
ἔμψυχον, οἶνόν τ᾽ οὐχὶ πίνουσιν μόνοι.
(Β.) Ἐπιχαρίδης μέντοι κύνας κατεσθίει,
τῶν Πυθαγορείων εἷς. (Α.) ἀποκτείνας γέ που·
οὐκέτι γάρ ἐστ᾽ ἔμψυχον.

προελθών τέ φησι·

        (Α.) πυθαγορισμοὶ καὶ λόγοι
λεπτοὶ διεσμιλευμέναι τε φροντίδες
c   τρέφουσ᾽ ἐκείνους, τὰ δὲ καθ᾽ ἡμέραν τάδε· |
ἄρτος καθαρὸς εἷς ἑκατέρῳ, ποτήριον
ὕδατος· τοσαῦτα ταῦτα. (Β.) δεσμωτηρίου
λέγεις δίαιταν. πάντες οὕτως οἱ σοφοὶ
διάγουσι καὶ τοιαῦτα κακοπαθοῦσιν; (Α.) οὔ·
τρυφῶσιν οὗτοι πρὸς ἑτέρους. ἆρ᾽ οἶσθ᾽ ὅτι
Μελανιππίδης ἑταῖρός ἐστι καὶ Φάων
καὶ Φυρόμαχος καὶ Φᾶνος, οἳ δι᾽ ἡμέρας
δειπνοῦσι πέμπτης ἀλφίτων κοτύλην μίαν;

καὶ ἐν Πυθαγοριζούσῃ·

---

198 *PAA* 399660. This is probably the same man as the one
who, according to the comic poet Alexis (fr. 248, quoted at
4.165e), ran through his inheritance in five days, in which case the
point must be that he eats dogs because he now has no money to
buy anything else. That he was actually a Pythagorean seems unlikely.   199 Phyromachus is probably the gluttonous parasite
mentioned by various authors preserved at 6.245e; 8.343b;
10.414d–e. Nothing else is known of Melanippides (*PAA* 638480),

BOOK IV

(A.) Because the Pythagoreans, according to what we
    hear,
don't eat fish or anything else that's
alive; and they're the only people who don't drink
    wine.
(B.) But Epicharides[198] eats dogs,
even though he's one of the Pythagoreans. (A.) After
    he kills them, I imagine;
then it's not alive anymore.

And further on he says:

            (A.) Pythagorean terms and over-subtle
arguments and finely-chiselled thoughts
provide their nourishment, and on a daily basis they
    have the following:
a single loaf of high-quality bread for both of them
    and a cup
of water. That's it. (B.) You're talking about
a prison diet! Do all these wise men live
like this and endure such misery? (A.) No;
these people have a luxurious existence compared
    with others. Don't you realize that
Melanippides is a disciple, and Phaon
and Phyromachus and Phanus?[199] And that once
    every four days
they get a single cup of barley groats for dinner?

Also in *The Female Pythagorean* (Alex. fr. 201, encompassing both quotations):

Phaon, or Phanus; but most likely none of the men referred to in
the fragment were actually Pythagoreans.

273

d   (Α.) ἡ δ᾽ ἑστίασις ἰσχάδες καὶ στέμφυλα |
    καὶ τυρὸς ἔσται· ταῦτα γὰρ θύειν νόμος
    τοῖς Πυθαγορείοις. (Β.) νὴ Δί᾽, ἱερεῖον μὲν οὖν
    ὁποῖον ἂν κάλλιστον, ὦ βέλτιστ᾽, ἔχῃ.

καὶ μετ᾽ ὀλίγα·

    ἔδει θ᾽ ὑπομεῖναι μικροσιτίαν, ῥύπον,
    ῥῖγος, σιωπήν, στυγνότητ᾽, ἀλουσίαν.

τούτων δ᾽ ὑμεῖς, ὦ φιλόσοφοι, οὐδὲν ἀσκεῖτε, ἀλλὰ καὶ
τὸ πάντων χαλεπώτατον λαλεῖτε περὶ ὧν οὐκ οἴδατε
καὶ ὡς κοσμίως ἐσθίοντες ποιεῖτε τὴν ἔνθεσιν κατὰ
e   τὸν ἥδιστον Ἀντιφάνη· οὗτος γὰρ ἐν | Δραπεταγωγῷ
λέγει·

        κοσμίως ποιῶν τὴν ἔνθεσιν
    μικρὰν μὲν ἐκ τοὔμπροσθε, μεστὴν δ᾽ ἔνδοθεν
    τὴν χεῖρα, καθάπερ αἱ γυναῖκες, κατέφαγεν
    πάμπολλα καὶ ταχύτατα,

ἐξὸν κατὰ τὸν αὐτὸν τοῦτον ποιητὴν ἐν Βομβυλιῷ
λέγοντα δραχμῆς ὠνήσασθαι τὰς προσφόρους ὑμῖν
τροφάς,

                σκόροδα, τυρόν, κρόμμυα,
κάππαριν < . . . > πάντα ταῦτ᾽ ἐστὶν δραχμῆς.

Ἀριστοφῶν δ᾽ ἐν Πυθαγοριστῇ·

f   πρὸς τῶν θεῶν, οἰόμεθα τοὺς πάλαι ποτέ, |
    τοὺς Πυθαγοριστὰς γινομένους ὄντως ῥυπᾶν

(A.) You'll be dining on dried figs, olive pomace,
and cheese; this is what the Pythagoreans
customarily sacrifice. (B.) By Zeus, the meal features
    the
finest sacrificial offering there is, my very good sir!

And after a bit:

We had to endure limited food, dirt,
cold, silence, sullenness, and no baths.

But you, my philosophers, practice none of this; and what
is worst of all, you chatter about topics you are ignorant of,
and when you eat, you put the food in your mouths in a decent way, to quote the very entertaining Antiphanes, who
says in *The Slave-Catcher* (fr. 87):

By making what he put in his mouth look decently
small from the front, while having the interior of his
    hand
full, like women do, he gobbled down
a lot of food very rapidly.

But, as this same poet says in *The Bumblebee* (fr. 63),
you could have purchased the food that suits you for a
drachma:

garlic, cheese, onions,
pepper . . . all this costs a drachma.

Aristophon in *The Pythagorean* (fr. 9):

Do we, by the gods, think that the ancient
    Pythagoreans,
who really were Pythagoreans, were dirty

ἑκόντας ἢ φορεῖν τρίβωνας ἡδέως·
οὐκ ἔστι τούτων οὐδέν, ὡς ἐμοὶ δοκεῖ·
ἀλλ' ἐξ ἀνάγκης, οὐκ ἔχοντες οὐδὲ ἕν,
τῆς εὐτελείας πρόφασιν εὑρόντες καλὴν
ὅρους ἔπηξαν τοῖς πένησι χρησίμους.
ἐπεὶ παράθες αὐτοῖσιν ἰχθῦς ἢ κρέας,
κἂν μὴ κατεσθίωσι καὶ τοὺς δακτύλους,
162   ἐθέλω κρέμασθαι δεκάκις. ‖

οὐκ ἄκαιρον δ' ἐστὶν μνημονεῦσαι καὶ τοῦ εἰς ὑμᾶς
ποιηθέντος ἐπιγράμματος, ὅπερ παρέθετο ὁ Δελφὸς
Ἡγήσανδρος ἐν ἕκτῳ Ὑπομνημάτων·

ὀφρυανασπασίδαι, ῥινεγκαταπηξιγένειοι,
    σακκογενειοτρόφοι καὶ λοπαδαρπαγίδαι,
εἱματανωπερίβαλλοι, ἀνηλιποκαιβλεπέλαιοι,
    νυκτιλαθραιοφάγοι, νυκτιπαταιπλάγιοι,
b   μειρακιεξαπάται ⟨καὶ⟩ συλλαβοπευσιλαληταί, |
    δοξοματαιόσοφοι, ζηταρετησιάδαι.

Ἀρχέστρατός τε ὁ Γελῷος ἐν τῇ Γαστρολογίᾳ—ἣν
μόνην ὑμεῖς ῥαψῳδίαν οἱ σοφοὶ ἀσπάζεσθε, μόνον
τοῦτο πυθαγορίζοντες τὸ σιωπᾶν, δι' ἀσθένειαν λόγων
τοῦτο ποιοῦντες, ἔτι τε τὴν Σφοδρίου τοῦ κυνικοῦ
Τέχνην Ἐρωτικὴν καὶ τὰς Πρωταγορίδου Ἀκροάσεις
Ἐρωτικὰς Περσαίου τε τοῦ καλοῦ φιλοσόφου Συμ-

---

200 A mark of a haughty contempt for others; see 2.35d n.
201 The quotation is finally offered at 4.163c–d.

because they wanted to be, or enjoyed wearing rough
    robes?
None of this is true, in my opinion.
Instead, they didn't have anything, so they were
    forced to
find a good excuse for their shabbiness
and impose standards that worked for the poor.
But serve them some fish or meat,
    and if they don't consume their fingers along with it,
I'm willing to be hanged ten times.

This is not a bad time to mention as well the epigram
(anon. *FGE* 1752–7) directed against you that Hegesander
of Delphi quoted in Book VI of his *Commentaries* (fr. 2,
FHG iv.413):

Sons-of-eyebrow-raisers,[200] noses-stuck-into-beards,
    coarse-beard-growers and sons-of-casserole-dish-
        snatchers,
garments-about-their-face-wrappers, barefoot-and-
    with-a-lamp-oil-look,
    nighttime-secret-eaters, nighttime-sidestreet-
        trodders,
boy-deceivers and syllable-question-chatterers,
    foolish-belief-philosophers, sons-of-virtue-seekers.

Archestratus of Gela in his *Gastrology*[201]—this is the only
epic poem you clever people appreciate, while the only Pythagorean rule you honor is to keep quiet, which you do
because you have nothing to say; you also appreciate the
Erotic Technique of Sphodrius the Cynic, the *Erotic Lectures* of Protagorides (*FGrH* 853 T 2), and the *Drinking-
Party Dialogues* of the noble philosopher Persaeus (*FGrH*

ATHENAEUS

ποτικοὺς Διαλόγους συντεθέντας ἐκ τῶν Στίλπωνος
καὶ Ζήνωνος Ἀπομνημονευμάτων, ἐν οἷς ζητεῖ, ὅπως
c ἂν μὴ κατακοιμηθῶσιν | οἱ συμπόται, πῶς²³ ταῖς
ἐπιχύσεσι χρηστέον πηνίκα τε εἰσακτέον τοὺς ὡραί-
ους καὶ τὰς ὡραίας εἰς τὸ συμπόσιον καὶ πότε αὐτοὺς
προσδεκτέον ὡραϊζομένους καὶ πότε παραπεμπτέον
ὡς ὑπερορῶντας, καὶ περὶ προσοψημάτων καὶ περὶ
ἄρτων καὶ περὶ τῶν ἄλλων ὅσα τε περιεργότερον περὶ
φιλημάτων εἴρηκεν ὁ Σωφρονίσκου φιλόσοφος, ὃς
περὶ ταῦτα τὴν διάνοιαν ἀεὶ στρέφων πιστευθείς, ὥς
φησιν Ἕρμιππος, ὑπ' Ἀντιγόνου τὸν Ἀκροκόρινθον
d κωθωνιζόμενος ἐξέπεσεν | καὶ αὐτῆς τῆς Κορίνθου,
καταστρατηγηθεὶς ὑπὸ τοῦ Σικυωνίου Ἀράτου, ὁ πρότερον ἐν τοῖς Διαλόγοις Πρὸς Ζήνωνα διαμιλλώμενος
ὡς ὁ σοφὸς πάντως ἂν εἴη καὶ στρατηγὸς ἀγαθός,
μόνον τοῦτο διὰ τῶν ἔργων διαβεβαιωσάμενος ὁ καλὸς τοῦ Ζήνωνος οἰκετιεύς. χαριέντως γὰρ ἔφη Βίων ὁ
Βορυσθενίτης θεασάμενος αὐτοῦ χαλκῆν εἰκόνα, ἐφ'
ἧς ἐπεγέγραπτο "Περσαῖον Ζήνωνος Κιτιᾶ," πεπλανῆ-
e σθαι²⁴ τὸν ἐπιγράψαντα· δεῖν γὰρ οὕτως | ἔχειν, "Περ-
σαῖον Ζήνωνος οἰκετιᾶ." ἦν γὰρ ὄντως οἰκέτης γεγο-

²³ καὶ πῶς ACE   ²⁴ πεπλανῆσθαι εἶπε A

²⁰² Stilpon of Megara (late 4th/early 3rd century BCE) was the
head of the Megarian school and one of the teachers of Zeno of
Citium (for whom, see 4.158b n.; 5.186c–d). Persaeus was his
slave and eventually his student; see below.
²⁰³ Socrates.

278

584 F 6 = fr. 452, *SVF* i.101), which were compiled from the *Memoirs* of Stilpon and Zeno,[202] in which he tries to keep the guests at the symposium from falling asleep by asking how toasts should be made, and at what point good-looking young men and women should be introduced into the party, and when one ought to put up with their acting affectedly and when they ought to be kicked out for ignoring others, as well as questions about the items eaten along with the meal, and bread, and other matters, including whatever rather elaborate remarks Sophroniscus' son the philosopher[203] made about kisses (cf. X. *Mem.* 2.6.32–3). Persaeus was constantly turning his attention to subjects of this sort; and when, according to Hermippus (fr. 91 Wehrli), he was entrusted with Acrocorinth by Antigonus, he got drunk and was expelled from Corinth itself when Aratus of Sicyon out-generalled him[204]—although before this he maintained in his *Dialogues Addressed to Zeno* that the wise man would necessarily be a good general as well, which is the only point the actions of Zeno's noble slave established![205] Because when Bion of Borysthenes (fr. 73 Kindstrand) saw a bronze statue of him on which the words "Persaeus (the student) of Zeno of Citium" (*Zēnōnos Kitia*) had been inscribed, he wittily remarked that the stone-cutter had made a mistake, for it should have been as follows: "Persaeus the slave of Zeno" (*Zēnōnos oiketia*). Be-

---

[204] The events described took place in 244–243 BCE, and the Antigonus in question is Antigonus Gonatas (reigned *c.*277/6–239), whose son Persaeus had tutored. After he lost Acrocorinth, Persaeus committed suicide.   [205] If the wise man will necessarily be a good general, then the fool will presumably be a bad one—as Persaeus proved by losing Acrocorinth.

ATHENAEUS

νὼς τοῦ Ζήνωνος, ὡς Νικίας ὁ Νικαεὺς ἱστορεῖ ἐν τῇ
Περὶ τῶν Φιλοσόφων Ἱστορίᾳ καὶ Σωτίων ὁ Ἀλεξανδρεὺς ἐν ταῖς Διαδοχαῖς. δύο δὲ συγγράμμασι τοῦ
Περσαίου ἀπηντήκαμεν τῆς σοφῆς ταύτης πραγματείας τοιοῦτον ἔχουσι τὸ ἐπίγραμμα Συμποτικῶν Δια-
λόγων. Κτησίβιος δ᾽ ὁ Χαλκιδεὺς ὁ Μενεδήμου γνώριμος, ὥς φησιν Ἀντίγονος ὁ Καρύστιος ἐν τοῖς Βίοις,
f ἐρωτηθεὶς | ὑπό τινος τί περιγέγονεν ἐκ φιλοσοφίας
αὐτῷ, ἔφη "ἀσυμβόλῳ δειπνεῖν." διὸ καὶ ὁ Τίμων που
πρὸς αὐτὸν ἔφη·

    δειπνομανές, νεβροῦ ὄμματ᾽ ἔχων, κραδίην δ᾽
        ἀκύλιστον.

ἦν δ᾽ εὔστοχος ὁ Κτησίβιος καὶ χαρίεις περὶ τὸ
163 γελοῖον· διὸ καὶ πάντες αὐτὸν ἐπὶ τὰ συμπόσια ||
παρεκάλουν· οὐχ ὥσπερ σύ, κυνικέ, ὁ μηδέποτε ταῖς
Χάρισιν, ἀλλ᾽ οὐδὲ ταῖς Μούσαις θύσας. φυγοῦσα σε
καὶ τοὺς σοὶ παραπλησίους ἡ Ἀρετὴ Ἡδονῇ παρα-
κάθηται, ὥς φησι Μνασάλκης ὁ Σικυώνιος ἐν Ἐπι-
γράμμασιν·

    ἅδ᾽ ἐγὼ ἁ τλάμων Ἀρετὰ παρὰ τῇδε κάθημαι
        Ἁδονῇ αἰσχίστως κειραμένα πλοκάμους,
b   θυμὸν ἄχει μεγάλῳ βεβολημένη εἴπερ ἅπασιν |
        ἁ κακόφρων Τέρψις κρεῖσσον ἐμοῦ κέκριται.

Βάτων δ᾽ ὁ κωμικὸς ἐν Ἀνδροφόνῳ φησί·

    τῶν φιλοσόφων τοὺς σώφρονας ἐνταυθοῖ καλῶ,

280

cause he was in fact Zeno's slave, according to Nicias of
Nicaea in his *Inquiry Concerning the Philosophers* and
Sotion of Alexandria in his *Successions* (fr. 21 Wehrli). I
have come across two books of this clever treatise by
Persaeus, which bear the title *Symposium Dialogues*. According to Antigonus of Carystus in his *Lives* (p. 102
Wilamowitz), when someone asked Menedemus' acquaintance Ctesibius of Chalcis what good he had got out of
philosophy, he said (*SSR* III.H.1): "I didn't pay for my dinners." This is why Timon (*SH* 790) said about him somewhere:

> dinner-crazed, with a fawn's eyes and a firm heart.[206]

Ctesibius always knew the right remarks to make and was
amusingly witty, which is why everyone used to invite him
to their drinking parties. Not like you, Cynic, who never
made a sacrifice to the Graces, or to the Muses either! Virtue therefore ran away from you and those like you, and is
sitting next to Pleasure, as Mnasalces of Sicyon says in the
Epigrams (*HE* 2667–70):

> Here I, wretched Virtue, sit, beside Pleasure
>   here, with my long hair shamefully cropped,[207]
> stricken with tremendous grief in my heart, if in fact
>   everyone
> prefers heedless Enjoyment to me.

The comic poet Baton says in *The Murderer* (fr. 2):

---

[206] A parody of *Il.* 1.225.
[207] As if she were an aristocratic woman abruptly reduced to
being another woman's slave.

τοὺς ἀγαθὸν αὐτοῖς οὐ διδόντας οὐδὲ ἕν,
τοὺς τὸν φρόνιμον ζητοῦντας ἐν τοῖς περιπάτοις
καὶ ταῖς διατριβαῖς ὥσπερ ἀποδεδρακότα.
ἄνθρωπ᾽ ἀλάστωρ, διὰ τί συμβολὰς ἔχων
c   νήφεις; τί τηλικοῦτον ἀδικεῖς τοὺς θεούς; |
τί τἀργύριον, ἄνθρωπε, τιμιώτερον
† σαυτοῦ τέθεικας ἢ πέφυκε τῇ φύσει;
ἀλυσιτελὴς εἶ τῇ πόλει πίνων ὕδωρ·
τὸν γὰρ γεωργὸν καὶ τὸν ἔμπορον κακοῖς.
ἐγὼ δὲ τὰς προσόδους μεθύων καλὰς ποῶ.
ἔπειθ᾽ ἕωθεν περιάγεις τὴν λήκυθον
καταμανθάνων τοὔλαιον, ὥστε περιφέρειν
ὡρολόγιον δόξει τις, οὐχὶ λήκυθον.

Ἀρχέστρατος δέ, ὦ Κύνουλκε, ὃν ἀντὶ τοῦ Ὁμήρου
προσκυνεῖς διὰ τὴν γαστέρα,

d   ἧς οὐ λαμυρώτερον | οὐδέν,

ὁ Τίμων σου, περὶ τοῦ κυνὸς τοῦ θαλαττίου ἱστορῶν
γράφει καὶ ταῦτα·

  ἀλλ᾽ οὐ πολλοὶ ἴσασι βροτῶν τόδε θεῖον ἔδεσμα
  οὐδ᾽ ἔσθειν ἐθέλουσιν ὅσοι κουφαττελεβώδη

---

[208] The speaker probably went on to maintain that he, as a
"good citizen," used oil lavishly, thus stimulating the local econ-
omy in a second way.   [209] A more complete version of the
line is given at 7.279f.

[210] A number of additional verses from the same fragment are
preserved at 7.310c–e.

I'm summoning the prudent philosophers here,
the ones who never allow themselves anything good,
and who seek for "the wise man" in their walks
and their discussions as if he were a runaway slave.
Miserable creature—if you have money to contribute
    to a party,
why are you sober? Why do you wrong the gods so
    much?
Why do you value your cash, sir,
† more than yourself or what it's really worth?
You're no use to the city if you drink water,
because you're hurting the farmer and the trader;
whereas I increase their income by getting drunk.
Next, as soon as the sun rises you're carrying your
    flask around
and constantly checking the oil, with the result that
    someone's likely
to think you're carrying around a water-clock rather
    than an oil-flask![208]

But Archestratus (fr. 24.13–20 Olson–Sens = *SH* 154.13–
20), Cynulcus, whom you worship in place of Homer at the
urging of your belly—

    than which nothing is more greedy,

as your Timon (*SH* 781)[209] puts it—offers the following information about the shark in his writings:[210]

    But few mortals know about this divine food,
    and those mortals who have the sense of a foolish
        locust

283

ψυχὴν κέκτηνται θνητῶν εἰσίν τ' ἀπόπληκτοι,
ὡς ἀνθρωποφάγου τοῦ θηρίου ὄντος. ἅπας δὲ
ἰχθὺς σάρκα φιλεῖ βροτεήν, ἄν που περικύρσῃ·
ὥστε πρέπει καθαρῶς ὁπόσοι τάδε μωρολογοῦσι
τοῖς λαχάνοις προσάγειν καὶ πρὸς Διόδωρον
e   ἰόντας |
τὸν σοφὸν ἐγκρατέως μετ' ἐκείνου πυθαγορίζειν.

ἦν δ' ὁ Διόδωρος οὗτος τὸ μὲν γένος Ἀσπένδιος,
Πυθαγορικὸς δὲ δόξας εἶναι ὑμῶν τῶν κυνικῶν τρόπον
ἔζη, κομῶν καὶ ῥυπῶν καὶ ἀνυποδητῶν. ὅθεν καὶ
Πυθαγορικὸν τὸ τῆς κόμης ἔδοξαν εἶναί τινες ἀπὸ τοῦ
Διοδώρου προαχθέν, ὥς φησιν Ἕρμιππος. Τίμαιος δ'
ὁ Ταυρομενίτης ἐν τῇ ἐνάτῃ τῶν Ἱστοριῶν περὶ αὐτοῦ
γράφει οὕτως· Διοδώρου τοῦ τὸ γένος Ἀσπενδίου τὴν
ἐξηλλαγμένην εἰσαγαγόντος κατασκευὴν καὶ τοῖς Πυ-
f θαγορείοις πεπλησιακέναι | προσποιηθέντος· πρὸς ὃν
ἐπιστέλλων ὁ Στρατόνικος ἐκέλευσε τὸν ἀπαίροντα τὸ
ῥηθὲν ἀπαγγεῖλαι

τῷ περὶ θηροπέπλου μανίας ὕβρεώς τε
    περιστάσιμον
στοὰν ἔχοντι Πυθαγόρου πελάτᾳ.

Σωσικράτης δ' ἐν τρίτῳ Φιλοσόφων Διαδοχῆς βαθεῖ
πώγωνι χρήσασθαι τὸν Διόδωρον ἱστορεῖ καὶ τρί-

---

211 For an extensive collection of anecdotes about the lyre-

and are insane refuse to consume it,
on the ground that this beast eats human beings. But
    every
fish likes human flesh, if it encounters it somewhere.
Therefore it is clearly appropriate that those who talk
    this nonsense
keep company with vegetables and go to the wise
Diodorus and temperately play the Pythagorean
    along with him.

This Diodorus was an Aspendian by birth, and was thought
to be a Pythagorean but lived as you Cynics do, growing
his hair long and going dirty and barefoot. As a result,
some people believed that having long hair was a Pythagorean habit, since it was promoted by Diodorus, according
to Hermippus (fr. 24 Wehrli). Timaeus of Tauromenium
writes the following about him in Book IX of his *Histories*
(*FGrH* 566 F 16): Diodorus, an Aspendian by birth, introduced their strange way of life and pretended to have been
associated with the Pythagoreans. Stratonicus[211] sent him
a message and told the slave as he was taking it away to
announce what he had been told to say

to the dependant of Pythagoras who occupies a stoa
    crowded with witnesses
to his madness in wearing animal skins and to his
    insolence.

Sosicrates in Book III of his *Succession of Philosophers* (fr.

player Stratonicus of Athens (Stephanis #2310; *c*.410–360 BCE),
see 8.347f–52d; and cf. Philetaer. fr. 14 (quoted at 4.169e).

βωνα ἀναλαβεῖν κόμην τε φορῆσαι[25] κατά τινα τῦφον
τὴν ἐπιτήδευσιν ταύτην εἰσαγαγόντα, τῶν πρὸ αὐτοῦ
164 Πυθαγορικῶν λαμπρᾷ τε ἐσθῆτι ἀμφιεννυμένων || καὶ
λουτροῖς καὶ ἀλείμμασι κουρᾷ τε τῇ συνήθει χρω-
μένων. εἰ δ᾽ ὑμεῖς ὄντως, ὦ φιλόσοφοι, τὴν αὐτάρκειαν
ἀσπάζεσθε καὶ τῶν δείπνων τὰ εὐτελῆ, τί ἐνταῦθα
παραγίνεσθε μηδὲ κληθέντες; ἢ ὡς εἰς ἀσώτιον μαγειρικὰ σκεύη καταλέγειν μαθησόμενοι; ἢ ὡς τὸν Διο-
γένους Κεφαλίωνα ἀποστοματιοῦντες; κατὰ γὰρ τὸν
Σοφοκλέους Κηδαλίωνά ἐστε

μαστιγίαι, κέντρωνες, ἀλλοτριοφάγοι.

ὅτι δ᾽ ὑμεῖς οἱ φιλόσοφοι περὶ τὰ δεῖπνα ἀεὶ τὸν νοῦν
b ἔχετε, δέον ὑμᾶς ἐπιφαγεῖν αἰτῆσαι | ἢ ἐπεσθίειν τι
τῶν κυνικῶν βρωμάτων (οὐδὲ γὰρ

χαριτογλωσσεῖν ἡμᾶς θέμις),

δῆλον ἐξ ὧν καὶ Ἄλεξις ἐν τῷ ἐπιγραφομένῳ Λίνῳ
ἱστορεῖ. ὑποτίθεται δὲ τὸν Ἡρακλέα παρὰ τῷ Λίνῳ
παιδευόμενον καὶ κελευσθέντα ἀπὸ βιβλίων πολλῶν
παρακειμένων λαβόντα ἐντυχεῖν. ἐκεῖνος δ᾽ ὀψαρτυτι-
κὸν λαβὼν βιβλίον ἐν χεροῖν περισπουδάστως ἐκρά-
τει. λέγει δὲ οὕτως ὁ Λίνος·

25 φορῆσαι καὶ A: ἐφόρει tantum CE

---

212 Cf. D.L. 6.80; no fragments of the work survive.
213 Or "some dogs' food."   214 Cf. 4.169b.

20, *FHG* iv.503) records that Diodorus had a thick beard, adopted an inexpensive cloak, and wore his hair long, and introduced this way of life as a sort of affectation, since the Pythagoreans before him wore clean clothes, bathed, anointed themselves with oil, and wore their hair in the normal style. But if you, my philosophers, are in fact so eager for mere sufficiency and inexpensive dinners, why are you here uninvited? Is it because you're visiting a spendthrift's house (*asōtion*) to learn to make a list of cooking utensils? Or to recite Diogenes' *Cephalion*?[212] Because you are, to quote Sophocles' *Cedalion* (fr. 329),

> fit to be whipped or tortured, eaters of other people's food.

That you philosophers always have your minds on dinner parties, when you should be asking for some Cynics' food[213] to consume (*epiphagein*) or to go on consuming (*epesthiein*)[214]—for it is not (adesp. tr. fr. *92a)

> right that we speak kindly (*charitoglōssein*)—

is clear from what Alexis records in his play entitled *Linus* (fr. 140).[215] The gist of it is that Heracles was being educated in Linus' house and was ordered to pick up one of the many books lying beside him and read it; and he picked up a cookbook and was holding it in his hands with great enthusiasm. Linus says the following:

[215] Linus was a mythical singer who taught Heracles to play the lyre. When he tried to punish his student, Heracles killed him ([Apollod.] *Bib*. 2.4.9). Magnus' claim that Alexis asserts in vv. 10–12 that philosophers concern themselves more with fine food than with anything else ignores the obvious irony of the remark.

(Λι.) βιβλίον

c ἐντεῦθεν ὅ τι βούλει προσελθὼν γὰρ λαβέ, |
ἔπειτ᾽ ἀναγνώσει—(Ηρ.) πάνυ γε. (Λι.)
  διασκοπῶν
ἀπὸ τῶν ἐπιγραμμάτων ἀτρέμα τε καὶ σχολῇ.
Ὀρφεὺς ἔνεστιν, Ἡσίοδος, τραγῳδίαι,
Χοιρίλος, Ὅμηρος, † Ἐπίχαρμος, συγγράμματα
παντοδαπά. δηλώσεις γὰρ οὕτω τὴν φύσιν
ἐπὶ τί μάλισθ᾽ ὥρμηκε. (Ηρ.) τουτὶ λαμβάνω.
(Λι.) δεῖξον τί ἐστι πρῶτον. (Ηρ.) ὀψαρτυσία,
ὡς φησι τοὐπίγραμμα. (ΛΙ.) φιλόσοφός τις εἶ,
d εὔδηλον, ὃς παρεὶς τοσαῦτα γράμματα |
Σίμου τέχνην ἔλαβες. (Ηρ.) ὁ Σῖμος δ᾽ ἐστὶ τίς;
(Λι.) μάλ᾽ εὐφυὴς ἄνθρωπος. ἐπὶ τραγῳδίαν
ὥρμηκε νῦν καὶ τῶν μὲν ὑποκριτῶν πολὺ
κράτιστός ἐστιν ὀψοποιός, ὡς δοκεῖ
τοῖς χρωμένοις, τῶν δ᾽ ὀψοποιῶν ὑποκριτής

             *   *   *

(Λι.) βούλιμός ἐσθ᾽ ἄνθρωπος. (Ηρ.) ὅ τι βούλει
  λέγε·
πεινῶ γάρ, εὖ τοῦτ᾽ ἴσθι.

Ταῦτα τοῦ Μάγνου ἑξῆς καταδραμόντος ἀποβλέψας ὁ Κύνουλκος εἰς τοὺς παρόντας τῶν φιλοσόφων
e ἔφη· |

---

216 Not the early Athenian tragic poet (*TrGF* 2), since the tra-
gedians are referred to collectively at the end of v. 5, but the
Samian epic poet.

(Linus) Yes, go over
and pick any papyrus roll you like out of there
and then read it— (Heracles) Absolutely! (Linus)
    examining them
quietly, and at your leisure, on the basis of the labels.
Orpheus is in there, Hesiod, tragedies,
Choerilus,[216] Homer, † Epicharmus, prose treatises
of every type. This way you'll show me
what subject you're naturally inclined to. (Heracles)
    I'm picking this one!
(Linus) First show me what it is. (Heracles) It's a
    cookbook,
according to the label. (Linus) It's obvious that you're
    quite
a philosopher, since you passed by works like these
    and
chose Simus'[217] trade. (Heracles) Who's Simus?
(Linus) A very clever person. He's now turned
to tragedy; and he's far and away the best cook
among the actors, according to the people
who employ him, and the best actor among the cooks.

*   *   *

(Linus) This guy can't stop eating! (Heracles) Say
    what you want;
I'm hungry, that's for sure!

After Magnus ran through these quotations in order,
Cynulcus glanced at the philosophers present and said:

[217] Stephanis #2275; otherwise unknown.

εἶδες τὴν Θασίαν ἅλμην, οἷ᾽ ἅττα βαΰζει,
ὡς εὖ καὶ ταχέως ἀπετείσατο καὶ παραχρῆμα.
οὐ μέντοι παρὰ κωφὸν ὁ τυφλὸς ἔοικε λαλῆσαι,

ὡς ὁ Κρατῖνος ἐν τοῖς Ἀρχιλόχοις ἔφη. ἐπιλανθανό-
μενος γὰρ ἐν οἷς ποιεῖται δικαστηρίοις τῶν καλῶν
ἰάμβων αὐτοῦ τὰς ἐπιδείξεις ὑπὸ τῆς ἐμφύτου γαστρι-
μαργίας καὶ ἡδυλογίας κολάβρους ἀναγινώσκει καὶ

μέλη πάραυλα κἀκρότητα κύμβαλα.

f καὶ μετὰ | τὰς καλὰς ταύτας ἀμουσολογίας περιέρ-
χεται τὰς οἰκίας ἐξετάζων ὅπου δεῖπνα λαμπρὰ παρα-
σκευάζεται, ὑπὲρ τὸν Ἀθηναῖον Χαιρεφῶντα ἐκεῖνον,
περὶ οὗ φησιν Ἄλεξις ἐν Φυγάδι·

ἀεί γ᾽ ὁ Χαιρεφῶν τιν᾽ εὑρίσκει τέχνην
καινὴν πορίζεταί τε τὰ δεῖπν᾽ ἀσύμβολα.
ὅπου γάρ ἐστιν ὁ κέραμος μισθώσιμος
ὁ τοῖς μαγείροις, εὐθὺς ἐξ ἑωθινοῦ
165 ἕστηκεν ἐλθών· κἂν ἴδῃ μισθούμενον ‖
εἰς ἑστίασιν, τοῦ μαγείρου πυθόμενος
τὸν ἑστιῶντα, τῆς θύρας χασμωμένης
ἂν ἐπιλάβηται, πρῶτος εἰσελήλυθεν.

οὐκ ὀκνεῖ δ᾽ ὁ ἀνὴρ οὗτος, καθάπερ καὶ ὁ καλὸς

---

218 An allusion to Archilochus, who spent part of his life on
Thasos and was known for his bitter, pungent wit, and to whom
Magnus is thus compared. The precise meaning of the final verse

Did you see how this Thasian brine-sauce[218] barks?
How well and quickly he got his revenge, with no
    delay!
But the blind man isn't likely to talk to a deaf one,

as Cratinus said in *Archilochuses* (fr. 6). For his innate
gluttony and garrulousness (*hēdulogia*) make him forget
the court where he is putting his lovely iambs on display,
and he reads us his wild Thracian songs and his (adesp. tr.
fr. 93)

    badly-piped tunes and ill-coordinated cymbals.

And after these lovely displays of bad taste, he goes around
from one house to the next, checking to see where a brilliant dinner party is being prepared, and outdoing the
famous Chaerephon of Athens,[219] about whom Alexis says
in *The Fugitive* (fr. 259):

    Chaerephon is always coming up with some new
    trick and getting his dinners without contributing any
        money.
    For the minute the sun comes up, he goes and stands
    in the place where the cooks rent their
    earthenware. If he sees something being rented
    for a feast, he asks the cook
    who the host is; and if he finds the door
    open, he's the first one in.

Just like our fine Magnus, this fellow does not hesitate to

is obscure; but the basic sense must be that the preceding attack
has accomplished nothing, if only because of the stupidity of its
intended audience.   [219] See 4.134e n.

Μάγνος, καὶ ὑπερορίους ἀποδημίας ποιεῖσθαι τῆς γαστρὸς χάριν, ὡς <ὁ> αὐτὸς Ἄλεξις εἴρηκεν ἐν Συναποθνήσκουσιν·

> ἐπὶ δεῖπνον εἰς Κόρινθον ἐλθὼν Χαιρεφῶν
> ἄκλητος· ἤδη γὰρ πέτεται διαπόντιος·
> οὕτω τι τἀλλότρι' ἐσθίειν ἐστὶ γλυκύ. |

b

καὶ Θεόπομπος δ' ἐν Ὀδυσσεῖ ἔφη·

> Εὐριπίδου τἄριστον, οὐ κακῶς ἔχον,
> τἀλλότρια δειπνεῖν τὸν καλῶς εὐδαίμονα.

Γελασάντων οὖν πάντων ἐπὶ τούτοις ὁ Οὐλπιανὸς ἔφη· πόθεν δὲ καὶ ἡδυλογία τοῖς ἡδονικοῖς τούτοις ἁμαρτολόγοις; πρὸς ὃν ὁ Κύνουλκος· ἀλλ', ὦ χοιρίον εὐάρτυτον, Φρύνιχος ὁ κωμῳδιοποιὸς ἐν τῷ Ἐφιάλτῃ μνημονεύει τοῦ ἡδυλόγου διὰ τούτων·

> ἔστιν δ' αὐτούς γε φυλάττεσθαι τῶν νῦν
> χαλεπώτατον ἔργον. |

c

> ἔχουσι γάρ τι κέντρον ἐν τοῖς δακτύλοις,
> μισάνθρωπον ἄνθος ἥβης·
> εἶθ' ἡδυλογοῦσιν ἅπασιν ἀεὶ κατὰ τὴν
> ἀγορὰν περιόντες.
> ἐπὶ τοῖς <δὲ> βάθροις ὅταν ὦσιν, ἐκεῖ
> τούτοις οἷς ἡδυλογοῦσι

---

220 The second verse = E. fr. 894, although Theopompus' "dine on" has probably replaced a word such as "flee" (thus Nauck) in the tragic original.   221 Used at 4.164e.

travel outside the country to gratify his belly, as the same Alexis says in *Men Who Were Dying Together* (fr. 213):

> Chaerephon went to Corinth for dinner
> uninvited. Now he's flying over the sea;
> that's how sweet it is to eat other people's food.

Theopompus as well said in *Odysseus* (fr. 35):[220]

> The best remark Euripides made, and it isn't bad at
>   all,
> is that the man who's really fortunate dines on other
>   people's food.

Everyone laughed at these remarks, but Ulpian said: Where did these pleasure-loving language-butchers find the word *hēdulogia* ("garrulousness")[221]? Cynulcus answered him: In fact, you well-seasoned pig (= adesp. com. fr. *108, unmetrical), the comic poet Phrynichus mentions the garrulous man *(hēdulogos)* in *Ephialtes* (fr. 3), in the following verses:

> The most difficult job we have today is to protect
>   ourselves from them.
>   For they have a kind of sting in their fingers,[222]
>   a hostile bloom of youth.
> They always speak pleasantly *(hēdulougousin)* to
>   everyone, as they circulate through the
>   marketplace.
> But when they're in their seats, they rip long
>   scratches there into

---

[222] I.e. an extended middle finger or its ancient equivalent (perhaps the little finger).

μεγάλας ἀμυχὰς καταμύξαντες καὶ
συγκύψαντες ἅπαντες
γελῶσι.

τὸ δὲ χαριτογλωσσεῖν Αἰσχύλος εἴρηκεν ἐν Προμηθεῖ
Δεσμώτῃ·

d   γνώσῃ δὲ τάδ' ὡς ἔτυμ', οὐδὲ μάτην |
χαριτογλωσσεῖν ἔνι μοι.

πάλιν τε εἰπόντος τοῦ Οὐλπιανοῦ· τίνα δ' ἐστίν, ἄνδρες φίλοι, τὰ μαγειρικὰ σκεύη; τούτων γὰρ ἐμνημο-
νεύσατ' ἐν τοῖς Ἀρκαδικοῖς δείπνοις μνήμης ἠξιω-
μένων. καὶ τὸ ἀσώτιον ποῦ κεῖται; ἀσώτους μὲν γὰρ
οἶδα διαβοήτους· ἕνα μὲν οὖ μνημονεύει Ἄλεξις ἐν
Κνιδίᾳ·

Διόδωρος οὑπίτριπτος ἐν ἔτεσιν δύο
σφαῖραν ἀπέδειξε τὴν πατρῴαν οὐσίαν·
e   οὕτως ἰταμῶς ἅπαντα κατεμασήσατο. |

ἐν δὲ Φαίδρῳ φησί·

σχολῇ γε, νὴ τὸν Ἥλιον, σχολῇ λέγεις.
Ἐπιχαρίδης ὁ μικρὸς ἐν πένθ' ἡμέραις

---

223 Ulpian did not ask about this word (used at 4.164b), and
perhaps his second question has dropped out of the text, particularly since he poses two questions at the same time below.
224 At 4.149a. But Ulpian's question also recalls Magnus' de-
nunciation of the philosophers' presence in Larensius' house at
4.164a, where he uses the other word asked about here.

the people to whom they speak pleasantly
(*hēdulougousin*), and they all put their heads
together and laugh.

Aeschylus used the verb *charitoglōssein*[223] in *Prometheus
Bound* (293–4):

You will know that these words are true, and that it is
not
in my nature to speak kindly (*charitoglōssein*) to no
purpose.

And again Ulpian said: What, my friends, are the utensils
used by cooks? For you referred to these as worthy of mention in your discussion of Arcadian dinners.[224] And where
is the word *asōtion* ("spendthrift's house") attested? Because I am aware that spendthrifts (*asōtoi*) are widely
discussed. Alexis mentions one in *The Girl from Cnidus*
(fr. 110):

In two years that damned Diodorus[225]
turned the property he inherited from his father into
a ball;[226]
that's how recklessly he ate it all up.

And he says in *Phaedrus* (fr. 248):

Slowly, by the Sun, you're talking about doing it
slowly!
In five days little Epicharides[227]

[225] *PAA* 329550.
[226] I.e. that he then let roll away from him (thus Arnott)? The
image is used again below.
[227] See 4.161b n.

σφαῖραν ἐπόησε τὴν πατρῴαν οὐσίαν·
οὕτω συνεστρόγγυλεν ἰταμῶς καὶ ταχύ.

καὶ Κτήσιππος δ᾽ ὁ Χαβρίου υἱὸς εἰς τοσοῦτον ἦλθεν
ἀσωτίας ὡς καὶ τοῦ μνήματος τοῦ πατρός, εἰς ὃ
Ἀθηναῖοι χιλίας ἀνάλωσαν δραχμάς, τοὺς λίθους
πωλῆσαι εἰς τὰς ἡδυπαθείας. Δίφιλος γοῦν ἐν τοῖς
f   Ἐναγίζουσί φησι· |

εἰ μὴ συνήθης Φαιδίμῳ γ᾽ ἐτύγχανεν
ὁ Χαβρίου Κτήσιππος, εἰσηγησάμην
νόμον ⟨ἄν⟩ τιν᾽ οὐκ ἄχρηστον, ὡς ἐμοὶ δοκεῖ,
ὥστ᾽ ἐπιτελεσθῆναί ποτ᾽ αὐτῷ τοῦ πατρὸς
τὸ μνῆμα, κατ᾽ ἐνιαυτὸν ἕνα ⟨ . . . ⟩ λίθον
ἀμαξιαῖον. καὶ σφόδρ᾽ εὐτελὲς λέγω.

Τιμοκλῆς δ᾽ ἐν Δημοσατύροις φησίν·

166   οὐδ᾽ ὁ Χαβρίου Κτήσιππος ἔτι τρὶς κείρεται, ‖
ἐν ταῖς γυναιξὶ λαμπρός, οὐκ ἐν ἀνδράσιν.

καὶ Μένανδρος δ᾽ ἐν Ὀργῇ περὶ αὐτοῦ τάδε λέγει·

καίτοι νέος ποτ᾽ ἐγενόμην κἀγώ, γύναι·
ἀλλ᾽ οὐκ ἐλούμην πεντάκις τῆς ἡμέρας
τότ᾽, ἀλλὰ νῦν· οὐδὲ χλανίδ᾽ εἶχον, ἀλλὰ νῦν·

---

[228] *PAA* 587475. Chabrias (*PA* 15086) was an important Athenian general who died in combat in 357/6 BCE, hence the use of
public funds to construct his monument. Phaedimus (*PA* 13925) is
otherwise unknown.

turned the property he inherited from his father into
    a ball;
that's how recklessly and rapidly he rolled it up.

Ctesippus the son of Chabrias[228] too became such a spendthrift that he sold the stones of his father's tomb, on which
the Athenians spent 1000 drachmas, to finance his high living. Diphilus, at any rate, says in *Men Who Offer Sacrifice
To the Dead* (fr. 37):

If Ctesippus son of Chabrias didn't happen to be
related to Phaedimus, I'd have proposed
quite a useful law, I think,
requiring that he complete
his father's tomb, one massive stone . . .
per year. And I mean very cheap . . .

Timocles says in *The People's Satyrs* (fr. 5):

And Ctesippus son of Chabrias doesn't get his hair
    cut three times a day anymore,
a fellow who's distinguished among women but not
    among men.

And Menander says the following about him in *Wrath* (fr.
264):

And yet I too was once a young man, woman.
But I didn't bathe five times a day
back then, as I do now, or wear a fine wool robe, as I
    do now,

οὐδὲ μύρον εἶχον, ἀλλὰ νῦν· καὶ βάψομαι
καὶ παρατιλοῦμαι, νὴ Δία, καὶ γενήσομαι
b   Κτήσιππος, οὐκ ἄνθρωπος, ἐν ὀλίγῳ χρόνῳ, |
κᾆθ᾽ ὡς ἐκεῖνος κατέδομαι καὶ τοὺς λίθους
ἀπαξάπαντας, οὐ γὰρ οὖν τὴν γῆν μόνην.

τάχ᾽ οὖν διὰ τὴν πολλὴν ταύτην ἀσωτίαν καὶ κιναι-
δίαν τοὔνομα αὐτοῦ παρέλιπε Δημοσθένης ἐν τῷ Περὶ
Ἀτελειῶν. χρὴ δὲ τοὺς τὰ πατρῷα κατεδηδοκότας
κατὰ τὸν Μενάνδρου Ναύκληρον οὕτως κολάζεσθαι.
φησὶν γάρ·

ὦ φιλτάτη Γῆ μῆτερ, ὡς σεμνὸν σφόδρ᾽ εἶ
τοῖς νοῦν ἔχουσι κτῆμα πολλοῦ τ᾽ ἄξιον.
c   ὡς δῆτ᾽ ἐχρῆν, εἴ τις πατρῴαν παραλαβὼν |
γῆν καταφάγοι, πλεῖν τοῦτον ἤδη διὰ τέλους
καὶ μηδ᾽ ἐπιβαίνειν γῆς, ἵν᾽ οὕτως ᾔσθετο,
οἷον παραλαβὼν ἀγαθὸν οὐκ ἐφείσατο.

Πυθοδήλου δέ τινος ἀσώτου μνημονεύει Ἀξιόνικος ἐν
Τυρρηνῷ οὕτως·

                ὁ Πυθόδηλος οὑτοσὶ
ὁ Βαλλίων προσέρχετ᾽ ἐπικαλούμενος
μεθύουσά τ᾽ ἐξόπισθεν ἡ σοφωτάτη
d   Ἀποτυμπανισχὰς κατὰ πόδας πορεύεται. |

---

229 To look younger and thus become appealing to adult men;
cf. the reference to "sexual perversity" below.
230 *PAA* 794095.

or wear perfume, as I do now. I'm going to dye my
   hair
and pluck my beard,[229] by Zeus, and rapidly
turn into Ctesippus rather than a man.
And then I'll consume every single one
of my stones, as he did, and not just my land.

It was therefore perhaps on account of this enormous extravagance and sexual perversion that Demosthenes omitted his name in his *On Exemptions from Taxation* (*Or.* 20,
= *Against Leptines*). Individuals who squander their inheritance should be punished in the way described in
Menander's *The Shipowner* (fr. 247). For he says:

O dearest mother Earth, what a grand
and valuable possession you are for anyone with some
   sense!
It ought, in fact, to be a rule that whoever squanders
any land he inherits from his father has to sail the sea
   forever
and never set a foot on land, to make him understand
what a wonderful thing he had—and threw away.

Axionicus mentions a profligate named Pythodelus[230] in
The Etruscan (fr. 1), as follows:

                              Here comes
Pythodelus, whose nickname's Big Dick;[231]
and behind him, drunk, the clever
Apotumpanischas[232] is dogging his steps.

[231] Greek *Balliōn*, from *ballion* ("phallus").
[232] *Apotumpanismos* was a form of execution (see 4.134b n.),
and Ischas (literally "Dried Fig," i.e. "Sweetie") is attested as a
prostitute's name.

Πολύευκτον δ᾽ Ἀναξανδρίδης ἐν Τηρεῖ κωμῳδῶν·

(A.) ὄρνις κεκλήσῃ (φησί). (B.) διὰ τί, πρὸς τῆς
   Ἑστίας;
πότερον καταφαγὼν τὴν πατρῴαν οὐσίαν,
ὥσπερ Πολύευκτος ὁ καλός; (A.) οὐ δῆτ᾽, ἀλλ᾽
   ὅτι
ἄρρην ὑπὸ θηλειῶν κατεκόπης.

Θεόπομπος δ᾽ ἐν τῇ δεκάτῃ τῶν Φιλιππικῶν, ἀφ᾽ ἧς
τινες τὸ τελευταῖον μέρος χωρίσαντες, ἐν ᾧ ἐστι τὰ
περὶ τῶν Ἀθήνησι δημαγωγῶν, < . . . > Εὔβουλόν
e φησι τὸν δημαγωγὸν ἄσωτον γενέσθαι. τῇ | λέξει δὲ
ταύτῃ ἐχρήσατο· καὶ τοσοῦτον ἀσωτίᾳ καὶ πλεονεξίᾳ
διενήνοχε τοῦ δήμου τοῦ Ταραντίνων ὅσον ὁ μὲν περὶ
τὰς ἑστιάσεις εἶχε μόνον ἀκρατῶς, ὁ δὲ τῶν Ἀθηναίων
καὶ τὰς προσόδους καταμισθοφορῶν διατετέλεκε.
Καλλίστρατος δέ, φησίν, ὁ Καλλικράτους <ὁ> δημα-
γωγὸς καὶ αὐτὸς πρὸς μὲν τὰς ἡδονὰς ἦν ἀκρατής,
τῶν δὲ πολιτικῶν πραγμάτων[26] ἐπιμελής. περὶ δὲ τῶν
Ταραντίνων ἱστορῶν ἐν τῇ δευτέρᾳ <καὶ> πεντηκοστῇ
τῶν Ἱστοριῶν γράφει οὕτως· ἡ πόλις ἡ τῶν Ταραν-

---

[26] πραγμάτων ἦν A: ἦν om. CE

---

[233] Perhaps the well-known orator and politician Polyeuctus
son of Sostratus of the deme Sphettos (*PAA* 778285; Berve i #650),
although the period of his greatest public prominence probably
came after the end of Anaxandrides' career.
[234] Or perhaps "Chicken," i.e. "Rooster."

BOOK IV

Anaxandrides mocks Polyeuctus[233] in *Tereus* (fr. 46) and says:

> (A.) You'll be called "Bird."[234] (B.) Why, by Hestia?
> Because I gobbled up the property I inherited from
>   my father,
> like the noble Polyeuctus? (A.) Not at all, but
>   because
> you're a male who's been reduced to mincemeat by
>   females.

Theopompus in Book X of his *History of Philip* (*FGrH* 115 F 100), the final portion of which, containing the discussion of the Athenian demagogues, is treated as spurious by some authorities, . . . claims that the demagogue Eubulus[235] was a spendthrift. He said specifically the following: He has outdone the people of Tarentum in profligacy and greed[236] to such an extent that, whereas the only matter in which they failed to exercise self-control was feasts, the Athenians have spent their revenues on mercenaries. And he says that the demagogue Callistratus son of Callicrates[237] was also a reckless hedonist, but was nonetheless careful about public business. In his report on the people of Tarentum in Book LII of his *Histories* (*FGrH* 115 F 233) he writes the following: The city of Tarentum

[235] *PAA* 428495; he was prominent in the late 350s and 340s BCE. Theopompus' Book X appears to have treated events in 352.

[236] For the Tarentine love of feasting, drinking, and luxury generally, cf. 4.156a; 12.522d–f.

[237] *PAA* 561575. Callistratus was executed sometime before 355 BCE and was thus one of Eubulus' immediate predecessors rather than his contemporary.

f τίνων σχεδὸν | καθ᾽ ἕκαστον μῆνα βουθυτεῖ καὶ δημο-
σίας ἑστιάσεις ποιεῖται. τὸ δὲ τῶν ἰδιωτῶν πλῆθος
αἰεὶ περὶ συνουσίας καὶ πότους ἐστί. λέγουσι δὲ καί
τινα τοιοῦτον λόγον οἱ Ταραντῖνοι, τοὺς μὲν ἄλλους
ἀνθρώπους διὰ τὸ φιλοπονεῖσθαι καὶ περὶ τὰς ἐργα-
σίας διατρίβειν παρασκευάζεσθαι ζῆν, αὐτοὺς δὲ διὰ
τὰς συνουσίας καὶ τὰς ἡδονὰς οὐ μέλλειν, ἀλλ᾽ ἤδη
βιῶναι.

Περὶ δὲ τῆς ἀσωτίας καὶ τοῦ βίου Φιλίππου καὶ
167 τῶν ἑταίρων αὐτοῦ ἐν τῇ ἐνάτῃ καὶ τεσσαρακοστῇ ‖
τῶν Ἱστοριῶν ὁ Θεόπομπος τάδε γράφει· Φίλιππος
ἐπεὶ ἐγκρατὴς πολλῶν ἐγένετο χρημάτων οὐκ ἀνάλω-
σεν αὐτὰ ταχέως, ἀλλ᾽ ἐξέβαλε καὶ ἔρριψε, πάντων
ἀνθρώπων κάκιστος ὢν οἰκονόμος οὐ μόνον αὐτός,
ἀλλὰ καὶ οἱ περὶ αὐτόν· ἁπλῶς γὰρ οὐδεὶς αὐτῶν
ἠπίστατο ζῆν ὀρθῶς οὐδὲ σωφρόνως οἰκεῖν οἰκίαν. τοῦ
δ᾽ αὐτὸς αἴτιος ἦν ἄπληστος καὶ πολυτελὴς ὤν, προ-
χείρως ἅπαντα ποιῶν καὶ κτώμενος καὶ διδούς· στρα-
b τιώτης γὰρ ὢν λογίζεσθαι τὰ προσιόντα καὶ | τἀναλι-
σκόμενα δι᾽ ἀσχολίαν οὐκ ἠδύνατο. ἔπειτα δ᾽ οἱ
ἑταῖροι αὐτοῦ ἐκ πολλῶν τόπων ἦσαν συνερρυηκότες·
οἱ μὲν γὰρ ἐξ αὐτῆς τῆς χώρας, οἱ δὲ ἐκ Θετταλίας, οἱ
δὲ ἐκ τῆς ἄλλης Ἑλλάδος, οὐκ ἀριστίνδην ἐξει-
λεγμένοι, ἀλλ᾽ εἴ τις ἦν ἐν τοῖς Ἕλλησιν ἢ τοῖς
βαρβάροις λάσταυρος ἢ βδελυρὸς ἢ θρασὺς τὸν
τρόπον, οὗτοι σχεδὸν ἅπαντες εἰς Μακεδονίαν ἀθροι-
σθέντες ἑταῖροι Φιλίππου προσηγορεύοντο. εἰ δὲ καὶ
μὴ τοιοῦτός τις ⟨ὢν⟩ ἐληλύθει, ὑπὸ τοῦ βίου καὶ τῆς

sacrifices oxen and holds public feasts nearly every month. The citizen masses are constantly occupied with parties and drinking. The people of Tarentum have a saying along the lines that, because other people work hard and spend their time on business, they are preparing to live, whereas they themselves, because of their parties and the good times they have, are not getting ready to live but already doing so.

As for the profligate lifestyle of Philip[238] and his companions, Theopompus writes the following in Book XLIX of his *Histories* (*FGrH* 115 F 224): When Philip got his hands on large amounts of money, he did not just spend it quickly, but threw it away and wasted it, and was the worst manager in the world. And it was not just Philip, but also his circle; for, simply put, none of them knew how to live properly or manage a household responsibly. Philip himself was responsible for this, because he was greedy and extravagant, and did everything off-hand, be it accumulating money or disposing of it; for the fact that he was a soldier meant that he had no spare time to calculate his income and expenses. On top of this, his companions had streamed in from many places; some were from Macedon itself, others from Thessaly, and some from the rest of Greece. Nor had they been selected on the basis of merit. Instead, if anyone in the Greek or barbarian world had a sexually depraved, disgusting, or arrogant character, practically all such men gathered in Macedon and came to be called Philip's companions. And if someone was different from this when he arrived, the Macedonian lifestyle and the

[238] Philip II (King of Macedon 360/59–336 BCE), whose career was at the center of Theopompus' *Histories*.

ATHENAEUS

διαίτης τῆς Μακεδονικῆς ταχέως ἐκείνοις ὅμοιος ἐγί-
c νετο. τὰ μὲν γὰρ οἱ | πόλεμοι καὶ αἱ στρατεῖαι, ‹τὰ δὲ›
καὶ αἱ πολυτέλειαι θρασεῖς αὐτοὺς εἶναι προετρέποντο
καὶ ζῆν μὴ κοσμίως, ἀλλ᾽ ἀσώτως καὶ τοῖς λῃσταῖς
παραπλησίως. Δοῦρις δ᾽ ἐν ἑβδόμῳ Μακεδονικῶν περὶ
Πασικύπρου λέγων τοῦ ἐν Κύπρῳ βασιλέως ὅτι ἄσω-
τος ἦν γράφει καὶ τάδε· Ἀλέξανδρος μετὰ τὴν Τύρου
πολιορκίαν Πνυταγόραν ἀποστέλλων ἄλλας τε δωρεὰς ἔδωκε καὶ χωρίον ὃ ᾐτήσατο. πρότερον δὲ τοῦτο
Πασίκυπρος βασιλεύων ἀπέδοτο δι᾽ ἀσωτίαν πεντή-
d κοντα ταλάντων Πυμιάτωνι²⁷ | τῷ Κιτιεῖ, ἅμα τὸ
χωρίον καὶ τὴν αὑτοῦ βασιλείαν· καὶ λαβὼν τὰ χρήματα κατεγήρασεν ἐν Ἀμαθοῦντι. τοιοῦτος ἐγένετο
καὶ Αἰθίοψ ὁ Κορίνθιος, ὥς φησι Δημήτριος ὁ Σκήψιος, οὗ μνημονεύει Ἀρχίλοχος· ὑπὸ φιληδονίας γὰρ
καὶ ἀκρασίας καὶ οὗτος μετ᾽ Ἀρχίου πλέων εἰς Σικελίαν ὅτ᾽ ἔμελλεν κτίζειν Συρακούσας τῷ ἑαυτοῦ συσ-
σίτῳ μελιτούττης ἀπέδοτο τὸν κλῆρον ὃν ἐν Συρα-
κούσαις λαχὼν ἔμελλεν ἕξειν. εἰς τοσοῦτον δ᾽ ἀσωτίας
e ἐληλύθει καὶ Δημήτριος ὁ Δημητρίου τοῦ Φαληρέως |
ἀπόγονος, ὥς φησιν Ἡγήσανδρος, ὥστε Ἀρισταγό-
ραν μὲν ἔχειν τὴν Κορινθίαν ἐρωμένην, ζῆν δὲ πολυτελῶς. ἀνακαλεσαμένων δ᾽ αὐτὸν τῶν Ἀρεοπαγιτῶν
καὶ κελευόντων βέλτιον ζῆν, "ἀλλὰ καὶ νῦν," εἶπεν,
"ἐλευθερίως ζῶ. καὶ γὰρ ἑταίραν ἔχω τὴν καλλίστην

²⁷ πυμάτωνι ACE: Πυγμαλίωνι Kaibel (cf. D.S. 19.79.4)

304

way they behaved soon made him resemble them. For
wars and military campaigns, on the one hand, and an
extravagant lifestyle, on the other, encouraged them to be
arrogant and to live not in an orderly way but like spendthrifts and bandits. Duris, when he describes the Cyprian
king Pasicyprus as profligate in Book VII of his *History of
Macedon* (*FGrH* 76 F 4), writes the following: When Alexander dismissed Pnytagoras[239] after the siege of Tyre, he
gave him gifts, including a fortified place he asked for.
Previous to this, when Pasicyprus was king, his profligacy
forced him to sell the place to Pymiaton of Citium for 50
talents, and he sold his kingship along with it. After he got
the money, he spent his old age in Amathus. Aethiops of
Corinth, whom Archilochus (fr. 293 West[2]) mentions, was
also this sort of person, according to Demetrius of Scepsis
(fr. 73 Gaede). For as a result of his hedonistic lack of self-
control, as he was sailing to Sicily along with Archias, who
was preparing to found the city of Syracuse,[240] he sold his
mess-mate the section of land in Syracuse he had drawn by
lot and was going to own for a honey cake. Demetrius the
descendant of Demetrius of Phaleron[241] sank so far into
profligacy, according to Hegesander (fr. 8, *FHG* iv.415),
that he took Aristagora of Corinth as his lover and lived extravagantly. When the Areopagites summoned him and
told him to live a better life, he said: "But at the moment
I'm living the life of a free man. I've got an extremely beau-

---

[239] Pnytagoras (Berve i #642) was the king of the city of Salamis in Cyprus; the siege of Tyre took place in 332 BCE. Cf. D.S.
19.79.4 (where Pymiaton's name has, however, been garbled).

[240] *c*.734 BCE.   [241] *PAA* 312160 (mid- to late-3rd century); he was the dictator's grandson.

καὶ ἀδικῶ οὐδένα καὶ πίνω Χῖον οἶνον καὶ τἄλλ'
ἀρκούντως παρασκευάζομαι, τῶν ἰδίων μου προσόδων
εἰς ταῦτα ἐκποιουσῶν, οὐ καθάπερ ὑμῶν ἔνιοι δεκαζό-
f μενος ζῶ καὶ μοιχεύων." καὶ τῶν τὰ τοιαῦτα | πρατ-
τόντων καὶ ἐπ' ὀνόματός τινας κατέλεξε. ταῦτα δ'
ἀκούσας Ἀντίγονος ὁ βασιλεὺς θεσμοθέτην αὐτὸν
κατέστησεν. τοῖς δὲ Παναθηναίοις ἵππαρχος ὢν ἱκρί-
ον ἔστησε πρὸς τοῖς Ἑρμαῖς Ἀρισταγόρᾳ μετεωρότε-
ρον τῶν Ἑρμῶν, Ἐλευσῖνί τε μυστηρίων ὄντων ἔθηκεν αὐτῇ θρόνον παρὰ τὸ ἀνάκτορον, οἰμώξεσθαι
168 φήσας τοὺς κωλύσοντας. ‖ ὅτι δὲ τοὺς ἀσώτους καὶ
τοὺς μὴ ἔκ τινος περιουσίας ζῶντας τὸ παλαιὸν ἀνε-
καλοῦντο οἱ Ἀρεοπαγῖται καὶ ἐκόλαζον, ἱστόρησαν
Φανόδημος καὶ Φιλόχορος ἄλλοι τε πλείους. Μενέδη-
μον γοῦν καὶ Ἀσκληπιάδην τοὺς φιλοσόφους νέους
ὄντας καὶ πενομένους μεταπεμψάμενοι ἠρώτησαν πῶς
ὅλας τὰς ἡμέρας τοῖς φιλοσόφοις συσχολάζοντες,
κεκτημένοι δὲ μηδέν, εὐεκτοῦσιν οὕτω τοῖς σώμασι·
καὶ οἱ ἐκέλευσαν μεταπεμφθῆναί τινα τῶν μυλωθρῶν.
b ἐλθόντος δ' ἐκείνου | καὶ εἰπόντος ὅτι νυκτὸς ἑκάστης
κατιόντες εἰς τὸν μυλῶνα καὶ ἀλοῦντες δύο δραχμὰς
ἀμφότεροι λαμβάνουσι, θαυμάσαντες οἱ Ἀρεοπαγῖται
διακοσίαις δραχμαῖς ἐτίμησαν αὐτούς. καὶ Δημόκρι-

---

242 For Chian wine, see 1.28d–f.

243 Antigonus Gonatas (reigned c.277/6–239 BCE).

244 An Athenian magistrate charged with supervising the
lawcourts; see [Arist.] Ath. 3.4 with Rhodes ad loc.

245 Located along the Panathenaic Way where it enters the

tiful lover, I do no one any wrong, and I drink Chian wine[242] and arrange everything else in the way that suits me; and my personal income makes this possible, and I don't live on bribes and illicit sexual affairs, as some of you do." And he listed some of those who behaved this way by name. When King Antigonus[243] heard this, he appointed him as a *thesmothetēs*.[244] When Demetrius was serving as a cavalry commander, he set up a spectator's stand for Aristagora next to and higher than the Herms[245]; and when the Mysteries were being celebrated in Eleusis, he put a chair next to the temple for her and told the people who wanted to keep him from doing this to go to hell. That in the old days the Areopagus Council[246] used to summon spendthrifts and others with no visible means of support and punish them is recorded by Phanodemus (*FGrH* 325 F 10), Philochorus (*FGrH* 328 F 196), and many others. When the philosophers Menedemus and Asclepiades,[247] for example, were impoverished young men, the Areopagites summoned them and asked how it was, given that they spent their days lounging about with the philosophers and had no property, that they were in such good physical shape. They asked for a certain miller to be summoned. When he came, he reported that they went to his mill every night and threshed grain, and were paid two drachmas apiece; the Areopagites were astonished and gave them

northwest corner of the Agora near the Royal Stoa and the Stoa Poicile.

[246] The highest legal and political authority in Athens before Ephialtes' reforms in the late 460s BCE.

[247] I.e. Menedemus of Eretria (*c*.339–*c*.265 BCE) and Asclepiades of Phlius (d. 278); for their friendship, cf. D.L. 2.126, 137.

τον δ᾽ οἱ Ἀβδηρῖται δημοσίᾳ κρίνοντες ὡς κατεφθαρ-
κότα τὰ πατρῷα, ἐπειδὴ ἀναγνοὺς αὐτοῖς τὸν Μέγαν
Διάκοσμον καὶ τὰ περὶ τῶν ἐν Ἅιδου εἰπὼν εἰς ταῦτα
ἀνηλωκέναι, ἀφείθη. οἱ δὲ μὴ οὕτως ἄσωτοι κατὰ τὸν
Ἄμφιν

c   πίνουσ᾽ ἑκάστης ἡμέρας δι᾽ ἡμέρας, |

διασειόμενοι τοὺς κροτάφους ὑπὸ τοῦ ἀκράτου, καὶ
κατὰ τὸν Δίφιλον κεφαλὰς ἔχοντες τρεῖς ὥσπερ Ἀρτε-
μίσιον, πολέμιοι τῆς οὐσίας ὑπάρχοντες, ὡς Σάτυρος
ἐν τοῖς Περὶ Χαρακτήρων εἴρηκεν, κατατρέχοντες τὸν
ἀγρόν, διαρπάζοντες τὴν οἰκίαν, λαφυροπωλοῦντες τὰ
ὑπάρχοντα, σκοποῦντες οὐ τί δεδαπάνηται ἀλλὰ τί
δαπανηθήσεται, οὐδὲ τί περιέσται ἀλλὰ τί οὐ περιέσται, ἐν τῇ νεότητι τὰ τοῦ γήρως ἐφόδια προκατανα-
d λίσκοντες, | χαίροντες τῇ ἑταίρᾳ οὐ τοῖς ἑταίροις, καὶ
τῷ οἴνῳ οὐ τοῖς συμπόταις. Ἀγαθαρχίδης δ᾽ ὁ Κνίδιος
ἐν τῇ ὀγδόῃ πρὸς ταῖς εἰκοσταῖς τῶν Εὐρωπιακῶν,
Γνώσιππον, φησίν, ἄσωτον γενόμενον ἐν τῇ Σπάρτῃ
ἐκώλυον οἱ ἔφοροι συναναστρέφεσθαι τοῖς νέοις.
παρὰ δὲ Ῥωμαίοις μνημονεύεται, ὥς φησι Ποσειδώνιος ἐν τῇ ἐνάτῃ καὶ τεσσαρακοστῇ τῶν Ἱστοριῶν,
Ἀπίκιόν τινα ἐπὶ ἀσωτίᾳ πάντας ἀνθρώπους ὑπερ-
ηκοντικέναι. οὗτος δ᾽ ἐστὶν Ἀπίκιος ὁ καὶ τῆς φυγῆς
e αἴτιος | γενόμενος Ῥουτιλίῳ τῷ τὴν Ῥωμαϊκὴν Ἱστο-

---

248 I.e. productively.
249 Bradford p. 96; otherwise unknown.

308

200 drachmas as a reward. So too when the people of
Abdera tried Democritus (68 B 0c D–K) for having squan-
dered his inheritance, he read them his *Great Diakosmos*
and the sections about what goes on in Hades, and said that
this was what the money had been spent on, and he was
acquitted. People who are not profligate in this way,[248] as
Amphis (fr. 43) puts it, merely

> drink all day every day,

rattle their brains with unmixed wine, have three heads
like a miniature statue of Artemis, as Diphilus (fr. 123) puts
it, and are enemies of their own property, as Satyrus says in
his *On Character Types* (fr. 27 Schorn), because they tram-
ple their own fields; pillage their own house; sell their own
possessions as if they were plunder; consider not what they
have spent but what they are going to spend, and not what
is going to be left over but what is not going to be left over;
use up in advance while they are still young the money that
ought to support them in their old age; and take pleasure in a courtesan *(hetaira)* rather than in their companions *(hetairoi)*, and in the wine rather than the people
they drink it with. Agatharchides of Cnidus says in Book
XXVIII of his *History of Europe* (*FGrH* 86 F 12): When
Gnosippus[249] became a spendthrift in Sparta, the ephors
prevented him from spending time with the young men.
According to Posidonius in Book XLIX of his *Histories*
(*FGrH* 87 F 27 = fr. 78 Edelstein–Kidd), the Romans remember a certain Apicius as having outdone everyone in
the world in his profligacy. This is the Apicius who was also
responsible for the exile of Rutilius,[250] who published his

[250] In 92 BCE. For Rutilius, see also 6.274c–e.

ρίαν ἐκδεδωκότι τῇ Ἑλλήνων φωνῇ. περὶ δὲ Ἀπικίου
ἑτέρου καὶ αὐτοῦ ἐπὶ ἀσωτίᾳ διαβοήτου ἐν τοῖς πρώτοις εἰρήκαμεν. Διογένης δ᾽ ὁ Βαβυλώνιος ἐν τοῖς
Περὶ Εὐγενείας, τὸν Φωκίωνος υἱόν, φησί, Φῶκον οὐκ
ἦν ὃς οὐκ ἐμίσει Ἀθηναίων. καὶ ὁπότε ἀπαντήσειέ τις
αὐτῷ ἔλεγεν "ὦ καταισχύνας τὸ γένος". πάντα γὰρ
ἀνάλωσε τὰ πατρῷα εἰς ἀσωτίαν καὶ μετὰ ταῦτα
ἐκολάκευε τὸν ἐπὶ τῆς Μουνιχίας· ἐφ᾽ ᾧ πάλιν ὑπὸ
f   πάντων | ἐπερραπίζετο. ἐπιδόσεων δέ ποτε γινομένων
παρελθὼν καὶ αὐτὸς εἰς τὴν ἐκκλησίαν ἔφη, "ἐπιδίδωμι
κἀγώ"· καὶ οἱ Ἀθηναῖοι ὁμοθυμαδὸν ἀνεβόησαν, "εἰς
ἀκολασίαν." ἦν δ᾽ ὁ Φῶκος καὶ φιλοπότης. νικήσαντος
γοῦν αὐτοῦ ἵπποις Παναθήναια ὡς ὁ πατὴρ εἱστία
τοὺς ἑταίρους, συνελθόντων εἰς τὸ δεῖπνον λαμπρὰ
μὲν ἦν ἡ παρασκευὴ καὶ τοῖς εἰσιοῦσι προσεφέροντο
ποδονιπτῆρες οἴνου δι᾽ ἀρωμάτων. οὓς ἰδὼν ὁ πατὴρ
169 καλέσας ‖ τὸν Φῶκον, "οὐ παύσεις," ἔφη, "τὸν ἑταῖρον
διαφθείροντά σου τὴν νίκην;" οἶδα δὲ καὶ ἄλλους
ἀσώτους πολλούς, περὶ ὧν ὑμῖν καταλείπω ζητεῖν,
πλὴν Καλλίου τοῦ Ἱππονίκου, ὃν καὶ οἱ τῶν παίδων
οἴδασι παιδαγωγοί. περὶ δὲ τῶν ἄλλων ὧν φθάνω
προβεβληκὼς εἴ τι λέγειν ἔχετε, ἀναπεπταμένας ἔχω

---

251 *PA* 15081. Phocion "the good" (*PA* 15076; Berve i #816;
402/1–318 BCE) was elected general 45 times and was known for
his independence and incorruptibility.
252 I.e. to the man in charge of the Macedonian garrison established in the Piraeus by Antipater in 322 BCE.
253 Plutarch (drawing on the same source) offers a more co-

History of Rome (*FGrH* 815 T 7a) in Greek. We discuss another Apicius, who was also famous for his profligacy, in Book I (7a–c). Diogenes of Babylon says in his *On Nobility* (fr. 52, *SVF* iii.220–1): There was no Athenian who did not loathe Phocus the son of Phocion,[251] and everyone who met him used to say: "You disgrace to your family!" This was because he used up his entire inheritance on profligate behavior and afterwards sucked up to the Munychia commander,[252] for which everyone once again abused him. Once when people were making voluntary contributions to the state, he stepped forward in the Assembly and said "I'm also making a contribution"; and the Athenians shouted with one voice: "Yes—to profligacy!" Phocus also liked to drink. After he won the horse race at the Panathenaic festival, for example, his father gave a feast for his friends; when they gathered for dinner, the preparations were brilliant, and as the guests entered the house they were offered foot-washing basins full of spiced wine. When his father saw them, he called Phocus over and said: "Stop your friend from spoiling your victory!"[253] I also know of many other spendthrifts, but I leave it up to you to raise questions about them, with the exception of Callias son of Hipponicus,[254] about whom even the slaves who educate our sons know something. But if you have anything to say on the other topics about which I have had the first word, the gates of my ears are open wide![255] So speak up;

herent version of the story at *Phoc.* 20.1–2: Phocion was a guest at a party given by someone else to celebrate Phocus' victory, and communicated his disapproval of its lavishness to his son.

[254] *PAA* 554480 (*c.*490–after 446 BCE); cf. 4.184d.

[255] Perhaps a reminiscence of a lost anapaestic line.

τῶν ὤτων τὰς πύλας. ὥστε λέγετε· ἐπιζητῶ γὰρ καὶ
⟨ὅπερ ὁ⟩ Μάγνος εἴρηκε τὸ ἐπεσθίειν καὶ τὸ ἐπιφαγεῖν.

Καὶ ὁ Αἰμιλιανὸς ἔφη· τὸ μὲν ἀσώτιον ἔχεις παρὰ
b Στράττιδι ἐν Χρυσίππῳ λέγοντι οὕτως· |

εἰ μηδὲ χέσαι γ᾽ αὐτῷ σχολὴ γενήσεται,
μηδ᾽ εἰς ἀσωτεῖ τραπέσθαι, μηδ᾽ ἐὰν
αὐτῷ ξυναντᾷ τις, λαλῆσαι μηδενί.

μαγειρικὰ δὲ σκεύη καταριθμεῖται Ἀνάξιππος ἐν Κι-
θαρῳδῷ οὕτως·

ζωμήρυσιν φέρ᾽, οἷσ᾽ ὀβελίσκους δώδεκα,
κρεάγραν, θυείαν, τυρόκνηστιν παιδικήν,
στελεόν, σκαφίδας τρεῖς, δορίδα, κοπίδας
τέτταρας.
c οὐ μὴ πρότερον οἴσεις, θεοῖσιν ἐχθρὲ σύ, |
τὸ λεβήτιον, τἀκ τοῦ λίτρου· πάλιν ὑστερεῖς;
καὶ τὴν κύβηλιν τὴν ἀγωνιστηρίαν.

τὴν χύτραν δ᾽ Ἀριστοφάνης ἐν Σκηνὰς Καταλαμ-
βανούσαις κακκάβην εἴρηκεν οὕτως·

τὴν κακκάβην γὰρ κᾶε τοῦ διδασκάλου.

κἀν Δαιταλεῦσι·

⟨ . . . ⟩ κἄγειν ἐκεῖθεν κακκάβην.

312

because I would like further information about the words *epesthiein* and *epiphagein* that Magnus used.[256]

Aemilianus said: You have the word *asōtion* ("spend-thrift's house")[257] in Strattis' *Chrysippus* (fr. 54), where he says the following:

> if he's not going to have the leisure to shit,
> or to enter a spendthrift's house, or to
> speak to anyone who bumps into him.

Anaxippus offers an enumeration of cooks' utensils in *The Citharode* (fr. 6), as follows:

> Bring me a soup-ladle! And fetch 12 skewers,
> a meat-hook, a mortar, a small cheese-grater,
> an ax-handle[258], three bowls, a flaying-knife, and four
>   cleavers!
> Fetch the little cauldron, the one from the spice-
>   market,
> first, you bastard! Are you running behind again?
> And the contest-ax![259]

Aristophanes refers to a cookpot as a *kakkabē* in *Women Occupying Tents* (fr. 495), as follows:

> for he burned his teacher's *kakkabē*.

Also in *Banqueters* (fr. 224):

> and to be bringing a *kakkabē* from there.

---

[256] At 4.164b.   [257] Like what follows, a response to the questions posed by Ulpian at 4.165d.
[258] Perhaps to be used as a rolling pin.
[259] Obscure.

Ἀντιφάνης δ' ἐν Φιλοθηβαίῳ·

πάντ' ἐστὶν ἡμῖν· ἥ τε γὰρ συνώνυμος
τῆς ἔνδον οὔσης ἔγχελυς Βοιωτία
d   μιχθεῖσα[28] κοίλοις ἐν βυθοῖσι κακκάβης |
χλιαίνετ', αἴρεθ', ἕψεται, παφλάζεται.

βατάνιον δ' εἴρηκεν Ἀντιφάνης ἐν Εὐθυδίκῳ·

ἔπειτα πουλύπους τετμημένος
ἐν βατανίοισιν ἐφθός.

Ἄλεξις ἐν Ἀσκληπιοκλείδῃ·

οὕτως δ' ὀψοποιεῖν εὐφυῶς
περὶ ⟨τὴν⟩ Σικελίαν αὐτὸς ἔμαθον ὥστε τοὺς
δειπνοῦντας εἰς τὰ βατάνι' ἐμβάλλειν ποῶ
ἐνίοτε τοὺς ὀδόντας ὑπὸ τῆς ἡδονῆς.

e   πατάνιον δὲ διὰ τοῦ π Ἀντιφάνης ἐν Γάμῳ· |

πατάνια, σεῦτλον, σίλφιον, χύτρας, λύχνους,
κορίαννα, κρόμμυ', ἅλας, ἔλαιον, τρύβλιον.

Φιλέταιρος Οἰνοπίωνι·

ὁ μάγειρος οὗτος Πατανίων προσελθέτω.

καὶ πάλιν·

[28] τμηθεῖσα 14.622f

314

Antiphanes in *The Man Who Loved Thebes* (fr. 216.1–4):[260]

> We've got everything; for the Boeotian eel,
> whose name is the same as the woman's inside,
> is mixed up inside the hollow depths of a *kakkabē*
> and is getting hot, swelling up, stewing, and
>   spluttering.

Antiphanes uses the word *batanion* ("casserole-dish") in *Euthydicus* (fr. 95):

> then an octopus cut into pieces
> and stewed in *batania*.

Alexis in *Asclepiocleides* (fr. 24):

> I myself learned to cook
> so beautifully in Sicily that
> I sometimes make the dinner-guests gnaw on
> the *batania* because they like the food so much.

But Antiphanes uses *patanion*, with a *pi*, in *The Marriage* (fr. 71):

> *patania*, a beet, silphium, cookpots, lamps,
> coriander, onions, salt, oil, a bowl.

Philetaerus in *Oenopion* (fr. 14, encompassing both quotations):

> Let this cook named Pataniōn come over here!

And again:

315

πλείους Στρατονίκου τοὺς μαθητάς μοι δοκεῖ
ἕξειν Πατανίων.

ἐν δὲ Παρασίτῳ ὁ Ἀντιφάνης καὶ τάδε εἴρηκεν·

               (Α.) ἄλλος ἐπὶ τούτῳ μέγας
ἥξει τις ἰσοτράπεζος εὐγενής— (Β.) τίνα
λέγεις; (Α.) Καρύστου θρέμμα, γηγενής, ζέων— |
(Β.) εἶτ᾽ οὐκ ἂν εἴποις; ὕπαγε. (Α.) κάκκαβον
   λέγω·
σὺ δ᾽ ἴσως ἂν εἴποις λοπάδ᾽. (Β.) ἐμοὶ δὲ
   τοὔνομα
οἴει διαφέρειν, εἴτε κάκκαβόν τινες
χαίρουσιν ὀνομάζοντες εἴτε σίττυβον;
πλὴν ὅτι λέγεις ἀγγεῖον οἶδα.

Εὔβουλος δ᾽ ἐν Ἴωνι καὶ βατάνια καὶ πατάνια λέγει
ἐν τούτοις·

τρύβλια δὲ καὶ βατάνια καὶ κακκάβια καὶ
λοπάδια καὶ πατάνια πυκινὰ † ταρβα † καὶ
οὐδ᾽ ἂν λέγων λέξαιμι. ‖

Ἡδυσμάτων δὲ κατάλογον Ἄλεξις ἐποιήσατο ἐν
Λέβητι οὕτως·

(Α.) μὴ προφάσεις ἐνταῦθά μοι, μηδ᾽ "οὐκ
   ἔχω".
(Β.) ἀλλὰ λέγ᾽ ὅτου δεῖ· λήψομαι γὰρ πάντ᾽ ἐγώ.

---

261 See 4.163f n.

I think Pataniōn's going to have more students
than Stratonicus![261]

But in *The Parasite* Antiphanes (fr. 180) says the following:

> (A.) After this will come another large
> one, as big as the table, a noble—(B.) What
> are you talking about? (A.) child of Carystus, born of
>   the earth, boiling—
> (B.) Tell me! Spit it out! (A.) I'm referring to a
>   *kakkabos*;
> you might perhaps refer to it as a *lopas* ("casserole-
>   dish"). (B.) Do you think the name
> makes any difference to me, if some people like
> to call it a *kakkabos*, or a *sittubos*[262]?
> But I understand you're referring to a vessel.

Eubulus uses both *batania* and *patania* in *Ion* (fr. 37), in
the following lines:

> bowls and *batania* and *kakkabia* and
> *lopadia*[263] and *patania*, one after another [corrupt]
>   and
> I couldn't name them if I tried.

Alexis produced a list of spices in *The Cauldron* (fr.
132), as follows:

> (A.) Don't offer me any excuses here, and no "I
>   don't have it"!
> (B.) Tell me what you need; I'll buy everything.

---

[262] An otherwise unattested word, probably invented by the
poet.
[263] A diminutive of *lopas*; cf. Antiph. fr. 180.5 (above).

(A.) ὀρθῶς γε· πρῶτον μὲν λάβ᾽ ἐλθὼν σήσαμα.
(Β.) ἀλλ᾽ ἔστιν ἔνδον. (Α.) ἀσταφίδα κεκομμένην,
μάραθον, ἄνηθον, νᾶπυ, καυλόν, σίλφιον,
κορίαννον αὖον, ῥοῦν, κύμινον, κάππαριν, |
ὀρίγανον, γήτειον, ἄννηττον[29], θύμον,
σφάκον, σίραιον, σέσελι[30], πήγανον, πράσον.

ἐν δὲ Παννυχίδι ἢ Ἐρίθοις· μάγειρον δὲ ποιεῖ λέ-
γοντα·

κύκλῳ δεήσει περιτρέχειν με καὶ βοᾶν,
ἄν του δέωμαι. δεῖπνον αἰτήσεις με σὺ
ἤδη παρελθών· οὐκ ἔχων δὲ τυγχάνω
οὐκ ὄξος, οὐκ ἄνηθον, οὐκ ὀρίγανον,
οὐ θρῖον, οὐκ ἔλαιον, οὐκ ἀμυγδάλας,
οὐ σκόροδον, οὐ σίραιον, οὐχὶ γήτειον, |
οὐ βολβόν, οὐ πῦρ, οὐ κύμινον, οὐχ ἅλας,
οὐκ ᾠόν, οὐ ξύλ᾽, οὐ σκάφην, οὐ τήγανον·
οὐχ ἱμονιάν, οὐ λάκκον εἶδον, οὐ φρέαρ·
οὐ στάμνος ἐστί· διακενῆς δ᾽ ἔστηκ᾽ ἐγὼ
ἔχων μάχαιραν, προσέτι περιεζωσμένος.

κἂν Πονήρᾳ·

                    τῆς ὀριγάνου
πρώτιστον ὑποθεὶς εἰς λοπάδα νεανικὴν
τὸ τρίμμ᾽ ἐπιπολῆς εὐρύθμως διειμένον

---

[29] ἄννηττον Kassel–Austin: ἄνοιττον Pollux: σκόροδον A
[30] πέπερι Pollux

BOOK IV

(A.) Alright. First go buy sesame seeds—
(B.) I have some inside. (A.) chopped raisins,
fennel, dill, mustard, silphium-stalk, silphium,
dried coriander, sumach-fruit, cumin, pepper,
marjoram, *gētion*[264], anise, thyme,
sage, grape-must, hartwort, rue, leeks.

Also in *The All-Night Festival or Hired Workers* (fr. 179);
he represents a cook as saying:

I'm going to have to run in circles and scream
if I need anything. The minute you arrive, you're
going to ask for dinner. But as it happens, I've got
no vinegar, no dill, no marjoram,
no grape-leaves, no oil, no almonds,
no garlic, no grape-must, no *gēteion*,
no hyacinth bulbs, no fire, no cumin, no salt,
no eggs, no firewood, no bowl, no frying pan;
I've seen no well-rope, no cistern, and no well;
there's no water-jar; and I'm standing here for no
    reason
with my butcher's knife and wearing my apron.

Also in *The Miserable Woman* (fr. 193):

                              after you first
put the marjoram sauce, evenly
soaked on top with vinegar, into a small

[264] See 4.131e n.

ὄξει σιραίῳ χρωματίσας καὶ σιλφίῳ
πυκνῷ πατάξας.

d ἐπεσθίειν εἴρηκε Τηλεκλείδης | Πρυτάνεσιν οὕτως·

τυρίον ἐπεσθίοντα.

ἐπιφαγεῖν δ' Εὔπολις Ταξιάρχοις ·

  ἐπιφαγεῖν μηδὲν ἄλλ' ἢ κρόμμυον
λέποντα καὶ τρεῖς ἁλμάδας.

καὶ Ἀριστοφάνης Πλούτῳ·

πρὸ τοῦ δ' ὑπὸ τῆς πενίας ἅπαντ' ἐπήσθιον[31].

τῶν δὲ μαγείρων διάφοροί τινες ἦσαν οἱ καλούμενοι
τραπεζοποιοί. εἰς ὅτι δὲ οὗτοι προσελαμβάνοντο σαφῶς παρίστησιν Ἀντιφάνης ἐν Μετοίκῳ·

  προσέλαβον ἐλθὼν τουτονὶ
e τραπεζοποιόν, ὃς πλυνεῖ σκεύη, λύχνους |
ἑτοιμάσει, σπονδὰς ποήσει, τἄλλ' ὅσα
τούτῳ προσήκει.

ζητητέον δὲ εἰ καὶ ὁ τραπεζοκόμος ὁ αὐτός ἐστι τῷ
τραπεζοποιῷ. Ἰόβας γὰρ ὁ βασιλεὺς ἐν ταῖς Ὁμοι-

---

[31] ἅπανθ' ὑπήσθιεν Ar.[R]: ἅπαντα γ' ἤσθιεν Ar.[V]

[265] In the fragments of Teleclides and Eupolis the prefix *ep*-
appears to carry the sense "in addition" (sc. to the bread or other
starch consumed as the main course), although it is not clear that

casserole-dish, color it with grape-must and beat it up with a lot of silphium.

Teleclides uses the word *epesthiein*[265] in *Prytaneis* (fr. 27.3),[266] as follows:

eating in addition *(epesthionta)* a little cheese.

Eupolis uses *epiphagein* in *Taxiarchs* (fr. 275):

to eat *(epiphagein)* nothing else except a peeling onion and three brined olives.

Also Aristophanes in *Wealth* (1005):

Previously I used to eat *(epēsthion)* anything because of my poverty.

The men referred to as *trapezopoioi* ("table-makers") were different from cooks. The fact that they too were hired is established by Antiphanes in *The Resident Alien* (fr. 150):

I went and hired this
trapezopoios here, who's going to wash the dishes, get the lamps
ready, prepare the libations, and do whatever else he's supposed to.

We also need to consider the question of whether the *trapezokomos* ("table-setter") is the same as the *trapezopoios*. For King Juba in his *Similarities* (*FGrH* 275 F 14) claims

---

Athenaeus or his source took it that way; cf. 4.164b. In the line from Aristophanes' *Wealth*, manuscript R's *hup-* rather than Athenaeus' *ep-* probably represents the correct reading.

[266] Two additional verses probably from the same fragment are quoted at 11.485f.

ότησι τὸν αὐτὸν εἶναί φησι ⟨τὸν⟩ τραπεζοκόμον καὶ
τὸν ὑπὸ Ῥωμαίων καλούμενον στρούκτωρα, παρατιθέμενος ἐκ δράματος Ἀλεξάνδρου ᾧ ἐπιγραφὴ Πότος·

εἰς αὔριόν με δεῖ λαβεῖν αὐλητρίδα.
f   τραπεζοποιόν, δημιουργὸν λήψομαι· |
ἐπὶ τοῦτ᾽ ἀπέστειλ᾽ ἐξ ἀγροῦ μ᾽ ὁ δεσπότης.

ἐκάλουν δὲ τραπεζοποιὸν τὸν τραπεζῶν ἐπιμελητὴν
καὶ τῆς ἄλλης εὐκοσμίας. Φιλήμων Παρεισιόντι·

περὶ τοὐπτάνιον οὐ γίγνεθ᾽ ἡ σκευωρία·
τραπεζοποιός ἐστ᾽ ἐπὶ τοῦ διακονεῖν.

ἔλεγον δὲ καὶ ἐπιτραπεζώματα τὰ ἐπιτιθέμενα τῇ
171 τραπέζῃ βρώματα. Πλάτων Μενελάῳ· ‖

ὡς ὀλίγα λοιπὰ τῶν ἐπιτραπεζωμάτων;

ἐκάλουν δὲ καὶ ἀγοραστὴν τὸν τὰ ὄψα ὠνούμενον, νῦν
δ᾽ ὀψωνάτωρα, ὡς Ξενοφῶν ἐν δευτέρῳ Ἀπομνημονευμάτων οὑτωσὶ λέγων· διάκονον δ᾽ ἂν καὶ ἀγοραστὴν
τὸν τοιοῦτον ἐθέλοιμεν προῖκα λαβεῖν; παρὰ δὲ Με-
νάνδρῳ ἐστὶ κοινότερον ἐν Φανίῳ·

φειδωλὸς ἦν καὶ μέτριος ἀγοραστής.

ὀψώνην δ᾽ εἴρηκεν Ἀριστοφάνης ἐν Ταγηνισταῖς διὰ
b   τούτων· |

---

267 Latin structor.   268 Two additional verses of the same
fragment are given at 14.641b.

that the *trapezokomos* is identical with what the Romans call a *strouktōr*[267], and he cites from the play by Alexander entitled *The Drinking Bout* (fr. 3):

> Tomorrow I have to hire a pipe-girl.
> I'll hire a *trapezopoios*, one who works free-lance;
> this is what my master sent me from the country for.

They referred to the man who took care of the tables and organized everything else as the *trapezopoios*. Philemon in *The Man Who Tried To Sneak In* (fr. 64):

> Your authority doesn't extend to the kitchen;
> a *trapezopoios* is in charge of the serving.

They also used the word *epitrapezōmata* for the food put on the table *(epi- . . . tēi trapezēi)*. Plato in *Menelaus* (fr. 76.2):[268]

> How is it there's so little left of the *epitrapezōmata*?

And they referred to the man who bought the food *(opsa)*, for whom the modern term is the *opsōnatōr*[269], as an *agorastēs* ("marketer, buyer"), as Xenophon shows in Book II of the *Memorabilia* (1.5.2), where he says the following: Would we be willing to accept a man like this as a servant or an *agorastēs*, even as a gift? The word appears in a more general sense in Menander's *Phanion* (fr. 390):

> He was a thrifty, moderate shopper *(agorastēs)*.

Aristophanes uses the word *opsōnēs* ("*opson*-man," i.e. "*opson*-buyer") in *Frying-Pan Men* (fr. 517), as follows:

[269] Latin *obsonator*.

ὡς οὐψώνης διατρίβειν
ἡμῖν τἄριστον ἔοικε.

παροψωνεῖν δ᾽ ἔφη Κρατῖνος ἐν Κλεοβουλίναις οὕτως·
< . . . > παραγοράζειν δὲ Ἄλεξις ἐν Δρωπίδῃ. εἰλέα-
τροι δὲ καλοῦνται, ὥς φησι Πάμφιλος, οἱ ἐπὶ τὴν
βασιλικὴν καλοῦντες τράπεζαν παρὰ τὸ ἐλεόν. Ἀρτεμίδωρος δ᾽ αὐτοὺς δειπνοκλήτορας ὀνομάζει. ἐκάλουν
δέ, φησί, καὶ τοὺς προγεύστας ἐδεάτρους[32], ὅτι προ-
ήσθιον τῶν βασιλέων πρὸς ἀσφάλειαν. νῦν δὲ ὁ
ἐδέατρος ἐπιστάτης γέγονε τῆς ὅλης διακονίας. ἦν δ᾽
c   ἐπιφανὴς καὶ ἔντιμος ἡ χρεία. Χάρης γοῦν | ἐν τῇ
τρίτῃ τῶν Ἱστοριῶν Πτολεμαῖόν φησι τὸν Σωτῆρα
ἐδέατρον ἀποδειχθῆναι Ἀλεξάνδρου. μήποτε δὲ καὶ ὃν
νῦν καλοῦσι Ῥωμαῖοι προγεύστην τότε οἱ Ἕλληνες
προτένθην ὠνόμαζον, ὡς Ἀριστοφάνης ἐν προτέραις
Νεφέλαις διὰ τούτων·

(Στ.) πῶς οὐ δέχονται δῆτα τῇ νουμηνίᾳ
ἀρχαὶ τὰ πρυτανεῖ᾽, ἀλλ᾽ ἔνη τε καὶ νέα;
(Φε.) ὅπερ οἱ προτένθαι γὰρ δοκοῦσί μοι παθεῖν·

32 ἐδεάτρους Valckenaer: αιδεελαιατρους A: ἐλεάτρους CE

270 The quotation has fallen out of the text. According to D.L.
1.89, Cleobulina wrote riddles in dactylic hexameter.
271 Cf. 4.173a.   272 For Artemidorus, see 1.5b n.
273 Apparently derived here from *edō* ("eat") + *tēreō* ("guard,
watch"), although the correct form of the noun may be *eleatros/
eileatros* (see above).

since the *opsōnēs* seems
to be delaying our dinner.

Cratinus used the word *paropsōnein* ("to buy extra *opson*")
in *Cleoboulinas* (fr. 99), as follows . . . [270] Alexis uses
paragorazein ("to do extra shopping") in *Drōpides* (fr. 62).
According to Pamphilus (fr. III Schmidt), the men who
summon guests to the King's table are referred to as
eileatroi, from *eleon* ("cook's table").[271] But Artemidorus
calls them *deipnoklētores* ("dinner-callers").[272] And they
used to refer, he says, to the men who tasted his food in advance *(hoi progeustai)* as *edeatroi*[273], because they ate before the Kings did, to ensure their safety; but today the
edeatros has become the supervisor of the dinner service
generally. The office was a distinguished and honorable
one. Chares, for example, says in Book III of his *Histories*
(*FGrH* 125 F 1) that Ptolemy Soter[274] was appointed as Alexander's *edeatros*. But perhaps the Greeks in those days
called the individual to whom the Romans refer today as a
progeustēs[275] a *protenthēs*, as Aristophanes does in the first
Clouds (1196–1200),[276] in the following lines:

> (Strepsiades) Then why don't the magistrates accept
>   the sureties
> on New Moon Day, but on the Old-and-New Day[277]?
> (Pheidippides) I think the same thing happens to
>   them as to the food-inspectors *(protenthai)*—

[274] Reigned 323–283 BCE, but originally one of Alexander's
generals (Berve i #668). [275] The word (used above) is
Greek. [276] Actually from the second, revised version of the
play. [277] I.e. the final day of the preceding month, as opposed to the first day of the month (New Moon Day).

ATHENAEUS

d ἵν᾽ ὡς τάχιστα τὰ πρυτανεῖ᾽ ὑφελοίατο, |
   διὰ τοῦτο προυτένθευσαν ἡμέρᾳ μιᾷ.

μνημονεύει αὐτῶν καὶ Φερεκράτης ἐν Ἀγρίοις·

                              μὴ θαυμάσῃς·
τῶν γὰρ προτενθῶν ἐσμεν. ἀλλ᾽ οὐκ οἶσθα σύ.

καὶ Φιλύλλιος ἐν Ἡρακλεῖ·

βούλεσθε δῆτ᾽ ἐγὼ φράσω τίς εἰμ᾽ ἐγώ;
ἡ τῶν προτενθῶν Δορπία καλουμένη.

εὑρίσκω δὲ καὶ ψήφισμα ἐπὶ Κηφισοδώρου ἄρχοντος
Ἀθήνησι γενόμενον, ἐν ᾧ ὥσπερ τι σύστημα οἱ προ-
e τένθαι εἰσί, καθάπερ καὶ οἱ παράσιτοι | ὀνομαζόμενοι,
ἔχον οὕτως· Φῶκος εἶπεν· ὅπως ἂν ἡ βουλὴ ἄγῃ τὰ
Ἀπατούρια μετὰ τῶν ἄλλων Ἀθηναίων κατὰ τὰ πάτρια, ἐψηφίσθαι τῇ βουλῇ ἀφεῖσθαι τοὺς βουλευτὰς
τὰς ἡμέρας ἅσπερ καὶ αἱ ἄλλαι ἀρχαὶ αἱ ἀφεταὶ ἀπὸ
τῆς ἡμέρας ἧς οἱ προτένθαι ἄγουσι πέντε ἡμέρας. ὅτι
δ᾽ εἶχον οἱ ἀρχαῖοι καὶ τοὺς προγεύστας καλουμένους
Ξενοφῶν ἐν τῷ ἐπιγραφομένῳ Ἱέρωνι ἢ Τυραννικῷ
φησιν· ὁ τύραννος οὐδὲ σιτίοις καὶ ποτοῖς πιστεύων
f διάγει, ἀλλὰ | καὶ τούτων ἀντὶ τοῦ ἀπάρχεσθαι θεοῖς

---

278 Dorpia (personified here, and probably the prologue
speaker) was the first day of the Apatouria festival, which included
public feasting.
279 Probably 366/5 BCE, although another man named Cephisodorus was eponymous archon in 323/2. The Phocus who pro-

326

in order to embezzle the sureties as quickly as
  possible,
they start tasting them one day early.

Pherecrates as well mentions them in *Savages* (fr. 7):

> Don't be surprised;
> because we're some of the food-inspectors
>   (*protenthai*). But you're unaware of this.

Also Philyllius in *Heracles* (fr. 7):

> Do you want me to tell you who I am?
> I'm known as Dorpia, and I belong to the food-
>   inspectors (*protenthai*).[278]

I also find a decree passed in Athens during the archonship
of Cephisodorus,[279] in which the *protenthai* are something
like a college, as the men referred to as *parasitoi* are.[280] It
runs as follows: Phocus made the motion: In order that the
Council may celebrate the Apatouria festival in the traditional manner along with the other Athenians, that it be
decreed by the Council that its members are to be released
from their duties during the days when the other officials
who receive such releases are, for five days beginning on
the day when the *protenthai* begin to celebrate the festival.
Xenophon in his work entitled *Hieron or The Life of the
Tyrant* (4.2) says that the ancients also had the individuals
referred to as *progeustai*: The tyrant spends his life uncertain about what he eats and drinks; and rather than making
preliminary offerings to the gods, they first order their ser-

posed the decree may well be the individual discussed in 4.168e–
9a (where see n.).   [280] Cf. 6.234d–5e.

τοῖς διακονοῦσι πρῶτον κελεύουσιν ἀπογεύεσθαι διὰ
τὸ ἀπιστεῖν μὴ καὶ ἐν τούτοις κακόν τι φάγωσιν ἢ
172 πίωσιν. Ἀναξίλας δ' ἐν Καλυψοῖ φησιν· ||

    προγεύσεταί σοι πρῶτον ἡ γραῦς τοῦ ποτοῦ.

τοὺς δὲ τὰ πέμματα προσέτι τε τοὺς ποιοῦντας τοὺς
πλακοῦντας οἱ πρότερον δημιουργοὺς ἐκάλουν. Μένανδρος Ψευδηρακλεῖ· καταμεμφόμενος δὲ τοὺς μα-
γείρους ὡς ἐπιχειροῦντας καὶ οἷς μὴ δεῖ φησιν·

    μάγειρ', ἀηδής μοι δοκεῖς εἶναι σφόδρα.
    πόσας τραπέζας μέλλομεν ποιεῖν, τρίτον
    ἤδη μ' ἐρωτᾷς. χοιρίδιον ἓν θύομεν,
b   ὀκτὼ ποήσοντες τραπέζας, δύο, ἢ μίαν, |
    τί σοι διαφέρει τοῦτο; παράθες † σημίαν. †
    οὐκ ἔστι κανδύλους ποεῖν οὐδ' οἷα σὺ
    εἴωθας εἰς ταὐτὸν καρυκεύειν μέλι,
    σεμίδαλιν, ᾠά. πάντα γὰρ τἀναντία
    νῦν ἐστιν· ὁ μάγειρος γὰρ ἐγχύτους ποεῖ,
    πλακοῦντας ὀπτᾷ, χόνδρον ἕψει καὶ φέρει
    μετὰ τὸ τάριχος, εἶτα θρῖον καὶ βότρυς·
    ἡ δημιουργὸς δ' ἀντιπαρατεταγμένη
    κρεάδι' ὀπτᾷ καὶ κίχλας τραγήματα.
c   ἔπειθ' ὁ δειπνῶν μὲν τραγηματίζεται, |

---

281 For *kandulos* and *karukē* (below), see 4.132f n.

328

vants to have a taste of these items, out of suspicion that they may eat or drink something harmful in them. Anaxilas says in *Calypso* (fr. 10):

> First the old woman will take an initial taste
> (*progeusetai*) of your drink for you.

In the old days they referred to the people who produced pastries *(pemmata)* as well as flat-cakes as *dēmiourgoi* ("artisans"). Menander in *The Fake Heracles* (fr. 409); he finds fault with the cooks for meddling with matters they should not, saying:

> Cook, I think you're extremely obnoxious.
> As for how many tables we're going to prepare, this is
> now the third time you're asking me. We're
>   sacrificing one little pig;
> whether we're going to prepare eight tables, or two,
>   or one—
> what difference does it make to you? Serve [corrupt]!
> It's not a matter of making *kanduloi*[281] or the kinds of
>   dishes
> you're used to, when you combine honey, flour,
> and eggs in a *karukē*. Everything's the other way
> around now. The cook makes moulded cakes,
> bakes flat-cakes, and boils wheat pudding and serves it
> after the saltfish, followed by a fig-leaf pastry and
>   grapes,
> whereas the artisan-woman (*hē dēmiourgos*) who's
>   lined up opposite him
> roasts bits of meat and thrushes for snacks.
> The result is that the guest who comes for dinner has
>   a snack;

μυρισάμενος δὲ καὶ στεφανωσάμενος πάλιν
<σύμμεικτα> δειπνεῖ τὰ μελίπηκτα ταῖς κίχλαις.

ὅτι δὲ ἐκεχώριστο τὰ τῆς ὑπουργίας, πεμμάτων μὲν
προνοουσῶν τῶν δημιουργῶν, ὀψαρτυτικῆς δὲ τῶν
μαγείρων, Ἀντιφάνης διεσάφησεν ἐν Χρυσίδι οὕτως·

τέτταρες δ᾽ αὐλητρίδες
ἔχουσι μισθὸν καὶ μάγειροι δώδεκα,
καὶ δημιουργοὶ μέλιτος αἰτοῦσαι σκάφας.

Μένανδρος Δημιουργῷ·

d   (Α.) τί τοῦτο, παῖ; διακονικῶς γάρ, νὴ Δία, |
προελήλυθας. (Β.) ναί. πλάττομεν γὰρ πλάσματα
τὴν νύκτα τ᾽ ἠγρυπνήκαμεν· καὶ νῦν ἔτι
ἀπόητα πάμπολλ᾽ ἐστὶν ἡμῖν.

πεμμάτων δὲ πρῶτόν φησιν μνημονεῦσαι Πανύασσιν
Σέλευκος, ἐν οἷς περὶ τῆς παρ᾽ Αἰγυπτίοις ἀνθρωπο-
θυσίας διηγεῖται, πολλὰ μὲν ἐπιθεῖναι λέγων πέμματα, πολλὰς δὲ νοσσάδας ὄρνις, προτέρου Στησιχόρου
ἢ Ἰβύκου ἐν τοῖς Ἄθλοις ἐπιγραφομένοις εἰρηκότος
φέρεσθαι τῇ παρθένῳ δῶρα

e   σασαμίδας | χόνδρον τε καὶ ἐγκρίδας
ἄλλα τε πέμματα καὶ μέλι χλωρόν.

---

282 A prostitute's name.
283 I.e. the funeral games of Pelias.
284 See 3.110b n.

330

then after he's put on perfume and another garland,
he dines on a combination of honey cakes and
    thrushes.

That the different aspects of the service were kept separate, with the artisan-women (*dēmiourgoi*) worrying about
the pastries (*pemmata*) and the cooks about the other
dishes, is made quite clear by Antiphanes in *Chrysis*[282] (fr.
224), as follows:

> four pipe-girls
> are employed and twelve cooks,
> and artisan-women (*dēmiourgoi*) requesting bowls of
>   honey.

Menander in *The Artisan* (fr. 110):

> (A.) What's going on, slave? Because you've come
>   outside, by Zeus,
> looking busy. (B.) Yes; for we're producing moulded
>   shapes
> and haven't slept all night. And now we still
> have an immense amount left to do.

Seleucus (*FGrH* 634 F 2 = fr. 65 Müller) claims that
Panyassis (fr. 12 Bernabé) is the first author to mention
pastries (*pemmata*), in the passage where he describes
how the Egyptians sacrificed human beings, saying that
they put many *pemmata* and nestling birds on the altars.
But before him Stesichorus (*PMG* 179(a)) or Ibycus in the
work entitled *The Games*[283] says that the gifts brought for
the girl were:

> sesame cakes, wheat pudding, honey-and-oil cakes[284],
> and other pastries (*pemmata*) and pale honey.

ὅτι δὲ τὸ ποίημα τοῦτο Στησιχόρου ἐστὶν ἱκανώτατος
μάρτυς Σιμωνίδης ὁ ποιητής, ὃς περὶ τοῦ Μελεάγρου
τὸν λόγον ποιούμενός φησιν·

ὃς δουρὶ πάντας
νίκασε νέους δινάεντα βαλὼν
Ἄναυρον ὕπερ πολυβότρυος ἐξ Ἰωλκοῦ·
f   οὕτω γὰρ Ὅμηρος ἠδὲ Στασίχορος ἄεισε λαοῖς. |

ὁ γὰρ Στησίχορος οὕτως εἴρηκεν ἐν τῷ προκειμένῳ
ᾄσματι τοῖς Ἄθλοις·

θρῴσκων μὲν ἄρ' Ἀμφιάραος ἄκοντι δὲ
νίκασεν Μελέαγρος.

οὐκ ἀγνοῶ δὲ καὶ περὶ Δηλίων ἃ Ἀπολλόδωρος ὁ
Ἀθηναῖος εἴρηκεν ὅτι μαγείρων καὶ τραπεζοποιῶν
παρείχοντο χρείας τοῖς παραγινομένοις πρὸς τὰς ἱερουργίας, καὶ ὅτι ἦν αὐτοῖς ἀπὸ τῶν πράξεων ὀνόματα
173   Μαγίδες καὶ Γογγύλοι, || ἐπειδὴ τὰς μάζας, φησὶν
Ἀριστοφάνης[33], ἐν ταῖς θοίναις δι' ἡμέρας τρίβοντες
παρεῖχον ὥσπερ[34] γυναιξὶ γογγύλας μεμαγμένας. καλοῦνται δὲ καὶ μέχρι νῦν τινες αὐτῶν Χοίρακοι καὶ
Ἀμνοὶ καὶ Ἀρτυσίλεῳ καὶ Σήσαμοι καὶ Ἀρτυσίτραγοι
καὶ Νεωκόροι[35] καὶ Ἰχθυβόλοι, τῶν δὲ γυναικῶν Κυ-

33 Ἀριστοφάνης Schweighäuser: Ἀριστοτέλης ACE
34 ὥσπερ ἐν A
35 Kaibel suggested Ἀρτοτράγοι καὶ Κρεωβόροι, while
Gulick proposed emending the final word to Κρεωκόροι.

As for the fact that this poem is by Stesichorus, the poet Simonides (*PMG* 564) will do quite well as a witness when he says, in the course of telling the story of Meleager:

> who defeated all
> the young men with his spear and drove them over
> the eddying Anaurus out of Iolcus full of grapes.
> For this is how Homer and Stesichorus sang the song
>   to the people.

Because Stesichorus puts it this way in his poem *The Games* (*PMG* 179(b)), mentioned above:

> Amphiaraus was victorious in the long jump,
>   Meleager with the javelin.

Nor am I unfamiliar with what Apollodorus of Athens (*FGrH* 244 F 151) has to say about the inhabitants of Delos, which is that they worked as cooks and *trapezopoioi*[285] for visitors attending the sacred rites, and that because of what they did, some of them were named Magis[286] or Gongulis ("Round"), since Aristophanes (cf. *Pax* 27–8) claims that at their feasts they worked the barley-cakes all day long and served them kneaded round (*gongulai*), as one would for women. Even today some of them are called Choirakos[287], Amnos ("Lamb"), Artusileōs ("Public Seasoner"), Sēsamos ("Sesame Seed"), Artusitragos ("Goat-Seasoner"), Neōkoros ("Temple Warden"), and Ichthubolos ("Fish-Spearer"); some of the women are named Kuminanthē ("Cumin-Flower"); and they are all collec-

---

[285] Cf. 4.170d–e.

[286] Elsewhere a type of cake; cognate with *massō*, "knead."

[287] Cognate with *choiros*, "piglet."

μινάνθαι, κοινῇ δὲ πάντες Ἐλεοδύται διὰ τὸ τοῖς
ἐλεοῖς ὑποδύεσθαι διακονοῦντες ἐν ταῖς θοίναις. ἐλεὸς
δ᾽ ἐστὶν ἡ μαγειρικὴ τράπεζα. Ὅμηρος·

b   αὐτὰρ ἐπεί ῥ᾽ ὤπτησε καὶ εἰν ἐλεοῖσιν ἔθηκε[36]. |

ὅθεν καὶ Πολυκράτων ὁ Κρίθωνος Ῥηναιεὺς δίκην
γραφόμενος οὐ Δηλίους αὐτοὺς ὀνομάζει, ἀλλὰ τὸ
κοινὸν τῶν Ἐλεοδυτῶν ἐπῃτιάσατο. καὶ ὁ τῶν Ἀμφι-
κτυόνων δὲ νόμος κελεύει ὕδωρ παρέχειν ἐλεοδύτας,
τοὺς τραπεζοποιοὺς καὶ τοὺς τοιούτους διακόνους σημαίνων. Κρίτων δ᾽ ὁ κωμῳδιοποιὸς ἐν Φιλοπράγμονι
παρασίτους τοῦ θεοῦ καλεῖ τοὺς Δηλίους διὰ τούτων·

       Φοίνικα μεγάλου κύριον βαλλαντίου
c   ναύκληρον ἐν τῷ λιμένι ποιήσας ἄπλουν |
       καὶ † φορμιῶσαι ναῦς ἀναγκάσας δύο,
       εἰς Δῆλον ἐλθεῖν ἠθέλησ᾽ ἐκ Πειραιῶς
       πάντων ἀκούων διότι παρασίτῳ τόπος
       οὗτος τρία μόνος ἀγαθὰ κεκτῆσθαι δοκεῖ,
       εὔοψον ἀγοράν, † παντοδαπαν οὐκουντ᾽ † ὄχλον,
d   αὐτοὺς παρασίτους τοῦ θεοῦ τοὺς Δηλίους. |

Ἀχαιὸς δ᾽ ὁ Ἐρετριεὺς ἐν Ἀλκμαίωνι τῷ σατυρικῷ

---

[36] Other witnesses have ἔχευεν.

[288] Otherwise unknown. Rhenaea is a tiny island very close to
Delos.
[289] This is most naturally taken as a reference to the regula-

tively referred to as Eleodutai because they get under the tables *(eleois hupoduesthai)* when they serve the food at the feasts. A cook's table is an *eleos*. Homer *(Il.* 9.215):

> but after he roasted it and placed it on tables *(eleoi).*

This is why, when Polycraton son of Crithon of Rhenaea[288] sued them, he did not refer to them as Delians, but brought charges against the "Eleodutid state." And the Amphictyonic law[289] requires that water be provided by *eleodutai,* meaning the *trapezopoioi* and other servants of that sort. The comic poet Crito in *The Busybody* (fr. 3) refers to the Delians as the parasites of the god, in the following verses:

> After he made a Phoenician shipowner, who
>   controlled
> a large purse, give up his voyage
> and forced him to [corrupt] two ships,
> he wanted to leave Piraeus and go to Delos,
> because he heard that this appears to be the only
> place in the world that has three good features for a
>   parasite:
> a marketplace full of fine food; a population that
>   [corrupt];
> and the Delians themselves, who are parasites of the
>   god.

Achaeus of Eretria in the satyr play *Alcmeon (TrGF* 20 F

tions for Apollo's shrine at Delphi, which was controlled by an Amphictyonic (literally "Dwelling-Around," i.e. "Regional") League of Greek states. But perhaps the term is used loosely (and uniquely) here to refer to the magistrates who oversaw Delos.

καρυκκοποιοὺς καλεῖ τοὺς Δελφοὺς διὰ τούτων·

κἀρυκκοποιοὺς προσβλέπων βδελύσσομαι,

παρόσον τὰ ἱερεῖα περιτέμνοντες δῆλον ὡς ἐμαγεί-
ρευον αὐτὰ καὶ ἐκαρύκκευον. εἰς ταῦτα δὲ ἀποβλέπων
καὶ Ἀριστοφάνης ἔφη·

ἀλλ᾽ ὦ Δελφῶν πλείστας ἀκονῶν
Φοῖβε μαχαίρας
καὶ προδιδάσκων τοὺς σοὺς προπόλους.

κἂν τοῖς ἑξῆς δ᾽ ὁ Ἀχαιός φησιν·

τίς ὑποκεκρυμμένος μένει,
† σαραβάκων † κοπίδων συνομώνυμε; |

ἐπισκώπτουσι γὰρ οἱ σάτυροι τοὺς Δελφοὺς ὡς περὶ
τὰς θυσίας καὶ τὰς θοίνας διατρίβοντας. Σῆμος δ᾽ ἐν
τετάρτῃ Δηλιάδος, Δελφοῖς, φησί, παραγινομένοις εἰς
Δῆλον παρεῖχον Δήλιοι ἅλας καὶ ὄξος καὶ ἔλαιον καὶ
ξύλα καὶ στρώματα. Ἀριστοτέλης δ᾽ ἢ Θεόφραστος ἐν
τοῖς Ὑπομνήμασι περὶ Μαγνήτων λέγων τῶν ἐπὶ τοῦ
Μαιάνδρου ποταμοῦ ὅτι Δελφῶν εἰσιν ἄποικοι τὰς
αὐτὰς ἐπιτελοῦντας αὐτοὺς ποιεῖ χρείας τοῖς παρα-
γιγνομένοις τῶν ξένων, λέγων οὕτως· | Μάγνητες οἱ
ἐπὶ τῷ Μαιάνδρῳ ποταμῷ κατοικοῦντες ἱεροὶ τοῦ θεοῦ,
Δελφῶν ἄποικοι, παρέχουσι τοῖς ἐπιδημοῦσι στέγην,
ἅλας, ἔλαιον, ὄξος, ἔτι λύχνον, κλίνας, στρώματα,
τραπέζας. Δημήτριος δ᾽ ὁ Σκήψιος ἐν ἕκτῳ καὶ δεκάτῳ
Τρωικοῦ Διακόσμου ἐν τῇ Λακωνικῇ φησιν ἐπὶ τῆς

12) refers to the inhabitants of Delphi as *karukkē*[290]-makers, in the following lines:

> When I see these *karukkē*-makers, I'm disgusted,

inasmuch as it is clear that, when they trimmed the meat, they used to cook it and make *karukkē*. This is what Aristophanes (fr. 705) is referring to when he says:

> But, O Phoebus, you who sharpen the largest number
> of butcher's knives belonging to the people of Delphi
> and teach your servants in advance.

And in the lines that follow, Achaeus says (*TrGF* 20 F 13):

> Who remains hidden underneath,
> O you who share the name of [corrupt] cleavers?;

for the satyrs are mocking the Delphians for spending all their time on sacrifices and feasts. Semus says in Book IV of the *History of Delos* (*FGrH* 396 F 7): When the Delphians visited Delos, the Delians supplied them with salt, vinegar, oil, firewood, and bedding. Aristotle (fr. 772) or Theophrastus asserts in the *Commentaries* that the Magnesians who live along the Maeander River are colonists of the Delphians, and represents them as providing the same services for visiting foreigners. He says the following: The Magnesians who live along the Maeander River devote themselves to the god;[291] are colonists of the Delphians; and supply their visitors with shelter, salt, oil, and vinegar, as well as a lamp, couches, bedding, and tables. Demetrius of Scepsis says in Book XVI of the *Trojan Catalogue* (fr. 10 Gaede) that shrines were founded along

---

[290] See 4.132f n.   [291] Apollo.

όδοῦ τῆς καλουμένης Ὑακινθίδος ἱδρῦσθαι ἥρωας
174 Μάττωνα καὶ Κεράωνα ὑπὸ τῶν ἐν τοῖς ‖ φιδιτίοις
ποιούντων τε τὰς μάζας καὶ κεραννύντων τὸν οἶνον
διακόνων. ὁ δ᾽ αὐτὸς ἱστορεῖ κἂν τῷ τετάρτῳ καὶ
εἰκοστῷ τῆς αὐτῆς πραγματείας Δαίτην ἥρωα τιμώμε-
νον παρὰ τοῖς Τρωσίν, οὗ μνημονεύειν Μίμνερμον.
κἂν Κύπρῳ δέ φησι τιμᾶσθαι Ἡγήσανδρος ὁ Δελφὸς
Δία Εἰλαπιναστήν τε καὶ Σπλαγχνοτόμον.

      Πολλῶν δὲ τοιούτων ἔτι λεγομένων ἐκ τῶν γειτόνων
τις ἐξηκούσθη ὑδραύλεως ἦχος πάνυ τι ἡδὺς καὶ
τερπνός, ὡς πάντας ἡμᾶς ἐπιστραφῆναι θελχθέντας
b ὑπὸ τῆς | ἐμμελείας. καὶ ὁ Οὐλπιανὸς ἀποβλέψας πρὸς
τὸν μουσικὸν Ἀλκείδην, ἀκούεις, ἔφη, μουσικώτατε
ἀνδρῶν, τῆς καλῆς ταύτης εὐφωνίας, ἥτις ἡμᾶς ἐπ-
έστρεψεν πάντας κατακηληθέντας[37]; καὶ οὐχ ὡς ὁ παρ᾽
ὑμῖν τοῖς Ἀλεξανδρεῦσι πολὺς ὁ μόναυλος ἀλγηδόνα
μᾶλλον τοῖς ἀκούουσι παρέχων ἢ τινα τέρψιν μουσι-
κήν. καὶ ὁ Ἀλκείδης ἔφη· ἀλλὰ μὴν καὶ τὸ ὄργανον
τοῦτο[38], εἴτε τῶν ἐντατῶν αὐτὸ θέλεις εἴτε τῶν ἐμ-
c πνευστῶν, Ἀλεξανδρέως ἐστὶν ἡμεδαποῦ εὕρημα, |
κουρέως τὴν τέχνην· Κτησίβιος δ᾽ αὐτῷ τοὔνομα.
ἱστορεῖ δὲ τοῦτο Ἀριστοκλῆς ἐν τῷ Περὶ Χορῶν
οὑτωσί πως λέγων· ζητεῖται δὲ πότερα τῶν ἐμπνευ-

---

37 κατακηληθέντας ὑπὸ τῆς μουσικῆς A
38 τοῦτο ἡ ὕδραυλις ACE

---

292 Cf. Polemon fr. 40 Preller, quoted at 2.39c.
293 The hydraulic organ; the obscurity of the reference re-

the so-called Hyacinthis Road in Sparta for the heroes
Mattōn ("Kneader") and Keraōn ("Mixer") by the servants
who produce the barley-cakes and mix the wine for the
common messes.[292] The same authority records in Book
XXIV of the same work (fr. 14 Gaede) that the Trojans worship a hero named Daitēs ("Feaster"), whom Mimnermus
(fr. 18 West²) mentions. Hegesander of Delphi (fr. 30,
FHG iv.419) says that Zeus is worshipped on Crete under
the epithets Eilapinastēs ("Companion at the Feast") and
Splanchnotomos ("Cutter-Up of Entrails").

While many remarks of this sort were still being made,
we heard an extremely pleasant and enjoyable sound produced by a hydraulic organ coming from one of the neigh-
boring houses, and we were all entranced by the music and
turned our attention to it. Ulpian looked at Alceides the
musician and said: Do you hear, most musical sir, this
lovely tone, which captured our attention and brought us
under its spell? This is not like the single pipe *(monaulos)*,
which is common among you Alexandrians and gives the
audience more pain than musical pleasure. And Alceides
said: But in fact this instrument[293], whether you prefer to
consider it a string or a wind instrument, was invented by
one of our Alexandrian countrymen, who was a barber by
trade; his name was Ctesibius.[294] Aristocles records this in
his *On Choruses* (fr. 12, *FHG* iv.332), where he says something along the following lines: The question arises as to

quired a superlinear gloss ("the water-organ") that eventually
made its way into the text.

[294] Ctesibius (*fl.* 270 BCE; see below) was an important inventor of pneumatic devices. Cf. 11.497d–e. According to Vitruvius
9.8.2, his father was a barber.

στῶν ἐστιν ὀργάνων ἡ ὕδραυλις ἢ τῶν ἐντατῶν. Ἀριστόξενος μὲν οὖν τοῦτο οὐκ οἶδε. λέγεται δὲ Πλάτωνα
μικράν τινα ἔννοιαν δοῦναι τοῦ κατασκευάσματος
νυκτερινὸν ποιήσαντα ὡρολόγιον ἐοικὸς τῷ ὑδραυ-
λικῷ οἷον κλεψύδραν μεγάλην λίαν. καὶ τὸ ὑδραυλικὸν
δὲ ὄργανον δοκεῖ κλεψύδρα εἶναι. ἐντατὸν οὖν καὶ
καθαπτὸν οὐκ ἂν νομισθείη, | ἐμπνευστὸν δὲ ἂν ἴσως
ῥηθείη διὰ τὸ ἐμπνεῖσθαι τὸ ὄργανον ὑπὸ τοῦ ὕδατος.
κατεστραμμένοι γάρ εἰσιν οἱ αὐλοὶ εἰς τὸ ὕδωρ καὶ
ἀρασσομένου τοῦ ὕδατος ὑπό τινος νεανίσκου, ἔτι δὲ
δικνουμένων ἀξόνων[39] διὰ τοῦ ὀργάνου ἐμπνέονται οἱ
αὐλοὶ καὶ ἦχον ἀποτελοῦσι προσηνῆ. ἔοικεν δὲ τὸ
ὄργανον βωμῷ στρογγύλῳ, καί φασι τοῦτο εὑρῆσθαι
ὑπὸ Κτησιβίου κουρέως ἐνταῦθα οἰκοῦντος ἐν τῇ
Ἀσπενδίᾳ ἐπὶ τοῦ δευτέρου Εὐεργέτου, διαπρέψαι τέ
φασι μεγάλως. τουτονὶ οὖν καὶ τὴν αὐτοῦ | διδάξαι
γυναῖκα Θαΐδα. Τρύφων δ' ἐν τρίτῳ Περὶ Ὀνομασιῶν

d

e

39 ἀξόνων Dalechamp: ἀξινῶν ACE

295 An important early 4th-century authority on music, cited
by Athenaeus at e.g. 4.174e; he predates the invention of the water-organ.
296 Sc. when a sundial would be useless. Hydraulic clocks were
in fact another of Ctesibius' inventions (Vitruv. 9.8.4).
297 A primitive form of water-clock used in Athens' lawcourts.
298 Athenaeus' account of how the hydraulic organ functioned
is badly garbled. The pipes did not touch the water, but were connected to a domed chamber inside the organ. The upper portion
of this chamber contained air, while the lower portion contained

whether the hydraulic organ is a wind instrument or a string instrument. Aristoxenus[295] knows nothing about it; but it is said that Plato provided some idea of how one might be constructed, when he built a clock that would work at night[296] which resembled a hydraulic organ and was, as it were, a very large *klepsudra*.[297] The hydraulic organ thus appears to be a type of *klepsudra*. It could not therefore be considered a string or a percussion instrument, but might perhaps be said to be a wind instrument, because the pressure of the water causes air to move in and out of it. For the pipes are set down into the water; and when pressure is exerted on the water by a young man, and when, furthermore, the slider-valves move around inside the instrument, air moves through the pipes and they produce a pleasant sound.[298] The instrument resembles a round altar; they say that it was discovered by a barber named Ctesibius who lived there in Aspendia during the reign of the second Euergetes[299] and was very prominent. They also say that he taught his wife Thais to play. Tryphon says in Book III of *On Terminology* (fr. 111 Velsen)—the

water; pressure was maintained on the air in the chamber by a combination of an external cistern, in which the water level was higher than it was within the chamber, and a piston-pump, by means of which additional air was added. Keys and sliders allowed pressurized air to be forced out through one or more pipes, producing music. Cf. Vitruv. 10.8; West, *AGM* 114–18 (with a helpful drawing).

[299] Ptolemy VIII (reigned 170–163, 145–116 BCE). Ctesibius in fact appears to have lived during the reign of Ptolemy II Philadelphus. As Alceides claims at 4.174b that Ctesibius was an Alexandrian, Aspendia (otherwise unknown) is apparently to be understood as an area within the city.

(ἐστὶ δὲ τὸ σύγγραμμα περὶ αὐλῶν καὶ ὀργάνων)
συγγράψαι φησὶ περὶ τῆς ὑδραύλεως Κτησίβιον τὸν
μηχανικόν. ἐγὼ δὲ οὐκ οἶδα εἰ περὶ τὸ ὄνομα σφάλ-
λεται. ὁ μέντοι Ἀριστόξενος προκρίνει τὰ ἐντατὰ καὶ
καθαπτὰ τῶν ὀργάνων τῶν ἐμπνευστῶν, ῥᾴδια εἶναι
φάσκων τὰ ἐμπνευστά· πολλοὺς γὰρ μὴ διδαχθέντας
αὐλεῖν τε καὶ συρίζειν, ὥσπερ τοὺς ποιμένας. καὶ
f τοσαῦτα μὲν ἔχω σοι ἐγὼ λέγειν περὶ τοῦ ὑδραυλικοῦ |
ὀργάνου, Οὐλπιανέ· γιγγραίνοισι γὰρ οἱ Φοίνικες, ὥς
φησιν ὁ Ξενοφῶν, ἐχρῶντο αὐλοῖς σπιθαμιαίοις τὸ
μέγεθος, ὀξὺ καὶ γοερὸν φθεγγομένοις. τούτοις δὲ καὶ
οἱ Κᾶρες χρῶνται ἐν τοῖς θρήνοις, εἰ μὴ ἄρα καὶ ἡ
Καρία Φοινίκη ἐκαλεῖτο, ὡς παρὰ Κορίννῃ καὶ Βακ-
χυλίδῃ ἔστιν εὑρεῖν. ὀνομάζονται δὲ οἱ αὐλοὶ γίγγροι
ὑπὸ τῶν Φοινίκων ἀπὸ τῶν περὶ Ἄδωνιν θρήνων· τὸν
γὰρ Ἄδωνιν Γίγγρην καλεῖτε ὑμεῖς οἱ Φοίνικες, ὡς
175 ἱστορεῖ Δημοκλείδης. ‖ μνημονεύει τῶν γίγγρων αὐλῶν Ἀντιφάνης ἐν Ἰατρῷ καὶ Μένανδρος ἐν Καρίνῃ
Ἄμφις τ᾽ ἐν Διθυράμβῳ λέγων οὕτως·

(Α.) ἐγὼ δὲ τὸν γίγγραν γε τὸν σοφώτατον.
(Β.) τίς δ᾽ ἔσθ᾽ ὁ γίγγρας; (Α.) καινὸν ἐξεύρημά
  τι
ἡμέτερον, ὃ θεάτρῳ μὲν οὐδεπώποτε

---

300 There is nothing like this in the preserved works of
Xenophon, and the text should probably be emended to read
"Tryphon" (thus Bapp) or "Xenophanes" (thus Bergk).

treatise discusses pipes and instruments—that the mechanical engineer Ctesibius wrote a treatise on the hydraulic organ; I am uncertain as to whether he is mistaken about the name. Aristoxenus (fr. 95 Wehrli) in fact prefers string and percussion instruments to wind instruments, asserting that wind instruments are too easy; because many people play pipes or pan-pipes without taking lessons, as for example shepherds. This is all I can tell you, Ulpian, about the hydraulic organ. According to Xenophon,[300] the Phoenicians used to play *gingrainoi* pipes, which are about nine inches[301] long and produce a piercing, mournful sound. The Carians play them for their laments—unless "Caria" means "Phoenicia" here, as it does sometimes in Corinna (*PMG* 686) and Bacchylides (fr. 40). The Phoenicians refer to the pipes as *gingroi* because of the laments they offer for Adonis; for you Phoenicians[302] refer to Adonis as Gingrēs, according to Democleides (*FGrH* 794 F 8). Antiphanes mentions *gingras* pipes in *The Doctor* (fr. 107), as do Menander in *The Carian Female Dirge-Singer* (fr. 203) and Amphis in *The Dithyramb* (fr. 14), where he says the following:

(A.) But I . . . the *gingras*, the cleverest instrument
    there is.
(B.) What's a *gingras*? (A.) It's a new discovery
of mine, which I never put on display

[301] Literally "one span," the length of a fully extended hand from the tip of the thumb to the tip of the little finger.
[302] Ulpian is from Tyre, and this portion of Alceides' remarks is therefore a pointed if oblique attack on him.

ἔδειξ', Ἀθήνησιν δὲ κατακεχρημένον
ἐν συμποσίοις ἤδη 'στί. (Β.) διὰ τί δ' οὐκ ἄγεις
b εἰς τὸν ὄχλον αὐτό; (Α.) διότι φυλὴν περιμένω |
σφόδρα φιλονικοῦσαν λαχεῖν τιν'. οἶδα γὰρ
ὅτι πάντα πράγματ' ἀνατριαινώσει κρότοις.

καὶ Ἀξιόνικος ἐν Φιλευριπίδῃ·

οὕτω γὰρ ἐπὶ τοῖς μέλεσι τοῖς Εὐριπίδου
ἄμφω νοσοῦσιν, ὥστε τἄλλ' αὐτοῖς δοκεῖν
εἶναι μέλη γιγγραντὰ καὶ κακὸν μέγα.

πόσῳ δὲ κρεῖττον, ὦ Οὐλπιανὲ σοφώτατε, τὸ ὑδραυ-
c λικὸν τοῦτο ὄργανον τοῦ καλουμένου νάβλα, | ὅν φησι
Σώπατρος ὁ παρῳδὸς ἐν τῷ ἐπιγραφομένῳ δράματι
Πύλαι Φοινίκων εἶναι καὶ τοῦτον εὕρημα. λέγει δ'
οὕτως·

οὔτε τοῦ Σιδωνίου νάβλα
λαρυγγόφωνος ἐκκεχόρδωται κτύπος[40].

καὶ ἐν Μυστάκου δὲ Θητίῳ φησί·

νάβλας ἐν ἄρθροις γραμμάτων οὐκ εὐμελής,
ᾧ λωτὸς ἐν πλευροῖσιν ἄψυχος παγεὶς
d ἔμπνουν ἀνίει μοῦσαν. † ἐγρέτου † δέ τις |
τὸν ἡδονῆς μελῳδὸν εὐάζων χορόν.

[40] κτύπος anon. ap. Casaubon: τύπος A

344

in the theater, although it's being used now at
    drinking parties
in Athens. (B.) Why don't you introduce it
to the population generally? (A.) Because I'm waiting
    for a tribe
that really wants to win the prize to draw my name;
    for I know
it'll turn everything upside down with the applause it
    gets.

Also Axionicus in *The Man Who Loved Euripides* (fr. 3):

They're both so crazy about Euripides'
songs that everything else sounds like
gingras-music to them and a great disaster.

And how much better, my brilliant Ulpian, this hydraulic
organ is than the so-called *nablas*[303], which also, according
to the parodist Sopater in his play entitled *The Gates* (fr.
15), was invented by the Phoenicians! He says the following:

Nor has the deep-throated sound
of the Sidonian *nablas* left the strings.

And in *Mustakos' Wage* (fr. 10) he says:

A *nablas* isn't well-designed in the way its notes are
    articulated,
since a piece of lifeless lotus-wood stuck in its ribs
produces living music. But let someone [corrupt]
the pleasant musical chorus by crying *"Euai!"*

___

[303] Cognate with Hebrew *nebel* (a harp or lute of some sort).

Φιλήμων ἐν Μοιχῷ·

(Α.) ἔδει παρεῖναι, Παρμένων, αὐλητρίδ᾽ ἢ
νάβλαν τιν᾽. (Πα.) ὁ δὲ νάβλας τί ἐστιν < . . . >;
(Α.) < . . . > οὐκ οἶδας, ἐμβρόντητε σύ;
(Πα.) μὰ Δία. (Α.) τί φῄς; οὐκ οἶσθα νάβλαν;
    οὐδὲν οὖν
οἶσθας ἀγαθὸν σύ <γ᾽>. οὐδὲ σαμβυκίστριαν;

καὶ τὸ τρίγωνον δὲ καλούμενον ὄργανον Ἰόβας ἐν
τετάρτῳ Θεατρικῆς Ἱστορίας Σύρων εὕρημά φησιν
εἶναι, ὡς καὶ τὸν καλούμενον λυροφοίνικα < . . . >
e   σαμβύκην. | τοῦτο δὲ τὸ ὄργανον Νεάνθης ὁ Κυζι-
κηνὸς ἐν πρώτῳ Ὥρων εὕρημα εἶναι λέγει Ἰβύκου τοῦ
Ῥηγίνου ποιητοῦ, ὡς καὶ Ἀνακρέοντος τὸ βάρβιτον.
ἐπεὶ δὲ ἡμῶν τῶν Ἀλεξανδρέων κατατρέχεις ὡς ἀμού-
σων καὶ τὸν μόναυλον συνεχῶς ὀνομάζεις ἐπιχω-
ριάζοντα παρ᾽ ἡμῖν, ἄκουε καὶ περὶ αὐτοῦ ἃ νῦν ἔχω
σοι λέγειν ἐν προχείρῳ. Ἰόβας μὲν γὰρ ἐν τῷ προειρημένῳ συγγράμματι Αἰγυπτίους φησὶν λέγειν τὸν
μόναυλον Ὀσίριδος εἶναι εὕρημα, καθάπερ καὶ τὸν
καλούμενον φώτιγγα πλαγίαυλον, οὗ καὶ αὐτοῦ παρα-
f   στήσομαι | μνημονεύοντα ἐλλόγιμον ἄνδρα. ἐπιχωρι-
άζει γὰρ καὶ ὁ φῶτιγξ αὐλὸς παρ᾽ ἡμῖν. τοῦ δὲ
μοναύλου μνημονεύει Σοφοκλῆς μὲν ἐν Θαμύρᾳ οὕ-
τως·

304 For the *sambukē*, see 4.129a n.   305 A type of harp;
see West, *AGM* 72.   306 A type of bowl-lyre, first men-

Philemon in *The Seducer* (fr. 45):

> (A.) There should have been a pipe-girl there,
>   Parmenon, or
> a *nablas*. (Parmenon) What's a *nablas*? . . .
> (A.) . . . You don't know, you lunatic?
> (Parmenon) No, by Zeus, I don't. (A.) What do you
>   mean? You don't know about a *nablas*? In that
>   case, you don't
> know about anything good. Are you also
>   unacquainted with *sambukē*-girls?[304]

Juba claims in Book IV of his *History of the Theater* (*FGrH* 275 F 15) that the instrument referred to as a *trigōnos*[305] was invented by the Syrians, along with the so-called Phoenician lyre . . . a *sambukē*. Neanthes of Cyzicus reports in Book I of his *Annals* (*FGrH* 84 F 5) that this instrument was invented by the poet Ibycus of Rhegium, in the same way that the *barbitos*[306] was invented by Anacreon. But since you run us Alexandrians down for our lack of musical ability and consistently describe the single pipe as something we commonly use, listen to what I have available to tell you now about it. Juba says in the treatise mentioned above (*FGrH* 275 F 16) that the Egyptians claim that the single pipe was invented by Osiris, as was the flute[307] referred to as a *phōtinx*, which is mentioned by a prominent authority I will cite later.[308] The *phōtinx* pipe is commonly used in our country. But Sophocles mentions the single pipe in *Thamyris* (fr. 241), as follows:

---

tioned—although not necessarily invented—by Anacreon (*PMG* 472, quoted at 4.182f); see West, *AGM* 57–9.   [307] Literally "transverse pipe."   [308] Posidonius, cited at 4.176c.

ᾦχωκε γὰρ κροτητὰ πηκτίδων μέλη
λύρᾳ μοναύλοις † τε χειμωντεως
ναος στέρημα κωμασάσης. †

Ἀραρὼς δ' ἐν Πανὸς Γοναῖς·

176   ἁρπάσας μόναυλον εὐθὺς πῶς δοκεῖς; ||
κούφως ἀνήλλετο.

Ἀναξανδρίδης δ' ἐν Θησαυρῷ·

                    ἀναλαβὼν
μόναυλον ηὔλουν τὸν ὑμέναιον.

καὶ ἐν Φιαληφόρῳ·

(Α.) τὸν μόναυλον ποῖ τέτροφας; οὗτος Σύρε.
(Β.) ποῖον μόναυλον; (Α.) τὸν κάλαμον.

Σώπατρος Βακχίδι·

καὶ τὸ μόναυλον μέλος ἤχησε.

Πρωταγορίδης δ' ὁ Κυζικηνὸς ἐν δευτέρῳ Περὶ τῶν
b   Ἐπὶ Δάφνῃ Πανηγύρεων φησιν· παντὸς δὲ ὀργάνου |
κατὰ μίτον ἧπται, κροτάλων, † ὑπὸ φανοῦ † πανδούρου, τῷ τε ἡδεῖ μοναύλῳ τὰς ἡδίστας ἁρμονίας ἀναμι-
νυρίζει. Ποσειδώνιος δ' ὁ ἀπὸ τῆς στοᾶς φιλόσοφος ἐν
τῇ τρίτῃ τῶν Ἱστοριῶν διηγούμενος περὶ τοῦ Ἀπα-
μέων πρὸς Λαρισαίους πολέμου γράφει τάδε· παρα-

---

309 Cf. 4.183f.   310 Probably some type of lute; cf. Poll.
4.60 (identified as an Assyrian name); West, *AGM* 80.

For gone are the songs struck from harps *(pēktides)*
with lyre and single pipes [corrupt]
[corrupt].

Araros in *The Birth of Pan* (fr. 13):

> He grabbed a single pipe very quickly, let me
>   assure you!
> And he started leaping about lightly.

Anaxandrides in *The Treasure* (fr. 19):

> He picked up
> a single pipe and started playing the wedding song.

Also in *The Phiale-Bearer* (fr. 52):

> (A.) What have you done with my single pipe?
>   Hey Syrus!
> (B.) What do you mean, your "single pipe"? (A.) The
>   reed.

Sopater in *Bakchis* (fr. 2):

> and he made the single-pipe song resound.

Protagorides of Cyzicus says in Book II of *On the Festivals in Daphne* (*FGrH* 853 F 2a):[309] He has tried every instrument, one after another: the cymbals, [corrupt], the *pandoura*[310]; and he produces lovely droning harmonies on the lovely single pipe. Posidonius the Stoic philosopher in Book III of his *Histories* (*FGrH* 87 F 2 = fr. 54 Edelstein–Kidd), when he describes the war the inhabitants of Apamea fought against the people of Larisa[311],

---

[311] Probably in 145 BCE.

ζωνίδια καὶ λογχάρι᾽ ἀνειληφότες ἰῷ καὶ ῥύπῳ κε-
κρυμμένα, πετάσια δ᾽ ἐπιτεθειμένοι καὶ προσκόπια
σκιὰν μὲν ποιοῦντα, καταπνεῖσθαι δ᾽ οὐ κωλύοντα
τοὺς τραχήλους, ὄνους ἐφελκόμενοι γέμοντας οἴνου
c καὶ βρωμάτων παντοδαπῶν, | οἷς παρέκειτο φωτίγγια
καὶ μοναύλια, κώμων οὐ πολέμων ὄργανα. οὐκ ἀγνοῶ
δὲ ὅτι Ἀμερίας ὁ Μακεδὼν ἐν ταῖς Γλώσσαις τιτύ-
ρινόν φησι καλεῖσθαι τὸν μόναυλον. ἴδε ἀπέχεις, καλὲ
Οὐλπιανέ, καὶ τὸν τῆς φώτιγγος μνημονεύοντα· ὅτι δὲ
ὁ μόναυλος ἦν ὁ νῦν καλούμενος καλαμαύλης σαφῶς
παρίστησιν Ἡδύλος ἐν τοῖς Ἐπιγράμμασιν οὑτωσὶ
λέγων·

<τοῦτο> Θέων ὁ μόναυλος ὑπ᾽ ἠρίον ὁ γλυκὺς
οἰκεῖ
d αὐλητής, μίμων κἠν θυμέλῃσι Χάρις. |
† τυφλὸς ὑπαὶ γήρως εἶχεν καὶ Σκίρπαλον υἱὸν
νήπιόν τ᾽ ἐκάλει Σκίρπαλος Εὐπαλάμου·
ἀείδειν δ᾽ αὐτοῦ τὰ γενέθλια, τοῦτο γὰρ εἶχεν
πανμαρπᾶν ἥδυσμα σημανέων. †
ηὔλει δὴ Γλαύκης μεμεθυσμένα παίγνια
Μουσέων
ἢ τὸν ἐν ἀκρήτοις Βάτταλον ἡδυπότην

---

312 Cf. 4.182d (citing Artemidorus).   313 Cf. 4.175e.
314 Much of the epigram is desperately corrupt, but the first
and last lines are sound and serve to support Alceides' claim that a
monaulos can also be called a *kalamaul(ēt)ēs*. Theon is Stephanis
#1205.   315 Stephanis #545 (3rd century BCE).

writes the following: They took up daggers and spears covered with rust and dirt; put broad-brimmed hats and visors, which provided shade but did not prevent air from circulating around their necks, on their heads; and dragged along donkeys loaded with wine and food of every sort, beside which lay flutes *(phōtingia)* and single pipes, which are instruments intended for wandering drunk through the streets rather than for war. Nor am I unaware that Amerias of Macedon in his *Glossary* (p. 9 Hoffmann) says that the single pipe is referred to as a *titurinos*.[312] So there you are, my good Ulpian; you have the man who mentions the *phōtinx*.[313] That the word *monaulos* (here "player of a single pipe") was used for the man referred to today as a *kalamaulēs* (literally "reed-piper") is established clearly by Hedylus in his *Epigrams* (*HE* 1877–86), where he says the following:[314]

> Beneath this mound dwells Theon the sweet piper,
> who
> played the single pipe *(monaulos)* and was Grace
> itself on the mime stage.
> † After old age blinded him he had a son named
> Scirpalus,
> and Scirpalus called his little child the son of
> Eupalamus;
> and to sing at his birthday feast; for he had this
> [corrupt] .†
> Indeed, he used to sing Glauce's[315] trifles, which were
> drunk on the Muses,
> or about Battalus,[316] who enjoys drinking unmixed
> wine,

ἢ καὶ Κώταλον ἢ καὶ Πάκαλον. ἀλλὰ Θέωνα
τὸν καλαμαυλήτην εἴπατε, "χαῖρε Θέων".

e ὥσπερ οὖν τοὺς τῷ καλάμῳ αὐλοῦντας καλαμαύλας |
λέγουσι νῦν, οὕτω καὶ ῥαππαύλας, ὥς φησιν Ἀμερίας
ὁ Μακεδὼν ἐν ταῖς Γλώσσαις, τοὺς τῇ ῥάππῃ[41] αὐ-
λοῦντας. γινώσκειν δὲ βούλομαί σε, ἀνδρῶν λῷστε
Οὐλπιανέ, ὅτι Ἀλεξανδρέων μουσικώτεροι ἄλλοι γενέσθαι οὐχ ἱστόρηνται, καὶ οὐ λέγω περὶ κιθαρῳδίαν
μόνην, ἧς καὶ ὁ εὐτελέστατος παρ' ἡμῖν ἰδιώτης προσέτι τε καὶ ἀναλφάβητος οὕτως ἐστὶ συνήθης ὡς τάχιστα ἐλέγχειν τὰ παρὰ τὰς κρούσεις ἁμαρτήματα
γινόμενα, ἀλλὰ καὶ περὶ αὐλούς εἰσι μουσικώτατοι οὐ
f μόνον τοὺς παρθενίους καλουμένους | καὶ παιδικούς,
ἀλλὰ καὶ τοὺς ἀνδρείους, οἵτινες καλοῦνται τέλειοί τε
καὶ ὑπερτέλειοι, καὶ τοὺς κιθαριστηρίους δὲ καὶ τοὺς
δακτυλικούς. τοὺς γὰρ ἐλύμους αὐλούς, ὧν μνημονεύει
Σοφοκλῆς ἐν Νιόβῃ τε κἀν Τυμπανισταῖς, οὐκ ἄλλους
τινὰς εἶναι ἀκούομεν ἢ τοὺς Φρυγίους, ὧν καὶ αὐτῶν
ἐμπείρως ἔχουσιν Ἀλεξανδρεῖς. οἴδασι δὲ καὶ τοὺς
διόπους ἔτι τε μεσοκόπους καὶ τοὺς καλουμένους ὑπο-
τρήτους. τῶν δ' ἐλύμων αὐλῶν μνημονεύει καὶ Καλ-

---

41 ῥάππῃ Gulick: καλάμη A

---

316 Stephanis #519 (4th century BCE).
317 I.e. those with the highest registers ("soprano" and "tre-
ble," respectively), in contrast to the "male" pipes referred to
below; see West, *AGM* 89–94, esp. 89–90.

or about Cotalus, or Pacalus. But as for Theon
the *kalamaulētēs*, say "Farewell, Theon."

In the same way, therefore, that people today refer to those
who play pipe-music (*aulountes*) on a reed-pipe (*kalamos*)
as *kalamaulai*, so too, according to Amerias of Macedon in
his *Glossary* (p. 14 Hoffmann), those who play pipe-music
(*aulountes*) on a *rhappē* are called *rhappaulai*. But I would
like you to be aware, my excellent Ulpian, that no other
people are recorded as being more musical than the
Alexandrians; I am not referring to singing only to the *kithara*, with which the most worthless, indeed uneducated
private citizen in our country is so familiar that he can in-
stantly detect any errors that occur when the notes are
struck. Their musical expertise also extends to the pipes,
and not just what are referred to as girls' pipes and boys'
pipes,[317] but also the male pipes, which are called both
teleioi ("fully-grown," i.e. "baritone") and *huperteleioi*
("more than fully-grown," i.e. "bass"), as well as *kithara*-
playing pipes and finger-pipes. As for *elumoi*-pipes[318],
which Sophocles mentions in both *Niobe* (fr. 450) and
Drummers (fr. 644), I hear that they are no different from
Phrygian pipes, with which the Alexandrians are also experienced. The Alexandrians are also familiar with pipes
with two holes,[319] as well as with the midsized variety and
those referred to as *hupotrētoi* ("under-hole") pipes. Callias mentions *elumoi*-pipes in *Men in Shackles* (fr. 23). Juba

[318] Unequal pipes, one of which was a horn-pipe; see West,
AGM 91–2.

[319] I.e. with two parallel tubes of different length or bore (thus
West, *AGM* 92)?

177 λίας ἐν Πεδήταις. Ἰόβας ‖ δὲ τούτους Φρυγῶν μὲν
εἶναι εὕρημα, ὀνομάζεσθαι δὲ καὶ σκυταλείας, κατ᾽
ἐμφέρειαν τοῦ πάχους. χρῆσθαι δ᾽ αὐτοῖς καὶ Κυπρίους φησὶ Κρατῖνος ὁ νεώτερος ἐν Θηραμένῃ. οἴδαμεν
δὲ καὶ τοὺς ἡμιόπους καλουμένους, περὶ ὧν φησιν
Ἀνακρέων·

τίς ἐρασμίην
τρέψας θυμὸν ἐς ἥβην τερένων ἡμιόπων ὑπ᾽
    αὐλῶν
ὀρχεῖται;

εἰσὶ δ᾽ οἱ αὐλοὶ οὗτοι ἐλάσσονες τῶν τελείων. Αἰσχύ-
182b λος γοῦν κατὰ[42] μεταφορὰν ‖ ἐν Ἰξίονί φησι·

τὸν δ᾽ ἡμίοπον[43]
c   ταχέως ὁ μέγας | καταπίνει.

εἰσὶν δ᾽ οἱ αὐτοὶ τοῖς παιδικοῖς καλουμένοις, οἷς οὐκ
οὖσιν ἐναγωνίοις πρὸς τὰς εὐωχίας χρῶνται. διὸ καὶ
τέρενας αὐτοὺς κέκληκεν ὁ Ἀνακρέων. οἶδα δὲ καὶ
ἄλλα γένη αὐλῶν τραγικῶν τε καὶ λυσιῳδικῶν καὶ
κιθαριστηρίων, ὧν μνημονεύουσιν Ἔφορός τ᾽ ἐν τοῖς
Εὑρήμασι καὶ Εὐφράνωρ ὁ Πυθαγορικὸς ἐν τῷ Περὶ

[42] A large section of text (177b–82b) that begins after the
fourth letter of the next word is out of place where it stands in the
manuscripts and was moved by Casaubon to early in Book 5. Apparently a number of pages containing either 177b–82b or 182b–
87b fell out of the exemplar (or the text from which it was de-

(*FGrH* 275 F 81) says that they were invented by the Phrygians and are also referred to as baton-pipes, because they are the same thickness.[320] Cratinus the Younger says in *Theramenes* (fr. 3) that the Cyprians played them. I am also familiar with what are called half-hole pipes, about which Anacreon (*PMG* 375) says:

> Who turned his
> attention to lovely youth and is dancing to the
>   accompaniment of soft
> half-hole pipes?

These pipes are smaller than the baritone *(teleioi)* variety. Aeschylus, at any rate, says metaphorically in *Ixion* (fr. 91):

> The large pipe
> quickly consumes the half-hole.

These are the same as the so-called boys' pipes, which are played at feasts because they are inappropriate for contests. This is why Anacreon (above) refers to them as "soft." I am also familiar with other types of pipes used for tragedy, *lysiodēs*[321], and *kithara*-playing, which are mentioned by Ephorus in his *Inventions* (*FGrH* 70 F 3) and by Euphranor the Pythagorean in his *On Pipes*, as well as by

---

[320] Sc. as a Spartan message-baton *(skutalē)*, for which see Plu. *Lys.* 19.5–7.

[321] A type of mime in which a female entertainer wore male clothing or a male mask; cf. 5.211b–c; 14.620e.

---

scended) and were reinserted in the wrong place, and subsequent copyists failed to notice the problem.

[43] ἡμίοπον καὶ τὸν ἐλάσσονα A

Αὐλῶν, ἔτι δὲ καὶ Ἀριστόξενος[44] καὶ αὐτὸς ἐν τῷ Περὶ
Αὐλῶν. ὁ δὲ καλάμινος αὐλὸς τιτύρινος καλεῖται παρὰ
τοῖς ἐν Ἰταλίᾳ Δωριεῦσιν, ὡς Ἀρτεμίδωρος ἱστορεῖ ὁ
Ἀριστοφάνειος ἐν δευτέρῳ Περὶ Δωρίδος. ὁ δὲ μάγα-
d δις καλούμενος αὐλός. καὶ πάλιν· ὁ | μάγαδις ὀνομα-
ζόμενος ἐν ταὐτῷ ὀξὺν καὶ βαρὺν φθόγγον ἐπιδείκνυ-
ται, ὡς Ἀναξανδρίδης ἐν Ὁπλομάχῳ φησί·

   μαγάδι λαλήσω μικρὸν ἅμα σοι καὶ μέγα.

οἱ δὲ καλούμενοι λώτινοι αὐλοὶ οὗτοί εἰσιν οἱ ὑπὸ
Ἀλεξανδρέων καλούμενοι φώτιγγες. κατασκευάζονται
δ᾽ ἐκ τοῦ καλουμένου λωτοῦ· ξύλον δ᾽ ἐστὶ τοῦτο
γινόμενον ἐν Λιβύῃ. Θηβαίων δ᾽ εὕρημά φησιν εἶναι
Ἰόβας τὸν ἐκ νεβροῦ κώλων κατασκευαζόμενον αὐ-
e λόν. ὁ δὲ Τρύφων | φησὶ καὶ τοὺς καλουμένους ἐλεφαν-
τίνους αὐλοὺς παρὰ Φοίνιξιν ἀνατρηθῆναι. οἶδα δὲ ὅτι
καὶ μάγαδις ὄργανόν ἐστιν ἐντατὸν καθάπερ καὶ κι-
θάρα, λύρα, βάρβιτον. Εὐφορίων δὲ ὁ ἐποποιὸς ἐν τῷ
Περὶ Ἰσθμίων, οἱ νῦν, φησίν, καλούμενοι ναβλισταὶ
καὶ πανδουρισταὶ καὶ σαμβυκισταὶ καινῷ μὲν οὐδενὶ
χρῶνται ὀργάνῳ· τὸν γὰρ βάρωμον καὶ βάρβιτον, ὧν
Σαπφὼ καὶ Ἀνακρέων μνημονεύουσι, καὶ τὴν μάγαδιν
f καὶ τὰ τρίγωνα καὶ τὰς σαμβύκας ἀρχαῖα εἶναι. ἐν |

---

[44] Ἄλεξις ὧν A; cf. 14.634d

---

[322] Cf. 4.176c.
[323] Virtually identical material appears at 14.634d–e, where it

Aristoxenus himself in his *On Pipes*. The Dorians in Italy refer to a reed pipe as a *titurinos*, according to Artemidorus the student of Aristophanes in Book II of *On Doric*:[322] the pipe referred to as a *magadis*.[323] And again: The so-called *magadis* produces a high tone and a low tone simultaneously, as Anaxandrides says in *The Hoplite-Trainer* (fr. 36):

> I'll speak along with you soft and loud like a *magadis*.

The so-called *lōtinoi*-pipes are what the Alexandrians refer to as *phōtinges*.[324] They are made of what is called *lōtos*, which is a type of wood produced in Libya. Juba (*FGrH* 275 F 82) says that the Thebans invented pipes made from a fawn's leg.[325] Tryphon (fr. 112 Velsen) says that the Phoenicians bore what are referred to as ivory pipes. I am also aware that the *magadis* is a string instrument like the *kithara*, the *lura*, and the *barbiton*.[326] The epic poet Euphorion in his *On the Isthmian Games* (fr. 8, *FHG* iii.73 = fr. 180 van Groningen) says:[327] What are now referred to as *nablas*-, *pandoura*-, and *sambukē*-players are not playing a new instrument; the *barōmos* and the *barbiton*, which Sappho (fr. 176) and Anacreon (*PMG* 472) mention, as well as the *magadis*, the *trigōna*, and the *sambukai*, are

---

is attributed to Tryphon (fr. 110 Velsen). Exactly what a *magadis* was seems to have been disputed; cf. 14.634e–6c.

[324] Cf. 4.175e–f.

[325] I.e. from the bone (presumably the femur).

[326] The *kithara* was a box-lyre, while the *lura* and the *barbitos/barbiton* were different types of bowl-lyres.

[327] Cf. 14.635a–b, where Lesbothemis (below) is specifically identified as a sculptor.

γοῦν Μιτυλήνῃ μίαν τῶν Μουσῶν πεποιῆσθαι ὑπὸ
Λεσβοθέμιδος ἔχουσαν σαμβύκην. Ἀριστόξενος δ᾽
ἔκφυλα ὄργανα καλεῖ φοίνικας καὶ πηκτίδας καὶ μα-
γάδιδας σαμβύκας τε καὶ τρίγωνα καὶ κλεψιάμβους
καὶ σκινδαψοὺς καὶ τὸ ἐννεάχορδον καλούμενον. Πλάτων δ᾽ ἐν τρίτῳ Πολιτείας φησίν· "οὐκ ἄρα," ἦν δ᾽ ἐγώ,
"πολυχορδίας γε οὐδὲ παναρμονίου ἡμῖν δεήσει ἐν
183   ταῖς ᾠδαῖς τε καὶ μέλεσιν. "οὔ μοι," ἔφη, φαίνεται. ||
τριγώνων ἄρα καὶ πηκτίδων καὶ πάντων ὀργάνων ὅσα
πολύχορδα καὶ παναρμόνια < . . . > ἐστὶν δ᾽ ὁ σκινδαψὸς τετράχορδον ὄργανον, ὡς ὁ παρῳδός φησι
Μάτρων ἐν τούτοις·

οὐδ᾽ ἀπὸ πασσαλόφιν κρέμασαν, ὅθι περ
τετάνυστο
σκινδαψὸς τετράχορδος ἀνηλακάτοιο γυναικός.

μνημονεύει αὐτοῦ καὶ Θεόπομπος ὁ Κολοφώνιος ἐπο-
b   ποιὸς ἐν τῷ ἐπιγραφομένῳ Ἁρματίῳ· |

σκινδαψὸν λυρόεντα μέγαν χείρεσσι τινάσσων,
οἰσύινον προμάλοιο τετυγμένον αἰζήεντος.

καὶ Ἀναξίλας ἐν Λυροποιῷ·

ἐγὼ δὲ βαρβίτους τριχόρδους, πηκτίδας,

328 For the *nablas* and the *trigōnon*, see 4.175c–d with n. For
the *sambukē*, see 4.129a n.
329 Cf. 14.636b, where the same list is attributed to Phillis
(who probably drew it from Aristoxenus). The *phoinix* and *skin-*

ancient.[328] On Mitylene, for example, Lesbothemis represented one of the Muses as holding a *sambukē*. Aristoxenus
(fr. 97 Wehrli)[329] refers to *phoinikes, pēktides, magadides,
sambukai, trigōna, klepsiamboi, skindapsoi*, and the so-
called "nine-string" as foreign instruments. Plato says in
Book III of the *Republic* (399c–d): "So, then," I said,
"we're not going to need instruments with many strings or
that produce all types of harmonies for our songs and
tunes." "It doesn't look like it to me," he said. "Then of
trigōna, pēktides, and all the instruments that have many
strings and produce all types of harmonies . . . " The
skindapsos is an instrument with four strings, according to
the parodist Matro (fr. 6 Olson–Sens = *SH* 539) in the following lines:

> They did not hang it from a peg, where had been
> hung
> a four-stringed *skindapsos* belonging to a woman
> unconcerned with the distaff.

The epic poet Theopompus of Colophon also mentions it
in his poem entitled *The Little Chariot* (*SH* 765):

> brandishing in his hands a large, *lura*-like *skindapsos*
> made of withes from a vigorous willow.

Also Anaxilas in *The Lura-Maker* (fr. 15):

> But I used to build[330] three-stringed *barbitoi*,

dapsos are lyres of some sort; the *pēktis* is a type of harp; and nothing else is known about the *klepsiambos*.
   [330] The verb is preserved in the Doric form, but ought perhaps
to be emended to show the normal Attic ending.

κιθάρας, λύρας, σκινδαψὸν ἐξηρτυόμαν.

Σώπατρος δ᾽ ὁ παρῳδὸς ἐν τῷ ἐπιγραφομένῳ Μυ-
στά‹κου Θητίῳ› δίχορδον εἶναί φησι τὴν πηκτίδα
λέγων οὕτως·

c   πηκτὶς δὲ Μούσῃ γαυριῶσα βαρβάρῳ |
     δίχορδος εἰς σὴν χεῖρά πως κατεστάθη.

τῶν δὲ παριαμβίδων Ἐπίχαρμος ἐν Περιάλλῳ μνημονεύει οὕτως·

                              Σεμέλα δὲ χορεύει
     καὶ ὑπαυλεῖ σφιν † σοφὸς κιθάρᾳ παριαμβίδας·
         ἁ δὲ γεγάθει
     πυκινῶν κρεγμῶν ἀκροαζομένα.

τὸ δὲ ψαλτήριον, ὥς φησιν Ἰόβας, Ἀλέξανδρος ὁ
Κυθήριος συνεπλήρωσε χορδαῖς καὶ ἐγγηράσας τῇ
Ἐφεσίων πόλει ὡς σοφώτατον τῆς ἑαυτοῦ τέχνης
τουτὶ τὸ εὕρημα ἀνέθηκε ἐν Ἀρτέμιδος. μνημονεύει δ᾽
d   ὁ Ἰόβας καὶ τοῦ λυροφοίνικος καὶ τοῦ ἐπιγονείου, | ὃ
νῦν εἰς ψαλτήριον ὄρθιον μετασχηματισθὲν διασῴζει
τὴν τοῦ χρησαμένου προσηγορίαν. ἦν δ᾽ ὁ Ἐπίγονος
φύσει μὲν Ἀμβρακιώτης, δημοποίητος δὲ Σικυώνιος·
μουσικώτατος δ᾽ ὢν κατὰ χεῖρα δίχα πλήκτρου ἔψαλ-
λεν. πάντων οὖν τούτων τῶν προειρημένων ὀργάνων

---

331 The passage is corrupt, but *pariambides* appear to be referred to as a metrical form rather than a musical instrument.

BOOK IV

pēktides, *kitharai*, *lurai*, and a *skindapsos*.

The parodist Sopater says in his play entitled *Mustakos' Wage* (fr. 12) that the *pēktis* has two strings, putting it as follows:

A two-string *pēktis* that takes pride in a barbarian
Muse settled somehow into your hand.

Epicharmus mentions *pariambides* in *Periallos* (fr. 108), as follows:[331]

Semele is dancing
and a wise man † accompanies them with
pariambides on the pipes with a *kithara*; and she
is happy
when she hears the notes struck again and again.

According to Juba (*FGrH* 275 F 83), Alexander of Cythera[332] gave the harp (*psaltērion*) its full complement of strings, and when he grew old he dedicated it in Artemis' temple in Ephesus as the most brilliant invention his craft had produced. Juba (*FGrH* 275 F 84) also mentions the Phoenician *lura* and the *epigoneion*[333], which has now developed into the upright harp but preserves the name of the man who played it. Epigonus[334] was an Ambraciote by birth, but was made a citizen of Sicyon; he was extremely musical and played string instruments with his fingers without a pick. The Alexandrians have experience

---

[332] Stephanis #105.
[333] An instrument with 40 strings; perhaps a zither (thus West, *AGM* 78–9).
[334] Stephanis #855.

καὶ αὐλῶν ἐμπείρως ἔχουσι καὶ τεχνικῶς Ἀλεξανδρεῖς, καὶ ἐν οἷς ἄν μου θέλῃς ἀποπειραθῆναι ἐπιδεί-
ξομαί σοι ἐγὼ αὐτός, πολλῶν ἄλλων μουσικωτέρων
μου ἐν τῇ πατρίδι ὑπαρχόντων. Ἀλέξανδρος δὲ ὁ
e πολίτης | μου (οὗτος δ᾽ οὐ πρὸ πολλοῦ τετελεύτηκε)
δημοσίᾳ ἐπιδειξάμενος ἐν τῷ τριγώνῳ ἐπικαλουμένῳ
ὀργάνῳ οὕτως ἐποίησε πάντας Ῥωμαίους μουσομα-
νεῖν ὡς τοὺς πολλοὺς καὶ ἀπομνημονεύειν αὐτοῦ τὰ
κρούσματα. μνημονεύει δὲ τοῦ τριγώνου τούτου καὶ
Σοφοκλῆς ἐν μὲν Μυσοῖς οὕτως·

> πολὺς δὲ Φρὺξ τρίγωνος ἀντίσπαστά τε
> Λυδῆς ἐφυμνεῖ πηκτίδος συγχορδία,

f καὶ ἐν Θαμύρᾳ. Ἀριστοφάνης δ᾽ ἐν Δαιταλεῦσι | καὶ
Θεόπομπος ἐν Πηνελόπῃ, Εὔπολις δ᾽ ἐν Βάπταις φη-
σίν·

> ὃς καλῶς μὲν τυμπανίζεις
> καὶ διαψάλλεις τριγώνοις.

τοῦ δὲ καλουμένου πανδούρου Εὐφορίων μέν, ὡς προ-
είρηται, καὶ Πρωταγορίδης ἐν δευτέρῳ Περὶ τῶν Ἐπὶ
Δάφνῃ Πανηγύρεων. Πυθαγόρας δὲ ὁ γεγραφὼς περὶ
τῆς Ἐρυθρᾶς θαλάσσης τοὺς Τρωγλοδύτας φησὶ
184 κατασκευάζειν τὴν πανδούραν ‖ ἐκ τῆς ἐν τῇ θαλάσσῃ
φυομένης δάφνης. Τυρρηνῶν δ᾽ ἐστὶν εὕρημα κέρατά

---

335 Stephanis #102.
336 The fragment is quoted again at 14.635c.

with all these instruments I have just mentioned, as well as with pipes, and can play them skilfully; if you would like to test me on any of them, I myself will offer you a show, although many other people in my native land are better musicians than I am. My fellow-citizen Alexander[335] (he died not long ago) gave a public show on the instrument referred to as a *trigōnon* and made everyone in Rome so crazy about his music that many of them have memorized his songs. Sophocles also mentions the *trigōnon* in *Mysians* (fr. 412), as follows:[336]

> A Phrygian *trigōnos* sounds repeatedly, and the many strings
> of a Lydian *pēktis* accompany it with answering notes.

So too in *Thamyris* (fr. 239). Also Aristophanes in *Banqueters* (fr. 255) and Theopompus in *Penelope* (fr. 50). And Eupolis says in *Dyers* (fr. 88.1–2):

> You who play the drum well
> and produce notes on the strings of *trigōna*.

Euphorion refers to the so-called *pandouros*, as was noted earlier,[337] as does Protagorides in Book II of *On the Festivals in Daphne* (*FGrH* 853 F 2b).[338] The Pythagoras who wrote about the Red Sea says that the Troglodytes make the *pandoura* from the laurel tree that grows in the sea.[339] Horns and trumpets were invented by the Etruscans.

[337] At 4.182e.

[338] Cf. 4.176a–b.

[339] Identified as white mangrove by Hort; cf. Thphr. *HP* 4.7.2 (also discussing the Red Sea).

τε καὶ σάλπιγγες. Μητρόδωρος δ' ὁ Χῖος ἐν Τρωικοῖς
σύριγγα μέν φησιν εὑρεῖν Μαρσύαν καὶ αὐλὸν ἐν
Κελαιναῖς, τῶν πρότερον ἑνὶ καλάμῳ συριζόντων. Εὐφορίων δ' ὁ ἐποποιὸς ἐν τῷ Περὶ Μελοποιῶν τὴν μὲν
μονοκάλαμον σύριγγα Ἑρμῆν εὑρεῖν, τινὰς δ' ἱστορεῖν Σεύθην καὶ Ῥωνάκην τοὺς Μαιδούς, τὴν δὲ πολυ-
κάλαμον Σιληνόν, Μαρσύαν δὲ τὴν κηρόδετον. ταῦτα
b ἔχεις παρ' ἡμῶν τῶν Ἀλεξανδρέων, | Οὐλπιανὲ ὀνο-
ματοθήρα, τῶν περὶ τοὺς μοναύλους ἐσπουδακότων.
οὐ γὰρ οἶδας ἱστοροῦντα Μενεκλέα τὸν Βαρκαῖον
συγγραφέα ἔτι τε Ἄνδρωνα ἐν τοῖς Χρονικοῖς τὸν
Ἀλεξανδρέα, ὅτι Ἀλεξανδρεῖς εἰσιν οἱ παιδεύσαντες
πάντας τοὺς Ἕλληνας καὶ τοὺς βαρβάρους, ἐκλει-
πούσης ἤδη τῆς ἐγκυκλίου παιδείας διὰ τὰς γενο-
μένας συνεχεῖς κινήσεις ἐν τοῖς κατὰ τοὺς Ἀλεξάνδρου διαδόχους χρόνοις. ἐγένετο οὖν ἀνανέωσις πάλιν
παιδείας ἁπάσης κατὰ τὸν ἕβδομον βασιλεύσαντα
c Αἰγύπτου Πτολεμαῖον, τὸν | κυρίως ὑπὸ τῶν Ἀλεξαν-
δρέων καλούμενον Κακεργέτην. οὗτος γὰρ πολλοὺς
τῶν Ἀλεξανδρέων ἀποσφάξας, οὐκ ὀλίγους δὲ καὶ
φυγαδεύσας τῶν κατὰ τὸν ἀδελφὸν αὐτοῦ ἐφηβησάν-
των ἐποίησε πλήρεις τάς τε νήσους καὶ πόλεις ἀνδρῶν
γραμματικῶν, φιλοσόφων, γεωμετρῶν, μουσικῶν, ζω-
γράφων, παιδοτριβῶν τε καὶ ἰατρῶν καὶ ἄλλων πολ-

---

340 The satyr who was flayed alive by Apollo after he lost a
pipe-playing contest against him at Celaenae (e.g. Hdt. 7.26.3; X.
An. 1.2.8; [Appollod.] *Bib.* 1.4.2).

Metrodorus of Chios says in his *History of Troy* (*FGrH* 43
F 1) that Marsyas[340] invented the pan-pipe and the pipes in
Celaenae, and that previously people played pipe-music
on a single reed. The epic poet Euphorion in his *On Lyric
Poets* (fr. 10, *FHG* iii.74 = fr. 182 van Groningen) claims
that Hermes invented the pan-pipe made from a single
reed, although some authorities record that the Maedi
Seuthēs and Rhōnakēs[341] did this; that Silenus invented
the pan-pipe made from multiple reeds; and that Marsyas
invented the one held together with wax. This is what you
have from us Alexandrians, Ulpian the word-hunter, who
have devoted ourselves to the single pipes. Because you
are unaware that the prose-author Menecles of Barca
(*FGrH* 270 F 9), as well as Andron of Alexandria in his
Chronicles (*FGrH* 246 F 1), record that the Alexandrians
are the ones who educated all the Greeks and barbarians,
after systematic education disappeared as a result of the
constant disturbances that occurred in the times of Alexander's successors. There was accordingly a fresh revival of
all sorts of education in the period when Ptolemy VII[342]
was king of Egypt. The Alexandrians appropriately refer to
him as *Kakergetēs* ("Malefactor"),[343] because he butchered many of them, drove large numbers of those who had
been young men in his brother's time into exile, and filled
the islands and the cities with grammarians, philosophers,
mathematicians, musicians, painters, athletic trainers, and

---

[341] The Maedi were a Thracian people. Seuthēs and Rhōnakēs
are otherwise unknown.   [342] Referred to today as Ptolemy
VIII *Euergetēs* ("Benefactor") (reigned 145–116 BCE), the political rival of Ptolemy VIII (referred to below).

[343] Cf. 12.549d.

ATHENAEUS

λῶν τεχνιτῶν· οἱ διὰ τὸ πένεσθαι διδάσκοντες ἃ ἠπίσταντο πολλοὺς κατεσκεύασαν ἄνδρας ἐλλογίμους.
d ἔμελεν δὲ τοῖς πάλαι πᾶσιν Ἕλλησι μουσικῆς· |
διόπερ καὶ ἡ αὐλητικὴ περισπούδαστος ἦν. Χαμαι-
λέων γοῦν ὁ Ἡρακλεώτης ἐν τῷ ἐπιγραφομένῳ Προ-
τρεπτικῷ Λακεδαιμονίους φησὶ καὶ Θηβαίους πάντας
αὐλεῖν μανθάνειν Ἡρακλεώτας τε τοὺς ἐν τῷ Πόντῳ
καθ᾿ ἑαυτὸν ἔτι Ἀθηναίων τε τοὺς ἐπιφανεστάτους,
Καλλίαν τε τὸν Ἱππονίκου καὶ Κριτίαν τὸν Καλ-
λαίσχρου. Δοῦρις δ᾿ ἐν τῷ Περὶ Εὐριπίδου καὶ Σοφοκλέους Ἀλκιβιάδην φησὶ μαθεῖν τὴν αὐλητικὴν οὐ
παρὰ τοῦ τυχόντος, ἀλλὰ Προνόμου τοῦ μεγίστην
e ἐσχηκότος δόξαν. Ἀριστόξενος δὲ | καὶ Ἐπαμινώνδαν
τὸν Θηβαῖον αὐλεῖν μαθεῖν παρὰ Ὀλυμπιοδώρῳ καὶ
Ὀρθαγόρᾳ. καὶ τῶν Πυθαγορικῶν δὲ πολλοὶ τὴν αὐλητικὴν ἤσκησαν, ὡς Εὐφράνωρ τε καὶ Ἀρχύτας
Φιλόλαός τε ἄλλοι τε οὐκ ὀλίγοι. ὁ δ᾿ Εὐφράνωρ καὶ
σύγγραμμα Περὶ Αὐλῶν κατέλιπεν· ὁμοίως δὲ καὶ ὁ
Ἀρχύτας. ἐμφανίζει δὲ καὶ ὁ Ἀριστοφάνης ἐν τοῖς
Δαιταλεῦσι τὴν περὶ τὸ πρᾶγμα τοῦτο σπουδὴν ὅταν
λέγῃ·

344 Cf. 5.222a with n.
345 See 4.169a n.
346 *PAA* 585315 (*c.*460–403 BCE); associated with Socrates,
and ultimately one of the Thirty Tyrants.
347 A famous Theban piper (Stephanis #2149) also mentioned
at 14.631e.

numerous other professionals; because they were impoverished, they taught the subjects they knew and produced many distinguished men.[344] All the ancient Greeks studied music, and pipe-playing was therefore a matter of considerable interest. Chamaeleon of Heraclea, for example, says in his work entitled *The Exhortation* (fr. 3 Wehrli) that all Spartans and Thebans used to learn to play the pipes, as did the Heracleots who lived along the Black Sea in his own day, as well as the most distinguished Athenians, such as Callias son of Hipponicus[345] and Critias son of Callaeschrus.[346] Duris says in his *On Euripides and Sophocles* (*FGrH* 76 F 29) that Alcibiades did not learn to play the pipes from just anyone but from Pronomus[347], who had the finest reputation in this area. And Aristoxenus (fr. 96 Wehrli) says that Epameinondas of Thebes[348] learned to play the pipes from Olympiodorus and Orthagoras. Many Pythagoreans also played the pipes, such as Euphranor, Archytas (47 B 6), Philolaus (44 A 7), and quite a few others.[349] Euphranor even left behind a treatise *On Pipe-Playing*, and Archytas did as well. Aristophanes brings out the attention paid to this matter in *Banqueters* (fr. 232), when he says:

[348] The famous general (d. 362 BCE). Thebes was famous for its pipe-players; for Olympiodorus (Stephanis #1936) and Orthagoras (Stephanis #1957), see Nep. *Epam.* 2.1 and Pl. *Prt.* 318c, respectively.

[349] Philolaus of Croton was a contemporary of Socrates; Archytas of Tarentum dates to the first half of the 4th century; and Euphranor (D–K 56.3) is later than Archytas but otherwise almost entirely obscure. Nothing survives of the works referred to below.

ὅστις αὐλοῖς καὶ λύραισι κατατέτριμμαι
χρώμενος,
f   εἶτά με σκάπτειν κελεύεις; |

Φρύνιχος Ἐφιάλτῃ·

οὐ τουτονὶ μέντοι σὺ κιθαρίζειν ποτὲ
αὐλεῖν τ᾽ ἐδίδαξας;

καὶ τὴν Ἀθηνᾶν δέ φησιν Ἐπίχαρμος ἐν Μούσαις
ἐπαυλῆσαι τοῖς Διοσκόροις τὸν ἐνόπλιον. Ἴων δ᾽ ἐν
Φοίνικι ἢ Καινεῖ ἀλέκτορα τὸν αὐλὸν καλεῖ ἐν τούτοις·

ἐπὶ δ᾽ αὐλὸς ἀλέκτωρ
Λύδιον ὕμνον ἀχέων.

ἐν δὲ Φρουροῖς τὸν ἀλεκτρυόνα Ἰδαῖον εἴρηκε σύριγγα διὰ τούτων·

185   ῥοθεῖ δέ τοι σῦριγξ Ἰδαῖος ἀλέκτωρ. ||

ἐν δὲ τῷ δευτέρῳ Φοίνικι ὁ αὐτὸς Ἴων φησίν·

ἐκτύπουν ἄγων βαρὺν
αὐλὸν τρέχοντι ῥυθμῷ,

οὕτω λέγων τῷ Φρυγίῳ· βαρὺς γὰρ οὗτος· παρ᾽ ὃ καὶ
τὸ κέρας αὐτῷ προσάπτουσιν ἀναλογοῦν τῷ τῶν σαλπίγγων κώδωνι.

Ἐπὶ τούτοις τέλος ἐχέτω καὶ ἥδε ἡ βίβλος, ἑταῖρε
Τιμόκρατες, ἱκανὸν εἰληφυῖα μῆκος.

BOOK IV

I'm worn out from playing pipes and *lurai*—
and you're ordering me to dig?

Phrynichus in *Ephialtes* (fr. 2):

    Didn't you ever teach this fellow here to play
e the *kithara* and the pipes?

And Epicharmus says in *Muses* (fr. 92) that Athena accompanied the Dioscuri by playing an *enoplion* ("martial song")[350] on the pipes. Ion refers to the pipes as a rooster in *Phoenix or Caeneus* (*TrGF* 19 F 39), in the following words:

    pipes, like a rooster, making
    a Lydian hymn resound in accompaniment.

In *The Watchmen* (*TrGF* 19 F 45) he refers to the rooster as an Idaean pan-pipe, in the following words:

    A rooster, like an Idaean pan-pipe, produces a
      clamor.

And in his second *Phoenix* (*TrGF* 19 F 42) the same Ion says:

    I brought my bass pipes and
    was making them resound with a racing rhythm,

referring in this way to the Phrygian pipe, since this is a bass pipe. They accordingly attach the piece of horn to the pipes in much the same way as they do to trumpet bells.

    Let this book come to an end with these remarks, my friend Timocrates, since it has grown long enough.

---

[350] Cf. 1.16a; 14.630f.

E

185   Ἀλλ᾽ ἐπεὶ πολὺς οὕτως λόγος συμποσίων πέρι
διήντληται, ὦ Τιμόκρατες, ἐν τοῖς πρὸ τούτων, παρ-
ελίπομεν δὲ αὐτῶν τὰ χρησιμώτατα καὶ οὐ βαροῦντα
τὴν ψυχήν, ὠφελοῦντα δὲ καὶ τρέφοντα κατὰ παν-
δαισίαν, ἅπερ ὁ θεῖος Ὅμηρος παρεισήγαγε, μνημο-
νεύσω καὶ τὰ περὶ τούτων λεχθέντα ὑπὸ τοῦ πάντα
ἀρίστου Μασουρίου. ἡμεῖς γὰρ κατὰ τὸν καλὸν Ἀγάθωνα

b   τὸ μὲν πάρεργον ἔργον ὡς ποιούμεθα, |
        τὸ δ᾽ ἔργον ὡς πάρεργον ἐκπονούμεθα.

φησὶ δ᾽ οὖν ὁ ποιητὴς περὶ τοῦ Μενελάου τὸν λόγον
ποιούμενος·

        τὸν δ᾽ εὗρον δαινύντα γάμον πολλοῖσιν ἔτησιν
        υἱέος ἠδὲ θυγατρὸς ἀμύμονος ᾧ ἐνὶ οἴκῳ,

ὡς νενόμισται ἄγειν συμπόσια περὶ τοὺς γάμους τῶν
τε γαμηλίων θεῶν ἕνεκα καὶ τῆς οἱονεὶ μαρτυρίας. τὸ
δὲ πρὸς τοὺς ξένους συμπόσιον ὁ τῆς Λυκίας βασι-
c   λεὺς διδάσκει οἷον εἶναι δεῖ, τὸν Βελλεροφόντην |
μεγαλοπρεπῶς δεξάμενος·

370

BOOK V

Since we have completed such a long discussion of symposia, Timocrates, in the preceding books, but have omitted their most beneficial aspects, which do not burden the soul but benefit and nourish it like a great feast, and are the elements the divine Homer introduced into his poem, I will now recall what was said about these matters by the excellent Masurius.[1] For to quote the noble Agathon (*TrGF* 39 F 11), we

> are treating what is secondary as our main task,
> and working at our main task as if it were secondary.

The poet, then, says as he introduces his discussion of Menelaus (*Od.* 4.3–4):

> They found him giving a wedding feast for many
>   clansmen
> in his house in honor of his son and faultless
>   daughter,

since it is customary to hold symposia at wedding feasts both to honor the gods of marriage and as a witness, as it were, to the event. The king of Lycia teaches us what a symposium given for strangers ought to be like by entertaining Bellerophon magnificently (*Il.* 6.174):

[1] Masurius speaks for almost the entire Book.

371

ἐννῆμαρ ξείνισσε καὶ ἐννέα βοῦς ἱέρευσε.

δοκεῖ γὰρ ἔχειν πρὸς φιλίαν τι ὁ οἶνος ἑλκυστικόν,
παραθερμαίνων τὴν ψυχὴν καὶ διαχέων. διόπερ οὐδὲ
πρότερον ἠρώτων οἵτινες εἶεν ἀλλ' ὕστερον, ὡς τὴν
ξενίαν αὐτὴν τιμῶντες, ἀλλ' οὐ τοὺς ἐν μέρει καὶ καθ'
ἕκαστον ἡμῶν. τῶν δὲ νῦν δείπνων προνοοῦντες οἱ
νομοθέται τά τε φυλετικὰ[1] καὶ τὰ δημοτικὰ προσ-
έταξαν, ἔτι δὲ τοὺς θιάσους καὶ τὰ φρατρικὰ καὶ
πάλιν ⟨τὰ⟩ ὀργεωνικὰ λεγόμενα. πολλῶν γοῦν εἰσι
186 φιλοσόφων ἐν ἄστει σύνοδοι ‖ τῶν μὲν Διογενιστῶν,
τῶν δὲ Ἀντιπατριστῶν λεγομένων, τῶν δὲ Παναιτι-
αστῶν. κατέλιπε δὲ καὶ Θεόφραστος εἰς τὴν τοιαύτην
σύνοδον χρήματα, μὰ Δί' οὐχ ἵνα ἀκολασταίνωσι
συνιόντες, ἀλλ' ἵνα τὰ κατὰ τὸν τοῦ συμποσίου νόμον
σωφρόνως καὶ πεπαιδευμένως διεξάγωσι. συνεδεί-
πνουν δ' ὁσημέραι οἱ περὶ πρύτανιν σώφρονα καὶ
σωτήρια τῶν πόλεων σύνδειπνα. πρὸς γοῦν τοιοῦτο
συμπόσιόν φησιν ὁ Δημοσθένης ἀνενηνέχθαι τὴν
Ἐλατείας κατάληψιν· ἑσπέρα μὲν γὰρ ἦν, ἧκε δὲ
b ἀγγέλλων τις ὡς | τοὺς πρυτάνεις ὡς Ἐλάτεια κατεί-

----

[1] φυλετικὰ δεῖπνα ACE

----

[2] Dinners organized by a religious association (*orgeōn*).

[3] Diogenes of Babylon, Antipater of Tarsus (mentioned again
below), and Panaetius of Rhodes were all 2nd-century BCE heads
of the Stoic school, and the city referred to above must therefore be Athens. The reference would appear to date the docu-
ment from which much of the first section of this Book is drawn—

He entertained him for nine days and sacrificed nine
  bulls.

Because wine seems to draw people into friendship by
warming and relaxing the soul. This is why they did not ask
who their guests were immediately, but put this off until
later, as if they were honoring the act of hospitality itself
rather than particular people on an individual basis. The
lawgivers were anticipating today's dinner parties when
they mandated meals organized by tribes and commu-
nities, as well as cult-dinners, phratry-dinners, and also
those referred to as *orgeōnika*[2]. Many philosophic groups,
for example, get together in the city, such as the Dio-
genists, the so-called Antipatrists, and the Panaetiasts
(Panaet. fr. 29 van Straaten).[3] Theophrastus (fr. 36
Fortenbaugh) even left money behind for this sort of
meeting, not, by Zeus, in order that they could get together
and run wild, but so that they could do everything proper
symposium procedure requires in a decent, educated way.
The *prytaneis*[4] used to eat modest dinners together every
day, and these helped ensure the city's safety. Demosthenes (18.169) says that it was to a symposium of this sort,
for example, that the capture of Elateia was reported: For
it was evening, and a messenger came to the *prytaneis* and
informed them that Elateia had been captured.[5] The phi-

presumably Herodicus' *On Symposia* (Duering pp. 106–24; cf.
5.192b)—to around 145 BCE.   [4] A rotating subgroup of 50
members of the Athenian Council, who ran the city's affairs on a
day-to-day basis and took their meals together in the *tholos*.

[5] In 339 BCE, when Philip II of Macedon's unexpected capture
of the Phocian city of Elateia gave him a new route by which to
attack Thebes and eventually Athens.

λῆπται. καὶ τοῖς φιλοσόφοις δὲ ἐπιμελὲς ἦν συνάγουσι τοὺς νέους μετ' αὐτῶν πρός τινα τεταγμένον
νόμον εὐωχεῖσθαι. τοῦ γοῦν Ξενοκράτους ἐν Ἀκαδημείᾳ καὶ πάλιν Ἀριστοτέλους συμποτικοί τινες ἦσαν
νόμοι. τὰ δ' ἐν Σπάρτῃ φιδίτια καὶ τὰ παρὰ τοῖς
Κρησὶν ἀνδρεῖα μετὰ πάσης ἐπιμελείας αἱ πόλεις
συνῆγον. διὸ καί τις οὐ κακῶς ἔφη·

c   οὐ χρὴ συμποσίοιο φίλους ἀπέχεσθαι ἑταίρους |
     δηρόν· ἀνάμνησις δὲ πέλει χαριεστάτη αὐτή.

Ἀντίπατρος δ' ὁ φιλόσοφος συμπόσιόν ποτε συνάγων
συνέταξε τοῖς ἐρχομένοις ὡς περὶ σοφισμάτων ἐροῦ-
σιν. Ἀρκεσίλαον δέ φησιν εἰς συμπόσιον παρακλη-
θέντα καὶ συγκατακλιθέντα ἑνὶ τῶν βορῶς ἐσθιόντων,
αὐτὸν δὲ μηδενὸς ἀπολαῦσαι δυνάμενον, ἐπεί τις αὐτῷ
τῶν παρόντων ἐξέτεινεν, φάναι·

     εὖ σοι γένοιτο, Τηλέφῳ δ' ἀγὼ νοῶ.

d   ἔτυχε δ' ὁ κατοψοφαγῶν Τήλεφος καλούμενος. | ὁ δὲ
Ζήνων ἐπεί τις τῶν παρόντων ὀψοφάγων ἀπέσυρεν
ἅμα τῷ παρατεθῆναι τὸ ἐπάνω τοῦ ἰχθύος, στρέψας
καὶ αὐτὸς τὸν ἰχθὺν ἀπέσυρεν ἐπιλέγων·

---

6 Cf. 1.3f.
7 Presumably Herodicus.
8 Head of the Academy c.268–242/1 BCE.
9 An adaptation of E. *Tel.* fr. 707 (cf. Ar. *Ach.* 446).

losophers also did their best to gather a group of young men and feast them in a prescribed way. Works on the rules for symposia were produced by Xenocrates of the Academy (fr. 50 Isnardi Parente), for example, as well as by Aristotle (fr. 467).[6] The cities organized the common messes in Sparta and the men's meals in Crete very carefully. The anonymous remark is therefore apt:

> Friendly companions should not stay away from the
>   symposium
> too long; this is the best way to remember one
>   another.

The philosopher Antipater (fr. 14, *SVF* iii. 246) once organized a symposium and ordered the men who attended to discuss philosophic quibbles. He[7] says that when Arcesilaus[8] was invited to a symposium and lay down with someone who was gorging himself, he was unable to enjoy any of the food. When one of the guests offered him something, he said:

> Bless you; and may Telephus get what I have in mind
>   for him.[9]

The fellow gobbling down the food happened to be named Telephus. When one of the gluttons at a party ripped off the upper side of the fish the moment it was served, Zeno (fr. 291, *SVF* i.66) turned it over and ripped off the other side of the fish for himself, saying as he did so (E. *Ba.* 1129)[10]:

[10] From the description of the dismemberment of Pentheus. Cf. 8.344a, where a virtually identical story is told of Bion.

375

Ἰνὼ δὲ τἀπὶ θάτερ᾽ ἐξειργάζετο.

Σωκράτης δ᾽ ἰδών τινα ἀμέτρως τῇ ἐποψήσει χρώμενον, "ὦ παρόντες," ἔφη, "τίς ὑμῶν τῷ μὲν ἄρτῳ ὡς ὄψῳ χρῆται, τῷ δ᾽ ὄψῳ ὡς ἄρτῳ;"

e Ἡμεῖς δὲ νῦν περὶ τῶν Ὁμηρικῶν συμποσίων λέξομεν· ἀφορίζει γὰρ αὐτῶν ὁ ποιητὴς χρόνους, | πρόσωπα, αἰτίας. τοῦτο δὲ ὀρθῶς ἀπεμάξατο ὁ Ξενοφῶν καὶ Πλάτων, οἳ κατ᾽ ἀρχὰς τῶν ξυγγραμμάτων ἐκτίθενται τὴν αἰτίαν τοῦ συμποσίου καὶ τίνες οἱ παρόντες. Ἐπίκουρος δὲ οὐ τόπον, οὐ χρόνον ἀφορίζει, οὐ προλέγει οὐδέν. δεῖ οὖν μαντεύσασθαι πῶς ποτ᾽ ἄνθρωπος ἐξαπίνης ἔχων κύλικα προβάλλει ζητήματα καθάπερ ἐν διατριβῇ λέγων. Ἀριστοτέλης δὲ ἄλουτον καὶ κονιορτοῦ ἥκειν πλήρη τινὰ ἐπὶ τὸ συμπόσιόν φησιν ⟨ἀπρεπὲς εἶναι⟩. ἔπειθ᾽ ὁ μὲν Ὅμηρος f ἐκδιδάσκει τίνας κλητέον, | εἰπὼν ὡς τοὺς ἀρίστους τε καὶ ἐντίμους χρὴ καλεῖν·

κίκλησκεν δὲ γέροντας ἀριστῆας Παναχαιῶν.

οὐχ ὃν τρόπον Ἡσίοδος· οὗτος γὰρ ἀξιοῖ καὶ τοὺς γείτονας·

⟨ . . . ⟩ μάλιστα καλεῖν, ὅστις σέθεν ἐγγύθι ναίει.

τοῦτο γὰρ ὡς ἀληθῶς Βοιωτικῆς ἐστιν ἀναισθησίας

And Ino completed the work on the other side.

When Socrates (cf. X. *Mem.* 3.14.2–4) saw someone eating excessive amounts of the side-dish, he said: "Fellow guests, which of you is consuming bread as if it were the fanciest dish, and the fanciest dish as if it were bread?"

I will now say something about Homeric symposia; for the poet specifies the times when they are held, the individuals who attend, and the reasons for them. Xenophon (*Smp.* 1.2–4) and Plato (*Smp.* 172a–3a), who explain at the beginning of their treatises why the symposium is held and who is present, are right to imitate this; whereas Epicurus (p. 115 Usener) does not specify the place or the time, or provide any introduction, so that one is forced to divine for oneself how it is that someone is suddenly holding a cup and advancing topics for conversation as if he were speaking in a philosophical school. Aristotle (fr. 50)[11] says that it is inappropriate to attend a symposium unwashed and covered with dust. Next, Homer (*Il.* 2.404) instructs us about whom we ought to invite, saying that one should invite noble individuals in positions of authority:

> He summoned the elders, the best of the
> Panachaeans.

This is not Hesiod's style; he thinks (*Op.* 343) that one's neighbors should be invited:

> In particular invite whoever lives close to you.

This is assuredly a symposium marked by Boeotian stu-

---

[11] Cf. 5.178f, where the fragment (which seems out of place here) is given in a more complete form.

συμπόσιον καὶ τῇ μισανθρωποτάτῃ τῶν παροιμιῶν
187 ἁρμόττον· ||

τηλοῦ φίλοι ναίοντες οὔκ εἰσιν φίλοι.

πῶς γὰρ οὐκ ἄλογον τόπῳ τὴν φιλίαν καὶ οὐ τρόπῳ
κρίνεσθαι; τοιγαροῦν παρ᾽ Ὁμήρῳ μετὰ τὸ πιεῖν·

τοῖς δ᾽² ὁ γέρων πάμπρωτος ὑφαίνειν ἤρχετο
μῆτιν,

παρὰ δὲ τοῖς οὐ τὰ σώφρονα συμπόσια συνάγουσι·

τοῖς δ᾽ ὁ κόλαξ πάμπρωτος ὑφαίνειν ἤρχετο
μῶκον.

ἔτι δὲ ὁ μὲν Ὅμηρος ἡλικίαις εἰσάγει διαφέροντας
b καὶ ταῖς προαιρέσεσι τοὺς κεκλημένους, | Νέστορα
καὶ Αἴαντα καὶ Ὀδυσσέα, τὸ μὲν καθόλου σύμπαντας
τῆς ἀρετῆς ἀντεχομένους, εἴδει δὲ διαφόροις ὁδοῖς
ὡρμηκότας ἐπ᾽ αὐτήν. ὁ δ᾽ Ἐπίκουρος ἅπαντας εἰσ-
ήγαγε προφήτας ἀτόμων καὶ ταῦτ᾽ ἔχων παραδείγμα-
τα τήν τε τοῦ ποιητοῦ τῶν συμποσίων ποικιλίαν καὶ
τὴν Πλάτωνός τε καὶ Ξενοφῶντος χάριν. ὧν ὁ μὲν
Πλάτων τὸν μὲν Ἐρυξίμαχον ἰατρόν, τὸν δὲ Ἀριστο-
177 φάνη ποιητήν, ἄλλον δ᾽ ἀπ᾽ ἄλλης προαιρέσεως³ ||
σπουδάζοντας εἰσήγαγεν, Ξενοφῶν δὲ καί τινας ἰδιώ-

---

² δ᾽ is not found in the traditional text of Homer.
³ For the text problem here (hence the rearrangement), see
4.177a n.

pidity[12] and quite in accord with the most misanthropic of proverbs (*App. Prov.* 3.99):

Friends who live far away are not true friends.

Because is it not unreasonable to assess friendship by where someone is rather than by what they are like? In Homer (*Il.* 7.324), accordingly, after the drinking

The old man first of all began to weave a plan for them.

Whereas for those who celebrate immodest symposia (adesp. parod. fr. 3 Olson–Sens = incert. fr. 1 Brandt)

The parasite first of all began to weave flattery for them.

Furthermore, Homer introduces guests who differ in their ages and interests, such as Nestor, Ajax, and Odysseus, who are all utterly devoted to excellence (*aretē*) but pursue it by different paths. Whereas Epicurus' (p. 115 Usener) characters are all atom-prophets[13], despite the fact that he had as paradigms the poet's various types of symposia, as well as the graceful work of Plato and Xenophon. Of these men, Plato introduced the physician Eryximachus, the poet Aristophanes, and various other people with different interests into his account, while Xenophon mixed in

---

[12] Hesiod was from Boeotia.

[13] I.e. adherents of the atomist theories most often associated with Democritus.

ATHENAEUS

τας συνανέμιξε. πολλῷ τοίνυν κάλλιον Ὅμηρος ἐποί-
b ησε | καὶ διάφορα παρατιθέμενος συμπόσια· πᾶν γὰρ
ἐξ ἀντιπαραβολῆς ὁρᾶται μᾶλλον. ἐστὶν γὰρ αὐτῷ τὸ
μὲν τῶν μνηστήρων οἷον ἂν γένοιτο νεανίσκων μέθαις
καὶ ἔρωσιν ἀνακειμένων, τὸ δὲ τῶν Φαιάκων εὐσταθέ-
στερον μὲν τούτων, φιλήδονον δέ. τούτοις δ᾽ ἀντέθηκε
τὰ μὲν ἐπὶ στρατιᾶς, τὰ δὲ πολιτικώτερον τελούμενα
σωφρόνως. καὶ πάλιν αὖ διεῖλεν τὰ μὲν δημοθοινίαν
ἔχοντα, τὰ δ᾽ οἰκείων σύνοδον. Ἐπίκουρος δὲ συμπόσιον φιλοσόφων μόνων πεποίηται. ἐδίδαξεν δ᾽ Ὅμη-
c ρος καὶ | οὓς οὐ δεῖ καλεῖν, ἀλλ᾽ αὐτομάτους ἰέναι,
πρεπόντως ἐξ ἑνὸς τῶν ἀναγκαίων δεικνὺς τὴν τῶν
ὁμοίων παρουσίαν·

   αὐτόματος δέ οἱ ἦλθε βοὴν ἀγαθὸς Μενέλαος.

δῆλον γὰρ ὡς οὔτε ἀδελφὸν οὔτε γονέας οὔτε γυναῖκα
κλητέον οὔτ᾽ εἴ τις ἰσοτίμως τινὰς τούτοις ἄγει· καὶ
γὰρ ἂν ψυχρὸν εἴη καὶ ἄφιλον. καίτοι τινὲς στίχον
προσέγραψαν τὴν αἰτίαν προστιθέντες·

   ἤδεε γὰρ κατὰ θυμὸν ἀδελφεὸν ὡς ἐπονεῖτο,

d ὥσπερ δέον εἰπεῖν αἰτίαν δι᾽ ἣν ἀδελφὸς αὐτόματος |
ἂν ἥκοι πρὸς δεῖπνον, ⟨οὐδὲ⟩ πιθανῆς τῆς αἰτίας
ἀποδιδομένης. πότερον γάρ φησιν ὡς οὐκ ᾔδει τὸν

---

14 Agamemnon.   15 The verse is accepted by modern
editors.   16 The anonymous scholar (Aristarchus?) whose
arguments are being criticized.

380

some average citizens. Homer therefore did much better by offering us symposia of various sorts; for everything is understood better through contrast. Thus he has the Suitors' symposium, which is what one would expect when young men devote themselves to getting drunk and having love affairs, as well as the Phaeacians' symposium, which is quieter than the Suitors' but still devoted to pleasure. He contrasted these with the symposia that take place during military campaigns, on the one hand, and those that occur in a more civic setting and a sober fashion, on the other. Again, he distinguished between those that involve public feasting and a family gathering. Epicurus offered an account of a symposium attended only by philosophers. Homer (*Il.* 2.408) also taught us about who does not need to be invited but ought to come of his own accord, appropriately using one close relation to indicate the presence of others like him:

> But Menelaus good at the war-cry came to him[14] of
>   his own accord.

Because it is obvious that there is no need to issue an invitation to one's own brother, parents, or wife, or to anyone else who occupies the same position as they do, because this would be cold and unfriendly. And yet some authorities added a line (*Il.* 2.409) that supplies the reason:[15]

> For he knew in his heart that his brother was
>   troubled,

as if it were necessary to specify why a brother would come to dinner of his own accord, and as if a convincing explanation did not present itself. For does he[16] claim that Menelaus did not know that his brother was giving a feast?

ἀδελφὸν ἑστιῶντα; καὶ πῶς οὐ γελοῖον, ὁπότε περιφα-
νὴς ἦν ἡ βουθυσία καὶ πᾶσι γνώριμος; πῶς δ᾽ ἂν
ἦλθεν, εἰ μὴ ᾔδει; ἢ νὴ Δία Περισπώμενον, φησίν,
αὐτὸν εἰδὼς συνεγνωμόνει ὅτι μὴ κέκληκε καὶ συμ-
περιφερόμενος ἦλθεν αὐτόματος; ὥσπερ ὁ φήσας
ἄκλητον ἥκειν, ἵνα μὴ πρωίας ὑποβλέπωσιν ἀλλήλους, ὁ μὲν αἰδούμενος, ὁ δὲ μεμφόμενος. ἀλλὰ γελοῖ-
ον ἦν ἐπιλαθέσθαι τὸν Ἀγαμέμνονα | τοῦ ἀδελφοῦ,
καὶ ταῦτα δι᾽ ἐκεῖνον οὐ μόνον εἰς τὸ παρὸν θύοντα,
ἀλλὰ καὶ τὸν πόλεμον ἀναδεδεγμένον, καὶ κεκληκότα
τοὺς μήτε γένει προσήκοντας μήτε πατρίδι προσ-
ῳκειωμένους. Ἀθηνοκλῆς δ᾽ ὁ Κυζικηνὸς μᾶλλον Ἀρι-
στάρχου κατακούων τῶν Ὁμηρικῶν ἐπῶν εὐπαιδευ-
τότερον ἡμῖν φησι τοῦτον Ὅμηρον καταλιπεῖν, ὡς
τῆς ἀνάγκης ὁ Μενέλεως οἰκειοτέρως εἶχεν. Δημήτριος δ᾽ ὁ Φαληρεὺς ἐπαρίστερον τὴν τοῦ στίχου
παράληψιν ἐπειπὼν καὶ τῆς ποιήσεως ἀλλοτρίαν, | τὸν

ᾔδεε γὰρ κατὰ θυμὸν ἀδελφεὸν ὡς ἐπονεῖτο

μικρολογίαν ἐμβάλλειν τοῖς ἤθεσιν. οἶμαι γάρ, φησίν, ἕκαστον τῶν χαριέντων ἀνθρώπων ἔχειν καὶ οἰ-
κεῖον ‖ καὶ φίλον πρὸς ὃν ἂν ἔλθοι θυσίας οὔσης τὸν
καλοῦντα μὴ περιμείνας. Πλάτων δ᾽ ἐν τῷ Συμποσίῳ
περὶ τῶν αὐτῶν λέγει οὕτως· ἵνα καὶ τὴν παροιμίαν,
φησί, διαφθείρωμεν μεταβάλλοντες, ὡς ἄρα καὶ ἀγα-

---

17 I.e. "God of Grammarians"?
18 Apollo is speaking, urging Hector on.

Is this not laughable, given that the bull was slaughtered in plain sight and everyone was aware of it? And why would he have come, if he did not know? Or, he says, by Zeus Perispōmenos[17], does he claim that Menelaus knew about the feast, forgave his brother for not inviting him, and accommodated himself to the situation by coming of his own accord?—which is the same as saying that he came uninvited, so that they would not scowl at each other the next morning, one of them out of shame, the other out of resentment. It would be ridiculous, however, for Agamemnon to forget about his brother, especially because it was on his account that he not only was making sacrifice at the moment but had undertaken the war, and despite the fact that he had invited people who were not related to him by birth and had no connection with his fatherland. Athenocles of Cyzicus, who understands Homeric poetry better than Aristarchus does, offers what we consider the more scholarly explanation, that Homer passed over Menelaus since he was too closely related to Agamemnon for an invitation to be necessary. Demetrius of Phaleron (fr. 190 Wehrli = fr. 143 Fortenbaugh–Schütrumpf) pronounced the interpolation of the line awkward and foreign to the poet's style, saying that (*Il.* 2.409)

> For he knew in his heart that his brother was
>   troubled

attributes pettiness to the characters. Because I believe, he says, that every refined person has a relative or friend he could visit when a sacrifice occurs without waiting for the other man to invite him. Plato in his *Symposium* (174b–c) says the following about the same matters: So that, he says, we may change and thus corrupt the proverb, so that it says

383

θῶν ἐπὶ δαῖτας ἴασιν αὐτόματοι ἀγαθοί. Ὅμηρος μὲν
γὰρ κινδυνεύει οὐ μόνον διαφθεῖραι, ἀλλὰ καὶ ὑβρί-
σαι εἰς αὐτήν· ποιήσας γὰρ τὸν Ἀγαμέμνονα ἀγαθὸν
τὰ πολεμικά, τὸν Μενέλαον δὲ μαλθακὸν αἰχμητήν,
θυσίαν ποιουμένου τοῦ Ἀγαμέμνονος ἄκλητον ἐποίη-
σεν ἐλθόντα | τὸν χείρονα ἐπὶ τὴν τοῦ ἀμείνονος
δίαιταν. Βακχυλίδης δὲ περὶ τοῦ Ἡρακλέους λέγων ὡς
ἦλθεν ἐπὶ τὸν τοῦ Κήυκος οἶκόν φησιν·

στᾶ δ' ἐπὶ λάινον οὐδόν, τοὶ δὲ θοίνας ἔντυον,
    ὧδέ τ' ἔφα·
"αὐτόματοι δ' ἀγαθῶν
⟨ἐς⟩ δαῖτας εὐόχθους ἐπέρχονται δίκαιοι
φῶτες."

αἱ δὲ παροιμίαι ἡ μέν φησιν·

αὐτόματοι δ' ἀγαθοὶ ἀγαθῶν ἐπὶ δαῖτας ἴασιν,

ἡ δέ·

αὐτόματοι ⟨δ'⟩ ἀγαθοὶ δειλῶν ἐπὶ δαῖτας ἴασιν.

οὐ δεόντως γοῦν Πλάτων τὸν Μενέλεων | ἐνόμισεν
εἶναι δειλόν, ὃν ἀρηίφιλον Ὅμηρος λέγει καὶ μόνον
ὑπὲρ Πατρόκλου ἀριστεύσαντα καὶ τῷ Ἕκτορι πρὸ
πάντων πρόθυμον μονομαχεῖν, καίπερ ὄντα τῇ ῥώμῃ
καταδεέστερον, ἐφ' οὗ μόνου τῶν στρατευσαμένων
εἴρηκεν·

that good people go uninvited to meals given by good people. For Homer comes close to not just corrupting but abusing it; because he represents Agamemnon as a brave man in anything having to do with war, but Menelaus as a "cowardly spearman" (*Il.* 17.588);[18] but when Agamemnon was making a sacrifice, he represented the lesser man as going uninvited to the better man's residence. When Bacchylides (fr. 4.21–5) describes how Heracles came to Ceyx's house, he says:

> He stood at the stone threshold, and they were
>   preparing a feast; and he said the following:
> "Of their own accord just
> men come to the rich meals of good
> men."

One proverb says:

> Good men go to good men's feasts of their own
>   accord.[19]

Another says:

> Good men go to cowards' feasts of their own accord.

There was no need, at any rate, for Plato to consider Menelaus a coward, since Homer (*Il.* 17.1–8) refers to him as *arēiphilos* ("war-loving") and says that he was the only man who distinguished himself in the fight over the dead Patroclus and (*Il.* 7.94–105) was eager to fight a duel with Hector in front of everyone, although he was not as strong as him. Menelaus is also the only member of the expedition about whom Homer says (*Il.* 2.588):

[19] Cf. 1.8a.

ATHENAEUS

ἐν δ᾽ αὐτὸς κίεν ᾖσι προθυμίῃσι πεποιθώς.

εἰ δὲ ὁ ἐχθρὸς ὁ βλασφημῶν αὐτὸν εἴρηκε μαλθακὸν αἰχμητὴν καὶ διὰ τοῦτο Πλάτων τῷ ὄντι μαλθακὸν αὐτὸν ὑπολαμβάνει, οὐκ ἂν φθάνοι καὶ τὸν Ἀγαμέμνονα τιθεὶς ἐν τοῖς φαύλοις, ὃν | αὐτός φησιν εἶναι ἀγαθόν, εἴπερ εἰς αὐτὸν εἴρηται τοῦτο τὸ ἔπος·

d

οἰνοβαρές, κυνὸς ὄμματ᾽ ἔχων, κραδίην δ᾽ ἐλάφοιο.

οὐ γὰρ εἴ τι λέγεται παρ᾽ Ὁμήρῳ, τοῦθ᾽ Ὅμηρος λέγει. πῶς γὰρ ἂν εἴη μαλθακὸς Μενέλαος ὁ τὸν Ἕκτορα μόνος ἀπείρξας τοῦ Πατρόκλου καὶ Εὔφορβον ἀποκτείνας τε καὶ σκυλεύσας ἐν μέσοις τοῖς Τρωσί; τὸ δὲ μηδὲ τὸν στίχον ὃν ᾐτιᾶτο τελείως κατανοῆσαι ἄτοπον, δι᾽ οὗ | βοὴν ἀγαθὸς Μενέλαος λέγεται. τοῖς γὰρ ἀνδρειοτάτοις Ὅμηρος εἴωθεν ἐπιφωνεῖν, καλούντων τῶν παλαιῶν τὸν πόλεμον βοήν.

e

Πάντα δ᾽ ὢν ἀκριβὴς Ὅμηρος καὶ τὸ μικρὸν τοῦτο οὐ παρέλιπε τὸ δεῖν θεραπεύσαντα τὸ σωμάτιον καὶ λουσάμενον ἰέναι πρὸς τὸ δεῖπνον. ἐπὶ γοῦν τοῦ Ὀδυσσέως εἶπε πρὸ τῆς παρὰ Φαίαξι θοίνης·

αὐτόδιον δ᾽ ἄρα μιν ταμίη λούσασθαι ἄνωγεν[4]. |

f

ἐπὶ δὲ τῶν περὶ Τηλέμαχον·

[4] The traditional text of Homer has ἀνώγει.

He himself moved among them, confident in his
    courage.

And if his enemy slanders him by referring to him (*Il.*
17.588) as a "weak spearman," and Plato on that account
suspects that he actually was weak, he would not hesitate
to include Agamemnon, who he himself claims was brave,
among the worst men, given that the following line is spoken about him (*Il.* 1.225):[20]

    Heavy with wine, with a dog's eyes and a deer's heart!

Because if something is said in Homer, it is not necessarily
Homer who says it. For how could Menelaus be weak,
given that all by himself he kept Hector away from Patroclus, killed Euphorbus, and stripped him of his gear with
the Trojans all around?[21] But that he has not thought carefully though the line, in which Menelaus is referred to
as "good at the war-cry" *(boēn agathos)*, is curious; for
Homer's practice was to use this phrase for his bravest
characters, since the ancients referred to war as *boē*.[22]

Since Homer is precise about everything, he did not
omit the following small point, which is that one ought to
take care of one's body and bathe before going to dinner.
He said of Odysseus, for example, before the feast given by
the Phaeacians (*Od.* 8.449):

    At once, then, the housekeeper urged him to wash
      himself.

And concerning Telemachus' group (*Od.* 4.48):

---

[20] Achilleus is speaking.
summary of the action in *Iliad* 17.

[21] A somewhat inaccurate
[22] E.g. Theoc. 16.97.

ἔς ῥ᾽ ἀσαμίνθους βάντες ἐυξέστας λούσαντο.

ἀπρεπὲς γὰρ ἦν, φησὶν Ἀριστοτέλης, ἥκειν εἰς τὸ
συμπόσιον σὺν ἱδρῶτι πολλῷ καὶ κονιορτῷ· δεῖ γὰρ
τὸν χαρίεντα μήτε ῥυπᾶν μήτε αὐχμεῖν μήτε βορβόρῳ
χαίρειν καθ᾽ Ἡράκλειτον. δεῖ δὲ καὶ τὸν πρῶτον εἰς
ἀλλοτρίαν οἰκίαν ἐρχόμενον ἐπὶ δεῖπνον μὴ γαστρι-
179   σόμενον ‖ εὐθὺς ἐπὶ τὸ συμπόσιον χωρεῖν, ἀλλά τι
δοῦναι πρότερον τῷ φιλοθεάμονι καὶ κατανοῆσαι τὴν
οἰκίαν. οὐδὲ γὰρ τοῦτο παρέλιπεν ὁ ποιητής·

αὐτοὶ δ᾽ εἰσῆλθον⁵ θεῖον δόμον· οἱ δὲ ἰδόντες
θαύμαζον κατὰ δῶμα διοτρεφέος βασιλῆος.
ὥς τε γὰρ ἠελίου αἴγλη πέλεν ἠὲ σελήνης
δῶμα καθ᾽ ὑψερεφὲς Μενελάου κυδαλίμοιο.

καὶ Ἀριστοφάνης ἐν Σφηξὶ ποιεῖ τὸν ἄγριον γέροντα
b   καὶ φιλοδικαστὴν καταρρυθμιζόμενον εἰς βίον | ἥμε-
ρον ὑπὸ τοῦ παιδός·

παῦ· ἀλλὰ δευρὶ κατακλινεὶς προσμάνθανε
ξυμποτικὸς εἶναι καὶ ξυνουσιαστικός.

διδάξας τε αὐτὸν ὡς δεῖ κατακλίνεσθαί φησιν·

ἔπειτ᾽ ἐπαίνεσόν τι τῶν χαλκωμάτων,
ὀροφὴν θέασαι, κρεκάδι᾽ αὐλῆς θαύμασον.

⁵ The traditional text of Homer has αὐτοὺς δ᾽ εἰσῆγον.

They entered the polished bathtubs and washed
themselves.

Because it was inappropriate, says Aristotle (fr. 50), to
come to the symposium covered with sweat and dust; the
refined person should not be dirty or unwashed, or take
pleasure in muck, as Heracleitus (22 B 13) puts it. The
minute you arrive at another person's house for dinner, you
should not head straight for the symposium to stuff yourself, but should instead offer something to your contem-
plative faculty and examine the house. Because the poet
(*Od.* 4.43–6) did not leave this out:

They themselves entered the divine house and were
    amazed
as they gazed throughout the home of the Zeus-
    nourished king.
For like the light that shines from the sun or the
    moon
was the light throughout the high-roofed house of
    famous Menelaus.

And Aristophanes in *Wasps* (1208–9) represents the fierce
old man devoted to jury-duty as being converted to a tame
way of life by his son:

Cut it out! Lie down here and learn
how to behave at symposia and in company!

Again, after teaching him how he ought to lie down, he says
(1214–15):

Then praise one of the bronze objects;
take a look at the ceiling; express your amazement at
    the tapestries in the hall.

Καὶ πρὸ τοῦ θοινᾶσθαι δὲ ἃ δεῖ ποιεῖν ἡμᾶς διδάσκει πάλιν Ὅμηρος, ἀπαρχὰς τῶν βρωμάτων νέ-
c μειν τοῖς θεοῖς. οἱ γοῦν περὶ τὸν Ὀδυσσέα καίπερ |
ὄντες ἐν τῷ τοῦ Κύκλωπος σπηλαίῳ·

   ἔνθα δὲ πῦρ κείαντες ἐθύσαμεν ἠδὲ καὶ αὐτοὶ
   τυρῶν αἰνύμενοι φάγομεν.

καὶ ὁ Ἀχιλλεὺς καίπερ ἐπειγομένων τῶν πρέσβεων ὡς
ἐν μέσαις νυξὶν ἡκόντων ὅμως

                          θεοῖσι δὲ θῦσαι ἀνώγει
   Πάτροκλον, ὃν ἑταῖρον· ὁ δ' ἐν πυρὶ βάλλε
   θυηλάς.

καὶ σπονδοποιεῖταί γε τοὺς δαιτυμόνας·

d   κοῦροι μὲν κρητῆρας ἐπεστέψαντο ποτοῖο, |
     νώμησαν δ' ἄρα πᾶσιν ἐπαρξάμενοι δεπάεσσιν.
     αὐτὰρ ἐπεὶ σπεῖσάν τ'.

ἅπερ καὶ Πλάτων φυλάσσει κατὰ τὸ συμπόσιον· μετὰ
γὰρ τὸ δειπνῆσαι σπονδάς τέ φησιν ποιῆσαι καὶ τὸν
θεὸν παιωνίσαντας τοῖς νομιζομένοις γέρασι. παραπλησίως δὲ καὶ Ξενοφῶν. παρὰ δ' Ἐπικούρῳ οὐ σπον-
δή, οὐκ ἀπαρχὴ θεοῖς, ἀλλ' ὥσπερ Σιμωνίδης ἔφη
περὶ τῆς ἀκόσμου γυναικός,

e   ἄθυστα δ' ἱρὰ πολλάκις κατεσθίει. |

Moreover Homer teaches us what we ought to do before we feast, which is to offer the gods first fruits of the food. Although Odysseus' men, for example, are in the Cyclops' cave (*Od.* 9.231–2),

> We kindled a fire there and made sacrifice; and we
>   ourselves
> took some of the cheeses and ate them.

And although the members of the embassy are in a hurry and have come in the middle of the night, Achilleus nonetheless (*Il.* 9.219–20)

>   orders his companion Patroclus
> to make a sacrifice to the gods. And he threw the
>   gods' portion in the fire.

He also represents diners as making libations (*Il.* 9.175–7):

> The young men filled the mixing-bowls to the brim
>   with wine
> and distributed it, pouring a libation in everyone's
>   goblet.
> But after they poured libations . . .

Plato (*Smp.* 176a) retains these elements in his symposium; after they had dinner, he says, they made libations and sang a paean to the god, giving him his customary honors. Xenophon (*Smp.* 2.1) says something similar. In Epicurus (p. 115 Usener), on the other hand, there is no libation or offering of first fruits to the gods, but as Simonides (Semon. fr. 7.56 West[2]) said about the disorderly woman,

> She often consumes the offerings before the sacrifice
>   is complete.

ATHENAEUS

Τὴν γὰρ σύμμετρον κρᾶσιν τοῦ οἴνου ὑπὸ Ἀμφι-
κτύονος βασιλεύσαντος διδαχθῆναί φασιν Ἀθηναίους, καὶ διὰ τοῦτο ἱερὸν Διονύσου Ὀρθοῦ ἱδρύσασθαι·
τότε γὰρ ὀρθός ἐστι τῷ ὄντι καὶ οὐ σφαλερός, ὅταν
συμμέτρως καὶ κεκραμένως πίνηται.

> οἶνος γὰρ ἀνώγει
> ἠλεός, ὅς τ᾽ ἐφέηκε πολύφρονά περ μάλ᾽ ἀεῖσαι
> καί θ᾽ ἁπαλὸν γελάσαι, καί τ᾽ ὀρχήσασθαι
f   ἀνῆκεν, |
> καί τε⁶ ἔπος προέηκεν ὅ πέρ τ᾽ ἄρρητον ἄμεινον.

τὸν γὰρ οἶνον Ὅμηρος οὐκ ἠλεὸν ὥσπερ ἠλίθιον
καλεῖ καὶ ματαιοποιόν, οὐδὲ κελεύει σκυθρωπὸν εἶναι
μήτε ᾄδοντα μήτε γελῶντα μήτ᾽ ἐρρύθμως ποτὲ καὶ
πρὸς ὄρχησιν τρεπόμενον· οὐχ οὕτως ἀγροῖκος οὐδ᾽
ἐπαρίστερός ἐστιν, ἀλλ᾽ ᾔδει τούτων ἑκάστου καὶ
ποσότητος καὶ ποιότητος διαφοράν. ὅθεν οὐκ εἶπεν ὡς
ἄρα τὸν πολύφρονα ὁ οἶνος ποιεῖ ᾆσαι, ἀλλὰ μάλ᾽
180 ἀεῖσαι, τουτέστιν ‖ ἀμέτρως καὶ ἐπὶ πλεῖον ὥστε
προσοχλεῖν· οὐδέ τι γελάσαι μὰ Δί᾽ οὐδ᾽ ὀρχήσασθαι·
κοινὸν δ᾽ ἐπ᾽ ἀμφοτέρων λαβὼν τὸ ἁπαλὸν τὴν ἄναν-
δρον εἰς τοῦτο πρόπτωσιν ἐπιστομίζει·

> καί θ᾽ ἁπαλὸν γελάσαι καί τ᾽ ὀρχήσασθαι
> ἀνῆκεν.

⁶ The traditional text of Homer has τι.

392

They say[23] that the Athenians learned the proper way to mix wine from Amphictyon when he was their king, and that as a result they founded a temple of Upright Dionysus; because he is in fact upright and not stumbling when drunk[24] in a moderate mixture.

> For the crazy wine
> urges me to. It encourages even a thoughtful man to sing much
> and to laugh softly, and it causes him to dance
> and also elicits a word that was better left unspoken.
> (*Od*. 14.463–6)

Homer does not refer to wine as "crazy" in the sense that it is foolish or encourages thoughtless behavior; nor is he ordering us to scowl, or to refuse to sing, laugh, or occasionally dance along with music. He is not that unrefined or clumsy, but understands the distinctions of quantity and quality in all these matters. He accordingly did not say that wine makes a thoughtful man sing, but that it makes him "sing much," which is to say too loud and too long, so that he annoys people. Nor, by Zeus, does he simply say "to laugh" or "to dance"; instead he takes the word "softly" with both verbs[25] and tries to restrain the effeminate tendency toward this sort of thing:

> and it causes him to laugh softly and to dance (*Od*. 14.465).

[23] At 2.38c, this information is attributed to Philochorus (*FGrH* 328 F 5b).   [24] Sc. in the form of wine.

[25] This is to say that there ought to be no comma in the middle of line 465 and it ought to be translated as it is below.

παρὰ δὲ τῷ Πλάτωνι τούτων οὐδὲν ἔμμετρον, ἀλλὰ
πίνουσι μὲν τοσοῦτον ὥστε μηδὲ τοῖς ἰδίοις ποσὶν
ἵστασθαι. ὅρα γὰρ τὸν ἐπίκωμον Ἀλκιβιάδην ὡς
ἀσχημονεῖ· οἱ δ' ἄλλοι τὸν ὀκτακότυλον ψυκτῆρα
b πίνουσι, προφάσεως λαβόμενοι | ἐπείπερ αὐτοὺς προ-
είλκυσεν Ἀλκιβιάδης, οὐχ ὥσπερ οἱ παρ' Ὁμήρῳ·

αὐτὰρ ἐπεὶ σπεῖσάν τ' ἔπιόν θ' ὅσον ἤθελε
θυμός.

τούτων οὖν ἃ μὲν καθάπαξ περιγραπτέον, οἷς δὲ
συμμέτρως χρηστέον ὥσπερ ἀναθήμασί τισι μικρὸν
προσαποβλέψαντας, καθάπερ Ὅμηρος εἴρηκεν·

μολπή τ' ὀρχηστύς τε· τὰ γάρ τ' ἀναθήματα
δαιτός.

τὸ δ' ὅλον τὸ πρὸς τὰ τοιαῦτα νενευκὸς τοῖς μνηστῆρ-
c σι καὶ τοῖς Φαίαξιν ἔνειμεν, ἀλλ' οὐχὶ Νέστορι | οὐδὲ
Μενελάῳ· οὗ ἐν τῇ γαμοποιίᾳ μὴ συνέντες οἱ περὶ
Ἀρίσταρχον ὅτι συνεχοῦς οὔσης τῆς ἑστιάσεως καὶ
τῶν ἀκμαίων ἡμερῶν παρεληλυθιῶν, ἐν αἷς παρεί-
ληπτο μὲν ἡ γαμουμένη πρὸς τοῦ νυμφίου, πέρας δ'
εἶχεν ὁ τοῦ Μεγαπένθους γάμος, αὐτοὶ δὲ μονάζοντες
διῃτῶντο ὅ τε Μενέλαος καὶ ἡ Ἑλένη, μὴ συνέντες,
ἀλλ' ἐξαπατηθέντες ὑπὸ τοῦ πρώτου ἔπους·

---

26 About a half-gallon.   27 Literally "those about
Aristarchus, Aristarchus' circle," although it is almost certainly
Aristarchus himself who is referred to.

BOOK V

In Plato none of this is done in a moderate way; instead, they drink so much that they cannot stand on their own feet (*Smp.* 212d). Look how disgracefully Alcibiades behaves when he wanders in drunk, while the others drain a cooler that holds 8 *kotulai*[26] and offer the excuse that Alcibiades led them to do it (*Smp.* 213e–14a). Homer's characters behave differently:

> But after they poured a libation and drank as much as
>   their heart desired. (e.g. *Il.* 9.177)

Some of these behaviors, therefore, must be unequivocally ruled out, but others can be indulged in moderation, if we regard them as a bit like extras *(anathēmata)* of a sort, as Homer (*Od.* 1.152) says:

> song and dance; for these are the extras *(anathēmata)*
>   that go with a feast.

Homer generally assigned everything that tends in this direction to the Suitors and the Phaeacians, and not to Nestor and Menelaus. As for the wedding celebrated by the latter, Aristarchus[27] did not understand that, because the feasting went on constantly and the most significant days, during which the bride[28] was taken home by the bridegroom and Megapenthes' wedding was complete, were over, Menelaus and Helen were alone in the house. Because he did not understand this, but was deceived by the first verse (*Od.* 4.3),

[28] Hermione, Menelaus' daughter by Helen, who was being sent to Achilles' son Neoptolemus, whereas Menelaus' bastard son Megapenthes was marrying "Alector's daughter from Sparta."

τὸν δ' εὗρον δαινύντα γάμον πολλοῖσιν ἔτησιν,

d προσσυνῆψαν τοιούτους τινὰς στίχους· |

ὡς οἱ μὲν δαίνυντο καθ' ὑψερεφὲς μέγα δῶμα
γείτονες ἠδὲ ἔται Μενελάου κυδαλίμοιο
τερπόμενοι· μετὰ δέ σφιν ἐμέλπετο θεῖος ἀοιδὸς
φορμίζων· δοιὼ δὲ κυβιστητῆρε κατ' αὐτοὺς
μολπῆς ἐξάρχοντες ἐδίνευον κατὰ μέσσους,

μετενεγκόντες ἐκ τῆς Ὁπλοποιίας σὺν αὐτῷ γε τῷ
περὶ τὴν λέξιν ἁμαρτήματι. οὐ γὰρ ἐξάρχοντες οἱ
κυβιστητῆρες, ἀλλ' ἐξάρχοντος τοῦ ᾠδοῦ πάντως ὠρ-
e χοῦντο. τὸ γὰρ ἐξάρχειν τῆς φόρμιγγος ἴδιον. | διόπερ
ὁ μὲν Ἡσίοδός φησιν ἐν τῇ Ἀσπίδι·

θεαὶ δ' ἐξῆρχον ἀοιδῆς
Μοῦσαι Πιερίδες,

καὶ ὁ Ἀρχίλοχος·

αὐτὸς ἐξάρχων πρὸς αὐλὸν Λέσβιον παιήονα.

καλεῖ δὲ Στησίχορος μὲν τὴν Μοῦσαν ἀρχεσίμολπον,
Πίνδαρος δ' ἁγησίχορα τὰ προοίμια. Διόδωρος δ' ὁ
Ἀριστοφάνειος ὅλον τὸν γάμον περιέγραψε τοπάζων
πρώτας ἡμέρας εἶναι, καὶ τὸ λῆγον αὐτῶν, ἔτι δὲ καὶ

They found him giving a wedding feast for many
   kinsmen,

he added some lines of the following sort (*Od.* 4.15–19):

So the neighbors and kinsmen of famous Menelaus
were feasting throughout his great high-roofed home,
enjoying themselves. Among them a divine bard was
   singing
and playing the lyre. And a pair of tumblers separate
   from the others
led *(exarchontes)* the song, whirling about among
   them,

borrowing the lines from *The Forging of the Arms* (*Il.*
18.604–6, quoted below), along with the error in the language; because it was not the tumblers who led *(exarchontes)*, but they danced while the singer, of course, led
(exarchontos). For leading *(exarchein)* is an action peculiar
to the lyre. This is why Hesiod says in *The Shield* (205–6):

                              and the goddesses, the Pierian Muses,
   led *(exērchon)* the song.

Also Archilochus (fr. 121 West²):

I myself leading *(exarchōn)* the Lesbian paean
   accompanied by pipes.

Stesichorus (*PMG* 250) refers to the Muse as *archesi-
molpos* ("song-leading"), while Pindar (*P.* 1.4) calls his pre-
ludes *hagēsichora* ("dance-leading"). Aristophanes' student Diodorus marked the entire wedding as spurious,
hypothesizing that these were the initial days, and taking
no account of the fact that they were coming to a close, or

ATHENAEUS

f τὸ ἕωλον τῆς συμποσίας | οὐκ ἐπιλογιζόμενος. ἔπειτα
κελεύει γράφειν·

< . . . > δοιὼ δὲ κυβιστητῆρε καθ᾽ αὑτοὺς

ἐν τῷ δασεῖ γράμματι, σολοικίζειν ἀναγκάζων. τὸ μὲν
γὰρ κατ᾽ αὐτοὺς κατὰ σφᾶς ἐστιν αὐτούς, τὸ δὲ λέγειν
ἑαυτοὺς σόλοικον. ἀλλ᾽ ὅπερ εἶπον, ἡ τῶν ἀκροαμάτων
εἰς τὸ σῶφρον τοῦτο συμπόσιον εἰσαγωγὴ παρέγ-
γραφός ἐστιν ἐκ τοῦ Κρητικοῦ χοροῦ μετενηνεγμένη,
181 || περὶ οὗ φησιν ἐν Ὁπλοποιίᾳ·

ἐν δὲ χορὸν ποίκιλλε περικλυτὸς Ἀμφιγυήεις
τῷ ἴκελον, οἷόν ποτ᾽ ἐνὶ Κνωσσῷ εὐρείῃ
Δαίδαλος ἤσκησεν καλλιπλοκάμῳ Ἀριάδνῃ.
ἔνθα μὲν ἠΐθεοι καὶ παρθένοι ἀλφεσίβοιαι
ὠρχεῦντ᾽, ἀλλήλων ἐπὶ καρπῷ χεῖρας ἔχουσαι[7].

τούτοις γὰρ ἐπιβάλλει·

b πολλὸς δ᾽ ἱμερόεντα χορὸν περιίσταθ᾽ ὅμιλος |
τερπόμενος· <μετὰ δέ σφιν ἐμέλπετο θεῖος ἀοιδὸς
φορμίζων·>[8] δοιὼ δὲ κυβιστητῆρε κατ᾽ αὐτοὺς
μολπῆς ἐξάρχοντες ἐδίνευον κατὰ μέσσους.

[7] Most witnesses to the text of Homer have ἔχοντες.
[8] add. Kaibel

---

[29] Literally "by themselves."
[30] An ungrammatical construction of a sort supposedly typical
of the inhabitants of Soli, a city in Southern Italy. Cf. 5.189b.

of the possibility that it was the very end of the symposium.
He then suggests that we write:

> . . . and a pair of tumblers separate from the others
>   (*kath' heautous*)[29] (*Od*. 4.18),

with the rough breathing, forcing us into a solecism[30],
since *kat' autous*[31] means "separate from the others," and
using *heautous*[32] is a solecism. But as I was saying, the introduction of entertainment into this sober symposium
is an interpolation borrowed from the Cretan chorus,
about which Homer says in *The Forging of the Arms* (*Il*.
18.590–4):

> The famous crippled god worked a dancing-place
>   into it,
> like the one Daedalus once made
> in wide Cnossus for Ariadne of the lovely tresses.
> Young men and unmarried girls whose bride-price
>   was many oxen
> were dancing there, holding one another's hands at
>   the wrist.

And he adds to these verses (*Il*. 18.603–6):

> A large crowd surrounded the lovely chorus,
> enjoying themselves. Among them a divine bard was
>   singing
> and playing the lyre. And a pair of tumblers separate
>   from the others
> led the song, whirling about among them.

---

[31] As in the traditional version of the text.
[32] The reflexive form of the pronoun ("themselves").

τοῖς μὲν οὖν Κρησὶν ἥ τε ὄρχησις ἐπιχώριος καὶ τὸ
κυβιστᾶν. διό φησι πρὸς τὸν Κρῆτα Μηριόνην·

Μηριόνη, τάχα κέν σε καὶ ὀρχηστήν περ ἐόντα
ἔγχος ἐμὸν κατέπαυσε διαμπερές, εἴ σ᾽ ἔβαλόν
περ.

ὅθεν καὶ Κρητικὰ καλοῦσι τὰ ὑπορχήματα·

Κρῆτα μὲν καλέουσι τρόπον, τὸ δ᾽ ὄργανον
c   Μολοσσόν. |

οἱ δὲ λεγόμενοι Λακωνισταί, φησὶν ὁ Τίμαιος, ἐν
τετραγώνοις χοροῖς ᾖδον. καθόλου δὲ διάφορος ἦν ἡ
μουσικὴ παρὰ τοῖς Ἕλλησι, τῶν μὲν Ἀθηναίων τοὺς
Διονυσιακοὺς χοροὺς καὶ τοὺς κυκλίους προτιμώντων,
Συρακοσίων δὲ τοὺς ἰαμβιστάς, ἄλλων δ᾽ ἄλλο τι. ὁ δ᾽
Ἀρίσταρχος οὐ μόνον εἰς τὸ τοῦ Μενελάου συμπόσιον
ἐμβαλὼν οὓς οὐ προσῆκε στίχους καὶ τῆς Λακώνων
παιδείας ἀλλότριον ἐποίησε καὶ τῆς τοῦ βασιλέως
σωφροσύνης, ἀλλὰ καὶ τοῦ Κρητικοῦ χοροῦ τὸν ᾠδὸν
d | ἐξεῖλεν, ἐπιτεμὼν τὰ ποιήματα τὸν τρόπον τοῦτον·

πολλὸς δ᾽ ἱμερόεντα χορὸν περίσταθ᾽ ὅμιλος
τερπόμενος· δοιὼ δὲ κυβιστητῆρε κατ᾽ αὐτοὺς
μολπῆς ἐξάρχοντες ἐδίνευον κατὰ μέσσους.

ὥστ᾽ ἀνίατον γίνεσθαι παντάπασι τὸ ἐξάρχοντες, μη-
κέτι δυναμένης τῆς ἐπὶ τὸν ᾠδὸν ἀναφορᾶς σῴζεσθαι.

Dancing and tumbling are indigenous among the Cretans, which is why he says to the Cretan Meriones (*Il.* 16.617–18):

> Meriones, even if you are a dancer, my spear would have
> stopped you once and for all, if I had hit you.

This is why they refer to certain combinations of song and dance as "Cretan" (Pi. fr. *107b.2):

> They refer to the style as Cretan, but the instrument as Molossian.

According to Timaeus (*FGrH* 566 F 140), the so-called *Lakōnistai* ("Sparta-imitators") sang in rectangular choruses. Greek music was generally diverse, given that the Athenians preferred Dionysiac and cyclic choruses,[33] the Syracusans preferred iambic poets, and other peoples preferred other things. Aristarchus not only added verses to Menelaus' symposium that did not belong there, making it foreign to the Spartan way of life and the king's sober-mindedness, but also removed the singer from the Cretan chorus, cutting the passage down in the following way (*Il.* 18.603–6):

> A large crowd surrounded the lovely chorus,
> enjoying themselves. And a pair of tumblers separate from the others
> led the song, whirling about among them.

The result is that *exarchontes* ("leading") remains an impossible problem, since the word can no longer be made to

---

[33] Dramatic and dithyrambic choruses, respectively.

διότι δὲ οὐ πιθανὸν ἀκρόαμα παρὰ τῷ Μενελάῳ τυγ-
χάνειν δῆλον ἐκ τοῦ δι' ὁμιλίας ὅλον τὸ συμπόσιον
e περαίνεσθαι τῆς | πρὸς ἀλλήλους, ὄνομα δὲ μηδὲν
εἰρῆσθαι τοῦ ᾠδοῦ μηδὲ ᾠδὴν ἣν ᾖδε μηδὲ προσέχειν
τοὺς περὶ Τηλέμαχον αὐτῷ, καθάπερ δ' ἐν σιωπῇ τινι
καὶ ἠρεμίᾳ κατανοεῖν μᾶλλον τὸν οἶκον· καίτοι γε πῶς
οὐκ ἀπίθανον τοὺς τῶν φρονιμωτάτων υἱέας Ὀδυσσέως καὶ Νέστορος ἐπαριστέρους εἰσάγεσθαι, ὥστε
τρόπον ἀγροίκων τινῶν μὴ προσέχειν τοῖς παρεσκευα-
σμένοις ἀκροάμασιν; ὁ γοῦν Ὀδυσσεὺς προσέχει
τοῖς τῶν Φαιάκων ᾀσματοποιοῖς·

f   αὐτὰρ Ὀδυσσεὺς |
μαρμαρυγὰς θηεῖτο ποδῶν, θαύμαζε δὲ θυμῷ,

καίπερ ἔχων πολλὰ τὰ περιέλκοντα καὶ δυνάμενος
εἰπεῖν·

κήδεά μοι καὶ μᾶλλον ἐνὶ φρεσὶν ἤ περ ἀοιδαί[9].

πῶς οὖν οὐκ ἂν ἀβέλτερος εἴη ὁ Τηλέμαχος ᾠδοῦ
παρόντος καὶ κυβιστητῆρος προσκύπτων πρὸς τὸν
Πεισίστρατον καὶ τῶν σκευῶν διατιθέμενος; ἀλλ'
182 Ὅμηρος ‖ ὥσπερ ἀγαθὸς ζωγράφος πάντα ὅμοιον τῷ
πατρὶ τὸν Τηλέμαχον παρίστησι· πεποίηκεν γοῦν

---

[9] The traditional text of Homer has ἄεθλοι.

refer to the singer.[34] As for the fact that it is impossible to believe that entertainment is going on in Menelaus' house, this is apparent from their talking to one another throughout the symposium, while the singer and the song he sang are never named, and Telemachus and the others pay no attention to him but carefully observe the house (*Od.* 4.43–4), as if the setting were quiet and peaceful. And is it believable that the sons of men as thoughtful as Odysseus and Nestor would be presented as such boors that they act like clodhoppers and ignore the entertainment arranged for them? Odysseus, at any rate, pays attention to the Phaeacian musicians (*Od.* 8.264–5):

> But Odysseus
> watched how their feet twinkled, and his heart was
> full of wonder,

even though he had things distracting him and could say (*Od.* 8.154):

> My troubles are more on my mind than songs are.

Would Telemachus not be a dolt, therefore, if a singer and a tumbler were present, but he leaned over to Peisistratus and described the furnishings (*Od.* 4.69–75)? But like a good painter, Homer presents Telemachus as being exactly like his father; he represents them both, for example, as recognized by the tears they shed, Odysseus by Alcinoos

---

[34] As it could if it were in the genitive singular? But the argument is opaque.

ATHENAEUS

ἀμφοτέρους τὸν μὲν τῷ Ἀλκινόῳ, τὸν δὲ τῷ Μενελάῳ
διὰ δακρύων γνωριζομένους.

Ἐν δὲ τῷ Ἐπικουρείῳ Συμποσίῳ κολάκων ἐστὶν
ἄγυρις ἀλλήλους ἐπαινούντων, τὸ δὲ Πλάτωνος πλῆ-
ρές ἐστιν μυκτηριστῶν ἀλλήλους τωθαζόντων· τὸν
γὰρ περὶ Ἀλκιβιάδου λόγον σιωπῶ. παρὰ δ' Ὁμήρῳ
συγκεκρότηται τὰ σώφρονα συμπόσια. καί ποτε μὲν
b ἐπήνεσέ τις φήσας πρὸς τὸν Μενέλαον | ὡς οὐ τολμᾷ
λέγειν

   ἄντα σέθεν, τοῦ νῶι θεοῦ ὣς τερπόμεθ' αὐδῇ.

ὁ δ' ἐπελάβετό τινος τῶν οὐκ ὀρθῶς λεγομένων ἢ
γιγνομένων·

   καὶ νῦν, εἴ τί που ἔστι, πίθοιό μοι· οὐ γὰρ
      ἐγώ γε
   τέρπομ' ὀδυρόμενος μεταδόρπιος.

ὁ δὲ πάλιν·

187b Τηλέμαχε, ποῖόν σε ἔπος φύγεν ἕρκος ὀδόντων; ‖

οὔτε γὰρ κόλακα πρέπον ἐστὶν εἶναι οὔτε μυκτη-
c ριστήν. πάλιν Ἐπίκουρος ἐν | τῷ Συμποσίῳ ζητεῖ περὶ
δυσπεψίας ὥστ' οἰωνίσασθαι, εἶθ' ἑξῆς περὶ πυρετῶν.

---

35 In fact Odysseus is not recognized by Alcinoos, although the
hero's tears lead the king to ask more forcefully about his anonymous guest's identity than he has up to this point; and Helen
names Telemachus before Menelaus has a chance to do so (*Od.*
4.138–54).

404

(*Od*. 8.521–34) and Telemachus by Menelaus (*Od*. 4.113–
19).[35]

Epicurus' *Symposium* (p. 115 Usener) is made up of a
crowd of flatterers who praise one another, while Plato's is
full of sneerers mocking each other; I pass over in silence
what is said about Alcibiades.[36] In Homer, on the other
hand, moderate symposia are organized. At one point (*Od*.
4.160) someone[37] praised Menelaus and said to him that
he did not dare to speak

to your face, since the two of us delight in your voice
as in a god's.

And he attacked anything not said or done properly (*Od*.
4.193–4):

And now, if this might be, do what I say; because I
for my part
take no joy in tears after dinner.

He says again (*Od*. 3.230):

Telemachus, what sort of a word escaped the fence of
your teeth?

For one ought to be neither a flatterer nor a sneerer. Again,
Epicurus (fr. 57 Usener) poses questions in his *Symposium* about indigestion as a means of obtaining omens, and
then immediately after this discusses fevers. Why should I

[36] A reference to the description of his extreme drunkenness
at *Smp*. 212d–e?
[37] Both this quotation and the one that follows are spoken by
Peisistratus, while the speaker at *Od*. 3.230 is Athena disguised as
Mentor.

τὴν μὲν γὰρ ἐπιτρέχουσαν τῇ λέξει ἀρρυθμίαν τί δεῖ
καὶ λέγειν; Πλάτων δὲ—τὸν μὲν ὑπὸ τῆς λυγγὸς
ὀχλούμενον καὶ θεραπευόμενον ἀνακογχυλιασμοῖς
ὕδατος, ἔτι δὲ ταῖς ὑποθήκαις τοῦ κάρφους ἵνα τὴν
ῥῖνα κνήσας πτάρῃ, παρίημι· κωμῳδεῖν γὰρ ἤθελε καὶ
διασύρειν—χλευάζει τε τὰ ἰσόκωλα τὰ Ἀγάθωνος καὶ
τὰ ἀντίθετα, καὶ τὸν Ἀλκιβιάδην παράγει λέγοντα ὅτι
πασχητιᾷ. ἀλλ' ὅμως τοιαῦτα γράφοντες τὸν Ὅμηρον
d | ἐκβάλλουσι τῶν πόλεων. ἀλλ' οὔτε ἐκ θύμβρας, ἔφη
Δημοχάρης, λόγχη οὔτ' ἐκ τοιούτων λόγων ἀνὴρ ἀγαθὸς γίνεται. οὐ μόνον δ' Ἀλκιβιάδην διασύρει, ἀλλὰ
καὶ Χαρμίδην καὶ Εὐθύδημον καὶ ἄλλους πολλοὺς
τῶν νέων. τοῦτο δὲ κωμῳδοῦντός ἐστι τὴν Ἀθηναίων
πόλιν, τὸ τῆς Ἑλλάδος μουσεῖον, ἣν ὁ μὲν Πίνδαρος

Ἑλλάδος ἔρεισμα

ἔφη, Θουκυδίδης δ' ἐν τῷ εἰς Εὐριπίδην ἐπιγράμματι

< . . . > Ἑλλάδος Ἑλλάδα,

ὁ δὲ Πύθιος ἑστίαν καὶ πρυτανεῖον τῶν Ἑλλήνων.
e διότι τοίνυν | κατέψευσται τῶν νεανίσκων πάρεστι
σκοπεῖν ἐξ αὐτοῦ τοῦ Πλάτωνος. τὸν μὲν γὰρ Ἀλκι-

---

38 I.e. their ideal states; cf. Pl. R. 606e–7a. The implication is
that Epicurus expressed similar opinions.

39 Cf. 5.215c, where the remark is quoted in what appears to
be the original form and is an attack on Socrates and the political
values he is taken to represent.

40 I.e. in the dialogues for which these names serve as titles.

even mention the lack of discipline that permeates his style? As for Plato—I ignore the man who was troubled by hiccoughs and cured by gargling water, as well as by tickling his nose with a piece of straw to make him sneeze (*Smp.* 185d–e); for he wanted to mock and ridicule people—he makes fun of Agathon's balanced clauses and antitheses (*Smp.* 194e–7e), and brings in Alcibiades saying that he is afflicted with lust (*Smp.* 217a–d, 218b–19d). But even though they write things like this, they expel Homer from their cities.[38] As Demochares (fr. I.3, vol. II.342 Baiter–Sauppe) said,[39] a spearhead cannot be made out of savory, and neither can a good man be produced from words like these. It is not just Alcibiades he mocks, but also Charmides, Euthydemus[40], and many other young men; this marks him as someone intent on ridiculing the city of Athens, the *Mouseion* ("shrine of the Muses") of Greece, which Pindar (fr. 76.2) called

the stay of Greece,

while Thucydides refers to it in his epigram on Euripides (*AP* 7.45.3 = *FGE* 1054) as

the Greece of Greece,

and the Pythian god (Delphic Oracle Q198 Fontenrose) said that it was the Greeks' hearth and *prytaneion* ("civic center").[41] Plato himself reveals the reason he brings these false charges against the young men.[42] For as for

---

[41] Cf. 6.254b.   [42] Although Athenaeus (or Herodicus, whose work he is excerpting) does not say so explicitly, the point seems to be that Socrates' motives (which are jumbled together here with Plato's) involved sexual resentment and the like.

βιάδην φησὶν ἐν τῷ ὁμωνύμῳ διαλόγῳ παρακμά-
σαντα τότε πρῶτον ἄρξασθαι Σωκράτει λαλεῖν ὅτε
πάντες αὐτὸν κατέλιπον οἱ τοῦ σώματος ἐπιθυμηταί.
λέγει γὰρ ταῦτα κατ᾽ ἀρχὰς τοῦ διαλόγου. τὰ δ᾽ ἐν τῷ
Χαρμίδῃ ἐναντιώματα ἐξ αὐτοῦ τοῦ διαλόγου ὁ βουλόμενος εἴσεται. ποιεῖ γὰρ αὐτὸν ἀσυμφώνως ποτὲ
f   μὲν σκοτοδινιῶντα καὶ μεθυσκόμενον τῷ τοῦ | παιδὸς
ἔρωτι καὶ γινόμενον ἔξεδρον καὶ καθάπερ νεβρὸν
ὑποπεπτωκότα λέοντος ἀλκῇ, ἅμα δὲ καταφρονεῖν
φησι τῆς ὥρας αὐτοῦ.

Ἀλλὰ μὴν καὶ τὸ Ξενοφῶντος Συμπόσιον καίπερ
ἐπαινούμενον οὐκ ἐλάττους ἔχει τούτων ἐπιλήψεις.
Καλλίας μὲν γὰρ συνάγει τὸ συμπόσιον, ἐπειδήπερ
τὰ παιδικὰ αὐτοῦ Αὐτόλυκος Παναθήναια παγκράτιον
ἐστεφανώθη. καὶ εὐθὺς οἱ κατακλιθέντες τῷ παιδὶ
προσέχουσι τὸν νοῦν καὶ ταῦτα τοῦ πατρὸς παρα-
188 καθημένου. ‖ ὥσπερ γὰρ ὅταν φέγγος ἐν νυκτὶ παρῇ
πάντων προσάγεται τὰ ὄμματα, οὕτω καὶ τὸ Αὐτολύκου κάλλος πάντων ἐφέλκεται τὰς ὄψεις ἐφ᾽ ἑαυτό.
ἔπειτα τῶν παρόντων οὐδεὶς ἦν ὃς οὐκ ἔπασχέ τι τὴν
ψυχὴν ὑπ᾽ ἐκείνου· οἱ μέν γε σιωπηλότεροι ἐγίγνοντο,
οἱ δὲ καὶ ἐσχηματίζοντό πως. ἀλλ᾽ οὐχ Ὅμηρος
τοιοῦτόν τι εἰπεῖν ἐπεχείρησε καίπερ τῆς Ἑλένης
παρούσης, περὶ ἧς τοῦ κάλλους τις τῶν ἐναντίων αὐτῇ
b   τοιαῦτ᾽ εἶπεν ὑπὸ τῆς ἀληθείας ἐκνικώμενος· |

οὐ νέμεσις Τρῶας καὶ ἐυκνήμιδας Ἀχαιοὺς

Alcibiades, he says in the dialogue that bears his name (*Alc.1* 103a–b) that he first started to talk to Socrates when he was past his prime and everyone who lusted after his body had abandoned him; he says this at the beginning of the dialogue. And anyone who wants to can detect the contradictions in the *Charmides* from the dialogue itself; because he represents Socrates inconsistently, sometimes as dizzy and drunk with his love for the boy, and as out of his mind and like a fawn overcome by a powerful lion (*Chrm.* 155c–d), while he claims at the same time that he felt contempt for the boy's beauty (cf. *Chrm.* 154d–e).

Xenophon's *Symposium* as well, despite the praise it receives, has even more points that require censure. For Callias assembles the group, because his boy-love Autolycus was victorious in the *pancration* at the Panathenaic games (1.2); and the minute they lie down, they fix their attention on the boy, even though his father is sitting next to him. (1.9) For just as when a light appears at night and attracts everyone's eyes, so Autolycus' beauty drew everyone's glances to itself. The soul of everyone present was affected somehow by him; some of them grew quieter, while others altered their posture a bit. But Homer made no effort to say anything like this, even though Helen was present, about whose beauty one of her enemies said something along the following lines (*Il.* 3.156–8), since the truth got the better of him:

It is no cause for resentment that the Trojans and the
    well-greaved Achaeans

τοιῇδ᾽ ἀμφὶ γυναικὶ πολὺν χρόνον ἄλγεα
πάσχειν·
αἰνῶς ἀθανάτῃσι θεῇς εἰς ὦπα ἔοικεν.

εἶτά φησιν·

ἀλλὰ καὶ ὥς, τοίη περ ἐοῦσ᾽, ἐν νηυσὶ νεέσθω.

τὰ δὲ μειράκια τὰ ὡς τὸν Μενέλαον παραγενόμενα, ὁ
Νέστορος υἱὸς καὶ ὁ Τηλέμαχος, ἐν οἴνῳ ὄντες καὶ ἐν
c γαμικῷ συμποσίῳ διατρίβοντες καὶ τῆς | Ἑλένης
παρακαθημένης, ὡς πρέπον ἐστίν, ἡσυχίαν ἄγοντες
πρὸς τὸ περιβόητον ἐκκεκωφωμένοι κάλλος. ὁ δὲ Σωκράτης τίνος χάριν τῶν αὐλητρίδων ἀνεχόμενος καὶ
τοῦ ὀρχουμένου παιδὸς καὶ κιθαρίζοντος, ἔτι δὲ καὶ
τῆς κυβιστώσης γυναικός, ἀπρεπῶς τὸ μύρον ἀπεί-
πατο; οὐδεὶς γὰρ ἂν αὐτοῦ ἀγελαστὶ ἠνέσχετο κατὰ
νοῦν ἔχων ταῦτα τὰ ἔπη·

τοὺς ὠχριῶντας, τοὺς ἀνυποδήτους λέγεις,
ὧν ὁ κακοδαίμων Σωκράτης καὶ Χαιρεφῶν.

καὶ μὴν ἀσύμφωνα καὶ τὰ μετὰ ταῦτα τῇ αὐστη-
d ρότητι· | ὁ γὰρ δὴ Κριτόβουλος, μειράκιον ἀστεῖον,
γέροντα ⟨ὄντα⟩ καὶ διδάσκαλον αὐτοῦ τὸν Σωκράτη
σκώπτει πολὺ τῶν σιληνῶν αἰσχίονα λέγων εἶναι. ὁ
δὲ αὐτῷ διαμορφοσκοπεῖται καὶ κριτὰς ἑλόμενος τόν
τε παῖδα καὶ τὴν ὀρχηστρίδα προτίθησι νικητήρια
φιλήματα τῶν κριτῶν. τίς οὖν τῶν νέων ἐντυχὼν

suffer griefs for a long time for a woman like this;
she is remarkably like the immortal goddesses in
appearance.

Then he says (*Il.* 3.159):

But even so, whatever she is, let her go home in the
ships!

The boys visiting Menelaus, that is Nestor's son and
Telemachus, even though they are drinking wine and
spending time at a wedding symposium, and even though
Helen is sitting next to them, keep quiet, as they should,
having been struck dumb in the face of her notorious
beauty. But why does Socrates put up with the pipe-girls
and the boy who dances and plays the lyre (X. *Smp.* 2.1–2),
as well as the woman who does indecent tumbling tricks
(X. *Smp.* 2.8, 11), but refuse the perfume (X. *Smp.* 2.3)?
Because no one who had the following verses (Ar. *Nu.*
103–4) in mind would have put up with his behavior without laughing:

You're talking about the guys with pale complexions
and no shoes,
including the miserable Socrates and Chaerephon.

What follows is also inconsistent with his austerity. For (X.
Smp. 4.19–20) Critobulus, a quick-witted boy, mocks Socrates, who is an old man and his own teacher, and claims
that he is much uglier than the silens. But Socrates proposes a beauty contest with the boy, selects him and the
dancing-girl as judges, and proposes that the prize be the
right to kiss them. What young man, therefore, who en-

τούτοις οὐκ ἐπιτριβήσεται μᾶλλον ἤπερ εἰς ἀρετὴν
⟨ἂν⟩ προαχθείη;

Παρὰ δ᾽ Ὁμήρῳ ἐν τῷ τοῦ Μενελάου συμποσίῳ
προβάλλουσιν ἀλλήλοις ὥσπερ ἐν διατριβῇ ζητή-
ματα καὶ πολιτικῶς ὁμιλοῦντες τέρπουσιν | ἀλλήλους
καὶ ἡμᾶς. ὁ γοῦν Μενέλαος παραγενομένων ἐκ τοῦ
λουτρῶνος τῶν περὶ τὸν Τηλέμαχον καὶ τῶν περὶ τὴν
ἐδωδὴν παρατεθέντων παρακαλεῖ μεταλαμβάνειν λέγων τάδε·

σίτου δ᾽ ἅπτεσθον καὶ χαίρετον. αὐτὰρ ἔπειτα
δείπνου παυσαμένω[10] εἰρησόμεθ᾽ οἵ τινές ἐστόν.

ἔπειτα προσεπιδίδωσι τῶν παρακειμένων αὐτῷ φιλαν-
θρωπευόμενος·

ὣς φάτο, καί σφιν νῶτα βοὸς παρὰ πίονα
    θῆκεν |
ὄπτ᾽ ἐν χερσὶν ἑλών, τά ῥά οἱ γέρα πάρθεσαν
    αὐτῷ.

φαγόντες δ᾽ ἐκεῖνοι μετὰ σιωπῆς, ὡς πρέπει νέοις,
ἀλλήλοις ὁμιλοῦσιν ἠρέμα προσκύψαντες οὐ περὶ
ἐδεσμάτων, φησίν, οὐδὲ ⟨τῶν⟩ θεραπαινῶν τοῦ κεκλη-
κότος ὑφ᾽ ὧν ἐλούσαντο, περὶ δὲ τῶν κτημάτων τοῦ
ὑποδεξαμένου·

Ζηνός που τοιαῦτα δόμοις ἐν κτήματα κεῖται.

[10] The traditional text of Homer has πασσαμένω.

412

counters this passage will not be ruined by it rather than being drawn toward virtue?

At Menelaus' symposium in Homer they pose questions for one another as if they were in a school, and they provide pleasure for one another and us by talking in a civilized manner. When Telemachus and his companion appear after their bath, and the food and everything that accompanies it has been served, for example, Menelaus invites them to take their share, saying the following (*Od.* 4.60–1):

> Put your hands to the food, both of you, and enjoy it!
>   Then
> after you are done with dinner, we will ask you who
>   you are.

Then he kindly offers them an additional portion of what he was served himself (*Od.* 4.65–6):

> Thus he spoke; and he took in his hands the fat,
>   roasted back-slices of the bull
> that they served him as his portion of honor, and set
>   this beside them.

They eat in silence, as young men should, then put their heads together and converse quietly with one another (*Od.* 4.69–70), not about the food, according to the poet, or their host's slave-women, who washed them, but about the possessions of the man whose guests they are (*Od.* 4.74):

> Possessions like these are found in the house of Zeus,
>   I imagine.

βέλτιον γὰρ οὕτως φησὶν ὁ Σέλευκος γράφεσθαι.
189   Ἀρίσταρχος δὲ οὐ δεόντως γράφει· ‖

Ζηνός που τοιήδε γ᾽ Ὀλυμπίου ἔνδοθεν αὐλή.

οὐ γὰρ τῆς οἰκίας τὸ κάλλος μόνον ἀποθαυμάζουσι.
πῶς γὰρ ἤλεκτρον καὶ ἄργυρος καὶ ἐλέφας ἐν τοῖς
τοίχοις ἦν; ἀλλὰ τὰ μὲν περὶ τοῦ οἴκου εἰρήκασιν, ὡς
ἐστι δώματα ἠχήεντα· τοιαῦτα γὰρ δὴ τὰ ὑψόροφα καὶ
μεγάλα. περὶ δὲ τῶν σκευῶν τὸ

χρυσοῦ τ᾽ ἠλέκτρου τε καὶ ἀργύρου ἠδ᾽
    ἐλέφαντος.

οἷς εἰκότως ἐπιφέρεται·

b   Ζηνός που τοιαῦτα δόμοις ἐν κτήματα κεῖται, |
ὅσσα τάδ᾽ ἄσπετα πολλά· σέβας μ᾽ ἔχει
    εἰσορόωντα.

οὐκ ἔστιν δ᾽ ἀκόλουθον τῷ

Ζηνός που τοιήδε γ᾽ Ὀλυμπίου ἔνδοθεν αὐλὴ

ἐπιφέρειν

ὅσσα τάδ᾽ ἄσπετα πολλά,

σόλοικον ὂν τῷ ἀσυνήθει τῆς ἀναγνώσεως. ἔτι τοίνυν
οὐδ᾽ ἡ αὐλὴ ἁρμόττει ἐπὶ τοῦ οἴκου· ὁ γὰρ διαπνεό-
μενος τόπος αὐλὴ λέγεται, καὶ διαυλωνίζειν φαμὲν τὸ

---

43 Aristarchus' reading is accepted by all modern editors.

For Seleucus (fr. 22 Müller) says that the line is better written this way, whereas Aristarchus offers the wrong reading:[43]

> The court (*aulē*) of Zeus on Olympus is like this, I
>   imagine.

Because they do not just express amazement at the beauty of the house; for how could electrum, silver, and ivory (cf. *Od.* 4.73) be part of the walls? But they refer to the house itself, saying that it is an "echoing mansion" (*Od.* 4.72); because this is what large, high-roofed houses are like. But the line (*Od.* 4.73)

> of gold, electrum, silver, and ivory

concerns furnishings. These words are appropriately followed by (*Od.* 4.74–5):

> Possessions like these are found in the house of Zeus,
>   I imagine,
> so unspeakably numerous are they; awe grips me as I
>   look at them.

Whereas after

> The court (*aulē*) of Zeus on Olympus is like this, I
>   imagine,

the text cannot continue (*Od.* 4.75)

> so unspeakably numerous are they,

which would be a solecism produced by the peculiarity of the reading. The word *aulē*, moreover, is inappropriate for the house; for a place the breeze blows through is referred to as an *aulē*, and we use the verb *diaulōnizein* in

δεχόμενον ἐξ ἑκατέρου πνεῦμα χωρίον. ἔτι δὲ αὐλὸς
c μὲν τὸ ὄργανον, | ὅτι διέρχεται τὸ πνεῦμα, καὶ πᾶν τὸ
διατεταμένον εἰς εὐθύτητα σχῆμα αὐλὸν καλοῦμεν
ὥσπερ τὸ στάδιον καὶ τὸν κρουνὸν τοῦ αἵματος·

< . . . > αὐτίκα δ᾽ αὐλὸς ἀνὰ ῥῖνας παχὺς ἦλθε,

καὶ τὴν περικεφαλαίαν ὅταν ἐκ τοῦ μέσου πρὸς ὀρθὸν
ἀνατείνῃ αὐλῶπιν. λέγονται δὲ Ἀθήνησι καὶ ἱεροί
τινες αὐλῶνες, ὧν μέμνηται Φιλόχορος ἐν τῇ ἐνάτῃ.
καλοῦσι δ᾽ ἀρσενικῶς τοὺς αὐλῶνας, ὥσπερ Θουκυδίδης ἐν τῇ τετάρτῃ καὶ πάντες οἱ καταλογάδην συγ-
d γραφεῖς, οἱ δὲ ποιηταὶ θηλυκῶς. | Καρκίνος μὲν
Ἀχιλλεῖ·

βαθεῖαν εἰς αὐλῶνα περίδρομον στρατοῦ.

καὶ Σοφοκλῆς Σκύθαις·

κρημνούς τε καὶ σήραγγας ἠδ᾽ ἐπακτίας
αὐλῶνας.

ἐκδεκτέον οὖν καὶ τὸ παρὰ Ἐρατοσθένει ἐν τῷ Ἑρμῇ
θηλυκῶς εἰρῆσθαι

< . . . > βαθὺς διαφύεται αὐλών

---

44 Cf. Lyc. 40 with the *scholia*, which note the common use of
diaulos for a race the length of the stadium and back.

reference to a spot that gets a breeze from either side. The musical instrument, moreover, is called an *aulos* ("pipe") because air passes through it; and we refer to anything stretched out in an elongated form as an *aulos*, for example a stadium[44] or a stream of blood (*Od.* 22.18):

> Immediately a thick stream (*aulos*) of blood came out
>   of his nostrils.

We also call a helmet, when it extends straight up from the middle, an *aulōpis*.[45] Certain sacred *aulōnes* ("hollows") in Athens are referred to; Philochorus (*FGrH* 328 F 68) mentions them in Book IX. Some authorities have the word in the masculine, as for example Thucydides in Book IV (103.1)[46] and all prose-authors, whereas the poets have it in the feminine. Carcinus in *Achilles* (*TrGF* 70 F 1d):[47]

> into the deep hollow (fem.) surrounding the army.

Also Sophocles in *Scythians* (fr. 549):

> crags, caves, and hollows (fem.)
> along the shore.

We must therefore accept that the word is also feminine in Eratosthenes' *Hermes* (fr. 8, p. 60 Powell):

> a deep hollow runs through it,

[45] The word appears in Homer (e.g. *Il.* 5.182) in connection with helmets, although its precise sense is obscure.

[46] A personal name.

[47] The form of the adjective in this quotation and the one that follows makes it clear that the word is being treated as feminine.

ἀντὶ τοῦ βαθεῖα, καθάπερ λέγεται

< . . . > θῆλυς ἐέρση.

e πᾶν οὖν τὸ τοιοῦτον αὐλή τε καὶ αὐλὼν λέγεται. | νῦν
δὲ τὰ βασίλεια λέγουσιν αὐλάς, ὥσπερ Μένανδρος·

αὐλὰς θεραπεύειν καὶ σατράπας.

καὶ Δίφιλος·

αὐλὰς θεραπεύειν δ᾽ ἐστίν, ὡς ἐμοὶ δοκεῖ,
ἢ φυγάδος ἢ πεινῶντος ἢ μαστιγίου,

ἤτοι διὰ τὸ μεγάλους ἔχειν τοὺς πρὸ τῶν οἴκων ὑπ-
αιθρίους τόπους ἢ τῷ παραυλίζεσθαι καὶ παρακοι-
μᾶσθαι τοὺς δορυφόρους τοῖς βασιλείοις. Ὅμηρος δὲ
τὴν αὐλὴν ἀεὶ τάττει ἐπὶ τῶν ὑπαίθρων τόπων, ἔνθα ἦν
f ὁ τοῦ Ἑρκείου Ζηνὸς βωμός. ὁ μέντοι | γε Πηλεὺς
καταλαμβάνεται

αὐλῆς ἐν χόρτῳ· ἔχε δὲ χρύσειον ἄλεισον,
σπένδων αἴθοπα οἶνον ἐπ᾽ αἰθομένοις ἱεροῖσι·

ὁ δὲ Πρίαμος

αὐλῆς ἐν χόρτοισι κυλινδόμενος κατὰ κόπρον.

καὶ ὁ Ὀδυσσεὺς προστάττει τοῖς περὶ τὸν Φήμιον·

---

48 The word "dew" is normally feminine, but the masculine
form of the adjective is used with it in this phrase.

where the masculine *bathus* ("deep") appears rather than the feminine *batheia*, in the same way that (e.g. *Od.* 5.467)

female dew

is used.[48] Everything of this sort, therefore, is referred to as an *aulē* or an *aulōn*. But nowadays they refer to royal palaces as *aulai*, as for example Menander (fr. 436):

to be in attendance on courts *(aulai)* and satraps.

Also Diphilus (fr. 97):

To be in attendance on courts *(aulai)*, in my opinion, is
the mark of an exile, a pauper, or a good-for-nothing.

This is either because they have large, unroofed areas in front of the residence, or because the royal bodyguard sleep in the open air *(paraulizesthai)* and make their beds beside the palace. But Homer always uses the word *aulē* for unroofed areas where the altar of Zeus Herkeios ("of the Enclosure") was located. Thus Peleus is found (*Il.* 11.774–5)

in the part of the courtyard *(aulē)* where they fed the animals; he was holding a golden goblet
and pouring a libation of shining wine over burning sacrifices,

while Priam is represented (*Il.* 24.640)

rolling about in the dung in the part of the courtyard *(aulē)* where they fed the animals.

And Odysseus orders Phemius and the others with him (*Od.* 22.375–6):

190   ἀλλ᾽ ἐξελθόντες μεγάρων εὖ ναιεταόντων[11] ‖
ἐκ φόνου εἰς αὐλήν.

ὅτι δὲ ὁμοῦ τόν τε οἶκον καὶ τὰ κτήματα ἐπῄνεσεν ὁ
Τηλέμαχος ἐμφανίζει ὁ Μενέλαος·

τέκνα φίλ᾽, ἦ τοι Ζηνὶ βροτῶν οὐκ ἄν τις ἐρίζοι·
ἀθάνατοι γὰρ τοῦ γε δόμοι καὶ κτήματ᾽ ἔασιν.

Ἀλλὰ γὰρ ἐπανιτέον ἐπὶ τὸ συμπόσιον, ἐν ᾧ Ὅμηρος ἐπιδεξίως ἀφορμὴν εὗρεν λόγων, ὥστε κτῆσιν
συγκρῖναι φίλῳ[12]. οὐ γὰρ ὡς πρόβλημα προτείνει,
b   ἀλλ᾽ ἐπιχαρίτως παρείρας ὁ Μενέλαος, | ἐπειδὴ ἤκου-
σε τῶν ἐπαίνων, τὸ μὲν εἶναι πλούσιος οὐκ ἀρνεῖται·
κἀνταῦθα δὲ περιελὼν τὸν φθόνον, < . . . > πολλὰ γάρ,
φησίν, παθὼν ἔχειν αὐτόν. οὐ μέντοι γε ἀξιοῖ ἑαυτὸν
θεοῖς συγκρίνειν·

ἀθάνατοι γὰρ τοῦ γε δόμοι καὶ κτήματ᾽ ἔασιν.

ἐνδειξάμενος δὲ φιλάδελφον ἦθος καὶ μετ᾽ ἀνάγκης
φήσας ζῆν τε καὶ πλουτεῖν ἀντιπαρέθηκε τὸν τῆς
φιλίας λόγον·

ὧν ὄφελον τριτάτην περ ἔχων ἐν δώμασι μοῖραν
c   ναίειν, οἱ δ᾽ ἄνδρες σόοι ἔμμεναι οἳ τότ᾽ ὄλοντο |
Τροίῃ ἐν εὐρείῃ ἑκὰς Ἄργεος ἱπποβότοιο.

---

[11] The traditional text of Homer has ἔζεσθε θύραζε.
[12] φίλου A

Go out of the well-inhabited house
away from the slaughter into the courtyard *(aulē)*!

That Telemachus praised both the king's house and his possessions is made clear by Menelaus (*Od.* 4.78–9):

My dear children, certainly no mortal could rival
    Zeus;
for his house and possessions are immortal.

But we need to return to the symposium, where Homer cleverly invented a pretext for conversation, so as to produce a contrast between owning property and having a friend. For Menelaus does not treat this as a point requiring discussion, but graciously concedes the matter, after he hears their praise, and does not deny that he is rich. But afterward he removes any ground for resentment . . . ; for he says that he got his property "after suffering many things" (*Od.* 4.81). Moreover, he does not think it right to compare himself to the gods (*Od.* 4.79):

for his house and possessions are immortal.

And after making a show of the affection he felt for his brother (*Od.* 4.90–3) and saying that life and wealth were forced on him,[49] he balances against this his account of friendship (*Od.* 4.97–9):

Would that I lived in my house with only a third
of these things, and those men were alive who
    perished then
in wide Troy far from horse-pasturing Argos!

---

[49] A reference to a line (*Od.* 4.93a) known and rejected by the scholiast, as well as by modern editors.

τίς ἂν οὖν τῶν ἐκγόνων ἐκείνων τῶν ὑπὲρ τοῦ τοιούτου
τεθνηκότων οὐκ ἂν ἀνταξίαν δόξειεν τὴν ἐπὶ τῇ στερή-
σει τοῦ πατρὸς λύπην τῇ τοῦ πατρὸς εὐχαρίστῳ
μνήμῃ διορθουμένην; ὅπως δὲ μὴ δόξῃ κοινὸς εἶναι
πρὸς πάντας τοὺς παραπλησίως αὐτῷ τὴν εὔνοιαν
ἐνδεδειγμένους, ἐπήνεγκεν·

d   τῶν πάντων οὐ τόσσον ὀδύρομαι ἀχνύμενός περ |
    ὡς ἑνός, ὅς τέ μοι ὕπνον ἀπεχθαίρει καὶ ἐδωδήν.

ἵνα δὲ μὴ φαίνηται μηδενὸς τῶν ἐκείνου παραμελῶν,
ἐμνήσθη κατ᾽ ὄνομα·

               ὀδύρονταί νύ που αὐτὸν
    Λαέρτης θ᾽ ὁ γέρων καὶ ἐχέφρων Πηνελόπεια
    Τηλέμαχός θ᾽, ὃν ἔλειπε[13] νέον γεγαῶτ᾽ ἐνὶ οἴκῳ.

τοῦ δὲ δακρύσαντος πρὸς τὴν μνήμην ὁ μὲν ἐφίστησι
e κἂν τοσούτῳ ‹ . . . › τῆς Ἑλένης ἐπεισόδῳ κἀκείνης |
ἐκ τῆς ὁμοιότητος τεκμηραμένης—πάνυ γὰρ αἱ γυναῖκες διὰ τὸ παρατηρεῖσθαι τὴν ἀλλήλων σωφροσύνην
δειναὶ τὰς ὁμοιότητας τῶν παίδων πρὸς τοὺς γονέας
ἐλέγξαι. παρεμβάλλοντός τινα λόγον καὶ τοῦ Πεισι-
στράτου—χρὴ γὰρ καὶ τοῦτον μὴ παρεῖναι δορυφο-
ρήματος τρόπον—καὶ διαλεχθέντος εὐσχημόνως περὶ
τῆς αἰδοῦς τοῦ Τηλεμάχου, πάλιν ἐπιβάλλει ὁ Μενέ-

---

[13] The traditional text of Homer has λεῖπε.

What descendant of those who died on behalf of such a person would not feel that his grief for the loss of his father had been redeemed at full price by such a gracious mention of him? But so as not to seem to feel the same way about everyone who showed him similar goodwill, he added (*Od.* 4.104–5):

> For none of them all do I grieve as much, sorrowful
> though I am,
> as I do for one man, who makes sleep and food
> hateful to me.

And in order not to appear to be neglecting the man's relatives, he mentioned them by name (*Od.* 4.110–12):

> The old Laertes and
> thoughtful Penelope are grieving for him now, I
> imagine,
> and Telemachus, whom he left a newborn baby in his
> house.

When Telemachus bursts into tears at the mention,[50] Menelaus stops (*Od.* 4.116–20); in the meantime . . . by the entrance of Helen (*Od.* 4.121–2); and when she recognizes him because of his resemblance[51] (*Od.* 4.141–6)—because the fact that women keep a close watch on one another's modesty makes them very good at detecting the similarities between children and their parents—and Peisistratus as well interjects a speech (*Od.* 4.155–67); we ought not to overlook him, as if were simply a bodyguard—and makes some neat remarks about Telemachus' sense of decency (*Od.* 4.158–60), Menelaus again adds something about his

---

[50] Sc. of his father (*Od.* 4.113–14).   [51] Sc. to Odysseus.

λαος περὶ τῆς τοῦ Ὀδυσσέως φιλίας ὅτι μετὰ μόνου
καταγηρᾶναι μάλιστ᾽ ἂν ἤθελεν ἐκείνου. κατὰ δὲ τὸ
f εἰκὸς | οἱ μὲν δακρύουσιν, ἡ δ᾽ Ἑλένη Διὸς οὖσα
θυγάτηρ καὶ παρὰ τῶν ἐν Αἰγύπτῳ σοφῶν μεμαθη-
κυῖα πολλοὺς λόγους εἰς τὸν οἶνον ἐμβάλλει πανακὲς
τῷ ὄντι φάρμακον καὶ ἄρχεται διηγεῖσθαι τὰ περὶ τοῦ
Ὀδυσσέως μεταξὺ ταλασιουργίας ἁπτομένη, οὐ δι᾽
ἀρέσκειαν τοῦτο πράττουσα, ἀλλ᾽ οἴκοθεν ἔχουσα τὴν
191 τοιαύτην αἵρεσιν. ‖ ἡ γοῦν Ἀφροδίτη ἐρχομένη πρὸς
αὐτὴν μετὰ τὸ μονομάχιον εἰκάζεται·

γρηὶ δέ μιν εἰκυῖα παλαιγενέι προσέειπεν
εἰροκόμῳ, ἥ οἱ Λακεδαίμονι ναιεταούσῃ
ἤσκειν εἴρια καλά.

ἐμφανίζεται δ᾽ αὐτῆς οὐ παρέργως τὸ φίλεργον κἀκ
τούτων·

τῇ δ᾽ ἄρ᾽ ἅμ᾽ Ἀδρήστη κλισίην εὔτυκτον ἔθηκεν,
b Ἀλκίππη δὲ τάπητα φέρεν μαλακοῦ ἐρίοιο, |
Φυλὼ δ᾽ ἀργύρεον τάλαρον φέρε, τόν οἱ ἔδωκεν
Ἀλκάνδρη, Πολύβοιο δάμαρ ⟨ . . . ⟩.
τόν ῥά οἱ ἀμφίπολος Φυλὼ παρέθηκε φέρουσα
νήματος ἀσκητοῖο βεβυσμένον· αὐτὰρ ἐν[14] αὐτῷ
ἠλακάτη τετάνυστο ἰοδνεφὲς εἶρος ἔχουσα.

ἔοικε δὲ καὶ αὐτὴ τὴν ἑαυτῆς καλλιτεχνίαν συνορᾶν.
c τῷ γοῦν Τηλεμάχῳ πέπλον τινὰ δωρουμένη | φησί·

---

[14] The traditional text of Homer has ἐπ᾽.

424

friendship with Odysseus, to the effect that he was the one man he would particularly have liked to grow old with (*Od.* 4.168–82, esp. 178–80). As one might expect, they weep (*Od.* 4.183–6); but Helen, since she is a daughter of Zeus (cf. *Od.* 4.219, 227) and has learned many spells from the wise men in Egypt (cf. *Od.* 4.228–32), throws a drug into the wine that can in fact cure anything (*Od.* 4.220–1), and begins to tell stories about Odysseus (*Od.* 4.240ff), taking up her wool-working at the same time, something she did not for pleasure but because she developed a habit of this sort at home. When Aphrodite, for example, comes to her after the duel, she makes herself look (*Il.* 3.386–8)

> Like an ancient old woman she spoke to her,
> a wool-dresser, who worked beautiful wool for her
> when she lived in Sparta.

Her industry is carefully described in the following lines as well (*Od.* 4.123–6, 133–5):

> Adreste accompanied her and set her well-made
>   chair in its place;
> Alcippe brought a blanket made of soft wool;
> and Phylo brought a silver work-basket which
>   Alcandre,
> Polybus' wife, gave her . . .
> The servant-woman Phylo brought it and set it beside
>   her
> stuffed full of carded wool; a distaff holding
> dark-colored wool lay stretched out in the basket.

She herself appears to be conscious of her own skill at this craft. When she gives Telemachus a robe, at any rate, she says (*Od.* 15.125–7):

δῶρόν τοι καὶ ἐγώ, τέκνον φίλε, τοῦτο δίδωμι,
μνῆμ᾽ Ἑλένης χειρῶν, πολυηράτου ἐς γάμου
    ὥρην,
σῇ δ᾽¹⁵ ἀλόχῳ φορέειν.

αὕτη δ᾽ ἡ φιλεργία τὴν σωφροσύνην αὐτῆς κατα-
μηνύει· οὐ χλιδῶσα γὰρ οὐδὲ θρυπτομένη διὰ τὸ
κάλλος εἰσάγεται. εὑρίσκεται γοῦν περὶ ἱστὸν ὑφαί-
νουσα καὶ ποικίλλουσα·

d
τὴν δ᾽ εὗρ᾽ ἐν μεγάρῳ· ἡ δὲ μέγαν ἱστὸν
    ὕφαινε, |
δίπλακα μαρμαρέην, πολέας δ᾽ ἐνέπασσεν
    ἀέθλους
Τρώων θ᾽ ἱπποδάμων καὶ Ἀχαιῶν χαλκοχιτώνων,
οὓς ἕθεν εἵνεκ᾽ ἔπασχον ὑπ᾽ Ἄρηος παλαμάων.

Διδάσκει δ᾽ ἡμᾶς Ὅμηρος ὅτι δεῖ καὶ τοὺς κεκλη-
μένους ἐφ᾽ ἑστίασιν παρακαλεῖν ἀπανίστασθαι τοὺς
κεκληκότας. ὁ μὲν Τηλέμαχος τὸν Μενέλαον·

ἀλλ᾽ ἄγετ᾽ εἰς εὐνὴν τράπεθ᾽ ἡμέας, ὄφρα καὶ
    ἤδη
ὕπνῳ ὑπὸ γλυκερῷ ταρπώμεθα κοιμηθέντες.

e   ἡ δὲ προσποιουμένη Μέντωρ εἶναι Ἀθηνᾶ πρὸς τὸν |
Νέστορα·

ἀλλ᾽ ἄγε τάμνετε μὲν γλώσσας, κεράσασθε¹⁶ δὲ
    οἶνον,
ὄφρα Ποσειδάωνι καὶ ἄλλοις ἀθανάτοισιν

426

And I offer you this gift, my dear child,
something to remember me, from Helen's hands, for
    the time of your lovely marriage,
for your wife to wear.

This industry betrays her discretion; because she is not
introduced as someone who lives a luxurious life or has
grown conceited because of her beauty. She is found, for
example, weaving at her loom and working figures into it
(*Il.* 3.125–8):

He found her in the hall. She was weaving a large
    web,
making a bright double-robe; and she was working
    into it many struggles
between the horse-mastering Trojans and the bronze-
    armored Achaeans,
which they endured on her account at Ares' hands.

Homer teaches us that the guests at a meal should ask
their hosts for permission to leave the table. Telemachus
says to Menelaus (*Od.* 4.294–5):

But come—send us to bed, so that we may now
lie down and have the pleasure of sweet sleep.

And Athena pretending to be Mentor says to Nestor (*Od.*
3.332–4):

But come—cut out the tongues and mix some wine,
so that we can pour libations to Poseidon and the
    other

---

15 δ' is not in the traditional text of Homer.
16 The traditional text of Homer has κεράασθε.

427

ATHENAEUS

σπείσαντες κοίτοιο μεδώμεθα· τοῖο γὰρ ὥρη.

ἐν δὲ ταῖς τῶν θεῶν ἑορταῖς οὐδ᾽ ὅσιον εἶναι δοκεῖ πλείω χρόνον παραμένειν. γνωμικῶς γοῦν φησιν παρὰ τῷ Ὁμήρῳ ἡ Ἀθηνᾶ·

ἤδη γὰρ φάος οἴχεθ᾽ ὑπὸ ζόφον, οὐδὲ ἔοικε
δηθὰ θεῶν ἐν δαιτὶ θαασσέμεν, ἀλλὰ νέεσθαι.

καὶ νῦν δὴ νόμος ἐκ θυσιῶν τινων πρὸ ἡλίου δύνοντος
f | ἀπιέναι. καὶ παρ᾽ Αἰγυπτίοις δὲ τὸ παλαιὸν σωφρονικῶς διεξήγετο τὸ τῶν συμποσίων γένος, καθάπερ εἴρηκεν Ἀπολλώνιος ὁ περὶ τούτων γεγραφώς. καθήμενοι μὲν γὰρ ἐδείπνουν, τροφῇ τῇ λιτοτάτῃ καὶ ὑγιεινοτάτῃ χρώμενοι καὶ οἴνῳ τοσούτῳ ὅσος ἱκανὸς ἂν γένοιτο πρὸς εὐθυμίαν, ἣν ὁ Πίνδαρος αἰτεῖται παρὰ τοῦ Διός·

τί ἔρδων φίλος σοί τε, καρτερόβροντα[17]
Κρονίδα, φίλος δὲ Μοίσαις,
192   Εὐθυμίᾳ τε μέλων εἴην, τοῦτ᾽ αἴτημί σε. ||

τὸ δὲ Πλάτωνος συμπόσιον οὐ συνέδριόν ἐστιν, οὐ βουλευτήριον, οὐ λέσχη φιλοσόφων. Σωκράτης γὰρ οὐδὲ τοῦ συμποσίου ἀποστῆναι θέλει καίτοι Ἐρυξιμάχου καὶ Φαίδρου καὶ ἄλλων τινῶν ἀποστάντων, ἀλλ᾽ ἐγρήγορε μετ᾽ Ἀγάθωνος καὶ Ἀριστοφάνους καὶ πίνει ἐξ ἀργυροῦ φρέατος—καλῶς γάρ τις τὰ μεγάλα

17 καρτερόβρεντα Snell

428

immortals and think of bed; because it is time for
that.

It does not appear to be pious to remain too long at festivals in honor of the gods. The Homeric Athena, for example, says, as if it were a maxim (*Od.* 3.335–6):

> For now the light is gone into the darkness, and it is
> not proper
> to sit for a long time at the gods' feast, but to go
> home.

Even today, in fact, it is the rule to leave some sacrificial festivals before the sun sets. And in Egypt in ancient times symposia were conducted in a restrained manner, according to Apollonius (*FGrH* 661 F 2), who wrote about them. They sat when they dined, ate very simple, healthy food, and drank just enough wine to make them cheerful, which is what Pindar (fr. 155) requests from Zeus:

> Whatever I must do to become your friend, mightily
> thundering
> son of Cronus, and a friend of the Muses,
> and of Cheerfulness of songs—this is what I ask you
> for.

Plato's symposium is no board-meeting, council-meeting, or club-meeting of philosophers. For (*Smp.* 223b–d) Socrates does not want to leave the party, although Eryximachus, Phaedrus, and some of the others are gone, but stays awake along with Aristophanes and Agathon and drinks from a silver well—for one authority aptly applies

ποτήρια οὕτως ὠνόμασε—πίνει τ᾽ ἐκ τῆς φιάλης ἐπι-
δέξια. φησὶ δὲ καὶ μετὰ τοῦτο τοὺς μὲν δύο νυστάζειν,
b καταδαρθεῖν δὲ πρότερον τὸν | Ἀριστοφάνη, ἤδη δὲ
ἡμέρας ὑποφαινούσης τὸν Ἀγάθωνα· καὶ τὸν Σωκράτη κατακοιμήσαντα ἐκείνους ἀναστάντα ἀπιέναι
εἰς τὸ Λύκειον, ἐξόν, φησὶν ὁ Ἡρόδικος, εἰς τοὺς
Ὁμήρου Λαιστρυγόνας,

ἔνθα κ᾽ ἄυπνος ἀνὴρ δοιοὺς ἐξήρατο μισθούς.

Πᾶσα δὲ συμποσίου συναγωγὴ παρὰ τοῖς ἀρχαίοις τὴν αἰτίαν εἰς θεὸν ἀνέφερε, καὶ στεφάνοις
ἐχρῶντο τοῖς οἰκείοις τῶν θεῶν καὶ ὕμνοις καὶ ᾠδαῖς.
καὶ δοῦλος οὐδεὶς ἦν ὁ διακονήσων, ἀλλ᾽ οἱ νέοι τῶν
c ἐλευθέρων ᾠνοχόουν, ὡς ὁ τοῦ Μενελάου υἱὸς | καίτοι
νυμφίος ὑπάρχων καὶ ἐν αὐτοῖς τοῖς γάμοις. παρὰ δὲ
τῇ καλῇ Σαπφοῖ καὶ ὁ Ἑρμῆς οἰνοχοεῖ τοῖς θεοῖς. καὶ
τἆλλα δὲ πάντα παρεσκεύαζον τοῖς δειπνοῦσιν ἐλεύ-
θεροι· καὶ οἱ δειπνήσαντες ἀπελύοντο φωτὸς ὄντος. ἐν
ἐνίοις δὲ καὶ τῶν Περσικῶν συμποσίων ἐγίνοντό τινες
καὶ βουλαί, καθάπερ ἐν τῷ τοῦ Ἀγαμέμνονος κατὰ
τὴν στρατείαν. τὸ δὲ τοῦ Ἀλκινόου συμπόσιον, πρὸς ὃ
ἀποτέταται ⟨ὁ⟩ τοῦ Ὀδυσσέως λόγος·

d οὐ γὰρ ἐγώ γέ τί φημι τέλος χαριέστερον εἶναι |

52 At 11.461c, Chamaeleon (drawing in turn on unidentified
older authorities) is cited as the source of this information.
53 The action at *Od.* 4.3–12 is confounded with that at *Od.*
15.121–3, as also at 1.18b.

this term to large drinking cups[52]—and drinks from the libation-bowl as it is passed around from left to right. And he says that after this the two of them nodded off, and that Aristophanes was the first to fall asleep, while Agathon did only when day was breaking. After Socrates put them to bed, he got up and went off to the Lyceum—although, according to Herodicus, he could have gone to visit Homer's Laestrygonians (*Od.* 10.84),

> where a man who did not sleep could earn double
> wages.

Among the ancients, every time a group was assembled for a symposium this was regarded as being for a god's sake, and they wore garlands and sang hymns and songs appropriate to the gods in question. No slaves were there to serve them; instead, free young men poured the wine, as Menelaus' son does even though he is a bridegroom and his wedding feast is going on.[53] And in the noble Sappho (fr. 141)[54] Hermes pours wine for the gods. Free people also prepared everything else for the dinner-guests; and they left the meal while it was still light. At some Persian symposia, council-meetings took place,[55] as one does at Agamemnon's symposium during the expedition against Troy (*Il.* 2.402ff). Alcinoos' symposium, to which Odysseus' remark applies (*Od.* 9.5–7):

> For I declare that there is no greater height of
> happiness

[54] Quoted at 2.39a; 10.425c–d.
[55] Cf. 4.144a–b.

ἢ ὅταν εὐφροσύνη[18] μὲν ἔχῃ κατὰ δῆμον ἅπαντα,
δαιτυμόνες δ' ἀνὰ δώματ' ἀκουάζωνται ἀοιδοῦ,

ξένου ὑποδοχὴν ἔχει, ὄντων καὶ αὐτῶν τῶν Φαιάκων
τρυφερῶν. ὅπερ συμβάλλων τις πρὸς τὰ τῶν φιλοσόφων συμπόσια κοσμιώτερον ἂν εὕροι, καίτοι τοῦτο
περιέχον καὶ ἱλαρότητα καὶ παιδιὰν εὐσχήμονα. μετὰ
γὰρ τὸν ἀγῶνα τὸν γυμνικὸν ᾄδει ὁ ᾠδὸς ἀμφ' Ἄρεος
φιλότητα μῦθόν τινα χλεύῃ κεκραμένον, καίτοι εἰς τὴν
e   μνηστηροφονίαν ὑποθηκῶν | ὑποτιθεμένων τῷ Ὀδυσ-
σεῖ, ὡς τοῦ Κυλλοποδίωνος[19] τὸν ἀνδρειότατον Ἄρη
καταγωνισαμένου.

Ἐκαθέζοντο δὲ καὶ δειπνοῦντες οἱ τότε. πολλαχοῦ
γοῦν ὁ Ὅμηρός φησιν·

ἑξείης ἕζοντο κατὰ κλισμούς τε θρόνους τε.

ὁ γὰρ θρόνος αὐτὸ μόνον ἐλευθέριός ἐστι καθέδρα
σὺν ὑποποδίῳ, ὅπερ θρῆνυν καλοῦντες ἐντεῦθεν αὐτὸν
ὠνόμασαν θρόνον τοῦ θρήσασθαι χάριν, ὅπερ ἐπὶ τοῦ
καθέζεσθαι τάσσουσιν, ὡς Φιλητᾶς·

< . . . > θρήσασθαι δὲ πλατάνῳ γραίῃ[20] ὕπο.

f   ὁ δὲ κλισμὸς | περιττοτέρως κεκόσμηται ἀνακλίσει.
τούτων δ' εὐτελέστερος ἦν ὁ δίφρος· τῷ γοῦν Ὀδυσσεῖ
ἐπαίτῃ εἶναι δοκοῦντι

---

[18] The traditional text of Homer has ὅτ' ἐυφροσύνη.
[19] ὡς τοῦ Ἡφαίστου καὶ τοῦ Κυλλοποδίωνος A: ὡς τοῦ
Κυλλοποδίωνος tantum CE   [20] γραίῃ Bergk: γαίῃ ACE

432

than when joy prevails among all the people[56]
and feasters are in the house listening to a bard,

involves the entertainment of a guest, and the Phaeacians themselves were devoted to luxurious living. But if one were to compare this symposium with those of the philosophers, it would appear more orderly, even though it involves some humor and tasteful fun. Because after the athletic contest the bard sings a story (*Od.* 9.266–365) about Ares' lovemaking which involves a bit of mockery, although hints are also offered to Odysseus about the killing of the Suitors, since Clubfoot[57] defeats Ares, the paragon of masculinity.

People in those days sat at dinner. Homer, at any rate, says repeatedly (e.g. *Od.* 1.145):

They sat in rows on couches (*klismoi*) and chairs
  (*thronoi*).

Because a *thronos* is a chair used exclusively by free people and equipped with a footstool, which they referred to as a *thrēnus*, from which they got the word *thronos*, deriving it from *thrēsasthai*, which they use to mean "to sit down," as Philetas (fr. 14, p. 93 Powell = fr. 22 Sbardella) does:

to sit down beneath a gray plane-tree.

The *klismos* is more elaborately designed to allow one to recline. The *diphros* ("stool") was more humble than these. When Odysseus, for example, looks like a beggar, Homer (*Od.* 20.259) describes someone[58] as

---

[56] For the text, cf. 1.16d with n. wife Aphrodite was seduced by Ares.

[57] Hephaestus, whose [58] Telemachus.

δίφρον ἀεικέλιον (φησί) καταθεὶς ὀλίγην τε
τράπεζαν.

Οἱ δὲ κρατῆρες αὐτοῖς, ὥσπερ ἔχει καὶ τοὔνομα,
κεκραμένοι παρεστήκεσαν, ἐξ ὧν οἱ κοῦροι διακονού-
μενοι τοῖς μὲν ἐντιμοτάτοις ἀεὶ πλῆρες παρεῖχον τὸ
ποτήριον, τοῖς δ᾽ ἄλλοις ἐξ ἴσου διένεμον. ὁ γοῦν
193 Ἀγαμέμνων πρὸς τὸν Ἰδομενέα φησί· ‖

σὸν δὲ πλεῖον δέπας αἰεὶ
ἕστηχ᾽ ὥσπερ ἐμοί, πιέειν ὅτε θυμὸς ἀνώγοι.

προέπινον δ᾽ ἀλλήλοις οὐχ ὥσπερ ἡμεῖς (τοῦτο γὰρ
προεκπιεῖν ἐστιν), ἀλλὰ μεστὸν τὸν σκύφον·

πλησάμενος δ᾽ οἴνοιο δέπας δείδεκτ᾽ Ἀχιλῆα.

ὁσάκις δὲ καὶ τροφὰς ἐλάμβανον, προειρήκαμεν ἤδη
ὅτι δὴ τρεῖς ἦσαν διὰ τὸ τὸ αὐτό ποτε μὲν ἄριστον,
ποτὲ δὲ δεῖπνον ὀνομάζεσθαι. γελοῖοι γάρ εἰσιν οἱ
φάσκοντες ὅτι καὶ τέσσαρας ἐλάμβανον, ἐπεὶ ὁ ποιητὴς ἔφη·

< . . . > σὺ δ᾽ ἔρχεο δειελιήσας,

b οὐ νοοῦντες ὅτι | λέγει τὸν δειλινὸν διατρίψας χρόνον.
ὅμως δὲ οὐδεὶς δείξει παρὰ τῷ ποιητῇ τρίς τινα λαμ-
βάνοντα τροφάς. διαμαρτάνουσι δὲ πολλοὶ παρὰ τῷ
ποιητῇ ἐφεξῆς τιθέντες τούτους τοὺς στίχους·

59 I.e. with only a little wine in the cup, which was drained as
part of the toast.

setting up a shabby stool and a little table

for him.

Their mixing-bowls were, as the name suggests, set beside them full of wine mixed with water; the young men who did the serving kept the cups of the most distinguished guests constantly full and divided the wine equally among the others. Agamemnon, for example, says to Idomeneus (*Il.* 4.262–3):

> Your cup always stands
> full, like mine, to drink when your heart urges you to.

They toasted one another not in the way we do, for which the term is *proekpiein*,[59] but with a full cup (*Il.* 9.224):

> He filled a cup with wine and toasted Achilleus.

As for how many times a day they ate, we already noted earlier (1.11b–f) that there were three meals, because the same meal is sometimes referred to as *ariston* and at other times as *deipnon*. Those who claim that they ate four meals,[60] on the ground that the poet said (*Od.* 17.599):

> Leave after you have your evening meal (*deieliēsas*)!,

deserve to be laughed at, since they do not understand that the poet means "after you spend the afternoon" (*ton deilinon . . . chronon*). And in any case no one can point to anyone in the poet who eats three meals. Many authorities are wrong to place the following three verses (*Od.* 1.139–41 = 4.55–7) one after another in the poet:[61]

[60] Cf. 1.11e, where this opinion is attributed to Philemon.
[61] Cf. 1.8f with n.

σῖτον δ' αἰδοίη ταμίη παρέθηκε φέρουσα,
εἴδατα πόλλ' ἐπιθεῖσα, χαριζομένη παρεόντων·
δαιτρὸς δὲ κρειῶν πίνακας παρέθηκεν ἀείρας.

εἰ γὰρ εἴδατα παρέθηκεν ἡ ταμίη, δῆλον ὡς κρεάτων
λείψανα τυγχάνοντα, τὸν δαιτρὸν οὐκ ἔδει παρεισφέ-
ρειν. διόπερ τὸ δίστιχον ἀπαρκεῖ. ἀπαλλαγέντων δὲ
τῶν δειπνούντων αἱ τράπεζαι ἐβαστάζοντο, ὥσπερ
c παρὰ | τοῖς μνηστῆρσι καὶ τοῖς Φαίαξιν, ἐφ' ὧν καὶ
λέγει·

< . . . > ἀμφίπολοι δ' ἀπεκόσμεον ἔντεα δαιτός,

δῆλον ὡς τὰ ἀγγεῖα. καὶ γὰρ τῶν ὅπλων τὰ σκε-
παστικά, θώρακα καὶ κνημῖδας καὶ τὰ τούτοις ἐμφερῆ,
λέγουσιν ἔντη, καθάπερ ἀγγεῖα τῶν τοῦ σώματος
μερῶν ὄντα. τῶν δὲ ἡρωικῶν οἴκων τοὺς μείζονας
Ὅμηρος μέγαρα καλεῖ καὶ δώματα καὶ κλισίας, οἱ δὲ
νῦν ξενῶνας καὶ ἀνδρῶνας ὀνομάζουσι.

Τί οὖν ὀνομάσομεν, ἄνδρες φίλοι, τὸ συμπόσιον
ὅπερ Ἀντίοχος ὁ Ἐπιφανὴς μὲν κληθείς, Ἐπιμανὴς δ'
d ἐκ | τῶν πράξεων ὀνομασθείς; βασιλεὺς δ' ἦν οὗτος[21]
τῶν ἀπὸ Σελεύκου εἷς· περὶ οὗ φησι Πολύβιος τάδε,
ὡς ἀποδιδράσκων ἐκ τῆς αὐλῆς ἐνίοτε τοὺς θεραπεύ-
οντας οὖ τύχοι τῆς πόλεως ἀλύων ἐφαίνετο δεύτερος

---

[21] οὗτος τῶν Συριακῶν A: τῶν Συριακῶν tantum CE

---

[62] I.e. the first and the third.
[63] Antiochus IV (reigned 175–164 BCE).

And the respectful housekeeper brought bread and
set it by their side,
adding many dainties, favoring them from what she
had available.
And the carver picked up platters of meat and set
them by their side.

Because if the housekeeper served them dainties, it is obvious that these are leftover bits of meat, and there would
be no need for the carver to bring them anything else; so
the two verses[62] are enough. After the dinner-guests left,
the tables were carried out, as in the case of the Suitors and
the Phaeacians, about whom he says (*Od.* 7.232):

The servant-women cleared away all the equipment
(*entea*) for the feast,

obviously referring to the vessels; for they refer to protective armor, such as a chest-plate, greaves, and the like,
as *entē*, as if they were vessels that contain parts of the
body. Homer refers to the larger rooms in the heroes'
houses as *megara*, *dōmata*, and *klisiai*, which people today
call *xenōnes* and *andrōnes*.

What name, then, shall we use, my friends, for the symposium given by Antiochus[63], who was referred to as
Epiphanes, but whose actions earned him the title
Epimanes ("the Madman")? This fellow was one of the
Seleucid kings, and Polybius[64] says the following about
him: He sometimes left the palace and escaped his servants, and was seen wandering at random around the city

[64] From Book XXVI, which is otherwise lost; portions of the
same passage are cited at 10.439a, and cf. 2.45c.

καὶ τρίτος· μάλιστα δὲ πρὸς τοῖς ἀργυροκοπείοις
εὑρίσκετο καὶ χρυσοχοείοις εὑρησιλογῶν καὶ φιλο-
τεχνῶν πρὸς τοὺς τορευτὰς καὶ τοὺς ἄλλους τεχνίτας.
ἔπειτα καὶ μετὰ δημοτῶν ἀνθρώπων συγκαταβαίνων
ὡμίλει ᾧ τύχοι καὶ μετὰ τῶν παρεπιδημούντων
e συνέπινε τῶν εὐτελεστάτων. ὅτε | δὲ τῶν νεωτέρων
αἴσθοιτό τινας συνευωχουμένους, οὐδεμίαν ἔμφασιν
ποιήσας παρῆν ἐπικωμάζων μετὰ κερατίου καὶ συμφωνίας, ὥστε τοὺς πολλοὺς διὰ τὸ παράδοξον ἀφι-
σταμένους φεύγειν. πολλάκις δὲ καὶ τὴν βασιλικὴν
ἀποθέμενος ἐσθῆτα τήβενναν ἀναλαβὼν περιῄει κατὰ
τὴν ἀγορὰν ἀρχαιρεσιάζων καὶ τοὺς μὲν δεξιούμενος,
τοὺς δὲ καὶ περιπτύσσων παρεκάλει φέρειν αὐτῷ τὴν
ψῆφον, ποτὲ μὲν ὡς ἀγορανόμος γένηται, ποτὲ δὲ καὶ
ὡς δήμαρχος. τυχὼν δὲ τῆς ἀρχῆς καὶ καθίσας ἐπὶ
f τὸν ἐλεφάντινον δίφρον κατὰ | τὸ παρὰ Ῥωμαίοις ἔθος
διήκουε τῶν κατὰ τὴν ἀγορὰν γινομένων συναλ-
λαγμάτων καὶ διέκρινε μετὰ πολλῆς σπουδῆς καὶ
προθυμίας. ἐξ ὧν εἰς ἀπορίαν ἦγε τῶν ἀνθρώπων τοὺς
ἐπιεικεῖς· οἱ μὲν γὰρ ἀφελῆ τινα αὐτὸν εἶναι ὑπελάμ-
βανον, οἱ δὲ μαινόμενον. καὶ γὰρ περὶ τὰς δωρεὰς ἦν
194 παραπλήσιος· ‖ ἐδίδου γὰρ τοῖς μὲν ἀστραγάλους
δορκαδείους, τοῖς δὲ φοινικοβαλάνους, ἄλλοις δὲ χρυσίον. καὶ ἐξ ἀπαντήσεως δέ τισι συντυγχάνων οὓς μὴ
ἑωράκει ποτὲ ἐδίδου δωρεὰς ἀπροσδοκήτους. ἐν δὲ
ταῖς πρὸς τὰς πόλεις θυσίαις καὶ ταῖς πρὸς τοὺς θεοὺς

with one or two other men. Generally he was found in the silversmiths' and goldsmiths' shops, offering them ideas and discussing their craft with the engravers and the other workmen. Sometimes he would stoop to associating with whatever ordinary people he met, and he used to drink with the least distinguished visitors to the country. When he discovered that some young men were having a feast, he would burst in on them drunk, without any explanation, carrying a drinking horn and a *sumphōnia*;[65] many of them were so shocked that they got up and tried to run away. He would frequently take off his royal robes, put on a toga, and walk around the marketplace campaigning for office, shaking some people's hands, hugging others, and urging them to give him their vote, sometimes so that he could become a market-commissioner, sometimes a tribune. After he won the office and took his seat in the ivory chair,[66] as is the Roman custom, he listened to the cases involving transactions in the marketplace and made his decisions earnestly and eagerly. The result was that he baffled reasonable people, because some of them suspected that he was a fool, while others considered him crazy. Where presents were involved, he behaved in a similar way; he gave some people gazelle knucklebones, some dates, and others gold coins. And he sometimes gave individuals he had never seen before unexpected presents when they met accidentally. As for the sacrificial festivals he offered the cities, and the honors he showed the gods, he outdid all

[65] Probably a musical instrument of some sort; but the text might mean instead "accompanied by musicians." Cf. 5.195f, where there is a similar ambiguity.

[66] I.e. the *sedes curulis*, used by Roman magistrates.

τιμαῖς πάντας ὑπερέβαλλε τοὺς βεβασιλευκότας. τοῦτο δ' ἄν τις τεκμήραιτο ἔκ τε τοῦ παρ' Ἀθηναίοις
Ὀλυμπιείου καὶ τῶν περὶ τὸν ἐν Δήλῳ βωμὸν ἀνδρι-
άντων. ἐλούετο δὲ κἂν τοῖς δημοσίοις βαλανείοις ὅτε
b δημοτῶν ἦν τὰ βαλανεῖα | πεπληρωμένα, κεραμίων
εἰσφερομένων αὐτῷ μύρων τῶν πολυτελεστάτων. ὅτε
καί τινος εἰπόντος "μακάριοί ἐστε ὑμεῖς οἱ βασιλεῖς οἱ
καὶ τούτοις χρώμενοι καὶ ὀδωδότες ἡδύ," μηδὲν τὸν
ἄνθρωπον προσειπὼν ὅπου 'κεῖνος τῇ ἑξῆς ἐλούετο
ἐπεισελθὼν ἐποίησεν αὐτοῦ καταχυθῆναι τῆς κεφαλῆς
μέγιστον κεράμιον πολυτελεστάτου μύρου τῆς στα-
κτῆς καλουμένης, ὡς πάντας ἀναστάντας κυλίεσθαι
⟨τοὺς⟩ λουομένους τῷ μύρῳ καὶ διὰ τὴν γλισχρότητα
c καταπίπτοντας γέλωτα παρέχειν, καθάπερ | καὶ αὐτὸν
τὸν βασιλέα. ὁ δ' αὐτὸς οὗτος βασιλεὺς ἀκούσας τοὺς
ἐν τῇ Μακεδονίᾳ συντετελεσμένους ἀγῶνας ὑπὸ Αἰμι-
λίου Παύλου τοῦ Ῥωμαίων στρατηγοῦ, βουλόμενος
τῇ μεγαλοδωρίᾳ ὑπερᾶραι τὸν Παῦλον ἐξέπεμψε πρέσβεις καὶ θεωροὺς εἰς τὰς πόλεις καταγγελοῦντας
τοὺς ἐσομένους ἀγῶνας ὑπὸ αὐτοῦ ἐπὶ Δάφνης· ὡς
πολλὴν γενέσθαι τῶν Ἑλλήνων σπουδὴν εἰς τὴν ὡς
αὐτὸν ἄφιξιν. ἀρχὴν δ' ἐποιήσατο τῆς πανηγύρεως
d τὴν πομπείαν οὕτως ἐπιτελεσθεῖσαν. καθηγοῦντό |
τινες Ῥωμαϊκὸν ἔχοντες καθοπλισμὸν ἐν θώραξιν
ἀλυσιδωτοῖς, ἄνδρες ἀκμάζοντες ταῖς ἡλικίαις πεντα-
κισχίλιοι· μεθ' οὓς Μυσοὶ πεντακισχίλιοι. συνεχεῖς δ'

those who had been kings before him. One can see evidence of this in the Olympieum in Athens[67] and the statues around the altar on Delos. He used the public baths when the bathhouse was full of ordinary people, and jars of extremely expensive perfume were brought in for him. Once, when someone said "You kings are lucky, because you get to use these perfumes and smell good," he said nothing to him. But the next day he went over to where the fellow was bathing and had a huge pot of extremely expensive perfume, called *staktē*, dumped over his head; the result was that everyone taking a bath got up and rolled around in the perfume, or fell down because it was so slippery, which made everyone laugh, including the king himself. This same king heard about the games that had been celebrated in Macedon by the Roman general Aemilius Paulus;[68] and because he wanted to outdo Paulus in munificence, he sent off ambassadors and sacred delegates to the cities to announce the games he was going to hold at Daphne.[69] As a result, the Greeks were eager to visit him. He began the festival with a parade that proceeded in the following way: 5000 young men in the prime of life dressed in Roman chain-mail armor led the way, and behind them were 5000 Mysians. Immediately after them were 3000

[67] Work on the Olympieum was begun by the tyrant Peisistratus in the 6th century but abandoned when the dynasty collapsed, and Antiochus revived (but did not complete) the project.

[68] After his victory over the Macedonian king Perseus at Pydna in 168 BCE; cf. Plu. *Aem.* 28.7.

[69] A park outside of Antioch (one of the Seleucid royal capitals) controlled by the king; cf. 5.210e. The events referred to here took place in 166/5 BCE and were followed by a major military campaign in which Antiochus lost his life.

ἦσαν Κίλικες εἰς τὸν τῶν εὐζώνων τρόπον καθω-
πλισμένοι τρισχίλιοι, χρυσοῦς ἔχοντες στεφάνους.
ἐπὶ δὲ τούτοις Θρᾷκες τρισχίλιοι καὶ Γαλάται πεντακισχίλιοι. τούτοις ἐπέβαλλον Μακεδόνες δισμύριοι
καὶ χαλκάσπιδες πεντακισχίλιοι, ἄλλοι δὲ ἀργυρά-
σπιδες· οἷς ἐπηκολούθει μονομάχων ζεύγη διακόσια
e τεσσαράκοντα. | τούτων κατόπιν ἦσαν ἱππεῖς Νισαῖοι
μὲν χίλιοι, πολιτικοὶ δὲ τρισχίλιοι, ὧν οἱ μὲν πλείους
ἦσαν χρυσοφάλαροι καὶ χρυσοστέφανοι, οἱ δ᾽ ἄλλοι
ἀργυροφάλαροι. μετὰ δὲ τούτους ἦσαν οἱ λεγόμενοι
ἑταῖροι ἱππεῖς· οὗτοι δὲ ἦσαν εἰς χιλίους, πάντες
χρυσοφάλαροι. τούτοις συνεχὲς ἦν τὸ τῶν φίλων
σύνταγμα, ἴσον καὶ κατὰ τὸ πλῆθος καὶ κατὰ τὸν
κόσμον. ἐπὶ δὲ τούτοις ἐπίλεκτοι χίλιοι, οἷς ἐπηκολούθει τὸ καλούμενον ἄγημα, κράτιστον εἶναι δοκοῦν
f σύστημα τῶν ἱππέων, περὶ χιλίους. | τελευταία δ᾽ ἦν ἡ
κατάφρακτος ἵππος, οἰκείως τῇ προσηγορίᾳ τῶν ἵππων καὶ τῶν ἀνδρῶν ἐσκεπασμένων τοῖς ὅπλοις· ἦσαν
δὲ καὶ αὐτοὶ χίλιοι καὶ πεντακόσιοι. πάντες δ᾽ οἱ
προειρημένοι εἶχον πορφυρᾶς ἐφαπτίδας, πολλοὶ δὲ
καὶ διαχρύσους καὶ ζωοτάς. ἐπὶ δὲ τούτοις ἔξιππα μὲν
ἦν ἑκατόν, τέθριππα δὲ τεσσαράκοντα· ἔπειτα ἐλεφάντων ἅρμα καὶ συνωρίς· καθ᾽ ἕνα δὲ εἵποντο ἐλέφαντες
διεσκευασμένοι τριάκοντα καὶ ἕξ. τὴν δ᾽ ἄλλην πομ-
πὴν λέγειν ἐστὶ δυσέφικτον, ὡς ἐν κεφαλαίῳ δὲ λεκτέ-
195 ον. ἔφηβοι μὲν γὰρ ἐπόμπευσαν εἰς ὀκτακοσίους, ‖
χρυσοῦς ἔχοντες στεφάνους, βόες δ᾽ εὐτραφεῖς περὶ
χιλίους, θεωρίαι δὲ βραχὺ λείπουσαι τριακοσίων, ἐλε-

Cilicians equipped like light-armed troops and wearing gold garlands. After them were 3000 Thracians and 5000 Galatians; after them came 20000 Macedonians, 5000 carrying bronze shields and the rest carrying silver shields. 240 pairs of gladiators followed them; and behind them were 1000 Nisaean cavalry and 3000 citizen cavalry, most of whom had gold cheek-pieces[70] and wore gold garlands, while the others had silver cheek-pieces. After them were the so-called companion cavalry; there were about 1000 of them, all with gold cheek-pieces. Immediately after them was the contingent of Friends; there was the same number of them and they were outfitted in the same way. After them were 1000 picked men, who were followed by the so-called *agēma* ("guard"), which has a reputation for being the best cavalry unit; there were about 1000 of them. Last was the armored cavalry, with both horses and men covered with armor, as the name suggests; there were 1500 of them. All the individuals mentioned above wore purple military cloaks, often with gold threads running through them or embroidered figures. After them were 100 six-horse chariots and 40 four-horse chariots, and then a cart drawn by a team of elephants; 36 elephants fitted with ornamental trappings followed in single file. A complete description of the rest of the parade would be difficult to achieve, and a summary account is thus called for. About 800 ephebes marched in procession, wearing gold garlands, as well as about 1000 large bulls, slightly less than

[70] Sc. on their horses' bridles.

ATHENAEUS

φάντων δὲ ὀδόντες ὀκτακόσιοι. τὸ δὲ τῶν ἀγαλμάτων
πλῆθος οὐ δυνατὸν ἐξηγήσασθαι· πάντων γὰρ τῶν
παρ᾽ ἀνθρώποις λεγομένων ἢ νομιζομένων θεῶν ἢ
δαιμόνων, προσέτι δὲ ἡρώων εἴδωλα διήγετο, τὰ μὲν
κεχρυσωμένα, τὰ δ᾽ ἠμφιεσμένα στολαῖς διαχρύσοις.
καὶ πᾶσι τούτοις οἱ προσήκοντες μῦθοι κατὰ τὰς
b παραδεδομένας ἱστορίας ἐν διασκευαῖς | πολυτελέσι
παρέκειντο. εἴπετο δ᾽ αὐτοῖς καὶ Νυκτὸς εἴδωλον καὶ
Ἡμέρας, Γῆς τε καὶ Οὐρανοῦ, καὶ Ἠοῦς καὶ Μεσημ-
βρίας. τὸ δὲ τῶν χρυσωμάτων καὶ ἀργυρωμάτων πλῆθος οὕτως ἄν τις ὑπονοήσειεν ὅσον ἦν· ἑνὸς γὰρ τῶν
φίλων Διονυσίου τοῦ ἐπιστολιαγράφου χίλιοι παῖδες
ἐπόμπευσαν ἀργυρώματα ἔχοντες, ὧν οὐδὲν ἔλαττον
ὁλκὴν εἶχεν δραχμῶν χιλίων. βασιλικοὶ δὲ παῖδες
παρῆλθον ἑξακόσιοι χρυσώματα ἔχοντες. ἔπειτα γυ-
c ναῖκες ἐκ χρυσῶν | καλπίδων μύροις ἔραινον εἰς
διακοσίας. ταύταις δ᾽ ἑξῆς ἐπόμπευον ἐν χρυσόποσι
μὲν φορείοις ὀγδοήκοντα γυναῖκες, ⟨ἐν⟩ ἀργυρόποσι
δὲ πεντακόσιαι καθήμεναι, πολυτελῶς διεσκευασμέναι. καὶ τῆς μὲν πομπῆς τὰ ἐπιφανέστατα ταῦτα ἦν.
ἐπιτελεσθέντων δὲ τῶν ἀγώνων καὶ μονομαχιῶν καὶ
κυνηγεσίων κατὰ τριάκονθ᾽ ἡμέρας, ἐν αἷς τὰς θέας
συνετέλει, πέντε μὲν τὰς πρώτας ἐν τῷ γυμνασίῳ
πάντες ἐκ χρυσῶν ὁλκείων ἠλείφοντο κροκίνῳ μύρῳ·
d ἦν | δὲ ταῦτα πεντεκαίδεκα, καὶ κινναμωμίνου τὰ ἴσα
καὶ ναρδίνου. παραπλησίως δὲ καὶ ταῖς ἑξῆς εἰσεφέρετο τήλινον, ἀμαράκινον, ἴρινον, πάντα διαφέροντα
ταῖς εὐωδίαις. ἔστρωτο δὲ εἰς εὐωχίαν ποτὲ μὲν χίλια

444

300 sacred embassies, and 800 elephant tusks. It is impossible to give an account of all the statues; for images of every god or divinity mentioned or believed in by human beings, as well as of heroes, were carried along. Some were gilded, others dressed in robes that had gold threads running through them; and the stories that went with all of them lay next to them in expensive editions that followed the traditional accounts. Images of Night and Day, Earth and Sky, and Dawn and Noon followed them. One might arrive at a sense of the number of gold and silver vessels in the following way: 1000 slaves belonging to one of the king's friends, Dionysius the royal secretary, marched in the procession carrying silver vessels, none of which weighed less than 1000 drachmas; and 600 slaves belonging to the king passed by carrying gold vessels. Then came about 200 women who sprinkled the spectators with perfume from gold pitchers. Immediately after them in the procession came 80 women seated on litters with gold feet, and 500 on litters with silver feet, all expensively dressed. These were the most ostentatious parts of the parade. The athletic contests, gladiatorial combats, and hunts took 30 days to complete, during which time he staged spectacles, at the first five of which all the people in the exercise-yard anointed themselves with saffron perfume from gold basins. There were 15 of these, as well as an equal number filled with cinnamon and spikenard perfume. Likewise on the days that followed, fennugreek, marjoram, and iris perfumes, all deliciously scented, were brought in. On one occasion 1000 triclinia[71] were spread with bed-clothes for

71 Banqueting rooms with three couches.

ATHENAEUS

τρίκλινα, ποτὲ δὲ χίλια πεντακόσια μετὰ τῆς πολυτελεστάτης διασκευῆς. ὁ δὲ χειρισμὸς ἐγίνετο τῶν
πραγμάτων δι᾽ αὐτοῦ τοῦ βασιλέως· ἵππον γὰρ ἔχων
εὐτελῆ παρέτρεχε παρὰ τὴν πομπήν, τοὺς μὲν προ-
e   άγειν κελεύων, τοὺς δὲ ἐπέχειν. κατὰ | δὲ τοὺς πότους
αὐτὸς ἐπὶ τὰς εἰσόδους ἐφιστάμενος οὓς μὲν εἰσῆγεν,
οὓς δ᾽ ἀνέκλινε, καὶ τοὺς διακόνους δὲ τοὺς τὰς παραθέσεις φέροντας αὐτὸς εἰσῆγε. καὶ περιπορευόμενος
οὗ μὲν προσεκάθιζεν, οὗ δὲ προσανέπιπτε· καί ποτε
μὲν ἀποθέμενος μεταξὺ τὸν ψωμόν, ποτὲ δὲ τὸ ποτήριον ἀνεπήδα καὶ μετανίστατο καὶ περιῄει τὸν πότον
προπόσεις λαμβάνων ὀρθὸς ἄλλοτε παρ᾽ ἄλλοις, ἅμα
δὲ καὶ τοῖς ἀκροάμασι προσπαίζων. προϊούσης δ᾽ ἐπὶ
f   πολὺ | τῆς συνουσίας καὶ πολλῶν ἤδη κεχωρισμένων
ὑπὸ τῶν μίμων ὁ βασιλεὺς εἰσεφέρετο ὅλος κεκα-
λυμμένος καὶ εἰς τὴν γῆν ἐτίθετο ὡς εἷς ὢν δῆτα τῶν
μίμων· καὶ τῆς συμφωνίας προκαλουμένης ἀναπηδή-
σας ὠρχεῖτο καὶ ὑπεκρίνετο μετὰ τῶν γελωτοποιῶν,
ὥστε πάντας αἰσχυνομένους φεύγειν. ταῦτα δὲ πάντα
συνετελέσθη ἐξ ὧν τὰ μὲν ἐκ τῆς Αἰγύπτου ἐνοσφί-
σατο παρασπονδήσας τὸν Φιλομήτορα βασιλέα παι-
δίσκον ὄντα, ‹τὰ› δὲ καὶ τῶν φίλων συμβαλλομένων.
196   ἱεροσυλήκει δὲ καὶ τὰ πλεῖστα τῶν ἱερῶν. ||

Θαυμασάντων δὲ τῶν δαιτυμόνων τήν τε τοῦ βασιλέως διάνοιαν ὡς οὐκ Ἐπιφανής, ἀλλ᾽ ὄντως ἐπιμανὴς

---

72 See 5.193e n.
73 Ptolemy VI (reigned 180–145 BCE). Antiochus invaded

446

a feast, while on another there were 1500 and the arrangements were extremely lavish. The king handled all the details personally; for he trotted alongside the procession on an unremarkable horse, telling some groups to move forward and others to wait. At the drinking parties he stood at the entrance in person and escorted some people in; showed others to their couches; and personally gave directions to the servants carrying the dishes. He walked around and sat next to someone here, or lay down beside someone else there; and sometimes he set down a bit of food when he was in the middle of eating it, or a glass of wine, and leapt up, went off somewhere else, and circulated through the party, receiving toasts standing next to various people, while simultaneously laughing at the entertainment. When the party had gone on for a long time and many people had already left, the king was carried in by the mime-actors with his face entirely concealed, and was set on the ground as if he were actually one of them. When the *sumphōnia*[72] summoned him, he leapt up and began to dance and to act along with the clowns; everyone was so embarrassed that they tried to flee. This was all done in part with money he appropriated from Egypt after he broke his treaty with King Philometor[73], who was only a boy, and in part with funds contributed by his friends. He also plundered most of the temples.

After the members of the dinner party expressed their astonishment at both the state of the king's mind, which suggested that he was not Epiphanes but *epimanēs*

Egypt twice in 169–168, originally with the support of Ptolemy VI, who was locked in a struggle with his brother Ptolemy VIII, but the Romans ordered him out of the country shortly thereafter.

ὑπῆρχε, < . . . > προσέθηκεν ὁ Μασούριος περὶ τῆς ἐν
Ἀλεξανδρείᾳ γεγενημένης ὑπὸ τοῦ πάντα ἀρίστου
Πτολεμαίου τοῦ Φιλαδέλφου βασιλέως πομπῆς Καλ-
λίξεινον τὸν Ῥόδιον ἱστοροῦντα ἐν τῷ τετάρτῳ Περὶ
Ἀλεξανδρείας, ὅς φησι· πρὸ δὲ τοῦ ἄρξασθαι τὴν
κατασκευασθεῖσαν σκηνὴν ἐν τῷ τῆς ἄκρας περιβόλῳ
χωρὶς τῆς τῶν στρατιωτῶν καὶ τεχνιτῶν καὶ παρεπι-
b δήμων ὑποδοχῆς ἐξηγήσομαι· καλὴ γὰρ | εἰς ὑπερ-
βολὴν ἀξία τε ἀκοῆς ἐγενήθη. τὸ μὲν οὖν μέγεθος
αὐτῆς ἑκατὸν τριάκοντα κλίνας ἐπιδεχόμενον κύκλῳ,
διασκευὴν δ᾽ εἶχε τοιαύτην. κίονες διεστάθησαν ξύλι-
νοι πέντε μὲν κατὰ πλευρὰν ἑκάστην τοῦ μήκους
πεντηκονταπήχεις πρὸς ὕψος, ἑνὶ δὲ ἐλάττους κατὰ
πλάτος· ἐφ᾽ ὧν ἐπιστύλιον καθηρμόσθη τετράγωνον,
ὑπερεῖδον τὴν σύμπασαν τοῦ συμποσίου στέγην.
αὕτη δ᾽ ἐνεπετάσθη κατὰ μέσον οὐρανίσκῳ κοκκινο-
βαφεῖ περιλεύκῳ, καθ᾽ ἑκάτερον δὲ μέρος εἶχε δοκοὺς
c μεσολεύκοις ἐμπετάσμασι | πυργωτοῖς κατειλημμένας,
ἐν αἷς φατνώματα γραπτὰ κατὰ μέσον ἐτέτακτο. τῶν
δὲ κιόνων οἱ μὲν τέσσαρες ὡμοίωντο φοίνιξιν, οἱ δ᾽
ἀνὰ μέσον θύρσων εἶχον φαντασίαν. τούτων δ᾽ ἐκτὸς
περίστυλος ἐπεποίητο σῦριγξ ταῖς τρισὶ πλευραῖς
καμαρωτὴν ἔχουσα στέγην, ἐν ᾗ τὴν τῶν κατακειμένων ἀκολουθίαν ἑστάναι συνέβαινεν. ἧς τὸ μὲν
ἐντὸς αὐλαίαις περιείχετο φοινικέαις, ἐπὶ δὲ τῶν ἀνὰ
μέσον χωρῶν δοραὶ θηρίων παράδοξοι καὶ τῇ ποικι-
d λίᾳ καὶ τοῖς μεγέθεσιν ἐκρέμαντο. τὸ δὲ περιέχον |
αὐτὴν ὕπαιθρον μυρρίναις καὶ δάφναις ἄλλοις τε

("mad"),[74] . . . Masurius added an account of the procession in Alexandria organized by the universally excellent King Ptolemy Philadelphus,[75] about which Callixeinus of Rhodes offers a report in Book IV of *On Alexandria* (*FGrH* 627 F 2). He says: Before I begin, I am going to offer a description of the pavilion set up within the citadel, in a different spot from where the soldiers, craftsmen, and visitors from other cities were entertained; for it was extraordinarily beautiful and well worth hearing about. As for its size, it could hold 300 couches set in a circle, and it was decorated as follows. Five wooden columns 50 cubits[76] high stood at intervals along the long sides, and four along the shorter sides; a rectangular architrave was set on top of them and supported the entire roof over the symposium area. The center of the roof was draped with a canopy dyed red with an off-white border; in each section there were beams covered with towering white curtains, and painted cofferwork was set between the beams. Four columns were made to resemble palmtrees, while those in the middle were decorated like Dionysiac staffs. Outside the columns a peristyle gallery with a vaulted roof had been built along three sides of the structure; this is where the servants who accompanied the guests stood. The interior of the gallery was lined with dark red curtains, and a large and diverse collection of animal skins was hanging in the spaces between them. The open area around the gallery had been roofed with myrtle, laurel, and other branches

[74] Cf. 5.193d with n.
[75] Ptolemy II (reigned 285/3–246 BCE).
[76] About 75 feet.

ἐπιτηδείοις ἔρνεσιν ἐγεγόνει συνηρεφές. τὸ δ' ἔδαφος
πᾶν ἄνθεσι κατεπέπαστο παντοίοις. ἡ γὰρ Αἴγυπτος
καὶ διὰ τὴν τοῦ περιέχοντος ἀέρος εὐκρασίαν καὶ διὰ
τοὺς κηπεύοντας τὰ σπανίως καὶ καθ' ὥραν ἐνεστη-
κυῖαν ἐν ἑτέροις φυόμενα τόποις ἄφθονα γεννᾷ καὶ διὰ
παντός, καὶ οὔτε ῥόδον οὔτε λευκόιον οὔτ' ἄλλο ῥᾳδίως ἄνθος ἐκλιπεῖν οὐθὲν οὐδέποτ' εἴωθεν. διὸ δὴ καὶ
κατὰ μέσον χειμῶνα τῆς ὑποδοχῆς τότε γενηθείσης
e   παράδοξος ἡ φαντασία[22] | τοῖς ξένοις κατέστη· τὰ
γὰρ εἰς μίαν εὑρεθῆναι στεφάνωσιν οὐκ ἂν δυνηθέντα
ἐν ἄλλῃ πόλει ῥᾳδίως, ταῦτα καὶ τῷ πλήθει τῶν
κατακειμένων ἐκεχορήγητο εἰς τοὺς στεφάνους ἀφθόνως καὶ εἰς τὸ τῆς σκηνῆς ἔδαφος κατεπέπαστο χύδην, θείου τινὸς ὡς ἀληθῶς ἀποτελοῦντα λειμῶνος
πρόσοψιν. διέκειτο δὲ ἐπὶ μὲν τῶν τῆς σκηνῆς παρα-
στάδων ζῷα μαρμάρινα τῶν πρώτων τεχνιτῶν ἑκατόν.
ἐν δὲ ταῖς ἀνὰ μέσον χώραις πίνακες τῶν Σικυωνικῶν
f   ζωγράφων, ἐναλλὰξ δ' ἐπίλεκτοι | εἰκασίαι παντοῖαι
καὶ χιτῶνες χρυσοϋφεῖς ἐφαπτίδες τε κάλλισται, τινὲς
μὲν εἰκόνας ἔχουσαι τῶν βασιλέων ἐνυφασμένας, αἱ
δὲ μυθικὰς διαθέσεις. ὑπεράνω δὲ τούτων θυρεοὶ περι-
έκειντο ἐναλλὰξ ἀργυροῖ τε καὶ χρυσοῖ. ἐν δὲ ταῖς
ἐπάνω τούτων χώραις οὔσαις ὀκταπήχεσιν ἄντρα κατεσκεύαστο κατὰ μὲν τὸ μῆκος τῆς σκηνῆς ἓξ ἐν
ἑκατέρᾳ πλευρᾷ, κατὰ πλάτος δὲ τέτταρα· συμπόσιά
τε ἀντία ἀλλήλων ⟨ἐν⟩ αὐτοῖς τραγικῶν τε καὶ κωμι-

[22] φαντασία τότε A

that would serve the purpose. The entire floor had been strewn with flowers of every kind; for the fact that the air in Egypt is temperate, and the gardeners there cultivate plants that grow elsewhere only in limited quantities and in particular seasons, means that the country produces enormous quantities of flowers at every time of year, and the general rule is that no flower, including roses, snowdrops, or anything else, ever completely stops blooming. The fact that the party took place in mid-winter therefore meant that the guests were astonished by what they saw; because flowers that could not easily have been found combined in a single garland in any other city had been arranged in garlands in immense numbers for the large crowd of guests and strewn in heaps on the floor of the pavilion, making it look as if it were truly a divine meadow. 100 marble statues by the most important artists stood by the pilasters that supported the canopy; in the spaces between these were paintings by Sicyonian artists,[77] alternating with select images of every sort, tunics with gold woven into the fabric, and beautiful military cloaks, some with royal portraits woven in, others with mythological subjects. Oblong shields that alternated between silver and gold were set around the room above these. And in the space over them, which was eight cubits high, caves had been constructed; there were six of these along each long side of the room, and four along the short sides. Set opposite one another in the caves were symposia being celebrated by characters drawn from

---

[77] For the Sicyonian school, see Plin. *Nat.* 35.75.

197 κῶν καὶ σατυρικῶν ‖ ζώων ἀληθινὸν ἐχόντων ἱμα-
τισμόν, οἷς παρέκειτο καὶ ποτήρια χρυσᾶ. κατὰ μέσον
δὲ τῶν ἄντρων νύμφαι ἐλείφθησαν, ἐν αἷς ἔκειντο
Δελφικοὶ χρυσοῖ τρίποδες ὑποστήματ' ἔχοντες. κατὰ
δὲ τὸν ὑψηλότατον τόπον τῆς ὀροφῆς ἀετοὶ κατὰ
πρόσωπον ἦσαν ἀλλήλων χρυσοῖ, πεντεκαιδεκαπή-
χεις τὸ μέγεθος. ἔκειντο δὲ κλῖναι χρυσαῖ σφιγ-
γόποδες ἐν ταῖς δυσὶ πλευραῖς ἑκατόν· ἡ γὰρ κατὰ
πρόσωπον ἀψὶς ἀφεῖτ' ἀναπεπταμένη. ταύταις δ' ἀμ-
b φίταποι ἁλουργεῖς ὑπέστρωντο ǀ τῆς πρώτης ἐρέας,
καὶ περιστρώματα ποικίλα διαπρεπῆ ταῖς τέχναις
ἐπῆν. ψιλαὶ δὲ Περσικαὶ τὴν ἀνὰ μέσον τῶν ποδῶν
χώραν ἐκάλυπτον, ἀκριβῆ τὴν εὐγραμμίαν τῶν ἐνυ-
φασμένων ἔχουσαι ζῳδίων. παρετέθησαν δὲ καὶ τρίποδες τοῖς κατακειμένοις χρυσοῖ διακόσιοι τὸν ἀ-
ριθμόν, ὥστ' εἶναι δύο κατὰ κλίνην, ἐπ' ἀργυρῶν
διέδρων. ἐκ δὲ τῶν ὄπισθεν πρὸς τὴν ἀπόνιψιν ἑκατὸν
ἀργυραῖ λεκάναι καὶ καταχύσεις ἴσαι παρέκειντο.
c ἐπεπήγει δὲ τοῦ συμποσίου ǀ καταντικρὺ καὶ ἕτερα
κλίνη πρὸς τὴν τῶν κυλίκων καὶ ποτηρίων τῶν τε
λοιπῶν τῶν πρὸς τὴν χρῆσιν ἀνηκόντων[23] κατασκευασμάτων ἔκθεσιν· ἃ δὴ πάντα χρυσᾶ τε ἦν καὶ διά-
λιθα, θαυμαστὰ ταῖς τέχναις. τούτων δὲ τὴν μὲν κατὰ
μέρος κατασκευὴν καὶ τὰ γένη μακρὸν ἐπεφαίνετό μοι
δηλοῦν· τὸ δὲ τοῦ σταθμοῦ πλῆθος εἰς μύρια τάλαντα
ἀργυρίου τὴν σύμπασαν εἶχε κατασκευήν. ἡμεῖς δὲ

[23] ἀνηκόντων καὶ A

tragedy, comedy, and satyr play; they wore real clothing, and gold drinking cups lay beside them. Niches[78] had been left in the middle of the caves, with gold Delphic tripods on stands set in them. At the highest point of the roof were gold eagles that faced one another and were 15 cubits high. 100 gold couches with feet shaped like sphinxes were set along the two sides of the pavilion; the front end of the hall was left open. Purple double-pile carpets made of first-quality wool were spread over the couches, and on top of these were embroidered quilts of remarkable workmanship. Smooth Persian carpets with fine designs of living creatures worked into them covered the space in the center where people walked around. 200 gold tripods on silver stands were set beside the guests, so that there would be two per couch; behind these were set 100 silver basins and an equal number of pitchers for them to wash with. Another couch had been erected facing the symposium to display the cups and drinking vessels and the other items that were needed; these were all made of gold, had inset jewels, and were of extraordinary workmanship. It seemed to me that offering a detailed account of the craftsmanship of these vessels and listing all the types would be an enormous undertaking; but the total weight of all the dinner vessels taken together was 10000 talents of silver.[79] Now

[78] The Greek says "nymphs"; either this is an otherwise unattested extended use of the word in the sense "features typical of shrines of the nymphs," or the word is corrupt.

[79] Around 300 tons.

ἐπειδὴ τὰ κατὰ τὴν σκηνὴν διεληλύθαμεν, ποιησό-
d μεθα καὶ τὴν τῆς πομπῆς | ἐξήγησιν. ἤγετο γὰρ διὰ
τοῦ κατὰ τὴν πόλιν σταδίου. πρώτη δ' ἐβάδιζεν ⟨ἡ⟩
Ἑωσφόρου· καὶ γὰρ ἀρχὴν εἶχεν ἡ πομπὴ καθ' ὃν ὁ
προειρημένος ἀστὴρ φαίνεται χρόνον. ἔπειθ' ἡ τοῖς
τῶν βασιλέων γονεῦσι κατωνομασμένη. μετὰ δὲ ταύτας αἱ τῶν θεῶν ἁπάντων, οἰκείαν ἔχουσαι τῆς περὶ
ἕκαστον αὐτῶν ἱστορίας διασκευήν. τὴν δὲ τελευταίαν
Ἑσπέρου συνέβαινεν εἶναι, τῆς ὥρας εἰς τοῦτον συν-
αγούσης τὸν καιρόν. τὰ δὲ κατὰ μέρος αὐτῶν εἴ τις
εἰδέναι βούλεται, τὰς τῶν πεντετηρίδων γραφὰς λαμ-
e βάνων | ἐπισκοπείτω. τῆς δὲ Διονυσιακῆς πομπῆς
πρῶτοι μὲν προῇεσαν οἱ τὸν ὄχλον ἀνείργοντες σιλη-
νοί, ⟨οἱ μὲν⟩ πορφυρᾶς χλαμύδας, οἱ δὲ φοινικίδας
ἠμφιεσμένοι. τούτοις δ' ἐπηκολούθουν σάτυροι καθ'
ἕκαστον τοῦ σταδίου μέρος εἴκοσι, λαμπάδας φέροντες κισσίνας διαχρύσους. μεθ' οὓς Νῖκαι χρυσᾶς
ἔχουσαι πτέρυγας. ἔφερον δ' αὗται θυμιατήρια ἑξαπήχη κισσίνοις διαχρύσοις κλωσὶ διακεκοσμημένα,
ζῳωτοὺς ἐνδεδυκυῖαι χιτῶνας, αὐταὶ δὲ πολὺν κόσμον
f χρυσοῦν περικείμεναι. | μετὰ δὲ ταύτας εἵπετο βωμὸς
ἑξάπηχυς διπλοῦς κισσίνῃ φυλλάδι διαχρύσῳ πεπυ-
κασμένος, ἔχων ἀμπέλινον χρυσοῦν στέφανον μεσο-
λεύκοις μίτραις διειλημμένον. ἐπηκολούθουν δ' αὐτῷ
παῖδες ἐν χιτῶσι πορφυροῖς, λιβανωτὸν καὶ σμύρναν,
ἔτι δὲ κρόκον ἐπὶ χρυσῶν μαζονόμων φέροντες ἑκατὸν
εἴκοσι. μεθ' οὓς σάτυροι τεσσαράκοντα ἐστεφανωμένοι κισσίνοις χρυσοῖς στεφάνοις· τὰ δὲ σώματα οἱ

454

that I have given a full account of everything connected with the pavilion, I will also describe the procession. It was held in the stadium in the city. The first unit to march was dedicated to the morning star, because the procession began when the aforementioned star appears. Next came the unit named for the royal couple's parents.[80] After these came units dedicated to all the gods, with paraphernalia appropriate to the gods' individual stories. It happened that the last unit was dedicated to the evening star, since the season put the end of the procession at this time of day. If anyone wants to know the individual details about these units, he can get the records of the penteteric festivals and consult them. At the head of the Dionysiac procession came silens, who forced the crowd back; some of them wore purple military cloaks, others dark red ones. They were followed by satyrs, 20 of whom were posted in each part of the stadium, and who carried gilded torches decorated with ivy. After them came Victories with gold wings. They were carrying incense-burners six cubits long that were decorated with gold ivy-branches; were dressed in embroidered tunics; and were themselves covered with a great deal of gold jewelry. A double altar six cubits long followed them; it was covered with gilded ivy-leaves and had a gold grapevine-garland with off-white ribbons wrapped around it. After this came 120 boys dressed in purple tunics and carrying frankincense and myrrh, as well as saffron on gold platters. Behind them were 40 satyrs wearing gold garlands made to look like ivy; some had smeared

---

[80] Ptolemy I Soter and Berenice I, parents of Ptolemy II and Arsinoe II Philadelphus, who were brother and sister, and married sometime in the mid-270s BCE; cf. 14.621a.

198 μὲν ἐκέχριντο ὀστρείῳ, τινὲς δὲ μίλτῳ καὶ χρώμασιν ‖
ἑτέροις. ἔφερον δὲ καὶ οὗτοι στέφανον χρυσοῦν ἐξ
ἀμπέλου καὶ κισσοῦ εἰργασμένον. μεθ᾽ οὓς σιληνοὶ
δύο ἐν πορφυραῖς χλαμύσι καὶ κρηπῖσι λευκαῖς. εἶχε
δ᾽ αὐτῶν ὁ μὲν πέτασον καὶ κηρύκειον χρυσοῦν, ὁ δὲ
σάλπιγγα. μέσος δὲ τούτων ἐβάδιζεν ἀνὴρ μείζων ‹ἢ›
τετράπηχυς ἐν τραγικῇ διαθέσει καὶ προσώπῳ, φέρων
χρυσοῦν Ἀμαλθείας κέρας· ὃς προσηγορεύετο Ἐνι-
αυτός. ᾧ γυνὴ περικαλλεστάτη ‹καὶ ἴση› κατὰ τὸ
b μέγεθος εἵπετο πολλῷ χρυσῷ καὶ διαπρεπεῖ ǀ ‹ . . . ›
κεκοσμημένη, φέρουσα τῇ μὲν μιᾷ τῶν χειρῶν στέφανον περσαίας, τῇ δ᾽ ἑτέρᾳ ῥάβδον φοίνικος· ἐκαλεῖτο δὲ αὕτη Πεντετηρίς. ταύτῃ δ᾽ ἐπηκολούθουν
Ὧραι ‹αἱ› τέσσαρες διεσκευασμέναι καὶ ἑκάστη φέρουσα τοὺς ἰδίους καρπούς. ἐχόμενα τούτων θυμιατήρια δύο κίσσινα ἐκ χρυσοῦ ἑξαπήχη καὶ βωμὸς
ἀνὰ μέσον τούτων τετράγωνος χρυσοῦ. καὶ πάλιν
σάτυροι στεφάνους ἔχοντες κισσίνους χρυσοῦς, φοινικίδας περιβεβλημένοι· ἔφερον δ᾽ οἱ μὲν οἰνοχόην
χρυσῆν, οἱ δὲ καρχήσιον. μεθ᾽ οὓς ἐπορεύετο Φι-
c λίσκος ὁ ποιητὴς ἱερεὺς ὢν Διονύσου ǀ καὶ πάντες οἱ
περὶ τὸν Διόνυσον τεχνῖται. τούτων δ᾽ ἐφεξῆς ἐφέροντο Δελφικοὶ τρίποδες, ἆθλα τοῖς τῶν ἀθλητῶν
χορηγοῖς, ὁ μὲν παιδικὸς ἐννέα πηχῶν τὸ ὕψος, ὁ δὲ

---

81 A horn of plenty.
82 An Egyptian tree.
83 "Five-year Interval," referring (on Greek inclusive reckon-

their bodies with sea-purple, others with vermilion and other colors. They were carrying a gold garland made of grapevines and ivy. After them came two silens in purple military cloaks and high white boots. One of them wore a broad-brimmed hat and was carrying a gold herald's staff, while the other carried a trumpet. Between them walked a man who was over four cubits tall, wore tragic clothing and a mask, and was carrying a golden horn of Amaltheia;[81] he was called "The Year." A beautiful woman followed him; she was as tall as he was, was decked out in a great deal of gold and a striking . . . , and was carrying a garland of persea[82] in one hand and a palm-branch in the other. Her name was Pentetēris.[83] She was followed by the four Seasons, who were elaborately costumed and each of whom carried the crops appropriate to her. Next after them were two incense-burners six cubits long made of gold and decorated with ivy; between them was a rectangular altar made of gold. Then came more satyrs wearing gold garlands made to resemble ivy and dressed in dark red robes; some were carrying a gold pitcher, others a *karchēsion*.[84] After them marched the poet Philiscus,[85] who was a priest of Dionysus, and all the artists associated with Dionysus. Immediately after them were carried Delphic tripods, which were prizes for the *chorēgoi*[86] responsible for the athletes; the one for the boys' events was nine cubits high,

---

ing) to the period between games and festivals we would say were celebrated every fourth year.

[84] A type of drinking cup; see 11.474d–5c, and cf. below.

[85] The tragedian Philiscus of Corcyra (*TrGF* 104 T 4).

[86] See 3.103f n. The men referred to here were presumably responsible for organizing various classes of competitions.

πηχῶν δώδεκα ὁ τῶν ἀνδρῶν. μετὰ τούτους τετράκυκλος πηχῶν τεσσαρεσκαίδεκα, ὀκτὼ δὲ τὸ πλάτος,
ἤγετο ὑπὸ ἀνδρῶν ὀγδοήκοντα καὶ ἑκατόν, ἐπὶ δὲ
ταύτης ἐπῆν ἄγαλμα Διονύσου δεκάπηχυ σπένδον ἐκ
καρχησίου χρυσοῦ, χιτῶνα πορφυροῦν ἔχον διάπεζον
d καὶ ἐπ' αὐτοῦ κροκωτὸν | διαφανῆ· περιεβέβλητο δὲ
ἱμάτιον πορφυροῦν χρυσοποίκιλον. προέκειτο δὲ αὐτοῦ κρατὴρ Λακωνικὸς χρυσοῦς μετρητῶν δεκαπέντε
καὶ τρίπους χρυσοῦς, ἐφ' οὗ θυμιατήριον χρυσοῦν καὶ
φιάλαι δύο χρυσαῖ κασσίας μεσταὶ καὶ κρόκου. περι-
έκειτο δ' αὐτῷ καὶ σκιὰς ἐκ κισσοῦ καὶ ἀμπέλου καὶ
τῆς λοιπῆς ὀπώρας κεκοσμημένη, προσήρτηντο δὲ
καὶ στέφανοι καὶ ταινίαι καὶ θύρσοι καὶ τύμπανα καὶ
μίτραι πρόσωπά τε σατυρικὰ καὶ κωμικὰ καὶ τραγικά.
e τῇ δὲ τετρακύκλῳ | < . . . > ἱερεῖς καὶ ἱέρειαι καὶ
πέρυσι τελεσταὶ[24] καὶ θίασοι παντοδαποὶ καὶ τὰ λῖκνα
φέρουσι. μετὰ δὲ ταύτας Μακέται αἱ καλούμεναι
Μιμαλλόνες καὶ Βασσάραι καὶ Λυδαί, κατακεχυμέναι
τὰς τρίχας καὶ ἐστεφανωμέναι τινὲς μὲν ὄφεσιν, αἱ δὲ
μίλακι καὶ ἀμπέλῳ καὶ κισσῷ· κατεῖχον δὲ ταῖς χερσὶν αἱ μὲν ἐγχειρίδια, αἱ δὲ ὄφεις. μετὰ δὲ ταύτας
ἤγετο τετράκυκλος πηχῶν ὀκτὼ πλάτος ὑπὸ ἀνδρῶν
f ἑξήκοντα, | ἐφ' ἧς ἄγαλμα Νύσης ὀκτάπηχυ καθή-
μενον, ἐνδεδυκὸς μὲν θάψινον χιτῶνα χρυσοποίκιλον,
ἱμάτιον δὲ ἠμφίεστο Λακωνικόν. ἀνίστατο δὲ τοῦτο
μηχανικῶς οὐδενὸς τὰς χεῖρας προσάγοντος καὶ

---

[24] πέρυσι τελεσταὶ Schweighäuser: περσειστελεται A

while the one for the men was 12 cubits high. After them
came a four-wheeled cart 14 cubits long and eight cubits
wide pulled by 180 men. On it was a statue of Dionysus ten
cubits high pouring libation from a gold *karchēsion* and
wearing a purple tunic that stretched to its feet and a thin
saffron robe over this; a purple robe with gold spangles was
wrapped around its shoulders. In front of the statue lay a
gold Spartan mixing-bowl with a capacity of 15 amphoras
and a gold tripod, on which rested a gold incense-burner
and two gold libation bowls full of cassia[87] and saffron. The
statue was surrounded by a canopy decorated with ivy,
grapevines, and other types of fruit; garlands, ribbons,
Dionysiac staffs, drums, strips of cloth, and satyric, comic,
and tragic masks were fastened to it. And to the cart . . .
priests and priestesses, the previous year's initiates, and
Dionysiac groups of all sorts carrying winnowing fans.[88]
After them came the Macedonian women referred to as
Mimallones, Bassarai, and Lydians, with their hair undone
and some wearing snakes wrapped around their heads,[89]
others smilax, grapevines, and ivy; and some held daggers
in their hands, others snakes. After them came a four-
wheeled cart eight cubits wide pulled by 60 men. On it was
a seated statue of Nysa[90] eight cubits high wearing a yellow
tunic with gold spangles, with a Spartan robe wrapped
around her. A mechanical device made the statue stand up

---

[87] Chinese cinnamon.

[88] Sacred to Dionysus.

[89] As if they were maenads.

[90] The mountain where Dionysus was said to have been born;
here personified.

σπεῖσαν ἐκ χρυσῆς φιάλης γάλα πάλιν ἐκάθητο. εἶχε
δὲ ἐν τῇ ἀριστερᾷ θύρσον ἐστεμμένον μίτραις. αὕτη δ᾽
ἐστεφάνωτο κισσίνῳ χρυσῷ καὶ βότρυσι διαλίθοις
πολυτελέσιν. εἶχε δὲ σκιάδα καὶ ἐπὶ τῶν γωνιῶν τῆς
τετρακύκλου κατεπεπήγεσαν λαμπάδες διάχρυσοι
199 τέτταρες. ‖ ἑξῆς εἵλκετο ἄλλη τετράκυκλος μῆκος
πηχῶν εἴκοσι, πλάτος ἑκκαίδεκα, ὑπὸ ἀνδρῶν τρι-
ακοσίων· ἐφ᾽ ἧς κατεσκεύαστο ληνὸς πηχῶν εἴκοσι
τεσσάρων, πλάτος πεντεκαίδεκα, πλήρης σταφυλῆς.
ἐπάτουν δὲ ἑξήκοντα σάτυροι πρὸς αὐλὸν ᾄδοντες
μέλος ἐπιλήνιον, ἐφειστήκει δ᾽ αὐτοῖς Σιληνός· καὶ δι᾽
ὅλης τῆς ὁδοῦ τὸ γλεῦκος ἔρρει. ἑξῆς ἐφέρετο τετράκυκλος μῆκος πηχῶν εἴκοσι πέντε, πλάτος τεσσαρεσ-
καίδεκα· ἤγετο δὲ ὑπὸ ἀνδρῶν ἑξακοσίων· ἐφ᾽ ἧς ἦν
b ἀσκὸς τρισχιλίους ‖ ἔχων μετρητάς, ἐκ παρδαλῶν[25]
ἐρραμμένος· ἔρρει δὲ καὶ οὗτος κατὰ μικρὸν ἀνιέμενος
κατὰ πᾶσαν τὴν ὁδόν. ἠκολούθουν δ᾽ αὐτῷ σάτυροι
καὶ σιληνοὶ ἑκατὸν εἴκοσι ἐστεφανωμένοι, φέροντες οἱ
μὲν οἰνοχόας, οἱ δὲ φιάλας, οἱ δὲ Θηρικλείους μεγάλας, πάντα χρυσᾶ. ἐχόμενος ἤγετο κρατὴρ ἀργυροῦς
ἑξακοσίους χωρῶν μετρητὰς ἐπὶ τετρακύκλου ἑλκο-
μένης ὑπὸ ἀνδρῶν ἑξακοσίων. εἶχε δὲ ὑπὸ τὰ χείλη
καὶ τὰ ὦτα καὶ ὑπὸ τὴν βάσιν ζῷα τετορευμένα καὶ
c διὰ μέσου ἐστεφάνωτο ‖ στεφάνῳ χρυσῷ διαλίθῳ.
ἑξῆς ἐφέρετο κυλικεῖα ἀργυρᾶ δωδεκάπηχη δύο, ὕψος
πηχῶν ἕξ· ταῦτα δ᾽ εἶχεν ἄνω τε ἀκρωτήρια καὶ ἐν

[25] παρδαλῶν δερμάτων ACE

without anyone touching it; pour a libation of milk from a gold libation bowl; and sit down again. It held a Dionysiac staff garlanded with strips of cloth in its left hand; and the goddess wore a gold ivy-garland set with precious stones made to resemble grape-clusters. The statue was fitted with a canopy, and four gilded torches had been fastened to the corners of the cart. Another four-wheeled cart 20 cubits long and 16 cubits wide was pulled along immediately behind this one by 300 men. A wine-press 24 cubits high, 15 cubits wide and full of grapes had been constructed on top of it. 60 satyrs were trampling the grapes and singing a grape-pressing song to the accompaniment of pipes, and Silenus was supervising them; the grape-must ran everywhere in the street. Immediately after it came a four-wheeled cart 25 cubits long and 14 cubits wide, pulled by 600 men. On this was a wineskin with a capacity of 3000 amphoras, stitched together from leopard skins; it too flooded the street as it was slowly allowed to empty out. It was followed by 120 satyrs and silens wearing garlands, some carrying wine-pitchers, some libation bowls, and others Thericleian drinking cups;[91] all the vessels were made of gold. Close behind them came a silver mixing-bowl with a capacity of 600 amphoras on top of a four-wheeled wagon pulled by 600 men. It had figures worked in relief beneath the brim and handles and around the base, and a gold garland set with jewels ran around its middle. Immediately after it came two silver cup-stands 12 cubits long and six cubits high; they had elaborate ornaments

[91] See 11.470e–2e.

ταῖς γάστραις κύκλῳ καὶ ἐπὶ τῶν ποδῶν ζῷα τρι-
ημιπήχη καὶ πηχυαῖα πλήθει πολλά. καὶ λουτῆρες
μεγάλοι δέκα καὶ κρατῆρες ἑκκαίδεκα, ὧν οἱ μείζους
ἐχώρουν μετρητὰς τριάκοντα, οἱ δ᾿ ἐλάχιστοι πέντε.
εἶτα λέβητες[26] βαλανωτοὶ εἴκοσι τέσσαρες ἐπ᾿ ἐγγυθήκαις πάντες καὶ ληνοὶ ἀργυραῖ δύο, ἐφ᾿ ὧν ἦσαν
d βῖκοι εἴκοσι τέσσαρες, τράπεζά τε ὁλάργυρος | δω-
δεκάπηχυς καὶ ἄλλαι ἑξαπήχεις τριάκοντα. πρὸς δὲ
τούτοις τρίποδες τέσσαρες, ὧν εἷς μὲν εἶχε τὴν περίμετρον πηχῶν ἑκκαίδεκα, κατάργυρος ὢν ὅλος, οἱ δὲ
τρεῖς ἐλάττονες ὄντες διάλιθοι κατὰ μέσον ὑπῆρχον.
μετὰ τούτους ἐφέροντο Δελφικοὶ τρίποδες ἀργυροῖ
ὀγδοήκοντα τὸν ἀριθμόν, ἐλάττους τῶν προειρημένων,
ὧν αἱ γωνίαι < . . . > τετράμετροι· ὑδρίαι εἴκοσι καὶ ἕξ,
ἀμφορεῖς Παναθηναϊκοὶ δεκαέξ, ψυκτῆρες ἑκατὸν ἑξ-
ήκοντα· τούτων ὁ μέγιστος ἦν μετρητῶν ἕξ, ὁ δὲ
e ἐλάχιστος | δύο. ταῦτα μὲν οὖν ἦν ἅπαντα ἀργυρᾶ.
ἐχόμενοι δὲ τούτων ἐπόμπευον οἱ τὰ χρυσώματα φέροντες, κρατῆρας Λακωνικοὺς τέτταρας ἔχοντας στεφάνους ἀμπελίνους < . . . > τετραμέτρητοι ἕτεροι,
Κορινθιουργεῖς δύο—οὗτοι δ᾿ εἶχον ἄνωθεν καθήμενα
περιφανῆ τετορευμένα ζῷα καὶ ἐν τῷ τραχήλῳ καὶ ἐν
ταῖς γάστραις πρόστυπα ἐπιμελῶς πεποιημένα· ἐχώρει δ᾿ ἕκαστος μετρητὰς ὀκτώ—ἐπ᾿ ἐγγυθήκαις. καὶ
ληνός, ἐν ᾗ ἦσαν βῖκοι δέκα, ὁλκεῖα δύο, ἑκάτερον
f χωροῦν μετρητὰς πέντε, κώθωνες | διμέτρητοι δύο,
ψυκτῆρες εἴκοσι δύο, ὧν ὁ μέγιστος ἐχώρει μετρητὰς

on top and large numbers of figures a cubit-and-a-half or a cubit high around their sides and on their feet. There were also ten large basins and 16 mixing-bowls, the largest of which had a capacity of 30 amphoras, the smallest of five. Then came 24 cauldrons that could be bolted shut, all set on stands *(enguthēkai)*[92]; two silver wine-presses with 24 transport-jars on top of them; a table 12 cubits long made entirely of silver; and 30 other tables six cubits long. In addition there were four tripods, one with a circumference of 16 cubits and made entirely of silver, while the other three were smaller but had precious stones set in their centers. After these came 80 silver Delphic tripods smaller than the ones mentioned earlier; their corners . . . with a capacity of four amphoras; 26 water-jars; 16 Panathenaic amphoras; and 160 wine-cooling vessels, the largest of which had a capacity of six amphoras, the smallest of two. All these vessels were made of silver. Close behind them marched the men who carried the gold vessels, which were four Spartan mixing-bowls with grapevine garlands . . . Others with a capacity of four amphoras, two of Corinthian workmanship—these had seated figures in high relief on the upper part and carefully executed figures in low relief on the neck and sides, and each had a capacity of eight amphoras—on stands. Also a wine-press with ten transport jars on it; two large basins, each with a capacity of five amphoras; two *kōthōnes*[93] with a capacity of two amphoras; and 22 wine-

---

[92] This item in the catalogue is quoted again at 5.209f.

[93] A type of drinking cup; see 11.483b–4c, where this item in Callixeinus' catalogue is quoted again.

---

[26] λέβητες ἓξ A

τριάκοντα, ὁ δὲ ἐλάχιστος μετρητήν. ἐπόμπευσαν δὲ
τρίποδες χρυσοῖ μεγάλοι τέτταρες· καὶ χρυσωματο-
θήκη χρυσῆ διάλιθος πηχῶν δέκα ὕψος, ἔχουσα
βασμοὺς ἕξ, ἐν οἷς καὶ ζῷα τετραπάλαιστα ἐπιμελῶς
πεποιημένα, πολλὰ τὸν ἀριθμόν· καὶ κυλικεῖα δύο καὶ
ὑάλινα διάχρυσα δύο· ἐγγυθῆκαι χρυσαῖ τετραπήχεις
200   δύο, ἄλλαι ἐλάττους τρεῖς, || ὑδρίαι δέκα, βωμὸς
τρίπηχυς, μαζονόμια εἴκοσι πέντε. μετὰ δὲ ταῦτα
ἐπορεύοντο παῖδες χίλιοι καὶ ἑξακόσιοι ἐνδεδυκότες
χιτῶνας λευκούς, ἐστεφανωμένοι οἱ μὲν κισσῷ, οἱ δὲ
πίτυι· ὧν διακόσιοι μὲν καὶ πεντήκοντα χοεῖς εἶχον
χρυσοῦς, τετρακόσιοι δὲ ἀργυροῦς, ἕτεροι δὲ τριακόσιοι καὶ εἴκοσι ψυκτήρια ἔφερον χρυσᾶ, οἱ δὲ ἀργυρᾶ. μεθ᾽ οὓς ἄλλοι παῖδες ἔφερον κεράμια πρὸς τὴν
τοῦ γλυκισμοῦ χρείαν, ὧν εἴκοσι μὲν ἦν χρυσᾶ,
πεντήκοντα δὲ ἀργυρᾶ, τριακόσια δὲ κεκηρογρα-
b   φημένα | χρώμασι παντοίοις. καὶ κερασθέντων ἐν ταῖς
ὑδρίαις καὶ πίθοις πάντες κοσμίως ἐγλυκάνθησαν οἱ
ἐν τῷ σταδίῳ.

Ἑξῆς τούτοις καταλέγει τετραπήχεις τραπέζας, ἐφ᾽
ὧν πολλὰ θέας ἄξια πολυτελῶς κατεσκευασμένα περι-
ήγετο θεάματα. ἐν οἷς καὶ ὁ τῆς Σεμέλης θάλαμος, ἐν
ᾧ ἔχουσαι χιτῶνας τινὲς διαχρύσους καὶ λιθοκολ-
λήτους τῶν πολυτιμήτων. οὐκ ἄξιον δ᾽ ἦν παραλιπεῖν
τήνδε τὴν τετράκυκλον, μῆκος οὖσαν πηχῶν εἴκοσι
c   δύο, πλάτος δεκατεσσάρων, ὑπὸ | ἀνδρῶν ἑλκομένην
πεντακοσίων· ἐφ᾽ ἧς ἄντρον ἦν βαθὺ καθ᾽ ὑπερβολὴν
κισσῷ καὶ μίλῳ. ἐκ τούτου περιστεραὶ καὶ φάσσαι καὶ

cooling vessels, the largest of which had a capacity of 30 amphoras, the smallest a capacity of one. Four large gold tripods followed in the procession; also a gold storage chest for gold vessels, which was set with precious stones and ten cubits tall, with six shelves on which were a large number of carefully executed figures four palms[94] high. Also two cup-stands and two gilded vessels made of glass; two gold stands four cubits high, and three other smaller ones; ten water-jars; an altar three cubits long; and 25 platters. After these items came 1600 boys wearing white tunics and garlands, some of ivy and some of pine. 250 boys held gold pitchers, 400 held silver pitchers, and another 320 carried gold wine-cooling vessels, while the others carried silver ones. After them came other boys carrying jars used for sweets, 20 of them made of gold and 50 of silver, while 300 had encaustic decoration in various colors. When the contents of the water-jars and the wine-casks were mixed together, everyone in the stadium got a slight whiff of the sweet smell.

Immediately after these items he lists tables four cubits long, on top of which numerous expensively prepared spectacles well worth seeing were carried around. Among these was Semele's[95] bedroom, in which some of the female figures wore gilded tunics set with precious stones. It would not be right to pass over this four-wheeled cart, which was 22 cubits long and 14 cubits wide and was hauled by 500 men. On top of it was a cave very deeply covered by ivy and smilax. Pigeons, ringdoves, and turtledoves

94 About 16 inches.
95 Semele was Dionysus' mortal mother.

ATHENAEUS

τρυγόνες καθ' ὅλην ἐξίπταντο τὴν ὁδόν, λημνίσκοις
τοὺς πόδας δεδεμέναι πρὸς τὸ ῥᾳδίως ὑπὸ τῶν θεω-
μένων ἁρπάζεσθαι. ἀνέβλυζον δὲ ἐξ αὐτοῦ καὶ κρου-
νοὶ δύο, ὁ μὲν γάλακτος, ὁ δὲ οἴνου. πᾶσαι δ' αἱ περὶ
αὐτὸν νύμφαι στεφάνους εἶχον χρυσοῦς, ὁ δὲ Ἑρμῆς
καὶ κηρύκειον χρυσοῦν, ἐσθῆτας δὲ πολυτελεῖς. ἐπὶ δὲ
d ἄλλης τετρακύκλου, ἣ περιεῖχε τὴν | ἐξ Ἰνδῶν κάθ-
οδον Διονύσου, Διόνυσος ἦν δωδεκάπηχυς ἐπ' ἐλέφαντος κατακείμενος, ἠμφιεσμένος πορφυρίδα καὶ στέφανον κισσοῦ καὶ ἀμπέλου χρυσοῦν ἔχων· εἶχε δ' ἐν ταῖς
χερσὶ θυρσόλογχον χρυσοῦν, ὑπεδέδετο δ' ἐμβάδας
χρυσορραφεῖς. προεκάθητο δ' αὐτοῦ ἐπὶ τῷ τραχήλῳ
τοῦ ἐλέφαντος σατυρίσκος πεντάπηχυς ἐστεφανωμέ-
νος πίτυος στεφάνῳ χρυσῷ, τῇ δεξιᾷ χειρὶ αἰγείῳ
κέρατι χρυσῷ σημαίνων. ὁ δὲ ἐλέφας σκευὴν εἶχε
e χρυσῆν καὶ περὶ τῷ τραχήλῳ | κίσσινον χρυσοῦν
στέφανον. ἠκολούθουν δὲ τούτῳ παιδίσκαι πεντακόσιαι κεκοσμημέναι χιτῶσι πορφυροῖς, χρυσῷ διε-
ζωσμέναι. ἐστεφάνωντο δὲ αἱ μὲν ἡγούμεναι ἑκατὸν
εἴκοσι χρυσοῖς πιτυΐνοις στεφάνοις, ἠκολούθουν δ'
αὐταῖς σάτυροι ἑκατὸν εἴκοσι, πανοπλίας οἱ μὲν ἀργυρᾶς, οἱ δὲ χαλκᾶς ἔχοντες. μετὰ δὲ τούτους ἐπορεύοντο ὄνων ἶλαι πέντε, ἐφ' ὧν ἦσαν σιληνοὶ καὶ σάτυροι ἐστεφανωμένοι. τῶν δὲ ὄνων οἱ μὲν χρυσᾶς, οἱ δὲ
f ἀργυρᾶς προμετωπίδας καὶ σκευασίας | εἶχον. μετὰ
δὲ τούτους ἐλεφάντων ἅρματα ἀφείθη εἴκοσι τέτταρα
καὶ συνωρίδες τράγων ἑξήκοντα, κώλων δεκαδύο, ὀρύ-
γων ἑπτά, βουβάλων δεκαπέντε, στρουθῶν συνωρίδες

flew out of this along the whole course of the procession, and wool ribbons were tied to their feet to make them easy for the spectators to catch. Two springs, one of milk and the other of wine, gushed forth from it; all the nymphs around it wore gold garlands, and Hermes carried a gold messenger's staff and wore expensive clothing.[96] On another four-wheeled cart, which contained the scene of Dionysus' return from India,[97] was a 12-cubit-tall Dionysus lying on an elephant and wearing a purple robe and a gold garland made to resemble ivy and grapevines. He held a gold thyrsus-lance in his hands and wore shoes with gold stitching on his feet. Sitting in front of him on the elephant's neck was a small satyr five cubits high wearing a gold garland made to resemble pine, and gesturing with his right hand with a gold goat-horn. The elephant had gold trappings and a gold garland made to resemble ivy around its neck. It was followed by 500 girls dressed in purple tunics and gold belts. The 120 who led the way wore gold garlands made to resemble pine, and were followed by 120 satyrs, some of whom wore silver armor, the others bronze. After them came five troops of donkeys with silens and satyrs wearing garlands mounted on them. Some of the donkeys had gold frontlets and gear, the others silver. After them 24 carts drawn by elephants were sent out, along with 60 teams of billy-goats, 12 teams of hornless goats, seven teams of oryxes[98], 15 teams of bubales, eight

---

[96] The scene depicted must have been the presentation of the baby Dionysus to the nymphs on Mt. Nysa by Hermes (e.g. *hHom.* 26.3–5; cf. 2.38d).　　　　[97] After his conquests there (D.S. 4.3.1).　　　　[98] Like bubales and most likely *onelaphoi* (literally "donkey-deer"; mentioned below), a type of African antelope.

ὀκτώ, ὀνελάφων ἑπτά, καὶ συνωρίδες τέσσαρες ὄνων
ἀγρίων, ἅρματα τέσσαρα. ἐπὶ δὲ πάντων τούτων ἀν-
εβεβήκει παιδάρια χιτῶνας ἔχοντα ἡνιοχικοὺς καὶ
πετάσους. παρανεβεβήκει δὲ παιδισκάρια διεσκευ-
ασμένα πελταρίοις καὶ θυρσολόγχοις, κεκοσμημένα
ἱματίοις καὶ χρυσίοις. ἐστεφάνωτο δὲ τὰ μὲν ἡνιο-
χοῦντα παιδάρια πίτυι, τὰ δὲ παιδισκάρια κισσῷ.
201 ἐπῆσαν δὲ καὶ συνωρίδες καμήλων ⟨ἕξ⟩, ἐξ ἑκατέρου ‖
μέρους τρεῖς· αἷς ἐπηκολούθουν ἀπῆναι ὑφ' ἡμιόνων
ἀγόμεναι. αὗται δ' εἶχον σκηνὰς βαρβαρικάς, ἐφ' ὧν
ἐκάθηντο γυναῖκες Ἰνδαὶ καὶ ἕτεραι κεκοσμημέναι ὡς
αἰχμάλωτοι. κάμηλοι δ' αἱ μὲν ἔφερον λιβανωτοῦ
μνᾶς τριακοσίας, σμύρνης τριακοσίας, κρόκου καὶ
κασίας καὶ κινναμώμου καὶ ἴριδος καὶ τῶν λοιπῶν
ἀρωμάτων διακοσίας. ἐχόμενοι τούτων ἦσαν Αἰθίοπες
δωροφόροι, ὧν οἱ μὲν ἔφερον ὀδόντας ἑξακοσίους,
ἕτεροι δὲ ἐβένου κορμοὺς δισχιλίους, ἄλλοι χρυσίου
b καὶ ἀργυρίου κρατῆρας ἑξήκοντα καὶ ψήγματα | χρυ-
σοῦ. μεθ' οὓς ἐπόμπευσαν κυνηγοὶ † β΄ † ἔχοντες
σιβύνας ἐπιχρύσους. ἤγοντο δὲ καὶ κύνες δισχίλιοι
τετρακόσιοι, οἱ μὲν Ἰνδοί, οἱ λοιποὶ δὲ Ὑρκανοὶ καὶ
Μολοσσοὶ καὶ ἑτέρων γενῶν. ἑξῆς ἄνδρες ἑκατὸν
πεντήκοντα φέροντες δένδρα, ἐξ ὧν ἀνήρτητο θηρία
παντοδαπὰ καὶ ὄρνεα. εἶτ' ἐφέροντο ἐν ἀγγείοις ψιτ-
τακοὶ καὶ ταῷ καὶ μελεαγρίδες καὶ φασιανοὶ ὄρνιθες
καὶ ἄλλοι Αἰθιοπικοί, πλήθει πολλοί.

Εἰπὼν δὲ καὶ ἄλλα πλεῖστα καὶ καταλέξας ζώων
c ἀγέλας ἐπιφέρει· πρόβατα Αἰθιοπικὰ ἑκατὸν | τριά-

teams of ostriches, seven teams of *onelaphoi*, four teams of onagers, and four four-horse chariots. Boys wearing charioteers' tunics and broad-brimmed hats were mounted on all of these; girls equipped with peltast shields and thyrsus-lances and dressed in robes and gold coins were mounted beside them. The boys who held the reins wore garlands of pine, the girls garlands of ivy. After them were six teams of camels, three on either side. They were followed by carts pulled by mules. The carts contained scenes depicting barbarian countries, and women from India and elsewhere sat on them dressed like war-captives. There were also she-camels loaded with 300 minas of frankincense, 300 minas of myrrh, and 200 minas of saffron, cassia, cinnamon, iris-root, and other spices. Behind them were Ethiopian tribute-bearers, some of whom carried 600 tusks, others 2000 ebony logs, and others 60 mixing-bowls full of gold and silver coins and gold-dust. After them marched † two † huntsmen holding gilded hunting-spears. Also 2400 dogs were led along; some were Indian, while the others were Hyrcanian, Molossian, and other breeds. Immediately behind them came 150 men carrying trees, from which wild animals of every sort were suspended, as well as birds. Then came an enormous number of parrots, peacocks, guinea-fowl, pheasants, and other Ethiopian birds, carried in cages.[99]

After he mentions many other things and lists various herds of animals, he adds: 130 Ethiopian sheep, 300

[99] This sentence is also preserved, in a slightly different form, at 9.387d.

κοντα, Ἀράβια τριακόσια, Εὐβοϊκὰ εἴκοσι, καὶ ὁλό-
λευκοι βόες Ἰνδικοὶ εἴκοσι ἕξ, Αἰθιοπικοὶ ὀκτώ, ἄρ-
κτος λευκὴ μεγάλη μία, παρδάλεις τέσσαρες καὶ
δέκα, πάνθηροι ἑκκαίδεκα, λυγκία τέσσαρα, ἄρκηλοι
τρεῖς, καμηλοπάρδαλις μία, ῥινόκερως Αἰθιοπικὸς εἷς.
ἑξῆς ἐπὶ τετρακύκλου Διόνυσος περὶ τὸν τῆς Ῥέας
βωμὸν καταπεφευγὼς ὅτε ὑπὸ Ἥρας ἐδιώκετο, στέφανον ἔχων χρυσοῦν, Πριάπου αὐτῷ παρεστῶτος
ἐστεφανωμένου χρυσῷ κισσίνῳ. τὸ δὲ τῆς Ἥρας
d   ἄγαλμα στεφάνην | εἶχε χρυσῆν. Ἀλεξάνδρου δὲ καὶ
Πτολεμαίου ἀγάλματα ἐστεφανωμένα στεφάνοις κισσίνοις ἐκ χρυσοῦ. τὸ δὲ τῆς Ἀρετῆς ἄγαλμα τὸ παρ-
εστὸς τῷ Πτολεμαίῳ στέφανον εἶχεν ἐλαίας χρυσοῦν.
καὶ Πρίαπος δ' αὐτοῖς συμπαρῆν ἔχων στέφανον
κίσσινον ἐκ χρυσοῦ. Κόρινθος δ' ἡ πόλις παρεστῶσα
τῷ Πτολεμαίῳ ἐστεφάνωτο διαδήματι χρυσῷ. παρέκειντο δὲ πᾶσι τούτοις κυλικεῖον μεστὸν χρυσωμάτων κρατήρ τε χρυσοῦς μετρητῶν πέντε. τῇ δὲ
τετρακύκλῳ ταύτῃ ἠκολούθουν γυναῖκες ἔχουσαι ἱμά-
e   τια πολυτελῆ | καὶ κόσμον· προσηγορεύοντο δὲ πό-
λεις, αἵ τε ἀπ' Ἰωνίας καὶ ⟨αἱ⟩ λοιπαὶ Ἑλληνίδες ὅσαι
τὴν Ἀσίαν καὶ τὰς νήσους κατοικοῦσαι ὑπὸ τοὺς
Πέρσας ἐτάχθησαν· ἐφόρουν δὲ πᾶσαι στεφάνους
χρυσοῦς. ἐφέρετο καὶ ἐπ' ἄλλων τετρακύκλων θύρσος
ἐνενηκοντάπηχυς χρυσοῦς καὶ λόγχη ἀργυρᾶ ἑξήκον-
τάπηχυς καὶ ἐν ἄλλῃ φαλλὸς χρυσοῦς πηχῶν ἑκατὸν
καὶ εἴκοσι διαγεγραμμένος καὶ διαδεδεμένος στέμ-

Arabian sheep, 20 Euboean sheep, and 26 all-white zebus, eight Ethiopian cows, a single large white bear, 14 leopards, 16 spotted wildcats, four caracals[100], three young leopards (?), one giraffe, and one Ethiopian rhinocerus. Immediately after them on a four-wheeled cart came Dionysus, who had fled to Rhea's altar when Hera was persecuting him;[101] he was wearing a gold garland, and Priapus was standing beside him wearing a gold garland made to resemble ivy. The statue of Hera wore a gold garland. Also statues of Alexander and Ptolemy[102] wearing ivy garlands made of gold. The statue of Virtue that stood next to Ptolemy wore a gold olive-garland. Priapus was also with them, wearing an ivy-garland made of gold. The city of Corinth stood next to Ptolemy wearing a gold diadem.[103] Beside all these figures lay a cup-stand full of gold vessels and a gold mixing-bowl with a capacity of five amphoras. This cart was followed by women who wore expensive robes and jewelry. They bore the names of cities, both the Ionian cities and all the other Greek cities in Asia and on the islands that had been subject to the Persians; they all wore gold garlands. Other carts carried a gold Dionysiac staff 90 cubits long and a silver spear 60 cubits long. On another cart was a gold phallus 120 cubits long; it was painted various colors and

[100] An African wildcat.　　　[101] When Dionysus was driven mad by Hera, the goddess Cybele (frequently confounded with Rhea) cleansed him and taught him her rites ([Apollod.] *Bib.* 3.5.1). Priapus (below) was an ithyphallic fertility deity often associated with Dionysus.

[102] I.e. Alexander the Great and Ptolemy I.

[103] Ptolemy had occupied the city (here personified), and also dominated the Aegean League of Islanders (see below).

μασι διαχρύσοις, ἔχων ἐπ᾽ ἄκρου ἀστέρα χρυσοῦν, οὗ
ἦν ἡ περίμετρος πηχῶν ἕξ. πολλῶν οὖν καὶ ποικίλων
f εἰρημένων | ἐν ταῖς πομπαῖς ταύταις μόνα ἐξελεξά-
μεθα ἐν οἷς ἦν χρυσὸς καὶ ἄργυρος. καὶ γὰρ διαθέσεις
πολλαὶ ἀκοῆς ἦσαν ἄξιαι καὶ θηρίων πλήθη καὶ
ἵππων καὶ λέοντες παμμεγέθεις εἴκοσι καὶ τέσσαρες.
ἦσαν δὲ καὶ ἄλλαι τετράκυκλοι οὐ μόνον εἰκόνας
βασιλέων φέρουσαι, ἀλλὰ καὶ θεῶν πολλαί. μεθ᾽ ἃς
χορὸς ἐπόμπευσεν ἀνδρῶν ἑξακοσίων· ἐν οἷς κιθαρι-
σταὶ συνεφώνουν τριακόσιοι, ἐπιχρύσους ἔχοντες
202 ὅλας κιθάρας καὶ στεφάνους χρυσοῦς. ‖ μεθ᾽ οὓς
ταῦροι διῆλθον δισχίλιοι ὁμοιοχρώματοι χρυσόκερῳ,
προμετωπίδας χρυσᾶς καὶ ἀνὰ μέσον στεφάνους ὅρ-
μους τε καὶ αἰγίδας πρὸ τῶν στηθῶν ἔχοντες· ἦν δ᾽
ἅπαντα ταῦτα χρυσᾶ. καὶ μετὰ ταῦτα Διὸς ἤγετο
πομπὴ καὶ ἄλλων παμπόλλων θεῶν καὶ ἐπὶ πᾶσιν
Ἀλεξάνδρου, ὃς ἐφ᾽ ἅρματος ἐλεφάντων ἀληθινῶν
ἐφέρετο χρυσοῦς, Νίκην καὶ Ἀθηνᾶν ἐξ ἑκατέρου
μέρους ἔχων. ἐπόμπευσαν δὲ καὶ θρόνοι πολλοὶ ἐξ
ἐλέφαντος καὶ χρυσοῦ κατεσκευασμένοι· ὧν ἐφ᾽ ἑνὸς
b ἔκειτο στεφάνη χρυσῆ, ἐπ᾽ ἄλλου | δίκερας χρυσοῦν,
ἐπ᾽ ἄλλου δὲ ἦν στέφανος χρυσοῦς, καὶ ἐπ᾽ ἄλλου δὲ
κέρας ὁλόχρυσον. ἐπὶ δὲ τὸν Πτολεμαίου τοῦ Σωτῆρος
θρόνον στέφανος ἐπέκειτο ἐκ μυρίων κατεσκευασμέ-
νος χρυσιῶν. ἐπόμπευσε δὲ καὶ θυμιατήρια χρυσᾶ
τριακόσια καὶ πεντήκοντα, καὶ βωμοὶ δὲ ἐπίχρυσοι
ἐστεφανωμένοι χρυσοῖς στεφάνοις· ὧν ἑνὶ παρεπεπή-
γεσαν δᾷδες χρυσαῖ δεκαπήχεις τέσσαρες. ἐπόμπευ-

wrapped in strips of gilt cloth, and had a gold star six cubits in circumference at its tip. Although many other items of different sorts were mentioned as part of these processions, I selected only those that included gold and silver. For there were many things put on display worth hearing about, including a large number of wild animals and horses, and 24 huge lions. There were also other four-wheeled carts, which did not only carry images of kings, because many carried images of gods. After them in the procession marched a chorus of 600 men, with 300 lyre-players among them playing in harmony and holding lyres entirely covered with gold and gold garlands. After them 2000 bulls, all the same color and with their horns gilded, passed through. They wore gold frontlets, garlands between their horns, and necklaces and aegises on their chests; all these items were made of gold. After this there was a procession dedicated to Zeus and a large number of other gods, and after all of them to Alexander, who was made of gold and carried on a cart pulled by real elephants, with Victory and Athena on either side of him. Many thrones made of ivory and gold were also carried in the procession; a gold crown lay on one of them, a gold double horn on another, a gold garland on another, and a horn of solid gold on another. A garland made of 10000 gold coins lay on the throne of Ptolemy Soter. 350 gold incense-burners were also carried in the procession, as were gilded altars decorated with gold garlands; four gold torches 10 cubits high had been fastened to one of them.

σαν δὲ καὶ ἐσχάραι ἐπίχρυσοι δύο, ὧν ἡ μὲν δωδεκάπηχυς τῇ περιμέτρῳ, τεσσαρακοντάπηχυς ὕψει, ἡ δὲ
πηχῶν πεντεκαίδεκα. ἐπόμπευσαν δὲ καὶ Δελφικοὶ

c τρίποδες | χρυσοῖ ἐννέα ἐκ πηχῶν τεσσάρων, ἄλλοι
ὀκτὼ <ἐκ> πηχῶν ἕξ, ἄλλος πηχῶν τριάκοντα, ἐφ᾽ οὗ
ἦν ζῷα χρυσᾶ πενταπήχη καὶ στέφανος κύκλῳ χρυσοῦς ἀμπέλινος. παρῆλθον δὲ καὶ φοίνικες ἐπίχρυσοι
ὀκταπήχεις ἑπτὰ καὶ κηρύκειον ἐπίχρυσον πηχῶν
τεσσαράκοντα πέντε καὶ κεραυνὸς ἐπίχρυσος πηχῶν
τεσσαράκοντα ναός τε ἐπίχρυσος, οὗ ἡ περίμετρος
πηχῶν τεσσαράκοντα· δίκερας πρὸς τούτοις ὀκτά-
πηχυ. πολὺ δὲ καὶ ζῴων πλῆθος ἐπιχρύσων συνεπόμ-

d πευεν, ὧν ἦν τὰ πολλὰ δωδεκαπήχη· | καὶ θηρία
ὑπεράγοντα τοῖς μεγέθεσι καὶ ἀετοὶ πηχῶν εἴκοσι.
στέφανοί τε χρυσοῖ ἐπόμπευσαν τρισχίλιοι διακόσιοι, ἕτερός τε μυστικὸς χρυσοῦς λίθοις πολυτελέσι
κεκοσμημένος ὀγδοηκοντάπηχυς· οὗτος δὲ περιετίθετο
τῷ τοῦ Βερενικείου θυρώματι· αἰγίς τε ὁμοίως χρυσῆ.
ἐπόμπευσαν δὲ καὶ στεφάναι χρυσαῖ πάνυ πολλαί, ἃς
ἔφερον παιδίσκαι πολυτελῶς κεκοσμημέναι· ὧν μία
δίπηχυς εἰς ὕψος, τὴν δὲ περίμετρον ἔχουσα ἑκκαί-

e δεκα πηχῶν. ἐπόμπευσε δὲ καὶ θώραξ χρυσοῦς |
πηχῶν δώδεκα καὶ ἕτερος ἀργυροῦς πηχῶν ὀκτωκαίδεκα[27], ἔχων ἐφ᾽ ἑαυτοῦ κεραυνοὺς χρυσοῦς δεκαπήχεις δύο καὶ στέφανον δρυὸς διάλιθον· ἀσπίδες
χρυσαῖ εἴκοσι, πανοπλίαι χρυσαῖ τέσσαρες καὶ ἑξήκοντα, κνημῖδες χρυσαῖ τριπήχεις δύο, λεκάναι χρυσαῖ δεκαδύο, φιάλαι πολλαὶ πάνυ τὸν ἀριθμόν, οἰ-

Two gilded braziers were also carried in the procession; one was 12 cubits in circumference and 40 cubits high, while the other was 15 cubits in circumference. Nine gold Delphic tripods about four cubits high were also carried in the procession, along with eight others about six cubits high, and another 30 cubits high that had gold figures five cubits high on it and a gold garland made to resemble grapevines around it. Seven gilded palmtrees eight cubits high also passed by, along with a gilded herald's staff 45 cubits long, a gilded lightning bolt 40 cubits long, and a gilded shrine 40 cubits in circumference; and in addition to these an eight-cubit double horn. A large number of gilded figures were also carried in the procession, many 12 cubits high; also extraordinarily large wild animals and eagles 20 cubits high. 3200 gold garlands were carried in the procession, along with another gold initiate's garland 80 cubits in size set with precious stones—this was placed around the doorway of Berenice's shrine—and likewise a gold aegis. An immense number of gold crowns were also carried in the procession by expensively dressed girls; one crown was two cubits high and 16 cubits in circumference. A gold breastplace 12 cubits long was also carried in the procession, along with another made of silver that was 18 cubits long and had two gold lightning bolts ten cubits long on it and a garland of oak-leaves set with jewels. Also 20 gold shields; 64 sets of gold armor; two sets of gold greaves three cubits high; 12 gold basins; a very large number of

---

[27] ιη´ (i.e. ὀκτωκαίδεκα) ἐννέα A

νοχόαι τριάκοντα, ἐξάλειπτρα μεγάλα δέκα, ὑδρίαι
δεκαδύο, μαζονόμια πεντήκοντα, τράπεζαι διάφοροι,
κυλικεῖα χρυσωμάτων πέντε, κέρας ὁλόχρυσον πηχῶν

f τριάκοντα. | ταῦτα δὲ τὰ χρυσώματα ἐκτὸς ἦν τῶν ἐν
τῇ τοῦ Διονύσου πομπῇ διενεχθέντων. εἶτ᾿ ἀργυρωμάτων ἄμαξαι τετρακόσιαι καὶ χρυσωμάτων εἴκοσι,
ἀρωμάτων δὲ ὀκτακόσιαι. ἐπὶ δὲ πᾶσιν ἐπόμπευσαν αἱ
δυνάμεις αἱ ἱππικαὶ καὶ πεζικαί, πᾶσαι καθωπλισμέ-
ναι θαυμασίως. πεζοὶ μὲν εἰς πέντε μυριάδας καὶ
ἑπτακισχιλίους καὶ ἑξακοσίους, ἱππεῖς δὲ δισμύριοι

203 τρισχίλιοι διακόσιοι. ‖ πάντες δ᾿ οὗτοι ἐπόμπευσαν
τὴν ἁρμόζουσαν ἑκάστῳ ἠμφιεσμένοι στολὴν καὶ τὰς
προσηκούσας ἔχοντες πανοπλίας. ἐκτὸς δ᾿ ὧν πάντες
οὗτοι εἶχον πανοπλιῶν καὶ ἄλλαι πλεῖσται ἦσαν ἀπο-
κείμεναι, ὧν οὐδὲ τὸν ἀριθμὸν ἀναγράψαι ῥάδιον·
κατέλεξε δ᾿ αὐτὸν ὁ Καλλίξεινος. ἐστεφανώθησαν δ᾿
ἐν τῷ ἀγῶνι καὶ στεφάνοις χρυσοῖς ⟨καὶ⟩ εἴκοσι
Πτολεμαῖος δὲ ὁ πρῶτος καὶ Βερενίκη εἴκοσι τρισὶν
ἐφ᾿ ἁρμάτων χρυσῶν καὶ τεμένεσιν ἐν Δωδώνῃ. καὶ

b ἐγένετο τὸ δαπάνημα τοῦ | νομίσματος τάλαντα δισ-
χίλια διακόσια τριάκοντα ἐννέα, μναῖ πεντήκοντα· καὶ
ταῦτ᾿ ἠριθμήθη πάντα τοῖς οἰκονόμοις διὰ τὴν τῶν
στεφανούντων προθυμίαν πρὸ τοῦ τὰς θέας παρελθεῖν. ὁ δὲ Φιλάδελφος Πτολεμαῖος υἱὸς αὐτῶν εἴκοσι
χρυσαῖς δυσὶ μὲν ἐφ᾿ ἁρμάτων χρυσῶν, ἐπὶ δὲ κιόνων
ἑξαπήχει μιᾷ, πενταπήχεσι πέντε, τετραπήχεσι ἕξ.

Ποία, ἄνδρες δαιτυμόνες, βασιλεία οὕτως γέγονε
πολύχρυσος; οὐ γὰρ τὰ ἐκ Περσῶν καὶ Βαβυλῶνος

libation bowls; 30 wine-pitchers; ten large unguent-flasks; 12 water-jars; 50 platters; various tables; five cup-stands for gold vessels; and a solid gold horn 30 cubits long. These gold vessels did not include those carried in the procession of Dionysus. Then there were 400 carts loaded with silver vessels, 20 loaded with gold vessels, and 800 loaded with spices. After all these the cavalry and infantry forces, all marvellously outfitted, moved in procession. There were about 57600 infantry and 23200 cavalry. All of them marched in the procession wearing the clothing that was right for them and outfitted in the appropriate armor. In addition to the suits of armor worn by all these men, there were a substantial number of others in storage; it is not very easy to offer a full count of them, but Callixeinus computed the number. Victors in the contest were honored with gold garlands and portrait-statues, and Ptolemy I and Berenice were honored with three portrait-statues carried on gold carts, as well as with sacred precincts in Dodona. The cost in coined money was 2239 talents and 50 minas, and the entire sum was paid to the officials in charge before the shows were over, as a result of the enthusiasm of those who provided the garlands. Ptolemy Philadelphus, their son, was honored with two gold portrait-statues carried on gold carts and set on columns, one six cubits high, while five were five cubits high, and six were four cubits high.

What kingdom, my fellow diners, has ever been so rich in gold? Certainly not the one that seized the wealth of

c λαβοῦσα χρήματα ἢ μέταλλα | ἐργασαμένη ἢ Πακτω-
λὸν ἔχουσα χρυσοῦν ψῆγμα καταφέροντα. μόνος γὰρ
ὡς ἀληθῶς ὁ χρυσορόας καλούμενος Νεῖλος μετὰ
τροφῶν ἀφθόνων καὶ χρυσὸν ἀκίβδηλον καταφέρει
ἀκινδύνως γεωργούμενον, ὡς πᾶσιν ἐξαρκεῖν ἀνθρώποις, δίκην Τριπτολέμου πεμπόμενον εἰς πᾶσαν γῆν.
διόπερ αὐτὸν καὶ ὁ Βυζάντιος ποιητὴς Παρμένων
ἐπικαλούμενος

Αἰγύπτιε Ζεῦ (φησί) Νεῖλε.

πολλῶν δὲ ὁ Φιλάδελφος βασιλέων πλούτῳ διέφερε
d καὶ περὶ πάντα ἐσπουδάκει | τὰ κατασκευάσματα
φιλοτίμως, ὥστε καὶ πλοίων πλήθει πάντας ὑπερ-
έβαλλεν. τὰ γοῦν μέγιστα τῶν πλοίων ἦν παρ' αὐτῷ
τριακοντήρεις δύο, εἰκοσήρης μία, τέσσαρες δὲ τρισ-
καιδεκήρεις, δωδεκήρεις δύο, ἑνδεκήρεις δεκατέσσα-
ρες, ἐννήρεις τριάκοντα, ἑπτήρεις ἑπτὰ καὶ τριάκοντα,
ἑξήρεις πέντε, πεντήρεις δεκαεπτά· τὰ δ' ἀπὸ τετρή-
ρους μέχρι τριημιολίας διπλάσια τούτων. τὰ δ' εἰς τὰς
νήσους πεμπόμενα καὶ τὰς ἄλλας πόλεις ὧν ἦρχε καὶ
e τὴν Λιβύην πλείονα ἦν τῶν τετρακισχιλίων. | περὶ δὲ
βιβλίων πλήθους καὶ βιβλιοθηκῶν κατασκευῆς καὶ
τῆς εἰς τὸ Μουσεῖον συναγωγῆς τί δεῖ καὶ λέγειν,
πᾶσι τούτων ὄντων κατὰ μνήμην; ἐπεὶ δὲ περὶ νεῶν

---

[104] Triptolemus offered Demeter information about her kid-
napped daughter, and she rewarded him with the secret of agri-
culture, which he spread throughout the world (e.g. Orph. 397 F

Persia and Babylon, or worked mines or controlled the river Pactolus, which carries gold-dust down from the mountains. Only the Nile, appropriately referred to as "flowing with gold," carries downstream not just immense amounts of food but pure gold that can be farmed without risk and that produces enough for the whole human race when it is sent out into the entire world like Triptolemus.[104] This is why, when the poet Parmenon of Byzantium (fr. 3, p. 237 Powell) invokes it, he says:

Egyptian Zeus, the Nile.

Philadelphus was richer than many kings and made a vigorous effort to win glory in everything he did, and as a result he outdid everyone in the number of ships he had. His largest ships, at any rate, were two "30s,"[105] one "20," four "13s," two "12s," 14 "11s," 30 "nines," 37 "sevens," five "sixes" and 17 "fives"; and there were twice this many in the range from "fours" to "triple one-and-a-halfs." The number of ships sent to the islands, the other cities he controlled, and Libya was greater than 4000. And what need is there to mention the immense number of books he owned, the number of libraries he developed, and the resources he brought together in the Museum, given that everyone remembers this? But since we are on the subject

Bernabé ap. Paus. 1.14.3; S. fr. 598; Olson on Ar. *Ach*. 47–8). Egypt was famous for its massive exports of grain, which made the Ptolemies (and later the Roman emperors) immensely rich.

[105] Ships in this period appear to be described by the number of men set to work each set of oars, which were divided into three superimposed banks. The "40" described below is the largest ship known in antiquity.

ATHENAEUS

κατασκευῆς εἰρήκαμεν, φέρ' εἴπωμεν (ἀκοῆς γάρ
ἐστιν ἄξια) καὶ τὰ ὑπὸ τοῦ Φιλοπάτορος βασιλέως
κατεσκευασμένα σκάφη. περὶ ὧν ὁ αὐτὸς Καλλίξεινος
ἱστορεῖ ἐν τῷ πρώτῳ Περὶ Ἀλεξανδρείας οὑτωσὶ λέ-
γων· τὴν τεσσαρακοντήρη ναῦν κατεσκεύασεν ὁ Φιλο-
f πάτωρ τὸ μῆκος ἔχουσαν διακοσίων | ὀγδοήκοντα
πηχῶν, ὀκτὼ δὲ καὶ τριάκοντα ἀπὸ παρόδου ἐπὶ πάροδον, ὕψος δὲ ἕως ἀκροστολίου τεσσαράκοντα ὀκτὼ
πηχῶν. ἀπὸ δὲ τῶν πρυμνητικῶν ἀφλάστων ἐπὶ τὸ τῇ
θαλάσσῃ μέρος αὐτῆς τρεῖς πρὸς τοῖς πεντήκοντα
πήχεις. πηδάλια δ' εἶχε τέτταρα τριακονταπήχη, κώ-
πας δὲ θρανιτικὰς ὀκτὼ καὶ τριάκοντα πηχῶν τὰς
204 μεγίστας, ‖ αἳ διὰ τὸ μόλυβδον ἔχειν ἐν τοῖς ἐγχει-
ριδίοις καὶ γεγονέναι λίαν εἴσω βαρεῖαι κατὰ τὴν
ζύγωσιν εὐήρεις ὑπῆρχον ἐπὶ τῆς χρείας. δίπρωρος δ'
ἐγεγόνει καὶ δίπρυμνος καὶ ἔμβολα εἶχεν ἑπτά· τούτων ἓν μὲν ἡγούμενον, τὰ δ' ὑποστέλλοντα, τινὰ δὲ
κατὰ τὰς ἐπωτίδας. ὑποζώματα δὲ ἐλάμβανε δώδεκα·
ἑξακοσίων δ' ἦν ἕκαστον πηχῶν. εὔρυθμος δ' ἦν καθ'
ὑπερβολήν. θαυμαστὸς δ' ἦν καὶ ὁ ἄλλος κόσμος τῆς
νεώς· ζῷα μὲν γὰρ εἶχεν οὐκ ἐλάττω δώδεκα πηχῶν
b κατὰ πρύμναν τε καὶ κατὰ πρῶραν, | καὶ πᾶς τόπος
αὐτῆς κηρογραφίᾳ κατεπεποίκιλτο, τὸ δ' ἔγκωπον
ἅπαν μέχρι τῆς τρόπεως κισσίνην φυλλάδα καὶ θύρ-
σους εἶχε πέριξ. πολὺς δ' ἦν καὶ ὁ τῶν ὅπλων κόσμος·
ἀνεπλήρου δὲ τὰ προσδεόμενα τῆς νεὼς μέρη. γενομένης δὲ ἀναπείρας ἐδέξατο ἐρέτας πλείους τῶν τετρα-
κισχιλίων, εἰς δὲ τὰς ὑπηρεσίας τετρακοσίους, εἰς δὲ

480

of shipbuilding, come—these things are worth hearing about—let me discuss the vessels constructed by King Philopator.[106] The same Callixeinus offers an account of them in Book I of *On Alexandria* (*FGrH* 627 F 1), where he says the following: Philopator built a "40" that was 280 cubits long, 38 cubits from gangway to gangway, and 48 cubits high to the top of the prow ornament; from the tip of the stern-ornament to its waterline was 53 cubits. It had four steering-oars, each 30 cubits long, and thranite oars[107] (which were the longest) 38 cubits long; because the oars had lead in the handles and were very heavy inboard, the way they were balanced made them easy to row with. The ship had two prows, two sterns, and seven rams; one was the chief ram, while the others were smaller, and some were set on the outrigger cheeks. It required 12 undergirds, each 600 cubits long. It was very well-proportioned. The rest of the ship's decoration was remarkable: it had figures no less than 12 cubits high on the stern and the prow; every part of it had been decorated in encaustic; and the entire portion of the ship that housed the oars was covered with ivy leaves and Dionysiac staffs down to the keel. The ship's gear was also elaborately decorated, and the other parts of the ship that could accept ornamentation were full of it. When a sailing-trial took place, it took more than 4000 rowers on board, along with about 400 crewmen and

[106] Ptolemy IV (reigned 221–204 BCE).
[107] The uppermost of the three banks of oars, and thus necessarily the longest.

τὸ κατάστρωμα ἐπιβάτας τρισχιλίους ἀποδέοντας
ἑκατὸν καὶ πεντήκοντα· καὶ χωρὶς ὑπὸ τὰ ζύγια
c πλῆθος ἀνθρώπων ἕτερον ἐπισιτισμοῦ τε | οὐκ ὀλίγον.
καθειλκύσθη δὲ τὴν μὲν ἀρχὴν ἀπὸ ἐσχαρίου τινός, ὅ
φασι παγῆναι πεντήκοντα πλοίων πεντηρικῶν ξυλείᾳ,
ὑπὸ δὲ ὄχλου μετὰ βοῆς καὶ σαλπίγγων κατήγετο.
ὕστερον δὲ τῶν ἀπὸ Φοινίκης τις ἐπενόησε τὴν καθολ-
κήν, τάφρον ὑποστησάμενος ἴσην τῇ νηὶ κατὰ μῆκος,
ἣν πλησίον τοῦ λιμένος ὤρυξε. ταύτῃ δὲ τοὺς θεμε-
λίους κατῳκοδόμησε λίθῳ στερεῷ πρὸς πέντε πήχεις
τὸ βάθος, καὶ διὰ τούτων φάλαγγας ἐπικαρσίας κατὰ
d πλάτος τῆς τάφρου διώσας συνεχεῖς τετραπήχυν | εἰς
βάθος τόπον ἀπολειπούσας. καὶ ποιήσας εἴσρουν ἀπὸ
τῆς θαλάσσης ἐνέπλησεν αὐτῆς πάντα τὸν ὀρυχθέντα
τόπον, εἰς ὃν ῥᾳδίως ὑπὸ τῶν τυχόντων ἀνδρῶν εἰσ-
ήγαγε τὴν ναῦν ‹ . . . › τὸ ἀνοιχθὲν κατ᾽ ἀρχὰς
ἐμφράξαντας μετεξαντλῆσαι πάλιν τὴν θάλασσαν
ὀργάνοις· τούτου δὲ γενομένου ἐδρασθῆναι τὸ πλοῖον
ἀσφαλῶς ἐπὶ τῶν προειρημένων φαλάγγων.

Κατεσκεύασεν δ᾽ ὁ Φιλοπάτωρ καὶ ποτάμιον πλοῖον, τὴν θαλαμηγὸν καλουμένην, τὸ μῆκος ἔχουσαν
ἡμισταδίου, τὸ δὲ εὖρος ᾗ πλατύτατον τριάκοντα πη-
e χῶν· τὸ δὲ ὕψος | σὺν τῷ τῆς σκηνῆς ἀναστήματι
μικρὸν ἀπέδει τεσσαράκοντα πηχῶν. τὸ δὲ σχῆμα
αὐτῆς οὔτε ταῖς μακραῖς ναυσὶν οὔτε ταῖς στρογ-
γύλαις ἐοικός, ἀλλὰ παρηλλαγμένον τι καὶ πρὸς τὴν
χρείαν τοῦ ποταμοῦ τὸ βάθος. κάτωθεν μὲν γὰρ ἁλι-
τενὴς καὶ πλατεῖα, τῷ δ᾽ ὄγκῳ μετέωρος· τὰ δ᾽ ἐπὶ τῶν

2850 marines on deck; apart from them, there was another large group of people and a considerable amount of provisions below deck. It was originally launched from a sort of platform, which they say was constructed with the wood from 50 "fives," and was hauled into the water by a large crowd of men accompanied by shouting and trumpets. Later a Phoenician conceived a way to launch it by digging a ditch near the harbor as long as the ship. He built a foundation for the ditch about five cubits deep out of hard rock, and all along its length he set transverse rollers, placing them continuously so that they left a space four cubits deep.[108] After he cut a channel from the sea, he filled the entire excavated area with sea-water, and easily brought the ship into it with common laborers ... After they barred the opening at its entrance, they drained out the sea-water again with mechanical pumps; when this was done, the ship sat securely on the rollers mentioned above.

Philopator also built a river-boat, the so-called *thalamēgos* ("house-boat"), which was half a stade long and 30 cubits wide at its broadest point; its height, including the pavilion when it was set up, was slightly less than 40 cubits. Its shape was unlike either long ships or round ships,[109] but had been altered a bit in its draft to make it usable on the river. For it was shallow and flat below, but rose up high

---

[108] The rollers were one cubit high, and thus decreased the effective depth of the ditch by that amount.

[109] Warships and merchant vessels, respectively.

ἄκρων αὐτῆς μέρη καὶ μάλιστα τὰ κατὰ πρῷραν
παρέτεινεν ἐφ᾽ ἱκανόν, τῆς ἀνακλάσεως εὐγράμμου
φαινομένης. δίπρῳρος δ᾽ ἐγεγόνει καὶ δίπρυμνος καὶ

f πρὸς ὕψος ἀνέτεινε διὰ τὸ μετέωρον ἄγαν | ἵστασθαι
πολλάκις ἐν τῷ ποταμῷ τὸ κῦμα. κατεσκεύαστο δ᾽
αὐτῆς κατὰ μὲν μέσον τὸ κύτος τὰ συμπόσια καὶ οἱ
κοιτῶνες καὶ τὰ λοιπὰ τὰ πρὸς τὴν διαγωγὴν χρη-
στήρια. πέριξ δὲ τῆς νεὼς περίπατοι κατὰ τὰς τρεῖς
πλευρὰς ἐγεγόνεσαν διπλοῖ. ὧν ἡ μὲν περίμετρος ἦν
πέντε πλέθρων οὐκ ἐλάττων, ἡ δὲ διάθεσις τοῦ μὲν

205 καταγείου περιστύλῳ παραπλήσιος, ‖ τοῦ δ᾽ ὑπερῴου
κρύπτη φραγμοῖς καὶ θυρίσι περιεχομένη πάντοθεν.
πρώτη δ᾽ εἰσιόντι κατὰ πρύμναν ἐτέτακτο προστὰς ἐξ
ἐναντίου μὲν ἀναπεπταμένη, κύκλῳ δὲ περίπτερος· ἧς
ἐν τῷ καταντικρὺ τῆς πρῴρας μέρει προπύλαιον κατεσκεύαστο δι᾽ ἐλέφαντος καὶ τῆς πολυτελεστάτης
ὕλης γεγονός. τοῦτο δὲ διελθοῦσιν ὡσανεὶ προσκή-
νιον ἐπεποίητο τῇ διαθέσει κατάστεγον ὄν. ᾧ πάλιν
ὁμοίως κατὰ μὲν τὴν μέσην πλευρὰν προστὰς ἑτέρα

b παρέκειτο ὄπισθεν, καὶ τετράθυρος ἔφερεν | εἰς αὐτὴν
πυλών. ἐξ ἀριστερῶν δὲ καὶ δεξιῶν θυρίδες ὑπέκειντο
εὐαερίαν παρέχουσαι. συνῆπτο δὲ τούτοις ὁ μέγιστος
οἶκος· περίπτερος δ᾽ ἦν εἴκοσι κλίνας ἐπιδεχόμενος.
κατεσκεύαστο δ᾽ αὐτοῦ τὰ μὲν πλεῖστα ἀπὸ κέδρου
σχιστῆς καὶ κυπαρίσσου Μιλησίας· αἱ δὲ τῆς περιστάσεως θύραι τὸν ἀριθμὸν εἴκοσι οὖσαι θυΐναις
κατεκεκόλληντο σανίσιν, ἐλεφαντίνους ἔχουσαι τοὺς
κόσμους. ἡ δ᾽ ἐνήλωσις ἡ κατὰ πρόσωπον αὐτῶν καὶ

with its bulk; and its ends, especially toward the prow, were quite extended, and its curve appeared graceful. It had two prows and two sterns, and projected up because of the fact that the waves in the river often rise quite high. Dining-rooms, bedrooms, and the other facilities necessary to make life onboard possible were constructed in the center of its hull. A pair of covered walkways ran around the ship on three sides. One was at least five *plethra*[110] around, while the other, below decks, was arranged like a peristyle courtyard, and the one on the upper level was arranged like a closed courtyard surrounded by screens and windows. As you came on board at the stern, there was an initial vestibule that was open in front and had a row of columns set around it. In the portion of the vestibule toward the prow an entrance-way made of ivory and very expensive wood had been constructed. After you passed through this, there was a roofed area whose structure resembled a theatrical stage-building. There was, once again, another entrance-way in the central side of this room, in the rear. A gateway with four doors led into it, and windows to the left and right provided fresh air. The largest room was connected to the ones just described; it had a row of columns set around it and room for 20 couches. Most of it had been constructed of split cedar and Milesian cypress; the 20 doors in the portico had been joined together from planks of citron-wood and decorated with ivory. The decorative

---

[110] Approximately 500 feet.

τὰ ῥόπτρα ἐξ ἐρυθροῦ γεγονότα χαλκοῦ τὴν χρύ-

c σωσιν | ἐκ πυρὸς εἰλήφει. τῶν δὲ κιόνων τὰ μὲν
σώματα ἦν κυπαρίσσινα, αἱ δὲ κεφαλαὶ Κορινθιουργεῖς, ἐλέφαντι καὶ χρυσῷ διακεκοσμημέναι. τὸ δὲ
ἐπιστύλιον ἐκ χρυσοῦ τὸ ὅλον· ἐφ᾽ οὗ διάζωσμα ἐφήρ-
μοστο περιφανῆ ζῴδια ἔχον ἐλεφάντινα μείζω πηχυ-
αίων, τῇ μὲν τέχνῃ μέτρια, τῇ χορηγίᾳ δὲ ἀξιο-
θαύμαστα. ἐπέκειτο δὲ καὶ στέγη καλὴ τῷ συμποσίῳ
τετράγωνος κυπαρισσίνη· γλυπτοὶ δ᾽ αὐτῆς ἦσαν οἱ
κόσμοι, χρυσῆν ἔχοντες τὴν ἐπιφάνειαν. παρέκειτο δὲ

d | τῷ συμποσίῳ τούτῳ καὶ κοιτὼν ἑπτάκλινος· ᾧ συν-
ῆπτο στενὴ σῦριγξ κατὰ πλάτος τοῦ κύτους χωρίζου-
σα τὴν γυναικωνῖτιν. ἐν δὲ ταύτῃ συμπόσιον ἐννεάκλινον ἦν, παραπλήσιον τῇ πολυτελείᾳ τῷ μεγάλῳ,
καὶ κοιτὼν πεντάκλινος. καὶ τὰ μὲν ἄχρι τῆς πρώτης
στέγης κατεσκευασμένα τοιαῦτ᾽ ἦν. ἀναβάντων δὲ τὰς
παρακειμένας πλησίον τῷ προειρημένῳ κοιτῶνι κλί-
μακας οἶκος ἦν ἄλλος πεντάκλινος ὀρόφωμα ῥομ-
βωτὸν ἔχων· καὶ πλησίον αὐτοῦ ναὸς Ἀφροδίτης

e θολοειδής, | ἐν ᾧ μαρμάρινον ἄγαλμα τῆς θεοῦ. κατ-
εναντίον δὲ τούτου ἄλλο συμπόσιον πολυτελὲς περί-
πτερον· οἱ γὰρ κίονες αὐτοῦ ἐκ λίθων Ἰνδικῶν συν-
έκειντο. παρὰ ⟨δὲ⟩ καὶ τούτῳ τῷ συμποσίῳ κοιτῶνες,
ἀκόλουθον τὴν κατασκευὴν τοῖς προδεδηλωμένοις
ἔχοντες. προάγοντι δὲ ἐπὶ τὴν πρῷραν οἶκος ὑπέκειτο
Βακχικὸς τρισκαιδεκάκλινος περίπτερος, ἐπίχρυσον
ἔχων τὸ γεῖσον ἕως τοῦ περιτρέχοντος ἐπιστυλίου·

studs on their fronts and the knockers, made of red bronze, had been treated with fire to make them seem to be gilded. The column-shafts were of cypress-wood, while the capitals were of Corinthian workmanship and had been ornamented with ivory and gold. The entire architrave was made of gold, and a frieze that contained striking ivory figures more than a cubit high was attached to its top; the workmanship of the figures was indifferent, but the amount of money spent on them was astonishing. The dining-room had a beautiful square[111] ceiling of cypress-wood; its ornamentation was carved and gilded. Next to this dining-room was a bedroom large enough for seven couches. A narrow passageway that ran the width of the ship was connected to this room and divided off the women's quarters; these included a dining-room large enough for nine couches, which was decorated as expensively as the large one, and a bedroom large enough for five couches. This was how the first deck was constructed. When you went up the ladders located near the bedroom mentioned above, there was another room large enough for five couches with a rhombus-shaped[112] ceiling; close to it was a rotunda-like shrine of Aphrodite that contained a marble statue of the goddess. Opposite this was another lavish peripteral dining-room; its columns were of Indian marble. Next to this dining-room were bedrooms decorated like the areas described above. As you moved forward toward the prow, there was a peristyle room dedicated to Dionysus large enough for 13 couches, with a cornice gilded up to the level of the architrave that ran

111 Perhaps "coffered."
112 Perhaps "made of rhombus-shaped panels."

στέγη δὲ τῆς τοῦ θεοῦ διαθέσεως οἰκεία. ἐν δὲ τούτῳ
κατὰ μὲν τὴν δεξιὰν πλευρὰν ἄντρον κατεσκεύαστο,
f οὗ χρῶμα μὲν | ἦν ἔχον τὴν πετροποιίαν ἐκ λίθων
ἀληθινῶν καὶ χρυσοῦ δεδημιουργημένην· ἵδρυτο δ' ἐν
αὐτῷ τῆς τῶν βασιλέων συγγενείας ἀγάλματα εἰκονι-
κὰ λίθου λυχνέως. ἐπιτερπὲς δ' ἱκανῶς καὶ ἄλλο συμπόσιον ἦν ἐπὶ τῇ τοῦ μεγίστου οἴκου στέγῃ κείμενον,
σκηνῆς ἔχον τάξιν· ᾧ στέγη μὲν οὐκ ἐπῆν, διατόναια
206 δὲ τοξοειδῆ διὰ ποσοῦ τινος ἐνετέτατο διαστήματος, ||
ἐφ' ὧν αὐλαῖαι κατὰ τὸν ἀνάπλουν ἁλουργεῖς ἐνεπε-
τάννυντο. μετὰ δὲ τοῦτο αἴθριον ἐξεδέχετο τὴν ἐπάνω
τῆς ὑποκειμένης προστάδος τάξιν κατέχον· ᾧ κλῖμαξ
τε ἑλικτὴ φέρουσα πρὸς τὸν κρυπτὸν περίπατον παρέκειτο καὶ συμπόσιον ἐννεάκλινον, τῇ διαθέσει τῆς
κατασκευῆς Αἰγύπτιον· οἱ γὰρ γεγονότες αὐτόθι κίονες ἀνήγοντο στρογγύλοι, διαλλάττοντες τοῖς σπον-
δύλοις, τοῦ μὲν μέλανος, τοῦ δὲ λευκοῦ παράλληλα
b τιθεμένων· εἰσὶ δ' αὐτῶν | καὶ αἱ κεφαλαὶ τῷ σχήματι
περιφερεῖς, ὧν ἡ μὲν ὅλη περιγραφὴ παραπλησία
ῥόδοις ἐπὶ μικρὸν ἀναπεπταμένοις ἐστίν. περὶ δὲ τὸν
προσαγορευόμενον κάλαθον οὐχ ἕλικες, καθάπερ ἐπὶ
τῶν Ἑλληνικῶν, καὶ φύλλα τραχέα περίκειται, λωτῶν
δὲ ποταμίων κάλυκες καὶ φοινίκων ἀρτιβλάστων καρ-
πός· ἔστι δ' ὅτε καὶ πλειόνων ἄλλων ἀνθέων γέγλυ-
πται γένη. τὸ δ' ὑπὸ τὴν ῥίζαν, ὃ δὴ τῷ συνάπτοντι
πρὸς τὴν κεφαλὴν ἐπίκειται σπονδύλῳ, κιβωρίων ἄν-
c θεσι καὶ φύλλοις ὡσανεὶ καταπεπλεγμένοις | ὁμοίαν
εἶχε τὴν διάθεσιν. τοὺς μὲν οὖν κίονας οὕτως Αἰγύ-

around the room; the ceiling was appropriate to the god's character. A cave had been constructed on the right side of the room; its exterior featured stonework of actual jewels and gold. Portrait-statues of the royal family fashioned from translucent marble were set inside it. Another very pleasant dining-room designed like a tent was located directly above the largest room. It lacked a roof, but cross-supports had been stretched into a bow-shape a considerable distance above it, and when the ship was under sail, purple curtains were suspended from them. After this came an atrium that occupied the area above the vestibule one deck down. Next to this was a spiral staircase that led to the enclosed walkway, and a dining-room large enough for nine couches. It was decorated in the Egyptian style; because the columns in it increased in diameter from the bottom to the top, with drums of different sizes that alternated between black and white. The shape of their capitals is round, and their general appearance is like roses that have barely opened. No volutes or rough foliage surround what is referred to as the basket[113], as on Greek columns, but there are instead water-lily flowers and dates from palms that have just fruited; and sometimes many other types of flowers have been carved. The portion of the column below the "root" (which rests, of course, on top of the drum that attaches to the capital) is made to resemble the flowers and leaves, seemingly intertwined, of Egyptian beans. This is how the Egyptians make their columns; and

[113] The body of the capital.

πτιοι κατασκευάζουσι· καὶ τοὺς τοίχους δὲ λευκαῖς
καὶ μελαίναις διαποικίλλουσι πλινθίσιν, ἐνίοτε δὲ καὶ
τοῖς ἀπὸ τῆς ἀλαβαστίτιδος προσαγορευομένης πέτρας. πολλὰ δὲ καὶ ἕτερα κατὰ μέσον τῆς νεὼς τὸ
κύτος ἐν κοίλῃ καὶ κατὰ πᾶν αὐτῆς μέρος οἰκήματα
ἦν. ὁ δὲ ἱστὸς ἦν αὐτῆς ἑβδομήκοντα πηχῶν, βύσσι-
νον ἔχων ἱστίον ἁλουργεῖ παρασείῳ κεκοσμημένον.
πᾶς δ' ὁ τοῦ βασιλέως τοῦ Φιλαδέλφου πλοῦτος
d φυλαχθεὶς < . . . > κατελύθη | ὑπὸ τοῦ τελευταίου
Πτολεμαίου τοῦ καὶ τὸν Γαβινιακὸν συστησαμένου
πόλεμον, οὐκ ἀνδρὸς γενομένου ἀλλ' αὐλητοῦ καὶ
μάγου.

Περὶ δὲ τῆς ὑπὸ Ἱέρωνος τοῦ Συρακοσίου κατα-
σκευασθείσης νεώς, ἧς καὶ Ἀρχιμήδης ἦν ὁ γεωμέ-
τρης ἐπόπτης, οὐκ ἄξιον εἶναι κρίνω σιωπῆσαι, σύγγραμμα ἐκδόντος Μοσχίωνός τινος, ᾧ οὐ παρέργως
ἐνέτυχον ὑπογυίως. γράφει οὖν ὁ Μοσχίων οὕτως·
Διοκλείδης μὲν ὁ Ἀβδηρίτης θαυμάζεται ἐπὶ τῇ πρὸς
τὴν Ῥοδίων πόλιν ὑπὸ Δημητρίου προσαχθείσῃ τοῖς
e τείχεσιν | ἐλεπόλει, Τίμαιος δ' ἐπὶ τῇ πυρᾷ τῇ κατα-
σκευασθείσῃ Διονυσίῳ τῷ Σικελίας τυράννῳ, καὶ
Ἱερώνυμος ἐπὶ τῇ κατασκευῇ τῆς ἁρμαμάξης, ᾗ συν-
έβαινε κατακομισθῆναι τὸ Ἀλεξάνδρου σῶμα, Πολύ-

---

114 Ptolemy XII Neos Dionysus (reigned 80–58, 55–51 BCE),
who was temporarily expelled from his throne and later restored
by Aulus Gabinius, whose troops he then used to suppress revolts.
He was not in fact the last Ptolemy.

they vary the color of their walls with white and black bricks, and occasionally also with bricks made from the stone referred to as alabaster. There were many other rooms in the space in the center of the ship's hold and in every other part of it. Its mast was 70 cubits high and had a linen sail ornamented with a purple topsail. All King Philadelphus' wealth, although preserved . . . was dissipated by the last Ptolemy[114], who was also responsible for the Gabinian war and was not a real man but a pipe-player and a charlatan.

I do not think it right to keep quiet about the ship constructed by Hieron of Syracuse[115], for which the mathematician Archimedes served as supervisor, given that a certain Moschion (*FGrH* 575 F 1) published a treatise on the subject, which I recently studied with some care. Moschion, therefore, writes as follows: Diocleides of Abdera[116] is admired for the siege-engine brought up against the walls of the city of Rhodes by Demetrius,[117] Timaeus (*FGrH* 566 F 112) for the pyre built for Dionysius the tyrant of Sicily,[118] Hieronymus (*FGrH* 154 F 2) for the construction of the wagon that carried Alexander's body down to the sea,[119] and Polycleitus (*FGrH* 128 F 4) for the

[115] Hieron II (reigned *c*.271–216 BCE).

[116] Otherwise unknown, but presumably an author rather than an engineer, given what follows.

[117] I.e. for his literary description of the siege-engine. Demetrius of Macedon (Berve i #258; 336–283 BCE) besieged Rhodes for a year in 305–4, winning the nickname Poliorcetes ("Besieger of Cities").

[118] Presumably Dionysius I (*d*.367 BCE).

[119] In 323 BCE; Ptolemy I Soter then took the corpse to Egypt.

κλειτος δ' ἐπὶ τῷ λυχνίῳ τῷ κατασκευασθέντι τῷ
Πέρσῃ· Ἱέρων δὲ ὁ Συρακοσίων βασιλεύς, ὁ πάντα
Ῥωμαίοις φίλος, ἐσπουδάκει μὲν καὶ περὶ ἱερῶν καὶ
γυμνασίων κατασκευάς, ἦν δὲ καὶ περὶ ναυπηγίας
f   φιλότιμος πλοῖα σιτηγὰ | κατασκευαζόμενος, ὧν ἑνὸς
τῆς κατασκευῆς μνησθήσομαι. εἰς ὕλην μὲν ξύλωσιν
ἐκ τῆς Αἴτνης παρεσκεύαστο ἑξήκοντα τετρηρικῶν
σκαφῶν πλῆθος[28] ἐξεργάσασθαι δυναμένην. ὡς δὲ
ταῦτα ἡτοιμάσατο γόμφους τε καὶ ἐγκοίλια καὶ σταμῖνας καὶ τὴν εἰς τὴν ἄλλην χρείαν ὕλην τὴν μὲν ἐξ
Ἰταλίας, τὴν δ' ἐκ Σικελίας, εἰς δὲ σχοινία λευκέαν
μὲν ἐξ Ἰβηρίας, κάνναβιν δὲ καὶ πίτταν ἐκ τοῦ Ῥοδα-
νοῦ ποταμοῦ καὶ τἆλλα πάντα τὰ χρειώδη πολλα-
χόθεν. συνήγαγε δὲ καὶ ναυπηγοὺς καὶ τοὺς ἄλλους
τεχνίτας καὶ καταστήσας ἐκ πάντων Ἀρχίαν τὸν Κο-
ρίνθιον ἀρχιτέκτονα παρεκάλεσε προθύμως ἐπιλαβέ-
σθαι τῆς κατασκευῆς, προσκαρτερῶν καὶ αὐτὸς τὰς
207 ἡμέρας. ‖ τὸ μὲν οὖν ἥμισυ τοῦ παντὸς τῆς νεὼς ἐν
μησὶν ἓξ ἐξειργάσατο < . . . > καὶ ταῖς ἐκ μολίβου
ποιηθείσαις κεραμίσιν ἀεὶ καθ' ὃ ναυπηγηθείη μέρος
περιελαμβάνετο, ὡς ἂν τριακοσίων ὄντων τῶν τὴν
ὕλην ἐργαζομένων τεχνιτῶν χωρὶς τῶν ὑπηρετούντων.
τοῦτο μὲν οὖν τὸ μέρος εἰς τὴν θάλασσαν καθέλκειν
προσετέτακτο, τὴν λοιπὴν κατασκευὴν ἵν' ἐκεῖ λαμ-
b   βάνῃ. ὡς δὲ περὶ τὸν καθελκυσμὸν αὐτοῦ τὸν εἰς τὴν |
θάλασσαν πολλὴ ζήτησις ἦν, Ἀρχιμήδης ὁ μηχα-

____

[28] τὸ πλῆθος A: πλῆθος tantum CE

492

lampstand made for the Persian king. But Hieron the king of Syracuse, who was always a friend of the Romans, devoted attention to building temples and wrestling-schools, but was also interested in winning a reputation for naval construction by building grain-transport ships. I will offer an account of the construction of one of these. For the materials, he had enough wood to produce the hulls of 60 "fours" collected from Mt. Aetna. He likewise prepared wooden pegs, belly-timbers, rib-timbers, and whatever other material was needed for other purposes, getting some items from Italy and others from Sicily, along with esparto for ropes from Spain, hemp and pitch from the Rhone valley, and everything else that was needed from many other places. He also recruited shipwrights and other craftsmen, and after he selected Archias of Corinth out of the whole group to be his chief builder, he ordered him to begin the project without delay; he himself devoted his days to it. Half of the whole ship[120] was completed in six months . . . and any section that was built was immediately sheathed with sheets of lead, as one would expect, given that 300 craftsmen were working on the materials, not counting their assistants. He had given orders to drag this section down to the sea, so that the rest of the work could be done there. After considerable discussion about how it could be dragged down to the sea, the engineer Archimedes moved it down there by himself with the assistance of

120 I.e. the lower half of the hull.

νικὸς μόνος αὐτὸ κατήγαγε δι᾽ ὀλίγων σωμάτων·
κατασκευάσας γὰρ ἕλικα τὸ τηλικοῦτον σκάφος εἰς
τὴν θάλασσαν κατήγαγε. πρῶτος δ᾽ Ἀρχιμήδης εὗρε
τὴν τῆς ἕλικος κατασκευήν. ὡς δὲ καὶ τὰ λοιπὰ μέρη
τῆς νεὼς ἐν ἄλλοις ἓξ μησὶ κατεσκευάσθη καὶ τοῖς
χαλκοῖς ἥλοις πᾶσα περιελήφθη, ὧν οἱ πολλοὶ δεκά-
μνοοι ἦσαν, οἱ δ᾽ ἄλλοι τούτων ἡμιόλιοι. διὰ τρυ-
πάνων δ᾽ ἦσαν οὗτοι ἡρμοσμένοι τοὺς σταμῖνας συν-
έχοντες· μολυβδίναις δὲ κεραμίσιν ἐπεστεγνοῦντο
πρὸς τὸ ξύλον, ὑποτιθεμένων ὀθονίων μετὰ πίττης. ὡς
οὖν τὴν ἐκτὸς ἐπιφάνειαν ἐξειργάσατο, τὴν ἐντὸς δια-
c   σκευὴν ἐξεπονεῖτο. ἦν δὲ ἡ ναῦς τῇ | μὲν κατασκευῇ
εἰκόσορος, τριπάροδος δέ· τὴν μὲν κατωτάτω † ἔχων †
ἐπὶ τὸν γόμον, ἐφ᾽ ἣν διὰ κλιμάκων πυκνῶν ἡ κατά-
βασις ἐγίνετο· ἡ δ᾽ ἑτέρα τοῖς εἰς τὰς διαίτας βουλομένοις εἰσιέναι ἐμεμηχάνητο· μεθ᾽ ἣν ἡ τελευταία τοῖς
ἐπὶ τοῖς ὅπλοις τεταγμένοις. ἦσαν δὲ τῆς μέσης παρόδου παρ᾽ ἑκάτερον τῶν τοίχων δίαιται τετράκλινοι
τοῖς ἀνδράσι, τριάκοντα τὸ πλῆθος. ἡ δὲ ναυκληρικὴ
δίαιτα κλινῶν μὲν ἦν πεντεκαίδεκα, θαλάμους δὲ τρεῖς
εἶχε τρικλίνους, ὧν ἦν τὸ κατὰ τὴν πρύμναν ὀπτα-
νεῖον. ταῦτα δὲ πάντα δάπεδον εἶχεν ἐν ἀβακίσκοις
συγκείμενον ἐκ παντοίων λίθων, ἐν οἷς ἦν κατεσκευ-
d   ασμένος | πᾶς ὁ περὶ τὴν Ἰλιάδα μῦθος θαυμασίως·
ταῖς τε κατασκευαῖς καὶ ταῖς ὀροφαῖς, καὶ θυρώμασι
δὲ πάντα ἦν ταῦτα πεπονημένα. κατὰ δὲ τὴν ἀνωτάτω
πάροδον γυμνάσιον ἦν καὶ περίπατοι σύμμετρον
ἔχοντες τὴν κατασκευὴν τῷ τοῦ πλοίου μεγέθει, ἐν οἷς

a few workmen; for by constructing a screw-windlass he moved a hull of this size down to the sea. Archimedes was the first person to discover how to build a screw-windlass. So the rest of the ship was constructed in another six months, and the whole thing was fastened together with bronze spikes, many weighing ten minas,[121] the others one-and-a-half times that much. Augers were used to put these spikes in place, and they held the ribs together; the spikes were covered by lead sheathing attached to the wood, with strips of linen smeared with pitch set under the sheathing. After completing the exterior, he began building the interior. The ship was designed like a "20," but had three gangways. The lowest [corrupt] to the cargo hold, which you could descend to by means of a large number of ladders. The second gangway had been designed for anyone who wanted to enter the living quarters. After this was the final one, for the armed troops. The middle gangway led to 30 cabins for the men, each large enough for four couches, along both sides of the ship. The captain's quarters were large enough for 15 couches and contained three rooms large enough for three couches; the room toward the stern served as a kitchen. All these areas had mosaic floors made from a variety of stones, in which the entire story of the *Iliad* was represented; this was an amazing sight. All the fixtures, ceilings, and doorways were elaborately worked. The upper gangway led to an exercise-room and promenade-decks built proportionate to the size of the ship. Garden-beds of all sorts, remarkably full of plants

---

[121] About 10 pounds.

κῆποι παντοῖοι θαυμασίως ἦσαν ὑπερβάλλοντες ταῖς
φυτείαις, διὰ κεραμίδων μολυβδινῶν κατεστεγνωμέ
νων ‹ἀρδευόμενοι›, ἔτι δὲ σκηναὶ κιττοῦ λευκοῦ καὶ
ἀμπέλων, ὧν αἱ ῥίζαι τὴν τροφὴν ἐν πίθοις εἶχον γῆς
πεπληρωμένοις, τὴν αὐτὴν ἄρδευσιν λαμβάνουσαι
e καθάπερ | καὶ οἱ κῆποι. αὗται δὲ αἱ σκηναὶ συνεσκία
ζον τοὺς περιπάτους. ἑξῆς δὲ τούτων Ἀφροδίσιον
κατεσκεύαστο τρίκλινον, δάπεδον ἔχον ἐκ λίθων ἀχα
τῶν τε καὶ ἄλλων χαριεστάτων ὅσοι κατὰ τὴν νῆσον
ἦσαν· τοὺς τοίχους δ᾽ εἶχε καὶ τὴν ὀροφὴν κυπαρίτ
του, τὰς δὲ θύρας ἐλέφαντος καὶ θύου· γραφαῖς ‹δὲ›
καὶ ἀγάλμασιν, ἔτι δὲ ποτηρίων κατασκευαῖς ὑπερ
βαλλόντως κατεσκεύαστο. τούτου δ᾽ ἐφεξῆς σχολα
στήριον ὑπῆρχε πεντάκλινον, ἐκ πύξου τοὺς τοίχους
f καὶ τὰ θυρώματα κατεσκευασμένον, βιβλιοθήκην |
ἔχον ἐν αὐτῷ, κατὰ δὲ τὴν ὀροφὴν πόλον ἐκ τοῦ κατὰ
τὴν Ἀχραδίνην ἀπομεμιμημένον ἡλιοτροπίου. ἦν δὲ
καὶ βαλανεῖον τρίκλινον πυρίας χαλκᾶς ἔχον τρεῖς
καὶ λουτῆρα πέντε μετρητὰς δεχόμενον ποικίλον τοῦ
Ταυρομενίτου λίθου. κατεσκεύαστο δὲ καὶ οἰκήματα
πλείω τοῖς ἐπιβάταις καὶ τοῖς τὰς ἀντλίας φυλάτ
τουσι. χωρὶς δὲ τούτων ἱππῶνες ἦσαν ἑκατέρου τῶν
τοίχων δέκα· κατὰ δὲ τούτους ἡ τροφὴ τοῖς ἵπποις
208 ἔκειτο καὶ τῶν ἀναβατῶν καὶ τῶν παίδων τὰ σκεύη. ‖
ἦν δὲ καὶ ὑδροθήκη κατὰ τὴν πρῷραν κλειστή, δισχι
λίους μετρητὰς δεχομένη, ἐκ σανίδων καὶ πίττης καὶ
ὀθονίων κατεσκευασμένη. παρὰ δὲ ταύτην κατεσκεύ
αστο διὰ μολιβδώματος καὶ σανίδων κλειστὸν ἰχθυο-

and watered by means of concealed lead plates,[122] were in them. There were also screens of white-berried ivy and grapevines, whose roots drew their nourishment from large pots full of dirt, and which were watered in the same way as the garden-beds. These screens provided shade for the walkways. Immediately after them was a shrine of Aphrodite large enough for three couches; its floor was made of agates and other beautiful stones found on the island[123]. Its walls and ceiling were of cypress; its doors were of ivory and citron-wood; and it was lavishly decorated with paintings and statues, as well as with elaborate drinking vessels. Next after this was a study large enough for five couches. Its walls and doors were of box-wood; it contained a collection of books; and a concave sundial modelled on the one in Achradina[124] was set in the ceiling. There was also a bathroom large enough for three couches that contained three bronze tubs and a multi-colored wash-basin with a capacity of five amphoras made of Tauromenian marble. There were also additional rooms for the marines and the men who kept an eye on the bilge. Aside from these, there were ten horse-stalls along each side of the ship; fodder for the horses was stored in the same area, along with the equipment for the riders and grooms. There was also a covered watertank near the prow; it held 2000 amphoras and was constructed of wooden planks, pitch, and strips of linen. Next to it was a covered fishtank constructed of lead and wooden planks; it

122 I.e. lead piping?   123 Sicily.

124 Achradina was part of the city of Syracuse, and the sundial in question had been constructed by the tyrant Dionysius I (see 5.206e n.); cf. Plu. *Dion* 29.3.

τροφεῖον· τοῦτο δ᾽ ἦν πλῆρες θαλάττης, ἐν ᾧ πολλοὶ
ἰχθύες ἐνετρέφοντο²⁹. ὑπῆρχον δὲ καὶ τῶν τοίχων
ἑκατέρωθεν τρόποι προεωσμένοι, διάστημα σύμμετρον ἔχοντες· ἐφ᾽ ὧν κατεσκευασμέναι ἦσαν ξυλοθῆ-
και καὶ κρίβανοι καὶ ὀπτανεῖα καὶ μύλοι καὶ πλείους
b ἕτεραι διακονίαι. ἄτλαντές | τε περιέτρεχον τὴν ναῦν
ἐκτὸς ἑξαπήχεις, οἳ τοὺς ὄγκους ὑπειλήφεσαν τοὺς
ἀνωτάτω καὶ τὸ τρίγλυφον, πάντες ἐν διαστήματι
⟨συμμέτρῳ⟩ βεβῶτες. ἡ δὲ ναῦς πᾶσα οἰκείαις γραφαῖς ἐπεπόνητο. πύργοι τε ἦσαν ἐν αὐτῇ ὀκτὼ σύμ-
μετροι τὸ μέγεθος τοῖς τῆς νεὼς ὄγκοις· δύο μὲν κατὰ
πρύμναν, οἱ δ᾽ ἴσοι κατὰ πρῷραν, οἱ λοιποὶ δὲ κατὰ
μέσην ναῦν. τούτων δὲ ἑκάστῳ παρεδέδεντο κεραῖαι
δύο, ἐφ᾽ ὧν κατεσκεύαστο φατνώματα, δι᾽ ὧν ἠφίεντο
λίθοι πρὸς τοὺς ὑποπλέοντας τῶν πολεμίων. ἐπὶ δὲ
c τῶν πύργων ἕκαστον | ἀνέβαινον τέτταρες μὲν καθω-
πλισμένοι νεανίσκοι, δύο δὲ τοξόται. πᾶν δὲ τὸ ἐντὸς
τῶν πύργων λίθων καὶ βελῶν πλῆρες ἦν. τεῖχος δὲ
ἐπάλξεις ἔχον καὶ καταστρώματα διὰ νεὼς ἐπὶ κιλλι-
βάντων κατεσκεύαστο· ἐφ᾽ οὗ λιθοβόλος ἐφειστήκει,
τριτάλαντον λίθον ἀφ᾽ αὑτοῦ ἀφιεὶς καὶ δωδεκάπηχυ
βέλος. τοῦτο δὲ τὸ μηχάνημα κατεσκεύασεν Ἀρχιμήδης. ἑκάτερον δὲ τῶν βελῶν ἔβαλλεν ἐπὶ στάδιον.
μετὰ δὲ ταῦτα παραρτήματα ἐκ τρόπων παχέων συγ-
d κείμενα διὰ ἁλύσεων χαλκῶν κρεμάμενα. | τριῶν δὲ
ἱστῶν ὑπαρχόντων ἐξ ἑκάστου κεραῖαι λιθοφόροι ἐξ-
ήρτηντο δύο, ἐξ ὧν ἅρπαγές τε καὶ πλίνθοι μολίβου
πρὸς τοὺς ἐπιτιθεμένους ἠφίεντο. ἦν δὲ καὶ χάραξ

was full of seawater, and a large number of fish were kept alive inside it. There were also beams that projected out from the sides of the ship at uniform intervals; wood-bins, baking shells, ovens, millstones, and many other service implements were set on top of them. Colossal statues six cubits high ran around the exterior of the ship; they supported the weight of the upper portions of the ship and the triglyph, and were set at uniform intervals. The entire ship had been decorated with suitable paintings. There were eight towers on it which matched the height of the ship's superstructure. Two were at the stern, the same number at the prow, and the rest in the middle of the ship. Two booms were attached to each of these and were fitted with boxes, which served to drop stones onto enemy ships that sailed in under the oars. Four young men in full armor were stationed on top of each tower, along with two archers; the entire interior of the towers was full of stones and missiles. A wall with battlements and decking had been constructed the length of the ship on trestles, and a stone-throwing machine that could throw a stone weighing three talents[125] or a missile 12 cubits long was mounted on it. Archimedes built this machine, which threw both types of missiles a stade.[126] After these came protective curtains made of heavy leather that hung from bronze chains. There were three masts, with two booms for moving stones attached to each; grappling hooks and lumps of lead were dropped from these onto attackers. There was also an iron palisade

[125] About 180 pounds.   [126] About 200 yards.

---

29 ἐνετρέφοντο Coraes: εὖ ἐτρέφοντο ACE

ATHENAEUS

κύκλῳ τῆς νεὼς σιδηροῦς πρὸς τοὺς ἐπιχειροῦντας
ἀναβαίνειν κόρακές τε σιδηροῖ[30], οἳ δι' ὀργάνων ἀφιέ-
μενοι τὰ τῶν ἐναντίων ἐκράτουν σκάφη καὶ παρέβαλ-
λον εἰς πληγήν. ἑκατέρῳ δὲ τῶν τοίχων ἑξήκοντα
νεανίσκοι πανοπλίας ἔχοντες ἐφειστήκεσαν καὶ τούτοις ἴσοι περί τε τοὺς ἱστοὺς καὶ τὰς λιθοφόρους
e   κεραίας. | ἦσαν δὲ καὶ κατὰ τοὺς ἱστοὺς ἐν τοῖς
καρχησίοις οὖσι χαλκοῖς ἐπὶ μὲν τοῦ πρώτου τρεῖς
ἄνδρες, εἶθ' ἑξῆς καθ' ἕνα λειπόμενοι· τούτοις δ' ἐν
πλεκτοῖς γυργάθοις διὰ τροχιλίων εἰς τὰ θωράκια
λίθοι παρεβάλλοντο καὶ βέλη διὰ τῶν παίδων. ἄγκυ-
ραι δὲ ἦσαν ξύλιναι μὲν τέτταρες, σιδηραῖ δ' ὀκτώ.
τῶν δὲ ἱστῶν ὁ μὲν δεύτερος καὶ τρίτος εὑρέθησαν,
δυσχερῶς δὲ ὁ πρῶτος εὑρέθη ἐν τοῖς ὄρεσι τῆς
f   Βρεττίας ὑπὸ συβώτου ἀνδρός· κατήγαγε δ' | αὐτὸν
ἐπὶ θάλατταν Φιλέας ὁ Ταυρομενίτης μηχανικός. ἡ δὲ
ἀντλία καίπερ βάθος ὑπερβάλλον ἔχουσα δι' ἑνὸς
ἀνδρὸς ἐξηντλεῖτο διὰ κοχλίου, Ἀρχιμήδους ἐξευρόν-
τος. ὄνομα δ' ἦν τῇ νηὶ Συρακοσία· ὅτε δ' αὐτὴν
ἐξέπεμπεν Ἱέρων, Ἀλεξανδρίδα αὐτὴν μετωνόμασεν.
ἐφόλκια δ' ἦσαν αὐτῇ τὸ μὲν πρῶτον κέρκουρος τρισχίλια τάλαντα δέχεσθαι δυνάμενος· πᾶς δ' ἦν οὗτος
ἐπίκωπος. μεθ' ὃν χίλια πεντακόσια βαστάζουσαι
ἁλιάδες τε καὶ σκάφαι πλείους. ὄχλος δ' ἦν οὐκ
ἐλάττων < . . . > μετὰ τοὺς προειρημένους ἄλλοι τε
ἑξακόσιοι παρὰ τὴν πρῷραν ἐπιτηροῦντες τὰ παραγ-

___
[30] σιδηροῖ κύκλῳ τῆς νεὼς ACE

500

that surrounded the ship and guarded against anyone who tried to board it, as well as iron hooks[127] which, when fired into the enemy's ships by catapults, got control of them and hauled them alongside, where they could be assaulted. 60 young men in full armor were stationed along each side of the ship, and an equal number were stationed around the masts and the booms used to transport stones. Men were also stationed at the masts in the mast-tops, which were made of bronze; three were assigned to the main mast, and two and one to the others, respectively. Slaves supplied them with stones and missiles, which were moved up to the crow's-nests in wicker baskets by means of blocks-and-tackle. There were four wooden anchors and eight made of iron. The second and third masts were found easily, but the main mast was located only with great difficulty, in the mountains of Bruttium by a swineherd. The engineer Phileas of Tauromenium transported it down to the sea. Although the bilge was very deep, it was emptied by one man using a screw-pump, which Archimedes invented. The ship's name was the Syracosia; but when Hieron sent it off,[128] he changed its name to the Alexandris. As for the vessels that accompanied it, there was, first of all, a cargo-galley with a capacity of 3000 talents, fully equipped with oars. After this, there were smaller craft capable of carrying 1500 talents, and many other boats. The total number of men was at least . . . in addition to those mentioned above, another 600 were posted at the prow awaiting or-

[127] Literally "ravens," presumably called after their color and general shape.

[128] As a gift to the king of Egypt (hence the new name); see 5.209b, below.

209 γελλόμενα. ‖ τῶν δὲ κατὰ ναῦν ἀδικημάτων δικαστή-
ριον καθειστήκει ναύκληρος, κυβερνήτης, καὶ πρῳ-
ρεύς, οἷπερ ἐδίκαζον κατὰ τοὺς Συρακοσίων νόμους.
σίτου δὲ ἐνεβάλλοντο εἰς τὴν ναῦν μυριάδας ἕξ, ταρίχων δὲ Σικελικῶν κεράμια μύρια, ἐρίων τάλαντα
δισμύρια, καὶ ἕτερα δὲ φορτία δισμύρια· χωρὶς δὲ
τούτων ὁ ἐπισιτισμὸς ἦν τῶν ἐμπλεόντων. ὁ δ᾽ Ἱέρων
ἐπεὶ πάντας τοὺς λιμένας ἤκουεν τοὺς μὲν ὡς οὐ
b δύνατοί εἰσι τὴν ναῦν δέχεσθαι, ‖ τοὺς δὲ καὶ ἐπι-
κινδύνους ὑπάρχειν, διέγνω δῶρον αὐτὴν ἀποστεῖλαι
Πτολεμαίῳ τῷ βασιλεῖ εἰς Ἀλεξάνδρειαν· καὶ γὰρ ἦν
σπάνις σίτου κατὰ τὴν Αἴγυπτον. καὶ οὕτως ἐποίησε,
καὶ ἡ ναῦς κατήχθη εἰς τὴν Ἀλεξάνδρειαν, ἔνθα καὶ
ἐνεωλκήθη. ὁ δ᾽ Ἱέρων καὶ Ἀρχίμηλον τὸν τῶν ἐπιγραμμάτων ποιητὴν γράψαντα εἰς τὴν ναῦν ἐπίγραμμα χιλίοις πυρῶν μεδίμνοις, οὓς καὶ παρέπεμψεν ἰδίοις δαπανήμασιν εἰς τὸν Πειραιᾶ, ἐτίμησεν. ἔχει δ᾽
c οὕτως τὸ ἐπίγραμμα· ‖

τίς τόδε σέλμα πέλωρον ἐπὶ χθονὸς εἴσατο;
    ποῖος
κοίρανος ἀκαμάτοις πείσμασιν ἠγάγετο;
πῶς δὲ κατὰ δρυόχων ἐπάγη σανίς, ἢ τίνι
    γόμφοι
τμηθέντες πελέκει τοῦτ᾽ ἔκαμον τὸ κύτος,
ἢ κορυφαῖς Αἴτνας παρισούμενον ἤ τινι νάσων
ἃς Αἰγαῖον ὕδωρ Κυκλάδας ἐνδέδεται,

ders. The captain, the pilot, and the bow-officer served as a court for any crimes committed onboard, and made their decisions based on Syracusan law. 60000 measures of grain were loaded into the ship, along with 10000 jars of Sicilian saltfish, 20000 talents of wool, and 20000 talents of other merchandise; apart from all this, there were the provisions for everyone onboard. When Hieron began to get reports about all the harbors, saying that some were unable to accommodate his ship, while others were too dangerous, he decided to send it to Alexandria as a gift for King Ptolemy[129], because there was a shortage of grain in Egypt. He did so, and the ship put in to Alexandria and was hauled to the docks there. Hieron also honored the epigrammatic poet Archimelus, who wrote an epigram about the ship, with 1000 *medimnoi* of wheat, which Archimelus sent to the Piraeus at his own expense. The epigram (*SH* 202) runs as follows:

Who set these monstrous timbers on the earth? What
    sort
  of lord brought them here with untiring cables?
And how was the planking fixed in place on the
    trestles? Or with what
  ax were the pegs cut that made this hull,
as large as Aetna's peaks or one of the islands
  the Aegean water binds together as the Cyclades,

[129] Most likely Ptolemy III Euergetes (reigned 246–221 BCE).

d τοίχοις ἀμφοτέρωθεν ἰσοπλατές; ἦ ῥα Γίγαντες |
  τοῦτο πρὸς οὐρανίας ἔξεσαν ἀτραπιτούς·
 ἄστρων γὰρ ψαύει καρχήσια καὶ τριελίκτους
  θώρακας μεγάλων ἐντὸς ἔχει νεφέων.
 πείσμασι δ' ἀγκύρας ἀπερείδεται οἷσιν Ἀβύδου
  Ξέρξης καὶ Σηστοῦ δισσὸν ἔδησε πόρον.
 μανύει στιβαρᾶς κατ' ἐπωμίδος ἀρτιχάρακτον
  γράμμα, τίς ἐκ χέρσου τάνδ' ἐκύλισε τρόπιν·
e φατὶ γὰρ ὡς Ἱέρων Ἱεροκλέος Ἑλλάδι πάσᾳ |
  καὶ νάσοις καρπὸν πίονα δωροφορῶν,
 Σικελίας σκαπτοῦχος ὁ Δωρικός. ἀλλά,
  Πόσειδον,
 σῷζε διὰ γλαυκῶν σέλμα τόδε ῥοθίων.

 παρέλιπον δ' ἑκὼν ἐγὼ τὴν Ἀντιγόνου ἱερὰν τριήρη, ᾗ
ἐνίκησε τοὺς Πτολεμαίου στρατηγοὺς περὶ Λεύκολλαν
τῆς Κῴας, ὅπου δὴ καὶ τῷ Ἀπόλλωνι αὐτὴν ἀνέθηκεν·
ἥτις οὐδὲ τὸ τρίτον, τάχα δὲ οὐδὲ τὸ τέταρτον εἶχε τῆς
Συρακοσίας ἢ Ἀλεξανδρίδος ταύτης νεώς.

f Τοσαῦτ' οὖν καὶ περὶ τοῦ τῶν νεῶν καταλόγου | οὐκ
ἀπὸ Βοιωτῶν ἀρξάμενοι κατελέξαμεν, ἀλλ' ἀπὸ πανη-
γυρικῶν πομπῶν. καὶ ἐπεὶ τὸν καλὸν Οὐλπιανὸν οἶδα

---

130 In 480 BCE, when the Persians invaded Greece via a bridge
constructed over the Dardanelles.
131 Antigonus Gonatas, king of Macedon c.277/6–239. The
Ptolemy referred to below is Ptolemy II Philadelphus, and the
battle may have taken place in 254 BCE.
132 An allusion to the Homeric Catalogue of Ships (Il. 2.484–
779), which begins with a description of the Boeotian contingent.

whose walls are equally broad on both sides?
    Certainly Giants
  shaped this to travel paths in the heavens;
for its mastheads touch the stars and it raises its
    threefold
  bulwarks into the midst of the vast clouds.
Its anchors are attached by the cables with which
    Xerxes
  bound the double passage between Abydus and
    Sestus.[130]
A message freshly engraved on its stout shoulder
    reveals
  who rolled this keel to sea from the dry land;
for they say that Hieron son of Hierocles, the Dorian
  who controls the scepter of Sicily, did this,
    bringing a gift
of rich grain to all Greece and the islands. And so,
    Poseidon,
  keep these timbers safe as they travel through the
    gray surge of the sea.

I deliberately failed to mention Antigonus'[131] sacred trireme, with which he defeated Ptolemy's generals off Leu-
colla on Cos, where he in fact dedicated it to Apollo; it was
not one-third or perhaps even one-fourth the size of this
ship known as the Syracosia or Alexandris.

This is the extent of the catalogue of ships I have to offer, although I began not with Boeotians[132] but with festival processions. And since I know that our good Ulpian is
now going to ask me what this *enguthēkē* ("stand") men-

πάλιν προβαλοῦντα ἡμῖν, τίς αὕτη ἡ παρὰ τῷ Καλλι-
ξείνῳ ἐγγυθήκη, φαμὲν αὐτῷ ὅτι καὶ λόγος τις εἰς
Λυσίαν ἀναφέρεται τὸν ῥήτορα Περὶ Ἐγγυθήκης ἐπι-
γραφόμενος, οὗ ἡ ἀρχή· εἰ μὲν δίκαιον ἔλεγεν ἢ
μέτριον, ἄνδρες δικασταί, Λυσιμένης. ἐν ᾧ προελθών
φησιν· οὐκ ἂν ἐσπούδαζον περὶ αὐτῆς τῆς ἐγγυθήκης
δικαιολογεῖσθαι, ἢ οὔκ ἐστιν ἀξία τριάκοντα δρα-
210   χμῶν. ‖ ὅτι δὲ χαλκῆ ἦν ἡ ἐγγυθήκη ἑξῆς φησι·
πέρυσιν δὲ ἐπισκευάσαι αὐτὴν βουλόμενος ἐξέδωκα
εἰς τὸ χαλκεῖον· ἐστὶ γὰρ συνθετὴ καὶ σατύρων ἔχει
πρόσωπα καὶ βουκεφάλια < . . . > ἄλλο ἔτι μέγεθος τὸ
αὐτό. ὁ γὰρ αὐτὸς τεχνίτης πολλὰ σκεύη ταῦτὰ καὶ
ὅμοια ἐργάζεται. ἐν τούτοις ὁ Λυσίας εἰπὼν ὅτι καὶ
χαλκῆ ἦν ἡ ἐγγυθήκη, σαφῶς παρίστησιν, ὡς καὶ ὁ
Καλλίξεινος εἴρηκε, λεβήτων αὐτὰς ὑποθήματα εἶναι.
οὕτως γὰρ καὶ Πολέμων ὁ περιηγητὴς εἶπεν ἐν τρίτῳ
τῶν Πρὸς Ἀδαῖον καὶ Ἀντίγονον ἐξηγούμενος διάθε-
b   σιν ἐν Φλιοῦντι | κατὰ τὴν πολεμάρχειον στοὰν γε-
γραμμένην ὑπὸ Σίλλακος τοῦ Ῥηγίνου, οὗ μνημονεύουσιν Ἐπίχαρμος καὶ Σιμωνίδης, λέγων οὕτως·
ἐγγυθήκη καὶ ἐπ' αὐτῆς κύπελλον. Ἡγήσανδρος δὲ ὁ
Δελφὸς ἐν τῷ ἐπιγραφομένῳ Ὑπομνήματι Ἀνδριάν-
των καὶ Ἀγαλμάτων Γλαύκου φησὶ τοῦ Χίου τὸ ἐν
Δελφοῖς ὑπόστημα οἷον ἐγγυθήκην τινὰ σιδηρᾶν,
ἀνάθημα Ἀλυάττου· οὗ ὁ Ἡρόδοτος μνημονεύει ὑπο-

---

133 At 5.199c.   134 The word appears to be treated as an
Atticism at Luc. *Lex.* 2.

tioned by Callixeinus[133] is, I say to him that there is a
speech attributed to the orator Lysias entitled *On the
Enguthēkē* (fr. XLII Meddu) which begins: If Lysimenes
were arguing something just or reasonable, gentlemen of
the jury . . . And further on in it he says: I would not have
been eager to make a courtroom speech about the *enguthēkē* itself, which is not worth 30 drachmas. Immediately after this he says that the *enguthēkē* was made of
bronze: Last year I wanted to have it repaired, and I turned
it over to the foundry; for it is made of a number of pieces
and has satyrs' faces and bulls' heads on it . . . yet another
one of the same size; because the same craftsman produces many pieces that are the same or similar. When
Lysias says in these passages that the *enguthēkē* was made
of bronze, he clearly establishes (as Callixeinus says) that
these are support-stands for cauldrons.[134] For the travel-
writer Polemon said the same thing in Book III of his
To Adaeus and Antigonus (fr. 58 Preller), where he offers
a description of the subject of the painting in the
polemarch's stoa in Phlius done by Sillax of Rhegium[135],
whom Epicharmus (fr. 160) and Simonides (*PMG* 634)
mention. He says the following: an *enguthēkē* with a goblet on top of it. Hegesander of Delphi in his treatise entitled *On Statues of Men and Gods* (fr. 45, *FHG* iv.421–2)
says that the support-stand in Delphi made by Glaucus of
Chios is a sort of iron *enguthēkē* and was dedicated by
Alyattes[136]; Herodotus (1.25.2) mentions it, but refers to it

---

[135] Otherwise unknown.
[136] King of Lydia *c*.610–560 BCE.

ATHENAEUS

κρητηρίδιον αὐτὸ καλῶν. καὶ ὁ ⟨μὲν⟩ Ἡγήσανδρος
c ταῦτα λέγει· εἴδομεν δ᾽ αὐτὸ καὶ ἡμεῖς ἀνακείμενον | ἐν
Δελφοῖς ὡς ἀληθῶς θέας ἄξιον διὰ τὰ ἐν αὐτῷ ἐντετο-
ρευμένα ζῳδάρια καὶ ἄλλα τινὰ ζῴφια καὶ φυτάρια,
ἐπιτίθεσθαι ἐπ᾽ αὐτῷ δυνάμενα καὶ κρατῆρας καὶ
ἄλλα σκεύη. ἡ δ᾽ ὑπ᾽ Ἀλεξανδρέων καλουμένη ἀγγο-
θήκη τρίγωνός ἐστι, κατὰ μέσον κοίλη, δέχεσθαι
δυναμένη ἐντιθέμενον κεράμιον. ἔχουσι δὲ ταύτην οἱ
μὲν πένητες ξυλίνην, οἱ δὲ πλούσιοι χαλκῆν ἢ ἀργυρᾶν.

Εἰπόντες οὖν περὶ ἐγγυθήκης ἑξῆς πάλιν μνησθη-
σόμεθα φιλοδείπνων βασιλέων. ὁ γὰρ τῷ προειρη-
d μένῳ | Ἀντιόχῳ ὁμώνυμος βασιλεύς, Δημητρίου δ᾽
υἱός, ὡς ἱστορεῖ Ποσειδώνιος, ὑποδοχὰς ποιούμενος
καθ᾽ ἡμέραν ὀχλικὰς χωρὶς τῶν ἀναλισκομένων σω-
ρευμάτων ἑκάστῳ ἀποφέρειν ἐδίδου τῶν ἑστιατόρων
ὁλομελῆ κρέα χερσαίων τε καὶ πτηνῶν καὶ θαλαττίων
ζῴων ἀδιαίρετα ἐσκευασμένα, ἅμαξαν πληρῶσαι δυ-
νάμενα· καὶ μετὰ ταῦτα μελιπήκτων καὶ στεφάνων ἐκ
σμύρνης καὶ λιβανωτοῦ σὺν ἀνδρομήκεσι λημνίσκων
χρυσῶν πιλήμασι πλήθη. καὶ ἄλλος δ᾽ Ἀντίοχος
βασιλεὺς ἐπιτελῶν τοὺς ἐν Δάφνῃ ἀγῶνας ἐποιήσατο
e καὶ αὐτὸς ὑποδοχὰς | λαμπράς, ὡς ⟨ὁ⟩ αὐτός φησι
Ποσειδώνιος· τὸ μὲν γὰρ πρῶτον ἀναδόσεις ἐποιήσα-

137 The same passage of Posidonius is cited at 12.540b–c.
138 At 5.193d–5f.
139 Antiochus VII Sidetes reigned 139–129 BCE, the son of
Dematrius I.

508

as a *hupokrētēridion* ("mixing-bowl support-stand"). This is what Hegesander has to say. But I myself saw it set up as a dedication in Delphi, and it is well worth seeing because of the tiny figures worked in relief on it along with other small creatures and plants; mixing-bowls and other vessels can be placed on top of it. What the inhabitants of Alexandria refer to as an *angothēkē* ("vessel-stand") is triangular and has a hollow center, and can support an earthenware pot set on top of it. Poor people have one made of wood, whereas the rich have one of bronze or silver.

Now that I have discussed the *enguthēkē*, I will next make some further mention of kings who were fond of dinner parties. According to Posidonius (*FGrH* 87 F 9b = fr. 61b Edelstein–Kidd),[137] the king who shared a name with the Antiochus mentioned above[138] but was a son of Demetrius[139] gave receptions for large numbers of people every day. In addition to the heaps of food consumed, he allowed everyone at the feast to take away whole uncarved cuts of meat from land-animals, birds, and sea-creatures, enough to fill a cart, and after that large amounts of honey cakes, garlands made of myrrh, and frankincense with ribbons of pressed gold as long as a man is tall. A different King Antiochus[140] also held brilliant receptions when he was celebrating the games at Daphne, according to the same Posidonius (*FGrH* 87 F 21b = fr. 72b Edelstein–Kidd): He began by distributing whole cuts of meat to each

---

[140] Antiochus VIII Grypus (reigned 125/1–96 BCE). For Daphne (mentioned below), see 5.194c n. The same passage of Posidonius is quoted at 12.540a–b, which is the source of the supplement.

το κατ' ἄνδρα ὁλομελῶν βρωμάτων, μετὰ δὲ καὶ ζών-
των χηνῶν ⟨καὶ⟩ λαγωῶν καὶ δορκάδων. ἀνεδίδοντο δὲ
καὶ χρυσοῖ στέφανοι τοῖς δειπνοῦσι καὶ ἀργυρωμάτων πλῆθος καὶ θεραπόντων καὶ ἵππων καὶ καμήλων.
καὶ ἔδει ἀναβάντα ἐπὶ τὴν κάμηλον πιεῖν ἕκαστον καὶ
λαβεῖν τὴν ⟨κάμηλον καὶ τὰ ἐπὶ τὴν⟩ κάμηλον καὶ τὸν
παρεστῶτα παῖδα. καὶ οἱ κατὰ τὴν Συρίαν δὲ πάντες,
φησί, διὰ τὴν τῆς χώρας εὐβοσίαν ἀπὸ τῆς περὶ
τἀναγκαῖα κακοπαθείας συνόδους ἔνεμον πλείους, ἵνα
f   εὐωχοῖντο | συνεχῶς, τοῖς μὲν γυμνασίοις ὡς βαλα-
νείοις χρώμενοι, ἀλειφόμενοι ἐλαίῳ πολυτελεῖ καὶ μύ-
ροις, τοῖς δὲ γραμματείοις—οὕτως γὰρ ἐκάλουν τὰ
κοινὰ τῶν συνδείπνων—ὡς οἰκητηρίοις ἐνδιαιτώμενοι,
τὸ³¹ πλεῖον μέρος τῆς ἡμέρας γαστριζόμενοι ἐν αὑτοῖς
οἴνοις καὶ βρώμασιν, ὥστε καὶ προσαποφέρειν πολλά, καὶ καταυλούμενοι πρὸς χελωνίδος πολυκρότου
ψόφους, ὥστε τὰς πόλεις ὅλας τοῖς τοιούτοις κελάδοις
211 συνηχεῖσθαι. ‖

    Ἐπαινῶ δ' ἐγώ, ἄνδρες φίλοι, τὸ γενόμενον παρ'
Ἀλεξάνδρῳ τῷ βασιλεῖ τῆς Συρίας συμπόσιον. ὁ δ'
Ἀλέξανδρος οὗτος ὢν Ἀντιόχου τοῦ Ἐπιφανοῦς υἱὸς
ὑποβληθείς, διὸ εἶχον μῖσος πάντες ἄνθρωποι εἰς
Δημήτριον· περὶ οὗ ἱστόρησεν ὁ ἑταῖρος ἡμῶν Ἀθή-

---

³¹ καὶ τὸ ACE

---

141 The same passage of Posidonius is cited, with a few vari-
ants, at 12.527e–f.

man, and afterward he distributed live geese, hares, and gazelles. Gold garlands were also given out to the dinner-guests, along with large quantities of silver vessels, slaves, horses, and camels. Everyone was required to mount his camel, have a drink, and take the camel, plus what was on it, and the slave standing beside it. And everyone in Syria, he says (Posidon. *FGrH* 87 F 10 = fr. 62b Edelstein–Kidd),[141] because the natural wealth of their country kept them from having to work hard for the necessities of life, used to hold large numbers of parties, so that they could feast constantly. They used their wrestling-schools for bath-houses, and anointed themselves with expensive oil and perfumes; and they used their *grammateia*—this is how they referred to their communal dining-halls—as if they were their homes, and practically lived in them, stuffing their bellies full of wine and food in them for most of the day, to the extent that they even carried a large amount of food back home, and listening to pipe-music accompanied by the sound of the noisy lyre, to the extent that entire cities echoed with sounds of this sort.

But I have praise, my friends, for the symposium that took place in the house of Alexander king of Syria.[142] This Alexander was a supposititious child of Antiochus Epiphanes,[143] as a result of which everyone hated Demetrius; our companion Athenaeus offers a complete account of

---

[142] Alexander Balas (reigned 151/0–145 BCE), the son (or sup-posed son) of Antiochus IV Epiphanes. The Demetrius referred to below might be either Demetrius I (d. 150 BCE) or his son Demetrius II (*c*.161–125 BCE).

[143] There may be a gap in the text at this point.

ναιος ἐν τοῖς Περὶ τῶν Ἐν Συρίᾳ Βασιλευσάντων. τὸ
οὖν συμπόσιον τοῦτο τοιόνδε τι ἐγένετο. Διογένης ὁ
Ἐπικούρειος, ἕξιν ἔχων ἱκανὴν ἐν οἷς μετεχειρίζετο
λόγοις, τὸ μὲν γένος ἦν ἐκ Σελευκείας τῆς ἐν Βαβυ-
b λωνίᾳ, ἀποδοχῆς δ᾽ | ἐτύγχανε παρὰ τῷ βασιλεῖ
καίτοι τοῖς ἀπὸ τῆς στοᾶς λόγοις χαίροντι. ἐπολυώρει
οὖν αὐτὸν ὁ Ἀλέξανδρος καίπερ ὄντα τῷ βίῳ φαῦλον,
ἔτι δὲ βλάσφημον καὶ βάσκανον ἕνεκά τε τοῦ γελοίου
μηδὲ τῶν βασιλέων ἀπεχόμενον· καὶ αἰτησαμένῳ αὐτῷ φιλοσοφίας ἀλλοτρίαν αἴτησιν, ὅπως πορφυροῦν
τε χιτωνίσκον φορήσει καὶ χρυσοῦν στέφανον ἔχοντα
πρόσωπον Ἀρετῆς κατὰ μέσον, ἧς ἱερεὺς ἠξίου προσαγορεύεσθαι, συνεχώρησε καὶ τὸν στέφανον προσχα-
ρισάμενος. ἅπερ ὁ Διογένης ἐρασθείς τινος λυσιῳδοῦ
c γυναικὸς ἐχαρίσατο αὐτῇ. ἀκούσας | δ᾽ ὁ Ἀλέξανδρος
καὶ συνάγων φιλοσόφων καὶ ἐπισήμων ἀνδρῶν συμπόσιον ἐκάλεσε καὶ τὸν Διογένη· καὶ παραγενόμενον
ἠξίου κατακλίνεσθαι ἔχοντα τὸν στέφανον καὶ τὴν
ἐσθῆτα. ἄκαιρον δ᾽ εἶναι εἰπόντος νεύσας εἰσαγαγεῖν
ἐκέλευσε τὰ ἀκούσματα, ἐν οἷς καὶ ἡ λυσιῳδὸς εἰσῆλθεν ἐστεφανωμένη τὸν τῆς Ἀρετῆς στέφανον, ἐν-
δῦσα καὶ τὴν πορφυρᾶν ἐσθῆτα. γέλωτος οὖν πολλοῦ
καταραγέντος ἔμενεν ὁ φιλόσοφος καὶ τὴν λυσιῳδὸν
ἐπαινῶν οὐκ ἐπαύσατο. τοῦτον τὸν Διογένη ὁ μετα-

---

[144] This is the only surviving fragment of this work, which may
well have brought the historical Athenaeus to his Roman patron's
attention. [145] The reference would appear to be to Dioge-

BOOK V

this in his *On the Kings of Syria* (*FGrH* 166 F 1).[144] This symposium, then, proceeded as follows: The Epicurean philosopher Diogenes,[145] who had a good command of the doctrine he practiced, was born in Seleucia in Babylon and enjoyed the king's favor even though the king was fond of Stoic doctrines. Alexander showed him great respect, although he was poor and spoke irreverently and slanderously to get a laugh, and did not even spare the royal family. When Diogenes asked a favor foreign to philosophy, which was that he be allowed to wear a purple robe and a gold garland with Virtue's face in the middle of it, since he deserved to be called her priest, Alexander agreed and granted him the garland as well. Diogenes was in love with a woman who danced in men's clothing,[146] and he gave these items to her. When Alexander found out about this, he gathered a group of philosophers and other distinguished men and invited them to a symposium along with Diogenes. When Diogenes arrived, the king asked him to put on his garland and robe and lie down. Diogenes said that this was not a good time; Alexander nodded his head and ordered the entertainers to come in—and the woman came in along with them, with the garland of Virtue on her head and wearing the purple robe. There was a great outburst of laughter; but the philosopher stayed where he was and continued praising her performance. Af-

nes "of Babylon" (*c*.240–152 BCE; for the use of the term "Babylon" to refer to the region in which the city of Seleucia-on-the-Tigris was located, see Str. 16.743–4), although he was the head of the Stoa after Zeno of Tarsus and has apparently been confused with the Epicurean Diogenes of Tarsus (second half of the 2nd c. BCE).   [146] See 4.182c; 14.620e.

d λαβὼν τὴν βασιλείαν Ἀντίοχος, οὐκ ἐνέγκας | αὐτοῦ
τὴν κακολογίαν, ἀποσφαγῆναι ἐκέλευσεν. ὁ δ᾽ Ἀλέξανδρος προσηνὴς ἦν πᾶσι καὶ φιλόλογος ἐν ταῖς
ὁμιλίαις καὶ οὐχ ὅμοιος Ἀθηνίωνι τῷ περιπατητικῷ
φιλοσόφῳ, τῷ καὶ διατριβῆς προστάντι φιλοσόφου
Ἀθήνησί τε καὶ ἐν Μεσσήνῃ, ἔτι δὲ καὶ ἐν Λαρίσῃ τῆς
Θετταλίας, καὶ μετὰ ταῦτα τῆς Ἀθηναίων πόλεως
τυραννήσαντι. περὶ οὗ καθ᾽ ἕκαστα ἱστορεῖ Ποσειδώνιος ὁ Ἀπαμεύς, ἅπερ εἰ καὶ μακρότερά ἐστιν ἐκθήσομαι, ἵν᾽ ἐπιμελῶς πάντας ἐξετάζωμεν τοὺς φάσκον-
e τας εἶναι φιλοσόφους καὶ μὴ τοῖς τριβωνίοις | καὶ
τοῖς ἀκάρτοις πώγωσι πιστεύωμεν. κατὰ γὰρ τὸν
Ἀγάθωνα

εἰ μὲν φράσω τἀληθές, οὐχί σ᾽ εὐφρανῶ·
εἰ δ᾽ εὐφρανῶ τί σ᾽, οὐχὶ τἀληθὲς φράσω.

ἀλλὰ φίλη ⟨γάρ⟩, φασίν, ἡ ἀλήθεια, ἐκθήσομαι τὰ
περὶ τὸν ἄνδρα ὡς ἐγένετο.

Ἐν τῇ Ἐρυμνέως τοῦ περιπατητικοῦ σχολῇ διέτρι-
βέ τις Ἀθηνίων προσκαρτερῶν τοῖς λόγοις· ὅστις
Αἰγυπτίαν ὠνησάμενος θεράπαιναν ἐπεπλέκετο αὐτῇ.
ταύτης οὖν εἴτ᾽ ἐξ αὐτοῦ τεκούσης, εἴτ᾽ ἐξ ἄλλου τινός,
f ὁμώνυμος Ἀθηνίωνι | τῷ δεσπότῃ παρετρέφετο. γράμ-
ματα δὲ μαθὼν καὶ πρεσβύτην γενόμενον τὸν δεσπό-
την μετὰ τῆς μητρὸς ἐχειραγώγει καὶ ἀποθανόντα

ter Antiochus[147] inherited the kingdom, he was unable to tolerate Diogenes' abuse and ordered him executed. But Alexander was gentle to everyone and enjoyed discussing literature, and was unlike the Peripatetic philosopher Athenion,[148] who was the head of philosophical schools in Athens and Messene, as well as in Larisa in Thessaly, and afterward became a tyrant who controlled the city of Athens. Posidonius of Apamea (*FGrH* 87 F 36 = fr. 253 Edelstein–Kidd) offers a detailed account of him, which I am going to provide even if it is quite long, in order that we can make a careful examination of all those who claim to be philosophers and not simply put our confidence in their rough robes and untrimmed beards. As Agathon (*TrGF* 39 F 12) says:

> If I speak the truth, I won't make you happy;
> but if I make you at all happy, I won't speak the truth.

But because the truth, as they say, is something we ought to care about, I will offer you an account of how this man's tale unfolded.

A certain Athenion spent time in the school of the Peripatetic Erymneus and applied himself to his doctrines. He bought an Egyptian slave-girl and had sex with her; the woman's son, whether Athenion was the father or someone else was, shared his master Athenion's name and was brought up in his house. He learned to read and write, and after his master had grown old, he and his mother would lead him around by the hand; after the old man died, he in-

---

[147] Presumably a reference to Antiochus VII Sidetes (reigned 139–129 BCE), although this is too late for Diogenes of Babylon.
[148] *PAA* 110370.

κληρονομήσας παρέγγραφος Ἀθηναίων πολίτης ἐγένετο. γήμας τε παιδισκάριον εὔμορφον μετὰ τούτου
πρὸς τὸ σοφιστεύειν ὥρμησε μειράκια σχολαστικὰ
212 θηρεύων. καὶ σοφιστεύσας ‖ ἐν Μεσσήνῃ κἂν Λαρίσῃ
τῇ Θετταλικῇ καὶ πολλὰ ἐργασάμενος χρήματα ἐπαν-
ῆλθεν εἰς τὰς Ἀθήνας. καὶ χειροτονηθεὶς ὑπὸ τῶν
Ἀθηναίων πρεσβευτής, ὅτε εἰς Μιθριδάτην τὰ πράγματα μετέρρει, ὑποδραμὼν τὸν βασιλέα τῶν φίλων
εἷς ἐγένετο, μεγίστης τυχὼν προαγωγῆς. διόπερ μετ-
εώριζε τοὺς Ἀθηναίους δι᾽ ἐπιστολῶν ὡς τὰ μέγιστα
παρὰ τῷ Καππαδόκῃ δυνάμενος, ὥστε μὴ μόνον τῶν
ἐπιφερομένων ὀφλημάτων ἀπολυθέντας ⟨ἂν⟩ ἐν ὁμο-
b νοίᾳ ζῆν, ἀλλὰ καὶ τὴν δημοκρατίαν | ἀνακτησα-
μένους, καὶ δωρεῶν μεγάλων τυχεῖν ἰδίᾳ καὶ δημοσίᾳ.
ταῦτα οἱ Ἀθηναῖοι διεκόμπουν τὴν Ῥωμαίων ἡγεμο-
νίαν καταλελύσθαι πεπιστευκότες. ἤδη οὖν τῆς Ἀσίας
μεταβεβλημένης ὁ Ἀθηνίων ἐπανῆγεν εἰς τὰς Ἀθήνας
καὶ ὑπὸ χειμῶνος ἐνοχληθεὶς εἰς τὴν Καρυστίαν κατ-
ηνέχθη. τοῦτο μαθόντες οἱ Κεκροπίδαι ἔπεμψαν ἐπὶ
τὴν ἀνακομιδὴν αὐτοῦ ναῦς μακρὰς καὶ φορεῖον ἀργυ-
ρόπουν. ἀλλ᾽ εἰσῄειν ἤδη, καὶ σχεδὸν τὸ πλεῖστον
c μέρος τῆς πόλεως ἐπὶ τὴν ἐκδοχὴν αὐτοῦ ἐξεκέχυτο· |
συνέτρεχον δὲ πολλοὶ καὶ ἄλλοι θεαταὶ τὸ παράδοξον
τῆς τύχης θαυμάζοντες, εἰ ὁ παρέγγραφος Ἀθηνίων
εἰς Ἀθήνας ἐπ᾽ ἀργυρόποδος κατακομίζεται φορείου
καὶ πορφυρῶν στρωμάτων, ὁ μηδέποτε ἐπὶ τοῦ τρίβωνος ἑωρακὼς πορφύραν πρότερον, οὐδενὸς οὐδὲ
Ῥωμαίων ἐν τοιαύτῃ φαντασίᾳ καταχλιδῶντος τῆς

herited the property and was illegally enrolled as an Athenian citizen. He married a pretty girl and with her help began to hunt for boys to teach, so that he could become a sophist. After he had worked as a sophist in Messene and Thessalian Larisa and had made a lot of money, he returned to Athens. The Athenians elected him an ambassador when their allegiance was shifting to Mithridates[149], and by flattering the king he became part of his inner circle and attained tremendous eminence. He accordingly began to write to the Athenians and encourage them to believe that he had enormous influence with the Cappadocian[150] and that they could not only escape the debts that were pressing them and live in harmony, but also recover their democracy and get huge gifts privately and as a people. The Athenians started bragging about this, since they had been convinced that Rome's power had collapsed. After Asia had switched sides, Athenion began his return to Athens; but a storm caused him trouble and he landed at Carystia. When the Cecropids[151] learned of this, they sent warships and a litter with silver feet to bring him home. And now he was coming in, and almost the entire city had poured out to greet him! Many other spectators ran to join them, astonished at how strange fortune can be, if the illegally enrolled Athenion is being brought home on a litter with silver feet and purple bed-clothes, a man who had never seen purple on his rough robe before this, and even though no Roman ever insulted Attica with such a

[149] Mithridates VI Eupator Dionysus, king of Pontus. Athenion was elected ambassador in 88 BCE and became tyrant of Athens in 87.   [150] Mithridates.

[151] The Athenians.

ATHENAEUS

Ἀττικῆς. συνέτρεχον οὖν πρὸς τὴν θέαν ταύτην ἄνδρες, γυναῖκες, παῖδες, τὰ κάλλιστα προσδοκῶντες
παρὰ Μιθριδάτου, ὁπότε Ἀθηνίων ὁ πένης καὶ τὰς
d ἐρανικὰς ποιησάμενος | ἀκροάσεις διὰ τὸν βασιλέα
σιληπορδῶν διὰ τῆς χώρας καὶ πόλεως πομπεύει.
ὑπήντησαν δ᾽ αὐτῷ καὶ οἱ περὶ τὸν Διόνυσον τεχνῖται,
τὸν ἄγγελον τοῦ νέου Διονύσου καλοῦντες ἐπὶ τὴν
κοινὴν ἑστίαν καὶ τὰς περὶ ταύτην εὐχάς τε καὶ
σπονδάς. ὁ δὲ πρότερον ἐκ μισθωτῆς οἰκίας ἐξιὼν εἰς
τὴν Διέους οἰκίαν τοῦ τότε πλουτοῦντος ἀνθρώπου
ταῖς ἐκ Δήλου προσόδοις εἰσηνέχθη, κεκοσμημένην
στρωμναῖς τε καὶ γραφαῖς καὶ ἀνδριᾶσι καὶ ἀργυρωμάτων ἐκθέσει. ἀφ᾽ ἧς ἐξῄει χλαμύδα λαμπρὰν ἐπισύ-
e ρων καὶ περικείμενος | δακτύλιον χρυσίου ἐγγεγλυμ-
μένην ἔχοντα τὴν Μιθριδάτου εἰκόνα· προεπόμπευον
δ᾽ αὐτοῦ καὶ ἐφείποντο θεράποντες πολλοί. ἐν δὲ τῷ
τεμένει τῶν τεχνιτῶν θυσίαι τε ἐπετελοῦντο ἐπὶ τῇ
Ἀθηνίωνος παρουσίᾳ καὶ μετὰ κήρυκος προαναφωνή-
σεως σπονδαί. καὶ τῇ ὑστεραίᾳ πολλοὶ μὲν ἐπὶ τὴν
οἰκίαν ἐλθόντες ἀνέμενον αὐτοῦ τὴν πρόοδον· πλήρης
δ᾽ ἦν καὶ ὁ Κεραμεικὸς ἀστῶν καὶ ξένων καὶ αὐτόκλη-
τος εἰς τὴν ἐκκλησίαν τῶν ὄχλων συνδρομή. ὁ δὲ
μόλις προῆλθε δορυφορούμενος ὑπὸ τῶν εὐδοκιμεῖν
f παρὰ | τῷ δήμῳ θελόντων, ἑκάστου σπεύδοντος κἂν
προσάψασθαι τῆς ἐσθῆτος. ἀναβὰς οὖν ἐπὶ τὸ βῆμα
τὸ πρὸ τῆς Ἀττάλου στοᾶς ᾠκοδομημένον τοῖς Ῥωμαίων στρατηγοῖς στὰς ἐπὶ τούτου καὶ περιβλέψας
κυκληδὸν τὸ πλῆθος, ἔπειτ᾽ ἀναβλέψας, "ἄνδρες Ἀθη-

display of luxury. So they all came running together to see this sight, men, women, and children, expecting the best from Mithridates, if the result of the king's favor was that the pauper Athenion, who used to give subscription lectures[152], was being paraded through the countryside and the city like an arrogant buffoon. Dionysus' artists met him and invited the messenger of the new Dionysus to the public hearth and the prayers and libations that took place around it. The man who previously emerged from a rented house was transported to the residence of Dies[153] (a contemporary whose wealth came from money made on Delos), which was fitted out with bedding, paintings, statues, and a display of silver vessels. He left there with a brilliant robe trailing behind him and wearing a gold ring engraved with Mithridates' portrait. A large number of slaves marched in front of him and followed behind. Sacrifices in honor of Athenion's presence were carried out in the sacred precinct of the artists, and after a herald made a proclamation, libations were poured. The next day many people came to the house and waited until he came out. The Cerameicus was full of citizens and foreigners, and the crowd rushed into the Assembly-place without being summoned. He made his way forward with difficulty, escorted by a bodyguard of men who wanted to gain favor with the people; everyone was eager simply to touch his clothing. After he got up, then, onto the speaker's stand that had been built in front of the Stoa of Attalus for the Roman magistrates, he stood on top of it, looked around in a circle at the crowd, raised his eyes, and said: "Men of

---

[152] Lectures at which everyone who attended made a contribution to cover the speaker's fee.   [153] *PAA* 324020.

ναῖοι," ἔφη, "τὰ πράγματα μὲν βιάζεται καὶ τὸ τῆς
πατρίδος συμφέρον ἀπαγγέλλειν ἃ οἶδα, τὸ δὲ μέγεθος τῶν μελλόντων λέγεσθαι διὰ τὸ παράδοξον τῆς
περιστάσεως ἐμποδίζει με." ἀθρόως δ' ἐπιβοησάντων
213 αὐτῷ τῶν περιεστώτων θαρρεῖν καὶ λέγειν, ‖ "λέγω
τοίνυν," ἔφη, "τὰ μηδέποτε ἐλπισθέντα μηδὲ ἐν ὀνείρῳ
φαντασθέντα. βασιλεὺς Μιθριδάτης κρατεῖ μὲν Βιθυ-
νίας καὶ τῆς ἄνω Καππαδοκίας, κρατεῖ δὲ τῆς συνεχοῦς Ἀσίας ἁπάσης ἄχρι Παμφυλίας καὶ Κιλικίας.
καὶ βασιλεῖς μὲν αὐτὸν Ἀρμενίων καὶ Περσῶν δορυ-
φοροῦσι, δυνάσται δὲ τῶν περὶ τὴν Μαιῶτιν καὶ τὸν
ὅλον Πόντον κατῳκισμένων ἐθνῶν ἐν περιμέτρῳ τρισ-
μυρίων σταδίων. Ῥωμαίων δὲ στρατηγὸς μὲν Παμφυλίας Κόιντος Ὄππιος παραδοθεὶς ἀκολουθεῖ δέσμιος,
b | Μάνιος δὲ Ἀκύλλιος ὁ ὑπατευκώς, ὁ τὸν ἀπὸ Σικε-
λίας καταγαγὼν θρίαμβον, συνδέτην ἔχων ἁλύσει
μακρᾷ Βαστάρνην πεντάπηχυν πεζὸς ὑπὸ ἱππέως ἕλ-
κεται. τῶν δ' ἄλλων Ῥωμαίων οἱ μὲν θεῶν ἀγάλμασι
προσπεπτώκασιν, οἱ δὲ λοιποὶ μεταμφιεσάμενοι τε-
τράγωνα ἱμάτια τὰς ἐξ ἀρχῆς πατρίδας πάλιν ὀνομάζουσι. πᾶσα δὲ πόλις ταῖς ὑπὲρ ἄνθρωπον τιμαῖς
ὑπαντῶσα κατακαλεῖ αὐτὸν θεὸν βασιλέα· χρησμοὶ
δὲ πάντοθεν τὸ κράτος τῆς οἰκουμένης θεσπιῳδοῦσι.
c διὸ καὶ πρὸς | τὴν Θρᾴκην καὶ τὴν Μακεδονίαν με-
γάλα πέμπεται στρατόπεδα, καὶ τὰ τῆς Εὐρώπης
ἅπαντα μέρη ἀθρόα εἰς αὐτὸν μεταβέβληται. πάρεισι
γὰρ πρὸς αὐτὸν πρέσβεις οὐ μόνον ἐκ τῶν Ἰταλικῶν
ἐθνῶν, ἀλλὰ καὶ παρὰ Καρχηδονίων, συμμαχεῖν ἀξι-

Athens, the circumstances and the interest of my country require me to report what I know; but the magnitude of what I am going to say restrains me, because the situation is so extraordinary." When the bystanders all shouted that he should get his courage up and speak, he said: "Well then, what I have to tell you was never expected or even seen in a dream. King Mithridates is in control of Bithynia and Upper Cappadocia, as well as all Asia as far as Pamphylia and Cilicia. Armenian and Persian kings serve in his bodyguard, as do princes of the peoples who live around Lake Maeotis and all of Pontus in an area 30000 stades in circumference. The Roman magistrate in charge of Pamphylia, Quintus Oppius, was turned over to him and follows him in shackles, while the ex-consul Munius Aquilius, who celebrated a triumph after his campaign in Sicily, is dragged along on foot by a horseman, bound together by a long chain with a Bastarnian five cubits tall. As for the rest of the Romans, some of them are clinging to the gods' statues, while the rest have shed their square robes[154] and are once again identifying themselves by their country of origin. Every city meets the king with more than human honors, referring to him as a god; and oracles from everywhere prophesy his control of the entire inhabited world. He is therefore sending large armies to Thrace and Macedon, and every part of Europe without exception has come over to his side. For ambassadors are with him not just from the Italian peoples but also from the Carthaginians, begging to

[154] Their togas.

οῦντες ἐπὶ τὴν τῆς Ῥώμης ἀναίρεσιν." μικρὸν δ' ἐπι-
σχὼν ἐπὶ τούτοις καὶ ἐάσας τοὺς πολλοὺς συλλαλῆ-
σαι περὶ τῶν παραδόξως προηγγελμένων τρίψας τε τὸ
μέτωπον, "τί οὖν," εἶπε, "συμβουλεύω; μὴ ἀνέχεσθαι
d   τῆς ἀναρχίας, ἣν ἡ Ῥωμαίων σύγκλητος | ἐπισχε-
θῆναι πεποίηκεν, ἕως ⟨ἂν⟩ αὐτὴ δοκιμάσῃ περὶ τοῦ
πῶς ἡμᾶς πολιτεύεσθαι δεῖ. καὶ μὴ περιίδωμεν τὰ ἱερὰ
κεκλημένα, αὐχμῶντα δὲ τὰ γυμνάσια, τὸ δὲ θέατρον
ἀνεκκλησίαστον, ἄφωνα δὲ τὰ δικαστήρια καὶ τὴν
θεῶν χρησμοῖς καθωσιωμένην Πύκνα ἀφῃρημένην
τοῦ δήμου. μὴ περιίδωμεν δέ, ἄνδρες Ἀθηναῖοι, τὴν
ἱερὰν τοῦ Ἰάκχου φωνὴν κατασεσιγασμένην καὶ τὸ
σεμνὸν ἀνάκτορον τοῖν θεοῖν κεκλημένον καὶ τῶν
φιλοσόφων τὰς διατριβὰς ἀφώνους." πολλῶν οὖν καὶ
e   ἄλλων τοιούτων λεχθέντων | ὑπὸ τοῦ οἰκότριβος, συλ-
λαλήσαντες αὑτοῖς οἱ ὄχλοι καὶ συνδραμόντες εἰς τὸ
θέατρον εἵλοντο τὸν Ἀθηνίωνα στρατηγὸν ἐπὶ τῶν
ὅπλων. καὶ παρελθὼν ὁ περιπατητικὸς εἰς τὴν ὀρχή-
στραν ἴσα βαίνων Πυθοκλεῖ εὐχαρίστησέ τε τοῖς
Ἀθηναίοις καὶ ἔφη διότι "νῦν ὑμεῖς ἑαυτῶν στρατη-
γεῖτε, προέστηκα δ' ἐγώ. καὶ ἂν συνεπισχύητε, τοσοῦτον δυνήσομαι ὅσον κοινῇ πάντες ὑμεῖς." ταῦτ'
εἰπὼν συγκατέστησεν ἑαυτῷ τοὺς ἄλλους ἄρχοντας,
f   ὧν ἠβούλετο ὑποβαλὼν τὰ ὀνόματα. καὶ | μετ' οὐ
πολλὰς ἡμέρας τύραννον αὐτὸν ἀποδείξας ὁ φιλόσοφος καὶ τὸ τῶν Πυθαγορικῶν ἀναδείξας δόγμα ⟨τὸ⟩
περὶ τῆς ἐπιβουλῆς καὶ τί ἠβούλετο αὐτοῖς ἡ φιλο-
σοφία ἣν ὁ καλὸς Πυθαγόρας εἰσηγήσατο, καθάπερ

522

be his allies when he moves to destroy Rome." He paused for a moment at this point, and after allowing the crowd to discuss the unexpected news, rubbed his forehead and said: "So what do I advise? That you not put up with the anarchy[155] the Roman Senate has caused to continue until it decides how we ought to be governed! And let us not ignore the fact that our temples are locked, our gymnasia filthy, our theater deserted by the Assembly, our lawcourts mute, and the Pnyx, although consecrated by divine oracles, taken away from the people! Nor let us ignore the fact, men of Athens, that Iacchus' holy voice has been silenced, the sacred shrine of the two goddesses has been locked, and the philosophical schools are mute!" After this domestic slave[156] said many similar things, the crowd discussed the matter among themselves and raced off to the Theater, where they elected Athenion as a general in charge of the hoplites. The Peripatetic stepped forward into the orchestra, carrying himself like Pythocles (cf. D. 19.314), thanked the Athenians, and said: "Now you are generals over yourselves, and I am your representative. If you lend me your strength, I will be as powerful as all of you combined." After saying this, he appointed the other magistrates who would serve along with him, proposing the names of those he wanted. A few days later the philosopher revealed himself to be a tyrant, and showed them what the Pythagorean doctrine of treachery was and what the consequences were for them of the philosophy introduced by the noble Pythagoras, as is recorded by Theo-

[155] I.e. the lack of annual archons.
[156] The word refers specifically to a slave born and raised in the house rather than bought.

ἱστόρησε Θεόπομπος ἐν ὀγδόῃ Φιλιππικῶν καὶ Ἕρμιππος ὁ Καλλιμάχειος, εὐθέως καὶ οὗτος τοὺς μὲν εὖ
214 φρονοῦντας τῶν πολιτῶν—παρὰ τὰ Ἀριστοτέλους ‖
καὶ Θεοφράστου δόγματα· ὡς ἀληθῆ εἶναι τὴν παροιμίαν τὴν λέγουσαν "μὴ παιδὶ μάχαιραν"—ἐκποδὼν
εὐθὺς ἐποιήσατο, φύλακας δ᾽ ἐπὶ τὰς πύλας κατέστησεν, ὡς νύκτωρ πολλοὺς τῶν Ἀθηναίων εὐλαβουμένους τὸ μέλλον κατὰ τῶν τειχῶν αὑτοὺς καθιμήσαν-
τας φεύγειν. καὶ ὁ Ἀθηνίων ἱππέας ἐπαποστείλας οὓς
μὲν ἐφόνευσεν, οὓς δὲ καὶ δεδεμένους κατήγαγε, δορυφόρους ἔχων πολλοὺς τῶν καταφρακτικῶν καλουμένων. συνάγων δὲ καὶ ἐκκλησίας πολλάκις τὰ Ῥωμαί-
b ων φρονεῖν | προσεποιεῖτο < ... > καὶ πολλοῖς αἰτίας
ἐπιφέρων ὡς διαπεμπομένοις πρὸς τοὺς φυγάδας καὶ
νεωτερίζουσιν ἐφόνευεν αὐτούς· καὶ τὰς πύλας < ... >
τριάκοντα καταστήσας ἐφ᾽ ἑκάστης οὔτ᾽ εἰσιέναι τὸν
βουλόμενον οὔτ᾽ ἐξιέναι εἴα. ἀνελάμβανεν δὲ καὶ τὰς
οὐσίας πολλῶν καὶ τοσαῦτα χρήματα συνήθροισεν
ὡς καὶ φρέατα πληρῶσαι πλείονα. ἐξαπέστειλεν δὲ
καὶ ἐπὶ τὴν χώραν ὥσπερ ὁδοιδόκους τῶν ἀποχωρούν-
των, οἵτινες αὐτοὺς ἀνῆγον ὡς αὑτόν· καὶ ἀκρίτους
c ἀπώλλυεν προβασανίσας | καὶ στρεβλώσας. πολλοῖς
δὲ καὶ προδοσίας δίκας ἐπῆγεν ὡς τοῖς φυγάσι περὶ
καθόδου συνεργοῦσιν· ὧν οἱ μὲν διὰ τὸν φόβον πρὸ
τῆς κρίσεως ἔφευγον, οἱ δ᾽ ἐν τοῖς δικαστηρίοις κατ-
εδικάζοντο, αὐτοῦ τὰς ψήφους φέροντος. ἐνειργάσατο

pompus in Book VIII of the *History of Philip* (*FGrH* 115 F 73) and by Callimachus' student Hermippus (fr. 21 Wehrli). For immediately—and contrary to the teachings of Aristotle and Theophrastus[157]; how true the proverb (Diogen. 6.46) is that says "Don't (give) a child a knife!"—the fellow immediately got all the citizens with any sense out of the way and posted guards on the gates, since many Athenians, fearing what was going to happen, were lowering themselves from the walls with ropes and trying to escape. Athenion had cavalry sent after them and killed some and brought others back as prisoners; he also had a large bodyguard made up of what are referred to as *kataphraktikoi* ("men in mail"). He frequently convened Assemblies and pretended that . . . were in sympathy with Rome; and he charged many people with communicating with the exiles and planning a revolution, and put them to death. And he . . . for the gates . . . , he stationed 30 men at each and did not allow people to go in and out as they pleased. He also began to confiscate many people's property and accumulated so much money that it filled a large number of cisterns. He sent people out into the countryside who behaved like bandits to anyone trying to leave the land and brought them back to him; and he put them to death without a trial, after torturing them first and breaking them on the rack. He also brought charges of treason against many people, claiming that they were working with the exiles to try to bring them back. Some of these people were so terrified that they attempted to flee before the verdict was given, while others were found guilty in the law-

---

[157] The first two heads of the Peripatetic school.
[158] *PAA* 140490.

δ᾽ ἐν τῇ πόλει καὶ τῶν πρὸς τὸ ζῆν ἀναγκαίων ἔνδειαν
κριθίδια καὶ πυροὺς ὀλίγους διαμετρῶν. ἐξέπεμπε δὲ
καὶ ἐπὶ τῆς χώρας ὁπλίτας τοὺς θηρεύσοντας, εἴ τις
τῶν ἀνακεχωρηκότων ἐντός ἐστι τῶν ὅρων ἢ τῶν
d Ἀθηναίων τις εἰς | τὴν ὑπερόριον ἀποδημεῖ· καὶ τὸν
ληφθέντα ἀπετυμπάνιζεν, ὧν ἐνίους καὶ προκατανά-
λισκε ταῖς βασάνοις. ἐκήρυσσέν τε δύντος ἡλίου
πάντας οἰκουρεῖν καὶ μετὰ λυχνοφόρου μηδένα φοι-
τᾶν. καὶ οὐ μόνον τὰ τῶν πολιτῶν διήρπαζεν, ἀλλ᾽ ἤδη
καὶ τὰ τῶν ξένων, ἐκτείνας τὰς χεῖρας καὶ ἐπὶ τὰ ἐκ
Δήλου τοῦ θεοῦ χρήματα. ἐκπέμψας οὖν εἰς τὴν νῆσον
Ἀπελλικῶντα τὸν Τήιον, πολίτην δὲ Ἀθηναίων γενόμενον, ποικιλώτατόν τινα καὶ ἀψίκορον ζήσαντα βίον·
e ὅτε μὲν γὰρ ἐφιλοσόφει | τὰ περιπατητικά, καὶ τὴν
Ἀριστοτέλους βιβλιοθήκην καὶ ἄλλας συνηγόραζε
συχνὰς (ἦν γὰρ πολυχρήματος) τά τ᾽ ἐκ τοῦ Μητρῴου
τῶν παλαιῶν αὐτόγραφα ψηφισμάτων ὑφαιρούμενος
ἐκτᾶτο καὶ ἐκ τῶν ἄλλων πόλεων εἴ τι παλαιὸν εἴη καὶ
ἀπόθετον. ἐφ᾽ οἷς φωραθεὶς ἐν ταῖς Ἀθήναις ἐκινδύ-
νευσεν ἄν, εἰ μὴ ἔφυγεν. καὶ μετ᾽ οὐ πολὺ πάλιν
κατῆλθε, θεραπεύσας πολλούς· καὶ συναπεγράφετο
τῷ Ἀθηνίωνι ὡς δὴ ἀπὸ τῆς αὐτῆς αἱρέσεως ὄντι.
f Ἀθηνίων δ᾽ ἐπιλαθόμενος | τῶν δογμάτων τῶν τοῦ
περιπάτου χοίνικα κριθῶν εἰς τέσσαρας ἡμέρας διεμέ-
τρει τοῖς ἀνοήτοις Ἀθηναίοις, ἀλεκτορίδων τροφὴν
καὶ οὐκ ἀνθρώπων αὐτοῖς διδούς. Ἀπελλικῶν δὲ μετὰ

---

159 Contrast 1.3a.

courts, since Athenion himself cast the ballots. In addition, he created a shortage of the necessities of life in the city by measuring out a little barley and small amounts of wheat. And he sent hoplites into the countryside to hunt down anyone who returned to the country and was now inside its borders, as well as any Athenians who were attempting to get away across the border. He executed anyone who was captured on the plank, but tortured some of them to death beforehand. He also issued a proclamation that everyone was to stay inside after the sun went down and that no one was to go around accompanied by a slave carrying a lamp. Nor was it just the property of the citizens he seized but now that of foreigners as well, and he stretched out his hands to get hold of the god's money on Delos. He accordingly sent Apellicon of Teos[158] to the island. Apellicon was an Athenian citizen who had led a colorful and diverse life: he occasionally interested himself in Peripatetic philosophy; had purchased Aristotle's library[159] and a number of others (he was very rich); and had surreptitiously acquired the original copies of the ancient decrees from the Metroon[160], as well as any other old, rare documents he could get from other cities. He was caught red-handed at this in Athens and would have been in danger, had he not gone into exile. But he returned shortly thereafter, by playing up to a large number of people, and enlisted with Athenion, since he was a member of the same sect. Athenion had forgotten his Peripatetic doctrines and was measuring out a *choinix* of barley every four days to the foolish Athenians, giving them enough food for chickens but not for human

[160] Athens' official archives.
[161] A normal ration would be one *choinix* per day.

δυνάμεως ἐξορμήσας εἰς Δῆλον καὶ πανηγυρικῶς
μᾶλλον ἢ στρατιωτικῶς ἀναστρεφόμενος, καὶ προφυ-
λακὴν ἀμελεστέραν πρὸς τὴν Δῆλον μερίσας, μάλιστα δὲ τὰ ἐξόπισθε τῆς νήσου ἐάσας ἀφύλακτα καὶ
οὐδὲ χάρακα βαλόμενος ἐκοιμᾶτο. τοῦτο δὲ ἐπιγνοὺς ὁ
215 Ὀρόβιος στρατηγὸς Ῥωμαίων ‖ φυλάξας[32] ἀσέληνον
νύκτα καὶ ἐκβιβάσας τοὺς ἑαυτοῦ στρατιώτας, κοιμω-
μένοις καὶ μεθύουσιν ἐπιπεσὼν κατέκοψε τοὺς Ἀθηναίους καὶ τοὺς μετ᾽ αὐτῶν συστρατευομένους ὡς
βοσκήματα, ἑξακοσίους τὸν ἀριθμόν, ἐζώγρησε δὲ
καὶ περὶ τετρακοσίους. καὶ ὁ καλὸς στρατηγὸς Ἀπελλικῶν ἔλαθε φυγὼν ἐκ Δήλου. πολλοὺς δὲ καὶ συμφυ-
γόντας κατιδὼν ὁ Ὀρόβιος εἰς ἐπαύλεις συγκατέφλε-
ξεν αὐταῖς οἰκίαις καὶ πάντα αὐτῶν τὰ πολιορκητικὰ
b   ὄργανα σὺν τῇ ἑλεπόλει, | ἣν εἰς Δῆλον ἐλθὼν κατ-
εσκευάκει. στήσας οὖν τρόπαιον ἐπὶ τῶν τόπων ὁ
Ὀρόβιος καὶ βωμὸν ἐπέγραψε·

τούσδε θανόντας ἔχει ξυνὸς τάφος, οἳ περὶ
   Δῆλον
μαρνάμενοι ψυχὰς ὤλεσαν ἐν πελάγει,
τὴν ἱερὰν ὅτε νῆσον Ἀθηναῖοι κεράιζον
κοινὸν Ἄρη βασιλεῖ Καππαδόκων θέμενοι.

Καὶ Ταρσοῦ δὲ Ἐπικούρειος φιλόσοφος ἐτυράν-
νησε, Λυσίας ὄνομα· ὃς ὑπὸ τῆς πατρίδος στεφανηφό-
ρος αἱρεθείς, τουτέστιν ἱερεὺς Ἡρακλέους, οὐκ ἀπ-

---

[32] Ῥωμαίων καὶ φυλάσσων τὴν Δῆλον φυλάξας A

beings.[161] Meanwhile Apellicon set off for Delos with a
military force, but behaved like he was attending a festival
rather than going on campaign; after he set too careless
a watch in the direction of Delos-town, left the portion
of the island to his rear entirely unguarded, and did not
even set up a palisade, he went to sleep. When the Roman
general Orobius[162] found out about this, he waited for a
moonless night, disembarked his own soldiers, and fell on
the Athenians and their allies, who were asleep and drunk,
butchering 600 of them like cattle and capturing about 400
alive; the noble general Apellicon escaped in secret from
Delos. When Orobius realized that many of them had fled
in groups into farm-buildings, he burned them up, buildings and all, along with all their siege-machines, including
the "city-taker" Apellicon had constructed after he came
to Delos. Orobius accordingly set up a trophy in the area
and inscribed on the altar (anon. *FGE* 1796–9):[163]

A common grave holds these men, who lost their lives
    fighting in the sea around Delos
when the Athenians attempted to plunder the holy
    island,
    making war in common with the king of
    Cappadocia.[164]

In addition, an Epicurean philosopher by the name of
Lysias was tyrant of Samos. After his country chose him to
be a *stephanēphoros* (literally "garland-bearer"), which is

[162] Lucius Orbius, a distinguished Roman resident of Delos.
[163] The inscription in fact refers to a naval battle, or perhaps to
a skirmish (not mentioned by Posidonius) that took place when
Orbius' troops landed on the island.   [164] Mithridates.

c ἐτίθετο τὴν ἀρχήν, ἀλλ᾽ ἐξ ἱματίου τύραννος ἦν, |
πορφυροῦν μὲν μεσόλευκον χιτῶνα ἐνδεδυκώς, χλαμύδα δὲ ἐφεστρίδα περιβεβλημένος πολυτελῆ καὶ ὑπο-
δούμενος λευκὰς Λακωνικάς, στέφανον δάφνης χρυσοῦν ἐστεμμένος, καὶ διανέμων τὰ τῶν πλουσίων τοῖς
πένησι, πολλοὺς φονεύων τῶν οὐ διδόντων.

Τοιοῦτοί εἰσιν οἱ ἀπὸ φιλοσοφίας στρατηγοί. περὶ
ὧν Δημοχάρης ἔλεγεν· ὥσπερ ἐκ θύμβρας οὐδεὶς ἂν
δύναιτο κατασκευάσαι λόγχην, οὐδ᾽ ἐκ Σωκράτους
στρατιώτην ἄμεμπτον. ὁ γὰρ Πλάτων φησὶν τρεῖς
d στρατείας στρατεύσασθαι | Σωκράτη, τὴν μὲν εἰς
Ποτίδαιαν, τὴν δὲ εἰς Ἀμφίπολιν, τὴν δὲ εἰς Βοιωτοὺς
ὅτε καὶ συνέβη τὴν ἐπὶ Δηλίῳ μάχην γενέσθαι. μηδενὸς δὲ τοῦθ᾽ ἱστορηκότος αὐτὸς καὶ ἀριστείων φησὶν
αὐτὸν τετυχηκέναι πάντων ⟨τῶν⟩ Ἀθηναίων φυγόν-
των, πολλῶν δὲ καὶ ἀπολομένων. πάντα δὲ ταῦτα
ἐψευδολόγηται. ἡ μὲν γὰρ ἐπὶ Ἀμφίπολιν στρατεία
γέγονεν ἐπὶ Ἀλκαίου ἄρχοντος Κλέωνος ἡγουμένου ἐξ
ἐπιλέκτων ἀνδρῶν, ὥς φησι Θουκυδίδης. τούτων οὖν
τῶν ἐπιλέκτων ἀνάγκη εἶναι καὶ Σωκράτην, ᾧ πλὴν
τρίβωνος καὶ βακτηρίας οὐδὲν ἦν. τίς οὖν εἶπεν ἱστο-
e ριογράφος | ἢ ποιητής; ἢ ποῦ Θουκυδίδης τὸν Σωκρά-
τη παρενέχρωσε τὸν Πλάτωνος στρατιώτην;

---

165 A fashionable item.
166 Most of what follows appears to be drawn from Herodicus'
To the Man Who Likes Socrates (Duering pp. 18–24, 26–30); cf.
5.215f; 11.504e n.

to say a priest of Heracles, he did not surrender the office, but stopped wearing an ordinary robe and became a tyrant: he put on a purple and off-white tunic, threw an expensive horseman's mantle about his shoulders, put white Spartan shoes[165] on his feet and a gold garland made to resemble laurel on his head, and distributed the property of the rich to the poor, murdering many people who refused to surrender what they had.

This is what the political leaders who began by studying philosophy are like.[166] Demochares used to say about them:[167] A spearhead could not be made out of savory, and neither could an irreproachable soldier be made from Socrates. For Plato (*Ap*. 28e) says that Socrates served on three campaigns: the one against Potidaea, the one against Amphipolis, and the one against the Boeotians, when the battle at Delium took place. And although no one else records this, he also claims (*Smp*. 220e–1c) that Socrates won the prize for valor when all the Athenians ran away and many of them actually died. Everything he says is a lie. For the campaign against Amphipolis took place in the archonship of Alcaeus,[168] and Cleon commanded a force of select men, according to Thucydides (cf. 5.2.1). Socrates must therefore have been one of these select men, although he owned nothing except an inexpensive robe and a staff![169] What historian, then, or poet mentioned this? Or where did Thucydides allude to Socrates the Platonic

[167] Cf. 5.187d.

[168] 422/1 BCE. But perhaps there was also fighting there in 437–436, when the city was founded.

[169] Viz. because he is imagined here as the archetypal Greek philosopher.

τί γὰρ ἀσπίδι ξύνθημα καὶ βακτηρίᾳ;

πότε δὲ καὶ εἰς Ποτίδαιαν ἐστρατεύσατο, ὡς ἐν τῷ
Χαρμίδῃ εἴρηκεν ὁ Πλάτων φάσκων αὐτὸν καὶ τῶν
ἀριστείων τότε Ἀλκιβιάδῃ παραχωρῆσαι; τοῦτο οὔτε
Θουκυδίδου ἀλλ᾽ οὐδ᾽ Ἰσοκράτους εἰρηκότος ἐν τῷ
Περὶ τοῦ Ζεύγους. ποίας δὲ καὶ μάχης γενομένης
ἔλαβε τὰ ἀριστεῖα Σωκράτης καὶ τί πράξας ἐπιφανὲς
καὶ διάσημον; καθόλου μάχης μηδεμιᾶς συμπεσού-
f   σης, | ὡς ἱστόρηκε Θουκυδίδης. οὐκ ἀρκεσθεὶς δὲ
ταύτῃ τῇ τερατολογίᾳ ὁ Πλάτων ἐπάγει καὶ τὴν ἐπὶ
Δηλίῳ γενομένην, μᾶλλον δὲ πεπλασμένην ἀνδραγα-
θίαν. εἰ γὰρ καὶ τὸ Δήλιον ᾑρήκει Σωκράτης, ὡς
ἱστορεῖ Ἡρόδικος ὁ Κρατήτειος ἐν τοῖς Πρὸς τὸν
Φιλοσωκράτην, ἅμα τοῖς πολλοῖς ἀσχημόνως ἂν ἔφυ-
γε, Παγώνδου δύο τέλη περιπέμψαντος τῶν ἱππέων ἐκ
τοῦ ἀφανοῦς περὶ τὸν λόφον. τότε γὰρ οἱ μὲν πρὸς τὸ
216   Δήλιον ‖ τῶν Ἀθηναίων ἔφυγον, οἱ δ᾽ ἐπὶ θάλατταν,
ἄλλοι δὲ ἐπὶ Ὠρωπόν, οἱ δὲ ⟨πρὸς⟩ Πάρνηθα τὸ ὄρος·
Βοιωτοὶ δ᾽ ἐφεπόμενοι ἔκτεινον καὶ μάλιστα οἱ ἱππεῖς
οἵ τε αὐτῶν καὶ ⟨οἱ⟩ Λοκρῶν. τοιούτου οὖν κυδοιμοῦ
καὶ φόβου καταλαβόντος τοὺς Ἀθηναίους, μόνος Σωκράτης βρενθυόμενος καὶ τὠφθαλμὼ παραβάλλων
εἱστήκει ἀναστέλλων τὸ Βοιωτῶν καὶ Λοκρῶν ἱππικόν;
καὶ ταύτης τῆς ἀνδρείας αὐτοῦ οὐ Θουκυδίδης μέμνηται, οὐκ ἄλλος οὐδεὶς ⟨ . . . ⟩ ποιητής. πῶς δὲ καὶ τῶν

soldier?

> For what does a shield have in common with a
>   staff?[170]

And when did he participate in the campaign against Potidaea, as Plato asserts in the *Charmides* (153b–c), where he
claims that Socrates gave up the prize for valor in favor of
Alcibiades? Neither Thucydides nor Isocrates in his *On
the Team of Horses* (= *Or.* 16) mentions this. What sort of a
battle took place, for which Socrates won the prize for
valor? And what did he do that was notable or distinguished? Since no battle at all took place, according to
Thucydides! And as if he were not satisfied with this fairy-
tale, Plato adds the battle that took place at Delium—or
rather a false story of courage. For even if Socrates had
captured Delium, he would have behaved disgracefully
and run away along with many other people, as Crates' student Herodicus reports in his *To the Man Who Likes Socrates*, after (Th. 4.96.5, 7) Pagondas unexpectedly sent two
cavalry units around the hill. For then some of the Athenians fled to Delium, some to the sea, others to Oropus,
and some to Mt. Parnes; and the Boeotians, and particularly their cavalry and that of the Locrians, followed and
killed them. When the Athenians fell into such confusion
and terror, then, was it Socrates alone, acting haughty and
refusing to meet anyone's eye,[171] who stood his ground and
drove off the Boeotian and Locrian horse? But Thucydides

---

[170] A parody of A. fr. **61a, where the final word is "a drinking
cup."

[171] Adapted from Ar. *Nu.* 362 (quoted at Pl. *Smp.* 221b).

b ἀριστείων Ἀλκιβιάδῃ παραχωρεῖ | τῷ μηδ᾽ ὅλως κε-
κοινωνηκότι ταύτης τῆς στρατείας; ἐν δὲ τῷ Κρίτωνι ὁ
τῇ Μνημοσύνῃ φίλος Πλάτων οὐδὲ ποιήσασθαι πώ-
ποτε ἀποδημίαν τὸν Σωκράτη ἔξω τῆς εἰς Ἰσθμὸν
πορείας εἴρηκε. καὶ Ἀντισθένης δ᾽ ὁ Σωκρατικὸς περὶ
τῶν ἀριστείων τὰ αὐτὰ τῷ Πλάτωνι ἱστορεῖ.

οὐκ ἔστιν δ᾽ ἔτυμος ὁ λόγος οὗτος.

χαρίζεται γὰρ καὶ ὁ κύων οὗτος πολλὰ τῷ Σωκράτει·
ὅθεν οὐδετέρῳ αὐτῶν δεῖ πιστεύειν σκοπὸν ἔχοντας
Θουκυδίδην. ὁ γὰρ Ἀντισθένης καὶ προσεπάγει τῇ
c ψευδογραφίᾳ λέγων | οὕτως· "ἡμεῖς δὲ ἀκούομεν κἂν
τῇ πρὸς Βοιωτοὺς μάχῃ τὰ ἀριστεῖά σε λαβεῖν."
"εὐφήμει, ὦ ξένε· Ἀλκιβιάδου τὸ γέρας, οὐκ ἐμόν."
"σοῦ γε δόντος, ὡς ἡμεῖς ἀκούομεν." ὁ δὲ Πλάτωνος
Σωκράτης εἰς Ποτίδαιαν λέγει παρεῖναι καὶ τῶν ἀριστείων Ἀλκιβιάδῃ παρακεχωρηκέναι. προτερεῖ δὲ κατὰ πάντας τοὺς ἱστορικοὺς τῆς ἐπὶ Δήλιον στρατείας
ἡ περὶ Ποτίδαιαν, ἧς Φορμίων ἐστρατήγει.

Πάντ᾽ οὖν ψεύδονται οἱ φιλόσοφοι καὶ πολλὰ παρὰ
τοὺς χρόνους γράφοντες οὐκ αἰσθάνονται, καθάπερ
d οὐδ᾽ ὁ καλὸς Ξενοφῶν, ὃς ἐν | τῷ Συμποσίῳ ὑποτίθε-
ται Καλλίαν τὸν Ἱππονίκου Αὐτολύκου τοῦ Λύκωνος
ἐρῶντα καὶ νενικηκότος αὐτοῦ παγκράτιον ἑστίασιν

---

172 Plato's Socrates in fact explicitly excludes military service
from his account of his travels (or lack thereof).
173 Quoted at Pl. *Phdr.* 243a.

makes no mention of his bravery, and neither does any other . . . poet. And how can he give up the prize for valor in favor of Alcibiades, who took no part whatsoever in this campaign? But in the *Crito* (52b)[172] Plato, the friend of the goddess Memory, says that Socrates (*SSR* V.A F 200) never left Attica except for his trip to the Isthmus. Socrates' student Antisthenes gives the same account as Plato about the prize for valor;

But this story is not true. (Stesich. *PMG* 192.1)[173]

For this bastard too shows tremendous favoritism toward Socrates, and as a result no one who takes Thucydides as his guide should put any confidence in either of them. Because Antisthenes goes even further in his misrepresentation, saying the following: "We hear that you also won the prize for valor in the battle against the Boeotians." "Hush, stranger; the honor belongs to Alcibiades, not to me." "Because you gave it to him, so we hear." Whereas Plato's Socrates claims that he was present at Potidaea (*Chrm.* 153b–c) and gave up the prize for valor to Alcibiades (cf. *Smp.* 220e)[174]. But all historians agree that the expedition against Potidaea, when Phormio served as general, preceded the expedition against Delium.[175]

The philosophers thus lie about everything and fail to realize that much of what they write is full of anachronisms. The noble Xenophon is unaware of this, for example, in his *Symposium* (1.2), where he represents Callias the son of Hipponicus[176] as in love with Autolycus the son

174 In fact Alcibiades is speaking.
175 The former took place in 432 BCE, the latter in 424 BCE.
176 *PAA* 554500.   177 *PAA* 239835.

ποιούμενον καὶ σὺν τοῖς ἄλλοις δαιτυμόσι παρόντα
⟨αὐτὸν⟩ τὸν ἴσως μηδὲ γεννηθέντα ἢ περὶ τὴν παιδι-
κὴν ἡλικίαν ὑπάρχοντα. ἐστὶν δὲ οὗτος ὁ καιρὸς καθ'
ὃν Ἀριστίων ἄρχων ἦν· ἐπὶ τούτου γὰρ Εὔπολις τὸν
Αὐτόλυκον διδάξας διὰ Δημοστράτου χλευάζει τὴν
e   νίκην τοῦ Αὐτολύκου. | πάλιν ὁ Ξενοφῶν ποιεῖ τὸν
Σωκράτην λέγοντα ἐν τῷ Συμποσίῳ ταυτί· καίτοι
Παυσανίας γε ὁ Ἀγάθωνος τοῦ ποιητοῦ ἐραστὴς ἀπο-
λογούμενος ὑπὲρ τῶν ἀκρασίᾳ συγκαλινδουμένων εἴρηκεν ὡς καὶ στράτευμα ἀλκιμώτατον ἂν γένοιτο ἐκ
παιδικῶν καὶ ἐραστῶν. τούτους γὰρ ἂν ἔφη οἴεσθαι
μάλιστα ἂν αἰδεῖσθαι ἀλλήλους ἀπολιπεῖν, θαυμαστὰ
λέγων, εἴ γε οἱ ψόγου τε ἀφροντιστεῖν καὶ ἀναισχυν-
τεῖν πρὸς ἀλλήλους ἐθιζόμενοι, οὗτοι μάλιστ' αἰσχύ-
f   νονται αἰσχρόν τι ποιεῖν. ὅτι μὲν οὖν τούτων οὐδὲν |
εἴρηκεν Παυσανίας ἔξεστι μαθεῖν ἐκ τοῦ Πλάτωνος
Συμποσίου. Παυσανίου γὰρ οὐκ οἶδα σύγγραμμα,
οὐδ' εἰσῆκται παρ' ἄλλῳ λαλῶν οὗτος περὶ χρήσεως
ἐραστῶν καὶ παιδικῶν ἢ παρὰ Πλάτωνι· πλὴν εἴτε
κατέψευσται τοῦτο Ξενοφῶν εἴτ' ἄλλως γεγραμμένῳ
τῷ Πλάτωνος ἐνέτυχε Συμποσίῳ, παρείσθω· τὸ δὲ
κατὰ τοὺς χρόνους ἀστόχημα λεκτέον. Ἀριστίων, ἐφ'
οὗ τὸ συμπόσιον ὑπόκειται συνηγμένον, πρὸ τεσσά-
217   ρων ἐτῶν Εὐφήμου πρότερος ἦρξεν, ‖ καθ' ὃν Πλάτων
τὰ Ἀγάθωνος νικητήρια γέγραφεν, ἐν οἷς Παυσανίας
τὰ περὶ τῶν ἐρωτικῶν διεξέρχεται. θαυμαστὸν οὖν καὶ
τερατῶδες, εἰ τὰ μήπω ῥηθέντα, μετὰ δὲ τέτταρα ἔτη
ἐπιχειρηθέντα παρ' Ἀγάθωνι Σωκράτης παρὰ Καλλίᾳ

of Lycon[177] and as giving a feast for him after he won the pancration, and represents himself as present along with the other dinner-guests, although he may well not even have been born yet or was only a boy. This is the period when Aristion was eponymous archon;[178] because it was in his archonship that Eupolis staged his *Autolycus* (test. i), with Demostratus[179] as producer, and made fun of Autolycus' victory. Again, Xenophon in his *Symposium* (8.32–3) represents Socrates as saying the following: And yet Pausanias, the lover of the poet Agathon, says in defense of those who wallow in lust that the most valiant military unit would be made up of boys and their lovers; because, he said, he thought that they would be particularly ashamed to desert one another—which is an extraordinary thing to say, if the idea is that people who are used to ignoring hostile comments and behaving shamelessly with one another would be particularly ashamed of doing something shameful! But that Pausanias actually said none of this can be learned from Plato's *Symposium*. I know of no treatise written by Pausanias; and no author other than Plato introduces him talking about the use to which lovers and boys could be put. The question, however, of whether Xenophon has lied about this or happened on a *Symposium* by Plato with different contents, can be set aside; but the chronological error requires discussion. Aristion, in whose year the symposium is supposed to be held, was archon four years before Euphemus[180], in whose year Plato (cf. *Smp*. 173a) has set Agathon's victory celebration, where Pausanias spells out his views on erotic attraction. It

173 421/20 BCE.   179 *PAA* 319190.
180 Eponymous archon for 417/16 BCE.

δειπνῶν εὐθύνει ⟨ὡς⟩ οὐ δεόντως ῥηθέντα. ὅλως δὲ
λῆρός ἐστι τῷ Πλάτωνι τὸ Συμπόσιον. ὅτε γὰρ Ἀγάθων ἐνίκα, Πλάτων ἦν δεκατεσσάρων· ἐτῶν. ὁ μὲν γὰρ
ἐπὶ ἄρχοντος Εὐφήμου στεφανοῦται Ληναίοις, Πλάτων δὲ γεννᾶται ἐπὶ Ἀπολλοδώρου τοῦ μετ᾽ Εὐθύδημον ἄρξαντος· δύο δὲ καὶ ὀγδοήκοντα βιώσας ἔτη
b μετήλλαξεν ἐπὶ Θεοφίλου | τοῦ μετὰ Καλλίμαχον, ὅς
ἐστιν ὀγδοηκοστὸς καὶ δεύτερος. ἀπὸ δὲ Ἀπολλοδώρου καὶ τῆς Πλάτωνος γενέσεως τεσσαρεσκαιδέκατός
ἐστιν ἄρχων Εὔφημος, ἐφ᾽ οὗ τὰ ἐπινίκια Ἀγάθωνος
ἑστιῶνται. καὶ αὐτὸς δὲ ὁ Πλάτων δηλοῖ τὴν συνουσίαν ταύτην πρὸ πολλοῦ γεγονέναι, λέγων οὕτως ἐν
τῷ Συμποσίῳ· "εἰ νεωστὶ ἡγεῖ τὴν συνουσίαν γεγο-
c νέναι, ὥστε κἀμὲ παραγενέσθαι." "ἐγὼ γάρ," ἔφη. |
"πόθεν," ἦν δ᾽ ἐγώ, "ὦ Γλαύκων; οὐκ οἶσθ᾽ ὅτι πολλῶν
ἐτῶν Ἀγάθων οὐκ ἐπιδεδήμηκε;" καὶ προελθὼν φησιν·
"ἀλλ᾽ εἰπέ μοι, πότε ἐγένετο ἡ συνουσία αὕτη;" κἀγὼ
εἶπον ὅτι παίδων ἔτι ὄντων ἡμῶν, ὅτε τῇ τραγῳδίᾳ
ἐνίκησεν ὁ Ἀγάθων. ὅτι δὲ πολλὰ ὁ Πλάτων παρὰ
τοὺς χρόνους ἁμαρτάνει δῆλόν ἐστιν ἐκ πολλῶν· κατὰ
γὰρ τὸν εἰπόντα ποιητήν

ὅττι κεν ἐπ᾽ ἀκαιρίμαν
γλῶτταν ἔλθῃ,

τοῦτο μὴ διακρίνας γράφει. οὐ γὰρ ἀγράφως τι ἔλε-

---

181 430/29 BCE. The reference to the previous year's archon

is therefore remarkable and strange if, when Socrates is
having dinner at Callias' house, he censures as inappropriate remarks that have not yet been made and that were,
in fact, only ventured four years later at the party for
Agathon. But Plato's *Symposium* is complete nonsense;
because when Agathon took the prize, Plato was 14 years
old. For Agathon was crowned at the Lenaia during
the archonship of Euphemus, while Plato was born during the archonship of Apollodorus[181], who came after
Euthydemus. He lived 82 years and passed on in the
archonship of Theophilus,[182] who came after Callimachus
and is the 82nd archon;[183] and the 14th archon after
Apollodorus and the birth of Plato is Euphemus, in whose
year Agathon's victory-feast is celebrated. Plato himself
makes it clear that this party took place much earlier when
he says the following in his *Symposium* (172c): "If you
think that the party took place recently, so that I was there
too." "I certainly do," he said. "Where did you get that
idea, Glaucon?", I said. "Don't you realize that Agathon
hasn't been in the country for many years?" And further on
(173a) he says: "But tell me—when did this party take
place?" And I said that it happened when we were still
boys, when Agathon was victorious with his tragedy. That
Plato makes numerous chronological errors is clear from
many passages. For, as the poet says (adesp. *PMG* 1020),

whatever comes to

that follows serves to distinguish this Apollodorus from the Apollodorus who was eponymous archon in 350/49.

[182] 348/7 BCE.

[183] Sc. after Apollodorus.

γεν, ἀλλὰ † πάνυ ἐσκεμμένως, ὡς ἐν τῷ Γοργίᾳ
d γράφων | φησίν· "ἄθλιος ἄρα οὗτος ὁ Ἀρχέλαός ἐστι
κατὰ τὸν σὸν λόγον;" "εἴπερ γε, ὦ φίλε, ἄδικος." εἶτα
ῥητῶς εἰπὼν ὡς κατέχοντος τὴν Μακεδόνων ἀρχὴν
Ἀρχελάου προβὰς γράφει τάδε· καὶ Περικλέα τοῦτον
⟨τὸν⟩ νεωστὶ τετελευτηκότα. εἰ δὲ νεωστὶ τετελεύτηκε
Περικλῆς, Ἀρχέλαος οὔπω κύριός ἐστι τῆς ἀρχῆς· εἰ
δ' οὗτος βασιλεύει, πρὸ πολλοῦ πάνυ χρόνου ἀπέθανε
Περικλῆς. Περδίκκας τοίνυν πρὸ Ἀρχελάου βασιλεύει, ὡς μὲν ὁ Ἀκάνθιός φησιν Νικομήδης, ἔτη ἓν καὶ
e τεσσαράκοντα, Θεόπομπος | δὲ πέντε καὶ τριάκοντα,
Ἀναξιμένης τεσσαράκοντα, Ἱερώνυμος ὀκτὼ καὶ εἴκοσι, Μαρσύας δὲ καὶ Φιλόχορος τρία καὶ εἴκοσι. τούτων οὖν διαφόρως ἱστορουμένων λάβωμεν τὸν ἐλάχι-
στον ἀριθμὸν τὰ τρία καὶ εἴκοσι ἔτη. Περικλῆς δ'
ἀποθνῄσκει κατὰ τὸ τρίτον ἔτος τοῦ Πελοποννησια-
κοῦ πολέμου ἄρχοντος Ἐπαμείνονος, ἐφ' οὗ τελευτᾷ ⟨
. . . ⟩ Περδίκκας καὶ τὴν βασιλείαν Ἀρχέλαος δια-
δέχεται. πῶς οὖν νεωστὶ κατὰ Πλάτωνα τελευτᾷ Περικλῆς; ἐν δὲ τῷ αὐτῷ Γοργίᾳ ὁ Πλάτων τὸν Σωκράτη
f ποιεῖ λέγοντα· καὶ πέρυσιν βουλεύειν | λαχών, ἐπειδὴ
ἡ φυλὴ ἐπρυτάνευε καὶ ἔδει με ἐπιψηφίζειν, γέλωτα
παρεῖχον καὶ οὐκ ἠδυνάμην ἐπιψηφίσαι. τοῦτο ὁ Σωκράτης οὐ κατὰ ἀδυναμίαν ἐποίησεν, ἀλλὰ μᾶλλον
κατὰ ἀνδραγαθίαν· οὐ γὰρ ἠβούλετο λύειν δημοκρα-
τίας νόμους. παρίστησι δὲ τοῦτο σαφῶς ὁ Ξενοφῶν ἐν

an untimely tongue,

he shows no discrimination and writes it down. Because he never said anything without writing it down, but did so †quite deliberately, as he says when he writes in his *Gorgias* (471a): "So according to your argument, then, this Archelaus[184] is miserable?" "He is, my friend, if he's unjust." And then, after saying explicitly that Archelaus is in control of the Macedonian throne, further on he writes the following (503c): and this Pericles who died recently. But if Pericles is recently dead, Archelaus is not in control of the throne; and if Archelaus is king, Pericles died a very long time ago. Perdiccas, in fact, reigned for 41 years before Archelaus according to Nicomedes of Acanthus (*FGrH* 772 F *2), for 35 years according to Theopompus (*FGrH* 115 F 279), for 40 years according to Anaximenes (*FGrH* 72 F 27), for 28 years according to Hieronymus (*FGrH* 154 F 1), and for 23 years according to Marsyas (*FGrH* 135/6 F 15) and Philochorus (*FGrH* 328 F 126). Of the various numbers offered, let us take the smallest, which is 23 years. Pericles died in the third year of the Peloponnesian War, when Epameinon was eponymous archon,[185] in the year when . . . died . . . Perdiccas, and Archelaus inherits the kingship. How then could Pericles be recently dead, as Plato puts it? In the same *Gorgias* (473e–4a), Plato represents Socrates as saying: And last year when I was chosen by lot to be a member of the Council, when my tribe supplied the prytaneis and I had to put a question to the vote, I made everyone laugh, since I was unable to do it. Socrates did this not because he

---

[184] Archelaus, king of Macedon, reigned *c.*413–399 BCE.
[185] 429/8 BCE.

πρώτῳ Ἑλληνικῶν ἐκτιθεὶς οὕτως· τῶν δὲ πρυτάνεων
τινων οὐ φασκόντων προθήσειν τὴν διαψήφισιν παρὰ
218 τοὺς νόμους, αὖθις Καλλίξεινος ‖ ἀναβὰς κατηγόρει
αὐτῶν. οἱ δὲ ἐβόων καλεῖν τοὺς οὐ φάσκοντας· οἱ δὲ
πρυτάνεις φοβηθέντες ὡμολόγουν ἅπαντες προθήσειν
πλὴν Σωκράτους τοῦ Σωφρονίσκου. οὗτος δὲ οὐκ ἔφη,
ἀλλὰ κατὰ τοὺς νόμους πάντα ποιήσειν. οὗτός ἐστιν ὁ
διαψηφισμὸς ὁ γενόμενος κατὰ τῶν περὶ Ἐρασινίδην
στρατηγῶν, ὅτι τοὺς ἐν Ἀργινούσσαις ἐν τῇ ναυμαχίᾳ
ἀπολομένους οὐκ ἀνείλοντο. ἐγένετο δὲ ἡ ναυμαχία
ἐπὶ ἄρχοντος Καλλίου, τῆς Περικλέους τελευτῆς ὕστερον ἔτεσιν εἴκοσι καὶ τέτταρσιν.

b   Ἀλλὰ ‖ μὴν καὶ ὁ ἐν τῷ Πρωταγόρᾳ διάλογος, μετὰ
τὴν Ἱππονίκου τελευτὴν γενόμενος παρειληφότος ἤδη
τὴν οὐσίαν Καλλίου, τοῦ Πρωταγόρου ⟨μέμνηται⟩
παραγεγονότος τὸ δεύτερον οὐ πολλαῖς πρότερον ἡμέραις. ὁ δ᾽ Ἱππόνικος ἐπὶ μὲν Εὐθυδήμου ἄρχοντος
στρατηγῶν παρατέτακται μετὰ Νικίου πρὸς Τανα-
γραίους καὶ τοὺς παραβοηθοῦντας Βοιωτῶν καὶ τῇ
μάχῃ νενίκηκε. τέθνηκε δὲ πρὸ τῆς ἐπ᾽ Ἀλκαίου διδα-
σκαλίας τῶν Εὐπόλιδος Κολάκων οὐ πολλῷ χρόνῳ
c   κατὰ τὸ εἰκός· πρόσφατον ‖ γάρ τινα τοῦ Καλλίου τὴν
παράληψιν τῆς οὐσίας ἐμφαίνει τὸ δρᾶμα. ἐν οὖν
τούτῳ τῷ δράματι Εὔπολις τὸν Πρωταγόραν ὡς ἐπι-
δημοῦντα εἰσάγει, Ἀμειψίας δ᾽ ἐν τῷ Κόννῳ δύο πρό-

---

186 PAA 558605; Xenophon and our other sources consistently
spell his name Callixenus.

was unable, but rather because he was brave; for he was unwilling to violate the laws of the democracy. Xenophon makes this clear in Book I (7.14–15) of the *Hellenica*, where he makes the following remarks: When some of the prytaneis refused to put the question contrary to the laws, Callixeinus[186] mounted the speaker's stand again and began to denounce them. And other people were shouting that those who refused should be put on trial. The prytaneis were frightened and all agreed to put the question, with the exception of Socrates the son of Sophroniscus. He refused and said that he would do everything according to the laws. This is the vote that took place about Erasinides[187] and his fellow-generals, because they failed to recover the bodies of the men who died in the naval battle at Arginusae. The battle took place during the archonship of Callias,[188] 24 years after Pericles' death.

Likewise the conversation in the *Protagoras*, which takes place after Hipponicus' death, when Callias[189] has already inherited his property, refers (309c–d) to Protagoras as having arrived in Athens for a second time a few days earlier. But Hipponicus was general during the archonship of Euthydemus[190] and was stationed along with Nicias opposite the men of Tanagra and the other Boeotians who came to their assistance, and won the battle. He apparently died shortly before the performance of Eupolis' *Flatterers* (test. ii) during the archonship of Alcaeus,[191] for the play

---

[187] *PAA* 400045. Erasinides and a number of the other generals were executed.   [188] 406/5 BCE.   [189] See 1.22f n. Callias' father Hipponicus (below) is *PAA* 538910.

[190] 431/0 BCE. The events referred to here, however, took place in 426/5, and the correct archon's name is Euthynus.

τερον ἔτεσιν διδαχθέντι οὐ καταριθμεῖ αὐτὸν ἐν τῷ
τῶν φροντιστῶν χορῷ. δῆλον οὖν ὡς μεταξὺ τούτων
τῶν χρόνων παραγέγονεν. ὁ δὲ Πλάτων καὶ τὸν Ἠλεῖ-
ον Ἱππίαν συμπαρόντα ποιεῖ τῷ[33] Πρωταγόρᾳ μετά
τινων ἰδίων πολιτῶν, οὓς οὐκ εἰκὸς ἐν Ἀθήναις ἀσφα-
d λῶς διατρίβειν | πρὸ τοῦ τὰς ἐνιαυσίας ἐπὶ Ἰσάρχου
Ἐλαφηβολιῶνος συντελεσθῆναι σπονδάς. ὁ δὲ τὸν
διάλογον ὑφίσταται γινόμενον περὶ τοὺς καιροὺς τούτους καθ᾽ οὓς αἱ σπονδαὶ προσφάτως ἐγεγόνεσαν.
λέγει γοῦν· εἰ γὰρ εἶεν ἄνθρωποι ἄγριοι οἵους πέρυσι
Φερεκράτης ὁ ποιητὴς ἐδίδαξεν ἐπὶ Ληναίῳ. ἐδιδάχ-
θησαν δὲ οἱ Ἄγριοι ἐπ᾽ Ἀριστίωνος ἄρχοντος, ἀφ᾽ οὗ
ἐστιν ἄρχων Ἀστύφιλος, πέμπτος ὢν ἀπὸ Ἰσάρχου,
καθ᾽ ὃν αἱ σπονδαὶ ἐγένοντο. Ἴσαρχος γάρ, εἶτ᾽
e Ἀμεινίας, μεθ᾽ ὃν Ἀλκαῖος, εἶτ᾽ Ἀριστίων, | εἶτ᾽ Ἀστύ-
φιλος. παρὰ τὴν ἱστορίαν οὖν ὁ Πλάτων ἐν τῷ διαλόγῳ εἰς τὰς Ἀθήνας παράγει πολεμίους ὄντας τοὺς
περὶ τὸν Ἱππίαν, μὴ τῆς ἐκεχειρίας αὐτῆς μενούσης.

Κἂν ἄλλοις δ᾽ ὁ Πλάτων φησὶ Χαιρεφῶντα ἐρωτῆ-
σαι τὴν Πυθίαν εἴ τις εἴη Σωκράτους σοφώτερος· καὶ
τὴν ἀνελεῖν μηδένα. κἂν τούτοις δὲ μὴ συμφωνῶν
Ξενοφῶν φησι· Χαιρεφῶντος γάρ ποτε ἐπερωτήσαν-
τος ἐν Δελφοῖς ὑπὲρ ἐμοῦ, ἀνεῖλεν ὁ Ἀπόλλων ⟨πολ-
λῶν⟩ παρόντων μηδένα εἶναι ἀνθρώπων ἐμοῦ μήτε
f δικαιότερον μήτε | σωφρονέστερον. πῶς οὖν εὔλογον ἢ
πιθανὸν Σωκράτη τὸν ὁμολογοῦντα μηδὲν ἐπίστασθαι

---

[33] ποιεῖ ἐν τῷ A

makes it clear that Callias' inheritance of the property was a recent event. In this play, then, Eupolis introduces Protagoras as present in Athens, whereas Amipsias in his *Connus* (test. ii), staged two years earlier, does not include him in his chorus of thinkers. It is thus clear that he arrived between those dates. Plato (*Prt.* 314b–c, 315b–c) represents Hippias of Elis as being in Athens at the same time as Protagoras, along with some of his fellow-citizens, who are unlikely to have spent time in Athens without being in danger before the conclusion of the one-year truce in the month of Elaphebolion during the archonship of Isarchus.[192] But Plato assumes that the conversation took place around the time when the truce had recently been concluded. He says (*Prt.* 327d), at any rate: For if human beings were savages like the ones the poet Pherecrates put onstage last year at the Lenaia. *Savages* (test. i) was staged during the archonship of Aristion,[193] and the next archon after him was Astyphilus, who was the fifth archon after Isarchus, in whose year the truce was concluded. For there was Isarchus, then Ameinias, after him Alcaeus, then Aristion, and then Astyphilus. Plato is thus contradicting history when he introduces Hippias and his companions, who were from an enemy state, in Athens in his dialogue when no truce was in place.

Elsewhere (*Ap.* 21a) Plato says that Chaerephon asked the Pythia if anyone was wiser than Socrates, and she answered (Delphic Oracle H3 Fontenrose) that no one was. Here too Xenophon (*Ap.* 14) disagrees with him: For when Chaerephon inquired once in Delphi about me, Apollo

---

[191] 422/1 BCE.   [192] 424/3 BCE.
[193] 421/0 BCE.

σοφώτατον ἁπάντων ὑπὸ τοῦ πάντα ἐπισταμένου θεοῦ
ἀναρρηθῆναι· εἰ γὰρ τοῦτό ἐστι σοφία, τὸ μηδὲν
εἰδέναι, τὸ πάντα εἰδέναι φαυλότης ἂν εἴη. τίς δ᾽ ἦν
χρεία τῷ Χαιρεφῶντι παρενοχλεῖν τὸν θεὸν περὶ Σωκράτους πυνθανόμενον· αὐτὸς γὰρ ἦν ἀξιόπιστος ὑπὲρ
219   αὑτοῦ λέγων ὡς οὔκ ἐστι σοφός. ‖

βλὰξ γάρ τις ἦν τοιαῦτ᾽ ἐρωτῶν τὸν θεόν,

ὡς ἂν εἰ καὶ τοιαῦτα, τίνα τῶν Ἀττικῶν ἐρίων ἄλλ᾽
ἐστὶ μαλακώτερα, εἰ τῶν ἐν Βάκτροις καμήλων εἰσί
τινες δυνατώτεροι, ἢ εἰ Σωκράτους ἐστί τις σιμότερος;
τοὺς γὰρ τὰ τοιαῦτα πυνθανομένους εὐστόχως ἐπιρ-
ραπίζει ὁ θεός, ὡς καὶ τὸν πυθόμενον, εἴτ᾽ Αἴσωπός
ἐστιν ὁ λογοποιὸς ἢ ἄλλος τις,

πῶς ἂν πλουτήσαιμι, Διὸς καὶ Λητοῦς υἱέ;

χλευάζων ἀπεκρίνατο·

εἰ τὸ μέσον κτήσαιο Κορίνθου καὶ Σικυῶνος.

b   Ἀλλὰ μὴν οὐδ᾽ ὧν ὁ Πλάτων | εἴρηκε περὶ Σω-
κράτους τῶν κωμικῶν τις εἴρηκεν, οὔθ᾽ ὅτι μαίας
βλοσυρᾶς υἱὸς ἦν οὔθ᾽ ὅτι Ξανθίππη χαλεπὴ ἦν γυνή,
ἥτις καὶ νιπτῆρας αὐτοῦ κατέχει τῆς κεφαλῆς, οὔθ᾽ ὡς

---

194 Zenob. 3.57 explains the proverb "Might I have what is between Corinth and Sicyon" thus: "Applied to those pray to have

answered in the presence of many people that no human being was more just or moderate than me. Then how is it reasonable or believable that Socrates, who admitted that he knew nothing, was proclaimed the wisest person of all by the god who knows everything? For if knowing nothing is wisdom, knowing everything would have to be stupidity. And why did Chaerephon need to bother the god by asking questions about Socrates? Because Socrates himself deserved to be believed when he said of himself (Pl. *Ap.* 21b, 23a–b) that he was not wise.

> For the man who asked the god such things was a
>   fool (adesp. com. fr. *109),

as if you were to ask questions like: What wool is softer than the Attic variety? or Are any camels stronger than the Bactrian type? or Does anyone have more of a snub-nose than Socrates? For the god is quite right to rebuke people who ask things like this, as for example the man (it may have been the storyteller Aesop or someone else) who asked:

> How could I get rich, son of Zeus and Leto?

The god mockingly replied (Fontenrose, *The Delphic Oracle* p. 86):

> If you acquire the land between Corinth and
>   Sicyon.[194]

Likewise nothing Plato says about Socrates is men-

what is best and most expensive. Because the land between these cities is extremely productive."

547

Ἀλκιβιάδῃ συνεκοιμήθη ὑπὸ τὴν αὐτὴν γενόμενος
χλαῖναν. καίτοι ἀναγκαῖον ἦν τοῦτο ἐκκωδωνισθῆναι
ὑπὸ Ἀριστοφάνους τοῦ καὶ ἐν τῷ συμποσίῳ κατὰ
Πλάτωνα· οὐ γὰρ ἂν ἐσίγησε τοῦτ' Ἀριστοφάνης <
. . . > ὡς τοὺς νέους διαφθείροντος. Ἀσπασία μέντοι ἡ
c σοφὴ τοῦ Σωκράτους διδάσκαλος τῶν ῥητορικῶν |
λόγων ἐν τοῖς φερομένοις ὡς αὐτῆς ἔπεσιν, ἅπερ
Ἡρόδικος ὁ Κρατήτειος παρέθετο, φησὶν οὕτως·

"Σώκρατες, οὐκ ἔλαθές με πόθῳ δηχθεὶς φρένα
τὴν σὴν
παιδὸς Δεινομάχης καὶ Κλεινίου. ἀλλ'
ὑπάκουσον,
εἰ βούλει σοι ἔχειν εὖ παιδικά, μηδ' ἀπιθήσῃς
ἀγγέλῳ, ἀλλὰ πιθοῦ, καί σοι πολὺ βέλτιον
d ἔσται." |
κἀγὼ ὅπως ἤκουσα, χαρᾶς ὕπο σῶμα λιπαίνω
ἱδρῶτι, βλεφάρων δὲ γόος πέσεν οὐκ ἀθελήτως.
"στέλλου πλησάμενος θυμὸν Μούσης κατόχοιο,
ᾗ τόνδ' αἱρήσεις, ὡσὶν δ' ἐνίει ποθέουσιν·
ἀμφοῖν γὰρ φιλίας ἥδ' ἀρχή, τῇδε καθέξεις

195 Probably intended as a colloquial way of saying "who constantly said abusive things to him." For Xanthippe's vile temper,
see X. *Mem.* 2.2.7; *Smp.* 2.10; but Socrates himself was doubtless
an extremely aggravating spouse.   196 Cf. Pl. *Ap.* 23d.

197 *PAA* 222330; she lived with the Athenian politician Pericles after his marriage ended. Despite Plato, she certainly did not
teach Socrates rhetoric.

548

tioned by any comic poet: not the fact that he was the son
of a burly midwife (*Tht.* 149a), nor that Xanthippe was a
difficult wife who used to pour washing-water over his
head,[195] nor that he slept with Alcibiades under the same
robe (*Smp.* 219b–c). Yet Aristophanes, who was at the symposium, according to Plato, would have to have made a
great deal of noise about this, because Aristophanes would
not have kept silent about this, . . . on the ground that
he was corrupting the young men.[196] In fact, the wise
Aspasia[197], who taught Socrates rhetoric (cf. Pl. *Menex.*
235e), says the following in the verses Crates' student
Herodicus cites, which are attributed to her (*SH* 495.1–
10):[198]

> "Socrates, I did not fail to note that your heart is
>   stung with desire
> for the son of Deinomache and Cleinias.[199] Pay
>   attention
> if you want to be successful at seducing boys, and do
>   not disbelieve
> the messenger, but believe her, and you will be much
>   better off."
> When I heard this, I was so overjoyed that my body
>   shone
> with sweat, and tears fell from my eyes not against
>   my will.
> "Prepare yourself by filling your heart with a
>   dominating Muse,
> with whose help you will capture him, and pour her

---

[198] The author is in fact almost certainly Herodicus himself.
[199] Alcibiades.

αὐτόν, προσβάλλων ἀκοαῖς ὀπτήρια θυμοῦ."

κυνηγεῖ οὖν ὁ καλὸς Σωκράτης ἐρωτοδιδάσκαλον
ἔχων τὴν Μιλησίαν, ἀλλ' οὐκ αὐτὸς θηρεύεται, ὡς ὁ
Πλάτων ἔφη, λινοστατούμενος ὑπὸ Ἀλκιβιάδου. καὶ
e μὴν οὐ διαλείπει γε κλαίων | ὡς ἄν, οἶμαι, δυσημερῶν.
ἰδοῦσα γὰρ αὐτὸν ἐν οἵῳ ἦν καταστήματι Ἀσπασία
φησίν·

"τίπτε δεδάκρυσαι, φίλε Σώκρατες; ἦ σ' ἀνακινεῖ
στέρνοις ἐνναίων σκηπτὸς πόθος ὄμμασι
    θραυσθεὶς
παιδὸς ἀνικήτου; τὸν ἐγὼ τιθασόν σοι ὑπέστην
ποιῆσαι."

ὅτι δὲ ὄντως ἦρα τοῦ Ἀλκιβιάδου δῆλον ποιεῖ Πλάτων
f ἐν τῷ Πρωταγόρᾳ, καίτοι μικρὸν ἀπολείποντος | τῶν
τριάκοντα ἐτῶν. λέγει δ' οὕτως· "πόθεν, ὦ Σώκρατες,
φαίνει; ἦ δηλαδὴ ἀπὸ κυνηγεσίου τοῦ περὶ τὴν Ἀλκιβιάδου ὥραν; καὶ μήν μοι καὶ πρώην ἰδόντι καλὸς
ἐφαίνετο ὁ ἀνὴρ ἔτι· ἀνὴρ μέντοι, ὦ Σώκρατες, ὥς γε
ἐν ἡμῖν αὐτοῖς εἰρῆσθαι, καὶ πώγωνος ἤδη ὑποπιμ-
220 πλάμενος." ‖ "εἶτα τί δὴ τοῦτο; οὐ σὺ μέντοι Ὁμήρου
ἐπαινέτης εἶ, ὃς ἔφη χαριεστάτην ἥβην εἶναι τοῦ
ὑπηνήτου, ἣν νῦν Ἀλκιβιάδης αὐτὸς ἔχει;"

Πεφύκασι δ' οἱ πλεῖστοι τῶν φιλοσόφων τῶν κωμικῶν κακήγοροι μᾶλλον εἶναι, εἴ γε καὶ Αἰσχίνης ὁ
Σωκρατικὸς ἐν μὲν τῷ Τηλαύγει Κριτόβουλον τὸν

into his longing ears.
For she is the beginning of a friendship between the
   two of you, and you will use her to get control
of him, by offering his ears glimpses of your soul."

The noble Socrates thus goes hunting with the Milesian[200]
as his instructor in love, and is not himself the quarry, as
Plato (*Smp*. 219b) claimed, and caught in Alcibiades' net.
Nor does he stop wailing in the way someone would, I
think, if luck were against him. Because when Aspasia sees
the state he is in, she says (*SH* 495.11–14):

"Why have you been weeping, my dear Socrates?
   Does shattered desire
that dwells in your breast and falls like a lightning
   bolt at the glance of a boy
who cannot be conquered stir you up? I promised to
   tame him
for you."

Plato in his *Protagoras* (309a–b) makes it clear that Socrates was actually in love with Alcibiades, even though
Alcibiades was almost 30 years old. He says the following:
"Where have you come from, Socrates? No doubt from
hunting Alcibiades' youthful beauty? The man did indeed
still look handsome to me when I saw him recently. But
he's a man, Socrates, just between the two of us, and is already getting a full beard." "And what does that matter?
Don't you applaud Homer, who said (*Od*. 10.279) that the
loveliest stage of youth is when someone is just getting a
beard, which is the age Alcibiades himself is now?"

[200] Aspasia.

Κρίτωνος ἐπ' ἀμαθείᾳ καὶ ῥυπαρότητι βίου κωμῳδεῖ,
τὸν δὲ Τηλαύγην αὐτὸν ἱματίου μὲν φορήσεως καθ'
ἡμέραν ἡμιωβέλιον κναφεῖ τελοῦντα μισθόν, κωδίῳ δὲ
b ἐζωσμένον καὶ τὰ ὑποδήματα σπαρτίοις ἐνημμένον |
σαπροῖς καὶ † τελέσαντα † οὐ μετρίως διαγελᾷ. ἐν δὲ
τῇ Ἀσπασίᾳ Ἱππόνικον μὲν τὸν Καλλίου κοάλεμον
προσαγορεύει, τὰς δ' ἐκ τῆς Ἰωνίας γυναῖκας συλλή-
βδην μοιχάδας καὶ κερδαλέας. ὁ δὲ Καλλίας αὐτοῦ
περιέχει τὴν τοῦ Καλλίου πρὸς τὸν πατέρα διαφορὰν
καὶ τὴν Προδίκου καὶ Ἀναξαγόρου τῶν σοφιστῶν
διαμώκησιν. λέγει γὰρ ὡς ὁ μὲν Πρόδικος Θηραμένην
μαθητὴν ἀπετέλεσεν, ὁ δ' ἕτερος Φιλόξενον τὸν Ἐρύ-
ξιδος καὶ Ἀριφράδην τὸν ἀδελφὸν Ἀριγνώτου τοῦ
c κιθαρῳδοῦ, | θέλων ἀπὸ τῆς τῶν δηλωθέντων μοχθη-
ρίας καὶ περὶ τὰ φαῦλα λιχνείας ἐμφανίσαι τὴν τῶν
παιδευσάντων διδασκαλίαν. ἐν δὲ τῷ Ἀξιόχῳ πικρῶς
Ἀλκιβιάδου κατατρέχει ὡς οἰνόφλυγος καὶ περὶ τὰς
ἀλλοτρίας γυναῖκας σπουδάζοντος.

Ἀντισθένης δ' ἐν Θατέρῳ τῶν Κύρων κακολογῶν
Ἀλκιβιάδην καὶ παράνομον εἶναι λέγει καὶ εἰς γυναῖκας καὶ εἰς τὴν ἄλλην δίαιταν· συνεῖναι γάρ φησιν
αὐτὸν καὶ μητρὶ καὶ θυγατρὶ καὶ ἀδελφῇ, ὡς Πέρσας.
d ὁ δὲ Πολιτικὸς αὐτοῦ Διάλογος | ἁπάντων κατα-

---

201 *PAA* 585450; Critoboulus was another of Socrates' fol-
lowers.   202 An early Pythagorean.
203 Perhaps *PAA* 538910 (see 5.218b), certainly referred to below; but the reference is more likely to his grandson, *PAA* 538915,
who was Aeschines' contemporary.

BOOK V

Most philosophers have more abusive tongues than comic poets so, given that in his *Telauges* Socrates' student Aeschines (*SSR* VI.A F 84) mocks Critoboulus the son of Crito[201] for his ignorance and filthy lifestyle, and makes vigorous fun of Telauges[202] himself for paying a fuller half an obol per day to rent the robe he wore, and for wrapping himself in a sheepskin, fastening his shoes with rotten rope, and [corrupt]. In his *Aspasia* (*SSR* VI.A F 61) he refers to Hipponicus son of Callias[203] as a fool, and to Ionian women generally as grasping adulteresses. His *Callias* (*SSR* VI.A F 73) contains a comparison of Callias with his father, and mockery of the sophists Prodicus and Anaxagoras; for he says that Prodicus (84 A 4b D-K) produced Theramenes[204] as his student, while the other fellow[205] (59 A 22 D-K) produced Philoxenus the son of Eryxis[206] and Ariphrades[207] the brother of the citharode Arignotus, his goal being to use the depravity of the individuals he named and their greed for foul behavior to illustrate the sort of education provided by these teachers. And in his *Axiochus* (*SSR* VI.A F 56) he bitterly disparages Alcibiades as a drunk interested in other men's wives.

Antisthenes in *On the Second Cyrus*[208] (*SSR* V.A F 141) abuses Alcibiades, saying that he lacked respect for the law

---

[204] *PAA* 513930. Theramenes was a late 5th-century Athenian politician routinely denounced in our sources as an unscrupulous opportunist.   [205] Anaxagoras.   [206] The notorious glutton (*PA* 14707) referred to also at 1.6b.   [207] *PAA* 202305; Stephanis #399. Aristophanes repeatedly denounces him for his alleged devotion to cunnilingus (esp. *Eq.* 1278–89).

[208] Cyrus the Younger, whose revolt against his brother Artaxerxes II came to an end at the Battle of Cunaxa in 401 BCE.

δρομὴν περιέχει τῶν Ἀθήνησιν δημαγωγῶν, ὁ δ'
Ἀρχέλαος Γοργίου τοῦ ῥήτορος, ἡ δ' Ἀσπασία τῶν
Περικλέους υἱῶν Ξανθίππου καὶ Παράλου διαβολήν·
τούτων γὰρ τὸν μὲν Ἀρχεστράτου φησὶν εἶναι συμ-
βιωτὴν τοῦ παραπλήσια ταῖς ἐπὶ τῶν μικρῶν οἰκη-
μάτων ἐργαζομένου, τὸν δ' Εὐφήμου συνήθη καὶ
γνώριμον τοῦ φορτικὰ σκώπτοντος καὶ ψυχρὰ τοὺς
συναντῶντας. καὶ Πλάτωνα δὲ μετονομάσας Σάθωνα
ἀσύρως καὶ φορτικῶς τὸν ταύτην ἔχοντα τὴν ἐπι-
e γραφὴν διάλογον | ἐξέδωκε κατ' αὐτοῦ. τούτοις γὰρ
τοῖς ἀνδράσιν οὐδεὶς ἀγαθὸς σύμβουλος εἶναι δοκεῖ,
οὐ στρατηγὸς φρόνιμος, οὐ σοφιστὴς ἀξιόλογος, οὐ
ποιητὴς ὠφέλιμος, οὐ δῆμος εὐλόγιστος ἀλλ' ἢ Σωκράτης ὁ μετὰ τῶν Ἀσπασίας αὐλητρίδων ἐπὶ τῶν
ἐργαστηρίων συνδιατρίβων καὶ Πίστωνι τῷ θωρακο-
ποιῷ διαλεγόμενος καὶ Θεοδότην διδάσκων τὴν ἑταίραν ὡς δεῖ τοὺς ἐραστὰς παλεύειν, ὡς Ξενοφῶν παρίστησιν ἐν δευτέρῳ Ἀπομνημονευμάτων. τοιαῦτα γὰρ
f ποιεῖ αὐτὸν παραγγέλματα | τῇ Θεοδότῃ λέγοντα, ἃ
οὔτε Νικὼ ἡ Σαμία ἢ Καλλιστράτη ἡ Λεσβία ἢ
Φιλαινὶς ἡ Λευκαδία, ἀλλ' οὐδὲ ὁ Ἀθηναῖος Πυθόνι-
κος συνεωράκασιν πόθων θέλγητρα· οὗτοι γὰρ περὶ
ταῦτα ἠσχόληντο περιττῶς. ἐπιλείποι δ' ἄν μ' ὁ πᾶς

---

209 *PAA* 730515 and 765275, respectively.

210 *PAA* 211100; nothing else is known about this man, and the
name is common.

211 I.e. prostitutes in brothels.

both where women were concerned and in other aspects of
his life; because he claims that he had sex with his mother,
sister, and daughter, as the Persians do. His *Political Dialogue* (*SSR* V.A F 203) contains an attack on all the Athenian demagogues; his *Archelaus* (*SSR* V.A F 204) attacks
the orator Gorgias; and his *Aspasia* (*SSR* V.A F 142) slanders Pericles' sons Xanthippus and Paralus,[209] since he
claims that the former lived with Archestratus[210], whose
business was similar to that of women who work in little
rooms,[211] while the latter was an associate and close friend
of Euphemus[212], who made cheap, clumsy jokes at the expense of anyone he met. He also changed Plato's name to
Sathōn[213]—a filthy, low thing to do—and published a dialogue attacking him with that as the title (*SSR* V.A F 147).
As far as these people are concerned, no one appears to be
a good advisor, a wise general, a respectable teacher, a
helpful poet, or a rational people—except for Socrates,
who spent his time with Aspasia's pipe-girls in the brothels,
talked (X. *Mem.* 3.10.9–15) with Piston the breastplate-
maker[214], and taught the courtesan Theodote[215] how to
entrap her lovers, as Xenophon establishes in Book II of
the *Memorabilia* (3.11.1–18). For he presents him as offering Theodote the sort of instructions that neither Nico
of Samos, nor Callistrate of Lesbos, nor Philaenis of Leu-

---

[212] *PAA* 449458; nothing else is known of him.

[213] A crude colloquial term for a penis. Cf. 11.507a (also from
Herodicus).   [214] In Xenophon the name is Pistion.

[215] *PAA* 505035.   [216] *PAA* 795295; otherwise unknown.
Philaenis was believed to be the author of an explicit sexual man-
ual (referred to at 8.335d–e), and most likely the same is true of
the other individuals mentioned here as well.

ATHENAEUS

χρόνος, εἰ ἐκτίθεσθαι βουληθείην τὰς σεμνὰς τῶν
φιλοσόφων μέμψεις. κατὰ γὰρ αὐτὸν δὴ τὸν Πλάτωνα·
221 ἐπιρρεῖ δὲ ὄχλος μοι τοιούτων Γοργόνων ‖ καὶ Πη-
γάσων καὶ ἄλλων ἀμηχάνων πλήθει τε καὶ ἀτοπίᾳ
τερατολόγων τινῶν φύσεων. διόπερ κατασιωπήσομαι.
   Τοσαῦτα τοῦ Μασουρίου εἰπόντος καὶ ὑπὸ πάντων
θαυμασθέντος διὰ σοφίαν ὁ Οὐλπιανὸς σιωπῆς γενομένης ἔφη· δοκεῖτέ μοι, ἄνδρες δαιτυμόνες, σφοδροῖς
κατηντλῆσθαι λόγοις παρὰ προσδοκίαν βεβαπτίσθαι
τε τῷ ἀκράτῳ·

      ἀνὴρ γὰρ ἕλκων οἶνον, ὡς ὕδωρ ἵππος,
      Σκυθιστὶ φωνεῖ, κοὐδὲ κόππα γινώσκων·
   ⟨   *   *   *   ⟩
b   κεῖται δ' ἄναυδος ἐν πίθῳ κολυμβήσας, |
      κάθυπνος ὡς μήκωνα φάρμακον πίνων,

φησὶν ὁ Βυζάντιος Παρμένων. ἢ ἀπολελίθωσθε ὑπὸ
τῶν προειρημένων Γοργόνων; περὶ ὧν ⟨ὡς⟩ ὄντως
γεγόνασί τινα ζῷα ἀπολιθώσεως ἀνθρώποις αἴτια,
ἱστορεῖ Ἀλέξανδρος ὁ Μύνδιος ἐν δευτέρῳ Κτηνῶν
Ἱστορίας οὕτως· τὸ ζῷον[34] καλοῦσιν οἱ ἐν Λιβύῃ
Νομάδες, ὅπου καὶ γίνεται, κατώβλεπον. ἔστιν δέ, ὡς
μὲν οἱ πλεῖστοι λέγουσιν ἐκ τῆς δορᾶς σημειούμενοι,
προβάτῳ ἀγρίῳ ὅμοιον, ὡς δ' ἔνιοί φασι, μόσχῳ.
c ἔχειν δὲ λέγουσιν αὐτὸ τοιαύτην | ἀναπνοὴν ὥστε

   [34] τὴν γοργόνα τὸ ζῷον ACE

556

cas, nor Pythonicus of Athens[216] ever thought of as love-charms, although they expended tremendous effort on such matters. But all the time in the world would be insufficient, if I wanted to catalogue the philosophers' self-important fault-finding. To quote Plato (*Phdr.* 229d) himself: A crowd of such Gorgons, winged horses, and other impossible creatures, and a bizarre collection of monstrous forms presses upon me. I will therefore be quiet.

After Masurius completed this speech and everyone expressed amazement at his learning, there was a silence, and Ulpian said: My fellow-diners, it appears to me that you have been unexpectedly engulfed in a violent rush of words and drowned in unmixed wine.

> For a man who gulps down wine as a horse does
>   water
> speaks Scythian, and unable to recognize the letter
>   *koppa*
>
>   *   *   *
>
> He lies there, unable to speak, swimming in the
>   wine-jar,
> asleep, like someone who consumes opium,

says Parmenon of Byzantium (fr. 1, p. 237 Powell). Or have you been turned to stone by the Gorgons mentioned above? As for them, that there are actually creatures capable of turning people to stone is recorded by Alexander of Myndus in Book II of the *Inquiry into Flocks and Herds* (fr. I.6 Wellmann), as follows:[217] The Numidians in Libya, where the creature is found, refer to it as a *katōblepos*. Ac-

---

[217] Cf. Ael. *NA* 7.5.

πάντα τὸν ἐντυχόντα τῷ ζῴῳ διαφθείρειν. φέρειν δὲ
χαίτην ἀπὸ τοῦ μετώπου καθειμένην ἐπὶ τοὺς ὀφθαλ-
μούς, ἣν ὁπόταν μόγις διασεισαμένη διὰ τὴν βαρύ-
τητα ἐμβλέψῃ, κτείνει τὸν ὑπ' αὐτῆς θεωρηθέντα οὐ
τῷ πνεύματι, ἀλλὰ τῇ γιγνομένῃ ἀπὸ τῶν ὀμμάτων
φύσεως φορᾷ καὶ νεκρὸν ποιεῖ. ἐγνώσθη δὲ οὕτως. τῶν
μετὰ Μαρίου τινὲς ἐπὶ Ἰογόρθαν στρατευσαμένων
ἰδόντες τὴν γοργόνα δόξαντές τε διὰ τὸ κάτω νενευ-
κέναι βραδέως τε κινεῖσθαι ἄγριον εἶναι πρόβατον
d ὥρμησαν ἐπ' αὐτὸ | ὡς κατεργασόμενοι οἷς εἶχον
ξίφεσι. τὸ δὲ πτοηθὲν διασεισάμενόν τε τὴν τοῖς
ὄμμασιν ἐπικειμένην χαίτην παραχρῆμα ἐποίησε
τοὺς ὁρμήσαντας ἐπ' αὐτὸ νεκρούς. πάλιν δὲ καὶ
πάλιν τὸ αὐτὸ ποιησάντων ἑτέρων νεκρῶν τε γενη-
θέντων, ἀεὶ τῶν προσφερομένων ἀπολλυμένων, ἱστο-
ρήσαντές τινες παρὰ τῶν ἐπιχωρίων τὴν τοῦ ζῴου
φύσιν, μακρόθεν ἐνεδρεύσαντες αὐτὸ ἱππῆς τινες Νομάδες Μαρίου κελεύσαντος κατηκόντισαν ἧκόν τε
φέροντες πρὸς τὸν στρατηγὸν τὸ θηρίον. τοῦτο μὲν
e οὖν ὡς ἦν ἄρα τοιοῦτο | ἥ δορὰ ἥ τε Μαρίου στρατεία
μηνύει· ἐκεῖνο μέντοι τὸ λεγόμενον ὑπὸ τοῦ ἱστορΙο-
γράφου οὐκ ἔστι πιστόν, ὡς εἰσί τινες κατὰ τὴν
Λιβύην ὀπισθονόμοι καλούμενοι βόες διὰ τὸ μὴ ἔμ-
προσθεν αὐτοὺς πορευομένους νέμεσθαι, ἀλλ' εἰς τοὔ-
πίσω ὑποχωροῦντας τοῦτο ποιεῖν· εἶναι γὰρ αὐτοῖς
ἐμπόδιον πρὸς τὴν τοῦ κατὰ φύσιν νομὴν τὰ κέρατα
οὐκ ἄνω ἀνακεκυφότα, καθάπερ τὰ τῶν λοιπῶν ζῴων,
ἀλλὰ κάτω νενευκότα καὶ ἐπισκοτοῦντα τοῖς ὄμμασι.

cording to most authorities, who draw their conclusions from its skin, it resembles a wild sheep, although some say that it resembles a calf. They claim that its breath is capable of killing anything that encounters the creature; its hair hangs down from its forehead over its eyes, and whenever it shakes it aside (which is difficult, because it is so heavy) and looks at someone, it kills the man it sees, not with its breath but with the force naturally produced by its eyes, and strikes him dead. It was discovered in the following way. Some soldiers who accompanied Marius in his campaign against Jugurtha[218] saw the gorgon, and because it kept its head bent low and moved slowly, they concluded that it was a wild sheep and set off after it, intending to kill it with the swords they were carrying. It was startled and shook aside the hair that covered its eyes, and immediately struck the men who were charging forward toward it dead. After other men did the same thing repeatedly and were killed, since anyone who attacked it died, some of them asked the locals about the animal; and at Marius' orders, Numidian horsemen set an ambush a long way from it, killed it with javelins, and came to the general carrying the beast. That the creature was in fact as described is demonstrated both by its skin and by Marius' expedition. But the other story told by the historian is unbelievable, which is that there are cows in Libya referred to as *opisthonomoi* ("backward-grazers") because they do not move forward as they graze, but go backward as they do this. For they are

[218] *c.*107 BCE.

τοῦτο γὰρ ἄπιστόν ἐστιν, οὐδενὸς ἑτέρου ἐπιμαρτυ-
f ροῦντος ἱστορικοῦ. |

Ταῦτα τοῦ Οὐλπιανοῦ εἰπόντος ἐπιμαρτυρῶν ὁ Λαρήνσιος καὶ συγκατατιθέμενος τῷ λόγῳ ἔφη τὸν Μά-
ριον τῶν ζῴων τούτων δορὰς εἰς τὴν Ῥώμην ἀνα-
πεπομφέναι, ἃς μηδένα εἰκάσαι δεδυνῆσθαι τίνος εἰσὶ
διὰ τὸ παράδοξον τῆς ὄψεως· ἀνατεθεῖσθαί τε τὰς
δορὰς ταύτας ἐν τῷ τοῦ Ἡρακλέους ἱερῷ, ἐν ᾧ οἱ τοὺς
θριάμβους κατάγοντες στρατηγοὶ ἑστιῶσι τοὺς πολίτας, καθάπερ πολλοὶ τῶν ἡμεδαπῶν ποιηταὶ καὶ συγ-
222 γραφεῖς εἰρήκασιν. ‖ ὑμεῖς οὖν, ὦ γραμματικοί, κατὰ
τὸν Βαβυλώνιον Ἡρόδικον, μηδὲν τῶν τοιούτων ἱστο-
ροῦντες,

φεύγετ᾽, Ἀριστάρχειοι, ἐπ᾽ εὐρέα νῶτα θαλάττης
Ἑλλάδα, τῆς ξουθῆς δειλότεροι κεμάδος,
γωνιοβόμβυκες, μονοσύλλαβοι, οἷσι μέμηλε
τὸ σφὶν καὶ σφῶιν καὶ τὸ μὶν ἠδὲ τὸ νίν.
τοῦθ᾽ ὑμῖν εἴη, δυσπέμφελοι· Ἡροδίκῳ δὲ
Ἑλλὰς ἀεὶ μίμνοι καὶ θεόπαις Βαβυλών.

b κατὰ γὰρ τὸν κωμῳδιοποιὸν Ἀναξανδρίδην· |

ἡδονὴν ἔχει,
ὅταν τις εὕρῃ καινὸν ἐνθύμημά τι,
δηλοῦν ἅπασιν· οἱ δ᾽ ἑαυτοῖσιν σοφοὶ

---

219 Written to celebrate Ptolemy VIII's expulsion of many
scholars associated with the Museum in Alexandria; cf. 4.184b–c
with n.

prevented from grazing in the normal way by their horns, which do not curve upward, like the horns of other animals, but bend down and shade their eyes. This is unbelievable, and no other historian confirms it.

After Ulpian made these remarks, Larensius confirmed his report and expressed agreement, saying that Marius had sent skins from these creatures back to Rome and that, as a result of their strange appearance, no one had been able to figure out what animal they were from. He also said that these skins had been dedicated in the temple of Heracles, where generals celebrating triumphs offer the citizens a feast, as many of our people's poets and prose-authors say. So as for you, my grammarians, who do not inquire into anything like this, to quote Herodicus of Babylon (*FGE* 233–8 = *SH* 494):[219]

Flee, students of Aristarchus, over the wide back of
    the sea
        from Greece, you who are more cowardly than the
        brown deer,
buzzers-in-corners, masters of the monosyllable,
    concerned with
    sphin versus *spōin* and *min* versus *nin*.[220]
This is what I wish for you, storm-tossed ones. But
    may Greece
        and Babylon, child of the gods, always be there for
        Herodicus.

As the comic poet Anaxandrides (fr. 55) puts it:

It's a pleasure,

[220] Alternative forms of two Greek pronouns.

πρῶτον μὲν οὐκ ἔχουσι τῆς τέχνης κριτήν,
εἶτα φθονοῦνται. χρὴ γὰρ εἰς ὄχλον φέρειν
ἅπανθ᾽ ὅσ᾽ ἄν τις καινότητ᾽ ἔχειν δοκῇ.

ἐπὶ τούτοις τοῖς λόγοις ἀναχωροῦντες οἱ πολλοὶ λελη-
θότως διέλυσαν τὴν συνουσίαν.

when you come up with some new idea,
to show it to everyone. Whereas those who keep their
    cleverness to themselves
first of all have no one to evaluate their art,
and also are resented. For you have to offer the
    crowd
everything you think provides some novelty.

At those words most of the group left, and the party gradually broke up.

Index

INDEX

INDEX

fr. 64: 4.156f–7a; fr. 97: 5.189e; fr. 123: 4.168c

Diphilus of Siphnos, 3.115c, 120e–1a, 121b

Diyllos of Athens (*FGrH* 73), F1: 4.155a

Dorion, 3.118b–c

Dosiades of Crete (*FGrH* 458), F2: 4.143a–d

Dromeas, 4.132c

Duris of Samos (*FGrH* 76), 4.128a; F4: 4.167c–d; F12: 4.155c; F29: 4.184d; F37b: 4.155d

Earth, 4.166b; 5.195b

Epameinon, *Athenian archon*, 5.217e

Epameinondas of Thebes, 4.184e

Ephippus, *comic poet*, fr. 1: 3.112f

Ephippus of Olynthus (*FGrH* 126), F1: 3.120d–e; F2: 4.146c

Ephorus of Aeolian Cymae (*FGrH* 70), F3: 4.182b; F54: 4.154d–e

Epicharides, 4.161b, 165e

Epicharmus, 4.164c; fr. 3: 3.120c; fr. 16: 3.106f; fr. 24: 3.120d; fr. 30: 4.158c; fr. 34: 4.139b; fr. 38: 4.160d; *Wedding of Hebe*, test. ii: 3.110b; fr. 46: 3.110b; fr. 69: 3.106f–7a; fr. 92: 4.184f; fr. 94: 4.160d; fr. 101: 3.121b; fr. 108: 4.183c; fr. 109: 4.139b; fr. 159: 3.119b, d; fr. 160: 5.210b

Epicurus of Athens (Usener ed.), 5.177b; p. 115: 5.177a, 179d, 182b, 186e, 187b–c

Epigonus of Sicyon, 4.183d

Epilycus, fr. 4: 4.140a; fr. 5: 4.133b

Erasinides of Athens, 5.218a

Eratosthenes of Cyrene (Powell ed.), fr. 8: 5.189d; (Bernhardy ed.) pp. 233–4: 4.140a; p. 252: 4.154a

Eriphus, fr. 1: 4.134c; fr. 6: 4.137d

Erymneus of Athens, 5.211e

Eryximachus of Athens, 5.177a, 192a

Eryxis, 5.220b

Eubulus, *comic poet*, fr. *17: 3.110a; fr. 23: 3.107f; fr. 37: 4.169f; fr. 61: 3.108a; fr. 75: 3.108b; fr. 76: 3.108d; fr. 77: 3.112e–f; fr. 87: 3.108d–e; fr. 137: 3.113f

Eubulus of Athens, *demagogue*, 4.166d

Eucrates (*FHG* iv), p. 407: 3.111b–c

Euphemus, *Athenian archon*, 5.216f–17a

Euphemus of Athens, *vulgar joker*, 5.220d

Euphorbus, 5.178d

Euphorion of Chalcis (*FGH* iii), fr. 8: 4.183f; fr. 4: 4.154c; fr. 8: 4.182e–f; fr. 10: 4.184a

Euphranor, 4.182b, 184e

Eupolis, *Autolycus*, test. i: 5.216c; fr. 88.1–2: 4.183f; fr. 99.41–3: 3.123a–b; fr. 147:

INDEX

4.138f; *Flatterers,* test. ii:
 5.218b; fr. 275: 4.170d
Euripides, 4.134c, 165b, 175b;
 5.187d; *Med.* 332: 4.156f n.;
 Hipp. 219: 4.133b n.; 612:
 3.122b; *Supp.* 861–6: 4.158f–
 9a; *Ph.* 460–1: 4.160b n.; *Ba.*
 1129: 5.186d; (Kannicht ed.)
 fr. 20: 4.159c; fr. 324: 4.159b–
 c; fr. 576: 4.129f n.; fr. 892:
 4.158e; fr. 893: 4.158e–f; fr.
 894: 4.165b n.
Eurybius, 4.158a
Eurydice, *Macedonian princess,*
 4.155a
Eurypylus, 4.158a
Eurystheus, 4.157f–8a
Euthycles, fr. 1: 3.124b
Euthydemus, *son of Diocles of
 Athens, acquaintance of Socrates,* 5.187d
Euthydemus of Athens,
 diaetetic author, 3.118b; (*SH*)
 455: 3.116a–c, d
Euthydemus, *Athenian archon,*
 5.217a, 218b
Euthynus of Athens, 3.120a
Euxitheus, 4.157c

Galen of Pergamum, 3.115c
Giants, 5.209c
Glauce, 4.176d
Glaucus of Chios, 5.210c
Gnesippus, 4.151c
Gnosippus of Sparta, 4.168d
Gorgias of Leontini, 3.113e;
 5.220d
Graces, 4.163a
Graeae, 3.113e n.

Hadrian, 3.115b
Harmodius of Lepreum (*FGrH*
 319), F1: 4.148f
Hecataeus of Miletus (*FGrH* 1),
 F9: 4.148f; F322: 3.114c
Hecate, 3.110c; 4.139d n.
Hector, 5.178c, d
Hedylus of Samos (*HE*), 1877–
 86: 4.176c–d
Hegemon of Thasos, fr. 1:
 3.108c
Hegesander of Delphi (*FHG*
 iv), fr. 2: 4.162a–b; fr. 8:
 4.167d–f; fr. 10: 4.132c; fr. 29:
 3.107e; fr. 30: 4.174a; fr. 37:
 3.108a; fr. 45: 5.210b–c
Hegesianax of Alexandria Troas
 (*FGrH* 45), T3: 4.155b–c
Helen, 5.180c, 188a, c, 190d, f,
 191c–d
Hephaestion, 3.120e; 4.146c
Hephaestus, 3.108b; 4.136f;
 5.192e
Hera, 3.122c; 5.201c
Heracleides of Cumae (*FGrH*
 689), F2: 4.145b–6a
Heracleides of Syracuse, 3.114a
Heracleides of Tarentum
 (Guardasole ed.), fr. 69:
 3.120b–c
Heracleitus of Ephesus, 4.134b;
 (Diels–Kranz eds.) 22 B 13:
 5.178f
Heracleon of Beroea, 4.153b
Heracleon of Ephesus (Berndt
 ed.), p. 6: 3.111c
Heracles, 4.130b n., 153c, 157f–
 8a, 164b–d; 5.178b, 215b,
 221f

573

INDEX

Hermeias (*FGH* ii), fr. 2: 4.149d

Hermes, 3.112a; 4.130a, 184a; 5.192c, 200c

Hermippus, *comic poet,* fr. 10: 3.119c; fr. 40: 3.123f

Hermippus of Smyrna (Wehrli ed.), fr. 21: 5.213f; fr. 24: 4.163e; fr. 83: 4.154c–d; fr. 91: 4.162c

Herodicus of Babylon, 5.192b, 215f, 219c; (*SH*) 494: 5.222a

Herodotus of Halicarnassus, 1.25.2: 5.210c; 1.133: 4.143f–4b; 2.77.4: 3.114c; 2.92.5: 3.110c; 7.118: 4.146a–b; 7.119.2: 4.146b; 7.120: 4.146b; 9.16.1: 4.148e; 9.82: 4.138b–e; 9.110.2: 4.146b–c; 9.120.1: 3.119d

Hesiod, 3.116a, d; 4.164c; *Op.* 343: 5.186f; 590: 3.115a; *Asp.* 205–6: 5.180e

Hestia Prytanitis, 4.149e

Hicesius of Smyrna, 3.116e–f, 118a–b

Hieron I of Syracuse, 3.121d–e; 4.144c–e, 171e–f

Hieron II of Syracuse, 5.206d–9e

Hieronymus of Cardia (*FGrH* 154), F1: 5.217e; F2: 5.206e

Hippias of Elis, 5.218c, e

Hippolochus of Macedon, 3.126d–e, 127e; 4.128a–30d

Hipponicus of Athens, *father of Callias,* 5.218b

Hipponicus of Athens, *son of Callias,* 5.220b

Homer, 4.163c, 164c, 172e; 5.177a, 185a, 191d, 193c; *Il.* generally: 5.207d; 1.225: 4.162f n.; 1.225: 5.178d; 2.402ff: 5.192c; 2.404: 5.186e–f; 2.408: 5.177b–c; 2.588: 5.178c; 3.125–8: 5.191c–d; 3.156–9: 5.188a–b; 3.386–8: 5.191a; 3.409: 5.177c; 4.262–3: 5.192f–3a; 6.174: 5.185b–c; 7.94–105: 5.178c; 7.161: 4.129f; 7.324: 5.187a; 9.175–7: 5.179c–d; 9.177: 5.180b; 9.215: 4.173a; 9.219–20: 5.179c; 9.224: 5.193a; 11.774–5: 5.189f; 14.159ff: 3.122c; 16.617–18: 5.181b; 17.1–8: 5.178c; 17.588: 5.178a, c; 18.590–4: 5.181a; 18.603: 5.181a–b; 18.603–6: 5.181d; 24.640: 5.189f; *Od.* 1.139–41 = 4.55–7: 5.193b; 1.145: 5.192e; 1.152: 5.180b; 3.230: 5.182b; 3.332–6: 5.191e; 4.3: 5.180c; 4.3–4: 5.185b; 4.15–19: 5.180d; 4.18: 4.180f; 4.43–4: 5.181e; 4.43–6: 5.179a; 4.48: 5.178f; 4.60–1: 5.188e; 4.65–6: 5.188e–f; 4.69–70: 5.188f; 4.72: 5.189a; 4.73: 5.189a; 4.74: 5.188f; 4.74–5: 5.189a–b; 4.78–9: 5.190a; 4.81: 5.190b; 4.90–3: 5.190b; 4.97–9: 5.190b–c; 4.104–5: 5.190c–d; 4.110–12: 5.190d; 4.113–19: 5.182a; 4.116–22: 5.190d; 4.123–6: 5.191a–b; 4.133–5:

574

INDEX

Philemon of Athens, *grammarian*, 3.114d–e
Philemon of Syracuse, fr. 40: 3.123e; fr. 42: 4.133a–b; fr. 45: 4.175d; fr. 64: 4.170f
Philetaerus, 3.108c, 118d; fr. 14: 4.169e; fr. 16: 3.106e
Philetas of Cos (Dettori ed.), fr. 11: 3.114e; (Powell ed.) fr. 14: 5.192e
Philip II of Macedon, 4.155d, 166f
Philip III Arrhidaeus, 4.155a n.
Philiscus of Corcyra, 5.198b
Philistion of Locris (Wellmann ed.), fr. 9: 3.115d
Philochorus (*FGrH* 328), F68: 5.189c; F126: 5.217e; F196: 4.168a
Philolaus of Croton (Diels–Kranz eds.), 44 A 7: 4.184e
Philoxenus of Cythera (*PMG*), 836(b): 4.146f–7e; 836(b).40: 4.156e
Philoxenus of Leucas, 4.146f
Philoxenus son of Eryxis, 5.220b
Philyllius, fr. 4: 3.110f; fr. 7: 4.171d; fr. 15: 4.140a
Phocus, *son of Phocion of Athens,* 4.168e–f, 171e
Phrynicus, 3.115b; fr. 2: 4.184f; fr. 3: 4.165b–c; fr. 40: 3.110e
Phylarchus of Athens or Naucratis (*FGrH* 81), F2: 4.150d; F9: 4.150d; F44: 4.141f–2f
Phylo, 5.191b
Phyromachus, 4.161c

Pindar, *O.* 3.1: 4.137e n.; *P.* 1.4: 5.180e; (Maehler ed.) fr. 76.2: 5.187d; fr. *107b.2: 5.181b; fr. 155: 5.191f; fr. 164: 4.154e–f
Pisistratus, *son of Nestor,* 5.181f
Piston of Athens, 5.220e
Plato of Athens, *comic poet,* fr. 49: 3.119b; fr. 76.2: 4.170f–1a; fr. 78: 3.110d–e; fr. 92: 3.110d; fr. 189.4: 4.146f
Plato of Athens, *philosopher,* 4.174c; 5.177a, 178b; *Ap.* 21a: 5.218e; 21b: 5.218f–19a; 28e: 5.215c; *Cr.* 52b: 5.216b; *Tht.* 149a: 5.219a; *Smp.* 172a–3a: 5.186e; 172c: 5.217b; 173a: 5.217a, c; 176a: 5.179d; 185d–e: 5.187c; 194e–7e: 5.187c; 212d: 5.180a; 213e–14a: 5.180b; 217a–d: 5.187c; 218b–19d: 5.187c; 219b: 5.219d; 219b–c: 5.219b; 220e: 5.216c; 220e–1c: 5.215d; 223b–d: 5.192a; *Phdr.* 229d: 5.220f–1a; *Alc. 1* 103a–b: 5.187e; *Chrm.* 153b–c: 5.215e, 216c; 154d–e: 5.187f; 155c–d: 5.187f; *Prt.* 309a–b: 5.219e–20a; 309c–d: 5.218b; 314b–c: 5.218c; 315b–c: 5.218c; 327d: 5.218d; *Grg.* 471a: 5.217c–d; 473e–4a: 5.217e–f; 518b: 3.112d; *Menex.* 235e: 5.219b; *R.* 372c–d: 4.137f–8b; 399c–d: 4.182f–3a; 437d–e: 3.123e; *Lg.* 637a–b: 4.155f–6a
Pleasure, 4.163a

578

INDEX

Plutarch of Alexandria, 3.118f;
  4.128c n., 134d, 158d
Plutarch of Chaeronea, *Mor.*
  841f: 4.129d n.; *Phoc.* 20.1–2:
  4.169a n.
Pnytagoras, 4.167c
Polemarchus, 3.111c
Polemon of Ilium (Preller ed.),
  4.140b; fr. 39: 3.109a; fr. 58:
  5.210a; fr. 74: 3.109a; fr. 86:
  4.138e, 140b–c, d; fr. 89:
  3.108f
Polybius of Megalopolis, 5.193d
Polybus of Egyptian Thebes,
  5.191b
Polycleitus of Larisa (*FGrH*
  128), F4: 5.206e
Polycrates (*FGrH* 588), F1:
  4.139c–e
Polycraton of Rhenaea, 4.173b
Polyeuctus, 4.166d
Polysperchon, 4.155a n., c
Pontianus, 3.109b, 123e
Poseidon, 4.135f; 5.191e, 209e
Posidippus, fr. 17: 3.118b; fr.
  23: 4.154f–5a
Posidonius of Apamea (*FGrH*
  87), fr. 53: 4.153c–d; fr. 54:
  4.175b; fr. 57: 4.152f–3a; fr.
  61b: 5.210d; fr. 64: 4.153a; fr.
  67: 4.151e–2f; fr. 68: 4.154a–
  c; fr. 72b: 5.210e; fr. 73:
  4.153e; fr. 75: 4.153b–c; fr.
  78: 4.168d; fr. 253: 5.211d–
  15b
Priam, 5.189f
Priapus, 5.201c, d
Prodicus of Ceos, 5.220b
Pronomus, 4.184d

Protagoras of Abdera, 3.113e;
  5.218b–c
Protagorides, *erotic author,*
  4.162b
Protagorides of Cyzicus (*FGrH*
  853), F1: 4.150c; F2a:
  4.175a–b; F2b: 4.183f; F3:
  3.124d–e
Proteas of Macedon, 4.128e–9f
Ptolemy I Soter, 4.171c; 5.201d,
  202b, 203a
Ptolemy II Philadelphus,
  4.128b, 174d n.; 5.203b,
  206c, 209e
Ptolemy III Euergetes, 5.209b
  with n.
Ptolemy IV Philopator,
  5.203e–6a
Ptolemy VI Philometor, 5.195f
Ptolemy VII, 4.184b
Ptolemy VIII Euergetes, 4.174d
Ptolemy XII, 5.206d
Pymiaton of Citium, 4.167c–d
Pyrgion (*FGrH* 467), F1:
  4.143e–f
Pyrrhon of Elis, 4.160a
Pythagoras, *philosopher,* 3.108f;
  4.160f–4a; 5.213f
Pythagoras of Alexandria, 4.183f
Pythocles, 4.213e
Pythodelus, 4.166c
Pythonicus of Athens, 5.220f

Rhea, 5.201c
Rhinthon of Tarentum, fr. 1:
  3.111c
Rhōnakēs, 4.184a
Rutilius (*FGrH* 815), T7a:
  4.168e

579

INDEX

Sanchuniathon (*FGrH* 794), F5a: 3.126a

Sappho (Voigt ed.), fr. 141: 5.192c; fr. 176: 4.182e

Sarambus, 3.112e

Satyrus of Callatis (Schorn ed.), fr. 27: 4.168c

Seasons, 3.112b; 5.198b

Seleucus (Müller ed.), fr. 22: 5.188f; fr. 40: 3.114d; fr. 50: 3.114b; fr. 65: 4.172d; fr. 80: 4.155d–e

Semele, 4.183c; 5.200b

Semonides of Amorgos (West² ed.), fr. 7.56: 5.179d

Semus of Delos (*FGrH* 396), F*3: 3.123d; F7: 4.173e; F14: 3.109e–f

Seuthēs, *inventor of Pan-pipe*, 5.184a

Seuthēs of Thrace, 4.150f–1e

Silenus and Sileni, 4.184a; 5.188d, 197e, 198a, 199a, 200e

Sillax of Rhegium, 5.210b

Simonides of Ceos, 3.121e, 125a, b; 4.144c, e; (*FGE*) 1032–7: 3.125c–d; (*PMG*) 564: 4.172e; 634: 5.210b

Simus, 4.164d

Socrates of Athens, 4.158f, 162c n.; 5.186d, 187e, 188c–d, 192a–b, 215c–16c, 216e–f, 218e–20a; (*SSR*) I.C 159: 4.157e; V.A 200: 5.216b

Socrates of Cos (*FHG* iv), fr. 15: 3.111b

Socrates of Rhodes (*FGrH* 192), F1: 4.147e–8d

Solon of Athens (Ruschenbusch ed.), fr. 89: 4.137e

Sopater of Paphos, fr. 1: 4.158d–e; fr. 2: 4.176a; fr. 3: 4.160a–b; fr. 6: 4.160e–f; fr. 9: 3.109e; fr. 10: 4.175c–d; fr. 11: 3.119a; fr. 12: 4.183b–c; fr. 13: 4.160b–c; fr. 15: 4.175c; fr. 22: 3.119a

Sophilus, fr. 1: 3.123d; fr. 6: 3.125e; fr. 8: 3.125e; fr. 10: 4.158a

Sophocles, *El.* 61: 3.122c; *Tr.* 1079: 4.130b n.; (Radt ed.) fr. 19: 3.122f–3a; fr. 28: 3.122b–c; fr. 239: 4.183e; fr. 241: 4.175f; fr. 329: 4.164a; fr. 412: 4.183e; fr. 450: 4.176f; fr. 549: 5.189d; fr. 609: 3.110e; fr. 644: 4.176f; fr. 712: 3.119c

Sophron, fr. 13: 3.110c–d; fr. 26: 3.110b–c; fr. 27: 3.110c; fr. 28: 3.110c

Sosibius (*FGrH* 595), T3: 4.144e; F6b: 3.114f–15a

Sosicrates of Rhodes, (*FHG* iv) fr. 20: 4.163f–4a

Sosippus, 4.133f

Sotion of Alexandria (Wehrli ed.), fr. 21: 4.162e

Speusippus (Tarán ed.), fr. 10: 4.133b

Sphaerus (*FGrH* 585), F1: 4.141c

Sphodrius (*FGrH* 853), T2: 4.162b

Stesichorus of Himera (*PMG*), 179(a): 4.172d–e; 179(b):